BACK ROADS
and
BETTER ANGELS

A Journey into the Heart of American Democracy

FRANCIS S. BARRY

STEERFORTH PRESS

LEBANON, NEW HAMPSHIRE

Cataloging-in-Publication Data is available from the Library of Congress

ISBN 978-1-58642-388-9
Printed in the United States of America

A journey is called that because you cannot know what you will discover on the journey, what you will do with what you find, or what you find will do to you.

— James Baldwin, 1979

For Laurel, and all who risk the journey

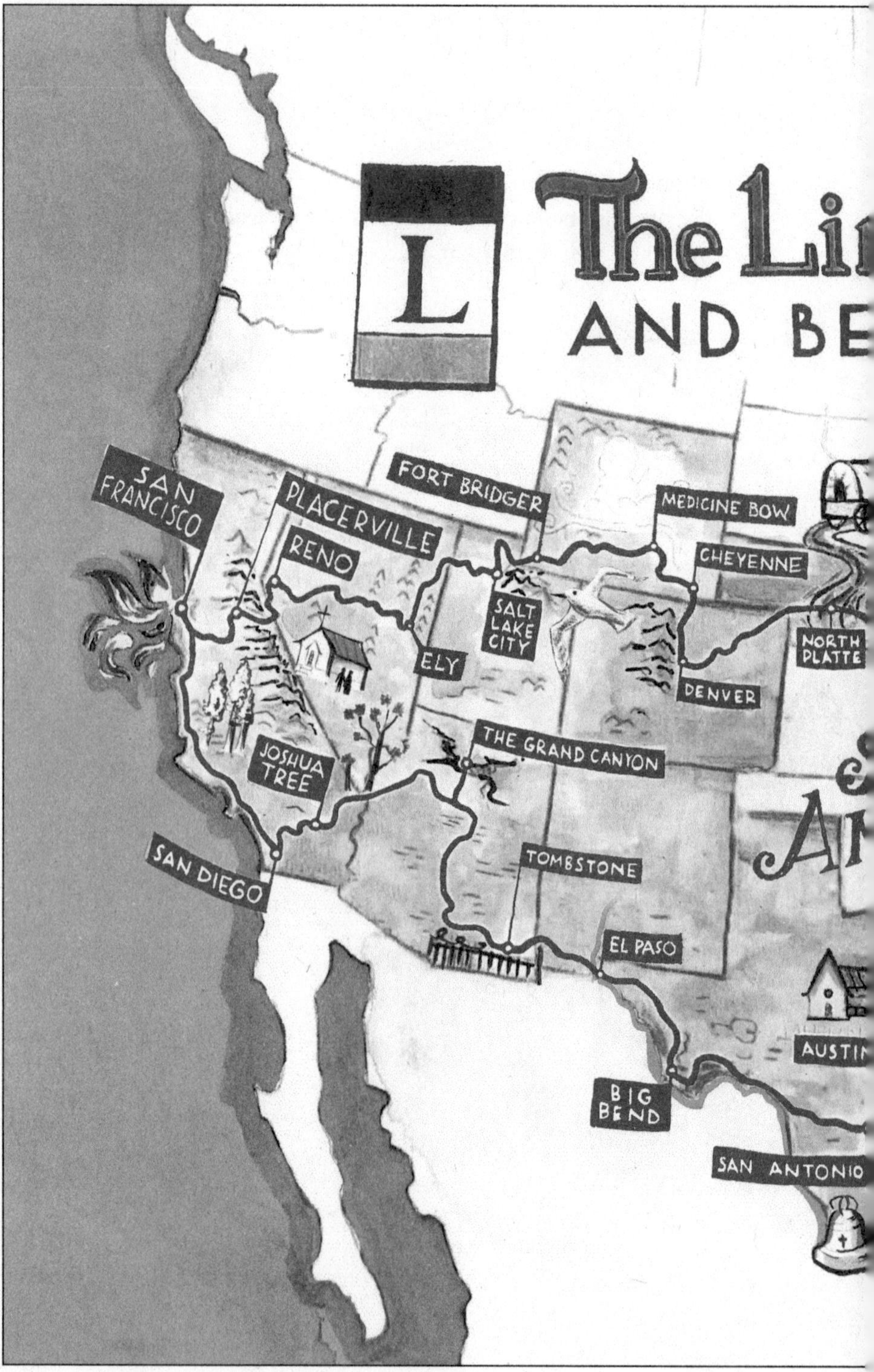

L
The Li
AND BE
SAN FRANCISCO
PLACERVILLE
RENO
FORT BRIDGER
MEDICINE BOW
CHEYENNE
SALT LAKE CITY
ELY
NORTH PLATTE
DENVER
JOSHUA TREE
THE GRAND CANYON
SAN DIEGO
TOMBSTONE
EL PASO
AUSTI
BIG BEND
SAN ANTONIO

oln Highway
OND
QICA
FIRST
CLINTON
FRANKLIN GROVE
AR RAPIDS
SOUTH BEND
PITTSBURGH
NEW YORK
CANTON
GETTYSBURG
WASHINGTON, D.C.
RICHMOND
FLOYD
ATLANTA
VICKSBURG
CHARLESTON
SAVANNAH
MARSHALL
MOBILE
MONTGOMERY
NEW ORLEANS
ORT ARANSAS

Contents

—

Prelude

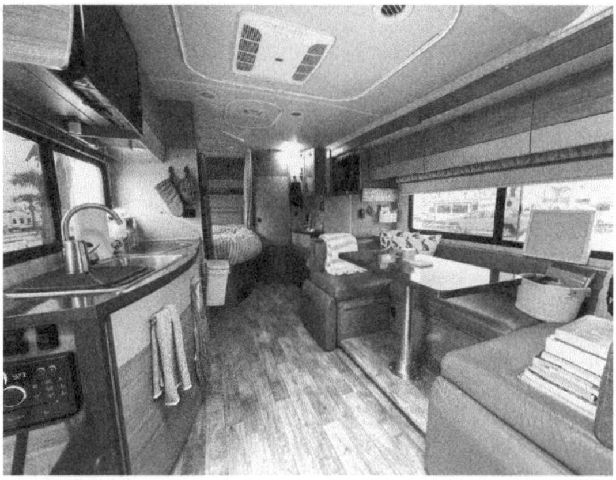

No, we're not going to Yellowstone.

That was the reply Laurel and I gave to the most frequent first question friends and family asked when they heard of our plan — a year into marriage and six months into a pandemic lockdown — to drive a motorhome across the country. They always seemed taken aback by our answer, as though we were traveling Egypt but passing on the pyramids, or crossing China without walking the Great Wall, or touring Ireland without having a pint at a pub. Who would dare? Snubbing Old Faithful on a road trip west — and through Wyoming, no less?

National parks occupy a sacred place in the American heart, and road trips have an unrivaled hold on the American imagination. The liberating pull of our open roads inspires romantic visions of the nation in its most idyllic form. When parents take the family wagon for a cross-country vacation, or kids cannonball like Kerouac and Cassady across the land, or retirees take the trip they've long dreamed about, national parks shape the itinerary and interstate highways speed the way. I had another kind of journey in mind.

The idea of driving the old Lincoln Highway — the nation's first transcontinental route, running from New York City to San Francisco — came to me in January 2016, when America seemed to be coming apart in ways I had never seen, as Donald Trump's presidential candidacy enthralled conservatives, enraged liberals, and sent both into delirium. After the election, Republicans rejoiced while many Democrats chanted "Not my president!" and spoke of impeachment even before his inauguration. In the months and years that followed, resentments deepened and passions burned hotter, each side increasingly unable to abide the other, with references to the Civil War growing more frequent.

On the left, a continual state of shock and disbelief mixed with fear and loathing — fear of what lay ahead for the country and loathing for what the Republican party had become: a toxic brew of intolerance, incompetence, ignorance, corruption, criminality, cowardice, racism, misogynism, and nativism, all debasing America's standing in the world and defiling our constitutional values. The left stopped using the word *deplorable*, but many never stopped thinking it. Yet with every new outrage there was hope that Trump had finally gone too far, only to see it forgotten within days or even hours, displaced by the next scandal more outrageous than the last, with the process repeating itself in an infuriating and exhausting loop.

On the right, a continual state of defiance and grievance mixed with fear and loathing — fear of what lay ahead for the country and loathing for what the Democratic Party had become: a toxic brew of elitism, socialism, and atheism, hostile to traditional family values, unconcerned with working people, overrun by political correctness, captive to gender and racial ideologies, blind to government dependence, hateful of American heroes, intolerant of dissent, disdainful of rural communities, and steeped in arrogance. No one had ever given voice to it all like Trump and his no-holds-barred brashness and braggadocio, which won him deep loyalty and admiration among many Republicans. The enemies he made and the battles he fought inspired a sense of hope on the right that what had been lost — factories, family farms, coal mines, traditional mores, the Protestant work ethic, the good ol' days however defined — could be regained.

As the pandemic stretched into the summer of 2020, and the passions aroused by the presidential election burned hotter, I realized that it was now or never for driving the Lincoln Highway. To avoid the need for hotels, I began researching RVs, which I knew almost nothing about. I'd ridden in one only once, at the end of senior year in college. About ten of us rented a motorhome to drive to the Kentucky Derby, and we broke down about halfway. The dealer agreed to deliver a replacement vehicle in a few hours, which turned into half the night. We didn't mind, since someone had the foresight to bring along a keg of beer. We didn't sleep and pulled into Churchill Downs at daybreak, not needing mint juleps but having them anyway and taking in the bacchanalia of the infield. This, it turns out, was not an accurate representation of RV life, except for the part about waiting on repairs.

After consulting with friends who had recently rented motorhomes, I zeroed in on the largest one I wanted to drive and the smallest one I wanted to live in: a twenty-five-foot Winnebago Navion with a full bed, toilet, shower, sink, stove, oven, dinette table, and even two televisions, plus a sleeping loft over the cab. Dealerships were sold out, listings were light, and long-term rentals were quite expensive — I was far from the only one to have the idea of RVing to escape the lockdown. But an online ad had just posted for a 2017 model with thirty thousand miles. I put in an inquiry without mentioning it to Laurel, who had scoffed at the whole idea of the trip. "Frank, there's a pandemic happening!" When she begins a sentence with my name, it usually means the matter is settled. But one of the many reasons I fell in love with her is her sense of adventure and openness to ideas of mine that fall somewhere between half-baked and harebrained.

The Winnebago's owner, Kim, replied the next morning. As we traded emails, I tried showing Laurel the listing, but she waved it off as ridiculous. Eventually, over dinner and a bottle of wine, with Taylor Swift's just-released *Folklore* playing, she agreed to look. It helped that when I initially raised the idea of the trip, I had proposed doing it in a van. The Winnebago was bigger than she had expected — about 150 square feet, the same size as Henry Thoreau's cabin at Walden Pond. If he could use a tiny cabin in the woods to "drive life into a corner," surely we could use a tiny cabin on wheels to drive life out of the corner Covid had put us into. I confessed to Laurel that I'd been emailing with the owner. She wasn't fazed.

I spoke with Kim the next morning to go over some additional questions, and she delivered the message I'd been fearing: She already had a buyer. Since I was her first inquiry, she would sell it to me, but the price was non-negotiable, and she needed a decision. Today.

Uh-oh.

As daily subway riders, neither Laurel nor I had ever bought a car. Were we really going to make our first motor vehicle purchase a Winnebago? The process was moving faster than I had expected. I hadn't even yet pitched my boss at Bloomberg News on the idea of taking the trip and writing a weekly column about it. I was putting the cart before the horse, and it was not an inexpensive cart. But the price was reasonable, and unless we wrecked it, it would hold most of its resale value.

I asked Laurel: *What do you think?* She didn't hesitate: "Let's do it!" I asked if she wanted to see the listing again, to be sure. "No. Just do it!" I asked again: *Are you positive?* "Frank, let's buy an RV!" She's the decisive one. It usually takes me a long time to make a major decision — we dated for seven years before I finally proposed — but with the world collapsing around us, it was easier to let go. I called Kim and told her: *We'll take it.*

Many people are not big on surprises, Laurel included. So before I go further, I should say a word about what, and what not, to expect in the pages ahead.

First, this is not another book about Trump, but like so much of American life now, he hovers around it. Nor is it a book to explain Republican voters to befuddled Democrats, a mission that liberal writers have spent two decades attempting with little success. In *What's the Matter with Kansas*, a bestseller published during the 2004 election, Thomas Frank looked back on his home state and painted its voting majority as suckers who fail to understand what's best for them, continually bamboozled by Republican candidates who sell them on cultural conservatism and then sell them out to Big Business. During the 2016 election, Democrats turned to J. D. Vance's memoir about his Appalachian roots, *Hillbilly Elegy*, but his attempt to particularize the Appalachian mind-set mostly reminded me of how much of it is shared by Americans of all regions and races. The book was another example of our national predilection for elevating and magnifying differences while ignoring and downplaying commonalities. Nevertheless, liberals swooned over Vance, until he ran for an Ohio Senate seat in 2022 as a Republican, whereupon his conciliatory tone turned combative and his disdain for Trump turned into fawning admiration — "kissing my ass" was how Trump put it — while Democrats reversed the other way, heaping contempt on him and the book they had once admired.

More books will be written to help coastal and urban readers understand middle and rural America, loaded with data and academic studies, but this is not one of them. Nor is it a collection of personal insights gleaned from familial connections to the heartland. Nearly all my extended family lives on the coasts. I do have one cousin in Cleveland, but he's estranged for reasons I don't entirely understand and that are not spoken of in our Irish-American family, leaving me only with vague recollections of whispers from long ago that conveyed more sadness than information. Since I am hardly able to explain my own family, and the cousin in Cleveland isn't the half of it, I won't be trying to explain anyone else's. Attempting to explain the American family is a doomed mission best left to novelists and poets. There is at least beauty in their failures.

My aim in writing this book is simpler: to invite you along with Laurel and me on a cross-country journey, in the hope that — by listening to people we meet along the way, digging into the landscape to uncover what it conceals, and remembering some of the domestic battles Americans have fought — we might view the country's challenges a little less rigidly, our fellow citizens a little more empathetically, our common history a little more clearly, our national resilience a little more appreciatively, our common inheritance a little more reverently, and our civic responsibilities a little more soberly. Cynics and partisans will dismiss the whole exercise as naive. I disagree. Our best hope in pursuing the Constitution's aim of "domestic tranquility" lies not in combing through research as sleuths but simply in listening more, judging less, and recognizing more of ourselves in one another — including the notion that conflicting views of what it means to be American is part of what it means to be American. "What is American history," wrote Steven B. Smith in *Reclaiming Patriotism in an Age of Extremes*, "but a series of debates over the meaning of our national identity."

We are not, of course, the first people to take to the road in search of answers. Cross-country travel has inspired a uniquely American genre of literature that explores the character of the country and the distances that separate it from its ideals. We are traveling in that tradition and will draw upon it for inspiration, but to guide the journey, we will track the same North Star that led the nation through our darkest hour: Abraham Lincoln, whose martyrdom has transcended our parties, a fate the poet Richard Henry Stoddard anticipated in his 1865 elegy.

One of the People! Born to be
Their curious epitome;
To share yet rise above
Their shifting hate and love.

We will hear from other American poets along the way, and since this is a road trip, we'll listen to music — American music in all its forms: rock, country, pop, punk, soul, jazz, blues, bluegrass, folk, hip-hop, Latin, all of them part of our shared heritage. (Listen along on streaming services via @fsbarry.) Song's unifying cultural force is why Lincoln, in his first inaugural address, declared that "the mystic chords of memory . . . will yet swell the chorus of the Union, when again touched, as surely they will be, by the better angels of our nature." We're going looking for those better angels and listening for those mystic chords in the hope of beginning to swell a chorus that has been drowned out by an earsplitting cacophony of anger and rage.

We could have no better guide than Lincoln, but we are not out to deify him. He was flawed and fallible, like all of us — and judged by modern standards, he was an abhorrent racist and sexist. Yet in looking unflinchingly at him, we can see paths that lead to greater understanding and a more perfect union. The alternative is deeply unsettling; as Gettysburg University professor Kent Gramm has written: "If we Americans can't find Lincoln, we are lost." Or worse. When the two major parties do not respect each other, when each views the other as an enemy that threatens the existence of the country, when each stridently condemns the other in moral terms and judges the other unfit for power, the prospect of a major breakdown in democratic governance — and the eruption of violence — should not be taken lightly.

Staving off such a nightmare begins, I believe, with considering both the tensions that have pulled the country apart since its inception and the elastic bands that have held us together. By doing so, it is my hope that we can better see the value of what I'd call patriotic pragmatism. A patriotic pragmatist is not so righteous as to reject compromise, not so modern as to damn all historical figures, not so defensive as to whitewash terrible wrongs, not so reckless as to tolerate political violence, not so feverish as to conflate party with deity, and not so blind as to fail to see through another's eyes. Patriotic pragmatists, guided by the three fundamental values of the Declaration of Independence and Constitution — freedom, equality, and democracy — may well determine whether the American people will, in Lincoln's phrase, "nobly save, or meanly lose, the last best hope of earth."

It's never wise to take a long road trip with an untrustworthy person, and trust begins with openness and transparency. So a quick word about my political background.

I'm a lifelong Democrat, but in my twenties I went to work for New York City's Republican mayor, Michael Bloomberg, which instantly made me a person of suspicion among some of my liberal friends. No matter that Bloomberg had only recently joined the Republican Party to run for mayor because he had no hope of winning the Democratic mayoral primary, or that he had hired an administration full of Democrats, or that he was pro-choice, pro–gay rights, pro–immigrant, pro–gun safety, and anti–death penalty. He had signed on to the party of George W. Bush and Dick Cheney, and for some, no virtue could ever redeem that sin, though his decision to leave the party in 2007 to become an independent seemed to help.

Over twelve years in city hall, I learned an enormous amount about government and politics and watched both parties engage in fights that had little to do with principle and everything to do with power. I wrote a book about one of those battles, over a proposal to replace closed party primaries with an open primary system, which *both* parties opposed. The one thing they agreed on was keeping independent voters shut out of the electoral process. That experience, and writing speeches for a mayor who didn't give a damn about party politics and was never afraid to buck both party lines, shaped my political outlook. When Bloomberg entered the Democratic presidential primary in 2020, I joined the campaign. Early each morning, I rode the subway to campaign headquarters in Times Square, exiting onto 42nd Street and the start of the Lincoln Highway, which served as a daily reminder for me of the campaign's core message: bringing the country back together.

So while I'm a Democrat, I've always taken to heart a truth spoken by John F. Kennedy: "Sometimes party loyalty asks too much." I will endeavor to be evenhanded on this trip, and I hope you will endeavor to be open-minded. When you read something you disagree with — and you will — stick with me. And know that Laurel is probably empathizing with you.

My bosses at Bloomberg gave me the green light to go out on the road, and Kim agreed to drive the Winnebago halfway to New York from her home in Florida. I left Manhattan at dawn in a one-way rental car and met her in the late afternoon in Fayetteville, North Carolina. After some paperwork and an orientation that I barely understood and quickly forgot, I got into the driver's seat and wondered if I had bitten off too much. I intended to stop for the night in Virginia, but once moving I dreaded the prospect of hitting morning traffic around Washington and Baltimore, so I decided to press on. After picking up Bojangles chicken and biscuits and a large

Dr Pepper, I ran on nervous energy, gripping tight the wheel, testing the stereo's maximum volume, and driving through the night. What I wouldn't have given to be lounging in the back with friends and a keg.

Finally, after thirty straight hours on the road, I arrived at our family house in upstate New York and kissed the ground — triumphant, exhausted, and apologetic, as Laurel rightly asked how I could do something so stupid. Her exasperation quickly gave way to excitement as she stepped inside the Winnebago, when it finally hit her: *It's really happening!*

We were RV people now. And the country was calling.

—1—

Manhattan Preamble

"Wrong ferry," the ferryman says, referring to the city-run ferry app Laurel has opened on her phone. "This is a private company, not that mess de Blasio is running over there — along with everything else."

I hadn't expected the very first words spoken by the very first person we encountered on our cross-country journey to be an attack on Mayor Bill de Blasio, but disparaging his haplessness — his much-hyped ferry has been plagued by long lines and breakdowns, infuriating but not surprising residents — is something of a bonding ritual for residents. Say this for him: Uniting New Yorkers on any topic is no small feat.

The ferryman is black, middle-aged, and, based on his eagerness to chat, probably lonely or bored, since only one other person is aboard a boat that, before Covid-19, would have been filled with commuters to Lower Manhattan. He says he was born in Harlem but now lives in Connecticut. "I still got family here, but I'm so glad not to be living in the city now," he says. I'm not sure if that's a comment on the pandemic or de Blasio. Probably both.

We're crossing the New York Harbor at dawn, from Jersey City to Wall Street. We had spent the previous night in an RV "park" — more of a weathered parking lot — abutting the ferry stop and a dockside restaurant. We thoroughly enjoyed the spot, since there is no surer way to a New Yorker's heart than through dining and transportation convenience, not to mention views of the skyline and Statue of Liberty. While there, I began getting the hang of connecting the water and electric lines, but I was so paranoid about flushing the toilet — I didn't want to fill the waste tank too quickly — that I reduced my fluid intake. This was in keeping with my general apprehension about the RV, born of inexperience and mechanical ignorance. The lengthy user's manual I read cover-to-cover produced more questions than answers. With all its moving parts, electrical intricacies, plumbing contraptions, and technical complexities, the Winnebago is like a god I do not understand and do not want to anger. Best to tread gingerly and call upon its great powers only when absolutely necessary.

Although I've been failing in my job of understanding the RV, Laurel has succeeded in her job of outfitting it with everything a home needs: cookware and tableware, bedding and bath items, hooks and hangers, and a wide variety of other items that I wouldn't have guessed necessary for such a small home, each seeming to require its own bin. We have bins to hold food and waste, linens and laundry, clothes and blankets, cleaning supplies and electronics. There is almost no household item that Laurel does not want to put in a bin, such is her desire for order. She tells me I'm messy (guilty), and I tell her we balance each other out.

We also purchased an array of outdoor living items: folding chairs, a collapsible table and tablecloth, hammock, flashlights, camp stove, lantern, outdoor rug, and even a retractable clothesline. As the gear piled up, we began to worry that we might run out of space — and that was before all the throw pillows arrived.

"Do we really need all these pillows?" I asked.

"Frank" — I knew the argument was already over — "yes, we do. Do we really need the solar shower you bought?" Touché.

To her credit, Laurel kept a running list of everything we were bringing and didn't try to sneak anything past me, as far as I know, which is more than I can say: I secretly stashed a small library of books under one of the dinette benches. If she had known about it, she might have told me to leave some behind — or bought another bin.

We have christened the Winnebago Charley in honor of the dog John Steinbeck brought with him on his trip around America that resulted in *Travels with Charley*, which may have sprung more from his imagination than his reportage. "He just sat in his camper," wrote his son many years later, "and wrote all that shit." But it was good shit, and scholars now mostly shrug at accusations of fabrication. There is truth in fiction, after all. Novelists have always known that. Politicians, too. The art is in the telling of the tale. I am neither novelist nor politician, though, just a man with a wife who really wants a dog, and who, when annoyed with me, threatens to leave me for a canine companion she would name Frank Junior. Charley the Winnebago is our compromise.

As we ferry across glassy water, day is breaking behind the skyline and beneath ashen clouds. It's September 11, 2020. I look across the harbor to the spot on the Manhattan shoreline where I had stood nineteen years earlier, when I was working three blocks south of the Twin Towers. On the way to the office that morning, I stopped into a record store in the World Trade Center to buy a copy of a Bob Dylan album being released that day, *Love and Theft*, a title that evokes a book of that name about the cultural influence of blackface minstrelsy. As the album played over the store's stereo, I lingered to listen. The opening lines of the second track, "Mississippi," which lifts its refrain from an old Louisiana prison song — Dylan's own love and theft — are now repeating in my mind, as my memories of 9/11 collide with the pandemic.

> *Every step of the way, we walk the line*
> *Your days are numbered, so are mine.*

I reached my office shortly before the first plane hit. Hearing of it on the news, I walked back outside, joining others who stood on the corner looking up at the Towers, all of us thinking it was a twin-engine accident. And then, the roar of the second plane overhead, the sonic boom of the crash. In the ensuing pandemonium, many rushed inside the nearest building. I headed south to Battery Park at the tip of the island, where I found two co-workers among the crowd. We had a clear view of the Towers and their unfathomable sights: people falling through the sky. When the first tower came down and the dust left us in darkness, I stood at the water's edge looking out at the bay Henry Hudson saw aboard the *Halve Maen* on September 11, 1609, but I could see no farther than a few feet. I knew the Statue of Liberty was out there. I just didn't know if I'd ever see it again.

Laurel and I are setting out on the anniversary of the darkest day the country had experienced since Pearl Harbor, but also a day that brought people together in ways that hadn't happened since World War II, and for the same purpose: to affirm our commitment to freedom and democracy. We aim to reach our destination by Election Day, our highest civic tradition, in a year that is testing our faith in democracy like never before in modern times.

As our ferry rounds the tip of Manhattan, Laurel and I look out on Governors Island and the spot where we met at a free outdoor concert in 2010. It was just a few days after I had stood on the island to watch Mayor Bloomberg, against a backdrop of the Statue of Liberty, deliver a speech defending the right of Muslims to build a mosque near the World Trade Center. Conservative politicians and media had been trying to block the mosque, and as they stoked outrage and fueled bigotry, many leading Democratic officials joined them or sat silently by. Not Bloomberg. It was, personally and professionally, the best week of my life.

Although the Lincoln Highway begins in Times Square, Laurel and I will begin the journey on foot in Lower Manhattan, which will give us a chance to encounter a variety of people whose lives or spirits intersected with Abe's and whom we will meet again down the road; to catch glimpses of some of the national fault lines we'll cross; and to begin collecting different strands of American life that we'll weave together in hopes of forming a tapestry worthy of discussion and reflection.

From a landing where ships carrying Africans once deposited their cargo at a slave market, Laurel and I walk up a deserted Wall Street to a building — the world's tallest when it opened in 1930 — with large gold letters that announce its lessee: Trump. It stands where the wall of Wall Street once did, built by the early Dutch settlers and their enslaved laborers to protect against attacks by the British and Indians. But the most dangerous threats can come from within: Where the wall once stood, enslaved Africans staged a revolt in 1712 that killed nine white residents. In the days that followed, seventy Africans were arrested and twenty were executed, three burned at the stake. The city adopted a law prohibiting the enslaved from meeting in groups larger than three. We will see battles over rights and liberties, and walls, all along the journey.

Across the street at the old J.P.Morgan building is another reminder of internal strife: blast marks from 1920, when a horse-drawn carriage pulling a hundred pounds of dynamite and five hundred pounds of cast iron exploded, killing forty people and injuring hundreds more. Investigators have never solved the case, though most evidence points to militant anarchists. Fifty years later, this same spot is where construction workers building the World Trade Center spent a lunch break beating up hundreds of young people protesting the Vietnam War and the shooting at Kent State

University by the Ohio National Guard, which killed four students and injured nine more. We will see violence and terrorism — political, cultural, religious, class — in big cities and small towns.

Here on the same block where hard hats attacked hippies, anarchists attacked capitalists, and Africans attacked their enslavers, George Washington took the oath of office on April 30, 1789. Reading his speech today, it is impossible not to marvel at its humility, unfathomable in a modern presidential speech. He described himself as "one, who, inheriting inferior endowments from nature and unpracticed in the duties of civil administration, ought to be peculiarly conscious of his own deficiencies." His one note of unwitting arrogance lay in a single phrase — "the pure and immutable principles of private morality" — that failed to envision a society capable of updating its moral underpinnings to accept blacks, women, Catholics, Jews, indigenous people, and others as full and equal citizens. We will see battles over the nation's mutating moral principles.

After his speech, Washington attended a service a few blocks north at St. Paul's Chapel on Broadway. As we follow his path, we pass Trinity Church, where Alexander Hamilton lies buried. "The only path to a subversion of the republican system of the Country," he wrote shortly after Washington's inauguration, "is by flattering the prejudices of the people, and exciting their jealousies and apprehensions, to throw affairs into confusion, and bring on civil commotion." We will see prejudices flattered, apprehensions excited, confusion created, and commotion stirred.

Past Trinity Church we walk along Zuccotti Park, now best known as the site of the 2011 Occupy Wall Street encampment, a proudly leaderless, ragtag group that capitalized on public anger at large banks in the aftermath of the Great Recession to air an amalgam of economic grievances and promote utopian ideals. This morning, some family members of 9/11 victims are starting to gather in the park to protest the annual commemoration at the World Trade Center. They are unhappy about a Covid precaution — audio recordings of family members, rather than family members themselves, will announce the name of each person killed — and so they are holding their own separate ceremony. The pandemic is even dividing a 9/11 remembrance. The sounds of protests will echo all along our route.

Lincoln passed through what is now the World Trade Center as he headed to a ferry that would bring him across the harbor, on his way to Washington, DC, to be inaugurated. He could not have imagined 110-story buildings (Trinity Church was the tallest building in the US at that time) nor the jet airplanes that would crash into them, but he would soon struggle to bear the kind of overwhelming grief — personal, national, historical — that is now enshrined at the World Trade Center Memorial. We will see tragedies enshrined and tragedies ignored.

When Lincoln first came to New York in 1860 to deliver a speech, he stayed at the Astor House hotel on Broadway beside St. Paul's Chapel, where we now stand. On the day before his speech, he boarded a ferry to Brooklyn to attend Sunday services at Plymouth Church, led by the Reverend Henry Ward Beecher, the militant abolitionist who had recently lionized John Brown for attempting to incite a slave rebellion at Harpers Ferry, Virginia. We will cross paths with Brown in Pennsylvania and wrestle with his legacy throughout our journey.

From Astor House, Lincoln walked to Cooper Union, a new college in Manhattan's East Village founded by the industrialist Peter Cooper, to deliver his speech. Laurel and I begin to retrace his steps, beginning in City Hall Park, where Washington and his soldiers joined city residents on July 9, 1776, to hear the reading of a declaration that had just arrived from Philadelphia: "When in the Course of human events . . ." After hearing it, the first act performed by these citizens of a newly independent nation was to march down Broadway to tear down a statue of King George III. Old reverence fell to new zeal. They would make their own heroes. We will see this impulse, and its blowback, again.

I look upon city hall's large second-floor windows enclosing the Governor's Room, where Lincoln attended a pre-inaugural reception in February 1861. Shortly prior to it, the city's Democratic mayor, Fernando Wood, proposed that the city secede from the state so that it could continue trading with the south. The city's economy was deeply intertwined with slavery: Shipbuilders made fortunes constructing vessels to carry southern cotton; bankers financed plantation owners; manufacturers sent their factory products south; and merchants got pieces of the action coming and going. "The City of New York belongs almost as much to the South as to the North," declared the *Saturday Evening Post*. Shortly before Lincoln's arrival, the New York Police Department seized thirty-eight cases of muskets bound for Savannah, leading Mayor Wood to issue an apology — to Georgia, for the "illegal and unjustifiable seizure of public property." We will see the scars and still-open wounds — north and south — of the Civil War.

By a statue of Horace Greeley ("Go West!"), Laurel and I unlock public bikes and ride north, stopping at the spot where Lincoln sat for a portrait in the temporary studio of photographer Mathew Brady, who positioned the camera on Lincoln's better side and lightly touched up his face, giving a stately appearance to a man often called homely, ugly, ungainly, and awkward — and that was by Republicans. Democrats dubbed him "the Illinois baboon." But in their newspapers and magazines, thanks to Brady, Americans saw a picture of dignity. (When people tell me I bear a passing resemblance to Lincoln — I'm six foot four with a long face, receding hairline, and gangly frame — I pretend they are referring to Brady's portrait and not the first-person descriptions.) "Brady and the Cooper Institute made me president," Lincoln would later say, or so claimed Brady three decades later. We will see the power of the media and popular culture to shape public consciousness.

A block up Broadway from Brady's studio and on the same side of the street, the Lafarge House hotel once stood beside the Winter Garden Theatre. On November 25, 1864, Confederates attempted to burn the Lafarge and nearly two dozen other city buildings in a bid to avenge Sherman's burning of Atlanta. As they put their plan in motion, a capacity crowd gathered at the Winter Garden to see a special production of *Julius Caesar*, with proceeds helping to fund a statue of William Shakespeare in Central Park. When the performance was interrupted by the sound of fire bells outside, the actor playing Brutus, Edwin Booth — a leading man of the American stage and a Lincoln supporter — broke from character to speak to the audience, urging calm. His two brothers in the cast, John Wilkes and Junius Brutus Jr., stood by, one of the only times the three Booth brothers ever appeared together on the same stage. Five months later, John Wilkes Booth would yell a line later attributed to Brutus — *Sic Semper Tyrannis!*, Ever thus to tyrants! — after firing a bullet into the back of Lincoln's head. When captured, his pocket diary recorded his final lament, that he was being hunted down "for doing what Brutus was honored for." We will see the enduring appeal of Brutus.

We pedal north to Cooper Union at Astor Place. When Lincoln arrived here, he would have known about the 1849 Astor Place Riot, instigated by a passion-fueled debate over who should be allowed to play the title role in *Macbeth*, one of his favorite plays — "I think nothing equals Macbeth," he wrote. "It is wonderful." The city's upper class preferred the formal English gentleman William Charles Macready. The working class and its Irish immigrants backed his more bravado-fueled American rival, Edwin Forrest, seeing Macready as a threat to America's cultural independence. "Working men, shall Americans or English rule in this city?" read a handbill by the American Committee, whose leaders included one of the most popular writers of the day, Ned Buntline. Full of ethnic and class resentment, they attacked the Astor Place Opera House, where Macready was appearing, and attempted to set it ablaze. When the police could not restore order, the militia arrived and fired into the crowd, killing more than twenty people. We will see the role of identity in fueling riots — and the ghost of Macbeth.

In the days before the 1860 election, Democrats took their own turn gathering at Cooper Union, declaring themselves a "white man's party." The *New York Herald* warned, "Irish and German laborers! If Lincoln is elected today you will have to compete with the labor of four million emancipated Negroes." Lincoln lost the city by an almost two-to-one margin, as city voters also overwhelmingly rejected a statewide referendum on black suffrage. But it was here at Cooper Union on Lincoln's birthday in 1908 that a group of interracial leaders gathered for a "Lincoln Conference on the Negro Question," out of which grew the National Association for the Advancement of Colored People (NAACP), its mission being "completion of the work . . . the Great Emancipator began." We will see how the struggle to complete that work continues.

At Cooper Union, the sun is rising over the hall where Lincoln delivered the speech in 1860 that catapulted him to the Republican nomination, a carefully researched refutation of the idea that the nation's founders would have supported the spread of slavery. The speech appeared in newspapers across the country, and its concluding line would be immortalized: "Let us have faith that right makes might." The words immediately following it, which have received less acclaim, deserve no less weight: "And in that faith, let us, to the end, dare to do our duty as we understand it." *As we understand it* — a public and prominent acknowledgment of fallibility, an admission that the course of action taken by Lincoln and Republicans might well be flawed. Here was George Washington's humility, alive and well. Rare though it was and is, we will see it again.

North to Union Square: When Lincoln's funeral procession passed by it, a six-year-old Teddy Roosevelt watched from a stately home while a fifteen-year-old descendant of Jewish refugees, Emma Lazarus, stood in the crowd. The statue in the harbor that inspired her famed poem was conceived in the aftermath of the Civil War by the French sculptor F. A. Bartholdi. And while its torch and crown became global icons, the broken shackles of slavery that lie at Lady Liberty's feet were mostly forgotten after Lazarus's verse transformed the monument's message from emancipation and equality to immigration and opportunity. While much was gained in that transformation, much was lost, too — for both black history and national unity. We will see it all along our journey: To transmit myth is to transmute it.

Behind Lincoln's statue stands the old Tammany Hall, once headquarters of the powerful Democratic party machine named for Tamanend, a Lenape Indian chief lionized by the colonists. The building is now being converted into office space, topped by a new glass dome inspired by the Lenape creation story of a great turtle shell rising from the sea. We will delve into mythology — what the writer Joseph Campbell called "the song of the imagination" — to better understand America's creation story and how it continues to evolve.

To the extent most New Yorkers know anything of the Lenape, it is the retelling of the city's own creation story, no less mythic: the buying of Manhattan for $24, a deal the Lenape believed would result in the land being shared, one of the earliest betrayals in a tragic relationship that lines every mile of the Lincoln Highway. Yet we will see how America has remained a land of communal aspirations — liberty and justice for all — and how the struggle to fulfill them still lies at the center of our national story, a story that inspired Woody Guthrie to write, while staying at a hotel for transients just around the corner from the start of the Lincoln Highway, a song that is both a patriotic and a protest anthem.

> *This land is your land, this land is my land*
> *From California, to the New York Island*

We've arrived at 42nd Street and Broadway, where a street sign marks the start of the Lincoln Highway. I once stood underneath it asking passersby if they could tell me how to get to the Lincoln Highway. Some didn't bother glancing in my direction, accustomed as they were to ignoring peddlers and panhandlers, but many tourists stopped and some New Yorkers did, too, if only to show off their knowledge of the city to a bewildered bumpkin. But no one, tourist or local, could tell me how to get to the Lincoln Highway. *Nope. Never heard of it. You mean the Lincoln Tunnel? Lincoln Center?* Only one man knew of it, a South Asian immigrant who lived alongside it in New Jersey, he proudly told me.

Most Americans have never heard of the Lincoln Highway, which zigzags its way across some thirty-four hundred miles of local roads from

Times Square to the foot of the Golden Gate Bridge. As a college student, I spent four years in South Bend, Indiana, without knowing that Lincolnway — the road we took to an out-of-the-way dusky tavern that didn't check IDs — was part of the national route dedicated in 1913 to honor Old Abe. How it came to be and what it still represents is important to our story. If you're going to come along for the ride, you should know a little about it. So before we get going, let me tell you the story of Crazy Carl Fisher.

— 2 —

Road as Idea

Carl Graham Fisher was ridiculed as "the stupidest boy in the school," he would later say with pride, because of an astigmatism that blurred his vision. After dropping out at age twelve to support his mother and siblings, his father having abandoned the family, he found work in grocery stores and bookstores, but it was through hawking newspapers, candy, tobacco, and peanuts that he learned the art of capitalism: Those who tipped him got a quick peek at a photo of a naked woman he kept hidden under his change apron.

In 1891 at age seventeen, Carl and his brother opened a bicycle repair shop, fixing flat tires as the cycling craze swept the nation, thanks to the introduction of the "safety" bicycle. With two wheels of equal size, the safety was faster and easier to ride than the high wheeler (also called the penny farthing), which had a seat atop a big front wheel that made it hard to balance over bumps, sending many riders tumbling. After testing a high wheeler, Mark Twain wrote, "Get a bicycle. You will not regret it, if you live."

As bicycle manufacturers proliferated in the 1890s, Carl expanded his shop from repair to sales. To advertise, he dreamed up outlandish stunts: throwing a bike from a tall building and giving a free one to the person who retrieved it; riding a bike across a tightrope stretched two stories high; building a bike twenty feet tall and riding it around town; and releasing a thousand balloons containing numbers, fifty of them entitling the finder to a free bike, creating a citywide scavenger hunt.

Bikes became immensely popular because they offered liberation from towns and trains, making it easy to travel distances that previously required a rail ticket, to do so on one's own schedule, and to stop where one pleased. Victorian society stood aghast at women shortening hemlines and donning bloomers to avoid their dresses getting caught in chains and wheels, but form trumped fashion and the bicycle opened new worlds to women who had few opportunities for exercise or escape. Susan B. Anthony said of it, "I think it has done more to emancipate women than any one thing in the world. It gives women a feeling of freedom and self-reliance. I stand and rejoice every time I see a woman ride by on a wheel." Transportation had never been so radical. In 1896, the *Detroit Tribune* predicted that history would prove the invention of the bicycle to be "the greatest event of the nineteenth century." And in one way, it was: There would be no Motor City without it.

Today it is difficult to comprehend how the bicycle, with its seemingly simple technology, preceded the automobile by only a few years, but the timing was not coincidental. Innovation is iterative, and bikes begat automobiles as their mechanics and engineers, Carl Fisher included, turned from two wheels to four. Many of the biggest names in the auto industry — Henry Ford, Louis Chevrolet, Horace and John Dodge, Henry Leland (Cadillac), and Max and Morris Grabowsky (GMC) — began their careers as bicycle mechanics or builders. The first car Henry Ford built in the shed behind his house, the quadricycle, ran on four wheels with pneumatic tires and a chain, all borrowed from bikes like the one he rode on his daily commute to Edison Illuminating Company, where he was chief engineer. The early auto pioneers also borrowed lights and horns from bicycles, and they benefited from the cycling industry's development of new technologies, including metal stamping and lightweight steel tubing. "Everything about the carriage is made on a bicycle basis," *Horseless Age* magazine explained to readers in 1897. During that decade, one-third of all US patents related to bicycles.

Automobiles were initially a recreational pastime, like cycling, only more expensive. Owners took their cars touring and racing, which critics charged was an ostentatious display of wealth that bred class resentment. "Nothing has spread Socialistic feeling in this country more than the use of automobiles," said Woodrow Wilson in 1906, while president of Princeton

University. "To the countryman they are a picture of arrogance of wealth with all its independence and carelessness." Carl knew better, converting his Indianapolis bike shop into one of the nation's first auto dealerships and becoming one of its best — and most outlandish — sellers.

To demonstrate the durability of a Stoddard-Dayton model from his showroom, he rolled it off the roof of a four-story building as a crowd looked on in wonder. After it landed in one piece, he drove it away to cheers. That was a warm-up for one of the great stunts of the century: In 1908, he replaced the basket of a hot-air balloon with a Stoddard-Dayton and flew it across Indianapolis — while sitting in the driver's seat. The sight stopped traffic and everything else. After two hours of floating, Carl landed in a field and drove back into the city, receiving a hero's welcome. Prior to the flight, however, he had secretly removed the car's engine to ensure liftoff and arranged to have an identical Stoddard-Dayton driven to the landing field so he could switch vehicles and make a triumphant return.

Among those gawking at the sky that day was a teenager, Jane Watts. When she and Carl got engaged the following year — he directed her to tell reporters she was twenty-four, and the wedding announcement was news to Carl's girlfriend of six years, who sued him for breach of promise. Nine other women sued on the same grounds, and marriage did not settle him down. "Living with Carl Fisher was like living in a circus," Jane would later say. "There was something going on — something exciting going on — every minute of the day. Sometimes it was very good. Sometimes it was very bad. Still, it was living."

Prior to marrying, Carl made a fortune building a network of factories to manufacture headlights powered by compressed gas rather than kerosene, and on a business trip to Dayton involving multiple flat tires and breakdowns, he had a brain flash: "I have a new hen coming off!" he would say when an idea struck him. This one would bring immortal fame: "What this country needs is a big racetrack to give manufacturers a chance to test their cars and equipment." By building it in Indiana, he could give the state's four hundred auto producers a leg up on the competition in Detroit and Cleveland, and give the public a chance to see, for a fee, the entirety of a race, rather than watching cars whiz past on local roads. The day after returning from Dayton, he scouted a 320-acre farm that became the Indianapolis Motor Speedway, which led to his most daring idea yet: a five-hundred-mile race, which no one had ever attempted, on a paved track, which no one had ever built. It became a national sensation and a smash success. And if paving a racetrack could capture the nation's imagination, Carl thought, imagine what paving a road all the way across America could do.

In 1912, a trip across the country required two to three months of driving ten-hour days, with nearly as much time spent looking under hoods as across landscapes. Of the nation's two and a half million total miles of road, more than 90 percent were dirt — mostly farmland wagon trails that were often impassable after rain. Drivers carried wood boards to help them get out of the mud, though heavy rains could form ponds. Few adventure seekers were hardy enough to attempt a cross-country trip, and no wonder.

In addition to primitive roads and frequent farm gates blocking them, no signs marked the way. Navigation required regular stops to ask for directions, but few people had any knowledge of the roads beyond their own towns, leading to endless wrong turns. No roadside motels existed. Travelers slept in ditches or pitched tents when reaching a hotel was not possible. No drive-through gas stations had yet opened, and fuel procured from barrels at pharmacies, hardware stores, and blacksmith shops came at great expense. But all of those challenges paled in comparison with the vehicle itself.

The most popular car in America, Ford's Model T, had an open carriage that exposed passengers to cold and rain, dust and dirt. Goggles were a must. It rode rough and loud: engine thrashing, pistons knocking, hood trembling, windows rattling. Tires regularly punctured, sprang leaks, and lost pressure, requiring frequent removal for patching and pumping. One early traveler driving from Cleveland to California and back counted 175 flats and 17 blowouts. Oil and water coolant levels needed to be checked every day. Bearings burned out. Radiators leaked. Fan belts slipped. Henry Ford expected buyers to be amateur mechanics, capable of futzing their way to a fix.

Even starting the engine was more art than science. The operator had to set the ignition timer jutting out from the steering shaft just right before getting out of the vehicle, bending over the front of the engine, pulling a choke wire if the engine was cold, and turning a hand crank from eight o'clock to one o'clock — "turning over the engine." Setting the spark lever too low could result in the engine kicking back, spinning the crank backward with force. If the operator cranked too far, or used an improper grip, a broken thumb, wrist, or arm might result. Doctors called these injuries "Ford fractures." In freezing temperatures, oil thickened in the crank case and prevented the engine from starting, even after the choke was used. "Warming up the engine" meant getting creative — placing a kerosene lamp underneath it, or even lifting the front tires onto blocks and starting a fire.

To move the vehicle, drivers worked a hand lever that served as the throttle along with three foot pedals, none of them an accelerator: the left to engage low gear, the right to brake, and the middle to — what else? — go in reverse. The brake pedal did not actually activate the rear wheel brakes; only the hand brake did that. The brake pedal only slowed the transmission. Drivers found the reverse pedal to be a more effective brake. Crashes were common.

Traveling hilly terrain created another problem: Gravity fed gas to the carburetor from a tank under the driver's seat. As long as the tank remained above the engine, all was well. But arriving at a steep hill while low on gas meant turning the vehicle around and ascending in reverse, to keep the gas flowing and the engine running. There was no gas gauge to alert drivers to a low tank, nor a rearview mirror. In a 1936 elegy to the Model T, E. B. White concluded that it was "obviously conceived in madness."

Driving was a laborious, expensive, dangerous, and maddening ordeal, but a joyous one. A hit song for Al Jolson in 1913 told of a young couple on a date in their Sunday best, taking a new car for a drive only to have continual engine trouble interrupt their romance, with the refrain going:

He'd have to get under, get out and get under
To fix up his little machine.
He was just dying to cuddle his queen,
But ev'ry minute, when he'd begin it,
He'd have to get under, get out and get under

Americans didn't mind getting their hands dirty — the freedom exceeded the frustration — and public support for good roads began to grow. Yet many states did not even have a road department. Carl Fisher believed that a cross-country road could be built for $10 million and cut the time and hassle of driving cross-country in half. But who would build it? He would.

Carl devised a plan to raise the money: asking every auto dealer, manufacturer, and parts supplier to chip in, and selling public memberships for $5. Of course, he also had a public relations angle: Construction would be complete in time for the opening of the 1915 Panama-Pacific International

Exposition in San Francisco, where the highway would end, so all the world would hear of it. And besides, it would be fun: "Let's build it," Carl implored an audience of auto industry executives in Indianapolis, "before we're too old to enjoy it!"

Goodyear's CEO, Frank Seiberling, pledged $300,000 on the spot, and $1 million was quickly raised. But the industry's biggest name, Henry Ford, wasn't interested. Carl tracked down Ford at the Michigan State Fair and cornered him at a pigpen, but Ford's board formally rejected the idea: "We believe it is better to spend our money in making the price of the cars low, as this will have the beneficial effect of putting more cars in use, and the more cars there are in use, the greater demand there will be for government building Good Roads." Carl saw the bigger picture. The sooner the public understood they could travel long distances by car, the more demand for vehicles would rise. A cross-country road would be a boon to the industry and an adventure for him, a chance to create the Next Big Thing.

When the president of the Packard Motor Company, Henry Joy, donated $150,000, he also offered Carl a suggestion: that he should lobby Congress to fund a highway plan rather than spending $1.7 million on a massive monument to Abraham Lincoln in Washington, DC. Joy loved Lincoln — his father had known Abe — and saw the coast-to-coast highway as a far more fitting tribute than any statue. "Let good roads be built in the name of Lincoln," he wrote to Carl. The idea for a monument to Lincoln in the nation's capital had been discussed for more than a decade, but lack of consensus had stymied a final plan. In 1913, the leading idea remained a Greek temple on the north bank of the Potomac River, atop marshland filled in with dredge from the river bottom, but the Republican Speaker of the House — Joe Cannon, a self-taught and cigar-chomping Illinoisan who had met Lincoln and revered him — had blocked it for years. "So long as I live," he said, "I'll never let a memorial to Abraham Lincoln be erected in that goddamned swamp."

The alternative idea for a memorial to Lincoln had originated with former congressman James McCleary, of Minnesota. The first Lincoln memorial commission created by Congress had sent him to Europe to study its monuments. He came back most impressed not by any sculpture but by an ancient road still in use: the Appian Way, the Roman Empire's first great highway. Seeing beauty in its twenty-three hundred years of service, he proposed an American version: the Lincoln Way, from the White House to Gettysburg.

Elected officials who stood to benefit from the road combined with auto industry interests to push for it. They came up with the perfect slogan — "For Lincoln, a finished memorial is not a fit memorial" — and won over Cannon's successor as House Speaker, Democrat Champ Clark. "Lincoln was a practical man; a great man, with practical ideas," Clark said. "If we are to expend that much money, we should expend it where it will do some good."

It is hard to believe that Lincoln would not have preferred the road over the temple, given his humility and lifelong support for transportation infrastructure. But when opponents argued the road would cost upward of $20 million, congressional support weakened and reformers killed it by crying corruption, claiming speculators had bought land options along the proposed route.

Like Henry Joy, Carl had long admired Lincoln, and after Congress passed on the Gettysburg road, he and Joy coopted the name. At a meeting in Joy's Detroit office on April 14, the anniversary of Lincoln's assassination, they made it official, founding the Lincoln Highway Association. Almost immediately, the mythologizing began: "The Lincoln Highway is to be something more than a road," Carl would say. "It will be a road with personality, a distinct work of which the Americans of future generations can point with pride — an economic but also artistic triumph." Theodore Roosevelt loved the idea: "I particularly liked your phrase 'tightening the Union,'" he wrote to Joy. "You use exactly the words to express the idea!"

There was just one problem: Fundraising had fallen well short of the $10 million goal, itself a gross underestimate of the true cost of such a mammoth undertaking. No matter. Later in 1913, after spending several months exploring the country and meeting with state and local leaders who lobbied to be included, the association's leaders published a route, although it was nothing more than a list of cities. They chose Halloween to officially dedicate the road in the hope that city fathers would turn a pagan ritual into a patriotic celebration, and it worked: Towns along the highway shot off cannons and fireworks, held dances and parades, and festooned shops in red, white, and blue. Several governors officially proclaimed it Lincoln Highway Day, with Wyoming governor Joseph Carey calling for "an old-time jollification to include bonfires and general rejoicing." Newspapers ran a proclamation by the association declaring its ideals, and religious leaders exalted its virtues in their sermons. The outpouring of pomp and praise from public officials and preachers was all the more impressive since there was hardly a highway to speak of. It had never been constructed, only mapped out of existing local roads, such as they were. The association's proclamation admitted as much.

> UPON ALL THE PEOPLE, especially the OFFICIALS of each state and county and upon the inhabitants thereof, within the borders of which is designated by these resolutions a section of the LINCOLN HIGHWAY, DOES REST THE PATRIOTIC BURDEN of establishing, broadening, straightening, maintaining, and beautifying to the end that it may become a proper MEMORIAL to the GREAT MARTYRED PATRIOT whose name it bears.

In other words, the association was telling Americans: *You build it — it's your patriotic duty.*

By 1915, almost none of the states and cities along the route had constructed any new road for the Lincoln Highway. The association, still without money to build it, attempted to conjure it, by laying a number of "seedling miles," short stretches of paved roadways that would give the public a chance to see how pleasant driving on them could be and inducing them to raise their taxes to pay for more of them. Although seedling miles didn't prompt much local action, they did help spur the Federal Aid Road Act, which provided $75 million in matching funds to encourage states to invest in roads and which was signed into law by the first honorary member of the association, the auto skeptic who'd had a conversion on the road to Washington, Woodrow Wilson, whose $5 membership check was dated September 11, 1913.

In 1919, a young lieutenant colonel who was on the verge of quitting the army decided at the last minute to join a 297-man convoy leaving Washington bound for San Francisco along the Lincoln Highway — "partly for a lark and partly to learn," Dwight Eisenhower later wrote in his memoirs. The convoy was designed to test the military response to a worst-case scenario: foreign occupation. Leading it in a white touring Packard was not the colonel-in-command but the field secretary of the Lincoln Highway Association and its chief evangelist, Henry C. Ostermann, who had been barnstorming the country on the Lincoln Highway almost continuously for years, holding hundreds of meetings annually with community leaders and newspaper editors to promote the highway's coming glory and offer small towns a chance to be part of something big and exciting. The idea for the convoy came to Ostermann after the United States entered World War I, as he helped move men and supplies from the hinterlands to the ports, since the army couldn't find its way through its own land. The Lincoln Highway, he realized, was a critical element of national defense, and a convoy across it would be a public relations bonanza for both the association and the army.

Three months before New York City held a ticker-tape parade for General John J. Pershing and twenty-five thousand returning soldiers, Ostermann and the army began what was effectively a two-month parade over thirty-three hundred miles, complete with a film crew and a fifteen-member marching band, sponsored by the Goodyear Tire and Rubber Company. The convoy offered communities the opportunity to see and cheer conquering young heroes, stirring up more excitement than a traveling circus. Local leaders hung bunting, rehearsed bands, organized receptions, wrote speeches, and planned dances, sometimes encouraging men to bring two dates, the soldiers needing dance partners, too.

"The old convoy had started me thinking about good, two-lane highways," Eisenhower later wrote, explaining his support for a federal interstate highway system — and he had plenty to think about. A summary of the army's after-action report painted a grim picture of the Lincoln Highway's condition: "It frequently was necessary to pull and push the vehicles by man-power over wide areas of gumbo mud in the central states and across the desert lands of the far west, for many hours at a time." The army concluded that the Lincoln Highway, six years after its dedication, "existed largely in the imagination and on paper."

And so it still does.

The Lincoln Highway has always been more a vision than a road. And like the Mississippi River it crosses, its path was never fixed. It shifted various times in the years following its inception, and it has continued to adapt to the changing landscape around it. The only thing set in stone on the Lincoln Highway is the spirit that envisioned it as an invitation to discovery, an offer of adventure, an affirmation of freedom, an appeal to unity, and a call to action, all wrapped together and shot out of a cannon, with no one knowing precisely where it would land but all confident it would aid the nation's advance. And so it did, too well for its own good. By 1925, national support for building numbered highways threatened to erase the first transcontinental route and the most famous road in America. "The government, so far as has been within its power, has obliterated the Lincoln Highway from the memory of man," wrote a bitter Henry Joy, who considered the highway to be "the greatest thing I ever did in my life," even as large parts of it remained unpaved.

On September 1, 1928, eight months after the Lincoln Highway Association disbanded, thousands of Boy Scouts who lived along the route dug holes and planted twenty-four hundred concrete posts, each weighing 220 pounds and standing about four feet high, and each displaying Lincoln's profile set in bronze above a letter *L* emblazoned in red, white, and blue, the colors helping drivers to spot the posts. Six years after the dedication of the Greek temple in Washington, these small Lincoln memorials appeared in hundreds of American communities, paid by for by the association in one of its final acts. They were both guideposts that marked the route and gravestones that marked the end of the association, but not the death of the highway, which continued to find its way into songs, radio programs, TV shows, movies, and novels.

The idea that has always underlain the Lincoln Highway — that we will be a stronger, more unified nation if we are connected to one another through personal interaction and experience — survives, because it is still true. The association's first slogan, *See America First*, played to patriotism at a time when it was faster, easier, and cheaper for those on the Atlantic coast to visit Paris by steamer than California by car and when few Americans had seen much of their vast homeland. Today, as airplanes and interstates render much of America invisible to travelers, as Democrats buy political books to understand places in "flyover country" they don't visit, as Republicans watch cable news hosts turn big cities into hellish caricatures, the Lincoln Highway represents an alternative route — one that brings us face-to-face with both the beauty and the brutality of our shared heritage and the ambition and freedom that have shaped it, with casualties left by the roadside that are too burdensome to carry, too big to bury, and too important to ignore.

Let's get going.

— 3 —

Lighting Out

Times Square, 8:00 A.M. Billboards flash but there are no tourists here, no souvenir sellers, no street dancers, no portrait artists, no comedy club hawkers, no cartoon character hustlers, no one ranting and raving, no one rushing and shoving, no cops on horseback, no scammers handing out CDs, not even the Naked Cowboy. It would be wonderful if it weren't so awful.

A lone hot dog vendor, a Latino immigrant, stands under a Sabrett umbrella.

"How's business?" I ask.

"Not good."

Not surprising. Even before the pandemic, who's buying a hot dog at this hour? But he has bills to pay, and there's nothing to be gained by staying home. "I'll take the special," I say — two dogs and a bottled water for $7. Having a dirty-water dog for breakfast in Times Square somehow seems like a fitting way to begin the journey. The first bite reveals otherwise — it's lukewarm at best. I'm hungry enough to keep eating. Laurel is not.

Walking across the first block of the Lincoln Highway on 42nd Street, we pass under the marquee of the New Victory Theater, the oldest operating theater in the city, opened in 1900 by Oscar Hammerstein, whose grandson (Oscar II) would write the musicals that made Broadway, some of them shining a spotlight on racism and injustice, especially *Showboat* and *South Pacific.*

When the pandemic darkened Broadway, the New Victory had been hosting Step Afrika's *Drumfolk*, a show inspired by the Stono Rebellion, a failed slave uprising outside Charleston, South Carolina, in 1739. Today the theater marquee reads, "Black Lives Matter."

Walking to Eighth Avenue, we pass no other people, save three men drinking a case of Keystone Light beer. Given the breakfast I just had, I'm in no position to judge.

We reach the Port Authority Bus Terminal, where my parents met in 1971 for a dinner outing with mutual friends. After the Port Authority became a magnet for prostitution and drug dealing, when people would ask my mother where she met my father, she would cheerfully reply, "Port Authority!" It never occurred to any of us that they met on the Lincoln Highway, but this will be my first road trip to the west since they packed my sister and me into our Volkswagen Vanagon for a camping tour of national parks.

We continue across 42nd Street through Hell's Kitchen, past the Tenth Avenue headquarters of Ironworkers Local 580, whose members performed heroic work during rescue and recovery efforts after 9/11, many of them developing severe health problems from the air they breathed. Downtown, the names of all who were killed are now being announced — "so many names," wrote Billy Collins in a poem ("The Names") that I have long kept affixed to my refrigerator, "there is barely room on the walls of the heart."

The annual reading of the names is a way to honor the cry that went up in the aftermath of the attacks, "Never forget," which carries an echo of William Faulkner's truth: "The past is never dead. It's not even past." And since we are forced to carry the past with us, we shrink its burdens down to a more tolerable size, sanding off the sharp edges that would otherwise jab at our anger, depression, loneliness, and guilt. We tuck what is left under our coats, revealing only occasional glimpses of it to others, often while exaggerating its bright spots or using humor to lighten its dark ones, the beginning of memory's metamorphosis into myth.

Approaching Eleventh Avenue, a FedEx warehouse sits on the site where Senator Daniel Patrick Moynihan once lived above the bar his mother opened and operated, back when the Irish of Hell's Kitchen helped stir the melting pot. Young Pat poured drinks for the longshoremen who would wander over from the docks on the Hudson River. Laurel and I are there now ourselves, boarding a ferry to Weehawken, New Jersey, just like the early Lincoln Highway travelers did, and back to Charley.

Laurel hasn't driven Charley yet and wisely decides not to start on

Jersey's high-trafficked roads. She navigates as we pass through Hoboken, a few blocks from where Francis Albert Sinatra Jr. came into the world. One of his hits, from 1946, is the perfect song to send us on our way: "The House I Live In," written by Abel Meeropol, a son of Jewish immigrants who fled Russia's anti-Semitic pogroms.

What is America to me? A name, a map, the flag I see,
a certain word "democracy" — What is America to me?

To combat anti-Semitism after World War II, B'nai B'rith, the Anti-Defamation League, and RKO Pictures turned the song into a short film starring Sinatra, in which he defends a Jewish boy under attack from his peers. But Meeropol was unhappy that the film excluded the verses he wrote promoting racial tolerance and challenging segregation. Other singers, including Paul Robeson and bluesman Josh White, made sure to include them.

The house I live in, my neighbors white and black
The people who just came here, or from generations back . . .
The words of old Abe Lincoln, of Jefferson and Paine,
Of Washington and Douglass, and the task that still remains

The task that still remains has not changed: to create a more perfect union, more closely aligned with the truths expressed in the Declaration of Independence, as self-evident as they are contested. Each generation engages in a struggle over how to accomplish the task, with each side always seeing itself on the right side of history, even while often failing to learn from it. As we pass the riverfront bluffs where Vice President Aaron Burr shot and killed Alexander Hamilton in an 1803 duel, we can see the truth in the old saying that history doesn't repeat itself, but it does often rhyme.

Earlier in the summer, Lin-Manuel Miranda, who wrote the blockbuster musical *Hamilton*, took flak from critics who charged him with white-washing the founding fathers' involvement in slavery and called for a boycott of the film version of *Hamilton*. With #CancelHamilton trending, Miranda responded with a humility rarely seen on social media, in the spirit of one of his characters, Washington: "All the criticisms are valid. The sheer tonnage of complexities & failings of these people I couldn't get. Or wrestled with but cut. I took 6 years and fit as much as I could in a 2.5 hour musical. Did my best. It's all fair game."

Musical theater is not a field that lends itself to historical precision, and few seemed to mind that Miranda took other liberties with the characters and plot — the whole show is premised on the suspension of disbelief. We don't expect playwrights and songwriters to be professional historians, but the art they create is a central part of the way the past is understood and remembered, and so criticism, as Miranda acknowledged, is fair play. But cancel his show from stage and screen?

It has become harder to have disagreements without one side elevating the matter to a question of high moral principle that requires an all-or-nothing, life-or-death resolution — not unlike the way men of Hamilton's era viewed their personal honor. Attempting to get someone "canceled" — ostracized, disgraced, silenced — is the modern equivalent of challenging someone to a duel, only without needing any courage, since it involves no personal risk; without meeting your opponent one-on-one, since a mob is always invited; and without allowing the person you have accused to take the first shot (as Burr did with Hamilton, or so most historians believe). Miranda's response to his critics was not unlike Hamilton's, who may have intentionally fired an errant shot and then stood by to accept his fate, hoping decency would triumph over bloodlust. The social media mob, never much for self-reflection, failed to recognize itself in the role of Burr — thankfully, their volleys only grazed Miranda — even as Miranda's Burr saw the error of his ways.

I was too young and blind to see.
I should've known, I should've known
The world was wide enough for both Hamilton and me

Burr's murder of Hamilton helped make dueling less socially acceptable but did not end it. Lincoln escaped numerous brushes with duels, sometimes with the mediation of friends, but at least once through his own contrition. In 1840, when he found himself challenged to a duel, he managed to defuse the argument by writing a letter expressing regret for his words while insisting he meant no offense — an example of how the prospect of dueling was an incentive for tempering accusations and, once hurled, offering words of conciliation. One doesn't need to wish dueling back to recognize, as people say things online that they would never say to someone's face, the steep cost of losing mechanisms for tempering the rage of righteousness and enforcing civility and rapprochement.

The Lincoln Highway winds through downtown Jersey City to Lincoln Park and a roadside statue of Abe by James Earle Fraser, who also designed the buffalo nickel. I've come here a few times on Abe's birthday for the annual commemoration held by the Jersey City Lincoln Association, formed in 1867, the nation's oldest. In 2017, a rabbi offered a prayer that Americans would "put aside our differences." Just getting people to listen to each other has been the stuff of miracles.

Abe is sitting on a bench, slightly slouched and gazing downward deep in thought — *Mystic Lincoln*, Fraser named it. This is the Lincoln who bore on his shoulders the weight of an endless war, the fate of a nation that began with such promise, and the loss of two young sons to disease. He nearly lost a third here in Jersey City, when his son Robert fell between train cars and was pulled to safety by, incredibly, Edwin Booth, brother to John Wilkes. To stand before it is to feel a bit of the sadness that Lincoln suffered much of his life — "melancholy dript from him as he walked," his law partner William Herndon wrote. At the base of the statue is the famous phrase Lincoln spoke at Cooper Union — "let us have faith that right makes might" — and also the note of humility that followed it: "to do our duty *as we understand it*."

Jersey City mayor Steve Fulop kindly agreed to meet me here. On a shaded park bench, he tells me his 9/11 story: He was twenty-four years old and working in Lower Manhattan at Goldman Sachs, with a lucrative career ahead of him. But as a descendant of Holocaust survivors — the Nazis sent thirty-five of his relatives to Auschwitz, twenty-eight of whom did not make it out alive — the attacks triggered a sense of duty to serve, and he enlisted in the Marine Corps. With two master's degrees, he could have entered as an officer. He's grateful he chose not to. "I was exposed to a lot of people that I would never have interacted with, from different backgrounds," he tells me. "There were some people in my boot camp that never met a Jewish guy before."

The military is still a force for breaking down racial and ethnic prejudices, and Jersey City has seen more than its share. In the hours after the 9/11 attacks, rumors spread that a handful of Muslims here celebrated on rooftops. There was no evidence of it, but the claim has survived. "I watched in

Jersey City, New Jersey," Donald Trump said in 2015, "where thousands of people were cheering as that building was coming down." Fulop's administration investigated the claim — "patently false" and "totally fabricated," he says. But where prejudice, bias, and suspicion exist, evidence is secondary to belief — and those beliefs, once formed, are hard to dislodge. The local government just to the south, Bayonne, spent years blocking a mosque from being built, until a federal lawsuit finally cleared the way in 2018.

"We had a similar situation," says Fulop. "We have one of the largest Coptic communities in the United States. It is similar to the Orthodox Jewish community: They dress differently, they look differently. They were building a church on a property that was desolate and barren, and they had pretty fierce community pushback. We pushed it through, because I thought it was on the right side."

It was the same way when the ultra-Orthodox Jewish community was moving in. "A lot of the types of things that people were saying, they weren't anti-Semitic," he says, "but if you listen to the rhetoric, you could hear an undercurrent." And when people get swept up in those kinds of undercurrents, no one is safe. Only months earlier, two black residents in Jersey City were charged with killing four people, including a police officer, in a kosher grocery store, after killing a Jewish cabdriver several days earlier. Outside the grocery store, they left a pipe bomb in a van that could have killed many more had it detonated.

Nationally, violent hate crimes have risen in recent years, and Fulop worries that the undercurrents are being normalized in ways that will be hard to reverse. Yet his more pressing day-to-day worry is about what happened after 9/11: good people getting taken in by false information. He tells me a story to illustrate his concern, about a police shooting that had occurred days earlier.

"Immediately you start to see on social media: unarmed boy shot in the back on Martin Luther King Drive. Lots of posts and retweets." He held a press conference to dispel the false information by describing what they knew: the man was an adult, he had a gun, and he was shot in the hand. It didn't matter. "That narrative with the unarmed boy still spread until the next day. Yes, we're in a moment where we're having a conversation around policing nationally and that's healthy, but it doesn't mean that every time the police use force it's unjustified or irresponsible. How people consume information is very dangerous today, and what they believe as a result of what they consume is very dangerous. That can ultimately have a meaningful impact in destroying our system of government, because there's so much distrust out there based on misinformation."

Falling for misinformation is a bipartisan problem. Each side can see it in the other, but not in themselves. There's a genetic reason for this: Our brains are wired for survival, and survival involves identifying with a group and sticking with it. We want to believe those we sympathize with, so we give them the benefit of the doubt, applying less scrutiny to their claims than those made by other groups — about whom we are ready to believe the worst. So it has always been, but never have we all had media platforms to amplify and broadcast these tendencies at all hours of the day and night.

"I believe we need nothing so much as to get rid of unjust suspicions of one another," Lincoln wrote in 1858. He was urging party unity while seeking an Illinois Senate seat, but the same sentiment would hold true for the whole country two years — and nearly two centuries — later.

Under the Pulaski Skyway we are greeted by a giant statue of Paul Bunyan — boots, beard, blue jeans, and red shirt — holding a roll of carpet advertising a local carpet company. The lumberjack-turned-carpet-salesman is a fitting gatekeeper to this journey, opening the door to a land where tall tales and folklore are entangled with commerce, though usually in ways that obscure rather than highlight the relationship.

After crossing the Hackensack and Passaic Rivers, I miss the turn toward Newark. There is no GPS route for the Lincoln Highway, and the map the highway association posted on its website is not compatible with Google Maps. Making matters worse for Laurel and me, it would be hard to say which of us has the weaker sense of direction, although both of us would quickly develop an opinion on the matter, and at various points both of us would seem to be correct. As we discuss what turn to take with heavy traffic around us, we have our first moment of tension. Whoever said getting lost is half the fun of a road trip has never driven an RV through the outskirts of Newark.

Laurel gets us back on course and into downtown Newark, where we stop at the Essex County Courthouse to see another Lincoln statue. As with Fraser's Lincoln in Jersey City, he is seated on a bench, but at ground level and big enough for others to sit beside him. Many have, especially kids, irking Abe's son Robert, who complained that it was being "used as a playground by the hoodlum children of the neighborhood."

At its dedication on Memorial Day 1911, thirty-five thousand people came for pomp and circumstance that included a speech by Theodore Roosevelt. "There never was a great cause more absolutely embodied in a great man than the cause of union and freedom," Roosevelt said, "and now I speak in no momentary fervor, but as expressing what I am sure will be the absolute verdict of history." History, however, confers few absolute verdicts, because moral laws are not static. Yet once a verdict is cast in bronze or set in stone — whether for Lincoln or Roosevelt, Robert E. Lee or Jefferson Davis — it is difficult to alter. In this case, the sculptor himself, Gutzon Borglum, complicates the statue. In addition to sculpting Mount Rushmore, he joined the Ku Klux Klan to carve a monumental paean to the Confederacy in Georgia's Stone Mountain. In Newark, even a courthouse monument to liberty and equality carries a reminder of racial oppression.

Unlike New York and other cities, Newark's George Floyd protests remained peaceful and orderly, a credit to its residents and mayor, Ras Baraka. More than any other city in America, Newark knows how destructive riots can be. The shadow of its epoch-making 1967 riots still lingers over its streets: twenty-six dead, more than a thousand injured, and 889 businesses damaged or looted, a tragedy that accelerated white flight and made Newark synonymous with urban failure and abandonment. Lincoln has sat through it all as witness, untouched by the riots and unmoved by white flight, still offering us a seat beside him, as C. K. Williams wrote in his poem, "newark black: 1940–1954."

The finally unrecognizable city, done in by us all.
Only the ever benevolent Lincoln, unblackened
by time or pollution, emblem of promise and hope,
patiently waited, patiently waits.

Mayor Baraka won election in 2014 only months after the death of his father, Amiri, the revolution-seeking writer and poet who merged beat generation cool with the hot rage of racial injustice and Marxism. Amiri was one of black America's leading voices, yet his legacy will forever be tied up with the poem he wrote after 9/11, "Somebody Blew Up America," which suggested Israelis knew of the terrorist attacks in advance.

Who knew the World Trade Center was gonna get bombed
Who told 4000 Israeli workers at the Twin Towers

To stay home that day
Why did Sharon stay home?

The poem was meant to be a broadside against the oppression of all groups, written in his incendiary style. But it trafficked in the same kind of conspiracy theorizing that has given rise to QAnon, turns mass shootings into hoaxes, and inspires the kinds of hate that left four people dead at a kosher grocery store. Nevertheless, Baraka remained admired on the left. He continued to speak at universities, the body of his work has not been thrown overboard, and the nation is stronger for both. The danger to society lies not in artists, sculptors included, who are tainted by hateful ideologies, but in audiences who can't recognize and condemn the hate without trying to silence them and censor their entire body of work.

Driving off from the courthouse we pass Newark Airport, where United Flight 93 departed on 9/11 bound for our destination, San Francisco. It was renamed Newark Liberty to honor the victims of the attacks, but beyond saying its name and reading their names, do we condemn the hatred the hijackers held in their hearts when it appears in different forms in our own parties? And do we defend the freedom the hijackers hated when we find someone's speech despicable?

Never forget. It is easier said than done.

Somehow I make another wrong turn. Lost again. Laurel looks at Google Maps, checks it against the Lincoln Highway map, and gets us back on course. She's getting down a system that won't lack for use.

The sun is descending as we pull into Rockingham Historic Site, the farmhouse outside Princeton where George Washington lived during the final months of the Revolutionary War. I had invited the mayor of neighboring Montgomery Township, Sadaf Jaffer, to meet me here, and she kindly accepted. Her mother is from Pakistan, her father from Yemen, and she's the first Muslim woman to serve as mayor of a US city. She's just come from a September 11 memorial service at her local firehouse. At a picnic table looking out at a field of solar panels glowing in the setting sun, I ask her about her 9/11 experience.

"I was a freshman at Georgetown University," she says. "Obviously shaken to the core, crying every day. And it was in those days after September 11 that I attended the Catholic service, the Orthodox service, the Muslim service, the Jewish service. Maybe the methodology that I'm using for Montgomery Mosaic was born out of that experience."

Montgomery Mosaic is an initiative she started to bring people together to watch documentaries about various forms of bias and hatred. "I would try to hold it at different houses of worship, and I would always ask how many people are in this space for the first time — usually somewhere between 70 to 90 percent of the people would raise their hands. And even for me, I hadn't been inside the synagogue. I hadn't been inside all of the different churches, and now I feel comfortable in all those spaces. I know those are communities that would protect me or help me if I needed it."

I ask her whether she has faced any bias because of her background and religion. "My opponents made flyers or campaign ads that said that I was dangerous and extreme," she says of her campaign. "When my opponent had a concession post on Facebook, the first comment on it was, 'I was born in this country and some Indian is going to tell me what to do? You can't fix stupid.' So it is an undercurrent."

Undercurrent, the same word Fulop had used. Jaffer says the bigotry has gotten much worse in recent years. "In 2001, we had a president who said, 'This is not about Islam — Islam is a religion of peace,' and research does show that political leadership makes a difference. If political leaders are using hateful rhetoric, then we see a rise in hate crimes."

But she isn't just blaming politicians. "I attribute it to the Islamophobia industry — a whole bunch of people whose main goal is to demonize Islam and scare the American public through books, shows, movies. There's been twenty years of people spreading misinformation, so a lot of people are convinced that they know more about Islam than I do, as someone who has a PhD in Islamic studies. And it's very, very hard to correct misinformation."

Washington himself felt the sting of misinformation, when forged letters appeared during the Revolutionary War showing him expressing fealty to the king. The letters haunted him for two decades, and on the final day of his presidency he wrote a letter rebutting them. The conversation with Jaffer puts me in the mind of another letter Washington wrote, to the Hebrew congregation of Newport, Rhode Island, when he declared that the new nation "gives to bigotry no sanction, to persecution no assistance" — and in a show of respect for Jews, he quoted Hebrew scripture: "Every one shall sit in safety under his own vine and fig tree, and there shall be none to make him afraid."

I ask Jaffer a question that I plan to put to others along the trip: What binds the country together? "An aspiration," she says. "That's what I tell my students and community members. When we have difficult incidents, that's what we have to hold on to, and we have to keep struggling. That's what it is to be American. The aspiration for a better tomorrow."

She's expressed a central Lincolnian idea, that America is a land of opportunity, not only for economic advancement but also for national progress on the great moral questions facing the world. For Lincoln, aspiration was part of our national identity, and there are no great aspirations without setbacks and failures. As Newark's mayor-turned-senator Cory Booker has said, "If this country hasn't broken your heart, then you don't love her enough."

As night falls, we arrive at Princeton University and park illegally near a 9/11 memorial garden. In a quad with chirping crickets, we meet our friend Owen, a sophmore, and a few of his classmates. I tell them a little about the Lincoln Highway, and given Woodrow Wilson's connection to it, I ask what they think of the university's decision, in the wake of the George Floyd protests, to remove his name from its School of Public and International Affairs.

Wilson grew up in Georgia, and his earliest memory was of hearing that Lincoln had been elected and there would be war. As a historian, he labored to justify the Confederate cause. "There is nothing to apologize for in the past of the South," he said in an 1896 speech, "absolutely nothing to apologize for." The 1915 film *Birth of a Nation* opened with quotes from his book *A History of the American People,* and, like the book, the film turned history upside down — showing black men stealing elections, disenfranchising whites, attacking whites, and sexually assaulting white women. When Wilson watched a special screening of the film in the White House, boosting its publicity, he saw his own words appear on screen: "The white men were roused by a mere instinct of self-preservation, until at last there had sprung into existence a great Ku Klux Klan, a veritable empire of the South, to protect the Southern country." It was not just 9/11 terrorists who hated the fullness of American freedom. *Never forget.*

Owen and his friends all supported removing Wilson's name. Every generation gets to choose its own heroes, and replacing the name of a Confederate apologist who resegregated the federal workforce, failed to address widespread violence against black communities, and never showed any significant evolution in his thinking isn't a case of erasing history but of understanding it and deciding which parts to celebrate.

Wilson is hardly the only historical figure we will encounter on this journey to ignite a fierce debate over the honors previous generations have bestowed upon them. Americans hold strong opinions on these honors and monuments without a common basis for judging them, leaving each side to accuse the other of either whitewashing grievous mistakes or "presentism," holding historical figures to current morality standards. I believe we can bring more light to these debates by asking two questions.

First, why was the honor bestowed? Was it to hold aloft acts and principles we still admire? And second, did the honoree, on the whole, help advance the nation toward a more perfect union and its promise of equality — or fight those leading the way? The questions are inspired by Frederick Douglass, who used the same basic method in evaluating Lincoln. In dedicating a statue of Lincoln in DC honoring emancipation, Douglass explained that judging Lincoln must be done in the context of the public opinion he faced. "Viewed from the genuine abolition ground," he said, "Mr. Lincoln seemed tardy, cold, dull, and indifferent; but measuring him by the sentiment of his country, a sentiment he was bound as a statesman to consult, he was swift, zealous, radical, and determined."

Wilson passes the first test, since Princeton honored him not for his neo-Confederate views but for his role in winning World War I and adopting a variety of progressive ideals. But he fails the second, and badly. Not only was he far behind public sentiment on matters of race, but he also dragged the country backward. I'm not sorry to see his name removed. Other public figures, as we will see down the road, present more difficult cases.

For all the public attention paid to removing Wilson's name, Owen and his friends don't mistake it for actual change, and they are skeptical that the activism following George Floyd's murder will last. "It's so easy now for social justice issues to become pop culture," says one of his buddies, Kakuyon. "It was literally cool to be like, 'Black Lives Matter.' And that's the only reason why it has that much momentum behind it. But I think burnout's a real thing. And I don't think anybody's really passionate about this stuff long-term." Owen agrees: "With social media, you become very passionate about certain issues. And then your mind just travels in the complete other direction as soon as you see something else, as soon as there's a new spark to the fire." And on their phones, sparks are always flying.

Owen's friend Mara talks about reposting political messages on social media and the pressure and judgment it entails: "Someone will say either, 'That's tokenism — you're just posting that to be performatory' — or if you don't post it, people will be like, 'You didn't post it, you don't care about this.' And there's no in between. It's so hard."

I ask them how optimistic they are about the country's future on a scale of one to ten, with ten being extremely optimistic and one being extremely pessimistic. I was expecting answers in the six to eight range. A five wouldn't have shocked me. Kakuyon and Owen say two. Mara puts it at three. Another friend, Ahmad, is an immigrant. I expect he'll have a higher answer, but no: He's a three. Maybe their answers are not unusual for students at the most elite colleges, but I'm not ready to dismiss them so quickly. Low expectations can be a self-fulfilling prophecy, breeding tolerance for failure and leading to a loss of faith in the American project and the institutions that sustain it. Their answers, while depressing me, affirm the purpose of our journey.

It's late and time for bed — we just need somewhere to park. There are no campgrounds nearby, the local church I had emailed to ask if we could park overnight didn't respond, and the Princeton security guard standing nearby may start asking questions. So we try every RVer's plan B: the Walmart parking lot. It seemed like a safe backup, but we arrive to find the store permanently closed and two guys outside it drinking. Fortunately, a Lowe's is nearby, and a security guard gives us a thumbs-up. I never thought I'd be so happy to be sleeping outside a strip mall.

As we get ready for bed, Laurel notices that the refrigerator has shut off. Uh-oh. She attempts to get it back on by pressing its buttons, but no luck. As I begin thinking about sour milk and a ruined breakfast, Laurel flips through the owner's manual and pinpoints the problem: "The gas line must not be connected," she says. But the manual offers no clues on connecting it, and we are both exhausted and frustrated. We give up and go to bed. Whatever tomorrow's breakfast turns out to be, it can't be worse than today's.

—4—

Liberty Bells

We are heading for Philadelphia today, grateful that New Jersey and New York are not among the eighteen states whose travelers are required to self-quarantine for fourteen days upon crossing into Pennsylvania. More than a thousand people died of Covid yesterday, but how many visitors from those eighteen states are following the guidance? And how many would-be visitors is it keeping away? In both cases, probably precious few. In a land of liberty, lockdowns have their limits.

Before leaving Princeton, I text Charley's previous owner, Kim, about the refrigerator. She tells us to light the stove to pull gas into the line. When the stove won't ignite, she suggests starting the generator to push gas into the line and using a match to draw it out — *presto*! We are now cooking — and cooling — with gas.

In downtown Trenton, the old Roebling wire plant, closed since 1974, still sits partly vacant, as do other buildings. The boast that local officials posted in 1935 on a bridge over the Delaware River in big block letters — "TRENTON MAKES THE WORLD TAKES" — has long hung like an albatross over the entrance to the city, now one of the poorest in the region. Yet innovative industry remains here: A company called TerraCycle is trying to take what the world discards and repurpose it, with the goal of making a zero-waste economy profitable.

Today TerraCycle is hosting the fifteenth annual Jersey Fresh Jam, a graffiti and hip-hop festival organized by aerosol artist Leon "Rain" Rainbow. When we arrive, painters are covering the exterior walls of TerraCycle's warehouse with brightly colored designs as Biz Markie's "Nobody Beats the Biz" plays:

> *. . . the rhythm, that is what I give 'em*
> *Reagan is the Pres but I voted for Shirley Chisholm*

By promoting local talent and attracting national MCs like Cappadonna from the Wu-Tang Clan — the group's name was inspired by a late-night visit to a kung fu theater at the start of the Lincoln Highway — Rain has put Trenton on the map among graffiti artists. "People know," he says of the talent here. "Like, 'Oh, Trenton, they got their own jam. Cats out there know how to paint.' "

Rain's art mostly steers clear of politics, but after participating in a peaceful George Floyd protest that descended into looting and violence, he had an idea. With donated paint from Sherwin-Williams, a grant from a local nonprofit, and permission from the city, he invited artists to turn boarded-up windows into painted statements about the city's resilience and resolve: "Spread Love," "Uplift Each Other," "Trenton Strong," "Old Ways Won't Open New Doors." "What we try to do," he says, "is just spread positive messaging." Graffiti is usually a sign of decay and disorder, but Rain has turned it into a visible rejection of them, highlighting the pride that he and others have in the city and the hope for the future they seek to inspire in others.

We see some of the painted plywood boards on our way to the statehouse where Lincoln addressed the legislature in 1861, playing to his audience by speaking of the inspiration he drew as a child from reading about Washington's attack on Trenton. "I recollect thinking then, boy even though I was," he said, "that there must have been something more than common that those men struggled for; that something even more than National Independence; that something that held out a great promise to all the people of the world to all time to come."

Lincoln had just seen the painting *Washington Crossing the Delaware* in New York, where a print hung at his hotel. The artist, Emanuel Leutze, was a German immigrant who painted it with the hope that Germans — living under divided rule in a collection of weak independent states — would see the power of Washington's unifying leadership and follow in America's steps. The painting became wildly popular in both Germany and America, and no one has ever cared that the flag flying in Washington's boat didn't exist at the time, or that his heroic posture is a preposterous exaggeration. What matters are the feelings it inspires: pride, faith, hope. Leon Rainbow is working in the tradition of Emanuel Leutze.

Across the Delaware River, just inland from where William Penn established a plantation worked by enslaved men and women, is Levittown, built at the dawn of the suburban age by the nation's largest home builder after World War II, Levitt & Sons. They turned fifty-seven hundred acres of broccoli and spinach farms into 17,300 homes, each furnished with the latest appliances and conveniences, and each within a five-minute walk of a park, recreation center, or school. "The Best Planned Community in America," they called it, made possible by the Federal Housing Administration's mortgage-backed guarantees that opened homeownership to millions of Americans, but not blacks, who were denied admission to white neighborhoods and denied mortgages in black ones.

"As a Jew, I have no room in my mind or heart for racial prejudice," William Levitt said. "But I have come to know that if we sell one house to a Negro family, then 90 to 95 percent of our white customers will not buy into the community. This is their attitude, not ours." At one of his first developments on Long Island, he also locked out Jews, despite being Jewish himself. Business was business.

In 1957, Daisy and William Myers, a young black couple who had just welcomed their third child, moved into a Levittown home with help from a Jewish family, the Weschlers. They were greeted by two hundred protestors who threw rocks that shattered their front window. Two days later, five hundred people gathered at a Veterans of Foreign Wars hall to find a way to force the Myerses out, even though William had served in the army during World War II. A cross burned in front of a local elementary school named in honor of Walt Disney, who had attended its dedication. Residents clashed with police and spoke of starting a KKK chapter. And a man rented an empty house behind the Myers's and turned it into a clubhouse, flying a Confederate flag, walking the dog he called "Nigger," and blaring "Dixie" and other songs intended to drive the Myerses out.

"We never considered moving away," Daisy recalled forty years later, and for all she endured and risked, her reflections focused on the neighbors, friends, and local churches who had supported them. "I think of all the beautiful people who came to help us out," she said, "and I throw out of my mind all the other stuff."

Congress finally passed the Fair Housing Act in 1968, banning racial discrimination in the selling or renting of properties. By that time, however, another generation of black Americans had been denied a chance to buy the newest and nicest homes — and watched as their neighbors moved out when they moved in, as Langston Hughes wrote in his poem, "Restrictive Covenants."

> *When I move / into a neighborhood / Folks fly.*
> *Even every foreigner / That can move, moves. / Why?*

Today, Levittown remains about 90 percent white. Racial and ethnic segregation in housing persists so stubbornly here and across America in part because of the growth in home prices that are reinforced by zoning regulations, clustering people by wealth and skin color. Americans are more racially segregated today than we were in 1990, and segregated housing brings segregated schools, segregated business districts, segregated community groups, and just about everything else, too — but not quite everything.

A few miles away is a land of make-believe built on the promise of integration and equality: Sesame Place, the children's theme park based on *Sesame Street*, whose creators aimed to portray a color-blind community, giving puppets the colors of the rainbow. To help poor city kids relate, they set it on an urban street with the action happening on an old brownstone stoop next to a garbage can inhabited by a character who showed that it was okay not to be happy all the time. "You'd be a grouch too if you lived in a trash can," Oscar says — an implicit endorsement of the need for better housing to lift spirits. The show featured regular kids, not actors, and the interracial cast was rare for television — so rare that Mississippi initially banned the show. Black celebrities made regular appearances, including Nina Simone singing:

> *Oh what a lovely precious dream*
> *To be young, gifted and Black*

Since the theme park is one of the few public venues that's open, we decide to stop by, and I'm struck by the diversity of the families. I had thought that, since the area is predominantly white, the crowd would be, too. That it's highly diverse is heartening, but discouraging, too. Another generation of children is growing up in an environment where integration exists mostly in a fantasyland, bonding them over little more than fictional characters they will soon outgrow.

Nine miles south, we drive through Linconia, founded by a white farmer in 1923 to give black city dwellers a chance to purchase their own land and homes. It's named for the highway it sat beside and the vision of the man who inspired it. Residents here faced down burning crosses and banks that wouldn't lend, building 125 homes on eighty acres. A generation later, as Levitt was blocking black buyers from his community, a developer named Morris Milgram purchased fifty acres adjoining Linconia and set out to build the nation's first interracial suburban community, Concord Park. It was not an easy sell. Whites were "terrified" of living in a majority-black neighborhood, he said, and so he tried to keep a white majority of 55 percent. Over the years, he developed what he called Milgram's Law, which still holds true in most of the country: "The consumer who fails to state his or her determination to seek housing in such a way as to end segregation will nearly always find housing that perpetuates segregation." Milgram understood, as Owen and his friends at Princeton are seeing, that progressive views on race do not change society, no matter how publicly they are aired. Only direct personal action does.

At a Wawa, I fill the tank while Laurel buys her favorite menu item: a cheddar cheese stuffed pretzel, enough to tide us over until dinner. As we arrive in Philadelphia and circle the country's largest city hall, we are running on low-sulfur diesel and empty calories.

When Lincoln came to Philadelphia from Trenton en route to his first inauguration, he visited the old statehouse where the Declaration of Independence and Constitution were debated and adopted. In a brief speech that fell on Washington's birthday, he touched on that "something" from the Revolution he had alluded to in Trenton: "I have often inquired of myself, what great principle or idea it was that kept this confederacy so long together. It was not the mere matter of the separation of the colonies from the mother land; but something in that Declaration giving liberty, not alone to the people of this country, but hope to the world for all future time."

Liberty. The word appears only once in the Declaration of Independence, but in its most important phrase, connecting "life" and "the pursuit of happiness" and giving each meaning. In the Constitution, too, it makes a lone appearance and again carries outsized importance, as part of the preamble describing why "We the people" are establishing a government: "to secure the Blessings of Liberty for ourselves and our Posterity." Here in Philadelphia, Lincoln said the nation had been held together by liberty and what it promised: "that in due time the weights should be lifted from the shoulders of all men, and that all should have an equal chance." For Lincoln, liberty and equality were as inseparable as the union itself.

In the room where Lincoln spoke, the Liberty Bell was on display. It was cast to mark the fiftieth anniversary of William Penn's charter and its promise of religious freedom, but the inscription on it, taken from the King James Bible, is a reference to the jubilee tradition of freeing slaves every fifty years: "Proclaim LIBERTY throughout all the land unto all of the inhabitants thereof." The quotation inspired abolitionists to adopt it as a symbol — the first reference to a "Liberty Bell" is credited to a member of the Anti-Slavery Society, R. G. Williams — and it should have become a great symbol of emancipation and racial equality. Instead, in 1847, one of the most popular writers of the era, George Lippard, concocted a story that the bell cracked when rung on July 4, 1776, turning it into a symbol of the American Revolution. The bell likely didn't ring at all that day, since the steeple was under repair, but the myth endured. Rather than go stare at it through a glass case, we go to South Philly to hear its echo.

We have no parking plan in Philadelphia, only an idea: an ACME supermarket. Fortunately, the manager says it's fine to stay overnight so long as we are gone in the morning. We picked this ACME because it's close to the row house where Adam Weiner lives, and he has kindly agreed to open his door so I can watch one of the livestream shows he performs with Will Donnelly, the guitarist from his band, Low Cut Connie. Laurel and I stumbled across the band years ago at a club on Manhattan's Lower East Side and were taken by the barrelhouse boogie-woogie rock 'n' roll that Weiner plays with uninhibited abandon. His livestream shows have been a pandemic hit, and tonight, he kicks off his set by paying tribute to Toots Hibbert, the reggae star who died this morning, belting out "Pressure Drop," Toots's song about karma and the weight of justice coming down.

Sitting in his living room after the show, in a black T-shirt that matches his hair, Adam talks about the work he's put into building a diverse audience.

"My agent said, 'You're the only band where, when you see the line on the street outside the club, you have absolutely no clue who's inside,'" he says. "We get booked on country, Americana festivals, Pride. We've done R&B events. We have fans that are black and white." That shouldn't be remarkable, but it is.

When his talent agency asked what acts he'd like to open for on tour, he suggested Janelle Monáe. Instead, the agency tried to book him on a Kings of Leon tour playing to large arenas, an incredible opportunity. Adam declined. "They were so confused. I said, 'Let me break this down for you. The appetizer has got to taste different than the entrée. And who needs another package of white rock bands? I want to play the clubs and festivals that the hip-hop acts play in. I want to perform in front of black people, and I want my white rock 'n' roll fans to watch a hip-hop show." This week, Monáe released a new song, "Turntables," that's featured in a documentary, *All In: The Fight for Democracy*, about the long and continuing struggle for voting rights. The song merges a hip-hop foundation (turntables) with biblical verse (Ecclesiastes) to express faith in a coming change, just as Pete Seeger had done in 1959 in "Turn! Turn! Turn!"

Tables 'bout to turn turn turn
Ain't no stoppin' till they turn turn turn

Rock 'n' roll is rooted in black churches and communities, and half a century ago it seemed that music might help unite and integrate the country. Weiner talks about his parents' generation. "Motown, Stax — that was white and black kids listening to the same music," he says. "And that was white and black kids going to the same clubs, listening to the same radio station. It doesn't happen now as much. That's sad." He blames the industry but also puts some onus on artists, who are more likely to post on social media about racial justice than to do the work — and take the risks — required to build diverse audiences. Securing the blessings of liberty can't be done by virtue signaling, and what Morris Milgram said about home buyers — those who don't intentionally disrupt segregation in their own lives end up perpetuating it — applies to artists, too.

I ask him about fan reaction to his song "Look What They Did," an elegy for Atlantic City and the false promise of casinos. It references Donald Trump making money as the city falls into decline, and it includes the lines:

Little creatures get the shit end of the stick
Dark features get you shot in the head

"Ninety-five percent positive," he says. But he also heard a lot of anger and indignation. "I responded to everyone with respect, and basically said, 'I'm proud of the song, but guess what? There's room for everybody here. We're allowed to disagree on things.' That's the nature of any meeting and collection of people, whether it's religious, political, or artistic. So I said, 'If you'll stick with me, I'll stick with you. You don't have to love everything I do.'" And the response? "Great. Not in every case, but most."

I put the same question to him that I put to Mayor Jaffer: What binds us together? "America is a project that's not finished, it's not absolute — we're writing the story as we go, so of course things are fucked up all the time." He smiles. "We're always kinda workin' on it, and sometimes we're movin' forward and sometimes we're movin' back, but it's a project that demands our best efforts, our best ideas, some real care, because of what an imperfect and incomplete project it is." Like Jaffer, he's touching on a very Lincolnian idea, one that we will explore further at Gettysburg, where Lincoln referred to the nation's "unfinished work."

Adam kindly offers to share his dinner, but I promised Laurel cheesesteaks. We get one at Pat's with Cheez Whiz — "wit wiz," in the native tongue — and one with provolone at Cosmi's. The absurdity of wearing masks to protect our health while eating like there's no tomorrow is not lost on us.

Leaving Philadelphia, the Lincoln Highway follows the Lancaster Turnpike, the nation's first long-distance road constructed of stone and gravel, built in 1794 with private funds and financed through toll stations. Tracking alongside it is the Main Line, a commuter rail corridor that became synonymous with white suburban affluence, owing partly to racially restrictive covenants. There are still half a million fewer people in Philadelphia than in 1950, and since 1990, the city's white population has shrunk by one-third — Milgram's Law writ large.

We pass two colleges within three miles of each other, each its own Main Line stop and each possessing a relic that speaks to the ongoing struggle for acceptance and integration. Haverford College, founded by Quakers, houses America's first formal petition against slavery, lodged by German Quakers in Philadelphia in 1688, though nearly a century would pass before Quaker authorities issued a proclamation banning slavery. Villanova College, founded by Catholics, is home to the Sister Bell to the Liberty

Bell. Cast with the same biblical line about liberty, it hung at Independence Hall in 1776 and for half a century after, until it was sold to a nearby Catholic church, St. Augustine's. In 1844, as anti-Catholic sentiment intensified in northern cities — a year earlier, the nation's first restrictive covenant appeared outside Boston, barring home sales to "any Negro or native of Ireland" — rumors spread that Catholics wanted to remove Bibles from schools. In fact, Catholics wished only to have their children read from their own Bibles rather than the King James Version. But mobs do not stop to consider misinformation. Members of the nascent Native American Party attacked Catholic homes and set St. Augustine's ablaze, leaving at least twenty dead.

When news of the Philadelphia riot reached Springfield, Lincoln supported a resolution in the state legislature denouncing it. "*Resolved*, That the guarantee of the rights of conscience, as found in our Constitution, is most sacred and inviolable, and one that belongs no less to the Catholic, than to the Protestant." From the rubble of their church, priests saved the fragments of their cracked bell and sent them to Villanova for recasting and safekeeping.

Today, while a million people make pilgrimages to see a bell dedicated to religious tolerance, few have ever heard of the sister it lost to religious intolerance. The two ought to sit side by side.

—5—

Hold Together

"Hear Me Baby. Hold Together." That's the pandemic plea we see in downtown Wayne, Pennsylvania, on the marquee of the 1928 theater named for Anthony Wayne, the Revolutionary War general who suffered severe losses in the area. It's a line from *Star Wars*, spoken by Han Solo to his spaceship as he's being attacked by the Emperor's forces during the Galactic Civil War, fought by rebel forces to restore democratic rule. The movie is about a boy's decision to confront rather than submit to darkness, beginning a journey into self-discovery that saves the world from an evil emperor, but there was much more to it than that. "It was really about the Vietnam War," George Lucas said years later of the film he wrote and directed, which carries echoes of the descent of the Roman Republic into monarchy, "and that was the period where Nixon was trying to run for a [second] term, which got me to thinking historically about how do democracies get turned into dictatorships? Because the democracies aren't overthrown; they're given away."

Hours after we pass through Wayne, a top Trump political appointee at the Department of Health and Human Services, Michael Caputo, accuses scientists at the Centers of Disease Control of "sedition" and warns of a looming battle. "When Donald Trump refuses to stand down at the inauguration, the shooting will begin," he says. "If you carry guns, buy ammunition, ladies and gentlemen, because it's going to be hard to get."

Hear me baby. Hold together.

Down the road in Berwyn, we drive under a banner draped across the road: "We are all in this together." Five miles farther, in Malvern, we stop at the Frazer Diner to consult a map. It's one of the last of the 1930s models built by Jerry O'Mahony, whose company in Elizabeth, New Jersey, turned out about two thousand prefabricated diners between 1917 and 1952. He designed them to look and feel like train cars at a time when the height of elegant white-glove food service could be found riding the rails. His dining cars were the poor man's Pullman, and they came to be called, simply, diners, and their immigrant owners turned them into the quintessential American eating experience.

With heavy hearts, we have resolved not to eat inside any diners or restaurants. Yesterday's headlines included news from the Centers for Disease Control that going to a restaurant triples the chances of contracting Covid, which would require a fourteen-day quarantine and end our hope of reaching San Francisco by Election Day. We could order to-go, but the joy of a diner is sitting at the counter or sinking into a booth, so we exit the parking lot back onto the Lincoln and soon see another banner reading, "We are all in this together." Must be a countywide campaign, I surmise. Farther along, there's another old-fashioned ice cream shop that looks identical to the one we just passed, except it's on the opposite side of the road. *That's strange*, I say to myself. Minutes later, could it be — another Anthony Wayne Theater with the same message on the marquee?

"Oh no," I say to Laurel, "we're going back the same way we came."

"You're just realizing that?" she asks incredulously.

"Why didn't you say anything?" I ask incredulously.

"I thought you knew where you were going," she says, setting up her punch line perfectly. "My mistake."

Hear me baby. Hold together.

I pull over and turn around, annoyed, embarrassed, and feeling a bit like Roy "Wrong Way" Riegels, the University of California football player who ran the ball seventy yards into the wrong end zone in the 1929 Rose Bowl, costing his team the game. The teammate who tried to tackle him was named player of the game. I decide not to mention that to Laurel.

At a campground in Lancaster adjoining Dutch Wonderland, an amusement park along a stream feeding the Conestoga River, we hook up to water and electric for the first time since leaving New York. We'll be able to take our first showers in three days, but I haven't yet figured out the hot-water heater, so they'll have to be cold showers, which is just as well: I'm paranoid about filling up the wastewater tank, so best to be quick. At the end of it, I feel more relieved than refreshed.

Around the same time, a few miles away in downtown Lancaster, the mother of twenty-seven-year-old Ricardo Muñoz is calling the county's crisis intervention center. Her son struggles with schizophrenia and bipolar disorder, hasn't taken his medication, and is being aggressive. His sister calls 911, asking that he be taken to a hospital. Minutes later an officer arrives. Muñoz charges out the front door with a knife. The officer turns and runs. Munoz gives chase. The officer turns and fires. Muñoz collapses on the sidewalk, dead.

As word spreads, protesters gather at the downtown police station demanding answers, and as the hours pass, the crowd grows and tensions rise. People hurl objects through windows, and police fire tear gas and rubber bullets — each side blaming the other for commencing the violence.

The following morning, as a hush hovers over Lancaster's stately Victorian homes, we park near the police station, where a man named David Watkins is sitting in the same spot he had been the night before, and for the same reason: to use the free Wi-Fi from the pizza shop next door. He was there when Ricardo Muñoz's family and supporters arrived and demanded to talk to the police, yelling that the officer didn't have a warrant. "The officer was responding to a domestic call," David says, relaying what he had heard, "and from what I got from the family, he just took matters into his own hands. Without even showing a warrant or anything like that." That isn't what happened, but Watkins, white and middle-aged, finds it believable based on his own experience being mistreated by local police. "I don't blame these people for coming out and protesting," he says. "I don't."

I walk across the street to where four people are finishing an interview with a local television reporter. *What happened?* I ask them. "We were chanting and I feel like we had good energy," says Nicole Vasquez of the crowd, about two hundred strong. What were they chanting?

What do we want? Justice! When do we want it? Now!
No justice, no peace! Fuck the racist police!

Another woman, Minister Jerona Rokins Green, says, "We all got hit with the tear gas and that's no joke. My throat still hurt. My whole face burning. She got hit with a rubber bullet" — she points to the woman beside her, who has a large red welt on her lower leg. In June, a protester in Washington lost his eye to a pepper-ball shot. Alaak Deu, twenty-one years old, holds up a rubber bullet. "At the end of the day," he says, "who's supposed to keep their peace when they're getting shot with this? What did they expect from an angry city?"

In addition to the police station, windows were smashed at the post office and some shops, too. One of the young people arrested, a white student at nearby Franklin & Marshall College, had her bail set at $1 million. Her father told a reporter he was "completely floored. It's really just vindictive. You want to have faith in the system because it's the only one we have, and then you experience this. I understand why my daughter would protest in the first place." If it can happen to her, he now knows, it can happen to anyone. *We're all in this together.*

Two blocks down from the police station is a cemetery that holds Thaddeus Stevens, the fiery abolitionist congressman who pushed Lincoln to emancipate enslaved people by proclamation, declaring weeks before Lincoln did so: "Abolition — Yes! abolish everything on the face of the earth, but this Union; free every slave — slay every traitor — burn every rebel mansion if these things be necessary to preserve this temple of freedom to the world and to our posterity." Stevens helped pass the Thirteenth Amendment and proposed breaking up plantations and distributing the land to freed slaves. "The whole fabric of southern society must be changed," he said, "and never can it be done if this opportunity is lost." Standing at his grave, I read the epitaph he wrote for himself.

> I repose in this quiet and secluded spot not from any natural preference for solitude, but finding other cemeteries limited as to race, by charter rules, I have chosen this that I might illustrate in my death the principles which I advanced through a long life: EQUALITY OF MAN BEFORE HIS CREATOR

In refusing to be buried in a whites-only cemetery, Stevens understood, like Morris Milgram and Adam Weiner, that integration requires intentionality.

We drive out of town past the Fulton Theatre, where Stevens delivered his "slay every traitor" speech, where an Underground Railroad stop had operated, and where the owners refused to screen *The Birth of a Nation*, which demonized a thinly disguised Stevens as a cowardly, lecherous, evil, and tyrannical monster. But the Fulton Theatre's history has a darker chapter, too. In 1763, when the site held the town workhouse and jail, local officials brought a group of Conestoga here to protect them from the Paxton Boys, a militia of mostly Scots-Irish formed by the pastor of Paxton Presbyterian Church. The militia had recently attacked the nearby Conestoga village, killing all six people who were present, in retaliation for raids by Native Americans on their community that left several dead. Although the Conestoga had not been involved in the raids, the settlers alleged they had acted as spies for the attackers, and after murdering the six, they "jubilantly paraded the scalps — their trophies of success — through Lancaster, and the townspeople laughed," wrote a local minister.

When Governor John Penn issued a proclamation forbidding anyone from harming the surviving fourteen members of the village, the Paxton Boys trampled it underfoot, believing the government was protecting Indians instead of them. A Paxton poet wrote:

> *Seeing then we've such good cause to hate 'em,*
> *what I intend's to extirpate 'em*

When the Paxton Boys returned to finish the massacre, the jailer wasn't there and the county sheriff stepped aside. In minutes, they slaughtered fourteen defenseless Conestoga, scalping each one. Although many in town knew who the killers were, no one was ever arrested.

In 2010, the three hundredth anniversary of the first European settlement in the area, a group of thirty Native American leaders from around the country joined several hundred residents to hear elected officials and leaders of nearby Presbyterian, Quaker, and Mennonite congregations offer a public apology for the Conestoga massacres, in the name of reconciliation and healing. The Paxton Presbyterian Church, however, did not send a representative. Perhaps its members wanted to protect the reputation of the minister they still lionized as "The Fighting Parson." But concern for historical figures is usually less about their good names than ours, less about history than the future, and less about factual accuracy than group power.

A favorite childhood camp counselor of mine, Emily, meets us at First Presbyterian Church in downtown York. She kindly offered to introduce us to the church's retired associate pastor, Guy Dunham. "We're still considered somewhat downtown," he says, giving me an orientation, "but if you go one block either way, it's the highest poverty in the city." Only forty-four thousand people live in York, down almost 50 percent since 1950, and one in three live in poverty. "York is losing more and more of its manufacturing base," he says. "Even Harley has taken it on the chin. Caterpillar moved out years ago. They were all major employers."

Still, Guy is optimistic about York's future and tells me about the old industrial area the city is developing into a tech sector with condos, an attempt to bring more residents and workers downtown. He speaks with a civic booster's pride of place and brims with historical anecdotes. In the cemetery beside the church, Guy points out the grave of James Smith, one of three Irish immigrants to sign the Declaration of Independence. York was an early stop on the Underground Railroad, he says, yet it also voted against Abraham Lincoln in both presidential elections. First Presbyterian was founded by men who held slaves, but it also had abolitionist pastors, including one who landed in jail after a fistfight with a southern sympathizer. And there's one story he's particularly eager to share.

In the 1960s, First Presbyterian took the progressive step of merging with a black church, one of only three such Presbyterian mergers in the country, he says. It seemed to go well, at least on the surface. But whites continued to exercise control over the liturgy, purse strings, staffing, and nearly everything else. Within a decade, he says, "a number of black families left. And the reason is that they never sensed that there was going to be any representation of African Americans" on staff or in the liturgy. It wasn't until 2019, more than fifty years after the merger, that the church made its first black hire, a director of youth and college ministries.

Integration requires more than a welcome mat. It requires power sharing. And giving up power to groups viewed as "other" does not come naturally. When I ask Guy what holds the country together, he says, "We really believe that diversity is a strength, not a weakness, and that's particularly true of the younger generation." Believing something and acting on it, however, are different things.

In *Star Wars*, Obi-Wan Kenobi explains "the Force" to Luke Skywalker by saying, “It’s an energy field created by all living things. It surrounds us and penetrates us. It binds the galaxy together.” What is the force that surrounds and penetrates us as Americans and binds the nation together? Guy’s answer moves us in the right direction, but we still have a way to go. Onward to Gettysburg.

—6—

For Us, the Living

Of all the wars ever waged, no battle has ever prompted a speech that so redefined and inspired a nation as the three days of fighting that took place in Gettysburg on July 1–3, 1863. In eloquence, economy, and effect, the 272 words Lincoln later spoke on a cemetery hillside here have never been surpassed. "The battle itself was less important than the speech," the abolitionist senator Charles Sumner said of the Gettysburg Address. "Ideas are more than battles." Nevertheless, Democrats and their newspapers panned it. "The cheeks of every American must tingle with shame as he reads the silly, flat and dishwatery utterances," the *Chicago Times* wrote. A Gettysburg newspaper attacked it, too, leading Union soldiers to destroy the printing press. Anger at partisan media and attempts to silence those on the other side are nothing new.

We enter town near the railroad depot where Lincoln stepped off a train from Washington on November 18, 1863. Gettysburg still looks much as it did then, and historic preservation is more than an architectural rule here. It's the town's main industry. The battlefield is big business — and it is still being fought over, no longer between blue and gray but instead between blue and red.

At a campground near the battlefield, it's time for the event I have been dreading: the inaugural Dumping of the Tanks. I attach the compressible six-foot sewage hose — known in RV circles as the Stinky Slinky — to

Charley's undercarriage and place the spout into the sewer hole. There are two separate tanks to empty, one containing black water (the toilet), and one containing gray water (the sink and shower). Squatting down with one hand holding the spout in place, I grab the tank handle and pull. *Gush!* Laurel and I are both pleasantly surprised that the smell is only barely perceptible, and though a pungent smell emerges with the gray water, it's not as bad as we'd expected. After completing the task, we feel a sense of accomplishment, like we're officially in the RV club now.

In the morning, I walk to the battlefield without Laurel, who is tied to her computer during working hours. Her job — she's part of a marketing team that promotes small businesses — leaves her little time to join me in exploring towns and talking with people during weekdays. If you miss her presence at various times along the journey, know that I do, too.

On Cemetery Ridge, I meet the director of the Civil War Institute at Gettysburg College, Peter Carmichael, the son of an Ecuadorian father and American mother, whose wavy gray hair makes him look more Hollywood than historian. We begin near the High Water Mark, the farthest point reached by Confederate soldiers during Pickett's Charge, where twelve to fourteen thousand Confederates attacked a Union line, half of them falling as casualties within an hour. The charge was not planned or led by General George Pickett — he stayed in the rear, directing the assault, ordered by General Robert E. Lee over the objections of General James Longstreet. Nor was it even a charge — soldiers marched in a line, stopping to fire. Nor was Pickett's the only division involved: Half of the soldiers were under the command of Generals James Johnston Pettigrew and Isaac Trimble, whose route to the ridge was more exposed than the one taken by Pickett's men. But while Pettigrew's and Trimble's troops came from a variety of states, Pickett's hailed from Virginia — and that made all the difference.

After the battle, newspapers in Richmond sought to transform failure into glory for their native sons, turning a disastrous decision into *Pickett's Charge* and turning the US Army's lowest moment into the "High Water Mark." In *Intruder in the Dust*, William Faulkner wrote of what the charge represented in the mind of a southern schoolchild — the promise and excitement of what might be, if the fight is undertaken: "For every Southern boy fourteen years old, not once but whenever he wants it, there is the instant when it's still not yet two o'clock on that July afternoon in 1863."

Peter begins by orienting me not geographically but politically. "When people understand how the battle took place, they see it from almost entirely the Confederate perspective," he says. "So the generals who capture people's attention here are Robert E. Lee, James Longstreet, George Pickett. There are not many people who can tell you even George Gordon Meade's name." General Meade commanded the Union forces and repulsed the Confederate attack. "One can go down Steinwehr Avenue, where there's a lot of touristy shops and shirts with Lee's face on it or other Confederate symbolism. There's a lot less for the northern side." There is a restaurant on Steinwehr called General Pickett's Buffet, but not even a snack stand named for Meade.

Peter points toward Meade's headquarters, a small white farmhouse with a white picket fence. "This should be a mandatory stop. People should want to see it. But no one's putting a flower there. No one's putting the US flag there. You go over to the Lee Monument, you'll see people placing Confederate flags and all kinds of things on it. It's so telling, I think shocking, that when people come here they look at that final act of this great three-day battle" — Pickett's Charge — "from the Virginia monument, from where Lee was at the very end of Pickett's Charge, a man who unquestionably violated his oath to this country. And people walk away looking at his great failure in the war with a degree of sympathy and sadness for him."

History is usually written by the victors. Not at Gettysburg.

"The success on this battlefield by the Union army went a very long way in achieving the two political goals of the war, union and emancipation. But for most people who come here, they're never engaging those ideas, because this isn't a battlefield. This is a commemorative landscape and a seductive place." Peter sweeps his arm across the vast field below us. "This place is spectacular in terms of its natural beauty, but the beauty often inhibits us from fully appreciating the carnage of the war and the political stakes, which were extraordinarily high. And as with any civil war, a spirit of vengeance, of bitterness, of brutality, animated the actions here. But that's not why people come to Gettysburg. They come for bedtime stories" — of brotherhood and fellowship, gallantry and heroism.

The seductive landscape obscuring the carnage and politics also omits any signs of the debates over Confederate monuments that played out here. Peter brings up one of the earliest, in 1888, at the twenty-fifth anniversary of the battle. The Confederate veterans of Pickett's division had initially refused to attend a reunion with the survivors of the Philadelphia brigade that defeated them, because their proposal for a Confederate monument at the High Water Mark had been rejected. After the Philadelphians promised to support it, Pickett's division relented, but they insisted on meeting on the Union side of the wall. The Union men refused, saying they hadn't let them over the wall in battle and wouldn't do so now. "So here's the compromise," says Peter, showing me a photo. "See how the Confederates are standing up on the rocks" — they are on the wall, above the Union men, reaching down to shake hands. "It's southern honor at work."

An officer in Pickett's division, William Aylett, gave a talk that day that touched on President Grover Cleveland's controversial order to return captured Confederate battle flags to the south, which Union veterans furiously opposed. "Southern men don't care who keeps those flags," Aylett declared. "The past went down in war, and we recognize now the flag of our fathers." He could speak with authority on the flag of their fathers — he was a great-grandson of Patrick Henry. But he hadn't absorbed Henry's most important legacy.

Generations of schoolchildren have memorized seven words from Henry's speech for independence — "Give me liberty or give me death!" (which he may not have ever spoken) — but few learn of his speeches attacking the Constitutional Convention delegates in Philadelphia: "What right had they to say, 'We the people'?" he asked. "Who authorized them to speak the language of 'We the People,' instead of 'We the states'? States are the characteristics, and the soul of a confederation."

Henry's speech foresaw that, if adopted, the new Constitution would elevate a central government above the states, and thus he opposed it. But once done, he stood against those, including Jefferson and Madison, who argued during the presidency of John Adams that states had the authority to reject federal laws they considered tyrannical or oppressive. In his last public speech, Henry attacked this theory of states' rights and pleaded for national unity: "If the administration have done wrong, let us all go wrong together rather than split into factions, which much destroy the Union upon which our existence hangs. Let us preserve our strength for the French, the English, the Germans, and whoever shall dare to invade our territory, and not exhaust it in civil commotions and intestine wars." Instead of using his final year of life to claim vindication for his views on the supremacy of the states, Henry had the humility to accept the fact he had lost the fight over that principle, and he refused to side with those who imperiled the nation by resurrecting it.

By the time of the 1888 reunion, more than one hundred memorial tablets and monuments had been placed on the battlefield, and all but two were to US Army soldiers — and Union veterans intended to keep it that way. At Little Round Top, one of the places where Confederates had sought to place a monument and were rebuffed, US general John Gobin denounced their effort by saying he was "tired of this gush and pretense for the glorification of the veteran simply because he wore a gray uniform with a southern flag printed on his badge. That badge meant treason and rebellion in 1861, and what it meant then it means now . . . I want to be distinctly understood, now and for all time, that the men who wore the gray were everlastingly and eternally wrong."

It was a common sentiment in the north. Here's General William T. Sherman: "We of the National Union Army were right and our adversaries were wrong." Here's Major Charles Holstein: "The war for the Union was a conflict between right and wrong — between truth and error." Here's Captain Clinton Spencer: "Disloyalty to the old flag was, is and always will be, TREASON, deep, dark, and damnable."

Confederate veterans remained just as adamant that they had been in the right, yet men on each side came here in 1888 to stretch out their hands in peace. "That they could forgive one another, that they could look to the future, that's a remarkable thing," says Peter. "Some might even say that there's evidence of American exceptionalism there. How many other civil wars don't end with the leaders of that war lined up and getting shot?" But forgiving did not mean forgetting — and for the north, it did not mean allowing the south to remember its cause with reverence. "There was well into the twentieth century," says Peter, "resistance by Union veterans to doing anything on this battlefield that would commemorate the actions of Confederate soldiers."

The resistance began to soften by the time a second reunion occurred on July 4, 1913. Three days after the Lincoln Highway Association's first formal meeting, President Wilson delivered a speech to an all-white group of Union and Confederate veterans that made no mention of slavery or emancipation, Jim Crow or segregation, nor any view on what became of Lincoln's "new birth of freedom." Instead Wilson suggested all was forgotten except the heroism, offering a bedtime story that ignored the simmering anger of black citizens deprived of their rights as well as the determination of southerners to deny the true cause of the war and basis of the Confederacy — slavery and white supremacy, as its leaders had often stated plainly, most memorably by Vice President Alexander Stephens: "Our new government is founded upon exactly the opposite idea [of the equality of races]; its foundations are laid, its corner-stone rests, upon the great truth that the negro is not equal to the white man; that slavery subordination to the superior race is his natural and normal condition. This, our new government, is the first, in the history of the world, based upon this great physical, philosophical, and moral truth."

Stephens was only echoing the secession resolutions adopted by states. Mississippi: "Our position is thoroughly identified with the institution of slavery." Louisiana: "The people of the slave-holding states are bound together by the same necessity and determination to preserve African slavery." Texas: "We hold as undeniable truths that the government of the various States, and of the confederacy itself, were established exclusively by the white race, for themselves and their posterity; that the African race had no agency in their establishment; that they were rightfully held and regarded as an inferior and dependent race; and in that condition only could their existence in this country be rendered beneficial and tolerable."

States seceded not only to preserve slavery but also to preserve its basis: white supremacy, a fact forthrightly stated by Edward Pollard in his 1868 book, *The Lost Cause Regained*: "The true question which the war involved," he wrote, "was the supremacy of the White race." And the conclusion of the war did not settle the question. In the postwar era, if the south "succeeds to the extent of securing the supremacy of the white man," Pollard wrote, "she really triumphs in the true cause of the war, with respect to all its fundamental and vital issues." Southerners adopted Pollard's phrase (the Lost Cause) and its mission (white supremacy), while also attempting to obscure the truth he acknowledged, by substituting a more palatable claim for the war's origin: states' rights.

In the Confederate constitution, however, states had no right to abolish slavery, and its central government was more powerful and controlling than the one it sought to replace, so much so that historian Richard Bensel would note that "a central state as well-organized and powerful as the Confederacy did not emerge until the New Deal and subsequent mobilization for World War II." Prior to secession, southerners had argued for an *expansion* of federal power to force northern states into stricter enforcement of the Fugitive Slave Act, and Jefferson Davis introduced a bill in the US Senate requiring all states to legalize slavery. The concept of states' rights was, from the beginning, political cover for white supremacy.

Five days before Woodrow Wilson's whitewashing speech, Virginia began erecting the first Confederate state monument at Gettysburg, in honor of

Robert Lee. (I've dropped his middle initial because it serves mostly to hamper our ability to see him with fresh eyes as a human, rather than an exalted mythic figure. Better for us to be on equal footing with him.) Northerners who supported the erection of Confederate monuments hoped they would strengthen the reconciliation process and promote national unity. But Virginians saw the Lee monument as a means of redeeming the Confederate cause. At its dedication four years later, the state's governor claimed the war had been fought over "rival conceptions of sovereignty" and called the monument "an undying expression of the high ideals in which we of the south would this day sanctify." With a southerner in the White House who supported this view, and Jim Crow in power across the south, the Lost Cause had indeed been regained.

"Most people did not believe the war was over slavery," Peter says of the visitors he encountered while working summers here from 1985 to 2000, the year Congress passed a law requiring the National Park Service to include mention of slavery on Civil War battlefields, over the objections of the Sons of Confederate Veterans. "I heard some egregious stuff, man" — including the worst slurs.

"The truly unique trait of Sapiens is our ability to create and believe fiction," the Israeli historian Yuval Noah Harari has written. "All other animals use their communication system to describe reality. We use our communication system to create new realities" — not only for entertainment but also for protection against shame, guilt, regret, and other feelings that stand in the way of pride, honor, and dignity. So it was that southern states never erected a monument to General Longstreet, who opposed Pickett's Charge, joined the Republican Party after the war, and supported Reconstruction and black voting rights. Southern whites who reviled him for that apostasy dotted their states with monuments to other Confederate generals, while writing Longstreet out of their history, except to unjustly blame him for the loss at Gettysburg. When a monument in his honor finally went up here in 1988, the Sons of Confederate Veterans insisted that it honored only his "war service," not his "postwar activities."

"There is at least a recognition now," says Peter, "that the legacy of slavery and emancipation is certainly felt today, and we have to be honest with that past. We see that in these Black Lives Matter protests, we see an awareness that racism is institutionalized. That's a sea change. I'm in awe of what's happened. I'm also concerned that in this understanding of the past and its relationship to today, that at times it becomes too simplistic, too judgmental. My fear is that the finger wagging, the presentism, the self-righteousness in looking at the past is bleeding into a way of seeing the world around us" — a way that increases animus and misunderstanding, rather than alleviating it.

"They are just what we would be in their situation," Lincoln said in 1854 of white southerners agitating for slavery's expansion. He recognized that perceptions of morality are rarely selfless — they are influenced by personal circumstance — and he had the humility to see that he and abolitionists might well have been enslavers under different circumstances. Can we see that the same truth holds for our differences today? One of Lincoln's favorite biblical lines, which he quoted in his second inaugural address, was "let us judge not, that we be not judged."

Lincoln's refusal to cast judgment even during wartime reflected one of his core convictions: Politics is rarely a good-versus-evil morality play. "The true rule," Lincoln said in 1848, during his one term in Congress, "in determining to embrace, or reject any thing, is not whether it have any evil in it; but whether it have more of evil, than of good. There are few things wholly evil, or wholly good. Almost every thing, especially of governmental policy, is an inseparable compound of the two; so that our best judgment of the preponderance between them is continually demanded." No three sentences better encapsulate the mind-set that saved the nation from a catastrophic fracture and that is sorely missing from political dialogue today.

"It is so important to reach out and acknowledge people's perspectives," Peter says. "When someone says to me, 'My great-great-great-great-grandpappy never owned slaves, and I'll be damned if someone's going to tell me he died for the cause of slavery.' That is an opportunity for me to say, 'You know what? You're right. Most Confederate soldiers did not own slaves. But there's a difference between what caused the war, and why men followed.' And then, if we get a nice conversation going, I might say, 'But you know a lot of non-slaveholders were invested in the system, in terms of their own social values and ideas about race.' You could get somebody there."

Peter sees hope for national progress in the Gettysburg Address, just not in the part that most people focus on. "When we point to the Gettysburg Address, we want to emphasize his call for liberty — overlooking the fact that he never used the word *emancipation*, he never mentioned *slave*. He was pointing in that direction, but his primary concern at Gettysburg was a war that still needed to be won. It's the lesson that we almost never pay any attention to: It's Lincoln the pragmatist, Lincoln the politician. And his reminder to the northern people was that the sacrifice of these men here would be squandered unless they continued to show the resolve and the determination to continue to send bodies into Union armies."

"It is for us the living," Lincoln said, "to be dedicated here to the unfinished work which they who fought here have thus far so nobly advanced." In the next sentence, he referred to "the great task remaining before us" (whose echo we heard in the lyrics of Abel Meeropol, "the task that still remains") but alluded to emancipation only obliquely, by calling for "a new birth of freedom." Lincoln was challenging Americans to win a war and transform the nation through inclusive language that labored — seemingly effortlessly — to avoid alienating potential opponents, including slaveholders in Maryland, Kentucky, and Tennessee. "It is a war speech, but we see the pragmatism to forge a political coalition," Peter says. "And Lincoln was able to do that — to bring together northern Democrats who never liked him, never agreed with his policies, but they understood what was at stake, and they came to ultimately accept that to save the Union, you've got to also take down slavery."

This side of Lincoln, the calculating politician who was slow on abolition and equal rights, is today held up by critics as a reason to strip his name from buildings. But Peter recognizes something else: the skill and temperament necessary to maintain the unity of a diverse and fractious nation while still pushing it toward its highest ideals. Says Peter: "We want the Lincoln who speaks of liberty for all. But when we can take him off that pedestal, we get a far more accurate assessment of Lincoln. Lincoln understood that democracy was no child's play. It's rough-and-tumble; it's in the gutter." And victory often requires strategic compromises. As the scholar and conservative intellectual Harry Jaffa wrote, "Lincoln never attempted to propose what was more than one step ahead of the great body of public opinion. But he always led the way." And his most extraordinary leadership quality — his humility — stood at the center of his Gettysburg Address.

In its ten sentences, Lincoln used the word *we* nine times and *us* three times. He never uttered the word *I*. "And in the place of his vanished ego," wrote the communications scholar Edwin Black, "he proposed a set of principles of which he became the personification" — an achievement Black called "the most sublime in our political history." But humility was not just a matter of syntax for Lincoln. "Lincoln's distinctive mark, one almost unique in the history of war leadership," Garry Wills wrote, "was his refusal to indulge in triumphalism, righteousness, or vilification of the foe." That refusal, born of his rejection of politics as a good-versus-evil morality play, was essential to his success in preserving and advancing the nation, yet rarely do we think of it as essential to ours.

"The big and important question that faced Americans after the war should face us now," Peter says. "And it's simply this: Can we have justice *and* reconciliation? Can you have it both ways?" Not without the humility to recognize shades of gray, and the need for blue and red to bleed together.

After saying good-bye to Peter, I walk through the Soldiers' National Cemetery, which Lincoln dedicated, where more than thirty-five hundred Union soldiers are buried, almost half unidentified. The night before Lincoln left Washington by train, he was visited by William Saunders, the Department of Agriculture's Scots-born horticulturist, who presented his design for the cemetery: graves grouped by state and arrayed in a semicircle around a central point, as the soldiers were around a common goal, with each grave marked with only a flat, rectangular, gray stone — no headstones, no sculptures, each death of equal importance, no matter the rank, an understated simplicity that would be the perfect complement to Lincoln's brief speech. Both Saunders and Lincoln found beauty and inspiration in spareness, and Lincoln took great interest in the design. "He was much pleased with the method of the graves," Saunders later wrote, "after I had explained the reasons, said it was an admirable and befitting arrangement." Future generations would seek greater glory for the dead in massive monuments — including to Lincoln, Jefferson, and Confederate heroes — that strained mightily to reach the transcendent heights of Saunders's landscape and Lincoln's speech, always falling short.

At the campground we test out Charley's passenger-side canopy for the first time —it unfurls smoothly — and I sit under its lights studying the next day's route. When I return inside, Laurel is sitting beside the toilet, trying to reattach the flush pedal, which somehow popped off. I stand over her as she makes a further study of the holes in the pedal that need to align with the plastic protrusions at the bowl's base. She tries to attach it again. And again. I take a turn on the floor and make the same study of the same holes, ending with the same result. The satisfaction we felt in successfully operating the Stinky Slinky has been replaced with dread, but Laurel figures out that we can still flush the toilet by manually twisting a small lever at the base of the bowl. It's just not an especially pleasant experience.

On our way out of town the next morning, we stop into the Ragged Edge Coffee House and meet its owner, Jake Schindel, who is president of the borough council, and Charles Gable, the borough manager. In the wake of George Floyd's murder, someone living near Gettysburg, South Dakota — their sister city — called with a question: Would they speak out against the South Dakota town's police department for displaying the Confederate battle flag on its uniforms and vehicles? Jake and Charles were reluctant to get involved in another city's politics, but when they began doing some research, they learned that their sister city was founded by Union soldiers and that it adopted the Confederate symbol only in 2009, after the election of President Obama. When they heard that it is also home to Selwyn Jones, George Floyd's uncle, Charles called him to ask if he supported the council sending a letter. He did.

Charles drafted a diplomatic letter explaining why they allow Confederate symbols and monuments on the battlefield — it is effectively an enormous museum — but not for any government use. "These Confederate symbols recognize our troubled past, but they do not honor that past — rather they now exist to teach the wrongs of the past." The South Dakota town removed the Confederate emblem, but whether the letter had anything to do with it, Charles and Jake can't say — they received no response. "Honestly, I'm a little disappointed by it," Charles says. "I had hoped that we would have heard something from someone."

At an RV repair shop just outside of town, a mechanic kindly agrees to see us about our toilet pedal. When he enters Charley, he's not wearing a mask, which we're not thrilled about, but contracting the virus is a risk we are willing to run for a working toilet. "Is it a Thetford?" he asks, referring to the toilet brand. We have no idea. He eyes it: "Yup. See it all the time." He explains that to get the pedal back on, the water pump needs to be on, so I flip the switch. He gets down on the floor and pops the pedal back in without too much difficulty, amazing us. "It'll probably keep happening," he says. "The plastic gets worn down and once it comes off, it keeps coming off." Uh-oh. "Just make sure you step straight on it, not from the side."

Every trip to the bathroom would now require some careful foot–eye coordination. When I ask what we owe him, he shakes his head — "Nothin'" — and walks off. We thank him profusely and feel, well, relieved.

—7—

Never Forget

Pioneers and gold rush prospectors who traveled west would tell their neighbors they were going to "see the elephant." The phrase seems to have originated with the excitement people would express when a traveling circus came to town, bringing the prospect of encountering new worlds. That sense of wondrous desire was captured in a song by James McMurtry, son of Larry, the novelist and screenwriter who demythologized the west and its cowboy heroes.

Please Papa can I go, down to Richmond to the traveling show
Please Papa don't say I can't, I just want to see the elephant

Outside Gettysburg, we turn into Mister Ed's Elephant Museum & Candy Emporium, its sign reading, "We believe in chocolate for breakfast." In 1967, Ed and Pat Gotwalt received a small wooden elephant as a wedding gift. They bought a few more elephant souvenirs on their honeymoon, giving birth to a hobby that grew into an obsession that led to a business. They now own perhaps the world's largest collection of elephant artifacts and figurines — twelve thousand items in all — plus elephant trinkets and knickknacks of every kind that are for sale, along with seven hundred flavors of candy, one hundred flavors of homemade fudge, and roasted peanuts. Opening an elephant museum to sell peanuts isn't any more ridiculous than what we had encountered yesterday: a shoe house built in 1948 as a marketing stunt by the largest shoe store owner in the country, Mahlon Haines, who handed a boot to an architect and said, "Build me a house like this."

The American appetite for absurdity feasts on snacks, souvenirs, and stunts. Ed once dressed as Santa Claus and took to the sky in a hot-air balloon, intending to land at his store, but when he crashed into treetops, the rescue made international news — far better publicity than he had dreamed possible. In 1976, he announced he would stay awake for seventy-six hours to celebrate America's bicentennial, and anyone coming to the store and finding him napping would get $100. Carl Fisher would've loved both stunts, and there was more than a little of Crazy Carl in Ed, who never made it beyond eighth grade. In more recent years, a near-death experience in a car accident led Ed to the local lecture circuit, speaking with community and spiritual groups on his topic of expertise: "Angels, Miracles, and Other Stuff."

Inside the shop, a wall holds a dictum written in large letters and ascribed to P. T. Barnum: "When entertaining the public, it is best to have an elephant." Maybe so, although Lincoln's law partner, William Herndon, claimed that "Barnum could make more money on Lincoln's dancing than he could on Jumbo." After picking up peanuts and fudge, Laurel and I take each other's photo while sticking our faces through an elephant cutout, above a sign reading, "I'll Never Forget Mister Ed's." As children we learn that elephants have long memories, but we rarely give any thought to what they use them for: distinguishing friends from foes and returning to old sources of food and water. In a word, survival.

In elephants as with humans, memory is a function of evolution, but for us, it is as much a process of reconstruction as it is an act of recollection. Our experiences and beliefs — about ourselves and our upbringing, our religion and politics, our successes and failures — shape how we remember the past. The more time passes, the more two people are unlikely to remember the same event the same way, because our brains are wired to filter and alter memories, often in ways that burnish our egos. Memory changes as we change. A nation's history, a people's collective memory, is no different. Such is the origin of myth.

Like memory, myths are malleable, and each generation shapes and reshapes them to serve its purposes. We have already seen this at work on Gettysburg Battlefield — the myth of the Lost Cause — and we will see it again and again along the route, for better and worse. As we do, I'd like to propose a way to view and evaluate our shared myths, and it centers on the same function that memory serves for elephants: survival — not for our own sake or the sake of any group, whether of race, ethnicity, religion, party, gender, sexual orientation, or anything else, but for national survival and what makes it possible: democracy and its promise of freedom and equality. How do we reckon with and adapt myths to ensure that they are bolstering the life and health of our democracy — and how do we protect ourselves from those whose actions, however unwittingly, risk its destruction? Pursuing answers to those questions will, I hope, lead us to the elephant. Keep an eye out for its footprints.

We pass two houses side by side, each with an American flag flying from its front porch, a small but well-manicured front yard, and a pickup truck in the driveway. One house displays "Patriots for Biden" signs. The other has a "Home of a Deplorable" sign and two Trump banners, one reading, "No More Bullshit," a testament to how, as beauty is in the eye of the beholder, bullshit is in the nose of the balloter.

It's day six of the trip, and we are finally stopping for our first proper lunch, Mim's Mighty Meaty Hoagies in Fayetteville, Pennsylvania. Laurel is on a work call, but I know she'll want her favorite sandwich: baloney on white. Inside, I examine the menu but don't see baloney. Who's ever heard of a deli without baloney? I see a newspaper article taped to the wall with the headline, "It's never too late to find God." I'd settle for baloney.

A woman appears at the counter. "Could I get baloney on a roll?" I ask.

"Baloney?"

"Yeah, baloney — do you have that?"

"We call that the All-American."

As with the two houses we had just passed: One person's baloney is another's patriotism.

We eat the hoagies, as mighty and meaty as advertised, in an empty parking lot for Lincoln Lanes, a bowling alley adorned with murals of the Lincoln Highway and a bowling pin above the front door emblazoned with "Lincoln." Abe would have loved it. "Abraham Lincoln was very fond of bowling," wrote an acquaintance of his during his one term in Congress. "He was a very awkward bowler but played the game with great zest and spirit . . . He accepted success and defeat with like good nature and humor."

Inside I meet Andre Bondarenko, twelve years the owner. When the state shut down businesses in March, he laid off nine employees. Now, he says, "A lot of people don't want to come back to work. They're waiting for another round of checks." It was a tough business to begin with.

In the 1990s, sociologist Robert Putnam used the dramatic decline in bowling leagues as a metaphor for the collapse of community in America, lamenting that the country Alexis de Tocqueville observed in 1831 — a nation of joiners — had fallen by the wayside. While de Tocqueville was writing mostly of the "intellectual and moral associations" formed to achieve some common goal — some social benefit beyond gathering to drink beer and roll balls, a great good though both are — he admired associations' tendency to bring people together in community on equal footing, precisely why Andre bought the business. He has aimed to create a bowling center devoted to families and Christian values, no alcohol or foul language permitted. Above one of the lanes in large letters there is a scripture reference, Hebrews 13:2 — "Do not forget to show hospitality to strangers, for by so doing some people have shown hospitality to angels without knowing it."

When I ask Andre what binds the country together, he has a one-word answer — God — and he sees the absence of faith at the core of the nation's problems. "The country has been divided so bad because everyone has taken God out of the picture — out of schools, out of their lives," he says. "If we don't get God back into our lives our country is gonna be in bad — there's gonna be a war is what's gonna happen. Good against evil, I can see it coming."

During the Civil War, Lincoln issued a proclamation announcing a national day of prayer and humiliation. "We have forgotten God," it read. But it did not speak of a battle between good and evil, believers and apostates, only of an entire nation that needed "to humble ourselves before the offended Power, to confess our national sins, and to pray for clemency and forgiveness."

"If people continue on the path that they're going on," Andre says, "this country will be destroyed."

"What path is that?" I ask.

"All the evil. All the fighting. All the hatred. I've never seen people hate as much as they hate right now. Just watch the news. People — they call it protesting, but they're destroying businesses that people have worked hard to establish, and what gives them the right to walk into somebody's business and rob and burn? And nobody does anything about it? Our government just sits there and watches like it's not a problem. Well, it is a problem."

It is hard for those of us who don't own a business to understand the outrage he feels when stores are vandalized and robbed. Democrats tend to lament the senselessness of it without wanting to condemn the perpetrators, as I heard from an art gallery manager in Lancaster while her glass window was being swept up from the sidewalk. Such tempered responses are born of a charitable impulse, but shrugging acquiescence to theft and property damage can carry high costs, not only for individual businesses and their employees but for public faith in the rule of law as well. One of democracy's most dangerous enemies is a violent mob, no matter how worthy its aims. To see that truth, it's time we meet up with Old Man Brown.

In Chambersburg, old homes press tight against the road, including the boardinghouse where John Brown stayed in 1859 as he plotted to spark a slave revolt by raiding a federal armory sixty miles south in Harpers Ferry, Virginia. He arrived here after three years in hiding, wanted by federal authorities for killing five pro-slavery settlers in Kansas. Announcing himself as Isaac Smith, he told the townsfolk he was looking to develop an iron mine and began surreptitiously collecting weapons and tools.

We pass over the Conococheague Creek where Brown waited, fishing pole in hand, to meet the man whose support he most desired, who had previously taken him into his house in Rochester, New York, shielding him from the authorities: Frederick Douglass. Over the course of a long conversation, Douglass told him he would not support the raid. "It would be an attack upon the federal government," Douglass said, "and would array the whole country against us." But Brown was a devout Calvinist who believed God had set him on this path.

After taking the armory and capturing several slaveholders — chief among them George Washington's great-grandnephew — Brown found himself surrounded by federal forces, led by two future Confederate generals, Robert Lee and J. E. B. Stuart. He was tried, convicted, and hanged. Witnessing the execution were Virginia Military Institute professor Thomas (later "Stonewall") Jackson and John Wilkes Booth, who had joined a Virginia militia company when rumors swirled that abolitionists planned to rescue Brown. Booth came away deeply impressed with

Brown's courage and dignity: "John Brown was a man inspired," he would later write, "the grandest character of the century!" On the night of the execution, Henry Wadsworth Longfellow wrote in his diary, "This will be a great day in our history, the date of a new Revolution quite as much needed as the old one."

Lincoln did not glorify Brown or his act. Instead he made known his disapproval, saying in a speech in Kansas: "Old John Brown has just been executed for treason against a state. We cannot object, even though he agreed with us in thinking slavery wrong. That cannot excuse violence, bloodshed, and treason." To Lincoln, no matter how worthy the cause, the concept of "right makes might" must be achieved "through the ballot box — the peaceful method provided by the Constitution."

Lincoln's condemnation of Brown, and Douglass's refusal here in Chambersburg to join him, are among history's most powerful examples of pragmatic patriotism. No one was more devoted to abolition than Douglass, and no one had spoken more eloquently against the spread of slavery and the Kansas-Nebraska Act than Lincoln, but both men refused to support an armed insurrection against the government even though its goal was morally correct. While Brown followed God, Douglass and Lincoln followed the Constitution. Their political restraint reflected a faith in democracy that was ultimately repaid, an enduring testament to its power.

Today Chambersburg bills itself as the only town north of the Mason-Dixon Line to be burned by the Confederate army — General Jubal Early burned it in 1864 — but when Union troops marched back into the charred town, they may well have been singing the most popular song of the war, a tribute to Old Man Brown put to an old Methodist melody. A New York poet, Julia Ward Howe, sought to make it more respectable, changing its title from "John Brown's Body" to "The Battle Hymn of the Republic," stripping all references to Brown, and revising the source of inspiration from Brown's soul to God's truth. Although erasing Brown and his tactics, she sanctified his cause, and her first line became the final words publicly spoken by America's prophet of nonviolent change, the Reverend Martin Luther King Jr., at the close of his Mountaintop sermon in Memphis. The next day, he was shot dead in the war that Brown had begun in violence and King was determined to finish in peace.

Mine eyes have seen the glory of the coming of the Lord

On our way to our campsite, in a clearing between cornfields, we pass a farmers market displaying an elephant statue. We have many miles to go before seeing the real thing and no guarantee of success. Today, Stewart Rhodes, the leader of the militant right-wing group Oath Keepers, which has five hundred thousand Facebook followers, urges Trump to declare a nationwide insurrection and impose martial law.

After winding through the ridges of the mountains, breaks in the forest give us occasional views across the valley. As we crest a hill, the pastoral scenery is replaced by a strip of national chains: fast-food joints, hotels, and gas stations. This is Breezewood — Gas Vegas, it's called — an unincorporated village with few residents that five million vehicles pass through each year, thanks to a quirk of federal law that forces interstate highway traffic onto the Lincoln Highway for a third of a mile. "When we get these thruways across the whole country, as we will and must," John Steinbeck wrote in *Travels with Charley*, as Eisenhower's interstates spread across the land, "it will be possible to drive from New York to California without seeing a single thing." Just the same chains at every exit: Gas Vegas, USA.

We have already gotten a feel for what has been lost by the time we pull into the Lincoln Motor Court, which was built around 1940, just as the state turnpike began siphoning away traffic. Twelve small cabins form a U shape around a common courtyard with a firepit and cornhole boards, to draw people out of their cabins and into conversation. We ring the office bell and are greeted by Robert Altizer, who bought the Lincoln Motor Court with his wife when they moved to the area in 1983.

"We brought it back from the ashes," Robert says. "But we didn't see any business for years. I loved it and didn't see why nobody else did. And then it finally came around again as a retro fad," thanks partly to a 2008 PBS documentary on the Lincoln Highway. "Come to find out, we're the last motor court still in operation on the Lincoln Highway. When I first moved here in 1983, there were twelve motor courts in Bedford County alone." He brings us inside one of the cabins, just large enough for a double bed and a day bed, a small bathroom, and a second sink in the living area. "The walls are one-inch-thick knotty pine, tongue-grooved — incredible," Robert says. "I couldn't possibly ever replace it." The deluxe cabins, which cost an extra $5, come with an old radio loaded with shows from the 1940s, like *The Lone Ranger* and *Dick Tracy*.

In many ways, the Lincoln Motor Court represents American travel at its most romantic. But amid these cute cabins, it is easy to miss a dark side. The 1962 edition of the *Green Book*, which informed black travelers where they might find lodging, listed only one option in Bedford County, and it's not this one, nor any of the other motor courts that once dotted the landscape. Driving off, we see a barn with murals on three sides, each depicting scenes from the Lincoln Highway in its early days: cars from the 1930s and travelers — all white — in formal dress. On the west side of the barn is a verse that we can just barely make out, through the peeling paint:

> *Times Square in the East / Golden Gate in the West*
> *For cross country travel / It was the best.*
> *Lincolnway!*

Lincolnway leads to a place that bookends our first day on the road: the Flight 93 National Memorial. Amid twenty-two hundred acres of wildflowers and woods, a granite walkway is flanked by concrete walls that jut outward like wings, tracking the flight path's final second on the morning of September 11, 2001. The walkway leads to a vista overlooking the site of impact off in the distance, where forty passengers and crew members perished, along with the four hijackers, after the terror and confusion of an upside-down nosedive at 563 miles an hour that ended in a fiery explosion and left behind few human traces, only a crater. It's now marked by a large sandstone boulder.

At the end of the walkway, crickets fill the field with song, a reedy, jangly, metallic, electric hum. It's their mating call, how they bring life into the world, but here it sounds like a trembling dirge, and their invisibility creates an eerie sense of absence. "There but for the grace of God go I" is the phrase we often turn to in such situations, to express our gratitude at escaping tragedy. But did God extend grace to us and not the passengers and crew? To see tragedies as irrespective of divine grace helps underscore that they are often the work of human hands, not God's.

Aboard the plane, the last words heard from thirty-two-year-old Todd Beamer, "Let's roll," became the day's most exalted phrase, a battle cry that captured the bravery and defiance we revere in heroes, especially martyrs. Fewer remember that before uttering the phrase, Beamer had asked a customer service representative for a phone company to join him in reciting the Lord's Prayer — begging forgiveness, forgiving enemies, and seeking deliverance from evil — as well as Psalm 23.

> *Yea, though I walk through the valley of the shadow of death, I will fear no evil: for thou art with me; thy rod and thy staff they comfort me.*

To recite this psalm, to sing this song, is to place all trust in God — an exercise in faith the hijackers were also engaged in, as some shouted "Allahu Akbar!" on the way to their death. The competing prayers of the hijacked and hijackers call to mind Lincoln's meditation on divine will, which he wrote following the war's bloodiest battle, at Antietam, the same month he issued the Emancipation Proclamation: "In great contests each party claims to act in accordance with the will of God. Both may be, and one must be, wrong. God can not be for and against the same thing at the same time."

In the Civil War, the north's victory vindicated the idea, now deeply ingrained in the American psyche, that God walks with those who fight for liberty. It is now difficult for Americans to imagine, as Lincoln did, a God who might possibly side against us in favor of a nation or group built on tyranny and repression. Ours is a God of freedom, equality, and democracy — the American trinity, we might say. And although the concept of the trinity is most often associated with Christianity, the fusing of threes to form a collective identity and value system can also be found in other religions, including Judaism (Abraham, Isaac, and Jacob), Hinduism (Brahma, Shiva, and Vishnu), and Buddhism (Buddha, dharma, sangha) as well as ancient Celtic and Roman beliefs — and in Islam, the holy month of Ramadan consists of three stages. I use *trinity* here in its most universal sense — secular, but still sacred — to capture the spiritualism of American patriotism.

Lincoln would now be called spiritual but not religious. He never belonged to a church and attended services infrequently, but he regularly invoked God, particularly during the war, and often used biblical language to evangelize America's founding texts and ideas. He described the Declaration of Independence as an "immortal emblem of Humanity" containing "sacred principles" that formed "my ancient faith." By making a civic religion of the highest of those sacred principles — freedom, democracy, equality — we are engaged in a constant struggle to live up to them, the noblest of all national callings. However often we fall short, however often we disagree over what they demand of us, our faith in them has always propelled us forward. So it was even on 9/11.

The visitor center reminds me of something I'd forgotten. Before Beamer and other passengers charged the cockpit, they discussed the matter and put it to a vote. An attack on democracy — likely the US Capitol itself — thwarted by democracy. Having just come from Gettysburg, where Lincoln lifted a war over secession to a war over ideas, we can see the legacy of his speech here in this field — in the spirit of equality that led to the vote, in the democratic action it produced, and in the great risk taken so that others might live, and live freely.

In recent years, however, instead of seeing the heroism of passengers as a personification of Lincoln's vision at Gettysburg, their story has been hijacked by those who lack Lincoln's faith in the people. In a 2016 essay published under a pseudonym, a former speechwriter for Mayor Rudolph Giuliani and national security adviser Condoleezza Rice, Michael Anton, used Flight 93 as a metaphor for a nation facing extinction unless it elected Donald Trump. "2016 is the Flight 93 election: charge the cockpit or you die," he wrote. "You may die anyway. You — or the leader of your party — may make it into the cockpit and not know how to fly or land the plane. There are no guarantees. Except one: if you don't try, death is certain."

Anton's essay went viral and became one of the most discussed commentaries of the election. American society was facing a "tidal wave of dysfunction, immorality, and corruption," he wrote, which he blamed in large measure on the usual suspects: "the ceaseless importation of Third World foreigners with no tradition of, taste for, or experience in liberty," words that might have been lifted from the lips of the mob that burned St. Augustine's in Philadelphia. He blamed immigrants for "importing poverty, crime, and alien cultures" and blamed Republicans for failing "to consider the possibility that the republic is dying." His complaint was more with modernity and pluralism than Democrats and liberalism, and he deployed the same rhetorical tools — fear and apocalypse — as fire-and-brimstone preachers.

There was sad irony in the article being published by the Claremont Institute, which was founded by students of a Lincoln scholar and admirer, the conservative intellectual Harry Jaffa. Anton's essay never mentioned Lincoln except to mock his rhetoric, calling immigration "the mystic chord that unites America's ruling and intellectual classes." The essay had none of Lincoln's magnanimous spirit, none of his humility in acknowledging that we may be wrong and our opponents right, and none of his commitment to democracy — Anton referred to the nation being governed by a bipartisan "junta." And where Lincoln referred to "the people" three times for emphasis at Gettysburg — "of the people, by the people, for the people"

— Anton referred only to *my* people ("I want my people to live") without explicitly saying who *his* people were, and without needing to. It was abundantly clear.

There is nothing more dangerous to the maintenance of democracy than the notion that the nation is doomed unless an election goes a particular way, thus justifying violence and authoritarianism. And it would be hard to conjure a more unseemly way to express it than enlisting the passengers of Flight 93. Yet even as Democrats lashed out against the essay, many — though loath to admit it or speak of it in such crass terms — were having similar feelings, only from the opposite perspective: that the country would not survive a Donald Trump presidency. Faith in the durability of the ideas that Lincoln captured at Gettysburg, in the midst of a war that had killed hundreds of thousands of Americans, ran low in both parties. Countering the weakening of faith was precisely Lincoln's purpose as he crafted his Gettysburg Address, urging people to "take increased devotion" to freedom, democracy, and equality.

How that devotion forms matters a great deal. Today President Trump delivers a speech announcing the creation of a 1776 Commission to foster a "pro-American curriculum" for schoolchildren. "Critical race theory, the 1619 Project, and the crusade against American history," he says, "is toxic propaganda — ideological poison that, if not removed, will dissolve the civic bonds that tie us together. It will destroy our country." And when faced with destruction of the country, anything is permissible — even, as Anton argued, charging the cockpit of a plane piloted by democratically elected officials.

The trouble with lionizing John Brown is that it inspires people like John Wilkes Booth and Michael Anton.

Driving off from the memorial, we have a spectacular view across the valley to the north, the last stretch of land covered by Flight 93. Twenty miles off in that distance lies another disaster site: Johnstown, where a dam break in 1889 sent a sixty-foot wave cascading down at forty miles an hour, destroying sixteen hundred homes and killing 2,208 people, many of them new arrivals from Eastern Europe who came to work in the town's booming steel and iron mills. Many of their bodies were never identified.

At that time, it was the nation's deadliest catastrophe and the biggest story since Lincoln's assassination a generation earlier. Accounts of the flood and its destruction filled newspapers, with shock turning to outrage directed at the gilded culprit, the South Fork Fishing and Hunting Club, which owned the lake and whose members included Pittsburgh titans like Andrew Carnegie, Henry Clay Frick, and Andrew Mellon. The club had failed to maintain the dam, but club members said the heavy rainstorm that led to its collapse was an act of God — and judges agreed, tossing out the lawsuits that sought to hold the rich and powerful to account. Many ministers across the country agreed, too, and they invoked the story of Noah's Ark to assert that the flood had been God's punishment for the sins of Johnstown, never mind that the town's most popular brothel had been untouched. "We think we know what struck us," countered the publisher of the *Johnstown Tribune*, George Swank, "and it was not the hand of Providence. Our misery is the work of man."

In the flood's wake, Carnegie donated $10,000 to relief efforts and later paid to construct a library in Johnstown. According to the "Gospel of Wealth," the essay he wrote evangelizing philanthropy, funding small works of mercy was a divine duty, but facing up to gross acts of injustice was not.

When we reach our campground, about thirty miles south of Pittsburgh, a neighbor comes over to greet us.

"How do you like your Navion?" he says.

"Just got it, but it's been great."

"We've had two," he says. "Loved them both, but we wanted something bigger because we wanted to stay put longer."

He introduces himself: Dick, retired and living in Florida. "You'll have no trouble in the Rockies," he says. "Up and over in that rig. Is it a V-6?"

"Yeah — it's turbo," I say. I know the engine has the word *turbo* in its name, and though I have no idea what it means, I'm trying to sound knowledgeable.

We're learning that RV owners love to talk about their rigs and hear about their neighbors'. But in this case, Dick just wants to engage in some Navion nostalgia, and soon I'm opening our undercarriage compartments so he can look at how its design had changed.

"You winterize this yourself?" he asks.

"No, we just got it a month ago."

"Well, it's real easy. Don't take it to the shop — they'll charge you an arm and a leg. Want me to show you how?"

"Sure."

"All you gotta do is —" He starts talking about fluids and tubes and completely loses me. "You change the oil yourself?"

"No, haven't had to yet."

He starts in again, talking about more fluids and tubes. Thank goodness he doesn't know I couldn't even reattach the toilet pedal.

On the next morning's drive into Pittsburgh, we pass just east of Homestead, where an 1892 strike at one of Carnegie's steel plants intensified the national debate over the power of wealth that arose after the Johnstown Flood. Carnegie's deputy, Henry Frick, demanded wage cuts from workers, refused to negotiate with their union, locked out workers, and hired a small army of Pinkerton detective agency men to guard and protect the mill, leading to a battle that left sixteen strikers and Pinkertons dead. Shortly afterward, Alexander Berkman attempted to assassinate Frick in what his fellow radical Emma Goldman called "the first Anarchist act of economic terror in the United States."

A few miles west of Homestead we cross a bridge named for one of Carnegie's fellow Pittsburgh industrialists, George Westinghouse, whose inventions revolutionized rail travel, increasing its efficiency and safety. But unlike Carnegie, his business practices set new standards for decency. He was one of the first large employers to implement half-days on Saturdays, and his factories provided safer and more sanitary working conditions than found in Carnegie's steel mills. He built houses for workers, which he provided at discounted prices; he established welfare, education, and cultural programs for workers; he hired the nation's first woman to earn a college degree in electrical engineering — and he declined to join the exclusive fishing club that evaded responsibility for destroying Johnstown.

The different responses to the challenges of capitalism by Carnegie (charity), Westinghouse (benevolence), workers (unionization), and Berkman (vigilantism) would shape the country for decades to come. We will encounter each response again as we push west, along with a subsequent response (reform) by a group who elevated monopoly power to new heights: progressive politicians. As we enter Pittsburgh through East Liberty, we get a preview of their handiwork and how Carnegie's and Westinghouse's legacies are helping to overcome it.

East Liberty was once the city's second downtown, having grown up around the rail tracks that delivered fortunes to Westinghouse and Carnegie and later inspired a neighborhood kid, Romare Bearden, to celebrate trains in his art. "Trains are so much a part of Negro life," said Bearden.

"Negroes lived near the tracks, worked on the railroads, and trains carried them north during the migration." Trains meant segregation, families pushed behind iron barriers, and discrimination in employment, but the train whistle also carried the sound of opportunity and liberation, commerce and prosperity.

East Liberty thrived until the 1960s, when the city's progressive leaders decided that competing with the advent of suburban shopping malls required the seizure and demolition of more than one thousand homes and six hundred businesses, no matter what their occupants said. In their place, the city built rental housing towers, tore up the street grid, redirected traffic to a ring road, created a centrally designed shopping plaza, and left space for suburban-style retail outlets and parking lots. It worked in reverse, of course — an "urban renewal" program that decimated a prosperous, safe, and middle-class neighborhood and business district, just as happened elsewhere. Decades of worsening decay and crime inspired more master plans that did little to right the city's wrongs.

It is not only conservatives like Michael Anton who, by lacking faith in the people, can threaten democracy.

The Lincoln runs through the heart of East Liberty, passing where the housing towers — "crack stacks," they came to be called, for the drug dealing around them — once stood, before they were knocked down, part of a revival effort spearheaded by a nonprofit group supported by local business, civic, and philanthropic leaders. Together, and with support from the city, the group has been re-stitching the urban fabric that progressive leaders ripped up, helping to refurbish and redevelop abandoned homes and lots and reduce crime with the help of off-duty police officers, a reversal of the narrow corporate aims that brought Pinkertons to Homestead.

A Google office building employing eight hundred people has taken over the old Nabisco plant on the Lincoln Highway. Other tech companies have followed Google, attracted by the presence of Carnegie Mellon University, a leading engineering school. Andrew Carnegie's philanthropic legacy is helping to extend Westinghouse's innovation legacy, thanks to bottom-up and community-driven leadership that combines their best qualities — Carnegie's generosity and Westinghouse's decency — to overcome one of the worst qualities of politicians: arrogance.

We approach downtown along a bluff overlooking a valley where the largest civilian disaster of the Civil War took place, a munitions explosion that killed seventy-six people, nearly all of them young girls. They had recently replaced the boys working there, since girls didn't smoke and thus didn't carry matches. Most of the bodies could not be identified, as the *Pittsburgh Gazette* reported: "The most appalling sight was the burning bodies. In some places they lay in heaps, and burnt as rapidly as pine wood, until the flames were extinguished by the firemen . . . The steel bands remaining from the hoop skirts of the unfortunate girls, marked the place where many of them perished."

It's the day after the anniversary of the explosion, September 17, 1862, the same date as the bloodiest battle of the Civil War, Antietam, whose battlefield is visited by several hundred thousand people annually. Few stop here to remember the women and girls who played a critical role in the war's supply chain, and there is not much to see. It's a park with a ball field and playground, a fitting monument to girls who had been denied their youth. Had they lived, what might they have achieved? And the same must be asked of the 750,000 people who died in the war. Westinghouse fought and survived. But what of the others? How might they have changed the course of the nation? The products they might have invented, the scientific discoveries they might have made, the art they might have created, the causes they might have advanced, the children they might have borne — all lost to history. We can count a war's casualties, but not its costs.

In a nearby cemetery, a small memorial stone honors those whose bodies were never identified after the munition explosion. A plaque reads, "Tread softly. This is consecrated dust. Forty-five pure patriotic victims lie here. A sacrifice to freedom and civil liberty. A horrid moment of a most wicked rebellion. Patriots! These are patriots' graves."

Consecrated dust. It is not just at Gettysburg where we can hear Lincoln: "We cannot dedicate — we cannot consecrate — we cannot hallow — this ground. The brave men" — and women and girls — "who struggled here, have consecrated it far above our poor power to add or detract." All we can do — whether here or in Shanksville, Lower Manhattan, Homestead, Johnstown, or East Liberty — is dedicate ourselves to "the unfinished work" that others "so nobly advanced" against forces hostile to freedom, democracy, and equality.

— 8 —

Point of View

When Lincoln arrived in Pittsburgh on Valentine's Day 1861, among the love letters he received was one that serves as a reminder that political vitriol did not begin with social media.

> Mr Abe Lincoln
> if you don't Resign we are going to put a spider in your dumpling and play the Devil with you you god or mighty god dam sunned of a bith go to hell and buss my ass suck my prick and call my Bolics your uncle Dick go dam a fool and goddam Abe Lincoln who would like you goddam you excuse me for using such hard words with you but you need it you are nothing but a goddam Black nigger
>
> yours & c
>
> Mr. A. G. Frick
>
> Tennessee Missouri Kentucky Virginia N. Carolina and Arkansas is going to secede Glory be to go on high.

There's no record of Lincoln's reaction to this missive, but in addressing a crowd outside his hotel that day, he took pains to argue that its sentiment was shared by only a small cabal, not half the country, and he urged people to "keep cool." The day prior, a live bomb had been discovered in Lincoln's train car. "If the great American people will only keep their temper, on both sides of the line," he said, "the troubles will come to an end."

As we arrive downtown, we are heading to a place I've always wanted to go: PNC Park, home of the Pirates, which opened in 2001 and is often considered the best baseball stadium of the modern era. That the stadium sits on the Lincoln Highway is fitting, since Abe played an early variation of the game called town-ball. A 1907 biography claimed he was playing the game when he learned of his nomination for president, all the better to mythologize him as the archetypal American. "All his comrades immediately threw up their hats and commenced to hurrah," the author asserted, apocryphally. "Abe grinned considerably, scratched his head and said 'Go on boys; don't let such nonsense spoil a good game.'" Not even a global pandemic can spoil it. Today is a double-header, but with all Major League games closed to fans, the closest we can get to the diamond is an adjacent parking lot, where we can stay overnight for $20 — not bad for Friday-night lodging.

To get there, we cross the Allegheny River on a bridge named for a native son, Andrew Warhola Jr., who dropped the third vowel of the family name after leaving for Manhattan to become an advertising illustrator. Warhol's critics derided his art as commercialism, but after growing up poor in the Great Depression, being accused of making money was no insult. Besides, national truths lay within his works, including in the soup and soda cans he celebrated. "What's great about this country is America started the tradition where the richest consumers buy essentially the same things as the poorest," he said. "A Coke is a Coke and no amount of money can get you a better Coke than the one the bum on the corner is drinking. All the Cokes are the same and all the Cokes are good."

Warhol saw growing social equality in the mass production of consumer goods, but others saw in him only dark nihilism that was rotting the culture. After an angry writer-actress fired three shots at him that left him gravely wounded, many joined with *Time* magazine — which called him a "guru of a nightmare world" — in believing the incident to be justice straight out of the Book of Galatians: You reap what you sow. The next day, when Robert F. Kennedy was shot and killed, voices inside both *Time* and *Life* blamed Warhol. The nightmare of rising gun deaths was only just beginning.

We've arrived in Pittsburgh on the first day of Rosh Hashanah and two years after a forty-eight-year-old white man with semi-automatic guns entered the Tree of Life synagogue and opened fire, yelling, "All Jews must die!" He killed eleven people and wounded six more — the deadliest attack on a Jewish community in American history. The man arrested for the massacre had posted online comments full of contempt for Jews, blacks, and immigrants. Two hours before the shooting, he wrote of the Hebrew Immigrant Aid Society, "HIAS likes to bring invaders in that kill our people. I can't sit by and watch my people get slaughtered."

My people — the same phrase Michael Anton had used in his Flight 93 essay. *Invaders* — the same word President Trump and conservative media figures have used dozens of times about unarmed émigrés moving north through Mexico, which the shooter referenced in social media posts. The word *invaders* is loaded with hostility and implies an attack intended to kill and conquer rather than adapt and contribute. Two days after the massacre, Trump used the word again, though not about the shooter's invasion of the sanctuary.

While Laurel works in Charley, I take a cab to the Tree of Life synagogue in Squirrel Hill, the center of the city's Jewish life. It's surrounded by a chain-link fence displaying artwork painted by teenagers — hands clasping, trees growing, flowers blooming, doves flying, hearts floating, many of the works carrying a written message: "Love conquers all." "You're not alone." "Together we stand." Local students painted most of them, but some are by kids in other communities who have survived the horror of mass shootings. One is by a thirteen-year-old from Auckland, New Zealand, where a gunman entered two mosques and opened fire, killing fifty-one people and injuring forty more. It shows eyes containing flags from every continent, and in between them it reads, "Look at the World from a Different Perspective." The synagogue shooter had written, "Open your Eyes! It's the filthy EVIL jews Bringing the Filthy EVIL Muslims into the Country!!" He could not see what the teenager did.

In the aftermath of the shooting here, a few young leaders came together to create the 412 Black Jewish Collaborative. "One of the things we were hearing over and over again," one of its founders, Josh Sayles, tells me, "especially from our black partners, was: 'Thank God the Jewish community is getting everything you need from the city, from faith leaders, from diverse community leaders. But we've got young black men dying in low-income neighborhoods several times a week, and no one is doing a thing for us.'" They formed the group to bring the two communities deeper into dialogue, and Josh organized a small delegation to go on a civil rights mission in the south. "I was absolutely blown away by the Lynching Memorial" in Montgomery, he says. "The atmosphere, the feeling in that space, was exactly how I felt in the Holocaust memorials in Germany."

The group has a rich history to draw upon. "If you talk to any Jewish person who lives in Pittsburgh of retirement age or older," says Josh, "they grew up in the Hill District," once one of black America's cultural capitals, known for its jazz and nightclubs — "the crossroads of the world," the poet Claude McKay called it, before the city bulldozed it in the name of urban renewal, leaving it awash in empty lots and saddled with segregation. A child born there to a black mother and a German father, August Wilson, became one of the nation's preeminent playwrights, and early into his Pittsburgh Cycle of ten plays, nine of them set in the Hill District, he attended a seder where he had a revelation: The gathering was more than a holiday meal. It was an exercise in communal memory that has been passed down for thousands of years, beginning with enslaved Jews in Egypt, and the words that are repeated each year help preserve a shared identity and sustain a common dream: *Next year in Jerusalem.*

"I find it criminal," he later reflected, "that we, after hundreds of years in bondage, do not celebrate our Emancipation Proclamation, that we do not have a thing like the Passover where we sit down and we remind ourselves that we are African people, that we were slaves. Because we try to run away, we try to hide that part of our past." The seder helped him see the unifying power of collective memory. "If we did something like that, it would say, 'This is who we are.' We would recognize the fact that we are Africans, we would recognize the fact that we were slaves, and we would recognize that since we have a common past, that we have a common future also."

A shared understanding of a common past is vital to success in building a common future, and Lincoln's experience with both blacks and Jews can aid us in keeping the struggle for inclusivity and pluralism at the center of it. Jews considered him a dear friend in part because he overrode Congress to appoint Jewish chaplains to the army during the Civil War, and he overrode a decision by General Grant — one that Grant would come to deeply regret — to ban Jews from several states under his control. Lincoln's assassination, though often recalled as coinciding with Good Friday, occurred during Passover, drawing comparisons to Moses leading the faithful out of bondage to the Promised Land, without making it there himself. The Bible calls that pilgrimage an exodus, but today some might call it an invasion.

From the neatly trimmed lawns of Squirrel Hill, where nearly half of residents are Jewish, I head to Homewood, which is 95 percent black and littered with abandoned lots, a legacy of the city's disastrous experiment with urban renewal, from which it is still recovering. One of the vacant lots holds a community garden worked by teenagers who grow tomatoes, corn, squash, peppers, eggplant, okra, watermelon, mint, and more. "The first week they hate me," says the program director, Ayanna Jones, of the student-employees she holds to exacting standards. "That second week, I have to push them off-site. They get off at three. At four thirty, they're still here working."

Throughout the summer, Ayanna talks to her gardeners about black history and black innovators in science and business. "These kids get the opportunity to hear something besides enslavement, so when they go back to school and slavery comes up, my kids have a foundation." She's instilling in them the kind of communal memory that fosters pride, ambition, and confidence.

One of her early students was Antwon Rose, a seventeen-year-old shot dead by a police officer in 2018 while running away from an arrest. On the day George Floyd was killed, she says, her kids didn't work. "We sat at the tent and those kids expressed some of the most profound statements, emotions, and feelings." She was proud that some of them participated in the protests, though she did not. "I'm not a protest person. I've been protesting since 1964. If it was successful, we wouldn't be where we're at now. I've been a Black Panther, I've been in the Black Liberation Army. I have lived through Emmett Till being killed all the way up to George Floyd, and I don't see any progress. But I did see participation by white folks that I never saw before. It was uncanny how white people took to the streets and made their voices heard. And that's what's going to make the change. It's not going to be a black change. It's going to be white people saying, 'We're tired of seeing what is being done to people because of the color of their skin and not the content of their character.'"

Earlier in the day, the country singer Tyler Childers released a new album, *Long Violent History*. In a video accompanying it, he asks his "white rural listeners" to imagine how they might react to regular headlines about police killings of innocent people in their own communities, an idea he sings about in the title track, which was partly inspired by the police killing of his fellow Kentuckian, Breonna Taylor.

How many boys could they haul off this mountain
Shoot full of holes, cuffed, and layin' in the streets
'Til we come in to town in a stark ravin' anger
Looking for answers and armed to the teeth

"On the whole, people want to do us right," Ayanna says. "But as a country, we have to do better. If we don't do better, Portland's just gonna be the tip of the iceberg."

Tonight in Portland, tear gas will again fill the streets as protestors square off against police in riot gear and gas masks, as they have been doing almost nightly since George Floyd's murder, sometimes resulting in vandalism, looting, arson, and even, just a few weeks ago, a homicide — of Aaron "Jay" Danielson, a Trump supporter, who was gunned down by a self-described anti-fascist, Michael Reinoehl. "I am 100% ANTIFA," Reinoehl had posted on social media. "We truly have an opportunity right now to fix everything. But it will be a fight like no other! It will be a war and like all wars there will be casualties." After he killed Danielson, he told a reporter, "That shot felt like the beginning of a war." Armed and resisting arrest, he was shot and killed by police.

Democrats have been muted about the murder of Danielson, while Republicans have been outraged, seeing it as a validation of antifa's danger. Stewart Rhodes, head of the right-wing militia Oath Keepers, tweeted, "Civil war is here, right now." Danielson's father had the opposite reaction. Democrats should "get together with the Republican side and put a stop to this violence," he tells a reporter. "If I can lose the life of my son, they can sit down at a table and be civil to each other and start to work something out. I deserve that as a citizen."

Laurel and I meet up at Klavon's Ice Cream Parlor in the Strip District, where blast furnaces once lit up the night sky so brightly that people said the city looked like "hell with the lid off." When the factories closed and wholesalers moved out, the area fell into decline, but it has recently been reborn with ethnic grocers, meat markets, and restaurants. We are Klavon's only customers, and as the owner shares some of its rich history — it opened in 1923 as a soda fountain and apothecary and reopened in 1999 after sitting vacant for twenty years — a father and son walk in and join the conversation. Ice cream has a way of bringing people together, and the son, nineteen, has a good story to share.

"I created this character," he says — Brandon Max is his name on TikTok — "to entertain people, to inspire people, to show people that it's okay to be different." That takes courage, given the cruelty that can dominate social media, but it has paid off: He's become a star by creating silly and uplifting videos. "I get some really nice comments from people saying that I've helped them through their anxiety or depression, or just that they were having a bad day and I cheered them up. But at the same time, of course, I'll have people throwing anti-Semitic comments toward me. It's just really, really ugly, but I don't listen to those people. I always stay positive and if I ever do respond, I just say, 'I'm sending you positive thoughts, I'm sorry you're having a bad day.'"

Brandon's artistic creations, like the art that adorns the fence around the Tree of Life synagogue, have a purpose. "All art is political," said August Wilson, "in the sense that it serves someone's politics." Wilson was making the same point W. E. B. Du Bois made in a 1926 speech to the NAACP: "All art is propaganda and ever must be, despite the wailing of the purists," which George Orwell later echoed: "All art is to some extent propaganda." Wilson, Du Bois, and Orwell all recognized that art is influenced and shaped, however subtly, by the artist's perspective. Creation cannot be separated from creator.

The word *propaganda* now carries a negative connotation because of its association with government disinformation, but its roots are religious. In 1622, Pope Gregory XV sought to bring missionary efforts under greater Vatican control by creating a new department to oversee them, Congregatio de propaganda fide. *Propaganda* is a Latin word meaning "multiplying" or "spreading" — hence the English derivative, *propagation*. It is a neutral term, but the Vatican imbued it with evangelism, giving the new department a motto from the Gospel of Matthew: "Go forth and teach all the people."

Today everyone on social media engages in the propagation of ideas — political, social, religious, cultural — with the intent to influence others. "Influencer" is a job title many aspire to, and it's a modern, secular, and democratized rebranding of the Vatican department. We have stripped propaganda of hierarchy but kept its purpose: to attract as many followers as possible. We are all propagandists now, evangelizing our lives and beliefs via the photos and messages we share with communities of fellow travelers, often posting idealized, filtered, and touched-up versions of our experiences, the better to enlarge our flocks.

The same social equality that Warhol found in soda and soup cans we can now see in social media platforms: Everyone can have them, we all get the same thing — and this time, they're free. We call them platforms since we stand upon them to hold forth to the world, but they are closer in spirit to pulpits, since they often radiate the missionary zeal of true believers, joined together in a giant Congregation of the Propagation of the Self.

Brandon's followers have grown by legions. "I was in front of the Apple store and a teen couple just literally screamed my name. And I went over to them and they asked me, 'Are you Brandon Max?'" The line attributed to Warhol about everyone in the future having fifteen minutes of fame — it hardly matters he never said it — perfectly presaged the democratization of celebrity that the digital media age would bring, and its fickle ephemerality. Brandon is worried his influence might wane. "I fear losing where I am right now every single day. I just want to continue doing what I'm doing" — using his creativity to influence and help others, propagating self in the service of society. It's a noble pursuit, social media at its most constructive, and yet in the fear he expresses of losing followers and the pressure to remain popular, we can see the difference between the cult of celebrity and the bonds of community, between the flavor of the month and friendships of a lifetime.

It's not for teenagers to worry about this — Brandon's rightly proud of what he's doing — but as the age of individuality reaches full maturity, the social equality it fosters must, for a nation to hold together, be paired with common bonds.

Down the street from Klavon's, we hear music coming from the back deck of Mullaney's Harp and Fiddle. Having had dessert but not dinner, we take a table and listen to a one-man band sing Irish ballads and Americana classics.

The pub is on the same avenue as the birthplace of Stephen Foster, a Scots-Irish descendant known as the "father of American music" for the popular songs he wrote in the mid-nineteenth century. Before there was recorded music, Foster's melodies and lyrics served as the country's first soundtrack. Although he began his career writing blackface minstrel songs in the tradition of T. D. Rice, who first performed the song "Jump Jim

Crow" in Pittsburgh in 1831, Foster turned away from minstrelsy as his career progressed, even writing songs that contained anti-slavery themes. One of them, "My Old Kentucky Home," about the cruelty of slavery and ripping enslaved people from their homes and families, later became a nostalgic reverie and prideful state anthem. Millions still sing it without thinking of its original message. For better and worse, song meanings change with those who sing them, just as statue meanings change with those who view them.

In 2018, city officials removed a statue of a seated and nattily dressed Foster holding a notebook with the words "Uncle Ned" written on it — the title of a song he wrote paying tribute, in a patronizing minstrel dialect, to an enslaved man. At his feet was a black man in rags strumming a banjo. Opponents called the statue condescending and exploitative. Proponents argued that it reflected the central influence black musicians had on Foster's work. There was truth in both, but the statue held more pain than pride.

The man on guitar here is singing a maudlin Irish ballad of family separation and state-sanctioned oppression, "The Fields of Athenry." But unlike "My Old Kentucky Home," there can be no mistaking its cry for freedom and justice, partly because its Irish writer, Pete St. John, was not trying to uplift another group but rather to uplift his own. In song, as in all art, there is no erasing one's point of view.

After eating dinner, we have another bar to get to — Cappy's Café in the Shadyshide neighborhood — to meet the city's second-term mayor, Bill Peduto, who is wearing a baseball cap emblazoned with the letter *C* — for Crawfords, the Negro League team that played in the Hill District and whose stars included Satchel Paige, who was finally allowed into Major League Baseball in 1948 at age forty-two. Even at that age, Joe DiMaggio called him "the best I ever faced, and the fastest." Paige was under no illusion about what segregation cost him in fame and fortune. "They said I was the greatest pitcher they ever saw. I couldn't understand why they couldn't give me no justice."

Peduto's Crawford cap is a political statement about racial justice, but he's concerned about how some are trying to achieve it. "There is a disconnect between the messages coming from the protesters and those that are coming from our predominantly black neighborhoods," he says. "Within our neighborhoods, public safety is a major concern. Reforming the police is a major concern, but police presence is something that they also want. With the protestors, the message is, 'Abolish the police' or 'Defund the police,' while in the community it's, 'We don't see enough police in our neighborhoods. Why are they only in the rich neighborhoods?'"

It's impossible not hear his exasperation with protesters. I ask him if extreme ideas carry more currency than they used to. "Yes, on both sides," he says. "This is the Democrats' Tea Party moment. The Republican party was lost to the Tea Party, and we're now in that phase of it where purity tests that would've made anybody unelectable are now being demanded of all candidates. You could have spent over thirty years working on issues like the environment and human rights and civil rights, and because you don't believe in abolishing the police, you're considered a fascist."

It's rare to hear a politician let loose on his own party's extremes, and he's on a tear. "Can I add another thing? What drives all this extremism is the threat of being primaried. It's not worrying whether you can be reelected, but whether you can win your own party primary, when you see your party becoming more extreme by the week." Next year, abandoned by liberal activists, he will lose his party primary.

On a cool and bright Saturday morning, Laurel and I walk across the Allegheny River to the Point, a park on the peninsula where the Allegheny and Monongahela Rivers meet to form the Ohio, which flows 981 miles westward to the Mississippi. The Ohio was the nation's original superhighway, carrying produce, raw materials, and finished goods across the country on steamboats manufactured here by Robert Fulton. As a young man, Lincoln chopped firewood to fuel the river's steamboats, and he earned his first dollar by ferrying passengers to an awaiting one. "I could scarcely credit that I, a poor boy, had earned a dollar in less than a day," he said. "The world seemed wider and fairer before me."

It was that same hope of economic opportunity that brought the Lincoln family across the Ohio River from Kentucky to Indiana. Lincoln wrote that his parents made the move "partly on account of slavery" — they were devout Baptists who believed it immoral — "but chiefly on account of the difficulty of land titles in Ky." Federal surveys guaranteed clear titles to land in the territories north of the river, whereas in Kentucky, disputes over titles often led to litigation, which favored the wealthy. In crossing the river with his family, a young Lincoln experienced the power of government to create economic opportunity for the poor and prohibit exploitation by the wealthy. Yet as Pittsburgh's experience with urban renewal shows — the old industrial neighborhood here on the Point was knocked down to build office towers while East Liberty and the Hill District were left to decay — government has often done the opposite for each group.

The park on the Point holds a re-creation of the British Fort Pitt. Inside it, a museum tells the story of the French and Indian War, or what more aptly would be called the French and British War over Indian Lands in Which Indian Tribes Picked Sides or Stayed Neutral and Sometimes Switched Allegiances. During the war, two Native Americans arrived at Fort Pitt to warn of further attacks if soldiers did not evacuate. "Out of our regard to them," wrote an American in his diary, "we gave them two Blankets and a Handkerchief out of the smallpox hospital. I hope it will have the desired effect." Whether it succeeded in killing anyone remains a matter of debate, but at a time when many Americans believe China intentionally released Covid as an act of aggression, it bears remembering that our own history includes one of the world's first episodes of biological warfare.

After France's surrender, the British issued the Proclamation Line of 1763, which prohibited colonists from moving west of the Allegheny Mountains onto lands acquired from the French. It was an attempt to make peace with a confederation of tribes that had continued fighting, in what became known as Pontiac's Rebellion. But if not for French lands, for what did the colonists fight? Many were already living past the line. Told that their land titles were void, they stayed, feeling betrayed by the Crown and willing to fight Native Americans who stood in their way. They had a supporter in George Washington, who called the proclamation line a "temporary expedient to quiet the Minds of the Indians & must fall of course in a few years." And so it did.

Overlooking the Point is Mount Washington. An old wooden funicular brings us up, providing spectacular views of the city. At the top is a statue of Washington and Guyasuta, the Seneca leader who led attacks on Fort Pitt during Pontiac's Rebellion. The sculpture depicts their meeting in 1770, some two hundred miles farther down the Ohio River, where Washington was surveying lands to claim, a reward for his service in the war against the French. Washington would soon gain title to ten thousand acres along the Ohio River and far more elsewhere, and he placed great value on the large tracts he claimed on this mission, later calling them "the cream of the country."

For generations, American students have learned that Washington was a surveyor without learning much about why he was engaged in the business: acquiring land for wealth, an obfuscation that hides the leading role he played in pushing Native Americans west. The Seneca called Washington by the same name they had called his great-grandfather: *Conotocarious*, which translates to "Town Taker." In 1790, in appealing for mercy and justice to President Washington, Seneca leader Cornplanter said, "To this day, when that name is heard, our women look behind them and turn pale, and our children cling close to the neck of their mothers."

There is no mention of that name or history here, nor of the fact that in 1775 the British government was threatening to void Washington's land claims, complicating the story of why he fought for independence. Instead, the sculpture, called *Point of View*, depicts Washington and Guyasuta facing each other while sitting down and leaning in almost nose-to-nose, conveying both intensity and equality. Washington faces west while Guyasuta holds his ground, even though, by the time of their meeting, Washington had already triumphed. The Proclamation of 1763 prohibiting settlements west of the Allegheny Mountains had been replaced by other treaties that extended the line farther west, just as Washington had predicted.

The artist's purpose in creating the Guyasuta-Washington sculpture was not merely to commemorate their meeting but to teach a lesson: that there is progress in civility. "They are listening to each other," explained the sculptor, Jim West. "They are having civil dialogue and putting their differences aside. That's the story. That's the lesson for us all, then and now." Yet it is hard to look at the statue and not wonder: What did it benefit Native Americans to listen and engage in civil dialogue? And how much listening was Washington really doing?

The statue reflects August Wilson's statement that "all art is political," while also serving as a reminder that different people can look at art and see different things, taking away lessons the artist never intended to convey. Art can reveal truth but not dictate it, which is precisely what makes public art, especially monuments, so effective at starting arguments.

After riding the funicular back down the mountain, we retrace our steps past Fort Pitt, where an American flag flies at half-staff in honor of Supreme Court justice Ruth Bader Ginsburg. She died yesterday, after dictating a final public statement: "My most fervent wish is that I will not be replaced until a new president is installed." In 2016, she had rebuked Republicans for taking much the same position when they refused to hold a vote on

President Obama's nomination to replace Antonin Scalia after his unexpected death. "The president is elected for four years not three years," she scolded them, "so the power he has in year three continues into year four. Maybe members of the Senate will wake up and appreciate that that's how it should be." With a different president in the White House, she had a deathbed conversion.

If we were more honest about how partisanship affects our point of view, it might be possible to temper, however modestly, some of the self-righteous rage that surrounds political maneuvers far smaller than Supreme Court nominations. Honesty about ourselves has a way of defusing anger with others, a truth often conveyed by a local kid sitting on the other side of the Allegheny River in bronze, tying his shoes: Fred Rogers.

Rogers grew up nearby in Latrobe and worked at a fledgling public television station in Pittsburgh while attending seminary school. His children's show probably wouldn't have been as popular had it been called "Minister Rogers Neighborhood," but he viewed it as a vehicle for his ministry and its mission, which he stated with characteristic simplicity: "Encourage children to feel good about themselves." He aimed to support children's emotional development, not their intellectual education, and he often did it through music, writing more than two hundred songs for the show, with the great jazz pianist Johnny Costa, also a Pittsburgh boy, improvising on the melody.

I have always wanted to live in a neighborhood with you

As the show became nationally syndicated in early 1968, black neighborhoods across America were erupting in violence, fueled in part by white flight and the same kinds of urban renewal programs that destroyed neighborhoods in Pittsburgh. During the show's first week, Rogers, a Republican, featured a black schoolteacher and a group of interracial students, sending a clear message that neighborhoods should welcome all people. At the same time, he invited François Clemmons, a man he had heard singing at his church, to become the first black character on a children's television show, a police officer. "I grew up in the ghetto, and I did not have a positive opinion of police officers," Clemmons later recalled. "Policemen were siccing dogs and water hoses on people. And I really had a hard time putting myself in that role. So I was not excited about being Officer Clemmons at all."

In 1969, as many areas of the country continued to resist desegregation, including of public swimming pools, Rogers invited Clemmons to stick his feet into a wading pool with him, while also sharing his towel, taking direct aim at the common fallacy among whites that blacks were dirty and prone to carry disease. "That scene touched me in a way that I was not prepared," said Clemmons. "I still was not convinced that Officer Clemmons could have a positive influence in the *Neighborhood* and in the real-world neighborhood. I think I was proven wrong."

The two re-created the scene in 1993 for Clemmons's final appearance on the show, and this time Fred went further, helping wipe Clemmons's feet dry, an act of sacrificial service imbued with meaning from the Christian faith they shared. The show — its title, songs, and sketches — evoked the universality of the commandment Jesus said was above all others, except love for God: "Love your *neighbor* as yourself." To do that, it helps to see yourself in your neighbors — to walk a mile in their shoes, as the adage goes. Rogers, who began his shows by taking off one pair of shoes and putting on another, encouraged children to do just that. And Clemmons, in an act of great compassion, would do it for Rogers.

In his memoir, Clemmons tells the story of what happened when Rogers heard that Clemmons had gone to a gay bar, in 1968. "If you're gay, it doesn't matter to me at all," Fred told him. "Whatever you say and do is fine with me, but if you're going to be on the show as an important member of the *Neighborhood*, you can't be out as gay." Rogers even suggested that Clemmons think about marriage, saying, "People do make some compromises in life." Clemmons said the talk "destroyed" him. He married, but it lasted only a few years, and when he came out soon after, Rogers supported him — and he remained on the show.

It is easy to judge Rogers for offering Clemmons private but not public support, but had he done otherwise, the show likely would have been canceled. As Lincoln's life shows, the price of progress for those in public life often requires coming to terms with public opinion. In his runs for the Senate and presidency, Lincoln made plain his personal moral opposition to slavery, while also stressing that he did not seek — as many in his party did — to abolish it. He could not afford to be that far in front of public opinion and still hope to have broad public support. Rogers was in a similar position. In an interview many years later, Clemmons said, "Lord have mercy, yes, I forgive him. More than that, I understand."

We leave Pittsburgh in the late afternoon to spend the night in another parking lot next to a sporting venue, this one open to fans: Pittsburgh's Pennsylvania Motor Speedway. Before going in, we sit outside with a beer and listen to the public address announcer hype up the night's races and urge people to follow masking rules so the track can avoid further trouble with the police: "We appreciate you leaving your politics out in the parking lot." At the end of our row in an open field, a pickup truck flies two flags: a Trump flag and one that melds the American and Confederate flags. We are both excited for the auto race — our first one — but I can't help but wonder: Were we black, would we feel safe sleeping here? I strongly suspect we'd have a different point of view.

— 9 —

Do Right

A sign for Janoski's Farm, family run since 1958, brings visions of cider donuts. I pump the brakes, but making a turn in an RV is like sliding a beer bottle down a bar: Do it too fast and you'll tip it over. We lean into the turn and pull into the lot, inventing a parking space next to rusted-out red 1950s Chevy pickup truck serving as a flowerpot. Flyers posted at the door tell us we are a week early for Pumpkinland, their fall festival with hayrides and a haunted barn, but pumpkins are displayed by the hundreds, and Laurel picks one out, along with a gourd. She loves this time of year — spooky season, she calls it — and on the kitchen counter she finds a spot for the beginnings of a Halloween display.

The feel of fall is with us as we wind through Pennsylvania's hilly western woodlands to the northern tip of West Virginia. A mile past the state line, just beyond the White Stallion Club tavern and before Gumby's Cigarette and Beer World, a thin flagpole stands in front of a house, bending in the breeze and flying the Confederate battle flag. This is Chester, population twenty-three hundred, once the northernmost point of the Confederacy, on the same latitude line as New York City. In 1861, when Virginians voted on secession, the tally in the county here was 23 in favor, 743 against. But still the flag waves.

The creation of the state of West Virginia was legally dubious, and its proponents knew it. "I will not stultify myself by supposing that we have any warrant in the Constitution for this proceeding," said Thaddeus Stevens, in voting to accept it as a state. Under Article IV of the Constitution, a new state can be formed out of an existing one only if the latter grants its permission, as Virginia did with Kentucky and Massachusetts did with Maine. Virginians who opposed seceding from the union, mostly from the west, lost at the state's convention and the referendum that followed. No matter. They formed their own state government and put statehood to a vote. It passed, and though no ballots were received from counties where Confederate sympathy ran strong, the provisional government declared the referendum valid, and the petition went to Congress for approval.

Lincoln's attorney general, Edward Bates, opposed splitting the state because the acting legislature was not "in truth or honesty" the government of Virginia. Some of Stevens's fellow abolitionists, like his friend Senator Charles Sumner, voted against the bill because it provided only for gradual emancipation of slaves, and thus would increase the number of slave states. But Lincoln's highest consideration was neither legal nor moral. It was tactical: winning the war and preserving the Union. He wrestled mightily with the matter, acknowledging that "the division of a state is dreaded as a precedent," but convinced himself of the bill's wisdom. "Mr. Lincoln probably thought it more convenient, to say the least," wrote the poet James Russell Lowell in 1864, "to have a country left without a constitution, than a constitution without a country."

We are bound together by more than the Constitution, which deserves reverence but not idolatry. It is imperfect. We occasionally modify it. It is our instrument, not our essence. And it exists to perpetuate and improve the nation, not the other way around. "The Union is older than the Constitution," Lincoln said in his first inaugural address, reminding Americans — especially in the south — that the nation was first formed with the Declaration of Independence and Articles of Confederation. The Constitution was adopted only "to form a more perfect union" — the nation's perpetual challenge.

Chester and its larger sister city across the river, East Liverpool, Ohio, once formed the pottery capital of the world, thanks to the rich deposits of yellow clay in the Ohio River that runs along their banks. More than two hundred pottery companies operated here, producing half the nation's ceramics. Pottery shops sold their wares to visitors who came to Chester to visit Rock Springs Park, an amusement park that opened in 1897, drawing people by boat and train from Pittsburgh, Wheeling, and across the region to its attractions and rides, including one of the great wonders of the age, a Ferris wheel, invented just down the river in Pittsburgh by George Washington Gale Ferris Jr. When a swimming pool and artificial lake opened in 1904, black visitors could swim in the lake, but not the pool.

The amusement park closed in 1970, and its lake was replaced by another: Little Blue Run Lake, the largest coal ash pond in the country, sixteen miles around. The coal company that built the pond told the surrounding communities they would be getting a beautiful lake for swimming, fishing, camping — even waterskiing! Imagine the soaring property values! The coal ash, they assured residents, would sink to the bottom and form a cement-like surface — nothing to worry about. Coal ash sinks, however, because it contains traces of metals, including arsenic, lead, and mercury. As the ash lake grew to nearly a thousand acres, it developed a bright teal color, giving rise to a local nickname: the Pennsylvania Caribbean. Over time, residents began noticing the smell of rotten eggs and the sight of groundwater carrying a white metallic film. The lake was leaking, seeping into the ground, contaminating the water table, and leaching its way into the Ohio River.

The company that owns the coal plant has bought out dozens of homes and farms in the vicinity of Little Blue Run. Often, it was the only potential buyer, leaving families to sell low. After years of fighting lawsuits by residents, the company is in the process of draining the lake.

"This must be it, right?" I ask Laurel, as we look out on an empty expanse of grassland.

She looks at a map on her phone: "It must be."

The company has placed a plastic liner over the lake bottom, added a foot of soil, seeded it, and inserted protruding pipes for water-quality measurements. It is not clear whether anyone will live on or farm this land again. Maybe someday it can be the public park the company had originally promised the community. But for now, it is fenced off, a beautiful landscape hiding corporate crime that has gone unpunished.

Across the river in East Liverpool, the Lincoln brings us to another place with a criminal legacy, this one a tourist attraction: the old funeral parlor where an undertaker embalmed the body of Charles Arthur "Pretty Boy" Floyd in 1934, after FBI agents shot him in the back outside of town. Ten thousand visitors came — some in mourning, some in relief, most in titillation — to see the country's "Public Enemy Number One," wanted for bank robberies and the murders of police officers, federal agents, and bootleggers, some he killed, some he may not have. During a Great Depression that left two million homeless, with banks foreclosing upon hundreds of thousands of farms and forcing families from their land, stories circulated that Floyd ripped up mortgage notes during bank robberies and shared his plunder with the poor. "I have robbed no one but moneyed men," he wrote on a postcard to the acting governor of his home state of Oklahoma. On paper containing the lyrics to his song, "Pretty Boy Floyd," Woody Guthrie wrote: "I love a good man outside the law just as much as I hate a bad man inside the law."

Some will rob you with a six-gun,
And some with a fountain pen.

A few doors down from the old funeral parlor is an old bank building, and above its columns is a name that takes me by surprise: the Lou Holtz/Upper Ohio Valley Hall of Fame. It's closed, which is a break for Laurel.

Holtz grew up here and coached the University of Notre Dame football team for eleven years, including the four I spent there. He won popular acclaim for his humorous aphorisms and folksy life lessons, his wispy frame and lispy voice packing his Horatio Alger view of the world with added punch. He has spent decades evangelizing his three rules of life: "Do right. Do your best. Show people you care." The second two are straightforward. The first is the puzzle at the center of democratic society.

A few weeks before we began our trip, Holtz delivered a speech at the Republican National Convention criticizing Trump's critics and protestors. "They don't have pride in our country," he said. "That's wrong." A few of his former players spoke out, telling Holtz he was wrong and mentioning Demetrius DuBose, an all-American linebacker under Holtz who was shot and killed in 1999 by San Diego police, who were called after a man found DuBose napping in his bed. DuBose, who had been crashing on a friend's couch in the condo next door, cooperated with their questioning and explained that he meant no harm. They told him to stand up so they could handcuff him. He asked why. They told him to comply, or they would spray him with Mace. He refused and said he was going to "go get the cops," believing he was being wrongly treated because of his race, his friend would tell police. They tried to tackle him. He threw them off and ran. They followed, one of the officers with his gun pulled. After they hit him with their nunchucks, he grabbed their nunchucks. The officers, fearing for their safety, shot him twelve times. The autopsy found traces of cocaine and Ecstasy in his system. The local district attorney reviewed the case and deemed the killing justified. The family didn't think so, and sued. They lost.

Do right. For some of DuBose's former Notre Dame teammates, that has meant supporting those protesting police violence. Not so their old coach. In the space between them, we can see much of the national debate over policing. DuBose *did wrong* by entering the neighbor's apartment and resisting arrest. But did the police *do right* by attempting to arrest and handcuff him when the misunderstanding was being explained, in drawing a gun in pursuit, and in firing their guns instead of retreating and de-escalating?

Do right. It's so easy to say. It is much harder to append, as Lincoln did, "as we understand it."

The day after Holtz's speech, Notre Dame's president, Father John Jenkins, gently rebuked him for calling Joe Biden "Catholic in name only," because of Biden's support for abortion rights. Jenkins's message was clear — *That's wrong* — but his words carried none of Holtz's righteous judgment: "We Catholics should remind ourselves that while we may judge the objective moral quality of another's actions, we must never question the sincerity of another's faith, which is due to the mysterious workings of grace in that person's heart. In this fractious time, let us remember that our highest calling is to love."

We can hold diametrically opposing views on the most contentious moral issues, including what constitutes a murder — whether of a fetus or of a football player — and still see in each other, if not divine grace, national fellowship. It's difficult, certainly. But are we *doing our best*? Are we *showing we care*? Are we acknowledging, as Lincoln did at Cooper Union, that we are capable of error and misjudgment?

In Spike Lee's 1989 movie, *Do the Right Thing,* about black and white relations and the gray in between, a white police officer strangles a black man to death, setting a neighborhood ablaze with anger, a drama intended to capture the zeitgeist of 1980s urban America that has instead, tragically, taken on a broader timelessness. In the final scene, Spike Lee's character, Mookie, throws a trash can through the window of a pizza shop owned by a racist, starting a riot but also possibly saving the owner's life — and maybe, just maybe, forcing more white people to stop ignoring the police killings of black people.

"Always do the right thing," an older man played by Ossie Davis had told Mookie.

"That's it?"

"That's it."

—10—

Pitchforks & Discourse

Candidate signs plaster the windows of Republican county headquarters in downtown Lisbon, Ohio, the birthplace of one of the party's modern founders: Mark Hanna, an industrialist who helped put William McKinley in the White House — and who, critics still say, helped robber barons plunder the masses. As I take a photo of the party's storefront, a man on a motorcycle rides by without a helmet, just a bandanna, as is permitted in Ohio and more than half of all states. It strikes me as foolishly dangerous — data shows that helmets save lives — but many motorcyclists understand the risks and don't want government taking the decision out of their hands. Having the liberty to control one's body stirs passionate debates, from abortion and euthanasia to mask and vaccine mandates. Two Lisbon natives have stood at the center of national debates over the wisdom and constitutionality of limits on liberty, and the first revolved around Lincoln.

In 1860, Lincoln ran on a platform of liberty for blacks in the western territories, and Republicans' most popular campaign song was "Lincoln and Liberty Too." During the war, however, the question arose: Did citizens possess the liberty to oppose the government's actions? In 1863, Major General Ambrose Burnside issued an order prohibiting anyone in his western military district from "declaring sympathy for the enemy." Violators would be arrested and possibly expelled to the Confederacy. "It must be understood that treason, expressed or implied," his order stated, "will not be tolerated."

The infringement on free speech enraged Democrats, none more so than Lisbon's Clement Vallandigham, who defended slavery, blamed abolitionism for causing the war, and advocated a negotiated peace that would divide the nation into four sections and require a congressional majority from each to pass a bill and elect a president. When he decried "a war for the purpose of crushing out liberty and erecting a despotism," he was arrested, tried in a military court, convicted, and sentenced to prison. Lincoln regarded the affair as regrettable — he ordered Burnside to commute the sentence to exile to the Confederacy — but the incident gave credence to the Democrats' charge that Lincoln was acting as "Caesar," "tyrant," "usurper," "dictator." Vallandigham had called him "King Lincoln." Democrats reminded the public that Lincoln had been a critic of the Mexican War. Should they not have the same free speech rights Lincoln did?

Fifty years later, in another federal crackdown on dissent, another Lisbon native took center stage, this time as judge. In 1918, Supreme Court justice John Hessin Clarke voted with the majority in upholding the convictions of Emma Goldman and Alexander Berkman under the Espionage Act of 1917, which prohibited Americans from urging resistance to the draft. Goldman and Berkman, who had organized resistance, were given the maximum sentence. The following year, Justice Clarke voted with the majority three times to uphold convictions of socialists under the Sedition Act of 1918, which broadened the categories of forbidden speech and increased the maximum sentence to twenty years. It passed the House by a nearly unanimous vote. Only a socialist Jewish immigrant from New York City's Lower East Side, Meyer London, opposed it.

In these cases of anarchists, socialists, and Confederate sympathizers — and with bandanna-wearing motorcyclists and anti-maskers — we can see the debates over liberty that have long shaped the American identity and how restrictions on liberty, and especially attempts to suppress speech, have been used to serve both conservative and liberal aims. Today, the suppression comes less through law than culture, as a poster taped to an ice cream stand window outside Minerva, Ohio, helps illustrate.

The poster is titled "How to Build Community," which is followed by a long string of friendly directives about helping, giving, sharing, listening, learning, and other practices of good neighborliness, beginning with "Turn off your TV." It predates social media, but the final instruction feels timeless: "Know that no one is silent but many are not heard. Work to change this."

In the wake of George Floyd's murder, the progressive publishing company that created the poster began selling an updated version called "Dismantle White Supremacy: Tools for Action." The final plea on the original poster — work to ensure all people are heard — has been replaced with "White folks need to listen more, talk less and support individuals, organizations and communities of color." Listening more is an unqualified good and an unquestionable need, but communities of color are not monoliths. They contain differing and often conflicting views on what it means to support them. Debating those differences is essential. The intimidation implicit in the sentence — *pipe down and fall in line* — is not a tool for building community, nor for promoting national unity, though during wartimes, our government has used it for exactly that purpose. We are not at war now, but sometimes it can feel that way. The more it does, the more likely we are to abrogate, or support politicians who abrogate, our right to speak freely and other constitutional protections that safeguard democracy.

Just beyond the ice cream stand is our campground. I park next to the office and remain inside Charley to make a phone call. An older woman and her husband drive by in their golf cart, staring. They circle the campground loop and drive by a second time, and it's now clear they're glaring. The golf cart stops, and the woman marches over to us.

"You lookin' for someone?" she asks, glowering. It's more of an accusation than a question.

"No, but thanks — I'm about to check in."

She says nothing and marches back to her cart.

On the "How to Build Community" poster, the commandments after "Turn off your TV" are "Leave your house" and "Know your neighbors." Say this for the woman: She's taking an interest in us. Thankfully, others are more welcoming. As we eat dinner at our picnic table, another woman walks by and says, friendly as can be, "I like your little motor home!"

It's not the first time a neighbor has called Charley little, and though we are still getting the hang of our little guy, tonight we take a big step. After reviewing the instruction manual to be certain of what I'm doing, I press the HEAT ELECTRIC button to turn on the hot-water tank. Laurel takes the first hot shower of the trip and comes out feeling rejuvenated — and wondering what took us so long to turn it on.

My general approach to Charley's amenities has been simple: If we don't attempt to use them, we can't break them. But each new step brings more confidence. At some point, I know, I'm going to have to face down the furnace.

A towering cow statue stands in front of Minerva Dairy, a family-owned creamery in Minerva, advertising "Butter Made Better." We see the statue again on Market Street, this time in a painting hanging on a wire fence around an empty lot beside a boarded-up bar, part of an exhibit by high school students who have put local twists on classic artworks. The artist has transformed the cow statue into a surrealistic portrait inspired by Salvador Dalí's *Persistence of Memory*, where clocks melt like cheese on a sunny seashore, "the camembert of time," said Dalí. Another painting, a play on Grant Wood's *American Gothic*, shows a farmer and daughter in front of a nearby historic mansion holding an enormous table fork, rather than a pitchfork, since the mansion is now a restaurant.

"I realized," Wood said about his time living in Paris in the 1920s, "that all the really good ideas I'd ever had came to me while I was milking a cow. So I went back to Iowa." For Wood, cows and consciousness had a more direct relationship than they did for Dalí, and he devoted himself to capturing the essence of the midwest, its land, people, and culture, giving rise to what came to be called Regionalism, a new American style at a time when the country's visual artists were only just beginning to emerge from the shadow of their European masters. It's fitting that one of the most distinctly American paintings, his *American Gothic*, contains a pitchfork, the symbol of both peaceful pastures and angry populism.

We pull over at the Robertsville Grange, #1784, a red-brick building in the shape of a church and built to play a similar role: bringing people together for mutual aid and benefit. Although its doors are locked, it's fitting to see a Grange lodge on the Lincoln Highway, since the movement sprang from a Lincoln creation: the Department of Agriculture, which he asked Congress to create, believing it would be "of great practical value to the country." In 1867, department leaders formed the National Grange of the Order of Patrons of Husbandry to help farmers support one another — a sort of federally inspired barn raising. Its founders, including William Saunders, who designed the national cemetery at Gettysburg, envisioned local chapters as cooperatives where farmers could share knowledge, pool resources, and advance their interests, helping to heal the deep scars left by the Civil War. Local Granges established stores to avoid retail markups and formed purchasing cooperatives to buy in bulk, sometimes jointly owning tools and machines. Their Declaration of Purposes read, "We propose meeting together, talking together, working together, buying together, selling together, and in general acting together for our mutual protection and advancement." Women were welcomed, but blacks were not.

Grange membership approached one million by 1875 but soon declined for the same reason that most communitarian societies struggle: Sharing resources is appealing in concept but challenging to manage. As the Grange transitioned into a more traditional civic and social organization — holding dances, offering classes, and raising money for those in need, activities it still conducts here in Robertsville — many Grange members traded collective economic action for collective political action, joining the more combative Farmers Alliance, which gave rise in the 1890s to the Populist Party, a coalition of farmers and laborers who took aim at corporations and corruption and pushed for federal ownership of railroads and telegraph lines. When the party folded, some members turned to the Socialist Party, and the Lincoln Highway rolls us into the city that landed its longtime leader, Eugene V. Debs, a ten-year prison sentence.

We park at a downtown Canton church not far from the place where Debs gave a speech in 1918 that is now often referred to as an antiwar speech, even though he went out of his way to not criticize US involvement in World War I, or the draft, or even Liberty Bonds. Instead he delivered a stump speech to more than a thousand supporters assembled for the Socialist state party convention. "It is extremely dangerous to exercise the constitutional right of free speech," Debs began, "in a country fighting to make democracy safe in the world." The crowd must have roared. Few sentences in political oratory have packed as much heft and humor.

Debs denounced war in general as a profit-seeking exercise foisted upon the poor by the rich, but he spent far more time attacking plutocrats like John D. Rockefeller (and his "blood-stained dollars"), politicians like Theodore Roosevelt ("a kaiser at heart"), the capitalist newspapers ("what a capacity they have for lying"), the two parties ("the gold dust boys of the ruling class"), and even labor leader Samuel Gompers ("loved and glorified by Wall Street"). He also defended socialists who had been unjustly imprisoned, including three local party leaders whom he had just visited in the county workhouse across the street from where he was speaking. Soon, he would be locked up, too, accused of violating the Sedition Act. His conviction and sentence were upheld by a unanimous Supreme Court that included Lisbon's John Hessin Clarke.

Today, if Debs were in Canton, which has a 30 percent poverty rate and a child poverty rate almost twice that, he might have looked for party recruits at the place near our parking spot, Refuge of Hope Ministries, which advertises "Meals, Shelter, Hope." I decide to stop in, and a friendly staff member tells me about their work with the single men who arrive seeking one of their fifty-eight beds and the meals they serve to anyone in need, each one preceded by a scripture reading, sermon, and prayer. "We believe that any lasting change that you're going to make in your life is through a relationship with Jesus Christ," the staff member says. Debs, who disdained organized religion, would have offered the hungry people here an alternative avenue for pursuing change.

From the shelter I walk a few blocks to the city's main thoroughfare, Market Avenue. Its wide median holds a promenade lined with trees and tables where young people sit on their lunch break, or so it appeared at first. I approach two men who are sitting together, both black. One is wearing a black leather jacket and red Ohio State hat. The other has a trim mustache and is dressed to the nines: brown suit, blue shirt, yellow tie, black loafers, flat cap, and dark sunglasses. "Just because I look like this doesn't mean I live like this," he says. He tells me his name, Anthony, and that he's been homeless since splitting from his wife four years earlier. His friend, Fred, is homeless, too.

When I tell them I've just visited Refuge of Hope, they unload their feelings. "They get paid for every head in there!" says Fred. I ask if staff members help them look for jobs and housing. "No, they don't," Fred says adamantly. "They don't help you out with no job, no housing, no nothing," he says. "They get paid and they don't care." Both have been kicked out of the shelter for policy violations. "And they got disrespectful people. They can say what they want to you, but you can't say nothing back." Power, as Debs knew, doesn't like to be challenged.

The staff member I spoke with, who seemed caring and earnest, twice used the phrase "love, compassion, and respect" to describe their approach, but Anthony and Fred resent the way they have been treated and tick off a litany of complaints, with each echoing the other at every turn, sometimes finishing the other's sentences. I don't know what goes on inside the shelter, but I'm struck by their solidarity. "This is my family," says Anthony, gesturing to Fred and the other men there. "We care about each other. We look after each other. We're a community. We're all we've got."

The median where they are sitting fronts the county courthouse, where a new statue — an old one, actually — will be erected, not of Debs, but of the town's most celebrated native son, William McKinley. It had long stood in California, but the town there voted to remove it, owing to McKinley's imperialism and role in removing Native Americans from the land. Canton gladly accepted it, since McKinley is the city's second-leading tourist attraction, after the Pro Football Hall of Fame. Which town is in the right?

William and his wife, Ida, lived in a house a few blocks from where Anthony and Fred sit. He fought for the Union in the Civil War, represented the area in Congress, served as governor, and after being elected president was, like his hero Lincoln, the victim of a political assassination. Canton seeks to honor him for all that and more. But the question of whether he, on balance, advanced the nation toward its highest ideals or dragged it backward is not one that should be shunted under the bunting of the front-porch campaign he conducted here in 1896.

In that election, Democratic and Populist nominee William Jennings Bryan championed minting silver currency to aid small borrowers against lenders. Bryan pitted the wealthy ("idle holders of capital") against farmers and workers ("struggling masses") and northern and eastern interests against southern and western ones. To Republicans, Bryan was inflaming the same class tensions that were fomenting anarchist violence and labor strife, and the same sectional tensions that thirty-five years earlier had brought war. "This country is in greater danger than it has been since 1861," the *New York Daily Tribune* wrote in the days before the election.

This story of the campaign, about populism versus business and silver versus gold, is true as far as it goes, but the focus on it obscures a crucial shift in national politics: For the first time since the end of the Civil War, Republicans dropped the plank in their party platform calling for the federal government to guarantee black suffrage. McKinley had vigorously supported federal enforcement of voting rights, but defeating the radical Bryan came first. Many northern Republican leaders applauded, including the *New York Times*, which hailed McKinley's "sagacity" in "appealing to a common patriotism to protect the nation's honor," just months after the Supreme Court upheld racial segregation in *Plessy v. Ferguson*. McKinley, in the name of national unity, abandoned political equality.

Black voters had little option but to stick with the Republican party. Among the leading candidates Bryan bested for the nomination was South Carolina senator "Pitchfork" Ben Tillman, one of the era's most bombastic racists, whose political rise began with a fiery speech at a Grange meeting. After losing the nomination, Tillman threw in behind Bryan. At the polls,

Bryan lost the battle for silver currency, but the Democratic Party's charge for white supremacy was strengthening.

In the White House, McKinley again appealed to national unity to rally support for war with Spain in Cuba, and, after the US victory, whites in Atlanta and Vicksburg celebrated Independence Day for the first time since the Civil War. Yet at that same time in Wilmington, North Carolina, the consequences of the Republican Party's decision to end its support for black voting rights were coming into full view: Whites were organizing to overthrow the black mayor and black-led municipal government.

In the run-up to Wilmington's 1898 election, Pitchfork Ben Tillman addressed a crowd of eight thousand people, explaining how whites had used any means necessary — including "by fraud and violence," as Tillman himself would boast — to take back power from blacks in South Carolina during Reconstruction. He urged North Carolinians to do the same, and to start by lynching a black newspaper editor. With him was a group of three hundred vigilantes known as the Red Shirts, their name likely serving as a defiant response to the northern politicians who "waved the bloody shirt" to protest southern attacks on blacks.

On Election Day in Wilmington, a mob of Red Shirts and local citizens terrorized black neighborhoods and blocked access to the polls, and with election officials stuffing ballot boxes, the white supremacist ticket prevailed. The city's mayor and other officials who had been in league with black leaders had not been up for reelection, and so two days later, more than two thousand vigilantes rampaged through the city, burning black newspaper buildings and killing dozens of black residents — perhaps more than a hundred, no one knows for sure — and forcing the remaining elected officials to flee. It was one of the deadliest acts of terrorism in American history.

Black leaders urged McKinley to publicly condemn the episode and send troops to restore the rightful government. He refused, as he had with other attacks on black officeholders, and no one was ever arrested. In the aftermath, when McKinley toured the south seeking support for a treaty concluding war with Spain, he visited the Tuskegee Institute and paid lip service to easing racial bitterness but said nothing about the Wilmington attacks or black voting rights. McKinley, who revered Lincoln and claimed his mantle, abandoned the "new birth of freedom" Lincoln spoke of at Gettysburg. As bigoted vigilantes bludgeoned it to death — and along with it, government of, by, and for the people — McKinley sat by silently, his progressive views on race eclipsed by his political ambitions. Where Lincoln rose to the occasion, McKinley shrank from it.

Most high school students learn of Bryan's "cross of gold" speech, but how many know of McKinley's silence in the face of the most violent coup in American history? Only one memory, the easier one, has persisted, though both are crucial to understanding national history. To reduce the story of the 1896 election to a triumph of big business over farmers, and eastern bankers over western miners, is to miss the steep price the country paid for McKinley pocketing thirty pieces of silver.

The only campaign speech McKinley made in 1896 came on Lincoln's birthday in Chicago. In praising Lincoln and his faith in the people, he noted how Lincoln rebuffed those who told him it was dangerous to stand among crowds. As president, McKinley took the same approach and met the same fate: assassination by an extremist, Leon Czolgosz, who shot him in a receiving line in Buffalo. Czolgosz told the authorities he was an anarchist who had been inspired by the teachings of Emma Goldman. "I killed the President because he was the enemy of the good people — the good working people," he said. "I am not sorry for my crime."

Goldman wrote a defense of Czolgosz, whom she saw as a hero trying to rescue the Republic from tyranny. "Not that this modern Caesar was the first to die at the hands of a Brutus," she wrote, likening Czolgosz to the same hero of the Roman Republic John Wilkes Booth had likened himself to, the same hero whose footsteps Timothy McVeigh believed he was following by bombing a federal office building in Oklahoma City in 1995, killing 168 people and wounding hundreds more. McVeigh wore a T-shirt emblazoned with Lincoln's face and the phrase *Sic Semper Tyrannis*.

After McKinley's assassination, many blamed Eugene Debs for the crime. In his 1918 speech here in Canton, he recalled that a group of local ministers in Ohio passed a resolution declaring him responsible and demanding that the mayor bar him from entering town to deliver a scheduled speech, which the mayor did. Debs defied the order and spoke.

Not long after New York State sent Czolgosz to the electric chair, with Westinghouse's alternating current zapping him dead, a song began circulating called "White House Blues." The original author and lyrics are lost, but as time passed and southern black singers passed it around and adapted its words and music, it acquired a playful tone and bouncy beat, not out of disrespect, but maybe out of familiarity. Political violence against blacks, after all, remained routine.

McKinley hollered, McKinley squalled
Doc said to McKinley, "I can't find that ball"

As we leave Canton, we can see a remnant of McKinley's legacy at one of the city's celebrated landmarks: the old auto dealership where the National Football League was founded. In its early years, black men were allowed to play, but in 1933 team owners quietly and informally banned them, without any disturbance by government. The ban held until 1946, when a team that had just left Ohio for Los Angeles, the Rams, signed Kenny Washington, who had starred at UCLA seven years earlier, winning the Douglas Fairbanks Award for the best college football player in America. When he went undrafted in 1940, NBC radio announcer Sam Balter, who attended the same high school as Washington — Lincoln High — criticized the owners on a national broadcast. "He would be the greatest sensation in pro league history," Balter lamented. "He was No. 1 on all your lists. None of you chose him."

Washington's teammate at UCLA, Jackie Robinson, became an American icon whose number, 42, has long been retired by Major League Baseball. But Washington, who re-integrated football a year earlier, is mostly forgotten. By the time he was drafted, his prime playing years were behind him, so he never became a star. No one wrote a hit song celebrating him, as Buddy Johnson did in 1949 for Robinson — "Did You See Jackie Robinson Hit That Ball?" — and as Chuck Berry would do in 1956 with "Brown Eyed Handsome Man." And while his number, 13, has been retired at UCLA since 1956, he has been largely ignored by the NFL, which has mostly swept its era of racial exclusion under the rug.

I hope Kenny Washington one day gets his due, including at Canton's Hall of Fame. I hope Eugene Debs's defense of free speech one day gets its due here, too — there is no statue of Debs in Canton. I hope that in remembering William McKinley, his presidential library gives visitors a chance to engage with the fullness of his record, which the new statue in front of the courthouse will only further obscure. But mostly I hope Anthony and Fred are able to find their way off the street.

— 11 —

The Fifth Voice

"Number two on the sides and three on top — a little fade."

At the Lincoln Way Barbershop on a busy commercial corridor between Canton and Massillon, Matthew Schuring is cutting hair. "Definitely slowed down," he says of business. "It's not terrible. You find guys stretching haircuts out a little bit longer than what they used to." I haven't had a cut in seven months. "Guys don't know if they're gonna have the money to spend, so everybody's pinchin' pennies." Well, not everyone. "If you have a 401(k) — they seem like they're happier than hell. They've got money coming in hand over fist. My retired clientele — they're making more money than I am, being retired! It's the younger guys, the non-union guys, they seem to be hurting more than anyone."

What do guys talk about when they're in the chair?

"Politics, obviously. Most of my customers swing more right. Hearin' a lot of guys sayin' that they used be Democrats and they're kinda feelin' left behind by the Democrats — just think they're gettin' too radical. And they just don't feel like the Democratic Party wants to represent them anymore. I feel the same way a little bit. I used to be not strictly Democrat — used to mix my ticket a little bit — but I leaned way more left, and I kinda feel like they left me behind."

He works out of a small red-brick building, the same one his father worked from for thirty years, adorned with a barber pole. In Europe, barber poles are traditionally red and white: the red for the bloodletting that barbers often performed, since it was thought to be therapeutic, and the white for the white bandages barbers applied after performing surgeries — or the teeth pulling and bone setting they did. No one knows for certain, nor is anyone quite sure why blue was added to the poles in America, but the best guess is the most obvious: patriotism. And it fits, since barbershops are linked to a distinctly American musical sound: a cappella quartets.

The music of barbershop quartets is now associated with old-timey white men in bright striped suits, ribboned hats, and handlebar mustaches, but it originated with black southerners in the late nineteenth century who harmonized on folk, popular, and religious songs — "cracking up a chord," they called it, often at barbershops, which served as social halls and fraternal clubhouses, and not just for black men. Lincoln's longtime barber in Springfield, William de Fleurville, was a Haitian immigrant, and as the historian Benjamin Quarles wrote, "Fleurville's shop was the informal social center for the men of the community; it was 'Lincoln's second home,' before his marriage in 1842. Frequently he would leave his law books there; he would have nobody in Springfield shave him except Billy."

What began in barbershops and living rooms found its way onto stages via minstrel singers in blackface. Audiences loved it, which moved the music into the ranks of professionals and recording artists, most of them white. As its popularity faded during the Great Depression and the big-band era swung onto the scene, two men in Tulsa formed a group, now called the Barbershop Harmony Society, to preserve and celebrate the music — and they excluded its originators. It wasn't until the mid-1960s that black men could join, and even then, the decision was left to local chapters, where exclusion often persisted. The society also excluded women, who formed their own club in the 1950s, the Sweet Adelines, which now has twenty thousand members around the world, about the same number as the men, who finally began permitting chapters to welcome women in 2018. The new openness is in accordance with the society's mission, "to bring people together in harmony and fellowship." To help do it, the society has long encouraged every quartet and chorus group to learn the same twelve standards, called the Barberpole Cat, a common songbook, so that members can sing with one another whenever they meet.

In any barbershop quartet — whether its members are male, female, mixed, transgender, nonbinary, gender-fluid, or anything else — the roles are the same, even as vocal ranges vary. A tenor sings the highest part, harmonizing above the lead, who sings second-highest and carries the melody. A baritone sings above and below the lead. And a bass takes the lowest notes and carries the beat. When pitch-perfect, they create a ringing chord that sounds like a fifth voice is singing — the "angel's voice," it's sometimes called, an audial phenomenon that melds the sounds into a unified whole and elevates them to higher plane. As the four singers move from tension to resolution and back again, a fifth voice emerges that cannot exist without the others. Hearing that fifth voice — the unifying force that makes a whole greater than the sum of its parts, and in so doing stirs and inspires us — is what we are after on this trip. The Lincoln Way barber, Matthew, believes there's more of it than we think.

"We're not all as evil as a lot of the media wants to portray us," he says. "We're a lot closer together than what anybody realizes. It's just certain issues people feel strongly on, but we probably agree on more than we disagree, you know?"

"Yeah, and it just doesn't get talked about as much."

"Exactly. There's not a whole lot of good news on the stations anymore. They tend to concentrate on all the negative. Keep people scared, keep people mad, keep people watching." That last sentence, just nine words long, captures the essence of what drives so much of modern media, and what so often prevents us from forming and hearing the fifth voice.

Laurel says she needs to pick up some essentials, so we stop at Target and she returns with pumpkin lights, a skeleton, and a candy bowl. The pandemic has not diminished her enthusiasm for spooky season.

In downtown Massillon, we pass the Lincoln Theatre, run by the Lions Club since 1982, when the group saved it from the wrecking ball. The Lions, born around the same time as the theater, 1915, are a Main Street echo of the Grange, founded by a small business owner to support and serve communities. But before the Lions existed, a Massillon business owner with the same goal had a more radical idea.

In the early 1890s, Jacob Coxey traveled back and forth from Massillon to his stone quarry in a buggy on bad roads, often passing men looking for work. "Well, it just didn't seem good sense," he explained. "There were all these men who needed work and here were roads needing fixing. The logical thing was for the government to get them together." When Coxey brought his idea for public works to the Populist Party's 1892 convention, where he served as a delegate, it was too wild a notion. And so when the Panic of 1893 threw the nation into a great depression, Coxey conceived of a publicity stunt to win attention for it: marching to Washington with the unemployed.

Leaving from Massillon on Easter Sunday 1894 and calling themselves the Commonweal of Christ, Coxey and 121 men, black and white, set out on the nation's first march on Washington, intending to present a petition calling for roadbuilding relief work and fiat currency, divorcing the dollar from both gold and silver, just as Lincoln had done — "the father of the legal tender," Coxey called him. Along the way, they would count on Americans to feed and join them. Coxey predicted their ranks would swell to a hundred thousand.

It was the biggest story in the country. Enthusiastic crowds greeted Coxey's Army along the route and gathered to hear speeches and songs by its six-piece band, but they arrived in Washington with only about five hundred people, led by a black flag bearer. Still, they were welcomed by a crowd of ten thousand, including many of the city's black residents. An article about their plans to gather on the capitol's steps carried the subheadline, "Won't Try to Go Inside." Most didn't even make it to the steps. Police blocked Coxey from reading his petition and arrested him for the attempt under a law that forbid unauthorized speeches on the capitol grounds. He was sentenced to twenty days in jail, plus a fine for walking on the grass.

Returning to Ohio, Coxey ran for governor as a Populist but received only 6 percent of the vote, the first of numerous failed bids for high office. It would be another four decades before the Democratic Party under Franklin Roosevelt swung behind his idea of hiring the unemployed to build roads. Four more decades would pass before the federal government, under President Richard Nixon, abandoned the gold standard for fiat currency. In between, labor and civil rights leaders led the March on Washington for Freedom and Jobs, where, on the steps of the Lincoln Memorial, during the one hundredth anniversary of the Emancipation Proclamation and Lincoln's call for a "new birth of freedom," Reverend King would deliver the most celebrated oration since the Gettysburg Address. In eloquence and effect, it far exceeded any speech Coxey might have imagined. And yet it did nothing to slow the nation's march toward the concentration of wealth, consolidation of corporations, and demise of local producers that McKinley's brand of economics helped accelerate and Coxey spent his life fighting.

One of the reporters to witness Coxey's march was Frank Baum, who may have had it in mind when he dreamed up the children's book he published six years later, *The Wonderful Wizard of Oz.* Some scholars came to see it as an allegorical critique of populism, with Dorothy as the noble commoner marching on a golden road (the gold standard) in silver slippers (Hollywood later made them ruby), which symbolized silver currency, as she made her way with a scarecrow (farmer), tinman (factory worker), and lion (cowardly politician) to the capital city of Oz (the abbreviation for ounces), where everyone's view of the world is tinted with green (the corrupting effect of money in politics) and the wizard (the president) is a fraud. They were in search of powers they already had, as E. Y. Harburg wrote:

> *With the thoughts that you'll be thinkin'*
> *You could be another Lincoln*
> *If you only had a brain.*

If Baum did find inspiration in Coxey's Army and populism, he left out of his story the same issue that many history books would ignore: race. But whether he had populists in mind doesn't much matter. The fairy tales that become part of a cultural landscape are not static in their meaning. Each generation interprets them in new ways — there are now theories that Baum's story was really a parable about God, atheism, and feminism — and each generation adds its own twists, as Hollywood did in dropping the original songs and adding new ones, including one added to the Barberpole Cat: "Somewhere Over the Rainbow."

At the end of the film, Judy Garland's Dorothy sees family friends she had imagined as the Lion, Scarecrow, Tinman, and Wizard, but she can't place them. "I wish I could remember, but I guess it doesn't matter anyway," she says. "We know each other now, don't we?"

Our memory of the past is less important than our relationships in the present. And while memory shapes us as citizens and voters, the more we can accept that our view of the past is hazy and incomplete; the more we can see that we share a history with people who seem to lack brains, hearts, and courage but in fact have had them all along; and the more we can recognize and guard against human nature's susceptibility to the spell of self-aggrandizing con artists, the more we can begin to hear the reverberations of the fifth voice.

— 12 —

Barnburners

Driving cross-country on local roads is an exercise in appetite restraint. We have passed up many spots with heavy hearts while also adopting a rule: Any restaurant shaped in the form of the food it sells or some related shape — like an igloo hut we pulled into in Everett, Pennsylvania — is a required stop. West of Massillon, fidelity to this rule necessitates a turn into a Twistee Treat stand that looks like a sugar cone topped with a vanilla-strawberry swirl. Tomorrow is National Ice Cream Cone Day — best to get started early — and besides, we are only channeling the Lincolns: Abe and Mary served ice cream at their second inaugural ball, offering their guests vanilla, chocolate, lemon, white coffee, burnt almond, and maraschino. No wonder he kept his address so brief.

At a railroad crossing gate in Wooster, we wait for the Norfolk Southern to arrive, its dulled air horn announcing the low rumble of its freight, its wheels keeping time to a steady rhythm that pulses through the American songbook.

"Can you get video of this?" I ask Laurel, who is working on her laptop.

"Okay, Steven Spielberg," she deadpans.

One of the challenges we have encountered is that while I've been behind the wheel taking in the sights, Laurel has been staring at her computer screen, concentrating on spreadsheets, presentations, and email. After numerous instances of me pointing out an eye-catching view and asking her to film it — interrupting her work and concentration — she began calling me Spielberg.

Wooster is home to two satellite campuses of Ohio State that are dedicated to agricultural studies and research, which befits its history as a land grant university that grew out of the Morrill Act signed by Lincoln in 1862. We're going to meet one of its graduates tomorrow, but first we stop at the College of Wooster to see a Lincoln statue that stands by its library. It was a Wooster man, Major Thomas Eckert, who rushed to the telegraph office the night of April 14, 1865, to send news to Ulysses Grant: "The President was assassinated at Ford's Theatre at 10 30 tonight & cannot live. The wound is a Pistol shot through the head." I walk around the library twice but see no Lincoln statue. Perhaps it's been moved inside, but the library is closed to visitors. No matter. It will appear, much to my surprise, farther down the road.

We camp for the night in Mansfield, home of the old Isaly's Dairy Company, begun here in 1914 by the son of Swiss immigrants as a milk and cheese processing operation. It expanded into the soda fountain and deli business and grew to four hundred stores across Ohio and Pennsylvania. In 1922, Isaly's concocted the Klondike Bar, a chocolate-coated square of ice cream that came in six flavors: vanilla, chocolate, strawberry, cherry, grape, and maple. Isaly's sold the rights to it in 1976, and it's now owned by Unilever, a British conglomerate that also owns Ben & Jerry's, Breyer's, and even Good Humor, all once independently owned by Americans. It takes some of the patriotism out of National Ice Cream Cone Day.

West of Mansfield the Lincoln Highway becomes Harding Way and leads us to Warren G. Harding's hometown, Marion. It's the centennial of his front-porch campaign, the last Ohioan elected president. The pandemic has canceled Marion's celebration, but the change Harding promised in 1920 — a "return to normalcy" — is in demand again, as pandemic restrictions continue. Another Harding phrase from that campaign is back on our lips, too: *America First.*

Harding began using the slogan in his 1914 Senate campaign. The next year, Woodrow Wilson adopted it to explain why he was keeping the United States out of World War I. After the war, its meaning took a darker turn, becoming synonymous with "100 percent Americanism" and the notion that blacks, Catholics, Jews, and others were less than fully loyal citizens and a blight on the purity of the nation's racial stock. Harding used it to attack "hyphenated-Americans" and the patriotism of those who disagreed with him. The Ku Klux Klan adopted it, too. In the years that followed, it became a politically palatable code word for isolationism, racism, nativism, anti-Semitism, and anti-Catholicism — and, as we will soon see, a justification for vigilantism.

Beyond Marion a red barn is painted with white and yellow letters: "Chew Mail Pouch Tobacco / Treat Yourself to the Best." It's the second one we've seen today. Some twenty thousand once dotted the country, and no state had more than Ohio. Workers in the steel, glass, and iron mills that filled the Ohio River Valley could not smoke tobacco — it was a fire hazard — but they could chew it. To advertise to the new auto travelers and bicyclists on the road, the brothers who started the tobacco business in West Virginia, Aaron and Samuel Bloch, turned barns into the first distinctly American public art exhibit, prefiguring America's great art form — mass advertising — as well as Wood's Regionalism and Warhol's pop art.

We park beside a barn to meet a friend of a friend, Chris Gibbs. He and an employee are using a front-end loader to level the ground before lining it with plastic to create a heavy-use-area pad for his livestock. Standing in mud all winter isn't good for cows' physical health, and walking through it each day isn't good for Chris's mental health.

"I'm born and raised here in Shelby County, a first-generation farmer," he says. "My mom and dad didn't farm and that was what I wanted to do, so I graduated from Ohio State University in agronomy. My wife and I started this farm in 1983 and we've grown it to 560 acres of corn, soybeans, and cattle. And this is going to be my legacy. This is what I've built for my kids, for my grandkids."

It's hard to raise a family on farming alone, so Chris had a day job at the Department of Agriculture, administering federal farm programs for thirty years before retiring in 2016. He also has a hobby: politics. "I spent twenty years inside the local Republican Party in Shelby County," he says. "I was chair of the local party between 2007 and 2015." In the 2016 presidential election, he supported Jeb Bush in the Republican primary and reluctantly voted for Trump in the general election. "I struggled with that, but I theorized: You know what, I'll get a Supreme Court nominee or maybe two out of it. That's been the Holy Grail for Republicans. And I theorized: There's nothing Trump can do that the institutions and our Congress can't fix. And when I say institutions, I'm talking about our judiciary, our intelligence services, the FBI, all of those institutions that we depend on — they're generally holding up pretty well. They're chinked, but they're holding up pretty well. But I never considered in my wildest dreams that Congress would cede its oversight responsibility as a separate and equal branch of government — and cede it not to the executive branch, but to a man. I never considered that, and that's what we have."

His breaking point came during Trump's 2018 summit with Vladimir Putin in Helsinki. "He threw the intelligence services overboard on foreign soil. I said, enough is enough. I'm done." But it wasn't just that. "About the same time, he started levying tariffs on all of our traditional trading partners, particularly China, South Asia, Mexico, Canada. These are trading partners where farmers built markets and relationships over the last three decades, one handshake at a time. Farmers went there and made sales. The US government didn't make sales. The government's job is to clear brush, so that we can go sell. And the moment Trump started to levy those tariffs, those countries had no choice but to retaliate — and they retaliated against our soft underbelly. And guess what our soft underbelly is?"

He's not asking me. He's setting up his answer, a rhetorical device found in the Bible that black preachers elevated to an art form. Chris is doing his own preaching, and he's just getting warmed up. That soft underbelly? "It's agriculture," he says. "And the price of soybeans — we lost 20 percent of our value overnight. Cattle and everything else just tanked, because we weren't able to sell into those other countries. And why is that important?"

I don't have to answer.

"About 95 percent of the people on the planet live outside of the US. So that means that agriculture has one business plan and one marketing plan: trade. It's what we do. It's the mechanism that agriculture uses to bring money back from foreign countries. And where does that money go?" He doesn't wait for me to guess. "It goes right into rural communities, because farmers don't sit on their money. We do not put it in the mattress. We spend it locally. The best way to get money into rural communities is to run it through a farmer, because where are we going to take it?" He's rolling. "The local hardware store, the tire store, the field store, the feed store, the truck store. And we're going to take it to our local schools through property taxes. And if we're not bringing it back from overseas, we're in trouble." Many farmers are in trouble. The number of farm bankruptcies has soared in recent years, and the number of farms has fallen by two hundred thousand, accelerating a decline long under way.

"When prices fell apart, when we lost those trading relationships, the president said, 'I have to make that up. I have to keep these people happy.'

And why is that?" We both know the answer. "Because the rural communities in Wisconsin, Minnesota, Michigan, western Pennsylvania, and Ohio are what got him elected by hairsplitting numbers of votes. So he gave the farmers $12 billion in the summer of 2018." Congress authorized Chris's former agency to direct $12 billion to farmers to compensate them for losses suffered due to tariffs. Trade aid, it's called.

"I went ape shit. I said, 'Listen, you start doing this, and that's going to adversely affect the good relationship that we've always enjoyed with taxpayers, when they figure out how much $12 billion is.'" In 2019, the bailout grew to $16 billion, and in 2020, to some $50 billion, four times the cost of the 2008–2009 auto bailout. "Where's all the money coming from?" He doesn't take a breath. "I know damn well — right from the printing press and right from the next generation. We have a reckoning coming."

Trump took credit for dispensing the money, but it was a Democratic House that passed it and sought credit for it, too.

"Both parties have been co-opted by the populist movement. And what is populism? In my view, it's a perennial search for a villain to slay with no plan of what to do with the body." He repeats the answer, like a preacher would, for emphasis. "It's a perennial search for a villain to slay with no plan of what to do with the body. On the left, I'm going to be very facetious, but who's the villain on the left?" Here we go. "Anybody that you perceive that has more than you do, because obviously they cheated to get it. Obviously they don't deserve it. And obviously they should give three-quarters of it away. A lot of hyperbole, but my point is this: What are you gonna do when you tear down all of the companies that hire people? What are you gonna do when you tear down the corporations that create jobs? What are you gonna do when you tear down the philanthropic folks? What's your plan?"

He has no answers to these questions, and that's the point — a fair one, but his diagnosis has missed the left's latest villains: the police and other law enforcement agencies, including Immigration and Customs Enforcement. He might also have asked: What do we do after we "abolish ICE"? And what do we do after we "defund the police"? There will be lots of bodies, but no plan.

Chris moves to the other side. "Who's the villain on the right? I'll be more specific, because I come from the right. I know these people, and it's much more insidious." The answer is personal for him. "Who are the villains? First villain: anybody that disagrees with the president. Our institutions, our FBI, our intelligence services are villains. The post office just became a villain. Mexico. Canada. Our traditional trading partners are villains. People with brown skin are villains. Health care is a villain. But what are you going to do when you've torn down those institutions? What are you going to do when you have torn down those trading relationships? What are you going to do when you've torn down people? When you've torn down our health care system? There's never a plan of what to do with the body. There's never a plan of what to replace it with."

There's an old story about a Dutch farmer who burned down his barn to get rid of the rats inside it, which gave rise to a term of derision for political groups that were, in the eyes of their opponents, dangerously reckless: *barnburners*. That the word has fallen out of our political lexicon — it's now used mostly to describe exciting sporting events — speaks to the difficulty both parties have in calling out the problem.

Last year, Chris decided to run against his local member of Congress, Jim Jordan. "Jim Jordan represents the hate and the destruction and the tearing down of people," he says. "And he represents what the Republican cult is all about. Now it's all about destruction, derision, division, dividing people, and tearing people down. And I wasn't going to be part of that because that's not where I came from." So he left the party.

"I had to declare my independence before I filed as an independent candidate. And so I wrote this statement, and when I got it finished, and I don't want to be dramatic, but it's actually true, I cried. Because I had spent twenty years in a party that I believed in. I spent twenty years with friends and neighbors and we believed in each other. And to see that wither away with a Donald Trump presidency was devastating. I felt like a jilted lover. Because the Republican Party, I found out, was so shallow. Their convictions were razor-thin. There was no fiscal conservatism. There was no such thing as free trade. That was all a joke. It's all about nationalism and protectionism. Pro-life was very shallow as well, because the moment we had Covid, the same Republicans who held up pro-life were saying that we could afford to get rid of senior citizens. This was not the party I grew up with. I grew up with a party that was lifting you up, that was talking about a thousand points of light and morning in America. That's what I subscribed to."

I finally see an opportunity for a question, and I seize it: "How has being an independent changed your view of politics?"

"If you're a member of a party, you are assigned values. You get a starter kit: pro-life, free trade, blah blah blah. When I became an independent —

this is such a nuance that I didn't see coming — I had to then justify each of those positions. I didn't have a starter kit anymore. Now all of a sudden, it's à la carte for me. I pick each one. And what I found out about myself is that I like a little bit from this side of the salad bar, and I like a little bit from that side. I can go down this side with the soup and I can go down that side with the cheese. I don't have to stay on one side or the other, because I'm my own person. I can have an independent thought, and I can listen to Democrats and Republicans."

"How did your friends in the party respond?"

"They are scared to death of associating with me because they think their other neighbors will look upon them poorly." He shares a story about sitting in a booth at a diner with his father. "We weren't there a minute, and one of the farmers that I've known for over forty years and farmed beside gets up out of his chair, and he comes to the table, and he looks me right square in the eye. And I reach out to shake his hand. He never raises his hand. He says, 'I always thought you were smarter than that' — and went right back to his table. I was at a soil and water conservation banquet after I'd left the party. My wife and I sat alone in a room of 150 people. People would walk away from me while I was talking to them. So what's the good news?"

Up until now, I could see his answers coming. On this one, I genuinely don't know.

"I got a whole lot less Christmas cards to send." He smiles, but he can't conceal the hurt he feels. "It is so disappointing to find the shallowness of people. People that I thought were my friends through the Republican Party establishment were only my friends because they were in proximity to me as a party leader. Once that leadership was gone, once I left the party, then those friends evaporated. And that's hard to take."

But he's hasn't lost faith. When I ask him what binds the country together, he says, "We're a good people. We believe in the Constitution, we believe in the Republic, we believe in our neighbors — and if we take that strength together, we can do anything in America." Spoken like a once, and maybe future, candidate.

We park in Lima across from the boarded-up Ohio Theatre, opened in 1927 with seating for eighteen hundred people. It was recently purchased by two television producers from Los Angeles who plan to restore the luster of the days when some of the nation's biggest live acts played here, including Guy

Lombardo, Gene Krupa, and Louis Prima, whose hits included — since this is National Ice Cream Cone Day — the best song ever written about ice cream, "Banana Split for My Baby."

Around the corner from the theater, a line of cars stretches around the block at the Kewpee Hamburgers drive-thru, a local institution for nearly a century. Above the entrance stands a Kewpee statue — a cherubic naked baby with a strand of hair, a play on Cupid created in 1909 by one of the nation's first female cartoonists, Rose O'Neill. As her comic strips grew in popularity, art begat commerce, and the Kewpie doll became one of the first mass-produced toys in the country, its image used to sell everything from cereal and soap to clothing and furniture.

There were once hundreds of Kewpee Hamburgers. Only five are left, three in Lima. Inside the art deco hut at a counter lined with red stools, I order two cheeseburgers but fail to notice the option of adding green olives until it's too late, an unfortunate rookie mistake. The patties are made from local beef, rolled fresh daily, and square — Dave Thomas's inspiration for Wendy's. Each is wrapped in paper printed with the Kewpee slogan: "We Cater to All the Folks." In Kewpee's early days, at least here in Lima, that message carried special meaning.

In the 1930s, Lima was the headquarters of the Black Legion, an offshoot of the Ku Klux Klan. Of Lima's forty thousand residents, about 10 percent belonged to the legion, perhaps a quarter of all adult men. Its national leader was a Lima resident, former Klansman Virgil Effinger, a veteran of the Spanish-American War who organized the legion into military units, adopted militant tactics, oversaw vigilante murders, plotted bombings, and worse.

In 1936, five years before the Nazis would send Jews to the gas chamber as part of their final solution, Effinger developed a plot to plant devices in every American synagogue that, when simultaneously triggered on Yom Kippur, would release mustard gas and kill, he hoped, one million Jews. The group collapsed the same year, after it kidnapped and murdered a Catholic man in Detroit, Charles Poole. Dozens of members were convicted for violent crimes, and the group was suspected of carrying out as many as fifty murders.

The following year, a young Humphrey Bogart starred in *Black Legion*, a film loosely based on Poole's murder. It was produced by the studio founded by Harry and Jack Warner, sons of Jewish émigrés who were determined to warn against Nazism abroad, fascism at home, and the xenophobia, racism, and religious bigotry feeding them. For the filmmakers, the Black Legion was a stand-in for all organizations that prey on fear and a warning about how decent people can be co-opted into the most despicable acts of vigilantism, often under the banner of America First.

"The Black Legion was originally America for Americans," recounted one Lima member years later. "They got a little carried away and were talking about raiding government arsenals and taking away arms and ammunition and starting a revolution against the government." He left the group when he was directed to bomb a theater showing a film it regarded as Catholic propaganda. He realized, if only belatedly: There was no plan of what to do with the bodies.

— 13 —

Engines of Hope

After ten days of channel surfing on the radio and hearing little besides overplayed hits, we broke down and subscribed to SiriusXM. Leaving Lima at dawn, I turn on E Street Radio and hear that today is Bruce Springsteen's birthday. To celebrate, the channel will be playing encore presentations of *My Home to Yours*, the radio show Bruce hosts offering "music for troubled times."

As we head toward the Indiana border, we hear Bruce say, "I've lived in the United States for seventy years now, and I have to admit I've often been disappointed in our failure to live up to our ideals. But I also have to say, I've never really been able to deny that there's a promise that constantly resides in the American people, that could make us the great democratic nation that we carry in our hearts and in our dreams. And if we put our hearts and our minds together and fought for the very ideals, those of equality, of liberty, of social justice, of compassion for our neighbors, we would find that this is where our strength resides. And we have it within in our power to create the kind of humane society we've always dreamt of. Now, all of this sounds corny when you say it. But it ain't corny when you do it."

We are driving through cornfields in what was once Great Black Swamp, glacially formed wetlands that stretched northeast from here to Lake Erie, 120 miles long and 30 to 40 miles wide — as large as the Everglades, full of elm and ash trees. Settlers pushed the Ottawa Indians to the edge of the swamp before draining it for farmland, even as they were building the Erie-Miami Canal to connect Toledo on Lake Erie to Cincinnati on the Ohio River.

We cross over what little is left of the canal in Delphos, Ohio. It came through shortly before the railroad did, and sitting on the intersection of the two transportation corridors, the town prospered. It could count more than one hundred factories in the late nineteenth century, churning out goods that traveled by rail in any direction: east to Pittsburgh, west to Chicago, south to St. Louis, and north to Toledo. The railroads carried travelers, too: It was possible to ride a train from Lima to Fort Wayne, Indiana, at speeds up to eighty miles per hour, powered by electric engines and overhead lines. It was one of hundreds of interurban rail lines that sprang up after the advent of electric streetcars in the 1880s, connecting small towns and big cities. Along with the safety bicycle, the interurbans brought social and commercial revolutions to small-town America, and no state had a more extensive interurban network than Ohio. Just about every town with a population of five thousand or more had a line, but they struggled to compete with automobiles and slowly died off.

In Delphos, the beautiful old train station fell to the wrecking ball in 1985, more than forty years after the end of passenger service. By that point, most of the factories were long gone. Main Street's historic facades are still full of character and charm, but some of the old buildings have sat vacant for decades. Two years ago, one was torn down. A year after we pass, six more will be demolished. It's the kind of place that Bruce Springsteen has spent his career writing and singing about in songs that have transcended the nation's partisan divide.

> *Now Main Street's whitewashed windows and vacant stores*
> *Seems like there ain't nobody wants to come down here no*
> *more . . .*
> *To your hometown*

There is still an agricultural processing plant along the tracks, owned by a global company headquartered in St. Louis, as well as a salad, dip, and dessert maker owned by a Dallas private equity firm. Economists evangelize efficiencies of scale of industrial concentration and consolidation, but for small towns, the decline of independently owned producers can leave their fates in the hands of a few outsiders. When market conditions change and global corporations decide to shut down or move operations, the local effects can be calamitous. Economists and business leaders call it the price of progress, but they are not the ones paying. When it's your hometown, and when you see vacant stores that were once full, dilapidated homes that were once grand, and public spaces that are no longer, the loss is personal. Chrissie Hynde of the Pretenders wrote about it after returning to her hometown of Akron in the early 1980s.

> *I went back to Ohio / But my city was gone*
> *There was no train station / There was no downtown*

When downtowns empty out, it is not only jobs that disappear. So too do social capital and civic infrastructure, as donations and support for communal activities and associations decline. The outposts of multinational corporations where residents work, shop, eat, and bank sometimes chip in a few peanuts, but without local ownership, profits go out of state and so do many of the best-paying jobs, hollowing out the middle class and giving refuge to one of democracy's most dangerous enemies: pessimism. But Delphos, like so many other places that have experienced this type of decline, is not taking it lying down.

On the Lincoln Highway in downtown Delphos is the Hope 214 Masonic Temple, home to the local freemasons, which has just posted on Facebook about a medical fundraiser for a 35-year-old woman battling cancer. Delphos also has a Kiwanis Club, Eagles Aerie, and Knights of Columbus Hall. Beside the Masonic Temple is the *Delphos Herald*, established in 1869 and still publishing as a weekly newspaper. Lehman's Furniture (est. 1959) and Lion Clothing (est. 1976) are both family-owned and going strong. And while it was canceled this year because of Covid, the town's big annual festival, Canal Days, will be back — the parade, car show, fishing derby, 5K run, livestock booths, live music, beauty pageant, basket bingo, beer tent, and all-you-can-eat pancake breakfast sponsored by the local Optimist Club. It's probably been a tough year for the club's membership recruitment.

Optimist clubs began in the early 1900s as business networks for ambitious men, merging two quintessentially American traits that Alexis de Tocqueville observed in his travels: an optimistic nature and a propensity for joining associations. The clubs soon became known for mentoring delinquent youths, and as chapters multiplied they extended to more civic activities. Membership has fallen by two-thirds over the past two decades, but there are still about sixty thousand members, all subscribing to the Optimist Creed, "Promise Yourself." It's a list of ten resolutions written a century ago aimed at fostering positive attitudes and selfless actions. Imagine how much stronger our communities and nation would be if more people who joined a social media platform followed Resolution Number Nine: "To give so much time to the improvement of yourself" — and of your community, club members today would add — "that you have no time to criticize others." It may sound corny when you say it, but it ain't when you do it.

For our better angels to triumph over our worst instincts, we need optimism. During the Civil War, it was Lincoln's optimistic conviction that right makes might, as much as any religious faith, that gave him the strength to persevere through the heavy toll of war as he battled depression. And in urging Americans to save "the last best hope of earth," Lincoln equated the nation with hope and tied their fates together, elevating a patriotic appeal for unity into a redemptive crusade for humanity.

In recent years, local advocates here have been pushing for a revival of passenger train service between Lima and Fort Wayne that would extend north to Chicago and south to Columbus, reducing travel time and bringing, so they hope, new residents, jobs, and companies to towns like Delphos. While nothing has come of it yet, they are pressing on — and in 2023, they will receive a federal planning grant allowing them to take the first steps.

"If we never try," Lincoln wrote to General George McClellan, urging him to be bolder, "we shall never succeed." I think he would've admired the Optimist Club, to say nothing of its all-you-can-eat pancake breakfast.

— 14 —

Sacred & Profane

Laurel is working on her laptop as we drive through Fort Wayne, Indiana, named for "Mad Anthony" Wayne, the army general we first encountered in Pennsylvania. I ask her for some navigational assistance, even though I don't need it.

"Can you keep an eye out for our turn?" I ask, setting up a joke.

"What street?" she replies, without looking up.

"Harry Baals Drive," I say, pronouncing Harry's last name the way he did: *balls*.

"Frank," she says as she keeps typing on her computer.

"I'm serious! It's named after Harry Baals — the old mayor."

She looks up from her work and tries to suppress a snicker, but can't.

When we reach the turn to our campground, the street sign reads, "H.W. Baals Drive." It originally read "Harry," but people kept stealing it. The initials are intended to be dignifying, but the joke can't be suppressed, especially since midwestern accents turn "Harry" into "Hairy." As humor goes, it may be a tad tawdry, but it's more silly than vulgar. When local officials asked the public to choose a name for a new government building, the runaway winner was, of course, Harry Baals. The voters were overruled.

It's easy to imagine Lincoln laughing along with the people, as a lover of both wordplay and bawdy jokes. Most of his stories, said his secretary, John Hay, were "unfit for family reading." He was a humor omnivore, enjoying barnyard banter, ethnic mimicry, and even, as one story goes, a farting joke. If it brought laughter, it was good. Acknowledging that people were shocked by his "low tastes," Lincoln defended them: "I tell you the truth when I say that a real smutty story, if it has the element of genuine wit in its composition, as most of such stories have, has the same effect on me that I think a good square drink of whiskey has to an old topper. It puts new life in me." According to his law partner, William Herndon, Lincoln often said, "If it were not for these stories, jokes, jests, I should die. They give vent — they are vents — of my moods and gloom."

H.W. Baals Drive takes us to a park and campground named after a legendary figure buried in Fort Wayne: John Chapman, better known as Johnny Appleseed. The city's annual Johnny Appleseed Festival was scheduled to take place here last weekend, but it fell victim to Covid. More than a hundred thousand visitors come each year to celebrate days of yore. Blacksmiths, candlemakers, and other artisans appear in period dress, and cooking must be done over open fires of wood or coal, not gas. There are no deep-fried Twinkies or funnel cakes, but there are apple desserts and apple drinks of every kind, except the one apple product that made John Chapman famous: hard cider.

The story we learn growing up about Johnny Appleseed is of a barefooted jolly wanderer who roamed the frontier spreading the gospel as he planted apple seeds. The fable is true enough, but few people ever ate Chapman's apples. They drank them. Apples grown from seeds are almost always mealy and sour — "spitters," they're called — because apples are extreme heterozygotes, like humans. They don't replicate themselves any more than we do. Growing a Red Delicious, for instance, doesn't happen by planting its seeds but rather only by grafting a branch of a Red Delicious tree onto another sapling.

Grafting plants was forbidden by the Christian sect that John Chapman followed, the New Church, or Swedenborgianism, which taught that the practice caused pain to plants. But apples from seeds worked just fine for making hard cider, and Johnny helped soak the frontier in alcohol. In 1830, the average American adult was consuming almost two standard-sized bottles (750ml) of eighty-proof liquor every single week, much of it in cider. We were a pie-eyed people, thanks in no small part to Johnny's trees. In 1840, cider and log cabins became symbols of the frontier spirit represented by the Whig Party's presidential candidate, William Henry Harrison, but a backlash was brewing.

In 1842, the teetotaling Lincoln gave a speech to the Washingtonian Temperance Society (never mind that George owned one of the largest whiskey distilleries in the nation). Lincoln was not a member, but neither was he a drinker. It made him feel "flabby and undone," as succinct a description of a hangover as has ever been uttered. But his remarks outraged some members of the audience. "I believe if we take habitual drunkards as a class," he said, "their heads and their hearts will bear an advantageous comparison with those of any other class." He lamented the temperance movement's moralizing, saying there was "too much denunciation against dram sellers and dram drinkers" and refuted the idea that abstainers had "any mental or moral superiority" over them. In the Illinois state legislature, Lincoln repeatedly voted against Prohibition, and when Stephen Douglas later accused him of being a tavern keeper in his earlier days, Lincoln denied the charge while also rejecting its moral scorn: "I don't know as it would have been a great sin," he said, "if I had been."

In the decades that followed, few temperance advocates embraced Lincoln's charitable approach to the issue, and most aimed their ire not at hard cider but at the liquor and beer they associated with German and Irish immigrants. When Congress and the states enacted Prohibition, they exempted homemade cider and wine to secure the votes of farmers, and the story of Johnny Appleseed moved from sotted to saccharine, with songs by Gene Autry, Bing Crosby, Walt Disney, and others portraying him as a manifestation of the grace and abundance God showered upon his favored land, an idea parodied by the fictional heavy-metal band Spinal Tap in the song "America."

Each religion, race and creed / Gets exactly what they need
God bless Johnny Appleseed

The Johnny Appleseed Festival takes seriously its mission to "provide a historically authentic re-creation of the time of Johnny Appleseed and the period in which he lived," yet it avoids the central element of Johnny's story, sanitizing history in an attempt to dictate decorum, just as officials did with the naming contest. Nevertheless, if people want a hearty drink after the festival, they can drive to the Mad Anthony Brewpub and order a Harry Baals Irish Stout.

At Johnny Appleseed Campground, I see an intriguing flyer: "If you like to ask hard questions and try your hand at giving the answers, come to the park on Wednesdays where we will be engaging in The Great Conversation." I arrive there to find several park staffers outnumbering the guests, though not the homeless men. On the sidewalk in colored chalk, I read what appears to be a conversation starter: "Should we give everyone Respect or should it be earned?" Beneath it, someone has written: "Always given."

"What do you think?" a staff member asks me, as I stand in front of it.

"I think everyone should be treated with a basic level of respect. But beyond that, you've got to earn it."

"Yeah, that's what I think, too," he says.

That was the end of the Great Conversation. But in a season of heightened tensions over race, I give the city credit for trying to bring people out of their houses and into dialogue, and I may have a second chance to engage. There is an event happening in another park tonight, called Sacred Conversations, organized by two local churches.

On the way, with Main Street to myself, I pass the county courthouse and read the inscription on its facade that quotes Lincoln's hero, Daniel Webster.

> *The People's Government.*
> *Made For The People. Made By The People.*
> *And Answerable To The People.*

Fort Wayne has a long history of celebrating Lincoln, who stopped in the city in 1861, but only to change trains. There was a Lincoln museum here until 2008, and a statue called *Lincoln the Hoosier Youth* stands in front of the Lincoln National Life Insurance building. One of his hands holds an ax and a book while the other pats the head of a dog, a nod to the tale (perhaps tall) of him saving the family pooch from drowning in the frozen waters of the Wabash River.

On the day of the statue's dedication in 1932, ten thousand people crowded into the streets. NBC carried the ceremony on a national radio broadcast. The same day, United Press ran a short story across its news wires about a black man in Crossett, Arkansas, named Frank Tucker, who was lynched by a mob of five hundred, with the UP reporting: "His body was left dangling in the air for 45 minutes. The crowd went home to dinner." No arrests were made.

The purpose of a lynching was not primarily punishment, as James H. Cone notes in *The Cross and the Lynching Tree*. It was to warn others who might consider challenging the social and political order of the fate they should expect. "The crucifixion of Jesus by the Romans in Jerusalem and the lynchings of blacks by whites in the United States are so amazingly similar," Cone wrote, "that one wonders what blocks the American Christian imagination from seeing the connection."

One of the nation's most notorious lynchings occurred fifty miles southeast of Fort Wayne in the town of Marion, two years before the dedication of *Lincoln the Hoosier Youth*. Three black men — Abram Smith, Thomas Shipp, and James Cameron — were beaten bloody and hung after a false allegation of rape. A photograph of Shipp and Smith hanging from a tree appeared in newspapers across America. It remained in circulation for years, and in 1937, it is believed to have inspired Abel Meeropol, whom we encountered in Hoboken, to write the poem "Strange Fruit," converting it into a song that Billie Holiday turned into a scorching, haunting, civil rights dirge. In 1999, *Time* magazine hailed it as "the song of the century."

Southern trees bear a strange fruit
Blood on the leaves and blood at the root
Black bodies swinging in the southern breeze
Strange fruit hanging from the poplar trees

If the photo of Shipp and Smith inspired Meeropol, he may have presumed the lynching occurred in the south — leaving one of the greatest songs of the civil rights era to stand as a monument to understatement, obscuring the geographic prevalence of the injustice it decried.

Northern lynching victims included a friend of Lincoln's, his shoemaker, William Donnegan, who was hauled out of his Springfield home in 1908 by a white mob attacking black residents, after it had been unable to lynch a black man accused of raping a white woman. "Lincoln freed you," the mob shouted, "we'll show you where you belong!" They cut Donnegan's throat and hung him from a pole. His crime? Owning property and being married to a white woman for thirty years. And the man accused of rape? He was freed, after the woman recanted her story. The shocking violence spurred an interracial group to announce, on Lincoln's one hundredth birthday, a national conference on racial equality at Cooper Union in Manhattan, out of which was born the NAACP, which began a long campaign to pass a federal law banning lynching.

No mention of Tucker's lynching was made at the dedication of *Lincoln the Hoosier Youth* — the dignitaries likely had not heard of it. But placing the Great Emancipator and a dog high on a pedestal while a black man had just been hung high from a light pole, and as Congress stonewalled efforts to pass an anti-lynching bill, captured the inherent flaw in all monuments: Their three-dimensional appearance conveys a one-dimensional history. And while it can be easy to dismiss lynchings as a thing of the past, a white supremacist murdered a black man in Fort Wayne in 2016.

On Main Street, I encounter no one on foot save a white woman at a well-trafficked intersection. She holds two handmade posters — one reading "Black Lives Matter," the other "No Justice No Peace." As cars whiz by, she tells me that she's out here every day. "I get a very good response," she says. A driver honks approval, right on cue. "But I'm at the point in my life" — her kids are grown — "where I can let a lot of things roll off, because I get some pretty hideous responses, too. I've had one gentleman say, 'There are dangerous people in this town. Be careful.'" She's undeterred: "I've lived a good life, and this is what matters."

I ask her what she thinks binds the country together, amid all the divisions we face.

"Hope for something better, I guess. We've always felt that we could do this" — she holds out her signs — "and make things better. A lot of countries don't have the ability to protest."

A mile away, in an open-air pavilion in Lakeside Park, about sixty people are gathered for the final installment of the Sacred Conversations series that the local Presbyterian and Unitarian churches have been holding. "Breathe in, breathe out," says the Reverend Misty-Dawn Shelly, pastor at the Unitarian Universalist church. "We are all tense. The tension in Louisville affects all of us."

She gives an update on the case of Breonna Taylor, a twenty-six-year-old emergency room technician in Louisville who was shot and killed by police officers after they broke down her apartment door at midnight with a no-knock warrant to search for drugs. Her boyfriend did not hear the officers announce themselves, feared for their lives, and fired his gun, striking an officer. They returned fire, squeezing off thirty-two rounds and striking Taylor eight times. Civil rights leaders have been trying to ban no-knock warrants for decades, as Gil Scott-Heron sang in his 1972 song, "No-Knock."

No-knock, the man will say
To protect people from themselves

Earlier this afternoon, a grand jury returned an indictment on charges of "wanton endangerment" against one of the three officers whose bullets did not strike Taylor but who fired his gun blindly. It returned no indictments against the other two officers, and Daniel Cameron, the state's first black attorney general, announced that his office's investigation found that both had been justified in returning fire, so there would be no charges against them.

"Breathe together," Reverend Shelly says again. "The last four weeks we've asked questions and felt discomfort. The one thing we keep doing is breathing together." At the previous weeks' meetings, they identified four action areas: education and economics; community involvement; multiracial relationship repair; and voting. Tonight's mission is to identify specific steps they can take in each. They split in four groups to brainstorm.

Fort Wayne is among the many places that calls itself the City of Churches, claiming more than 360 places of worship. But most congregations are fairly homogeneous, and tonight's group is nearly all white. "We say we want to be multicultural," says the Reverend Anne Eppling, pastor of First Presbyterian. She's talking about churches in general, not just hers. "But we're not willing to give up how we worship — that tradition, that music." The Reverend Guy Dunham had said the same in York. And singing together is not the same as speaking together. Dunham had told me that an interracial dialogue at his church this summer left many white congregants taken aback: "It was the first time that some of our white members heard our black members talk about racial profiling," he said. "Never dreamt that they had been victims of it on a regular basis."

A volunteer from each group announces their action plans. The education and economics group proposes that churches adopt schools and promote the *New York Times*'s 1619 Project. The community engagement group proposes to join activities that involve people of color while also creating a website promoting black-owned businesses. The interracial and intergenerational group proposes a Facebook group that draws in more diverse voices. And the voting group proposes to register voters with the League of Women Voters and Urban League. In 1980, the president of the national Urban League, Vernon Jordan, was shot in the back in Fort Wayne by a white supremacist. He survived, after six surgeries that kept him hospitalized for eighty-nine days.

As I'm listening to an almost entirely white audience discuss their well-intentioned ideas, I recall my phone conversation earlier in the day with former Philadelphia mayor Michael Nutter, whom I had hoped to meet in Philadelphia, but events intervened. I asked him why the killing of George Floyd struck such a chord with so many people like the ones here. "I just don't know that many people have actually watched somebody die. It's usually a gunshot or something like that — it's usually rather quick, you don't see it that closely. And I think lightbulbs started going off. Black people, we've been telling you about these things for literally hundreds of years, but somehow in that moment, it finally clicked."

Like the photo of Smith and Shipp, and the photo of Emmett Till lying disfigured in an open casket, and news footage of police dogs and fire hoses being turned on protest marchers, the video of George Floyd galvanized white people in ways that words could not. When it comes to racism, there has always been a strong streak of Doubting Thomas running through white America, until the evidence is so stark that it cannot be denied. Why? Nutter makes two related points.

First, the persistence of segregation in housing, education, and employment makes strangers of fellow citizens. "The reality is, white people don't have to be around black people. Most black people don't have that option," he says. "It's just easier for many whites to not have to pay attention or worry about what black people are doing, or how black people are affected. You see some stuff on TV and then, okay — that's that."

Second, he says, it can be difficult to discuss race. "Other than talking about money, there's possibly nothing more uncomfortable than talking about race and race relations," he says. "I think for many white people, it's, 'I didn't do it. I wasn't involved.' And for black people it's like, 'What the F? But you benefit from the privilege.' And a lot of white people think, 'Well okay, but we got laws now.' But that doesn't stop the guy from making a different decision about the mortgage application, or the job hiring. A lot of white people don't even want to believe that these things still go on — that there are things still in place that impede the ability of a certain group of folks to move forward."

The spirit of Doubting Thomas lives and always will. In the Gospel according to John — Matthew, Mark, and Luke never mention the story, which raises doubts of its own — the passage is usually taught as an exhortation to believe in a resurrection we did not witness and a God we cannot touch. But it can also be understood as a simpler plea: to open our eyes and reach out our hands to touch neighbors who have been wounded — and believe them, and believe *in* them, as embodiments of the divine.

"Here's the deal," Nutter told me, echoing the view of change I heard from Ayanna Jones in Pittsburgh: "The only people who can really do anything about racism in the United States of America are white people. Black people can't really do much about that. So they have to decide how much change they're willing to push for. They have to decide how they want things to be different."

There's some truth in that, but the decisions turn on interactions with those who have been wounded. Throughout our history, the biggest changes in legal rights and cultural norms — on matters of race, gender, sexual orientation, and religion — have always required coalition building. And the failure to attract the black community to these Sacred Conversations, and others like them, does not bode well for long-term change.

The meeting wraps up in time for people to join a protest march. In Louisville, one is already under way — and in about an hour, two police officers there, one white and one black, will be shot. A black man will be arrested on the scene and charged with wanton endangerment. The cycle of violence continues.

I head back to our campground, and a scan of the news brings other troubling developments. In a press conference earlier today, President Trump declined to say that he would commit to a peaceful transfer of power. "We're going to have to see what happens," he said. "I've been complaining very strongly about the ballots. And the ballots are a disaster" — a reference to his attempt to cast a cloud over mail-in ballots. His message, as *New York Times* columnist Tom Friedman noted, is not hard to decipher. "The president of the United States has told us, 'Either I win the election or I delegitimize the election,'" Friedman says in an interview. "Those are your choices, folks." He calls it a "six alarm fire" and sounds the loudest alarms he can: "I can't say this any more clearly: Our democracy is in terrible danger — more danger than it has been since the Civil War, more danger than after Pearl Harbor, more danger than during the Cuban missile crisis and more danger than during Watergate."

It is easy for Republicans to dismiss Friedman as a center-left commentator, but Stuart Stevens, who spent three decades electing Republicans all over the country, has been sounding the same warning — that Trump, should he lose, will claim he was cheated and seek to overturn the result, through force if necessary. Stevens is helping to lead a media campaign to defeat Trump, which they've named the Lincoln Project. Republicans attack the group, but this we know: Lincoln left little to doubt about how he would have answered the question put to Trump.

On August 23, 1864, when Lincoln faced the prospect of defeat, he wrote a letter that he signed and asked every cabinet officer to sign the back of, without letting them read it. "This morning, as for some days past," he wrote, "it seems exceedingly probable that this Administration will not be re-elected. Then it will be my duty to so co-operate with the President elect, as to save the Union between the election and the inauguration; as he will have secured his election on such ground that he can not possibly save it afterwards."

It was never an especially remarkable piece of Lincoln history — few books about him even make note of it — until now.

Back at Charley in Johnny Appleseed Park, I feel drained. I wish I had a hard cider in the refrigerator. Or better, a Harry Baals Irish Stout.

— 15 —

Uncle Sam's Band

Uncle Sam lies here, or so say the townsfolk of Merriam, Indiana. In a cemetery beside the highway, a gravestone bears the name of Samuel Wilson, a meat inspector who lived in Troy, New York, during the War of 1812, before ending up here late in life. Known as Uncle Sam, as the story goes, he stamped "US" on each barrel of meat, intertwining his nickname with the federal government. The people of Troy, however, say Wilson is buried there, and they seem to have the stronger claim, although the nickname "Uncle Sam" may have originated in the song "Yankee Doodle Dandy," or as a whimsical extension of the nation's initials having nothing to do with meatpacking. Whatever Uncle Sam's origins, his enduring fame owes much to another man known by a familial name: Uncle Abe.

Before secession, a different mythical figure overshadowed Uncle Sam as the personification of the country: Brother Jonathan, a name that may have originated as a tribute to the only colonial governor to support independence, Connecticut's Jonathan Trumbull. But as Brother Jonathan became associated with the divisive Know-Nothing Party, Uncle Sam's star rose, aided by a popular song by New Hampshire's Hutchinson Family Singers, ardent abolitionists and champions of women's rights, called "Uncle Sam's Farm." The lyrics encouraged the world's people, no matter how poor, to emigrate and settle the west, making no mention of Native Americans.

Laura Ingalls Wilder would later hear her father sing it on the family's journey to the Dakota territory. It was, she wrote, "the song he sang oftenest."

Come along, come along — make no delay;
Come from every nation; come from every way;
Our land is broad enough — don't be alarmed,
For Uncle Sam is rich enough to give us all a farm.

During the Civil War, Brother Jonathan's New England identity did nothing to promote national unity. Soldiers in the Irish Brigade sang "We'll Fight for Uncle Sam" to the tune of "Whiskey in the Jar," and Lincoln referred to "Uncle Sam" making tracks across the north and south. By war's end, cartoonists were taking images of Brother Jonathan — often tall, lanky, top-hatted — and rechristening him Uncle Sam, now the symbol of a unified nation. We don't know whether those features inspired the Republican cartoonist Thomas Nast to add a dash of Lincoln to his drawings, but in Nast's hands, Uncle Sam began sporting a beard.

After Uncle Sam acquired iconic form on World War I recruiting posters — "I want YOU," he declared, finger pointing and eyes glaring — his appearance in songs began to reflect more complicated views of his militarism. In the 1920s, Texas blues great Blind Lemon Jefferson sang of his power over men.

Uncle Sam was no woman,
but didn't he draft your man?

During World War II, the Texas-born trumpeter Oran "Hot Lips" Page took that lyric and added his own rejoinder in his song "Uncle Sam Blues."

Women ringin' hands and a-crying
All over the land.

At Woodstock in 1969, as the Vietnam War raged, Jefferson Airplane adapted it again, turning Page's rejoinder into:

40,000 guys in the service
Doin' somethin' they just don't understand

After the last US forces left Vietnam, another San Francisco band that played Woodstock, the Grateful Dead, recorded "U.S. Blues."

> *I'm Uncle Sam, that's who I am*
> *Been hidin' out, in a rock and roll band*

Wherever Uncle Sam is hiding out hardly matters. His origin as an instrument of national unity, and his extension into the realm of patriotic protest, transcends political parties. He lies comfortably here beside the Lincoln Highway, a kindred spirit.

We cut northwest through open farmlands to Goshen, settled by New England Protestants who named it after the fertile land given to Israelites by the Egyptian pharaoh. The Christian communities that arrived here saw themselves as walking in the footsteps of the early Jews, chosen by God and called to live in prayerful devotion before the Second Coming. To make room for them, the governor-pharaoh cast natives into exile, the culmination of three decades of indigenous removals, often the result of whiskey treaties, so called because of liquor's frequent role in obtaining signatures. When whiskey didn't work, signatures were forged. So it was here.

In 1838, the government rounded up 859 Potawatomi Indians across north-central Indiana, shackled their limbs, and sent them on a sixty-one-day, 660-mile march to the Osage River reservation in present-day Kansas, called Osawatomie. The journey came to be called the Trail of Death, for the forty-two people who perished along the way — a smaller-scale death march than the Trail of Tears of the same year, but a tragedy compounded by its descent into obscurity. Historians would record a Pottawatomi Massacre, but its victims were not natives. They were white pro-slavery settlers killed by John Brown and his band in Kansas territory in 1856, at a settlement along the Pottawatomie Creek.

The exclusion that the Potawatomi faced in Indiana was similar to the kind of exclusion some of Brown's men wished to bring to Kansas — not only of slavery but also of free black people. It was hardly an uncommon sentiment. Kentucky had banned free black people from the state in 1849 under penalty of imprisonment, and two years later Indiana's voters approved a state constitution excluding black people from taking up residence in the state.

Through much of the twentieth century, Indiana was full of "Sundown Towns." The name refers to signs found on the edge of many towns, and not just in the south: "Nigger, Don't Let the Sun Go Down on You in __." Often, no sign or ordinance was necessary for the edict to be clear, as it was here. In 2015, the Goshen city council adopted a resolution apologizing for its exclusionary past and declaring that "healthy communities are able to recognize past mistakes . . . and resolve to make improvements in the future." Lately, the council has discussed erecting an educational marker to acknowledge its history.

In downtown Goshen, a fountain holds a statue of Neptune, the Greek god of the sea, in front of the county courthouse. It is here because a Greek immigrant, James Polezoes, wished to express his gratitude to the community that took him in. In 1912, Polezoes opened a candy store across the street from the courthouse: Olympia Candy Kitchen, which is still operating. After some success, rather than pour his savings into a second business, he spent $1,000 on the statue and fountain and donated it to the town. Some two thousand people attended the dedication ceremony, but when it came time for Polezoes to speak, he was overcome with emotion. His American Dream had come true, in no small part because Uncle Sam afforded him the chance, unlike so many others, to settle here and pursue it.

Mishawaka is a city of fifty thousand that is usually overshadowed by its western neighbor, South Bend, though it made national news not long ago. In a *USA Today* interview, the actor Adam Driver, a local kid who earned an Oscar nomination for his role in the movie *Black KKKlansman*, said he was no stranger to white supremacy: "If anything, I was more aware of it as a kid growing up in Indiana, because there were always Klan rallies, like, every summer," he said. "There were people in the Klan who were in our neighborhood."

Baloney, said the St. Joseph County historian, sending reporters for the *South Bend Tribune* scurrying into the archives, where, sure enough, they found stories of KKK rallies and protests during Driver's formative years, beginning in the early 1990s. There were also stories of White Pride Fests held at the Mishawaka farm of a man who claimed to be the leader of the National Knights of the Ku Klux Klan and stories of two murders in South Bend tied to the KKK and white supremacy groups. One of the killings occurred in late December 1993, shortly after I had left South Bend to return home for Christmas break during my freshman year at Notre Dame. I don't recall ever hearing about the case, and apparently most others here didn't, either. "I stand corrected," the county historian admitted. "I was shocked. I would never have guessed that there were that many events. Shocked and saddened."

The Lincoln leads us into downtown South Bend, named for an almost ninety-degree bend in the St. Joseph River, and toward an intersection with the Dixie Highway, another Carl Fisher creation, though the inspiration for it had nothing to do with uniting the country. A year after dedicating the Lincoln Highway, Fisher needed to attract northern travelers to the South Florida resort community he was developing, Miami Beach. And so was born the Dixie Highway, running from Chicago and Detroit down through the old Confederacy. Sadly, it carried none of the Lincoln Highway's spirit. In Miami Beach, Fisher refused to sell property to Jews or blacks and barred them from the city's hotels, whose brochures advertised "Always a View, Never a Jew."

We stop at a traffic light in front of CJ's Pub, a South Bend institution known for its gluttonously sized burger: the twenty-ounce Golden Domer. I never attempted it during my four years living here, nor did I ever learn that one of the most extraordinary events in Notre Dame history occurred at this intersection.

In the 1920s, the local chapter of the KKK held its meetings on the third floor of a building where CJ's now stands. The Klan's Grand Dragon, David Curtis "D.C." Stephenson, lived in Indianapolis and dreamed of building a dominant political force by creating community social clubs, like the Lions, Optimists, and Grange, except with a bigoted mission. Leaders of local Klan chapters, called Klaverns, recruited members from churches, assisted by some forty thousand ministers who joined. Recuiting also involved organizing youth sports teams, parades, and picnics with family entertainment and "100 percent American" orchestras. Crowds sang old religious standards often set to new lyrics, like "The Bright Fiery Cross," sung to the tune of the "Rugged Old Cross."

> *Over all the USA the fiery cross we display*
> *The emblem of Klansmen's domain*
> *We'll be forever true to the Red, White and Blue*
> *And Americans always remain*

Indiana was home to few blacks and Jews but many Catholics, who the Klan also viewed as a dangerous threat to the nation's character and culture. Klan leaders fueled fear by spreading conspiracies about a Catholic takeover of America. The pope was living in Cincinnati! Guns were hidden in the basements of Catholic churches! Catholics had taken over the Departments of Justice and State! The Klan placed Protestant Bibles in public schools, sought to have Catholic teachers fired, and led boycotts of businesses owned by Catholics, Jews, immigrants, and blacks. Many shops posted signs on their windows identifying themselves as "100% American." To help spread their gospel, the Klan turned to radio and film and started a newspaper, *The Fiery Cross*, which grew to a circulation of about five hundred thousand.

The Klan's practice of cross burning connected the group to a medieval Scottish tradition and, by extension, to the Scots-Irish in the north of Ireland who opposed Catholic equality. But the Klan's cross burning sprang more from the Hollywood Hills than the Scottish Highlands. In his 1905 novel, *The Clansmen*, Thomas Dixon wanted to strengthen the Klan's claim to a shared heritage with Scottish clans. And so he took a piece of medieval lore — burning a cross as a signal to rally for battle and bloodshed — and placed it in the hands of the Klan after the Civil War. When his novel became the basis for *Birth of a Nation*, which helped revive the Klan, life imitated art.

By 1924, as a Mishawaka music publisher printed the song "Awake Ye Clansmen," no state had more Klan members than Indiana, some three hundred thousand, with Klaverns in all ninety-two counties. In May of that year, in the same month a Klan member in Congress secured passage of a bill severely restricting immigration, the Klan-backed candidate for governor of Indiana won the Republican primary in a landslide against the anti-Klan mayor of Indianapolis. But since the party convention held final say over nominations, Stephenson feared delegates might walk away from pro-Klan primary winners. To prevent that, he came up with a plan: provoking a confrontation with Catholics, which would allow him to paint them as aggressors and Protestants as victims. South Bend, with its large Catholic population, was the perfect place to stage it.

Notre Dame's president, Father Matthew Walsh, recognized the trap and urged students to remain on campus, but they ignored him. When figures in white robes and hoods appeared on downtown streets, students tore off their regalia, with some of the most violent de-robings occurring on the Lincoln Highway. The *South Bend Tribune* reported that the Klansmen were "roughly handled," likely an understatement.

Klan members retreated to their third-floor Klavern, where CJ's Pub now stands. About a hundred students followed, finding themselves standing at a grocery market across the street. Looking up at a cross lit with electric bulbs displayed in the window, and looking down at barrels of organic ammunition, they picked up potatoes — stereotypes be damned — and knocked out the window and bulbs. Among those throwing strikes, according to legend, was Harry Stuhldreher, the Notre Dame quarterback from Massillon, Ohio. When students rushed the Klavern, a Baptist minister greeted them on the stairwell, holding a revolver. After a few upperclassmen sat down with Klan leaders to broker a peace, students agreed to let the parade proceed if marchers put down their weapons and took off their hoods. The Klan reluctantly agreed.

In the end, Stephenson called off the parade because of rain and members drove home, though not before students smashed a windshield and destroyed some of the band's musical instruments. The police arrested eight people, six of them anti-Klan protestors, but students returned to campus triumphant, parading in their confiscated white robes and running a Klan banner up a flagpole while making obscene gestures and using colorful language, horrifying their prefects. Father Walsh declined to discipline any students.

In the next issue of the *The Fiery Cross*, the paper's propagandists called it the worst anti-Protestant riot in history and castigated Catholic students as unlawful, violent, dangerous hoodlums who lived up to the nickname often hurled derisively at their football team, the Fighting Irish. It was just as Walsh had feared — an embarrassing public setback for a university striving to gain cultural acceptance — and as Stephenson had hoped. At the Republican convention, delegates ratified the Klan-backed primary winners. At the Democratic convention, delegates rejected Catholic efforts to adopt an anti-Klan plank in their platform, which would have meant certain defeat. They instead took a middle course, declaring that the Republican party had been "delivered into the hands of an organization which has no place in politics and which promulgates doctrines . . . repugnant to the principles of government advocated by Lincoln."

At one of the first Republican state party conventions in 1856, Lincoln pushed for a plank forbidding discrimination "on account of religious opinions, or in consequence of place of birth." When it generated protests, he quieted critics by tying it to the promise of equality in the Declaration of Independence. The plank passed, and the national party soon adopted a similar one at its first national convention. While careful not to denounce the members of the anti-Catholic Know-Nothing movement — he wanted their votes —Lincoln made his views clear in a private letter to his friend Joshua Speed, writing:

> I am not a Know-Nothing. That is certain. How could I be? How can any one who abhors the oppression of negroes, be in favor of degrading classes of white people? Our progress in degeneracy appears to me to be pretty rapid. As a nation, we began by declaring that "all men are created equal.'" We now practically read it "all men are created equal, except negroes." When the Know-Nothings get control, it will read "all men are created equal, except negroes, and foreigners, and Catholics." When it comes to this I should prefer emigrating to some country where they make no pretence of loving liberty — to Russia, for instance, where despotism can be taken pure, and without the base alloy of hypocracy.

Two weeks before the 1924 election, Notre Dame's undefeated football team traveled to Manhattan's Polo Grounds to take on Army. Such long trips were born of necessity: The University of Michigan's football coach and athletic director, the anti-Catholic Fielding Yost, had long refused to schedule Notre Dame and blocked it from becoming a member of the Big 10 conference. At the Polo Grounds, a Notre Dame sophomore serving as a publicity assistant, George Strickler, talked up the team's four-man backfield to *New York Tribune* writer Grantland Rice, comparing it to the Rudolph Valentino silent film he had recently seen, *The Four Horsemen of the Apocalypse*. Rice handled the rest in a newspaper lede for the ages: "Outlined against a blue-gray October sky, the Four Horsemen rode again. In dramatic lore they are known as famine, pestilence, destruction and death. These are only aliases. Their real names are: Stuhldreher, Miller, Crowley and Layden." Whether Stuhldreher threw potatoes at the fiery cross in the third-floor window where CJ's now stands hardly matters. On a larger battleground — Notre Dame defeated Army, 13–7 — he struck a blow for equality by helping to push a small midwestern Catholic school to national acclaim.

That November, Democrats lost the 1924 elections in Indiana and nationally. Dozens of Klan members were elected to the US House and

Senate, and so many were elected to statehouses that the Klan commanded majorities in Colorado, Oregon, and Texas. But that November, too, the Notre Dame football team completed an undefeated season and earned an invitation to play in its first Rose Bowl, which university leaders saw as "an almost providential opportunity to counter the extremely negative Klan-inspired image of Notre Dame," wrote historian Robert E. Burns. Traveling there and back by train, the priest in charge of the trip concocted a public relations bonanza by organizing a whistle-stop tour that was as much about promoting Catholic Americanness as it was cheering for the Four Horsemen.

On New Year's Day, Notre Dame defeated Stanford to win its first national championship. The team returned to South Bend by January 12, the day the Klan's candidate, Ed Jackson, was sworn in as governor of Indiana. At the inauguration, native son William Herschell recited his most beloved poem.

Ain't God good to Indiana?
Folks, a feller never knows
Just how close he is to Eden
Till, sometime, he ups an' goes

Jackson's tenure was a failure rife with corruption, leading to his indictment for bribery. D. C. Stephenson went to prison for raping and murdering a young woman, who was not the first person he had sexually assaulted in a drunken rage. And the Klan here and elsewhere saw its membership collapse, though not its animating spirit, which would be reborn in new forms.

— 16 —

God, Country, Notre Dame

On the university's South Quad, two students — a boy and girl — are throwing a football. At Notre Dame, that's called flirting.

South Quad was built in the aftermath of the 1924 run-in with the Klan so as to house more students on campus rather than downtown, protecting them from further trouble. I spent two years in a dorm built in 1925 with a castle-like facade called Morrissey Manor, though there was nothing regal about its cramped rooms. The thirty guys who lived in the basement had only two showers among them, giving rise to a nickname they wore as a badge of honor: the Dirty Thirty. The basement also had a late-night snack stand with nachos and frankfurters and not much else. A friend of mine once patronized it nightly for weeks in what he called the Human Hot Dog Experiment. He was a science major and took his research seriously, and with mustard. The year before I graduated, a college magazine named Morrissey the worst residence hall in America. I loved it. Maybe it was good practice for RV life.

Behind Morrissey Manor is a replica of the log chapel built by Father Stephen Badin, a French immigrant and the first priest ordained in America, in 1793. He arrived here after a Potawatomi leader named Pokagon requested a priest to live among them. But for Pokagon's request, there may have been no Notre Dame and no Fighting Irish, at least not here. Yet as a student, I never learned of him. As Potawatomi citizen and American

Indian studies professor John N. Low has said, "History is not truth; it's memory. And a part of remembering is considering what we forgot."

We walk from South Quad to Main Quad, where a residence hall for priests and brothers is named for Father William Corby, who became president of the university after serving as chaplain of New York's Irish Brigade, the Fighting 69th, during the Civil War. A statue outside Corby Hall shows him giving absolution with one hand high in the air, just as he did on the Gettysburg battlefield. It's identical to one we saw of him at Gettysburg, but here, the hand gesture evokes a different kind of battle, and the statue is known as Fair Catch Corby — a companion to the mural known as Touchdown Jesus, which overlooks the campus cathedral: the football stadium. At Notre Dame, faith comes wrapped around a football.

At the stadium's 1930 dedication, the crowd roared for a special guest who had never before seen a football game: the world's most famous Catholic writer, the Englishman G. K. Chesterton. He was here to deliver a series of lectures on Victorian literature and English history, and while there is no record of what he said, there are scraps of notes from students with their remembrances, like drinking ale with him in a dorm, Prohibition be damned — "his stein was never empty for more than a minute" — and having to carry him down the stairs, his girth causing great difficulty, so the story goes. He later wrote a poem about the stadium's dedication, which vividly contrasts the blood and death of Nero's Roman coliseums with the joy and life inside the one overseen by the Virgin Mary from atop the Golden Dome. But there is something else he wrote that I would like to take with us on this journey.

In a 1905 letter lamenting the public's drift from its devotion to democracy, he summed up the problem of liberty without democracy and equality. It can lead to errors that impose our mistakes on others, such as thinking we have the liberty to enslave them. Only the humility to place our faith in one another — and not in our own moral certitude — can save us. "The answer to the question 'What is Wrong?' is, or should be, 'I am wrong,'" he wrote. "Until a man can give that answer his idealism is only a hobby." And when politics inflame passions, or religion inspires righteousness, hobbies can fall away.

In the front hallway of the Main Building beneath the Golden Dome, the murals of Christopher Columbus I saw as a student are now hidden behind tapestries. The university's president, Father John Jenkins, decided to cover them after concluding that many people now see them as demeaning toward Native Americans. "The murals' depiction of Columbus as beneficent explorer and friend of the native peoples," he wrote, "hides from view the darker side of this story, a side we must acknowledge." But hiding the murals from view helps obscure another dark story.

Two flights up, and two days before one of the university's law professors, Amy Coney Barrett, would be nominated for the Supreme Court, Jenkins is kind enough to sit down with me and talk about the role of faith in American political life. Without me mentioning them, he begins with the murals.

"In the 1880s, there was a strong anti-Catholic, anti-Irish sentiment in this country, and they were painted as a way of saying, 'Look, the first European immigrant to this country was a Catholic.'" In the university's early days, it banned celebrations of St. Patrick's Day, fearing potential violence from nativists, even as it sponsored on-campus Independence Day celebrations and invited surrounding communities to attend. As the nation approached the four hundredth anniversary of Columbus's landing in the Americas, the university hired an Italian artist, Luigi Gregori, to paint the murals to remind Catholic students of their Americanness. Nevertheless, bigotry toward Catholics remained, so more reminders followed, as Jenkins explains.

"Then the 'God, Country, Notre Dame'" — the words carved into the gothic basilica beside the Main Building, along with the names of every student killed in World War I — "That was kind of a way of saying, 'We Catholics can be patriots too, while we're faithful to our religion.'" Father Walsh served as a chaplain in that war and oversaw the integration of the memorial into the basilica, which was dedicated on Memorial Day 1924, eleven days after the Klan's attack on students.

On the other side of the Main Building is Washington Hall, a theater built in 1881. It's another example of the university saying, "See, we're Americans, too." After the Klan's ambush, Father Walsh gathered students in Washington Hall to warn them not to repeat the incidents. To drive home the point, he invited an immigrant — Knute Rockne, the football coach who would lead Notre Dame to a national championship that year — as a guest speaker . The university has always stood in the center of the two ideals that flank its Main Building: faith in God and faith in America.

"So when you look at the history of America and the history of Notre Dame and Catholics," says Jenkins, "this tension exists. There's this sort of fidelity to this transcendent faith, and this patriotism and fidelity to America. But I do think that this nation, if I look at its history, was deeply shaped by Christian faith broadly, and the values that arise from that." Yet some of the nation's founders, Jefferson included, were deists who saw Jesus as a moral teacher, not the resurrected Son of God. Other founders worked to exclude Catholics from public office. What happens, I ask him, when values conflict — not only among Christians, but many others, too? What then?

"It's the challenge of democracy, isn't it?" he says. "You have a set of commitments — moral commitments, religious commitments. You're trying to bring them into dialogue with a democratic process that makes decisions that shape our lives together. How can we make any decision on health care, on Social Security, on poverty programs, without a set of moral commitments?"

With Coney Barrett poised to join the Supreme Court, I ask him if we may see a return of anti-Catholic sentiment if part of the country views the Catholic majority on the Supreme Court as imposing its religious beliefs about abortion on the rest of the country.

"I honestly don't understand why a deep conviction about individual autonomy, which is behind a lot of the pro-choice arguments, why that's okay, that's not a problem — but a conviction about the dignity of every person, even in the womb, is deeply problematic and should be disqualified on religious grounds. I honestly don't understand the argument there."

No argument should be disqualified because of the religion of its speaker. But when speakers seek to make law based on moral values that are strenuously rejected by those of other faiths and creeds, the issue is not about the speakers' religion but rather about the essence of pluralism. In the Supreme Court's *Roe v. Wade* decision, the lone Catholic justice, William Brennan, voted with the majority. As he later explained, "I wouldn't under any circumstances condone an abortion in my private life. But that has nothing to do with whether or not those who have different views are entitled to have them and are entitled to be protected in their exercise of them. That's my job in applying and interpreting the Constitution."

In a 1984 speech at Notre Dame, New York governor Mario Cuomo took on the question of how a Catholic in elected office should consider the question. Cuomo, though personally opposed to abortion, said the burden lay with the clergy to convince the people, not with lawmakers to impose upon them, lest Catholics later find themselves on the other side of the law, as they had long been before. "We know that the price of seeking to force our beliefs on others," said Cuomo, "is that they might someday force theirs on us." But when "someday" seems distant and power is at hand, perspectives change.

In 1981, President Reagan delivered the commencement address at Notre Dame, a homecoming of sorts for the actor who had played George Gipp in the 1940 film *Knute Rockne: All American*. The film's subtitle evokes an honor bestowed upon the best college athletes, but the movie's producers had a larger idea in mind. The film opens in Sweden, with Rockne's father telling a group of men that he would be traveling to America and hoped to stay for the equal opportunity it promised his children. After "America the Beautiful" plays, the camera moves to a young Knute playing a racially integrated football game, and the entire movie unfolds as an homage to immigrants and the American Dream. Near the end, when Rockne testifies before Congress to defend the educational value of football, he doesn't talk about lessons in sportsmanship or hard work. He talks about national unity and understanding: "Now our boys at Notre Dame have played all over the country. And they've gotten to learn that southerners aren't lazy, northerners aren't cold, midwesterners aren't hicks, and Californians aren't big and dumb. They've learned from all sorts of Americans what America is. And in that process, they've found themselves."

The scene and speech were entirely fictitious and hardly the only liberty the screenwriters took. While Reagan's George Gipp was a model student, the real Gipp had dodged the draft during World War I and spent much of his time at Notre Dame playing pool and poker in South Bend bars. Gipp gambled on games, broke rules by playing professionally, and didn't bother registering for classes most semesters. When word reached the Holy Cross fathers that Gipp had gone to an off-limits dance club, they expelled him. Only the intercession of the city's businessmen, including two members of the Studebaker family, led to his reinstatement.

Rockne probably would have loved the movie's mythologizing of Gipp, since he likely invented the most famous story in all of college sports, his "win one for the Gipper" halftime speech. No one had ever called George Gipp "the Gipper," and no one had ever heard of the story before Rockne unveiled it in the locker room while losing to Army in 1928. Nevertheless, Reagan's sanitized Gipp aided the university's century-long effort to Americanize immigrant Catholics in the eyes of Protestants and helped catapult Reagan into politics. As Democratic political consultant Frank

Mankiewicz said, "If Ronald Reagan had played guys in the movies who fixed football games, instead of playing in them, he would never have been elected governor, let alone president. But he played heroes, and that's powerful as hell."

In his 1981 commencement speech here, Reagan put a new twist on the story of George Gipp. "Rockne could have used Gipp's dying words to win a game any time, but eight years went by following the death of George Gipp before Rock revealed those dying words," Reagan said, building the drama. "And then he told the story at halftime to a team that was losing, and one of the only teams he had ever coached that was torn by dissension and jealousy and factionalism. The seniors on that team were about to close out their football careers without learning or experiencing any of the real values that a game has to impart." In Reagan's telling, Rockne wasn't merely trying to inspire his players; he was trying to unite a group of self-centered individuals who weren't putting the team first, so that they would join "together in a common cause and attained the unattainable."

In this story, Reagan morphed from playing Gipp to Rockne, our national coach. "There will come times in the lives of all of us," he told the graduates, "when we'll be faced with causes bigger than ourselves, and they won't be on a playing field." It was as if he was writing the Cold War sequel to the movie, and his words echoed a commencement address given by William Sherman in 1865. Sherman's wife, Ellen, a devout Catholic, had moved the family to South Bend during the Civil War so their children could attend Notre Dame and its sister school for girls, St. Mary's. Just a week after addressing his troops for the final time, Sherman told the graduates here: "God knows there has been enough of fighting for a long spell, but it is the highest wisdom and the best policy . . . to be ready for that encounter at any moment." It was good advice, but the trouble is: Demagogues are forever telling us that the moment of encounter is upon us, and in the modern era, that drum has been beaten loudest and longest by an Irish Catholic who once served as Reagan's communications director, Pat Buchanan.

When Buchanan challenged President George H. W. Bush in the 1992 Republican party primary, his campaign slogan ("America First"), economic platform (attacks on trade), immigration proposal (a "Buchanan Fence" along the Rio Grande), hostility to pluralism (calling multiculturism a landfill), and militaristic rhetoric ("Buchanan's Brigade") would all foreshadow the party's future. "We were a little bit ahead of our time," Buchanan said in 2016, after Trump clinched the Republican nomination.

At the 1992 Republican National Convention in Houston, Buchanan spoke of "a religious war" and "cultural war," imploring listeners to "take back our cities, and take back our culture, and take back our country," echoing the cries made a century earlier by Protestants about Catholic immigrants like Buchanan's great-grandmother Anna Kerrigan, who arrived from County Cork during the Irish potato famine that supercharged the nativist movement. Around that time, in 1847, the name Abraham Lincoln, Esq., was recorded on a list of donors to a famine relief fund in the amount of 5 pounds. Irish immigrants would repay the debt many times over: Some two hundred thousand served in the Union army. When the leader of the Irish Brigade, Colonel Thomas Francis Meagher, visited Lincoln in the White House and complained that his men had been passed over for promotion, Lincoln dashed off a letter requesting a review and making it clear where his sympathies lay. For Lincoln, the fight in the Irish was indispensable to the preservation of the nation.

For Buchanan, however, the problem of immigration has been that immigrants no longer look and sound much like Anna Kerrigan, just as the Know-Nothings opposed immigrants who didn't look and sound like they came from Mother England. Ken Cuccinelli, the Trump administration's acting director of Citizenship and Immigration Services, remarked that Emma Lazarus's poem on the Statue of Liberty referred to "people coming from Europe" — like his Italian and Irish ancestors. To note that Cuccinelli is wrong — many came from outside Europe — is to miss the larger truth. When Lazarus wrote the poem and for decades after it, many Protestants viewed Italian and Irish Catholic immigrants as un-American and non-white threats to the country's democracy and identity, the same view that the Buchanan brigade has espoused of non-Europeans and, wherever they are from, Muslims.

In his 1992 convention speech, Buchanan declared that the religious and cultural wars he trumpeted were part of a wider war for "the soul of America." Joe Biden has regularly used that same phrase since the beginning of his 2020 presidential campaign, but from the other side of the aisle. To Buchanan and his supporters, as it was for the Know-Nothings and the KKK, the soul of the nation lies in shared background, shared language, shared religious traditions. "Anybody that believes a country can be maintained that has no ethnic core to it, or no linguistic core to it, I believe is naive in the extreme," Buchanan charged. But those characteristics are corporal, parts of the body politic. In most religions, as it was for the ancient Greeks, the soul transcends the body and mind and their features and functions, including ethnicity, language, and gender. The soul is not something we can see or hear or touch, nor a set of beliefs. An article of faith across religions is that what gives us life, our essence, is eternal, cosmic, heavenly — the godliness within.

Peering into America's soul starts with asking, *What breathed life into it?* It wasn't the English, whom we fought, or their language, which we made our own, or their religion, which many crossed an ocean to escape. And it wasn't, wrote Lincoln, the Constitution or the union of states. He believed both were necessary to our success and "great prosperity," but they were not the "primary cause" of it. "There is something back of these," he wrote, "entwining itself more closely about the human heart. That something, is the principle of 'Liberty to all' — the principle that clears the path for all — gives hope to all — and, by consequence, enterprise and industry to all." For Lincoln, the soul of the nation lay in that principle, just as it did for Chesterton. "America is the only nation in the world that is founded on a creed," Chesterton wrote. "That creed is set forth with dogmatic and even theological lucidity in the Declaration of Independence." He called America "a nation with the soul of a church."

Reagan's Notre Dame commencement speech was a celebration of the American creed and its power to triumph over Soviet communism. Toward the end of it, he quoted William Faulkner on the human condition. "He is immortal because he alone among creatures," Reagan said, "has a soul, a spirit capable of compassion and sacrifice and endurance." By tying the soul of humanity to the soul of the nation, Reagan used ecumenical language to conjure the nation's fifth voice and connect the Republican Party to Lincoln and all Americans to the better angels of our nature. That may be hard for Democrats to admit even two decades after Reagan's death, but as more Republican leaders follow in Buchanan's rather than Reagan's footsteps, acknowledging it has become not only more palatable but also more essential.

After talking with Father Jenkins, Laurel and I visit the office of an old colleague of mine from city government who works for the university. His window overlooks what used to be Brownson Hall, where my father lived during his year on campus as an Irish Christian Brother beginning a PhD program. I'm sad to see that it's recently been demolished — it was built in 1855 — and sadder still to see that the new building will be named for a donor rather than Brownson.

Orestes Brownson was the leading Catholic philosopher of his era, and he lived a life full of contradictions: attacking the evil of the priesthood shortly before converting to Catholicism, supporting the Civil War but opposing Lincoln's reelection, and fiercely criticizing wage labor and capitalism but seeing socialism as a great enemy. Threading through all his thought, however, was a constant mission: the uplifting and preservation of American society. Seeing the risk of a national breakup in the 1850s, he stressed the common bonds shared by Protestantism and Catholicism and worked to promote greater social and political unity. He published a book aimed at reconciliation, *The American Republic*, in the immediate aftermath of the war. He is mostly forgotten now, but in a 1843 Dartmouth commencement speech, Brownson spoke of the duty graduates owe to "their age and country," imploring them to "ask not what your age wants, but what it needs . . . and that go and do. Do it well." The echo of those words would find their way into the inaugural address of America's first Catholic president: "Ask not what your country can do for you, but what you can do for your country."

It was probably in his room in Brownson Hall where my father wrote a letter to the provincial of the Irish Christian Brothers notifying him of his intention to leave the order after twenty-five years, having entered the novitiate after his freshman year in high school. He mailed the letter on St. Patrick's Day — he believed in doing important things on important dates — and left campus and the brothers at the semester's end. He could not have imagined that seven months later he would meet a woman in New York City who had just left the convent after ten years and who had spent four summers at Notre Dame studying for a master's degree, their time on campus never overlapping. Three months after meeting, they got engaged on Shakespeare's birthday. Five months later, they wed.

My sister and I didn't learn of their decades in religious orders until we were about twelve and fourteen, and it was the shock of our lives. They had never lied about their past — they just told us they had always been teachers, which was true. Over the years, my mother opened up to us about why she became a nun — her feelings of being lost and lonely and believing the convent held the answers — and why she left: She got a taste of freedom at Notre Dame, where nuns lived independently and didn't have to wear their habits, and she began to recognize how unhappy she was in religious life, with all of its rules, restrictions, and hierarchical servitude. She loves telling stories about small rebellions against various holy-rolling Mothers Superior.

My father, born to Irish immigrants, said almost nothing about why he joined the brothers. His father being an alcoholic may have had something to do with it, and while there may have been abuse at home, our generation only heard the faintest whisper of it. We heard no more about why he decided to leave the brothers. Mostly, whenever we asked, we heard about the wonderful parts — playing sports and milking cows and taking classes at more colleges than we could count — as if there was no loneliness or darkness to the experience. He approached his own life story the same way generations had theirs, the same way Hollywood approached George Gipp's, the same way the university had conceived of the Columbus murals: Celebrate the light, hide the darkness.

My parents rarely argued, despite holding diverging views on culture, politics, and the church, including its teachings on the start of life. My mother supported *Roe v. Wade*, while my father opposed it. Although both were Democrats, they rarely voted the same way, Senator Moynihan excepted. Throughout American history, this was normal, including in the Lincolns' marriage. Abe believed slavery a moral wrong. Mary, who came from a family of slaveholders, defended the institution. They supported candidates from different parties, including in the 1856 presidential election, when Mary supported the Democrat Millard Fillmore in part because he would be better at "keeping foreigners within bounds," she wrote, mentioning the "wild Irish" domestic help she had to deal with.

Until recently, prospective spouses were not filtered out for their politics. In 1958, only about a quarter of Americans preferred that their child marry someone from a particular political party. By 2016, the number had doubled, and it has likely continued growing. Interparty marriages are declining even as acceptance of interfaith, interracial, and same-sex marriages reaches record levels.

My parents offer a small window into what is being lost. Theirs is a great love story, born of Notre Dame, which helped them find the inspiration and courage to leave the security of the garden and strike out for the wilderness, not knowing what they'd find but trusting the spirits that had stirred within. In leaving religious life, each drew closer to God, not through prayer or the works of mercy or weekly mass, though both continued to engage in those acts of faith, but simply through what each saw in the other's soul.

Leaving campus, Laurel and I stop at Rocco's, opened in 1951 and still run by the same family. It's a proper pizza parlor with booths, a jukebox, checkered tablecloths (green, not red), photographs of local celebrities, and a mural of what might be the Calabrian coast, where Rocco Ameduri was born and raised. Above the cash register, framed newspaper clippings tell his story, of a soldier in the Italian army taken prisoner in North Africa who learned to cook for Uncle Sam and began corresponding with a Calabrian immigrant living in South Bend, Julia Simeri. After he was deported back to Italy, she traveled there to marry him. He arrived in America two years later and began working as an assistant cook at Notre Dame. They saved enough to start a restaurant, serving the cheese and tomato sauce pies that few midwesterners had yet tasted. Rocco and Julia are both gone, and even though Covid has emptied the restaurant, their spirit is still here. Blaring from the jukebox is "*Che La Luna,*" a tarantella featured in the wedding scene of *The Godfather*, though this is Louis Prima's rollicking version, its 6/8 beat begging for hands to clap and feet to lift and voices to sing — *Oh! Ma-ma! La-la-la, la-la, la-la.*

At our campground, Hunt Brothers Pizza is for sale inside the office, one of the eight thousand locations where it's sold, many of them gas stations. We're now even more grateful for the prisoner of war whom Uncle Sam allowed to immigrate here. *Ain't God good to Indiana?*

— 17 —

Birth and Rebirth

On December 9, 1963, two weeks after President Kennedy's corpse was lowered into the ground, the *South Bend Tribune* announced a local death that had been equally unthinkable: "AUTO OUTPUT WILL END HERE: Studebaker Will Assemble Cars in Canada."

Clement and Henry Studebaker opened a blacksmith shop in South Bend in 1852 on what would become the Lincoln Highway, a block from where CJ's pub now stands. They soon began making wagons and buggies with their younger brother John before eventually moving on to what John had dismissed as "clumsy, dangerous, noisy brutes which stink to high heaven, break down at the worst possible moment, and are a public nuisance" — automobiles. Their vehicles would avoid some of those problems by running on electric power, but as gasoline allowed for faster and farther travel, they capitulated.

Hundreds of local auto companies sprang up in the first decade of the twentieth century, but most proved unable to compete with the efficiencies of scale that Ford and General Motors achieved. Studebaker was an exception. By the year of the Lincoln Highway's dedication, it was the nation's third-largest automaker, and the family shared its success with South Bend, financing the construction of churches, a YMCA, and a hospital expansion, and sponsoring dances, sports teams, choruses, hobby clubs, and other employee activities, including free English-language classes for immigrants.

After the Great Depression forced the company into bankruptcy, it emerged and thrived on government contracts during World War II, manufacturing B-17 engines and army vehicles, just as it had made wagons for the US Army during the Civil War. By 1950, it was the country's fourth-largest automaker, employing twenty-four thousand people. When the factory here shut thirteen years later, the city began a long and painful slide that left it, like so many other midwestern cities, a hollowed out shell of its former self.

Some say the closing was inevitable: Industry consolidation made it impossible to compete on cost with the three biggest players. Others blame management for not enduring strikes, as Ford and GM did, to keep a lid on wages. Others blame the United Auto Workers union for demanding too much. All three theories can be true. Regardless, the company was generous through the end: It donated a collection of thirty-three vehicles from across the company's history to the city of South Bend, giving rise to a museum.

The collection includes the last Studebaker ever produced, having rolled off the company's assembly line on St. Patrick's Day — the luck of the Irish — as well as the carriage the Studebakers purchased that carried the Lincolns and their guests to Ford's Theatre on April 14, 1865. One of the last people to see Abe at the White House was South Bend's congressman and Speaker of the House, Schuyler Colfax. The carriage now transports visitors back to that day, creating a physical connection to Lincoln in his final hours. Despite spending four years in South Bend, this is my first visit to the museum. It was worth the wait.

A few blocks south of the museum is Studebaker's six-story assembly-line building, which has sat vacant for decades, a hulking symbol of the city's decline. A Notre Dame graduate is now converting it into a tech campus that he hopes will employ several thousand people. That's only a fraction of the old factory's total, but some of the companies incubated here may grow into mini-Studebakers. Notre Dame hosts an incubator, too, and while we were on campus yesterday, I visited an old classmate who is working to create an environmentally friendly and lower-cost replacement for chrome, which is made with a toxic and carcinogenic compound. South Bend may not build the next generation of cars, but it might make them — and lots of other products — better and cheaper.

Former mayor Pete Buttigieg used the factory-turned-tech campus as the backdrop to announce his 2020 presidential candidacy, as he touted

South Bend as a "turnaround city." It's a slow process — downtown looks much the same as it did in the 1990s — but the redevelopment of the old plant reflects something else that I remember seeing here, through volunteering at a neighborhood center: pride in the city and hope for its future.

Nine days after Studebaker announced its closing in 1963, a resident named Charles Burkhart incorporated a company to manufacture signs, like the ones he had begun posting around a shell-shocked city, reading, "I believe in South Bend." The company is still operating, employing more than one hundred people.

On South Bend's ragged west side, the Lincoln Highway is home to the region's only abortion provider, a Whole Women's Health center. In a parking lot beside it, we meet a volunteer, April Lidinsky, a mother of two daughters and a professor of women's and gender studies at Indiana University South Bend. Abortion opponents are here, too, as they always are, trying to engage women in dialogue as they arrive and leave. Today's group is a mix of young and old, women and men, one man carrying a large wooden cross.

"We walk people in, shield them, help them feel that they're supported by the community," April says. The clinic only provides medical abortions, induced by two pills, for pregnancies up to ten and a half weeks, and the state imposes an eighteen-hour waiting period after the first visit to the clinic. Opening the clinic was a years-long struggle against groups that went to great lengths to block it — and who, when they lost, opened a competing clinic across the street, Women's Care Center, which offers free ultrasounds and counseling services, but not abortions.

"A few of us," April says, "reached out to leadership in the Women's Care Center and said, 'Could we make an argument that what's going on'" — she's referring to abortion opponents standing outside their center — "'is bad for our community?' If they really respect women and babies and want women to make a considered choice, then having to walk the gauntlet, having to be shouted at, that's bad, whatever your position on abortion."

One of the doctors at the pro-life center accepted the offer. "We ended up writing a viewpoint for our local paper. I would say it was a pleasant and respectful syntactical arm-wrestling match. Do you call people sidewalk counselors? Do you call them protesters? Do you use the phrase *pro-life*?" The unpleasantness came afterward: "I got flak from people I deeply respect on the left who said, 'By sitting down with them, you give them credence they don't deserve.' It was deeply painful to hear that criticism from people I respect, and I understand it." The reason people rarely stand publicly with opponents lies less in the difficulty of making new friends than in the ease of losing old ones.

In 2017, as women's marches were being planned across the country for the day after President Trump's inauguration, April helped organize the one in South Bend. Women who were pro-life asked if they could join. "I said, 'Absolutely. This is our march. You want to be part of it, show up.' So they did." Afterward, she followed up with two of the women. "I invited them over to my house and I went into this June Cleaver panic. I overperformed — sparkling house, I made three different kinds of baked goods. I'm like, really?" She laughs at herself. "They were very gracious and we had this wonderful conversation." But it did not go as she expected.

"I came in with all sorts of assumptions and said some version of, 'Well, surely we all agree that South Bend would be better if fewer abortions were needed. We know that means access to birth control and ramped-up sex ed.' And they were both like, 'Oh, April, honey.' It did not occur to me that very well-educated women would not believe in birth control. They are not interested in fewer abortions. They are interested in abolition in the same way I feel about the death penalty. Nobody's going to say, 'Let's get together and make it slightly less terrible.' No, I'm opposed. It is immoral, it's unethical to me. And so that's where I try to understand them. They do believe it's murder. And I mean" — I can see her trying to meet them halfway — "I don't think it's killing a baby, but it is stopping a life process certainly, the way miscarriages do all the time.'"

The women continued meeting and learned they shared "very little common ground except that we enjoyed each other a lot," April says, and that was enough to spark an idea: to write an op-ed together for the *South Bend Tribune*. It included an essential insight into bipartisan bridge building: "Meeting face to face, we must listen carefully, prioritizing the relationship above the message." Valuing relationships above righteousness requires a level of humility that is increasingly rare in a political environment that rewards indignation and absolutism, but as April and her co-authors wrote, it is full of promise: "This activism involves personal risk; it requires openness to admitting gaps in our knowledge, and our need for self-education. However, it can benefit every area of politics, regarding every difficult and deeply felt issue facing us today. We recommend this work, which is full of pleasure and rich with possibility."

She is trepidatious about Amy Coney Barrett's impending Supreme Court nomination, and for good reason: Coney Barrett will later vote with the court's majority in overturning *Roe*, allowing state legislatures to decide the issue — just as Ruth Bader Ginsburg had wanted half a century ago. Had states been able to control their abortion laws in the 1970s and perhaps beyond, Ginsburg argued in 2013, the issue may not have become so culturally polarizing. Her point — that the political and legislative process should have been allowed to unfold — formed the core of Lincoln's reaction to the most divisive court ruling of his day, *Dred Scott v. Sandford*, which held that black people could not be citizens and slavery must be permitted in federal territories. It was written by the nation's first Catholic Supreme Court justice, Roger Taney.

The debate over abortion is deeply rooted in the Civil War, since the court based its decision in *Roe* on the Fourteenth Amendment's guarantee of due process and equal protection under the law, which was intended to protect black citizens' civil rights. Once the court used it to establish reproductive rights, it was inevitable that battle lines would be drawn around different understandings of freedom. Abortion opponents often compare *Dred Scott*'s conclusion to *Roe*, arguing that the legal treatment of black people as less than human correlates to the legal treatment of the unborn as less than human. Their claim to be modern-day abolitionists galls pro-choice advocates, who consider abortion to be a matter of women's emancipation and equality. Each side sees the issue as a question of rights, just as abolitionists and Confederates did with slavery — only in this case, each side claims the role of liberator.

Lincoln strongly opposed the *Dred Scott* decision not only on moral and legal grounds but on procedural grounds, too. He believed that such weighty questions needed to be decided by the people, not a few judges, as did his fellow Republicans, who assailed the court mercilessly for overstepping its authority. In their debates during the 1858 Senate campaign, Senator Stephen Douglas took Lincoln to task for these attacks, accusing him of trying "to bring the Supreme Court into disrepute among the people . . . destroying public confidence in the court, so that people will not respect its decisions, but will feel at liberty to disregard them, and resist the laws of the land." Lincoln, he charged, was promoting mob rule.

Lincoln responded by rejecting violence and mocking Douglas for treating the court's rulings as holy writ, saying, "A decision of the court is to him a 'Thus saith the Lord.'" He went further in his first inaugural address, which contained a blunt denunciation of judicial rule: "If the policy of the Government upon vital questions affecting the whole people is to be irrevocably fixed by decisions of the Supreme Court, the instant they are made . . . the people will have ceased to be their own rulers, having to that extent practically resigned their Government into the hands of that eminent tribunal." A year later, Congress passed and Lincoln signed bills that flatly contravened *Dred Scott* by emancipating slaves in Washington, DC, and the existing territories. In effect, Lincoln and Congress said to the court: *Buzz off — matters of fundamental freedoms are the domain of elected leaders, not appointed judges.*

Democrats had a near-opposite response to *Roe*. For five decades, pro-choice politicians viewed the court's decision as settled law, absolving them of the need to act. They did little more than pay lip service to the idea of passing a bill codifying *Roe* and guaranteeing women's reproductive rights. Even during President Barack Obama's first two years in office, when Democrats held supermajorities in the House and Senate, they made no push to pass a bill — and never even introduced one. A NARAL Pro-Choice America leader later acknowledged the reason: They didn't have the votes. Democrats in Congress had no interest in sticking their necks out, and Democratic voters and activists placed no pressure on them to do so.

In Governor Mario Cuomo's speech at Notre Dame, he laid the onus on the Catholic Church for convincing the public that abortion is a moral wrong before expecting legislators to ban it. But he neglected to say what has proved equally true: There is also an onus on abortion-rights supporters to persuade their representatives to endorse it. That never happened. *Roe* provided a false sense of security that led Democrats to view the court as they did after *Dred Scott*: an adequate substitute for the will of the people.

Roe has allowed Republican politicians to avoid responsibility, too. Quietly, many would rather preserve the right to abortion for political reasons, given public support for it. If Republicans in Congress believe that abortion is murder, they must believe that murder is a lesser crime than ending the filibuster, because during the first two years of Trump's presidency, the Republican-controlled Senate opted to keep the arcane rule rather than save the unborn.

Legislators in both parties have lacked the courage of their convictions. The court has become a stand-in for Congress on fundamental rights, including gay rights, because members have been unwilling to stand up and be counted. For Lincoln, "of the people, by the people, for the people" did not mean legislative abdication and judicial genuflecting. It meant vigorous action by the people's elected representatives. And for Lincoln, like the founders, the Constitution's checks and balances did not require thinking of the judiciary as the first among equals — or even as an equal. Only two of the three branches include elected representatives, and it is their obligation to be the primary voice of the people. The court can and must constrain the people's voice to prevent a tyranny of the majority, but it cannot replace it. Democracy is not a passive activity, but for five decades, Democrats have mistaken silence for governance.

Lincoln's position — that the people must speak, lest the court speak for them — still holds wisdom.

We roll through Rolling Prairie and turn southwest toward Valparaiso, home to a university the KKK tried to buy in 1923, when the university was facing bankruptcy. The Klan hoped to create an "All-American" curriculum, faculty, and student body — Ku Klux College, they would call it, bringing the Klan new levels of prestige and respectability and creating "a monument to American ideals and principles." Local residents enthusiastically embraced the idea, and the two sides agreed on a price. A university official warned students that "hereafter Valparaiso will not be a place for the Kellys, Burkes, and Steins." Many Catholics dropped out. Blacks had never been permitted in the first place. Fortunately, the Klan failed to deliver the money, the plan collapsed, and Lutheran Church leaders stepped in to rescue the school.

Lutherans would also play a leading role in finally integrating the town almost half a century later. When a black woman, Barbara Cotton, moved her family here in 1969 with the help of a Lutheran family, she faced the same kinds of death threats and intimidation that Daisy and William Myers faced in Levittown a dozen years earlier. Like the Myers, she stayed, until her stepson was found dead on the side of the Lincoln Highway in 1980, killed by blunt trauma to the head and seemingly thrown from a moving vehicle. There was no sign saying, "Nigger, Don't Let the Sun Go Down on You," but there may as well have been.

In the same year that Barbara Cotton's stepson was killed, Indiana's John Mellencamp wrote a song about an interracial couple, but a record executive insisted he change the lyrics. That's how Jack of "Jack and Diane" stopped being black. If he had stayed black, imagine how this verse would have been received by radio stations and listeners, as images of teenage love became layered with racial resentments and fears.

> *Diane sitting on Jacky's lap, got his hands between her knees*
> *Jack he says, "Hey Diane, let's run off behind a shady tree*
> *Dribble off those Bobby Brooks let me do what I please"*

Integration came slowly to many Indiana communities, and resistance was common. The small town that inspired the movie *Hoosiers*, Milan, did not see its first black high school student until 1985. When a *Sports Illustrated* reporter asked a resident why, he was told, "They don't come and they wouldn't be welcome if they did." The movie became a national cultural landmark and a celebration of a state's love affair with basketball — Hoosier Hysteria — that goes back longer than anyone can remember. *Hoosiers* allowed Americans to swoon over an underdog without ever having to cast an eye on the racial segregation and exclusion that long defined Indiana basketball. But here in Valparaiso, Barbara Cotton's legacy endures. One of her sons has since returned to live here, and he is now serving his second term as a member of the Valparaiso city council. As Mellencamp sings: *Ain't that America?*

— 18 —

White City Blues

It's our third Friday night in a parking lot, this time at WGN-TV on Chicago's North Side. Our friend Terry is a morning news producer here and kindly cleared our stay with security. Inside the building's lobby, a display case celebrates the station's two biggest hits: *The Bozo Show*, which debuted as *Bozo's Circus* in 1960, and a program that later turned into a circus of its own, *The Phil Donahue Show*.

In the 1970s on WGN, Donahue challenged political leaders and economic thinkers to serious debates and invited the public to join in, turning the camera on his audiences and walking among them with a microphone, democratizing media. The son of a midwestern furniture salesman and a graduate of Notre Dame, Donahue was liberalism's answer to William F. Buckley and the Ivy League erudition of *Firing Line*. But Donahue understood that the future of news lay in entertainment, and the future of entertainment lay in its celebration of bad behavior, moral shock, and interpersonal conflict.

"This is a medium that rewards popularity," Donahue said of television in 1984, "and I don't want to be a dead hero. Besides, it doesn't do any good to talk if nobody's listening." Donahue's descent into tawdry spectacle gave rise to competitors who made him appear almost prudish. Geraldo Rivera, Morton Downey Jr., Jerry Springer, and others took the carnival barking to new lows, while talk radio hosts who adopted Donahue's model — merging news, entertainment, and audience participation — became insult-slinging provocateurs. Yet Donahue's spawn were not all boors. A young woman who filmed in Chicago rose to the top of the ratings by offering inspiration rather than titillation: Oprah Winfrey.

During a 1988 show about skinheads, Winfrey had an epiphany: "I realized in that moment that I was doing more to empower them than I was to expose them, and since that moment, I've never done a show like that again." She surpassed Donahue not only in popularity but also in purpose, demonstrating that it was possible to elevate a talk show into the realm of empowerment and self-help and away from group conflict and racial hatred. But she was an outlier, and the format was eventually eclipsed by an advance in technology that universalized it: social media, which allows everyone to host their own 24/7 talk shows, turning broadcasting into a birthright.

While social media can be a portal for discovery and empowerment, like Winfrey's show, much of it resembles the work of her competitors. Users mix the same strategies Donahue pioneered to attract audiences, playing to people's sense of outrage, anger, envy, and righteousness to escalate and magnify conflict. And the single microphone Donahue passed around to allow a select few to ask questions has been replaced by an infinite number of megaphones that allow everyone to make declarations, the more outlandish and provocative the better, blurring the line between civic dialogue and carnival barking beyond recognition. No one wants to be a dead hero.

Media has always held an outsized influence on politics and culture, allowing ordinary people to wield power over community and country without being elected to office or ordained to ministry. In an 1858 senatorial debate with Stephen Douglas, Lincoln said, "Public sentiment is everything. With public sentiment, nothing can fail. Without it, nothing can succeed. Consequently, he who moulds public sentiment, goes deeper than he who enacts statutes or pronounces decisions." As the 1860 presidential election approached, Lincoln secretly bought a failing German-language weekly newspaper, *Staats-Anzeiger* — his lawyer handled the transaction to ensure the public was not aware of his affiliation — and allowed its editor to run it under the condition that he faithfully espouse the Republican platform and tout its candidates. Lincoln's ownership remained secret. Denying it would've been dishonest. But hiding it? In the words of Mr. Dooley, the Chicago bartender invented in 1893 by newspaper columnist Finley Peter Dunne, "Politics ain't beanbag."

Although newspapers have lost much of their sway, media still "goes deeper" than lawmakers, even as it rests on new levels of superficiality that cater to ever-shorter attention spans. The "trash TV" Donahue pioneered paved the way for reality television, which helped catapult one of its stars — whose wealth and celebrity Donahue hyped in a 1987 interview — into the Oval Office, moving Washington under a Big Top and attracting record audiences to cheer in celebration, gape in horror, and argue in anger over whether we were watching the Great Santini or Bozo the Clown.

In the morning, we walk to Roscoe Village and down North Lincoln Avenue, which cuts diagonally through the neighborhood of Lincoln Park to our destination three miles away: Lincoln Park, the park. Along the way, we'll pass signs for the Lincoln Station Bar and Grill, Lincoln Tap Room, Lincoln Hall, Hotel Lincoln, Lincoln Dental Lounge, and the Lincoln Common shopping center. In the city where Lincoln secured the 1860 Republican nomination, his name appears on signs almost as frequently as Old Style beer.

On N. Lincoln, a white man in a black suit and black hat plays a racing blues solo on electric guitar, more Eddie Van Halen than Papa Charlie Jackson, the first successful self-accompanied musician to record the blues, which occurred in Chicago in 1924. The song he recorded, "Papa's Lawdy Lawdy Blues," held as clear a statement about human equality as has ever been written.

I ain't crazy 'bout no yellow
I ain't no fool 'bout no brown
'Cause you can't tell the difference, mama
when the sun go down
Lawd Lawd Lawd

Jackson had come north from New Orleans to play and record, the same opportunity that attracted so many others, not just the famous bluesmen like Jimmy and Mama Read, Buddy Guy, B. B. King, Jimmy Rogers, Muddy Waters, and Howlin' Wolf but also two of the greatest talents of the century: the Queen of Gospel, Mahalia Jackson; and the godmother of rock 'n' roll *and* soul, Sister Rosetta Tharpe, who mixed the sounds of the Pentecostal Church of God in Christ with blues and swing. She and other trailblazing women never got the respect or opportunities men did — her grave in Philadelphia didn't even get a headstone until 2008, thirty-five years after her death — but her songs are still being discovered. Her 1945 gospel-rock hit "Strange Things Happening Every Day" has found new life amid pandemic lockdowns — and not just the lockdowns.

A headline on the front page of today's *New York Times* reads, "At Pentagon, Fears Grow That Trump Will Pull Military into Election Unrest." On the record, military leaders call the idea preposterous, but off the record, they reveal their worries, and a former assistant secretary of defense echoes them: "The main fear is that Portland is Off Broadway and that Broadway would be something here" in DC, he says, referring to the political violence on the left in Portland. "The idea is that you are going to have a lot of kindling out there and Trump is doing nothing to keep that from getting more flammable."

Strange things happening every day.

The music that came north with black artists was old, but the name given to it was new, as one of Papa Charlie Jackson's acolytes and recording partners, Big Bill Broonzy, explained. "They didn't exactly call what they was playin' then blues, but it was," Broonzy said. "They called it reels — negro reels." And it wasn't just music; it was oral history. In reviewing Richard Wright's *Black Boy*, which parallel's Wright's own journey from the south to Chicago as part of the Great Migration, Ralph Ellison wrote, "The blues is an impulse to keep the painful details and episodes of a brutal experience alive in one's aching consciousness, to finger its jagged grain, and to transcend it, not by the consolation of philosophy, but by squeezing from it a near-tragic, near-comic lyricism."

Broonzy, born Lee Conley Bradley, said he learned such songs as a child in Arkansas from an uncle who had been a slave, but almost nothing he claimed about his biography was reliable, including where and when he was born or the stories he told about serving in World War I. Still, as Chicago's Studs Terkel said about Broonzy while hosting him on his radio show, a show that never treated guests like circus acts and aimed to enlighten rather than enrage, "Bill is speaking the truth — his truth." And truth lay in his songs, like "Black, Brown, and White," which he wrote in 1945, though no US record label would release until after his death in 1958.

They said, if you was white, should be all right
If you was brown, stick around
But as you black, oh brother — get back, get back, get back

At the 2009 inauguration of the first US president to call Chicago home, eighty-seven-year-old civil rights leader Reverend Joseph Lowery gave a benediction that concluded with an echo of Broonzy's song: "We ask you to help us work for that day when black will not be asked to get back; when brown can stick around; when yellow will be mellow; when the red man can get ahead, man; and when white will embrace what is right." Some conservatives denounced it as divisive and were outraged that President Obama smiled during it. But Lowery delivered it with the lightheartedness of someone who had heard Broonzy's song when the idea of a black president was "Just a Dream," as Broonzy sang in another song, a dream that required "near-tragic, near-comic lyricism" to sustain. Lowery closed his prayer by reciting the last verse of "Lift Every Voice and Sing," a song written by James Weldon Johnson and adopted by the NAACP in 1919 as the "Negro National Anthem." It was first sung by five hundred schoolchildren on Lincoln's birthday in 1900.

Farther down on N. Lincoln, we pass a small building that once housed the Lounge Ax, a rock club that closed in 2000 after hosting local talent like the Smashing Pumpkins, Urge Overkill, Liz Phair, and Wilco, which debuted one of its biggest songs here, about going home "Via Chicago." Its violent opening line — "I dreamed about killing you again last night" — is only a lover's lament, but Chicago is in the midst of murderous nightmare, the second-deadliest year in two decades. Eight in ten of the victims are black, and most of the rest are Latino. On May 31, the day George Floyd protests descended into looting, eighteen people were murdered in twenty-four hours, the city's deadliest day since it began keeping records in 1961.

Liberals have tended to see violence connected to the George Floyd protests as the work of a few bad apples, while conservatives have seen cities with a rotten core. Neither perspective is surprising: Liberals prefer to focus on killings by police rather than killings by criminals, while conservatives prefer to focus on killings by criminals rather than by police. Each has their ideological and political reasons, which are nearly impossible to separate from the issue of race. Rare is the person who raises a cry against both the disproportionate police brutality against blacks and the disproportionate numbers of violent crimes committed by blacks. To do the latter, even after doing the former, leads to charges of blaming the victim and racism, and not just for politicians. When the rapper Kendrick Lamar, whose parents moved out of Chicago to escape the trap of violent gangs, wrote a song called "The Blacker the Berry" decrying racism and its effects on black Americans, he was attacked by some on the left for its closing lines, when he dared turn the mirror around on the song's narrator, leading to charges of "false equivalency" and "what aboutism."

So why did I weep when Trayvon Martin was in the street?
When gang-banging make me kill a nigga blacker than me?

Across the street from the Lounge Ax, by an alleyway where the FBI gunned down the bank bandit John Dillinger, the marquee of the Biograph Theater reads, "Black Lives Matter," and a mural makes a demand: "Say Their Names." Black letters on a white board memorialize the names of black people whose killings, often by police, made national headlines and ignited protests, including Ahmaud Arbery, Michael Brown, Eric Garner, Trayvon Martin, Breonna Taylor, Tamir Rice, George Floyd, Freddie Gray, and Laquan McDonald. Toward the bottom on the right is a warning, written in red: "Without justice the list Will Go On."

As we say their names and work for justice, let's also say the names Serenity Arrington, age five, and Avion Aldridge, age seventeen, and Richard Soward, age twenty, and Rayalecio Turman, age forty-two, who were all murdered in Chicago this morning — and Omar Alvarado, fifteen, who will be murdered tonight. None will make the national news nor inspire protest marches. All are black or Latino, and chances are their killers — some of whom may spend the rest of their lives in prison — are, too. Without change, the list Will Go On.

Further down N. Lincoln, Oz Park holds statues of the Cowardly Lion, the Scarecrow, the Tin Man, Dorothy, and Toto. The thirteen-acre park was named in honor of the Chicagoan who wrote *The Wonderful Wizard of Oz* and lived nearby, L. Frank Baum. The city developed the park in the 1970s as part of an urban renewal plan that knocked down blocks of housing that had been home to low-income families, most black and Puerto Rican. *There's no place like home.*

In urging passage of the 1949 Housing Act that led to "slum clearance," Illinois's Democratic senator Paul Douglas wrote an article for *Collier's* arguing that tearing down old buildings was a matter of promoting morality and protecting personal safety. It was titled "Democracy Can't Live in These Houses." In 1968, a kid from Lincoln Park named Jose "Cha Cha" Jimenez, whose family had moved nine times in six years, had the opposite epiphany: Democracy *did* live in those houses, and residents had to show it.

After encountering the teachings of Malcolm X, Reverend King, and Thomas Merton while serving time for petty crime, Jimenez transformed his Lincoln Park street gang, the Young Lords, into a political organization modeled on the Black Panthers. They disrupted community meetings, smashed windows of the Department of Urban Renewal, and barricaded themselves into the McCormick Theological Seminary, demanding money for affordable housing. But they were no match for Democratic reformers.

Between the 1940s and today, Lincoln Park has gone from one of the poorest neighborhoods to one of the wealthiest, as its population has declined by about 30 percent and its housing stock has shrunk by about three thousand units. Much of the Puerto Rican community here moved west to Humboldt Park, where L. Frank Baum lived when he wrote *The Wonderful Wizard of Oz*. For Laurel and me, to stand at Oz Park is to see a pastoral oasis. But to those who once lived where an Emerald Garden now grows, it is a painful reminder of a government that stole their homes and crushed their community. And while there is no statue of the Wizard here, the park is a monument to the ruling powers who hid their hubris behind a curtain of beneficence, which people like Jimenez tried and failed to pull back, while white liberals sang along to E. Y. Harburg.

We hear he is a whiz of a wiz
If ever a wiz there was

We reach Lincoln Park, one of the earliest and grandest Lincoln monuments, named for him just two months after his assassination. A century later, it would be the backdrop for one of the nation's most carnivalesque political trials, and Lincoln would be invoked by the defense.

Our arrival in Chicago coincided with the premier of the Aaron Sorkin movie, *The Trial of the Chicago Seven*, about those arrested for protesting at the 1968 Democratic National Convention. At his sentencing, Abbie Hoffman said, "In 1861 Abraham Lincoln in his inaugural address said, and

I quote: 'When the people shall grow weary of their constitutional right to amend the government, they shall exert'" — Lincoln said "can exercise" — "'their revolutionary right to dismember and overthrow that government.' If Abraham Lincoln had given that speech in Lincoln Park, he would be on trial right here in this courtroom, because that is an inciteful speech. That is a speech intended to create a riot."

In fact, Lincoln's speech was intended to *quell* a riot: secession. And while Hoffman had a point — Lincoln recognized the right of the people to make revolution — he missed Lincoln's, which was to placate his opponents by showing that he was open to nearly any compromise to avoid a revolution, including a constitutional amendment guaranteeing slavery where it already existed. His strong moral opposition to slavery was secondary to his political devotion to the preservation of peace. But Hoffman turned Lincoln's conciliation into a call to arms.

In an 1856 speech here in Chicago, Lincoln said, "Our government rests in public opinion. Whoever can change public opinion can change the government." Yippies were trying to change public opinion, but by presenting themselves as revolutionaries committed to reordering society around a higher spiritual consciousness that rejected authority, private property, and capitalism, they appeared more aligned with the traditions of anarchists than progressives. Their utopian radicalism and shock value methods — including nominating a pig for president and threatening to release LSD into the water supply — treated democracy as a circus and politics as performance art, which frightened and angered much of the country and helped doom a Democratic nominee with strong civil rights credentials, Vice President Hubert Humphrey.

Although the Yippies soon flamed out, their style of political theater and approach to public opinion — confrontational, provocative, obscene — would take root, including their trolling of opponents. (They never had any intention of putting LSD in the water supply.) In the years that followed, embracing this idea of politics as an uninhibited spectacle would help make Donahue a star and Trump president. The carnival of modern politics first came into national view here, in Lincoln Park.

We meander through the park to a statue of Lincoln by Augustus Saint-Gaudens, the Dublin-born and New York City–raised sculptor whose young assistant, James Fraser, had given us *Mystic Lincoln* in Jersey City. "Lincoln stood tall in the carriage," Saint-Gaudens said of seeing him in New York City in 1861, "his dark uncovered head, bent in contemplative acknowledgement of the waiting people," just as he is here. He is stepping forward while leaning back — advancing, but with restraint.

In early summer 1894, Jane Addams stood where we now do at the height of a Pullman railroad strike, when more than a hundred thousand workers in twenty-seven states refused to operate trains carrying Pullman cars, all but shutting down the national economy. Addams walked here from Hull House, the home she founded to enlist urban missionaries to help provide social services, relief provisions, and educational and cultural opportunities to the huddled masses arriving in Chicago. Addams's father had been friends with Lincoln, and she credited Abe with helping to inspire Hull House through his faith in the people. "He made plain, once for all," she wrote, "that democratic government, associated as it is with all the mistakes and shortcomings of the common people, still remains the most valuable contribution America has made to the moral life of the world."

On her four-mile walk here, Hull passed close to Haymarket Square, where a bombing seven years earlier had killed seven police officers and at least four protesters and wounded dozens more. It was retaliation for an attack two days earlier at a lumberyard, where police fired into a crowd and killed four striking workers. Now, with federal troops on Chicago's streets to help break the Pullman strike, which began just days after several hundred unemployed laborers left Chicago to join Coxey's march on Washington, Addams feared the city would explode in violence again, and she came to Saint-Gaudens's statue "to look at and gain magnanimous counsel," she later wrote, from "the man who had won charity for those on both sides of an 'irrepressible conflict.'" She held divided sympathies, as Lincoln — who defended the railroads in many legal cases and defended the right of strikers, too — probably would have as well. "I know that in almost every case of strikes," Lincoln told striking machinists, "the men have just cause for complaint."

Addams knew the strikers had just cause, but she also admired George Pullman's experiment in welfare capitalism: The town he built for his workers included affordable homes with indoor plumbing and sanitation services, gaslit sidewalks and paved streets, a dairy and market, parks and playing fields, a library, a theater, and a church — all aimed at making residents upright citizens and loyal workers. But Pullman's thirteen thousand residents had to abide by the company's rules. They could only rent their homes, not buy them. The town had a curfew, there were no saloons, and Knights of Labor meetings were banned. The town had no mayor or council and was run by company-appointed agents, who banned public speeches.

Only a year before the strike, the town of Pullman and Hull House had both been major attractions for visitors to the World's Fair — the World's Columbia Exposition, it was called, in celebration of the four hundredth anniversary of Columbus's arrival in the Americas. The fair, like Hull House and Pullman, was an exercise in urban utopianism — an idealized city bathed in lights, centered on classical architecture, and landscaped with lush gardens, all conceived by the nation's leading architects and designers, including Saint-Gaudens.

The fair's "White City" was the birth of the City Beautiful movement and the idea that centrally planned aesthetic design on a monumental scale could save the soul of cities from the meanness of the masses and the chaos of the market by elevating the spirits of citizens and fostering a more moral and cultured society, the same mission Pullman and Addams were pursuing. And like their experiments in utopianism, the White City was a white-dominated affair. Blacks were excluded from operating exhibits, while the Native American exhibit depicted a variety of war cries, battle dances, body piercings, and other caricatures that drew crowds and reinforced images of primitive savages. The fair's organizers understood, presaging Phil Donahue, that the fair was a medium that rewarded popularity.

The White City burned to the ground at the height of the Pullman Strike, which left thirty dead, strikers blacklisted from future employment, and the union leader, Eugene Debs, imprisoned. During the World's Fair, people visited the White City, Pullman, and Hull House to see visions of the future. And in one way they did: The arrogance of top-down control exercised by white reformers would continue to plague American cities for generations to come.

We bid farewell to Saint-Gaudens's Lincoln and exit the park at Clark Street, or La Clark, as the Puerto Rican community here had called it before their homes were demolished to make way for a high-rise housing development that still stands: Carl Sandburg Village, named for the poet who gave Chicago its favored nickname — "city of broad shoulders" — and gave the country a six-volume, bestselling, Pulitzer Prize–winning biography of Lincoln that blended fact and myth into a work that was more literature than history. That his name adorns a housing development that displaced poor Puerto Ricans could be thought ironic — Sandburg was a friend of the working stiff and early supporter of civil rights — but as a clear-eyed witness of the American character and experience, it is fitting, too. "We are united in but one aim — getting the dollar," he wrote.

Cha Cha Jimenez's family was among those who saw their La Clark home flattened and replaced by eight towers and sixty townhomes across superblocks built with walls lining the sidewalks, designed to keep out undesirables who might intrude on its shops, swimming pools, and tennis court. Like the town of Pullman, Hull House, and the World's Fair, the development of Sandburg Village reflected a utopian vision, this one by urban planners who saw "towers in a park" as the modern medicine cities needed to restore their health, turning apartment complexes into self-contained communities, with private security guards protecting residents from the chaos of the people celebrated by Sandburg.

Each of the individual towers in Sandburg Village is named for a famous writer, all of them white. It was left to the Chicago Housing Authority to name a building for Lorraine Hansberry, on the west side of town, though there is still none named for Richard Wright, who lived in the city for a decade and wrote his first novel, *Lawd Today!*, here. During that time, Wright was employed as a postal worker. In his off hours, he sought inspiration at the Abraham Lincoln Centre, a South Side settlement house where writers often gathered. *Lawd Today!* takes place on Lincoln's birthday, and Lincoln makes regular appearances throughout the novel, via a radio broadcast that quotes from his second inaugural address and recounts battles between north and south, turning the Civil War's legacy into a backdrop for a day in the life of his alter ego, a black postal worker named Jake Jackson who left the south dreaming of the Promised Land only to find new forms of racism, poverty, and misery in Chicago.

The Great Migration that brought six million black citizens north between 1916 and 1970 was followed by a far greater migration: the twenty-five million Latin Americans who arrived between 1960 and 2010. Both waves followed the dream of a better life that Robert Johnson sang about in a song he recorded as Richard Wright was working on *Lawd Today!*, "Sweet Home Chicago." *There's no place like home.*

From Clark Street, we turn west toward Cabrini-Green, another slum-clearance project, this one for public housing. At its dedication in 1942, Mayor Edward Kelly evoked Lincoln's famous "house divided" speech. "I believe this government cannot endure, permanently half slave and half free," Lincoln said. Kelly gave it a modern spin: "We cannot continue as a nation, half slum and half palace," he warned, positioning housing conditions as Lincoln did slavery. "This project sets an example for the wide reconstruction of substandard areas which will come after the war."

Whether deliberate or not, Mayor Kelly's use of the word *reconstruction* reflected a mind-set among urban reformers that was not so different from the Radical Republicans who tried to reconstruct the south after the war. Both saw groups of people who could not be trusted to govern themselves and thus needed to become wards of the state. But where conservative resistance doomed southern reconstruction, liberal arrogance doomed urban reconstruction. Like Pullman before them, urban reformers failed because they refused to share power with those they believed they were helping, certain that they knew best.

In the late 1950s and early 1960s, the city cleared seventy acres around the Cabrini townhomes to construct towers-in-a-park for the working poor. At Sandburg Village, the design scheme allowed young professionals to close themselves off from their poorer neighbors. Here it worked in reverse. Residents of the more affluent neighborhoods surrounding Cabrini-Green stayed away, leaving fifteen thousand people marooned on an island of rising poverty, crime, and decay that became synonymous with urban failure.

In 1992, three days before the release of a horror movie set in Cabrini-Green, *Candyman*, seven-year-old Dantrell Davis was shot and killed while walking to school, forcing Mayor Richard Daley to show that the city was capable of governing itself. The plan that emerged was to knock down the towers and start again, this time with mixed-income buildings. At the press conference announcing the plan, Daley promised that residents being forced out would be given better housing — and better lives. He said of them, "I want to rebuild their souls." They would have settled for rebuilt homes. More than two decades after demolition began, less than one-third of the demolished units have been replaced.

Slowly, the area is being redeveloped, but large swaths are still empty, a colossal failure by urban reformers captured in three devastating lines by the Chicago poet Gwendolyn Brooks, who wrote of an apartment building where she worked that had been built for the 1893 World's Fair. In 1952, it was razed to make way for a building designed by the modernist architect Ludwig Mies van der Rohe, whose ideas also inspired the towers of Cabrini-Green.

Sit where the light corrupts your face
Miës Van der Rohe retires from grace
And the fair fables fall

For Brooks's generation, the "fair fables" of centralized urban planning — born of good intentions but doomed by arrogance — came crashing down around them. What began with great fanfare at the World's Fair ended here at Cabrini-Green, in a pile of rubble.

Liberal reformers have learned the lessons of Cabrini-Green and Sandburg Village and now promote mixed-income developments that are integrated with, rather than set off from, their surrounding neighborhoods. Some are even coming around on the need to eliminate or scale back another progressive-era achievement: zoning requirements that block the construction of multifamily homes, limiting supply and driving up costs. Liberal "YIMBYs" — Yes In My Backyard — now challenge government to permit more construction, rather than fighting it to stop "gentrification," a term sometimes wielded by progressives with the same conviction they once attached to "slum clearance," and for a similar purpose: to justify top-down planning of, and restrictions on, housing. But change has been slow, and not only because of zoning. Laws and regulations passed to protect the environment have also given homeowners considerable legal tools to kill housing projects and keep out unwanted — usually lower-income, often black and Latino — neighbors.

These problems are most acute in the bluest states and cities, where Democrats have yet to fully embrace the common lesson of the failed progressive utopian visions at Cabrini and Sandburg, Hull House and Pullman — a lesson underscored by the revival that has occurred in East Liberty, Pittsburgh: The strongest, healthiest, and most democratic communities are built from the ground up, and they are open to all without exclusions, whether in the form of restrictive covenants and redlining or their seemingly race-blind successors: thickets of zoning and environmental regulations. Until that changes, the lack of housing availability and affordability will continue to plague cities, with the highest costs paid by the poor.

Laurel and I end our day at a picnic table outside an empty Cubby Bear bar across from Wrigley Field. As we arrive, we look up to see a Cub hit a third-inning grand slam, giving them a lead against their crosstown rival, the White Sox. The two teams share the legend of Harry Carey, the announcer who began singing out-of-tune renditions of "Take Me Out to the Ballgame." Fans belt it out during every seventh-inning stretch, though few are aware that it was written from the perspective of a woman who prefers cheering for the home team and arguing with umpires to a night at the theater, making the song a celebration of women's liberation and equality.

The Cubs soon lose their lead and the game, but no matter: Their fans are still basking in the glow of their 2016 World Series victory. They blamed their 108-year title drought on a Greek immigrant, William Sianis, who bought the Lincoln Tavern in 1934 and renamed it the Billy Goat Tavern when a goat fell off a train and wandered in. When the Cubs owner denied entry to Sianis's goat during a World Series game, Sianis placed the curse that became an article of faith here, since belief in a just God precluded any other possibility. Fans tried all kinds of stunts to lift the curse — taking a goat to Wrigley Field in a limousine, making goat sausage, eating a goat in record time — to no avail. Maybe they should've just changed the tavern name back to Lincoln.

Community Building

Climbing out of bed early Sunday morning brings a disturbing sight: The toilet pedal is lying on the floor again. It must have happened when one of us got up in the middle of the night. I'm pretty sure only one of us got up, and it wasn't Laurel. I try to reattach it using the trick we were told in Gettysburg: Turn on the water pump. But it won't go on. When Laurel wakes up — and waking up to the sound of me cursing the toilet was not the Sunday morning she had envisioned — she takes a turn on the floor, with the same result. Making matters worse, RV service shops are closed on Sundays. We're shit out of luck.

On the outer rings of Chicago's suburbs is Batavia, where, six months after the Lincoln Highway's 1913 dedication, residents brought their shovels and picks to town to begin constructing the first stretch of concrete highway in the state. After a parade and speeches, community volunteers got to work. For their service, they received a paycheck signed by the governor redeemable for the coin emblazoned with Lincoln's face: a penny. The era of neighbors banding together to build public works lasted from time immemorial until only recently, when it was overtaken by the paralyzing combination of government regulations and insurance liability. It's a societal shift that doesn't get much attention, but it should.

A few years ago, my sister, Julie, told me about an elementary school playground that her community in Middlebury, Vermont, had built in

1990, much as our parents had helped construct a tire playground at our elementary school in the early 1980s. The Vermont playground came about the same way, a massive community effort involving hundreds of volunteers and thousands of hours of work. But after twenty-five years of wear and tear and a visit from an insurance agent, the school board decided it needed replacing. At a school board meeting, community members spoke with great emotion about their experience creating the original. But the board believed it was a safer bet to hire a private contractor for the job, costing taxpayers $250,000. Those who attended the meeting reluctantly supported the decision, and while some were disappointed, many felt an emotion even more debilitating: resignation. *That's just the way it is these days.*

We now pay taxes to provide services that we long provided as a community. Economists might say it's more efficient. But giving money to government or a nonprofit organization does not produce the same social capital as working collaboratively with neighbors. Forging civic bonds can't be outsourced, and fear of legal liability should not be accepted as barriers to creating them. ("Discourage litigation," Lincoln wrote. "Persuade your neighbors to compromise whenever you can.") When I asked Father Jenkins at Notre Dame what binds the country together, he replied, "This sense of building community, a sense of common ownership, and a sense of tolerance — coming together even despite differences, a common community."

Julie's story reminded me of a conversation I had while working in city hall. Former New York governor Mario Cuomo had an idea for a speech he wanted to offer Mayor Bloomberg, as news swirled that he might run for president as an independent. Over the phone, he delivered a fifteen-minute monologue that centered on a quote from Lincoln: "The legitimate object of government is to do for a community of people, whatever they need to have done, but can not do, at all, or can not, so well do, for themselves — in their separate, and individual capacities. In all that the people can individually do as well for themselves, government ought not interfere." Cuomo, with eloquence that made it hard to believe he wasn't reading from a carefully prepared text, argued that Lincoln's two sentences got to the heart not only of the purpose of government but also of what voters, whatever their party, want from their leaders.

Lincoln's first sentence is often taken by Democrats to justify expansionary policies — FDR and Obama both cited it — yet they rarely emphasize the second sentence. Even Cuomo, in his book *Why Lincoln Matters*, omitted the second Lincoln sentence while extolling the first. Including it would have required reckoning with the principle of limited government, which Democrats tend to dismiss as a self-interested desire for lower taxes. While that is often a factor, it can be secondary to a more primal desire: the freedom to do for ourselves and our communities what we are capable of handling on our own, whether it's building playgrounds or anything else. Some cities now even prohibit people from sharing food with the hungry without applying for government permits. Being told such jobs can only be done or approved by government can leave people feeling both powerless and disconnected from one another, weakening the bonds of community and citizenship.

As president, Lincoln encouraged Congress to revise and rewrite laws in plain language and reduce them to "one volume (or at most, two volumes)." There are now about seventy-five thousand pages of law added every single year, more than four times as many as were added in the 1960s.

After my call with Cuomo, a deputy mayor asked me, "Did you get in a single word?" He knew Cuomo, so he already knew the answer: hardly a one. But that was fine with me. It was a pleasure listening to him. Yet in looking back at the speech I ended up drafting, I'm disappointed to see that I quoted only the first Lincoln sentence, not the second. Understanding America's partisan divide requires recognizing, and respecting, both.

Past the last stop on the Chicago commuter rail line, a stone monument to the Lincoln Highway marks the entrance to DeKalb. On the side of an empty red-brick building, a mural recalls DeKalb's history as "a livewire city," a reference to its great invention, barbed wire. A local man, Joseph Glidden, came up with the idea in 1873 to stop his cattle from getting loose. The factory he built soon churned out nearly three hundred thousand miles of barbed wire annually, which earned him a fortune and played an instrumental role in settling the west. With hardly any wood on the prairie for fencing, farmers who laid claim to land under the 1862 Homestead Act signed by Lincoln had no way to control their livestock and mark their private property. Barbed wire made it possible for them to do both, not only keeping in cattle but also keeping out trespassers. Native Americans, who had long roamed freely across the land, called it the devil's rope. Cowboys hated it, too — it cut into their livelihood. The end of the open range, and the beginning of new battles over land and property rights, began here in DeKalb.

Down the road, more than ten silver grain bins and silos tower above the few trees standing nearby. American farmers long stored grain and grass in underground pits, but that began to change in the same year Glidden had his epiphany, when Fred Hatch returned to his family's dairy farm in northern Illinois with a degree from Illinois Industrial University (now the University of Illinois Champaign-Urbana). The university grew out of the Land Grand Act signed by Lincoln in 1862 to apply scientific techniques to improve agricultural production, and it didn't take long to pay off. With the fall harvest looming, Hatch — who was in the university's second graduating class — convinced his father to support a novel idea. Rather than putting the winter's feed into a hole in the ground, why not extend the hole upward in a structure made of floorboards and tar paper? Hatch believed that by vastly increasing storage space and keeping it away from the ground moisture that spoils feed, they would help to fatten the cows over the winter. It worked, and to deal with the small amount of feed spoiled by getting trapped in the corners of their tower, farmers switched to a circular design. By the early 1900s, more than half a million silos dotted the country.

About hallway across Illinois, the Lincoln crosses rail tracks and the road surface changes — our first stretch of dirt road. Between the rail line and cornfields, we roll slowly for several miles and reemerge onto pavement just before the Lincoln Highway National Headquarters, a two-story stone-and-brick building. Awaiting our arrival is John Nicholson, wearing a gray goatee, a tan button-up shirt, blue jeans darkened at the knees, and a camouflage baseball hat that rests above his ears.

"Franklin Grove's a nice little town," he says, welcoming us. He gestures toward the Lincolnway Café across the street, one of the only businesses on the town's commercial block. "Extremely good food. They close at three o'clock, though." It's now four o'clock — our dinner plan is dashed. "Are you driving the highway itself?"

"We are, and we're trying to stick to the original route."

"So often, roads followed the railroad. Didn't have to screw up the farm fields. The railroad came through in 1854, and this building went up six years later. It was built as a general store by H. I. Lincoln. Henry Lincoln. He was a sixteenth cousin of Abraham Lincoln."

I suppose when one shares a surname with one of history's epic figures, one traces the family tree as far as needed to establish a connection, but there's more than a name binding the two men. Abe also bought a general store as a young man, co-owning it with a partner. He had no head for business, however, and he spent much of his time reading while his partner seems to have spent much of his time drinking. As business flagged, Lincoln sold his share to his partner, but when his partner died and the business failed, Lincoln inherited the debt: $1,000. He called it his "national debt," and it took him more than a decade to repay it, but repay it he did. His distant cousin Henry fared better.

"It was a general store until about 1890, and this is where he sold his product," John says as he brings us into an open room, now a gift shop offering Lincoln Highway T-shirts, hats, mugs, key chains, books, and other Lincoln-related items. "After the general store, it was a post office for quite a while, and the local newspaper. When I moved here, a fellow that owned it used it as parts storage for a tractor supply business."

"Does the highway association own the building now?"

"No, our group does. It's called Farm Heritage. We started out with eight guys, expanded to ten, and now we're down to about six, because of some deaths. Unfortunately, one of them doesn't do much because of physical limitations, and another had a stroke. It's basically myself and three other guys doing most of it."

The building was little more than a shell before they began working on it. "All the wood you see, including the roof and floors, were pretty much all rotten. We had to chop it all apart and take it away. Then we ran seven beams across, very big beams. We tied the building back together, so to speak — squared it up. We had to bring the back wall in almost three inches. And then we put a new roof on and put a new floor in here — all cypress. Much easier to work with cypress than oak, and much more durable than pine. We made the whole thing as much out of cypress as we could, because it's so low-maintenance. Good thing, because we're all getting old and don't have a lot of time left, unfortunately."

He gives us a tour, pointing out rooms where H. I. Lincoln kept dry goods and explaining how wagons would load supplies in and out. On a landing, a Lincoln Highway poster catches my eye.

"Is that poster for sale?"

"It's yours," he says, handing it to me. "No charge."

We ascend to the second floor, an open room with high ceilings, wide-planked floors, good light, and lots of construction equipment. "Old

Mr. Lincoln decided the town needed a community area. It was built for dances, meetings, things like that. One of the first fundraisers for the Lincoln Highway was held up here. There was a stage right in front of you. They put on plays and music."

The room hasn't been used in many years, but John's group hopes to restore it to its original purpose. "Every third Friday, we have bands outside — about 150 people out on the street. And so we're going to make it so they can come up here. That's been a dream for several of us. Hopefully this winter, we're going to set up shop up here and get it remodeled."

"Where does the money come from?"

"We're selling raffle tickets for a Model T. We pop kettle corn, and we make maple syrup. We've got a huge sugar bush here in Franklin Grove. We tapped about a hundred maple trees and we took in twenty-four hundred gallons of sap. That got us about three hundred pints of syrup. We sell that as a fundraiser. Works out well."

"Has the association helped with the finances?"

"No. We did it just as a community project. And the people in town have helped out tremendously. We've had groups high as forty come over here to work."

The sense of pride and attachment that the community will feel toward this room when it's completed will be just as strong as the feelings my sister's Vermont neighbors had toward the playground they built. So much of volunteerism is now centered on performing acts of mercy and grace for individuals, which is noble. Governments at all levels support and incentivize it. Society celebrates it. But bonds of citizenship are forged out of shared community more than individual charity — by cooperating with others to shape our collective future and improve our collective prospects. To do for ourselves, not just for others. The essence of citizenship is not the selflessness found in the gospel. It's the conjoining of interests seen in the Declaration and Constitution.

"How much are the Model T tickets?" I ask.

"We sell two thousand $20 tickets."

"Can we buy one?"

"You bet."

Back in the gift shop, Laurel picks out a sweatshirt, I find a T-shirt, and John tells us how he came to be involved in this project.

"I'm from a town about twelve, fourteen miles south of here, but I came up here for school. I got out of school and married a local girl. She lived just a couple doors from us. I spent seven years with a big corporation and moved to the Chicago area, but that's no place to raise your kids. It's good when the kids can walk to school. Give me a gravel road. People think small towns don't do justice to the kids. Mine both came out really good. One's a school administrator and the other's a high-powered lawyer up in Twin City. Proud of my girls." And proud of his town, too. He moves seamlessly from talking about rehabbing the building to boosting the area.

"Ronald Reagan was raised about ten miles west of here, in Dixon. Walgreens got their start in Dixon. John Deere started just about twelve miles northwest of here. Grand Detour is where he developed his first self-scouring plow, they call it. The root structure of the grass makes it very difficult to plow" — the soil stuck to the plow, forcing farmers to make frequent stops to scrape it off — "so he developed a plow that would scour it."

Deere, who apprenticed as a blacksmith in my sister's town of Middlebury, only came to the area because he had more business sense than Lincoln, and fewer scruples. He fled his creditors, leaving behind piles of debt. His scouring plows vastly increased farmers' efficiency, accelerating the growth of farms across prairie lands and leading to what Lincoln dreamed of when he envisioned a steam-powered plow in an 1859 speech: agricultural production on an industrial scale, which the John Deere company would help lead. Today, while Joseph Glidden is long forgotten, John Deere is one of the most recognizable and celebrated names in America. A song by country singer Keith Urban places it in the heartland's holy trinity.

> *I learned everything I needed to know*
> *from John Cougar, John Deere, John 3:16*

As this John gives us a history lesson, he isn't just looking back.

"Southeast of town it's almost perfectly flat because the glaciers came through and they pushed up about a two-hundred-foot moraine. And so it held back the water, created this sixty-thousand-acre swamp — some of the best farm ground in the world. And we have 320-some-odd windmills scattered up on that moraine. And now we're getting into solar. I just zoned a thirteen-hundred-acre solar farm. It will have just nineteen permanent jobs, but that's nineteen jobs that we didn't have before, and it's going to be almost four hundred people in construction. And next week starts the zoning process on a fifty-seven-hundred-acre solar farm. Good revenue, keeps the schools open."

It's clear he's more than a casual observer of town affairs.

"I've been involved in politics for forty years, since Ronald Reagan got elected in 1980. He was the first politician that I admired. I happened to be the county board chairman. It used to be, you couldn't tell the R's and D's apart, and you didn't care. And now . . ." His voice trails off. "I had a friend growing up. I was very Republican, he was very Democrat, and he became the chairman of the Democratic Party here. We got along famously. He even put up campaign signs on my property, and I put up signs on his property. And I met with him last night — he owns a bar. We got chatting, and he said it's just not any fun anymore, because it's so tense. When you talk to somebody, there's no wiggle room. You don't talk things over and then go have a beer. Usually, you walk away not talking."

We thank him for spending some of his Sunday with us. "I hope you have a good trip," he says. "Hope you see a lot of good, small towns — hope you appreciate the small towns. And stay warm. It's going to go down to thirty-four Friday night."

Having missed the Lincolnway Café, we stop for dinner in Dixon at a chicken joint advertising "deep fried goodness." We order ours with fries and — in honor of Dixon's hometown hero, Ronald Reagan — a side of vegetables: ketchup. The Reagan administration's attempt to cut the cost of school lunches by allowing ketchup to count as a vegetable did not pass muster with Congress — it was even denounced by Senator John Heinz: "I need not add that I do know something about ketchup and relish," he said. But the hullaballoo it caused did reflect the never-ending debate over, paraphrasing Lincoln, what people should do for themselves and what government should do for them.

Reagan grew up two blocks from the Lincoln Highway and hitchhiked on it during the Great Depression, traveling east to Chicago and west to Iowa in search of work. Yet as I walk along the Rock River waiting for our dinner order, I see that the statue Dixon erected to him has him riding a horse. Too bad. Showing him sticking out his thumb and relying on the kindness of strangers would have reflected more of the spirit of community self-reliance that he brought to government.

On the other side of the Rock River from Reagan is the only known statue of Lincoln in uniform, commemorating the place where he camped during the 1832 Black Hawk War, as unnecessary a war as any ever waged. Black Hawk and the Sauk Indians had been forced west of the Mississippi River under the disputed terms of an 1804 treaty. When the Winnebago prophet, White Cloud, invited Black Hawk and his followers to return to Illinois and share a village not far from their ancestral land, he accepted, along with some one thousand followers among the Sauk, Fox, and Kickapoo, most of them women and children. The state and federal government viewed their return as an act of war. White Cloud's Winnebago community, aware of the calamity that could befall them, sent Black Hawk and his followers packing. When a Potawatomi village turned them away, too, they began retreating to the Mississippi — and toward the soldiers in the Illinois state militia and US Army who were tracking them.

While Lincoln camped here at Dixon, Black Hawk tried to surrender thirty miles east. That should have ended the affair before a war began. Instead, militiamen who were drunk or frightened or both shot the truce bearer, prompting Black Hawk to launch an attack that left a dozen militia members dead — some scalped, decapitated, and castrated. The next day, Lincoln's regiment marched to the battle site and helped bury the bodies. They would later find the corpses of an old woman and expectant mother, the latter sliced in the midsection, the infant left dangling from a tree.

Lincoln grew up hearing of Indian battles, especially about the grandfather he was named for, who was murdered by Indians while working in a field. Lincoln wrote, "The story of his death by the Indians, and of Uncle Mordecai, then fourteen years old, killing one of the Indians, is the legend more strongly than all others imprinted upon my mind and memory." Yet during the Black Hawk War, when the men in his unit threatened to kill an Indian who entered their camp bearing a letter of friendship, Lincoln told them he would fight or duel anyone attempting it. That ended the matter.

During his presidency, when the army sentenced 303 Dakota Indians to death after a war with Minnesota settlers that left hundreds of whites dead, Lincoln asked to review the evidence against them, enraging the state's voters and elected officials, who demanded the executions proceed: "Death to the Barbarians," one headline read. Having suffered embarrassing setbacks in the 1862 midterm elections, Lincoln had good reasons to steer clear of the matter. Instead he issued 264 pardons. When the governor later told him he could have carried the 1864 election more handily if he had not intervened, Lincoln replied, "I could not afford to hang men for votes." Lincoln hoped to go much further. "If we get through this war, and I live," he wrote to the Episcopal bishop of Minnesota, who had blamed government corruption for the massacre, "this Indian system shall be reformed!"

Had Lincoln been among the soldiers approached by Black Hawk's truce emissary, there may well have been no war. Instead, the army, with help from the Winnebago, Sioux, and other Indian nations, hunted Black Hawk's band into Wisconsin, leaving hundreds dead from battles, starvation, and drowning. After their second attempt at surrender was accepted, Black Hawk was escorted to prison by a young army lieutenant, Jefferson Davis, and held in captivity for nearly a year, while the federal government forced the Sauks, Fox, and Winnebagos — including those who had assisted the army's efforts — to abandon their lands and move deeper into Iowa, making way for new generations of settlers who would soon be using John Deere's plows, Fred Hatch's silos, and Joseph Glidden's barbed wire to farm and fence the frontier.

— 20 —

Abraham's Children

Ascending the bridge over the Mississippi River, a sense of awe washes over me — awe that we have made it to this east–west dividing line and at the history that has flowed beneath us. No river has carried more of the nation's cultural, political, and economic freight. Slavery and civil war, the agricultural and industrial revolutions, Indian wars and westward expansion — the river ran deep through them all, as it does through much of American letters, and not just works by the man dubbed the Lincoln of literature, Mark Twain, who grew up alongside it. Tennessee Williams, Herman Melville, William Faulkner, Langston Hughes, Edna Ferber, and many others found inspiration in its flow. "I feel that there is something in having passed one's childhood beside the big river," wrote T. S. Eliot, who grew up in St. Louis, "which is incommunicable to those people who have not."

Lincoln took two trips down the Mississippi River on flatboats he helped construct, each carrying goods to sell in New Orleans, and as in Twain's *Huckleberry Finn*, slavery loomed large over the journeys. Various accounts tell of Lincoln being repulsed by the brutal treatment of slaves, which led to the story that the trips shaped his view of slavery. More likely, the trips confirmed his lifelong opposition to it. Regardless, we do know this: On his first trip, while south of Baton Rouge, he and his partner were "attacked by seven negroes with intent to kill and rob" them, Lincoln later wrote. He and his partner managed to fight them off and escape, leaving him with scars above his right eye and left ear — but not, apparently, with any sense of vengeance. He never reported the incident to the authorities or attempted to find the attackers. "Violence and vindictiveness," writes historian David S. Reynolds, "did not come naturally to him."

Arriving on the other side of the Mississippi brings us into the land the United States purchased from France in 1803, even though the French never conquered or controlled it. They only sold their claim to it. In essence, President Thomas Jefferson was purchasing peace with France — removing it as a continental rival — not land. Native peoples controlled the land — the word *Mississippi* derives from the reverential term they used for it, meaning "Father of Waters" — and they were not ceding it without a fight. Nevertheless, ninety years after the ink dried on the Louisiana Purchase, a young writer, Katharine Lee Bates, could look down from Pikes Peak in Colorado, having taken a train there from the 1893 World's Fair in Chicago, and begin to write a poem about America that didn't mention native peoples who had been shunted at gunpoint onto reservations and deprived of basic rights. Instead, her verses were full of beauty and brotherhood, mountain majesties and fruited plains, shining seas and alabaster cities, halcyon skies and patriot dreams, and pilgrims and pioneers in love with liberty and mercy, blessed by God's grace. Yet amid all the celebratory grandeur of her verse, she also included a prayerful appeal — a petition to God acknowledging that living up to the nation's ideals was a work in progress, a verse that often falls out of public singings.

> *America! America! / God mend thine every flaw*
> *Confirm thy soul in self-control / Thy liberty in law!*

On the west side of the river in Clinton, Iowa, we pull into a parking lot to meet a mobile RV repairman, Al, who quickly gets our toilet pedal back on, albeit tenuously, and tells us to gingerly push left, toward the toilet, when pressing down. This is the second lesson in the physics of fruitful flushing that we have received, and we are grateful for it.

We mention to Al that an electric outlet under the dinette table has mysteriously stopped working. He opens it up, fiddles around, and declares it fixed. Although it can't be tested until we plug in at a campground, it's added to our bill. We may be flushing money down the toilet, but at least we're doing it with a working foot pedal.

Al mentions that Clinton once had more millionaires per capita than anyplace in America, back when it was known as the Lumber Capital of the World. Trees cut by lumberjacks in Wisconsin and Minnesota were floated downriver, milled here, and sent by rail across the country, providing settlers with materials to construct towns and homes. To get a longer look at the river, we drive onto the levee constructed after the Great Flood of 1965 and park near the Clinton Showboat, a 1935 tugboat-turned-theater that evokes the Mississippi River novel by Edna Ferber, *Show Boat*.

The theater is named for Clinton's native daughter, Lillian Russell, one of the Progressive era's most famous singers, actresses, and heartthrobs and a champion of women's suffrage. In 1922, President Harding put her celebrity to use, sending her on a fact-finding mission to Europe as part of his push for immigration restrictions. Upon her return, she recommended a five-year immigration holiday and urged Congress to save America from those who would ruin it. "The melting pot has become overcrowded," she said. "It has boiled too quickly and is running over. It were better to put out the fires under it and allow its contents to solidify before adding any more raw material. If we don't put up bars and make them higher and stronger, there no longer will be an America for Americans . . . The higher civilization of past ages, history teaches us, succumbed to such foreign invasions as now threaten us."

Invasions. It is not a word Lincoln ever used when referencing the flood of immigrants arriving in America, whom he called a "source of national wealth." He viewed immigrants much as Washington had. "I had always hoped that this land might become a safe & agreeable Asylum to the virtuous & persecuted part of mankind, to whatever nation they might belong," Washington wrote in 1788. In a speech marking Independence Day 1858, Lincoln spoke of immigrants having the same strong tie to founders like Washington as those who can trace their family trees back to them, because new arrivals could claim equal ownership of the "moral sentiment" of the statement that "all men are created equal." "That is the electric cord in that Declaration," he said, "that links the hearts of patriotic and liberty-loving men together." But in Lincoln's day, as in Russell's and ours, there are those who see immigrants as a short circuit that endangers the country.

Russell died shortly after her return to America, but her pleading was not in vain. Congress soon adopted quotas to severely limit the number of immigrants from outside Western Europe and extended to Japan the prohibition on Asian immigration. The KKK's Imperial Wizard called the 1924 immigration act "a stone wall around the nation so tall, so deep and so strong that the scum and riff-raff of the old world cannot get into our gates." There were only about 115 million people living in America at that time, a third of today's population. But immigration restrictions have never been about the number of people the country can hold, only their origin.

Many towns we have passed through on the Lincoln Highway have populations that have shrunk or stagnated over the past century, including most of Iowa's small towns. Clinton has lost 30 percent of its population since 1970, to say nothing of its millionaires, and it has struggled to deal with abandoned buildings — it's spending about $500,000 a year to tear them down. Immigrants account for only 2 percent of its population. Lillian Russell got her wish.

Past Clinton is DeWitt, both towns named for New York governor DeWitt Clinton, who built the Erie Canal, making him a hero to a young Lincoln, who dreamed of following in his footsteps. A block from its main street, a large ice cream cone juts out from a turquoise roof, Cups and Cones. The rule about restaurants shaped like their food must be followed.

"Do you want ice cream?" I ask Laurel as I tap the brakes.

"No, we haven't eaten lunch yet."

"I know, but we're getting lunch in a minute in town."

"I need real food," she says, reasonably.

"This is just a little appetizer," I counter, pulling over and parking. Suddenly she lights up.

"Look at the pootie!"

In the house beside us there's a dog in the window draped across the top of the sofa. As Laurel takes a photo, a second dog appears in a second window and adopts the same pose on the top of the same couch. "Ahhhhh!" she says, her heart melting. In college she had a Boston terrier named Tootie that she was forced to leave with her sister when she came to New York City after graduating. About a month after we met, she had to decide between returning to her beloved Tootie in Virginia and taking a full-time job in New York. I like to think I tipped the scales, but not infrequently she wonders aloud whether she made the right decision.

As I open my door to head out for ice cream, I ask again: "Are you sure you don't want a cone?"

"I'm gonna put you in that house," she replies with a smile, "and take the dogs with me."

Ice cream in hand, I park in the center of DeWitt, where the Lincoln Highway intersects with Highway 61, which runs from northern Minnesota to New Orleans, paralleling the Mississippi River and carrying much of American music with it, mostly black in origin. Tunes traveled upstream on boats, trains, cars, and radio waves, providing a soundtrack for the Great Migration and giving rise to one of the century's great inventions, rock 'n' roll. Robert Zimmerman, born near the route's northern terminus in Duluth, would later sing of it on his 1965 album, *Highway 61 Revisited.* Writing under the name Bob Dylan and smashing the conventions of popular music, he draped the highway in surrealism and centered the American journey on it, mythologizing it as a cultural cornerstone with biblical significance to the nation, the opening verse reimagining God's demand that Abraham sacrifice his son.

> *Abe says, "Where do you want this killin' done?"*
> *God says, "Out on Highway 61"*

The album's closing dream-state epic, "Desolation Row," which mentions T. S. Eliot and seems at least partly inspired by "The Wasteland," opens with a verse that evokes an ugly episode in Duluth that a young Bob heard while growing up, the 1920 lynching of three black workers in a traveling circus: Elias Clayton, Elmer Jackson, and Isaac McGhie. All were in their early twenties, murdered by a mob after an accusation that a nineteen-year-old white woman had been raped. No one was ever prosecuted for the murders, and a doctor found no evidence of assault. As in Marion, Indiana, entrepreneurs turned photographs of the lynching into a business opportunity, giving rise to Dylan's opening line: "They're selling postcards of the hanging."

At the intersection of the Lincoln and Highway 61, we stop into Urban Eats, where the sign reads, "Local people. Local farms. Real food." The owner asks if we're from the area, and we tell her we're from New York, just passing through. She walks back to the kitchen and returns with our soup and chili. "Now, you wouldn't turn down a piece of chocolate cake, would you? You need something to wash down the meal." We are overwhelmed by her generosity. And despite having just had ice cream, it would be rude to decline.

Driving into Cedar Rapids, downed trees and snapped trunks dot yards, awaiting chain saws. Branches line the roadside, awaiting collection. And blue tarps cover roofs, awaiting repair. The damage from an August windstorm that swept through here at 140 miles per hour — called a *derecho*, a Spanish word for "straight," like an uncurled twister — is still visible on nearly every block. Residents have organized via a Facebook page where they can offer food, shelter, and chain-saw services to those in need. The derecho brought people together in ways the pandemic has not.

In downtown Cedar Rapids, past the studio-turned-museum where Grant Woods completed *American Gothic*, and near the National Czech and Slovak Museum, we attend the unveiling of a new mural celebrating the city's immigrant roots. A city built on the backs of Bohemian workers is now working to cultivate a bohemian aesthetic. After eating a delicious sugar-sprinkled kolache, I introduce myself to the city's mayor, Brad Hart, who speaks proudly of the city's immigrants, old and new. "This whole theory that 'Oh, they're just freeloaders' is bull," he says. "I mean, it's unbelievable how many millions and millions of dollars that they are spending in our communities." He says immigration reform has been on the city's national legislative agenda for as long as he can remember. "We need to open more doors. I said when I was first campaigning that we need to be a more welcoming and engaged community. And anybody who wants to come to our community to be a part of it, come. We want you. And the more diverse, the better. Just makes us more interesting."

He stops. "Oh, the one thing you should know. Our city government is nonpartisan. Otherwise, there's no way I'd do this. In our town, either party, there's this craziness." He's a Republican but says party politics don't factor into the way government works. "The partisanship stays outside. And frankly, I will call somebody out if I think that they're making a decision based on a political party."

Over the course of our conversation, which touches on the city budget (he's proud of their bond rating), climate change (he boasts that Cedar Rapids was the first city in Iowa to hire a sustainability officer), and Covid protocols ("Just wear a mask, it's not that hard"), he strikes me as eminently pragmatic and earnest. I ask if he's considered running for a state or federal office. He says a council member had suggested it to him. "So first thing I did was Google 'running for office.' And it said something like, 'The first thing you have to do is contact your party official.' Like no, I don't. I said, 'Thank God I do not have to do that,' and I'm not doing that."

The very sort of people we need in state capitols and Congress — sensible and reasonable, levelheaded and dispassionate — are those who are most repulsed by the process of getting there. How can we change that? We'll return to that question a little farther down the road.

Cedar Rapids's embrace of multiculturalism includes an extraordinary distinction: Syrian immigrants here built America's first mosque, in 1934. When we arrive at what's called the Mother Mosque, Imam Taha Tawil greets us. He grew up in Jerusalem and came to Chicago to study theology when he was twenty-five. A professor told him they needed him in Iowa. He responded, "What is Iowa?" That was 1983.

As Imam Tawil brings me downstairs to the mosque's social room, he explains how it came to be. "The Muslims helped the Orthodox to build their church," he says. "And so the Muslims said: We want our own place." The Christian Orthodox returned the favor, helping them build the mosque. He points to a black-and-white photo of the two congregations standing together. "This is the imam at that time, and this is the Orthodox priest," he says. Each is wearing a suit and bow tie. "And you can't know which are the Muslim and which are the Christians. It's unity. That's America, man." He speaks in heavily accented and grammatically splintered English, but when he utters that last phrase — "That's America, man" — he sounds like Uncle Sam himself.

He is active in civic affairs, as a police department chaplain and a co-founder of an inter-religious council, which has helped win the mosque strong support from local residents. "In 2001, after this tragic incident of the towers and the hijack," he says, "suddenly we started having phone calls, letters, even bouquet of flowers were left at the steps, baskets of food, saying, 'We know you. You are not like them.' Even the Justice Department came in. The mayor, the governor came and show support to us as a community. It really gave a broad sense of confidence and sense of a protection that we are facing the tragedy together. And the State Department, they were so active in bringing Muslim delegates from Tunisia, France, Italy, Morocco, Egypt, et cetera. But after Mr. Trump and the ban on Muslim countries — and the sentiment of white supremacy and not accepting diversity or pluralism — we did not have much visitors from the Muslim world. After Mr. Trump win the election, things just start to be different." How so?

"It was like people, they want to go back to the old time — one faith. In Des Moines, many people sent letters of threat and hate to the Islamic centers. And so Grinnell College, that's between Des Moines and Cedar Rapids, a minister there said, 'We don't like what we hear. We want to come and support Muslims. And the Mother Mosque is the good, the place that represent Islam in America.' I said, 'Come on!' So many, many people came and show support. And then they hug the Mother Mosque in a human shield, showing that, hey, this is our heritage. And show that we are the one. We don't like politics, but it was not right what our president was doing, taking one side and slamming Muslims and talking bad about them. A father of a Gold Star marine who gave up his life came to visit us here. And Mr. Trump make many bad comments about him or his wife. Many Muslims are Republican because of family values. But people start to say, 'Hey, wait a minute. Why they are attacking us? That's not American. This is not right.'"

Cedar Rapids neighbors the congressional district represented by Steve King, who has a history of making comments with anti-Muslim and racist undertones that have sometimes become explicit. In 2019, he asked, "White nationalist, white supremacist, Western civilization — how did that language become offensive?" In mistaking the first two terms as synonymous with the third, he summed up how racism and nativism are mistaken for patriotism. To their credit, House Republican leaders stripped King of his committee assignments after that remark, and Republican voters defeated him in his primary reelection campaign.

Imam Tawil leads me upstairs to the worship hall and points toward the corner. "This is the direction for the prayer. That's where we face northeast. Why? Because the house of God is in Mecca. Who built it? Abraham and his son Ishmael."

He's giving me a brief tutorial in the origins of Islam and its view of Abraham's two sons, Isaac and Ishmael. Jews and Christians believe that when God ordered Abraham to kill a son, God spared Isaac, and they trace their lineage through him. Muslims believe that God's commandment led Ishmael, the older son, to depart on his own accord, settling in Mecca.

"God Almighty has the plan A and B. And so A, he started with Isaac and put Ishmael aside. Then the course of life went thousands of years. And to six hundred, God commissioned Prophet Muhammad, who is the son of Ishmael, to claim back the message of Abraham. So we are Abrahamic. That's why we look at the Jews and the Christian as cousins. We are from the same father."

He points out a painting of Mary on the wall. "There is a chapter in the Koran called Mary. Mary is the mother of Jesus. Amazing. That chapter starts with five Arabic letters. This is a few of them" — the letters stretch across Mary's midsection. "It was a nice inspiration that the painter brought these five Arabic letters and put them as a word in the womb of Mary, and it shows the spirit that God did blow into this word. And the word become flesh. That's how we say, Jesus is a word from God. He has a miraculous birth. And we have that in the Koran."

When many Americans think of Islamic theology, they are more likely to think of jihad than Jesus. "Many people does not know Islam. They don't know that we are Abrahamic and that we love Moses and Jesus and the scripture. But when we explain to them, they will be surprised, opening their eyes. 'Oh, do you believe in Jesus?' Yes, Jesus is a prophet and messenger. He is the Messiah that the Jews were waiting for. And we believe that he is alive in heaven and he will come back at the end of life. Yes, we do. So Muslim belief, Christian belief, Jewish belief, go together in a different understanding — but all is Abrahamic. He came to teach people that there is one God, there is a life after death, there is justice and compassion. We have to speak about justice and be kind to people. That's the Abrahamic message. Whoever follows Abraham must do this."

When I excuse myself to take a phone call, Imam Tawil, unbeknown to me, brings a cup of tea and some dates to Laurel, who is working in Charley. We are moved by his hospitality. He gives us a Koran and invites us to return. Before leaving, I ask him what binds the country together.

"This is a great country no doubt about it. And what will keep us together going forward as a great country is applying the law, applying the values that we came up with: freedom of speech, freedom of faith, that value of diversity, pluralism." *That's America, man.*

We come to a four-way stop with three other vehicles. Everyone waits. No one honks. As we keep waiting, Laurel and I trade wide-eyed glances. We've heard of "Iowa Nice," but this is hard to believe.

We pull over at a Victorian home with a tree down in its front yard. Beside it stands a skeleton in an open coffin with the word "Derecho" spraypainted in red. A black stretch limousine is parked at the curb. A banner reads: "No trespassing. We're tired of hiding the bodies." Ghosts and skulls decorate the front entrance. It's a former funeral parlor turned bed-and-breakfast that offers murder mystery dinners, ghost hunts, and haunted tours. It's closed today, but Laurel is happy just to be outside looking in on spooky season. And there is a ghost a little farther along in

Marshalltown, who — in the spirit of the fall season, with its frights, elections, and baseball — merits a moment.

In 1883, a young Marshalltown ballplayer named Billy Sunday got signed by the Chicago White Stockings, thanks to their player-manager from Marshalltown, Hall of Famer Cap Anson. The team included stars like Mike "King" Kelly, the son of Irish immigrants who was the likely inspiration for a poem as American as baseball itself.

And somewhere men are laughing,
and somewhere children shout,
But there is no joy in Mudville —
mighty Casey has struck out.

When the White Stockings didn't win the National League pennant in Billy Sunday's first season, ownership blamed booze, and Cap Anson enlisted Billy in keeping his teammates off it. Billy played seven seasons for several teams before going to work for the YMCA and beginning a career as a tent revival preacher who crusaded against "demon rum" and turned Christian faith into a test of masculine strength. "I'd like to put my fist on the nose of the man who hasn't gotten enough grits to be a Christian," he often said. His celebrity as a ballplayer and his natural athleticism helped make him a national sensation. Onstage he was an acrobatic apostle: running, sliding, shaking, gyrating, breaking chairs, and engaging in other histrionics that won legions of followers. He mocked liberals and evolutionists in a falsetto voice and shocked audiences with his sensationalized accounts of saloons, merging fire and brimstone with theater and sport into a gospel of fear and loathing and setting it all to music, staging the biggest choirs anyone had ever seen, often exceeding a thousand members who sang "Onward, Christian Soldier" and other militant songs, always ending with "The Battle Hymn of the Republic." For Billy Sunday, religion was war, and when the United States declared war on Germany in 1917, war became religion. Calling himself "God's recruiting officer," he beat the drum for holy battle, preaching that "Christianity and Patriotism are synonymous terms, and hell and traitors are synonymous."

Sunday had his critics, none fiercer than Carl Sandburg, who wrote a scathing poem denouncing Sunday and his ilk as bunkshooters "belching about hellfire" and driving people crazy with "gibberish about Jesus." But he was the era's most influential minister, and, more than any other, he helped push Prohibition across the line. In the 1920s, he accepted financial support from the KKK as it tried to piggyback on his success, and he on theirs. Rum was a demon, but bigotry was divine. His longtime musical director published the Klan's anthem, "The Bright Fiery Cross."

Billy Sunday died in 1935, but his brand of militant fundamentalism survived by embracing, of all things, evolution — not of humanity, but of its perceived enemies. In her book *The Evangelicals: The Struggle to Shape America*, historian Frances FitzGerald writes, "The fundamentalist warlords kept discovering new enemies, and whether they picked up on such commonly held prejudices as anti-Catholicism or anti-Semitism, or attacked the New Deal, the new enemy was always the worst threat to Christianity ever known. For fundamentalists, the world was always in a state of crisis, with Satan ever appearing in new guises." As existential threats to the country, Catholics gave way to Muslims, alcohol to abortion, Germans to Latinos, and — increasingly — communists to Democrats.

"We're in a time of war," evangelical pastor Rick Joyner said days after we set out on the Lincoln Highway. "We need to mobilize. We need to get ready." On *The Jim Bakker Show*, he announced he had a dream that "the Lord had seeded our country with veterans" and that "militias would pop up like mushrooms" to lead the new civil war against Black Lives Matter and other opponents of President Trump. In tonight's presidential debate, when Trump is pressed on whether he'll condemn white supremacists and militia groups threatening election violence, he says, "Proud Boys: Stand back and stand by."

Billy Sunday's approach to theology — machismo and militancy mixed with rage and racism and packaged in theatrics — is still with us. And while he is mostly a forgotten figure, when he is remembered at all it's often by people he would have despised, thanks to a song written by Robert Hunter for a band that celebrated the high times of hippie culture, "Ramble on Rose" by the Grateful Dead. It's a whimsical mash of mythology and folklore featuring characters real and imagined, with music seeming to serve, just maybe, as a redeeming force.

Just like Jack the Ripper, just like Mojo Hand
Just like Billy Sunday, in a shotgun ragtime band

After tonight's debate, I open a beer and play the song. That's America, man.

— 21 —

Building & Loan

"WELCOME TO NEVADA You are Traveling on the Original Lincoln Highway." The sign greeting visitors to this small Iowa town is a granite block resembling a large tombstone with Lincoln's face chiseled into it above a quotation: "I believe that a man should be proud of the city in which he lives, and that he should so live that his city will be proud that he lives in it. A. Lincoln." There is no evidence Lincoln ever said it, and the town may be in on the joke. Another sign promotes Nevada as the "26th best small town in America."

It's the first of October, and the weather is turning. Overnight temperatures will be dropping into the thirties, just as John had told us at Lincoln Highway Association headquarters. As we arrive for the night in Boone, Iowa, I have a night's work ahead of me, so the hour of confrontation has arrived. I pull out the owner's manual and begin making a study of the furnace, and after discussing the thermostat's settings with Laurel — heat powered by gas, electric, or gas and electric — she fiddles around with the settings, which prove to be remarkably simple, sets the temperature for fifty degrees, presses START, and presto! It kicks on. As with the hot water heater, my fear was entirely baseless. Almost.

Around midnight, as Laurel sleeps, the furnace suddenly shuts off and leaves behind a faint burning smell. Uh-oh. The indoor temperature begins dropping, but I have more work to do. I put on a coat and winter hat, but my teeth begin chattering, and when I finally lie down in bed after 3:00 A.M., my whole body is shaking. I can't sleep and begin to worry that I've got hypothermia. More likely, I realize, it's hypochondria, but I can't help but wonder: Is this how it ends — in Boone, Iowa, because I failed to learn how to run the furnace?

The next morning, I tell Laurel about the heat shutting off and the burning smell and ask her what we should do. Her solution is one that will prove effective time and again: "Just leave it alone," she says.

The Donna Reed Center and Heritage Museum lies on the Lincoln in Denison, Iowa. Donna grew up on a farm here, and her talent and beauty led to Hollywood stardom, the quintessential All-American girl now best remembered for playing Mary (Hatch) Bailey opposite Jimmy Stewart in Frank Capra's *It's a Wonderful Life*. Capra and Stewart had already teamed up in *Mr. Smith Goes to Washington*. "Our Jefferson Smith would be a young Abe Lincoln," Capra said of Stewart's character, "tailored to the rail-splitter's simplicity, compassion, ideals, humor." Capra had doubts about the wisdom of making a movie about Washington corruption as war was breaking out in Europe and Asia, but when he visited the Lincoln Memorial and saw a boy reading the Gettysburg Address and Lincoln's second inaugural address to an elderly man, he decided that "we must make the film if only to hear a boy read Lincoln to his grandpa." He put the scene in the movie, and it is Smith's visit to the Lincoln Memorial that convinces him not to give up his fight to do right.

Capra was still painting with a Lincoln palette in creating George Bailey, whose guardian angel (second class) shows him what his hometown would've looked like had he never been born, its people turned dark, mean, violent, and impoverished through Mr. Potter's greed. George's decision to sacrifice his dream of a high-flying career, and to forgo striking it rich with his friend Sam Wainwright, in order to serve his hometown had made all the difference, helping his neighbors build modest homes, stable families, and a strong community.

"Now, we can get through this thing all right," George says in the middle of the bank run that nearly destroys the Bailey Building and Loan and hands control of the town to Potter. "We've got to stick together, though. We've got to have faith in each other." In the abandoned old house that Donna Reed's Mary Bailey remakes into the family home, Capra hung a portrait of Lincoln.

On the way out of Denison, the highway passes what remains of the old Iowa Beef Packing operation, founded here in 1960 by two men who saw an opportunity to revolutionize the cattle industry by moving slaughtering out of urban areas, like Chicago and Omaha, closer to the cattle. In bringing the butcher shop to the farm, they also developed a "disassembly line" that accelerated and mechanized butchering, reducing the skills needed to do the job. They packed carcasses in boxes, reducing shipping weights by cutting off bones and waste. They bought directly from farmers, rather than stockyards, and they shipped by truck, over the newly built Interstate Highway System.

What Iowa Beef Packing did would come to be called "disruptive innovation," and it revolutionized the industry in ways that reduced prices for consumers and reduced wages for workers. But the march of technology isn't what closed the Denison plant five years ago, putting four hundred employees out of work in a town of eight thousand people. It was a decision by the global corporation that had purchased it, Tyson, which felt no obligation to the community. "Ideals without common sense can ruin this town," Old Man Potter said, in attacking George's father. "People were human beings to him," George countered angrily. "But to you, a warped, frustrated old man, they're cattle."

At least George could see the enemy. It's harder to fight a faceless distant corporation, which is one reason why few of today's George Baileys can resist the Sam Wainwrights. Helping more young people stay in their hometowns by fostering economic opportunity is a challenge that neither party has yet figured out. Each has been content to demonize China, Mexico, and other nations where American manufacturing jobs have moved, attack the wealthy who have done well through globalization, and promote "Buy American" schemes, as if any of them will have much effect on small towns like Denison.

This was a topic of much conversation on the Bloomberg 2020 presidential campaign, which made "place-based economics" a centerpiece of its economic agenda. The plan included initiatives to increase small-business creation and entrepreneurship in struggling towns; better connect local businesses with colleges and universities; expand the Earned Income Tax Credit for their workers; and offer special visas to skilled and educated immigrants who put down roots where others won't. This is not to plump for the plan, only to hope that it made a small contribution — losing campaigns must find solace somewhere — to the now burgeoning discussion about place-based economics. Not every small town will prosper, of course, but many can, which could help nudge politics away from divisive cultural issues toward more unifying economic ones.

On a stretch of dirt road, one of many we will travel in Iowa, a woman in an SUV pulls up alongside us as we're bumping along at about ten miles per hour. She rolls down her passenger-side window. "Are you looking for a campground?"

"No, we're just driving the Lincoln Highway."

"Oh, I thought you were lost."

"Not at the moment."

She smiles and speeds off.

As best I can tell, the Lincoln Highway doesn't run through any Indian reservations, but taking this trip without visiting one, especially while driving a Winnebago, would be unthinkable. And so we cross the Missouri River and follow it north, picking up the route the Omaha people took in the 1700s — *omaha* means "against the current" — as they searched for a new home, having been pushed out of the Ohio River Valley. In the early 1860s, they gave refuge to the Winnebago, who traveled down the same river, fleeing the starvation they faced on the bleak land in South Dakota they'd been forced onto after getting pushed out of Illinois, Wisconsin, Iowa, and Minnesota. The 1865 treaty granting the Winnebago this corner of northeast Nebraska tried to make farmers of them, as the federal government was always trying to do with native peoples, who had hunted and fished for millennia, their culture emphasizing communalism over individualism and subsistence over wealth. The question for tribes was never, how do we accumulate profits? But rather, how do we support our way of life?

In reading about the Winnebago, I was intrigued by its corporate subsidiary, Ho-Chunk Inc. *Ho-Chunk* is a shortened version of *Hunchungra*, the tribe's traditional name, meaning "People of the Big Voice." Its CEO, Lance Morgan, offered to meet me at a Dollar General store on the reservation. When we arrive, he's with John Snowball, a tribal council representative.

"This Dollar General was the first business to come here in thirty years," Lance says. It's now surrounded by a restaurant, coffee shop, farmers market, and soon-to-open law office, all part of a new housing and commercial development the tribe is building, called Ho-Chunk Village. It is easy to scorn Dollar General stores as bottom-feeding supermarkets — a suburban Atlanta county has banned them, fearful that they would tarnish its image — but its business model is to open stores in small markets that have been overlooked or dismissed by other national retailers. The Winnebago welcomed them with open arms.

We walk up to the new apartments and townhomes the tribe is building, about a hundred units around a village green with a statue garden. They designed it along "new urbanism" principles, Lance tells me, so everything is walkable. He points to the townhomes and says, "We elevated them so that it would be like a modern brownstone, with a basement apartment. They were built in pieces from a housing factory that we bought twenty years ago in Minnesota."

"You own a housing factory?"

"We have our own housing companies. We have our own construction companies. We have our own banks. We make our own money so we can do what we want with it. Usually a tribe has to ask the federal government for permission, and that system has never really worked for us."

"Permission for what?"

"Anything we do. Any type of housing we build, and it's always restricted to low-income, so it locks our community into poverty. That type of housing deteriorates the soul. It just becomes a perpetual downward cycle. And we're looking to flip that equation."

We walk into a townhome being finished, and it's bright, modern, and spacious. "What you have to understand," says Lance, "is that there are 350 low-income housing units in the community, none of which are owned by anybody. So you pay rent, you pay rent, you pay rent."

"Who owns the houses?"

"A tribal housing entity, and there's all these federal restrictions" on who can live there and their income. "As we became more prosperous, there was no place for our people to live. So it was ironic that the better off we did, the more our people were forced out of low-income housing and had to leave the reservation."

John is one of them. "I work in law enforcement," he says, "and there was no way that I could ever live on the reservation, because of my income."

"There was no private development," explains Lance. "And the waiting list for low-income housing is about three hundred people long. Some people wait for years. And if you're a workingman, you might as well forget about it because women and children are prioritized. My joke is: What do you call an Indian without a woman?" He pauses. "Homeless."

Not to laugh is to cry.

"We had to start building spec homes and hope people would buy them," Lance continues. "We give up to $65,000 in down payment assistance, which is funded with profits from Ho-Chunk Inc." Without it, few could afford to buy. "Nobody has any savings," he says.

"We were challenged by the tribe to build a hundred homes in five years. And we built 144" — for all segments of the community: families, young professionals, low-income, and seniors. "If you only have low-income people, then you don't have the variety that you need in your school district and community. Developing a middle class in our community has been one of the key drivers of what we're doing."

Lance is running a modern version of the Bailey Building and Loan, empowering people to escape run-down rental units and build equity and savings. There are fifty-six hundred members of the tribe, about two thousand living on the reservation and another five hundred within about twenty miles. They want more members to have the option of coming.

"It's really a special thing," says John, "that we can provide these opportunities for tribal members to build strong families on the reservation, and to build equity with these homes. This gave me the opportunity to move back to the reservation and purchase a home, which is amazing."

We walk upstairs and Lance points out the bedrooms: "The reason I wanted you to come up here is I don't think you have a concept of what tribal housing is actually like." I admit: I don't. "It's really old, it's done at the lowest possible cost, and it's super crowded. You have one bathroom for twelve people. This one has two and a half. So this is not what you anticipate when you visit a normal reservation." I can hear George Bailey taking it to Potter: "Is it too much to have them work and pay and live and die in a couple of decent rooms and a bath?" Lance suggests visiting a village in the Omaha Reservation, if we want to see the alternative — a federal Pottersville, the rural shadow of Cabrini-Green. "You'll see some tragic situations there. That's where we were heading, and we just took control. The tribe got some gaming money and we took some of it to start a separate corporate entity, and we've been able to drive the economic growth of the community."

The company has become a cash cow for the tribe. "We give the tribe 25 percent of our profits every year," Lance says. "We don't pay federal income tax, so the tribe essentially is our tax. But the tribe has allocated 30 percent of that to just make sure we build homes. Our return on equity is 4 to 6 percent, which is really modest for a corporation, but Ho-Chunk Inc. is a big entity. We're one of the largest real estate developers in Sioux City. If you go to Sioux City, we own the largest building downtown. We have just under fifteen hundred employees right now. Our first year, we had $400,000 in revenue. This year we'll do over $300 million in revenue. And it's completely non-gaming, diversified activity."

"Has Covid hurt your business?"

"No, we're actually having the best year in our history. We do a lot of government contracting, and the government's into spending money right now."

With a little bit of gambling revenue, the tribe has created a diversified financial portfolio that is doing what centuries of government welfare grants did not: allowing members to build and determine their own future, in no small part by turning government into an equal partner rather than a paternalistic patron. While the federal government always exhorted them to become capitalists, even as it disempowered them from doing so, the Winnebago are creating their own form of communal capitalism and succeeding where many others, from the Harmonists to the hippies, have failed.

"We're in the middle of a huge transition as a community," says Lance. "We have six, seven generations of real poverty. When we started the company twenty years ago, there were nine people with bachelor's degrees living in town. Now there's well over a hundred. John's wife just graduated from law school, and we have a law firm in town that has five tribal members in it."

"I think it's important to understand where we came from," John says. "We were placed here and they would say: 'We're going to take care of your food for you, and we're going to take care of your health, and we're going to take care of your housing.' And we're entering in the era where we're capable of doing it ourselves. The handout system was put upon us, and we're breaking free from that — saying, 'We don't want a handout anymore. We want to earn things and we want to create opportunities, not just give stuff away.' Because that was never us."

"Any Indian waiting for the federal government to rescue them," says Lance, "is going to be waiting a long time. And nobody else is coming to the rescue. They'll drive by and they'll feel sorry for us. They'll shake their head — 'The poor Indians' — but they won't do a damn thing to help us. So my attitude is, we're going to do what we want — fuck you."

Can't argue with that, but it's easier said than done — and politics on the tribal council is "pretty divided," John says. "When the tribe comes upon resources," he explains, "there's a decision whether we're going to invest it long-term or just hand it out to the people."

"And some people would prefer it to be distributed?"

"Yeah. And if we just give it out, then our town will never change. Our reservation will never change."

"I imagine the people on the other side say, 'Well, I'm hurting, I'm struggling.'"

"It creates some friction," Lance acknowledges. "I'm either a good guy or a bad guy, depending on your perspective." A few see both sides. "My own mother," he has joked, "says I'm a necessary evil, the corporate Indian."

Lance grew up in north Omaha, where he had a simple goal in life: "I wanted to quit being poor." The army reserves got him through the University of Nebraska, and a scholarship brought him to Harvard Law School. About a year after he started a prestigious job with a Minneapolis firm that unexpectedly involved a case for the Winnebago, the tribe asked him to start Ho-Chunk, which he's built into a regional economic powerhouse.

"The tribe has set up multiple quasi-independent corporate entities," he says. "Ho-Chunk is the biggest, but the college and casinos are corporate entities, the hospital is a separate corporate entity — we took it over two years ago. The Indian Health Service was running it and doing a poor job." It was the first IHS hospital in the nation to lose its Medicare and Medicaid reimbursements. "The tribe got tired of trying to ask them to fix it," Lance says, "so we're fixing it ourselves. You're always better off controlling your own destiny."

We pull into Veterans Memorial Park, where a covered grandstand rings a small field.

"What's this used for?" I ask.

"Oh, this is our big deal," says Lance. "Ten thousand people will be here in July for our powwow. A lot of tourists come, too. It's just an awesome event. See all the flagpoles? People will raise their veteran flags up. It's an honor to put your flag up. And there's a lot of people who served in the military. A lot." Lance included.

Native veterans were often denied the honors and respect they had earned, and a particularly infamous case involved a Winnebago: John R. Rice, who was killed in the Korean War after earning a Bronze Star and Purple Heart in World War II. His widow was white, but when several native people arrived for his burial in Sioux City, a cemetery employee halted the service and refused to let Rice's body share the same ground as whites, leaving his widow with his corpse. When the incident made national headlines, an outraged President Truman offered a plot at Arlington National Cemetery. Lance doesn't mention the story, but Rice was his great-uncle.

I ask Lance what binds the country together. "Normally Americans when challenged will rise up together as a group," he says, citing 9/11. "We've lost a little bit of our civility in the last few years, and I think that it's going to be a little bit difficult to change that back. And we all live in these echo chambers of self-reinforcing news, so it makes me a little bit nervous, but I think it'll come because America always finds a way to blend in the new groups, to figure out a way to coalesce, and to figure out a way to be successful. You'd be a fool to bet against America." It seems to me that his answer — a belief in his fellow citizens' ability to rise to any occasion — echoes what George Bailey told his panicking customers during the bank run: *We've got to have faith in each other.*

I thank Lance and John, and they wish us well on our trip.

"You're driving the right vehicle," Lance says — bringing up a topic I have been self-conscious about. Winnebago's corporate headquarters are in Iowa, so I ask him: "Does the tribe have any relationship with the Winnebago company — does it offer you any support?"

"Oh hell no! We got kicked out of Iowa a long time ago."

A mural on the exterior wall of Lincoln's Pub in Council Bluffs, Iowa, features Abe on the penny quaffing a large mug of beer, beside a Lincoln quotation: "Whatever you are, be a good one." He never said it, but the pub is a block away from a hotel where Lincoln stayed in 1859, out of which grew a great many myths about his role in choosing Council Bluffs as the starting point for the transcontinental railroad. The hotel where he stayed is long gone, and we are heading to more spacious accommodations: A Bass Pro Shop parking lot. Laurel has been excited for this stop all day and keeps telling me I'm in for a treat. I've never been to one and even with her evangelizing, I'm not prepared for its grandeur: a three-story timber-beamed ceiling that towers above an abundance of taxidermy — turkeys, deer, moose, rams, bears — and a pool fed by a waterfall amid murals of wilderness scenes. It's a hillbilly cathedral, and they're making a fast convert.

After finding a heavy flannel shirt on sale, I head for the thermal underwear section, not realizing that the traumatic night in Boone may be guiding my steps. I had not expected options, but there are lightweight, midweight, and heavyweight thermals, each described as a military-grade base layer with an advanced design used by US Special Operations Forces. Given their prices, I would have settled for something used by the Boy Scouts. I skip the bottoms, pick up a midweight top, and find Laurel to express my hesitation over the cost. "Buy it — they have good quality here," she says, which is all the convincing I need.

The store is part of a complex that includes a casino, an indoor arena, and a shopping plaza. Outside we can hear a band playing in the plaza. I've always wanted to visit Omaha for its music scene, having gone to many concerts by native son Conor Oberst and his band, Bright Eyes. Since Covid has killed live music, a classic rock band in a Council Bluffs shopping plaza is the best we can hope for. But as we walk over to see it, let's spare a moment for Bright Eyes, the Omaha Indian who helped launch the movement for Native American rights.

In 1879, a group of about thirty Ponca Indians were arrested and imprisoned in Omaha for the crime of leaving the desolate reservation they had been forced to accept in Indian Territory, later Oklahoma. Chief Standing Bear had lost two daughters on the march to the reservation, and within months of arrival, he had lost about one-third of the Ponca population to starvation and disease, including his son. He vowed to keep the promise he had made to his son to bury him in their ancestral homelands. In the dead of winter, he led a group on a five-hundred-mile walk to the Omaha Reservation in Nebraska, where the army rounded them up for the crime of leaving their reservation.

Disgusted by the idea of imprisoning peaceful Ponca people, General George Crook encouraged an Omaha newspaper editor to drum up public support for their release, and lawyers working pro bono filed a writ of habeas corpus. The district attorney argued that Standing Bear had no right to the writ because he was not, in a legal sense, a citizen or even a person under the Constitution. But if not a person, what, then, were the Ponca? "Are they wild animals, deer to be chased by every hound?" Standing Bear's lawyer asked.

At the conclusion of the trial but before issuing his ruling, the judge announced that he would grant Standing Bear's request to address the court. Wearing an eagle feather in his hair, a necklace of bear claws, deerskin moccasins, and a Thomas Jefferson medallion, he approached the bench, stopped, and raised his right hand. Speaking in his native tongue in a low voice and pausing for an interpreter — Bright Eyes — he said to the judge, "That hand is not the color of yours, but if I prick it, the blood will flow and I shall feel pain. The blood is of the same color as yours. God made me, and I am a man." The speech helped moved the judge to rule, for the first time in a US court, that an Indian was a person entitled to the Constitution's rights and protections.

The attention garnered by the trial and victory led to an East Coast speaking tour by Standing Bear and Bright Eyes, which marked the advent of the Indian rights movement, but change would come slowly. Later that same year, when Standing Bear's brother, Big Snake, left the Ponca Reservation to visit the Cheyenne Reservation — believing he had the legal right to move about freely — officers attempted to arrest him upon his return. In the scuffle that followed, he was shot and killed.

Five years later, in 1884, the Supreme Court ruled (7–2) that John Elk, a Winnebago man who had renounced his tribal membership and registered to vote in his Omaha neighborhood, was not a citizen of the United States — despite an 1866 civil rights law and the Fourteenth Amendment, both of which should have guaranteed him citizenship. Until 1924, when Congress passed the Indian Citizenship Act, Elk and many others found themselves, as Justice John Marshall Harlan wrote in dissent, "a despised and rejected class of persons with no nationality whatever." Legal recognition did little to change their status and improve their condition, but now, a century later, the Winnebago are doing it themselves.

We walk in the direction of the live music and learn it's a fundraiser for a woman hurt in a motorcycle crash. The band is called, and thankfully it seems to be an unrelated coincidence, Wrecked Becky. It's a large biker crowd — lots of black leather and beer, and no physical distancing or masks. We keep our masks on, drawing stares. From Laurel's wide eyes, I can tell she feels we're unwelcome and wants to leave. I hate the idea of being intimidated over something as a silly as a mask, but this does not seem like a hill worth dying on or divorcing over. As my thermal-wearing brothers and sisters in the US Special Operations Forces might advise: Discretion is the better part of valor.

— 22 —

Recognition & Respect

Driving out of Omaha, demonstrators of all ages line the sidewalks for miles, holding signs: "Abortion kills children." "Abortion hurts women." "Adoption: the Loving Option." "Life: The First Inalienable Right." "El aborto mata ninos." "Pray to end abortion." It's the thirty-third anniversary of LifeChain, "a peaceful, prayerful public witness of pro-life Americans, in honor of the pre-born" that happens in communities around the nation. Here, it's far larger than the Black Lives Matter march we had seen the night before, and far quieter. And unlike BLM, it is focused on a single concrete objective. As Amy Coney Barrett prepares for her confirmation hearing, the people here are poised for a triumph they have been working to achieve for thirty-three years and longer.

Omaha, one of the earliest cities to participate in LifeChain, has deep roots in social and political activism, from Standing Bear's trial in 1879 to the Populist Party convention of 1892 to Whitney Young's leadership of the Omaha Urban League in the 1950s. The Lincoln Highway passes one of the city's landmarks in social activism, Boys Town, the orphanage founded by Father Edward Flanagan in 1917. The leafy campus has the feel of an elite boarding school, though it's closed for Covid. The orphanage once housed eight thousand boys in racially and religiously integrated dormitories, where they learned the three R's and the Ten Commandments. "There are no bad boys," the Irish-born Flanagan said. "There is only bad environment, bad training, bad example, bad thinking." But what was once considered a bad environment that necessitated sending children to an orphanage was often simply poverty or single motherhood.

Lincoln's mother, Nancy Hanks, was born out of wedlock. Her mother had once been charged by a grand jury with fornication, and Lincoln described his grandmother as a "halfway-prostitute." Nancy was raised by relatives, but in the generations that followed, many like her would be needlessly and tragically forced into orphanages. "God bless my mother," Abe said, during one of the few instances when he spoke about his family background, "all that I am or ever hope to be I owe to her."

Among the countless American children removed from their family homes was one born in Omaha, Malcolm Little, whose parents were active in the local chapter of a Marcus Garvey–affiliated organization. After gun-toting KKK members smashed the windows of their home, they moved north and settled in Michigan, where Malcolm's father died in a streetcar accident, or so it was reported. The family believed he was killed by members of the Black Legion, the KKK-like group headquartered in Lima, Ohio. When his mother had a nervous breakdown, the state hospitalized her and placed her children into foster care. In his autobiography, Malcom X wrote, "I truly believe that if ever a state social agency destroyed a family, it destroyed ours. We wanted and tried to stay together. Our home didn't have to be destroyed. But the Welfare, the courts, and their doctor gave us a one-two-three punch. And ours was not the only case of this kind."

Without his family being broken, would Malcom have ended up in prison? Once there, like Eugene Debs before him and Jose "Cha Cha" Jimenz after him, he had his political epiphany, which is not the outcome the makers of the film *Boys Town* imagined. In an early scene meant to foreshadow what would become of the boys without Father Flanagan's intervention, a prisoner sings the blues of an old black spiritual.

> *Sometimes I feel like a motherless child*
> *A long ways from home*

When Malcom X returned to Omaha in 1964 to deliver a speech, he said, "We have a racist government in Washington that has the audacity to tell us that the south lost the Civil War." He spoke three weeks after the Senate broke a three-month filibuster of a civil rights bill and three days before President Johnson signed it into law. "We do not want integration," he said.

"We want complete recognition and respect as human beings." The two were not mutually exclusive ideas, but he was reminding his audience that of the two, the latter was more important — and the bill in Washington wouldn't achieve it. Eight months later, he was assassinated by Nation of Islam extremists.

Boys Town long ago moved children out of dormitories and into single-family homes run by married teachers, usually eight kids per home, creating a foster family. Today there are some four hundred thousand children in foster care, more than a quarter of them waiting to be adopted. Their numbers have risen as opioid addiction has ravaged families. Many churches have grown more involved in encouraging foster care, but the system remains plagued by failure and abuse. Studies and surveys have found that children in foster care are far more likely to be abused than other children and more likely to become victims of sex trafficking.

It is easy to hold a sign saying "Choose adoption," but it is harder to reckon with the fate that befalls many who already go unadopted, easier to focus on the womb than the wounded, who are often shielded from view. As new abortion bans and restrictions take effect in some states, the need for greater support for children in foster care — and for more complete recognition and respect for them — will only grow.

We turn south to Lincoln, our last detour before we reach San Francisco, in hopes it might help us answer the question that arose in talking to Mayor Hart in Cedar Rapids: How do we infuse politics with more pragmatism and less partisanship?

In downtown Lincoln, we pick up dinner at Honest Abe's, a burger joint where Lincoln photos and art line the wall, interspersed with the usual mix of apocryphal quotes: "Give me six hours to chop down a tree and I will spend the first four sharpening the axe" and "The best thing about the future is that it comes a day at a time." Lincoln is the American Confucius: any bit of pithy wisdom can be attributed to him with hardly anyone doubting its authenticity, such is his exalted status, and it can be employed by anyone on behalf of any cause — even a business advertising honesty.

The next afternoon, we drive to the home of state senator Adam Morfeld, a thirty-something Democrat who represents Lincoln. On the way, I miss the turn for his street. I slow down and consider entering a church parking lot but hesitate before turning, which prompts Laurel to tell me that there is traffic behind us, so I pass it and turn into the next street only to encounter tree limbs hanging low. I begin a K-turn, but turning around on a narrow city street isn't easy and must be done quickly, since we are near the intersection and another car could turn in. Laurel and I both check mirrors as I reverse. She warns me about a fire hydrant but says I'll clear it if I keep going back straight, which I do. I shift into forward, turn the wheel, gently press the gas, and — screeeech! We jump out. In making the turn, Charley's rear clipped the fire hydrant, breaking a taillight and dislodging the right bumper. The fire hydrant is fine, but Charley is a mess and I'm in shock. *Is this fixable? Did I just end the trip? Why didn't I turn into the church?* The temperamental toilet pedal is now the furthest thing from my mind.

After picking up the taillight pieces, we drive back to the church parking lot and I walk to Adam's house in a fog. As we sit in his backyard, I try to hide how distraught and distracted I am. Fortunately, he is friendly, easygoing, and accustomed to the questions that brought me here. "Anytime I go to a legislative conference or I talk to anybody out of state," he says, "the first thing they bring up is, 'Tell me about Nebraska's system.'" What really makes it different, he says, is not that it's unicameral but that it's nonpartisan, with elections that feature all candidates on the same ballot, regardless of party, and that are open to all voters, regardless of party. Voters adopted it in 1934 over the opposition of both parties, newspapers, bankers, and businessmen, thanks to the barnstorming support of US senator George Norris, a progressive Republican whose independence led him to support Al Smith's 1928 presidential campaign and Franklin Roosevelt's New Deal and who lined up support from labor unions and farmers, including the Nebraska State Grange. His party tried to defeat him in every election after his 1928 apostasy, finally succeeding in 1942, ending his thirty-year career in the Senate, which remains one of the most productive and nonpartisan in the body's history and which earned him a place in John F. Kennedy's book *Profiles in Courage*.

Adam talks about the practical consequences of structuring elections around voters rather than parties. "It builds incentives for you to reach across party lines and talk to everybody in your district and build a coalition," he says. "Whereas in a partisan primary, there's no incentive — you only dial Democrats or Republicans. It brings that mind-set that you represent everybody in your district and you generally have a more well-rounded understanding of the issues facing people. That's the first big difference."

"What's the second?"

"We choose our committee chairs and speaker by secret ballot. And so two-thirds of the legislators are Republicans, one-third are Democrats, but Democrats chair some of the most powerful committees." The committee selection process, he says, is like the election process. "It incentivizes being considered moderate, reasonable, and trustworthy, because there's no incentive for somebody to cast a vote that is truly secret for somebody they don't like. And so you're not just rallying people in your own party. You're going across the aisle and saying, 'Hey, I really want your support for this.'" He points to his own record. "I'm a pretty liberal Democrat, and I've been able to pass over twenty-five bills in a very conservative legislature. You just don't have the party-line voting. And there are no party caucuses. There's no minority leader, no majority leader. It's more people-centric coalitions and issue-centric coalitions."

For nearly a century, the Nebraska state legislature has had a reputation as one of the most civil and cooperative in the nation, and that tradition has mostly survived the hyper-partisanship that has come to define Washington and other state capitals. Of course, parties are not irrelevant here. "Some of the regular partisan flashpoints — like abortion, gun bills, things like that — those generally fall along the same party lines for the most part," Adam says. "But I would say 95 percent of the issues that would never have a chance in Nebraska" — if the legislature were partisan — "might have a chance."

In Pittsburgh, Mayor Bill Peduto had talked about how party primaries were incentivizing extremism. Here nonpartisan elections and committees incentivize moderation and cooperation by pushing candidates and elected officials to recognize and respect voters and colleagues regardless of party affiliation.

There's an old saying that people get the government they deserve. Or maybe we just get the government we design, and we have designed the very one that George Washington warned against in his farewell address, much of which he devoted to an attack on the "disorders and miseries" that parties inflict upon governments and people. He wrote that parties "incline the minds of men to seek security and repose in the absolute power of an individual; and sooner or later the chief of some prevailing faction, more able or more fortunate than his competitors, turns this disposition to the purposes of his own elevation on the ruins of public liberty." It was once common for public school students to read Washington's farewell address as part of their civic education, but no more.

The conversation with Adam eventually drifts to our road trip. "I grew up camping, but in a tent," he says. "My fiancée is like, 'Listen, I'll go camping with you, but you aren't getting me in a tent.'" So they compromised — Adam knows the benefits that come with it — and got an RV. He's amazed at all the ways people modify them and trick them out. "You got different solar panel arrays and inverters — I don't even know how to keep up. I'm just trying to figure out how to empty the waste thing, and make sure I have enough water."

That makes two of us. I want to warn him to beware of fire hydrants, but I can't bring myself to talk about it. When I return to Charley, Laurel can sense I'm in a dark place. She tells me not to beat myself up and offers words of encouragement: *It could've been worse. Accidents happen. RVing is bound to involve mishaps.* But I can't stop kicking myself and worrying that the accident will leave us stranded here — in Lincoln, of all places.

Early the next morning, we drive to an auto body repair shop that specializes in trucks — there are no RV service centers around. We arrive before it opens, and the only guy there kindly agrees to take a look. He jimmies the bumper around and tries to push it back in place but says we will need to order a new one, which would take weeks or months. I tell him about our cross-country trip, and he must sense my desperation. He jimmies it again: "Best I can do is maybe get it on there a little more directly, so it looks better." That might at least prevent it from hanging off and bouncing around. He walks back inside and comes out with a drill and duct tape. After a couple of screws and lots of duct tape, he's got the bumper back in place, including the cracked pieces of the taillights. We test the brake lights and turn signals and — presto! We are in business. I thank him profusely. He wishes us well and walks back into the shop. I follow him inside, expecting him to stop at the cashier's desk, but he keeps walking. "What do I owe you?" I ask.

"Nothing — get out of town and enjoy!"

I never caught his name, but I'm overwhelmed by his kindness. The only person more grateful than me is Laurel, whose endless patience I was testing with my gloominess. As the cloud above me lifts, an idea emerges: Maybe we can duct-tape the toilet pedal in place.

— 23 —

Remaking History

About halfway between Omaha and Fremont, the highway becomes a dirt road that leads to an intersection with nothing around but cornfields and what appears to be a blank billboard but is instead a screen for a drive-in movie theater under construction. At the concession stand being built, I meet the owners, Jeff and Jenny Karls, who tell me it was their own road trip, a family vacation on Route 66, that inspired them to open a drive-in. "Sitting at an Oklahoma drive-in and really enjoying the evening and seeing how family-friendly it is," Jenny says, "we were thinking, 'Somebody needs to bring this back.'" The last drive-in in the region closed in 2006. "And with me being an architect and him being into cars, it was that perfect marriage." They began studying the industry, attending drive-in conventions, pursuing financing, and scouting land. The theater will hold 540 cars — a $2 million project. "We always talked about spending our retirement at the drive-in," says Jeff. "I didn't think we'd spend it *on* the drive-in."

Four thousand drive-ins once dotted the country. Only about three hundred remain, but they have thrived during the pandemic, and the Karls see even better days ahead. "You've got the baby boomers that want to relive that experience from the '50s and '60s," says Jeff, "but you also have young millennials — an adventure-seeking, experience-seeking type of customer" — and young parents. "When we were at the Oklahoma drive-in, we pulled in, got parked, and got our chairs out. And in five minutes, the kids were gone. I'm like, 'Where did they go?' And they were playing with a Frisbee and football and running around. It has been that way every place we've gone. The crowd interacts. It brings out the best in people. It's a community center."

"A drive-in is just like a massive tailgate," says Jenny. "When most people talk about their experience at the drive-in, they sometimes can remember the movie, but they remember the starry sky, the concessions, playing on the playground, and all those things that create an experience. It's not just a movie." Sometimes, it's not a movie at all, as Pat Kirby sang sotto voce in the tender ballad "Moments to Remember," by the Four Lads, which reached number two on the charts in 1955.

The drive-in movie where we'd go
And somehow never watched the show

Just beyond the theater at a T in the road, the highway meets the Union Pacific Railroad. Across the tracks is a chicken slaughter and processing plant, Lincoln Premium Poultry. Costco opened it in 2019 to supply one of its most popular items, rotisserie chicken, which it sells at a loss to attract customers to its stores. Every week, the plant processes two million chickens that are raised in the region by local farmers who signed fifteen-year contracts to construct and operate five hundred industrial-sized henhouses — a boon for them. The contracts are better than the industry standard but still tilted heavily toward Costco, which saves about $35 million annually through the plant. The terms were effectively non-negotiable: Farmers cannot sell to any other buyer, and the company can pull out at any time, which could leave farmers holding millions of dollars in loans.

The deal worries the president of the Nebraska Farmers Union, John Hansen. "Here you have a retailer who will now — from cradle to grave — have complete control of the entire production system," he said after the company broke ground in 2018. "They'll own the birds, they'll control all of the particulars of the birds' genetics, the production. They'll own the feed mill and they'll have control of the processing plant. If this model works, what will it mean for the rest of the poultry industry? Will other retailers, like Walmart, be close behind?" Earlier in 2020, Walmart opened its first beef packing plant, in Georgia, after having already opened a dairy plant in Fort Wayne, Indiana.

The supply-chain consolidation being pursued by the nation's largest retailers is called vertical integration, and though it can resemble vertical annihilation, local farmers are fighting back. Next door to Lincoln Premium Poultry is a pork processing plant now owned by more than two hundred independent hog farmers who purchased it from Hormel in 2018 in an effort to compete with the handful of multinational corporations that dominate the market. In the 1970s, the four largest pork processors controlled about one-third of the market. Now they've got 70 percent of it, and two of them are subsidiaries of foreign corporations: Smithfield (China) and JBS (Brazil). The only way for family farms to compete with the industry's global giants is to band together, aggregate, and scale.

The pork plant co-op is a modern echo of the Grange and populist movements and their anti-monopolistic spirit — a spirit that, until recently, both major parties had largely ignored. Most of the farmers who share ownership of the co-op, I'm willing to wager, vote Republican. When Democrats can't attract farmers whose collectivism would bring a smile to the face of Marx and Engel, to say nothing of Mary Elizabeth Lease and Robert La Follette, the party has big problems in rural America.

In downtown Fremont we park at the Empress Theater, opened in 1915 but shuttered since 1977. Various efforts to revive it failed, though the current one, led by a nonprofit organization that teaches students documentary filmmaking, appears to be succeeding. A sign alludes to its dual mission: "Help us remake history." They are also trying to buck it. The pandemic and streaming services are accelerating the decline of the movie theater business, which threatens more than just an industry. Going to the movies, whether in a field or theater, is an escape to a place of fantasy, adventure and romance, where laughing and crying are expected, and the awkwardness of first dates is eased by simplicity — *Popcorn?* — and the safety of silence.

Laurel and I did not have our first date at a theater but did meet during a song about one, a favorite of hers, "Midnight at the Movies," by Justin Townes Earle. We saw Justin perform many times after that, in theaters, fields, and bars, but shortly before we left on the trip, and four days before our first wedding anniversary, he died of a fentanyl overdose, leaving Laurel — and many others — in tears. He was only thirty-eight years old.

When the Empress is reborn, it will be both a theater and community center. The nonprofit restoring it recognizes, just as the Karls have, that the enduring value of theaters is in their ability to bring people together, including those that Justin Townes Earle sang about in "Midnight at the Movies."

I ain't got nowhere to be
Ain't nobody at home waiting for me

From the Empress, we walk down a Main Street full of parked cars and open shops. New businesses — a brewery, nightclub, bakery — abut mainstays like Lou's Sporting Goods (est. 1967), Abe Krasne's Home Furnishings (est. 1968), Battiato Boot and Shoe Repair (est. 1919), and Sampter's (est. 1883), a clothing store run by the founder's great-grandson, Bob Missel. A year after we pass, Missel announced he would be closing the store, largely because of the explosion of online commerce, telling the *Fremont Tribune*, "I never thought my vendors would go into competition with me, but they have, and so the dynamics have changed." In a world of vertical integration, manufacturers are retailers and retailers are manufacturers. Consumers get lower prices, but many family businesses get squeezed out. "Retail's become tougher and tougher for a single independent merchant," Missel says.

Down the street in Fremont Park, we see a statue of a man whom the park's namesake, John C. Fremont, came to loathe: Lincoln. Although Lincoln stumped for Fremont in his 1856 presidential campaign (Lincoln received more than a quarter of the convention's vice presidential votes), Fremont would cause him nothing but problems throughout the war. After Lincoln appointed him to a high-ranking military post, Fremont declared martial law in Missouri and ordered the slaves of rebels to be freed — the war's first emancipation proclamation, thirteen months before Lincoln was ready to issue one. Lincoln wrote to Fremont, directing him to revoke his edict, fearing that it would "alarm our Southern Union friends, and turn them against us — perhaps ruin our rather fair prospects for Kentucky." Newspapers in the north howled in protest, arguing that Lincoln's reversal would demoralize the war effort, but he was not moved. "I think to lose Kentucky is nearly the same as to lose the whole game," he wrote, rescinding the order and soon replacing Fremont.

The statue of Lincoln here shows him holding the Gettysburg Address rather than the Emancipation Proclamation, which could have honored both men. But the company that produced the statue didn't customize it for the city of Fremont. It's the same statue we missed in Wooster, made by the W. M. Mullins Company, which manufactured cookie-cutter Civil War statues honoring both Union and Confederate soldiers, allowing towns north and south to look through a catalog and choose from a variety of designs. For the first time, towns could memorialize their dead and celebrate their cause at relatively low cost, at least in the near term. The long-term costs of mass production without regard for social cohesion — commerce above community and country — can stretch far beyond our grasp.

We are now following the Platte River — *la platte* being French for "the flat," which likely derived from *nebraska*, a native word for "flat river" or "shallow or broad water." We will be tracking the river and much of America's westward expansion for the next five hundred miles. Long before it was the Lincoln Highway, this was the Great Platte River Road. From the 1840s through the end of the Civil War, when the railroad replaced wagons, some four hundred thousand people followed it west. One of the earliest was John Fremont, thanks to his marriage to Jessie Benton, the daughter of the US Senate's strongest champion of westward expansion, Thomas Hart Benton. Fremont received several commissions to explore the west, funded by a federal government seeking to strengthen its claim to the Oregon territory, a large swath of the northwest also claimed by England. The expeditions had another mission, though it often went unspoken: to fuel support for the annexation of Mexican territory. John and Jessie wrote about the expeditions in reports and books that helped swell public interest in moving west and public support for national expansion.

On December 27, 1845, the *New York Morning News* carried an editorial by its politically influential publisher, John O'Sullivan, arguing that whatever the legal technicalities, the United States had a moral right to the Oregon territory: "That claim is by the right of our manifest destiny to overspread and to possess the whole of the continent which Providence has given us for the development of the great experiment of liberty and federated self-government entrusted to us."

The phrase he coined — *manifest destiny*, which he had also used five months earlier in urging the annexation of Texas— is familiar to anyone who stayed half awake during high school. It captured the central justification for westward expansion: that it was guided by the hand of God, who had anointed America to redeem the world through the spread of liberty and democracy. Under this ideology, war with Mexico was not a matter of conquest so much as divine liberation, with America serving as God's instrument. So it had been for every Indian battle and so it would be for every American war that followed, an idea Bob Dylan challenged so powerfully during the Cold War in his song "With God on Our Side."

Lincoln, too, opposed this worldview. What mattered to him was not the expansion of the nation's borders but of its central ideas. He saw America as the Puritan immigrant John Winthrop did: a "city on a hill" that would inspire the world with its example, though not through the Christian virtue of its citizens, as Winthrop believed, but through its commitment to freedom, democracy, and equality. In a speech on the House floor, Lincoln spoke of a people's "right to rise up" and overthrow a government, calling it "a most sacred right — a right which, we hope and believe, is to liberate the world." Liberating the world meant focusing inward and striving to live up to our ideals — not sending armies across borders. For this reason, he opposed the annexation of Texas, "inasmuch, as they were already a free republican people on our own model" — and opposed war with Mexico, too, which he believed unnecessary, since "Mexico was in no way molesting, or menacing the US." He viewed it as a "war of conquest brought into existence to catch votes." For his antiwar stance, Lincoln was dubbed "the Benedict Arnold of our district" by a hometown newspaper and denied renomination to Congress.

Even during the height of the Civil War, Lincoln refused to embrace the idea that American soldiers marched with God. According to the painter Francis B. Carpenter, when a minister told Lincoln he hoped that God was on their side, Lincoln gently rebuked him, saying, "I am not at all concerned about that, for I know that the Lord is always on the side of the right. But it is my constant anxiety and prayer that I and this nation should be on the Lord's side."

Although Lincoln frequently invoked an Almighty power, he did so as a supplicant who never pretended to know God's will. In his second inaugural address, he held out the possibility that God might favor the south. For him, faith in an unknowable God required holding even the firmest political views with humility and awareness of potential error. And it required showing mercy and understanding to one's opponents — including those who, like O'Sullivan, claimed God for the Confederacy.

As O'Sullivan was turning the spread of liberty and democracy (for whites) into a civil religion, another New Yorker, Joseph Smith, was spreading his own new religion grounded in the same fundamental idea: that America was chosen by God to usher in a new millennium of peace and prosperity. The Christian sect he founded taught that a group of Israelites sailed to the Americas around 600 B.C. and that Christ appeared to their descendants after his crucifixion, anointing America as the new Holy

Land to which he would return to redeem the world. Six weeks after O'Sullivan's newspaper editorial proclaiming manifest destiny, several hundred families who had joined the sect — Mormons, they would be called, after the book Smith said he received from a heavenly messenger — left their settlement in Illinois for Omaha, where they regrouped before heading out along the Platte River for a large salt lake in Mexico they had learned of from Fremont's accounts of his travels. While originally seeking to escape America and the persecution they had encountered everywhere they went, Mormons would greatly advance the cause of manifest destiny.

From the 1840s to the 1860s, more than seventy thousand Mormons took months-long journeys into the unknown, an exodus they likened to Jews leaving Egypt for the Promised Land, just as the Pilgrims and Puritans — and so many other Christian sects after them — had sought to build their own New Jerusalems in the wilderness, part of a long tradition of Americans seeing themselves as the new Chosen People. Lincoln, too, believed that America had divine purpose, but in calling Americans an "almost chosen people," he stopped short of claiming the fullness of God's favor, maintaining humility others did not.

For Lincoln, the sacred mission of America lay not in expanding empire or propagating revelation but in keeping faith with the American trinity: freedom, equality, and democracy, each limited and animated by the other. Fidelity to democracy must be restrained, unlike in popular sovereignty, by the equality promised in the Declaration of Independence. The right to individual freedoms must be negotiated, unlike in the vigilante abolitionism of John Brown, through democracy and the constitutional rule of law. And the promise of equality must be advanced, unlike in nativism and slavery, by a "free society," Lincoln said in an 1857 speech, "which should be familiar to all and revered by all, constantly looked to, constantly labored for, and even though never perfectly attained, constantly approximated, and thereby constantly spreading and deepening its influence, and augmenting the happiness and value of life to all people and of all colors everywhere."

Following the highway that followed the railroad that followed the wagon road that followed the river, we turn down a dirt road and roll slowly through six miles of cornfields and the town of Richland, home to about a hundred residents and a collection of large silos and grain bins, though the

Farmers Union Co-Op Association building sits abandoned, its window only half boarded up.

We return to pavement as we approach Columbus, where we stop at Glur's Tavern — the oldest in the west, or so it claims, dating to 1876, though some say it was 1879. After nearly getting run off the road today by a tractor-trailer truck that crossed over the yellow lines and came barreling toward us, we have earned a beer.

The tavern is inside a two-story white house on a corner lot. It's claim to fame is that William Frederick "Buffalo Bill" Cody drank here in the 1880s, and after the funeral of his friend and business partner, Frank North, he bought a round for the house, plunking down a $1,000 bill and giving the town a story that is still being told. Unlike most stories Cody told about himself — about fighting in the Mormon War, riding a record distance for the Pony Express, rafting down the Platte River, mining for gold at Pikes Peak, impressing the infamous killer John Slade, outrunning Indians and stealing a hundred of their ponies, all before he turned fifteen years old — this one seems to be true.

Cody created a mythical persona that embodied the mythical place he spent most of his life inhabiting and evangelizing — the Wild West — and all that it came to represent in his hands: the triumph of white civilization over Indian savagery, the rugged heroism of cowboys, the taming of the wilderness, the glorification of guns, and, though less well remembered and less recognized even at the time, the promise of reconciliation and national unity. The nation's divisions had deeply altered the course of Cody's life. He grew up in Bleeding Kansas, and the blood coursing through it included that of his father, who was stabbed at a public meeting for declaring himself against slavery even as he — like many others at that time — also expressed support for making Kansas an all-white state. When his father later died from the wound's complications, eleven-year-old Bill began a life that would become a testament to the power of what aspiring documentary filmmakers are learning to do at the Empress Theater: remake history.

Given his fondness for drink, a tavern would be a fitting place to tell his tall tale, but the Lincoln Highway will bring us to the spot where his legend began. For now, we cross over to a peninsula that Cody would've known well, between the Platte and Loup Rivers, and turn down a dirt road to Pawnee Camp, which appears closed for the season. There are no other campers and no staff. Grass grows on a basketball court. Rickety cabins are empty. Paint peels off every structure. When I turn on a waterspout, nothing comes out.

The deserted feel of Pawnee Camp carries an echo of the Pawnee's own retreat from this area, less because of settlers than the Lakota Sioux. The Pawnee lived and hunted along the Loup and Platte Rivers for centuries, battling rival tribes — especially the Apache, Cheyenne, Arapaho, and Lakota Sioux — for much the same prize Europeans and later Americans sought, control of the land and its bounty. After smallpox epidemics in the 1830s wiped out about half the Pawnee, more than six thousand people, other native nations exploited their weakness by stealing their food and horses and taking captive the warriors and women they did not kill. Lakota raids of the Pawnee became so routine in the 1840s that the Lakota stopped recording them. The raids eventually forced the Pawnee to retreat to Indian Territory, leaving behind the Platte River Valley that had long been their home, and leaving their land to be fought over by an American nation bent on a manifest destiny and a Lakota nation with its own vision of westward expansion.

The conflict between the Pawnee and Lakota highlights the oversimplification of history that reduces native peoples to victims of white theft, exploitation, and genocide. War and slavery both existed in North America before the arrival of Europeans. While native enslavement of other native peoples was not the same as plantation slavery, it was slavery nonetheless. And while native aims in war with other native nations were not the same as white aims in war with Indians, that made little difference to the casualties. Native nations often looked at each other much as settlers did: a people to be removed as an obstacle to survival and prosperity, no matter the human cost. Far from viewing Europeans and Americans as a universal evil, native nations sought to fashion trading relationships that maximized their access to new technology and their protection against rivals. They practiced realpolitik long before the term was coined in the mid-nineteenth century.

While occasional historical markers tell of battles between Native Americans and whites, almost always from the white perspective, there is little in the landscape that memorializes battles between native nations, which have hardly any hold on public memory or any place in popular culture. That history is still waiting to be remade.

— 24 —

Antiques & Ashcans

Kensinger Service and Supply opened in the 1930s in Grand Island, Nebraska. It's still selling gas, and it's the best place to stop to see what remains of the state's first model mile, or seedling mile, built in 1915, just as Carl Fisher and Henry Joy had hoped all Lincoln Highway towns would do. It's an original stretch of concrete, ten feet wide. A Model T Ford was five and a half feet wide. Two-way traffic meant pulling over onto the dirt. And that was luxury driving.

Grand Island's blocks of red-brick buildings give the city a sturdy charm and provide a natural setting for the antiques shops that line the street. The city serves as the starting and ending point of the "Junk Jaunt," a 350-mile yard sale that lines roads across the northwestern part of the state during the last weekend of each September, drawing visitors from around the country to the beauty of the Sand Hills. We stop into one of the larger antiques shops, Railroad Towne, where Laurel picks up a leather purse with an etching of a moose in a wilderness scene. It's gaudy and gauche and she loves it, but we are traveling light and carrying only what we need, so with great reluctance she puts it back down, and immediately regrets it.

Beyond the antiques stores in a Grand Island mall, a local kid saw the future in 1993, after buying the second issue of *Wired* magazine. Ev Williams would end up in Silicon Valley as a co-founder of Twitter, which began as a digital utopia — a community of free speech where good ideas would spread and good people would act on them. But by 2016, he had come to view Twitter much as Dr. Frankenstein did his science experiment.

In her book *How Civil Wars Start*, Barbara F. Walter writes, "social media created an avenue by which enemies of democracy can easily infiltrate society and destabilize it from within. The internet has revealed just how fragile a government by and for the people can be."

Today the US president uses Ev's co-creation to attack the media ("THE FAKE NEWS MEDIA IS THE REAL OPPOSITION PARTY"), suggest that Hillary Clinton should be prosecuted ("A Disgraceful Con Artist! Charges anyone?"), and allege that electing Democrats would spell the end of religion ("DEMS WANT TO SHUT YOUR CHURCHES DOWN, PERMANENTLY"). Overnight he had tweeted a message he has delivered before: "This will be the most corrupt Election in American history!"

Our campground is a county park adjacent to Grand Island's premier tourist attraction, the Stuhr Museum of the Prairie Pioneer. The museum features Railroad Town, a re-creation of an 1890s town facing the tracks of the Union Pacific and rendered in the soft glow of an old-timey reverie, a Colonial Williamsburg for the prairie, ever so quaint. Scattered through Railroad Town are a variety of homes that were moved here from around the area. One of them is the birthplace of Henry Fonda, who played the title role in 1939's *Young Mr. Lincoln*, Fonda's first collaboration with the director John Ford. In the movie, Fonda as Lincoln races to the head of an angry mob that's seeking to hang two men accused of murder. While standing in the doorway to the jail, he uses humor, reason, and bravado to persuade the men to go home. The incident never happened, but at a time when Congress was still refusing to pass an anti-lynching bill, Fonda and Ford sought to link it to Lincoln and build support for its passage.

As a boy in Omaha during the Red Summer of 1919, Fonda had stood in his father's printing shop and watched the mayor try to stop the lynching of a black man accused of rape, Will Brown. A mob of thousands stormed the county courthouse, set fire to it, dragged the mayor out of the building, attempted to hang him — he was cut down and saved by the police — and forced the jail guards to turn over Brown, whereupon they stripped him, beat him, hanged him, shot him, and burned him.

"It was the most horrendous sight I'd ever seen," Fonda later said. "We locked the plant, went downstairs, and drove home in silence. My hands were wet and there were tears in my eyes. All I could think of was that young black man dangling at the end of a rope."

Not until 2022 will Congress finally pass an anti-lynching bill, a mostly symbolic act akin to creating an antique-looking showpiece to impress others with faux historical appreciation. But which leaders are standing up to today's mobs — including online — and enacting safeguards around what often drives them: social media?

The toilet pedal has held for the past week, but we know we're on borrowed time. We arrive at an RV dealer before opening hours, and the manager kindly agrees to take a look. "Yup, see it all the time with Thetfords," he says. He doesn't have the part but could install a whole new unit — bowl and pedal — for about $200. Sold.

While we're waiting, I browse the store's supplies as employees talk about the prior night's vice-presidential debate. Doing most of the talking is a middle-aged white man who thinks Mike Pence wiped the floor with Kamala Harris, but it may not make a difference. "There's just too many uneducated people," he says. "My nineteen-year-old son called and said, 'I don't see how anyone could vote for Biden after watching this.'" While conservatives attack liberals for elitism, many share the common belief on the left: The problem is education. It's the only way each side can fathom how people on the other side could be so deluded.

His review of the debate continues, and he especially loved how Pence countered Harris's accusation of racism — she charged Trump with refusing to condemn white supremacists — by rejecting it and talking about racial disparities in prosecution and incarceration during Harris's time as district attorney and attorney general. He hushes his tone a little: "She's lockin' up her own kind and trying to call Pence a white supremacist." There are no black people here, which makes the hushed phrase *her own kind* even more racially freighted and uncomfortable. It would lead many on the left to accuse him of being racist, and maybe he is. Or maybe he just spoke crassly. One thing seems clear: He is offended that the charge of white supremacy has been cast upon his preferred political candidates.

He does not bring up Pence's response to the question, "If Vice President Biden is declared the winner and President Trump refuses to accept a peaceful transfer of power, what would be your role and responsibility as Vice President? What would you personally do?" Pence spent his two minutes talking about how they would win the election, how it was

Democrats who tried to overturn the 2016 election by impeaching Trump, and how mail-in voting was creating the potential for fraud.

In the final weeks of the 1864 election campaign, Lincoln addressed the question of whether, if defeated, he would attempt to "ruin the government." On the contrary, he said, "Whoever shall be constitutionally elected in November, shall be duly installed as President on the fourth of March; and that in the interval I shall do my utmost that whoever is to hold the helm for the next voyage, shall start with the best possible chance to save the ship."

Following the bend of the Platte River leads us to lunch at a Lexington taqueria owned by a couple from Mexico, Humberto and Norma Avalos. They were drawn here by the opportunity of working in a chicken processing plant that opened in 1990, when only 5 percent of the city's population was Latino. Residents tried to stop the plant from building housing for its workers, but without a referendum blocking unauthorized immigrants from housing — as happened in Fremont — it was whites who left in droves. Nevertheless, as new residents arrived, the number of businesses grew.

The Avaloses saved enough money from their factory years to open the taqueria. The restaurant's tables and booths are handcrafted from Mexico, with colorful intricate carvings. "What we have, we share — food, culture, everything," Humberto says. "We treat everyone the same. We offer the same food and prices to everyone." It is not hard to see the point he is driving at: their desire to be treated equally, too. He talks about respect — the respect he shows to all but that others do not always show. His eyes betray his hurt. He says there are bad people in every group, but to stereotype Mexicans and Hispanics as murders and rapists is wrong.

Humberto's words are being translated by a local priest who was brought here as a child from Mexico. After overstaying their tourist visa, his parents tried to gain legal status but got scammed by a lawyer. Risking deportation, they visited an immigration office, asked for help, and got it. Now he counsels families who fear — even more intensely than his parents did — that coming out of the shadows to begin the legalization process will lead to deportation.

Not every child brought here illegally grows up to become a priest, and not every person who comes here to work in a factory saves up their money to open a small business. But while their stories of hard work and faith are the norm — and always have been, among every immigrant group — touting good behavior does not sell news or win elections. It wasn't that way for the Irish or Germans, the Italians or Poles, the Chinese or Japanese, or Latin Americans, Africans, or Middle Easterners. Each group has faced fear, conflict, exclusion, bias, and violence, just as Native Americans did. If America is a melting pot, it is only because each group has pried the lid loose, while being jeered at and attacked as lazy ne'er-do-wells who are ruining the country, even as they toil long hours for low pay to build it. Not every lynching involves a noose.

The childhood home of Robert Henri sits on the Lincoln Highway in Cozad. It's been restored and preserved as a museum that celebrates his life as a leader of the Ashcan School of art, so named for its rejection of romanticized impressionism and its preference for the seamier side of life, ash cans and all, imbuing his work with a democratic spirit. Beginning in the 1890s, he sought to paint America as it was, stripping it of the gloss others brought to their subjects, often with the dark palette realism required.

Cozad sits on the 100th Meridian, which inspired one of the most profound works of realism ever created: a straight line on a map. A decade after the Union Pacific united the coasts, John Wesley Powell, a geologist, ethnologist, explorer, and Union army veteran who lost an arm at the Battle of Shiloh, drew a line that divided the nation in two — not by politics, but by climate. Powell was the first to note that the 100th Meridian roughly coincided with a change in climate: the humid east giving way to the arid west. East of the line, at least twenty inches of rain falls each year, the minimum necessary for agriculture without irrigation. West of it, less falls, often much less.

In drawing the line on a map, Powell gave Americans a visual of their country based not on state and territorial boundaries but on natural ones, and he argued that unregulated agricultural development west of the line was — to use a modern term — unsustainable. The Homestead Act of 1862, enacted before the nation understood its own geography, was a disaster in the making, he warned. What we now call the Great Plains was long called the Great American Desert, and there was simply not enough water to turn a desert into an oasis. The railroad financiers and politicians, however, had not laid thousands of miles of track at great expense to limit traffic. They wanted farmers and settlers, commerce and industry. Manifest destiny would not yield to climate science.

A generation after Powell died, a years-long drought turned the Great Plains's overgrazed and overfarmed land into America's worst environmental catastrophe: a decade of dust storms that carried off much of the Great Plains's topsoil and deposited it across the east, occasionally darkening skies from Chicago to New York, a dark coda to the 1862 Homestead Act. On the anniversary of Lincoln's assassination, 1934, in the midst of the Great Depression, high winds swept across the plains from Canada to Texas, lifting tons of dry soil five to six hundred feet in the air, moving at about sixty miles per hour — a dust blizzard that blinded eyes, filled lungs, struck terror into hearts, destroyed crops, suffocated cattle, and left half a million people homeless — Black Sunday, it was called, and the darkness continued. The two and a half million people who pulled up stakes for California and other verdant locations included Woody Guthrie, whose first album, *Dust Bowl Ballads*, would place him beside John Steinbeck as a definitive American voice.

Scientists have recently made a startling discovery: The line demarcating the arid west from the forested east has moved. As the climate warms, water evaporates from the soil more quickly, which has pushed the line 140 miles east, to about the 98th Meridian. Climate change is shrinking America's naturally arable land. But as it was during John Wesley Powell's day, private industry often trumps scientific evidence, and short-term economic gains are prioritized over long-term economic costs. Lake Powell, the artificial reservoir in Arizona and Utah that bears John Wesley's name, has dropped to a record low. Fed by the Colorado River and created to ensure that water flows to arid areas in Arizona, California, and Nevada, it's less than one-quarter full, a victim of climate change's consequences: lengthier droughts, diminished snowpack, and higher temperatures that accelerate evaporation.

In a biography of Powell, *Beyond the Hundredth Meridian*, Wallace Stegner wrote, "Science and Reason have always been on the side of Utopia; only the cussedness of the human race has not." But the shifting line on Powell's map highlights an important reality: The country is in a constant state of change, and our approach to its challenges — whether regarding climate, immigration, mobs, or anything else — must adapt, taking account of science and reason, lest we be left in darkness.

— 25 —

Wild West

We have been traveling rural roads that run straight as corn rows and making ninety-degree turns every couple of minutes. North then west, north then west, north then west, as we make our way up the river valley that leads to the Rocky Mountains, rising almost imperceptibly seven hundred feet in elevation from Kearney to North Platte, our destination for the night. It's common for travelers from the east to roll their eyes at the monotony of seemingly flat cornfields, and in the blur of an interstate, boredom slows down time. On back roads, where the land comes into clearer focus, patience comes easy.

Halfway to North Platte, a statue of a soldier stands by the roadside in front of a farmhouse. We pull onto the gravel shoulder and learn that it marks the site of the old Fort McPherson, where Buffalo Bill Cody arrived in May 1869, ten days after a Golden Spike connected the Union Pacific and Central Pacific in Utah, completing the transcontinental railroad. He came here to serve as a scout for the army's Fifth Cavalry, providing intelligence about the movements and strength of Indians, who continued to present threats to westward travelers despite the 1868 Treaty of Fort Laramie which ended a two-year period of Sioux raids on wagons and trains. The treaty required a cessation of raids in return for creating the Great Sioux Reservation and guaranteeing Sioux hunting rights in much of Nebraska, but many of the Lakota Sioux, including Sitting Bull, refused to accept its terms.

Not long after Cody's arrival, Edward Zane Carroll Judson came to Fort McPherson to deliver a temperance lecture or to find Wild Bill Hickock, or both. Hickok was a famed gunslinging gambler whose exploits battling Indians had been glorified in *Harper's* magazine. Judson was one of the nation's most popular writers, "the king of the dime novel," and he hoped to hear from Hickok about his adventures. Wild Bill either wasn't at the fort or wasn't interested in talking. Whatever the case, Judson needed a new source.

We have encountered Judson before, on the first day of this journey, under his pen name, Ned Buntline — the fellow who stirred up the nativist riot at Astor Place in Manhattan. He lived as daringly and dangerously as the characters in his dime novels (a dime being the typical price). In addition to shooting men in Tennessee and Maine, he was publicly flogged in New York City by a brothel madam, beaten up in Philadelphia by an ex-cop, and hung from a street pole by a lynch mob in Nashville before being cut down and saved. He helped found the xenophobic Know-Nothing Party, instigated anti-German Election Day violence in St. Louis, agitated for the invasion of Cuba, joined the Union army and was arrested for desertion, lectured on temperance while drinking heavily, and married at least eight women, one of them twice, sometimes not bothering with divorce papers. There is no accounting of mistresses. What Buntline did not do he invented, including fighting in the Mexican War and fending off pirates in the Caribbean, though he could fairly claim to have set off to sea at age thirteen: *Buntline* is a nautical term for the rope attached to a square sail, fitting for a man who followed the changing winds and loved sailing into a storm.

Buntline began his career as an acclaimed highbrow writer and literary critic, but he soon gave it up. "I found that to *make a living*," he lamented, "I must write 'trash' for the masses, for he who endeavors to write for the critical few, and do his genius justice, will go hungry." He began packing his stories with action and adventure, risk and romance, which brought money and fame. Many others in his wake would make the same decision, aiming for popularity, whatever the consequences — and whether Ned Buntline or Phil Donahue or their successors, there are always consequences.

Buntline's sentimental adventure tales captivated a young man who would also take a nautical term as a pen name, Samuel Clemens, who adopted the phrase riverboat men shouted — "mark twain!" — to signal a water depth sufficiently safe for passage: two (twain) fathoms (marks). But

Twain grew to despise Buntline's writing for the simplified fallacies and dangerous delusions it foisted upon the masses. When Tom Sawyer imagines himself as the pirate hero in a Buntline novel, Twain is showing Tom's juvenile attraction to violence and risk taking and their illusory personal glories. In children, it's endearing fantasy. In adults, it can lead down the path that Buntline followed in life.

Today in Michigan, thirteen members of a right-wing militia group are arraigned on charges of plotting to kidnap Democratic governor Gretchen Whitmer and storm the state capitol, motivated by anger over Covid restrictions and a desire to spark a civil war — referred to as the "boogaloo" by its proponents. One of the leaders, a marine reservist nicknamed Boogaloo Bunyan, flew a Confederate flag outside his house. "We wanted to cause as much a disruption as possible to prevent Joe Biden from getting into office," one of the men will later testify. "The plan was for us to basically be the ignition to it, and hopefully other states or other groups would follow."

Buntline's *Buffalo Bill, King of the Bordermen* — a novel masquerading as biography — turned Cody into the personification of the heroic frontiersman. It would be the first of more than 550 dime novels about Cody and lead him to a new career: acting out his life, at least as he told it, onstage. "Such a combination of incongruous drama, execrable acting, renowned performers, mixed audience, intolerable stench, scalping, blood and thunder," wrote the *Chicago Tribune* of his first show, written by Buntline, "is not likely to be vouchsafed to a city a second time, even Chicago." But audiences loved it, and by 1875, Cody's fame was such that, after Lieutenant Colonel George Armstrong Custer reported finding gold in the Black Hills, Cody lent his name to a prospecting company from Boston.

The next year, the army asked Cody to rejoin the Fifth Cavalry as it mobilized to confront the Sioux, Cheyenne, and other native peoples led by Sitting Bull, who had refused to accept the 1868 treaty and its land restrictions. The army intended to find them, corral them, move them onto the Great Sioux Reservation, and force them to accept a meager payment for mining and settlement rights on the reservation's Black Hills, which the Sioux held sacred. "Their lands were invaded by the gold-seekers," Cody would later say in their defense, making no mention of his own role in the invasion, "and when the US government failed to protect them, they thought it was time to do it themselves."

To corral the native holdouts, Lieutenant Colonel George Custer led the Seventh Cavalry out of Fort Abraham Lincoln in present-day North

Dakota, but when his troops discovered their village along the Little Bighorn River in Montana, he did not send an emissary to discuss peaceful surrender, nor wait for approaching reinforcements. Possibly seeking battlefield glory that would catapult him onto the front pages on the eve of the nation's centennial, he decided, like a character in a Ned Buntline novel, to hastily attack the village, which housed about eight thousand men, women, and children.

The native fighting force Custer encountered was much larger than what he had anticipated: about fifteen hundred strong, including Crazy Horse. Of the more than two hundred men Custer commanded, not one survived. Custer was left with a bullet through his head and an arrow through his penis. It was the worst army defeat of the Plains Wars and a shocking national humiliation that dampened centennial celebrations, lit the fires of vengeance, and created a new national martyr, all but erasing from history Custer's true glory: his courageous charge at Gettysburg, which helped save the battle for the United States.

Shortly after learning of Custer's fate, Cody prepared for a skirmish with a group of Cheyenne by donning a preposterous stage costume he had brought with him — a black velvet, silver-buttoned, lace-trimmed Mexican vaquero getup — merging his two jobs, scout and showman, into one. In the dustup that followed, he killed and scalped a young man, Yellow Hair, yelling out to cheers from the cavalry: "The first scalp for Custer!" Or so he would claim, greatly embellishing if not fabricating the incident for his next theatrical show, *The Red Right Hand, or Buffalo Bill's First Scalp for Custer*. It was hardly the show's only embellishment.

While glorifying himself, Cody would play an important role in mythologizing Custer and America's westward advance, a story that unfolds a little farther up the Lincoln Highway, in North Platte. Here at Fort McPherson, a national cemetery includes the graves of more than sixty men who were never made the heroes of dime novels or stage shows, nor even give much respect for their role in securing the US's westward expansion: buffalo soldiers. Native Americans gave the name to black soldiers, seeing in their dark curls a likeness to the animal they hunted and held sacred. The army formed the Ninth Cavalry of black soldiers after the Civil War and offered the command to Custer, but he refused it. And while Buffalo Bill rode with buffalo soldiers here in 1868, he never valorized them in his writings and shows — just the opposite. He infantilized them.

Buffalo soldiers' service to the nation had been all but forgotten in public memory by the late 1970s, when they were rescued by Bob Marley and Noel "King Sporty" Williams, whose song "Buffalo Soldiers" became one of reggae's most enduring hits, its bouncy beat and sparing refrain hooking audiences and transcending race, even if many give no thought to its message of black resilience and liberation, or to the tragic irony of black people joining a war to stamp out native freedom, in the hope of finally winning for themselves the freedom and equality promised in the Declaration of Independence, only to die disappointed. One of those buried here, First Sergeant George Jordan, spent his first seventeen years of life in slavery. He died after a thirty-year career in the army, when a hospital refused to admit him because of the color of his skin.

Stolen from Africa / Brought to America
Fighting on arrival / Fighting for survival

The Lincoln brings us down Buffalo Bill Avenue in North Platte, past the Wild West Arena and rodeo fairgrounds, to Buffalo Bill Ranch State Park and campground. The park was once part of a ranch Cody owned, and while living here in 1882, he helped organize an Independence Day celebration that featured horse races, shooting competitions, and the riding of a buffalo and steer, allowing North Platte to claim (along with a variety of other towns) the title of the world's first rodeo. The term *rodeo*, from the Spanish *rodear*, "to encircle or round up," didn't come into common usage until well into the twentieth century. Until then, they were called frontier days, stampedes, or cowboy contests — all of them owing a debt to Cody and the big idea that seemed to grow out of his Fourth of July celebration, the *Wild West*.

Buffalo Bill's Wild West was an epic pageant that incorporated "genuine" western relics into its performances, including the scalp Cody supposedly took. Crowds thrilled to Pony Express riding and cowboy competitions: lassoing, horse racing, trick riding, and sharpshooting, sometimes by Cody, his long blond locks and tall frame inspiring images of a pistol-packing Prince of Peace, at least for some, as e.e. cummings wrote.

onetwothreefourfive pigeonsjustlikethat
                                                  Jesus

he was a handsome man

Cody was a good shot, but when a rifle-toting young woman who stood under five feet tall auditioned, he knew he had a star. Phoebe Ann Moses — Annie Oakley, she called herself — was a deadeye. Her husband held seemingly impossible targets — a dime between his thumb and finger, a playing card facing sideways, a cigarette sticking out of his mouth — and she hit them, often while facing away from them and holding a rifle backward over her shoulder, sighting them in a mirror with one eye closed. For a show that touted "The Rifle as an Aid to Civilization," here was the west's belle ideal, even though she was from Ohio and never lived in the west. She taught women how to shoot, campaigned for equal pay, was the household's primary breadwinner, believed in women's emancipation from the home, and tried to enlist in the Spanish-American War — a feminist before the label gained currency, but also a Victorian lady who disliked bloomers and opposed women's suffrage. Today it is easy to look back on such opposition as backward and wrong, but she was an early example of the political diversity that has always existed within feminism.

Oakley helped persuade Sitting Bull to enlist in the *Wild West*, a coup for Cody that convinced many other Lakota to join, too, adding to the authenticity of the history being presented. A promotional photo of Cody and Sitting Bull, whose vision inspired the victory over Custer at Little Bighorn, was captioned "Foes in '76, Friends in '85." And it was true. Each man liked and respected the other. But Sitting Bull agreed to appear only before the crowd, not to take part in any of the re-created scenes, which always featured Indians encircling and attacking stagecoaches, wagon trains, and humble cabins while whooping war cries, as passengers and settlers valiantly fought them off, often buying time for the army to arrive — led by Cody riding a fine horse, though scouts generally rode mules, for their greater stamina and sure-footedness.

After sufficient time had elapsed, Cody sought permission from Custer's widow to portray the Battle of Little Bighorn in his show. She acquiesced and was pleased with the result: Cody turned Custer's attack into an Indian ambush. After a heroic fight, Custer was the last to die — and with no arrow sticking through his penis. "You have done so much to make him an idol among the children and young people," she told Cody.

In presenting Indians as the aggressors and settlers as the victims, Cody was only mirroring public sentiment, including in Longfellow's elegy to Custer.

In ambush the Sitting Bull
Lay with three thousand braves
Crouched in the clefts and caves,
Savage, unmerciful!

This reversal of reality — savage Indians attacking peaceful settlers who had no choice but to fight back in self-defense — allowed whites to claim moral righteousness in their westward push and to see themselves as both victims and victors. Cody, by staging it as drama, created the template for all Hollywood westerns to come, birthing stars, making fortunes, and writing national history, all at once. Ethel Merman in *Annie Get Your Gun* captured it in one line, from Irving Berlin.

There's no business like show business like no business I know

When Cody brought *Wild West* to New York in 1886 for three months, he billed it as "America's National Entertainment." Crowds flocked to it, including General Sherman, P. T. Barnum, and Mark Twain, who saw the show twice and was so inspired he wrote Cody a fan letter urging him to take it across the Atlantic to provide Europeans with an art form that was "purely and distinctly American." Cody heeded the advice, playing in England to more than one million spectators, including the queen, who so enjoyed it that she requested a private performance at Buckingham Palace. He then took it across Europe, always attracting large crowds. Generations of European children would play cowboys and Indians, having learned the same lessons as American children: that the noble savages had been defeated by a superior society and its rugged, gallant, God-fearing heroes. When Disneyland Paris opened in 1992, one of its featured shows was *Buffalo Bill's Wild West*, which ran until closing in 2020.

Over time, Cody scaled back some of the crudeness of the *Wild West*, and even publicly expressed some remorse. "I never scouted with a party of soldiers after Indians that I didn't feel a bit ashamed for myself and a whole heap sorrier for them," he said. In victory, when the defeated party is crushed into near oblivion, no longer a political or military threat, it is easy to be magnanimous. But the show went on, and it spawned dozens of imitation spectacles that, in the twentieth century, moved from stage to screen. Plots changed, but endings never did: The good guys rode off into the sunset on the back of justice, no matter what barbarities they had endured.

It took more than a century after Cody's *Wild West* began for popular audiences to see an even slightly more complex story in *Dances with Wolves*, the first major movie to reverse the traditional western narrative. It would never be made today, since it would be attacked for casting a "white savior," Kevin Costner, in the lead role. At the time, however, it was a groundbreaking plot that won high praise from native voices, who — for the first time — could see themselves in roles other than the ones Cody had first created. Costner, who also directed the movie, began to remake history, but it has been slow in coming.

The shadow of the *Wild West* still hovers over the country as the mythic inverse of the Lost Cause. Where the south refused to recognize the requirements of reconciliation and justice arising from defeat, the United States imagined that reconciliation and justice were part and parcel of victory. Cody, in presenting Native Americans as valiant warriors who accepted defeat, aimed to glorify — in addition to American victories — the achievement of peace. The mission of his show, Cody said, was to "bring the white and red races closer together." Like most others, Cody never fully grappled with the injustices Native Americans suffered — tomorrow we will encounter one of the worst — and what might be required for true reconciliation to occur.

— 26 —

Frontiers

At the Lincoln Highway Diner in North Platte, we order breakfast to go. Behind the counter hangs a poster of Lincoln titled "Perseverance," which recounts his many business and electoral failures. It is meant to inspire, and halfway through a heaping mound of greasy hash browns, it does.

In North Platte, the river splits into north and south forks. The Lincoln tracks the south fork to Paxton, where a lone traffic signal blinks yellow, perhaps less to protect pedestrians than to entice drivers into one of the four businesses here, three of them bars. We had heard about one of them, Ole's Big Game Steakhouse and Lounge, opened by a local kid, Rosser "Ole" Herstedt, as the curtain closed on Prohibition. We step inside to have a look at its knotty-pine walls adorned with animals native to the United States — bucks, steers, rams, antelope, elk, fox — and foreign: a lion, leopard, elephant, giraffe, zebra, dik-dik, python, and even a baboon. Encased in glass is the bar's prized possession, killed by Ole in 1969 while he was hunting on an ice floe between Alaska and Siberia: a polar bear. Also here is the animal that hunters before Ole nearly drove to extinction: the bison. The restaurant is as much a shrine to one man's exploits as it is an exhibit on humanity's need for collective restraint.

Past Ole's, a cattle feedlot stretches for a mile. For a state with more cattle than people, this is the first large-scale operation we've seen. As the landscape gets drier, we are moving from corn country to cattle country, to the town that was the terminus of the great cattle drives from Texas: Ogallala, named for the branch of the Sioux who once lived in the region. Across the United States, settlers named places for native tribes less in their honor than in their memory, a way for settlers to glorify and romanticize their own conquering success — like taxidermy hung on the wall, or a scalp raised high during a *Wild West* show. A town named for the Oglala was built to service a railroad the Oglala fought to stop, and its main business was transporting to Chicago's slaughterhouses the cattle that had displaced the bison the Oglala had hunted here for generations.

Ogallala now bills itself as the state's "Cowboy Capital," with a block-long replica of a frontier town built in 1964. There's a free cowboy museum, which helps bring people into the gift shop, restaurant, and saloon. During summer months, the saloon hosts campy musical revues with singing, dancing, and gunfighting — the ghost of *Buffalo Bill's Wild West*, no longer America's National Entertainment but still haunting towns and family vacations. In the hunt for greater understanding of our shared heritage, myths are the biggest of the big game — the most prized and valuable, and also the hardest to kill, if only because of the fear of what might replace them.

We need national myths. They help us understand our shared identity, they reflect our values, and they guide our ethics. And we need to be able to preserve those that ennoble our character, while hunting down those that diminish it and creating new ones where needed.

A dirt road shoots off the Lincoln Highway at California Hill, the first steep ascent that Oregon Trail travelers encountered on the way to their promised land. We had heard that wagon ruts are still visible on parts of trail, but as we walk through the prairie grass, we are astonished at how many we see and how fresh they appear: deep and wide, often with no grass growing in them, as though vehicles still come through. Up this hill came some sixty thousand wagons carrying four hundred thousand people. Though the settlers were glorified as rugged individuals, the journey west was an exercise in collective action. "The wagon was plainly a community vehicle: everything about it required traveling in groups," wrote Daniel Boorstin in his trilogy, *The Americans*. "To cross deep streams or climb steep slopes the ox teams had to be doubled and the wagons managed one at a time. Many ways were found to use the group's total resources to conquer obstacles and reduce risk."

Travelers were highly dependent on one another for survival, and together, they risked death daily — from native attacks, but more from disease, starvation, and hypothermia — to find a better life, one blessed by God or gold or other great gains. Many did not make it. Looking down at the ruts, Laurel and I are filled with awe. The idea that we have spent even a second worrying about a broken toilet pedal and a busted bumper now seems absurd.

In the distance, a freight train comes rumbling along the South Platte River, just beyond the Lincoln Highway and just before Interstate 80. Four generations of westward movement, all in one place. The fifth is flying miles overhead. What will be the sixth? It's a question that evokes a word with a singularly American meaning, *frontier*.

The word did not even appear in the first dictionary compiled by a native-born American, in 1798, and it did not burrow deep into the national psyche until a University of Wisconsin professor delivered a lecture at the 1893 World's Fair in Chicago titled "The Significance of the Frontier in American History." Frederick Jackson Turner developed the lecture after concluding, "The story of the peopling of America has not yet been written. We do not understand ourselves." For Turner, the lack of a coherent narrative meant a lack of a shared identity: "Until such a work is furnished, we shall have no real national consciousness."

Turner positioned westward expansion as the defining feature of the nation's identity and culture — a force for democracy, assimilation, individualism, and nationalism. He called the frontier "the line of most rapid and effective Americanization." The farther Americans pushed away from Europe geographically, battling and conquering an unforgiving wilderness, the more they forged their own character. "In the crucible of the frontier the immigrants were Americanized, liberated and fused into a mixed race," he declared, a wilderness forerunner of the urban melting pot metaphor.

Turner's thesis flipped on its head the usual understanding of America's origin story, replacing northern Pilgrims and southern planters with western settlers as the central characters and anchoring the story in the simple and solitary virtues of log cabin life that gave rise to a people who resembled Lincoln, whom he called in his lecture "the greatest frontiersmen." In Turner's telling, Native Americans were an afterthought, and expanding the frontier was a mostly peaceful affair, a triumph of perseverance and ingenuity. "The existence of an area of free land," he wrote, ignoring native claims to it, "its continuous recession, and the advance of American settlement westward, explain American development." By shunting Native Americans to the fringes of America's history, Turner was completing work begun by his father, who owned and edited a newspaper that had successfully sought to banish the Winnebago and Menominee Indians from their Wisconsin homes.

Across the street from the hall where Turner delivered his lecture, Buffalo Bill ran two shows a day in an arena that held eighteen thousand people. It was the fair's most popular attraction, thanks largely to the many Native Americans Cody employed — some of whom had been sitting in federal prison until he sprang them, not to freedom but to his employ, by promising federal officials that, as a condition of their release, he would hire them for his show and take them out of the country on a European tour, where they could cause the army no trouble. Such were the options for Native Americans: helping whites rewrite history in ways that dehumanized themselves, or remain imprisoned — behind bars or on a reservation.

Like Turner, Cody considered himself a historian and educator, and, like Turner, he saw the frontier as the American crucible. But where Turner saw a mostly peaceful triumph over nature, Cody saw a violent conquest over native people. "Without the bullet," Wild West programs read, "America would not be a great, free, united, and powerful country." And rather than diminishing natives' role in the story, as Turner did, Cody elevated them into fierce and powerful adversaries, thus magnifying American victories.

Although Cody's show was more faithful to central historical forces than Turner's thesis, it would be Turner's work that would dominate academia for generations, shape the "national consciousness," just as he had aimed to do, and permeate political rhetoric. One of his professors, Woodrow Wilson, invoked Turner's thesis in celebrating America's territorial acquisitions in the 1898 war with Spain: our "new frontiers beyond the seas . . . Who shall say where it will end." Nearly every president since has invoked the frontier as a symbol of any new challenge facing the country. Its enduring popularity lies in the unifying nature of the noble qualities it conveys — courage, industriousness, forward-mindedness — and the shared national mission it inspires: to advance, to lead, to be first among nations. And who forges across those frontiers? The pioneer, of course — rugged, fearless, independent, ambitious, the western echo of Horatio Alger's urban stories of boys pulling themselves up by their bootstraps and out of poverty through their own discipline and determination. The model for each archetype was — who else? — the poor boy born in the log cabin, Abe Lincoln, though it didn't hurt his prospects that he married a woman from one of the area's wealthiest families.

Of course, there was always another view of the frontier and the pioneer, one long ignored, disparaged, and dismissed, one that saw pioneers in much the same way that many now see those crossing the southern border: as migrants and invaders.

"Welcome to Colorful Colorado," a brown sign reads, though many people crossing the border are looking for the green signs of marijuana dispensaries. The first small town over the border, Julesburg, was once on the south side of the river, where the Pony Express route ran. It moved to the north side after the Sioux, Cheyenne, and Arapaho attacked it in 1864, killing about a dozen soldiers and several others (native casualties weren't recorded) and burning it to the ground. That attack and others like it were in retaliation for one of the worst massacres in US history, when seven hundred volunteers in the Colorado state militia under the command of Colonel John Chivington, a Methodist minister, laid waste to a Cheyenne village at Sand Creek, two hundred miles south of Julesburg.

Following the massacre, Chivington hailed it as a great victory against a fierce fighting force that was "900 to 1,000 warriors strong." His account may have become the official historical record but for a report filed by Captain Silas Soule to Major Edward "Ned" Wynkoop, which stated that Chivington and other officers "declared their intention to massacre the friendly Indians camped on Sand Creek." When Soule protested, his fellow soldiers threatened to hang him.

The Sand Creek village included at least four Cheyenne leaders who had met with Lincoln the previous year, when he invited a delegation of Apache, Arapaho, Caddo, Cheyenne, Comanche, and Kiowa leaders to the White House. Lincoln could not afford a western war while fighting a southern one, nor for the tribes to enlist with the Confederacy. "It is the object of this government to be on terms of peace with you, and with all our red brethren," Lincoln told them. "We make treaties with you, and will try to observe them." *Try.* He knew what was coming, and he told them as much: "If our children should sometimes behave badly, and violate these treaties, it is against our wish. You know it is not always possible for any father to have his children do precisely as he wishes them to do."

Lincoln could hardly control the army, no less settlers, but he sought to assure his visitors that the newer arrivals were peaceful. "Although we are now engaged in a great war between one another, we are not, as a race, so much disposed to fight and kill one another as our red brethren." That claim, given the tribes' experience with white people and the Civil War's rapidly rising casualty count, may have rung hollow to the native leaders, but they committed not to align with the Confederacy, and Lincoln gave them peace medals to take home, as symbols of friendship.

As Chivington's troops advanced at Summit Springs, one of those White House visitors, Black Kettle, raised high the American flag that had been given to him in a treaty negotiation. He told villagers not to be afraid and not to run — the army came in peace. He had been promised so by the army officer in command of a nearby fort, and even by the commander in chief himself. More than 150 years later, it is still difficult to read Soule's report of what happened next.

> I refused to fire and swore that none but a coward would. For by this time hundreds of women and children were coming towards us and getting on their knees for mercy . . . I tell you Ned it was hard to see little children on their knees have their brains beat out by men professing to be civilized. One squaw was wounded and a fellow took a hatchet to finish her, she held her arms up to defend her, and he cut one arm off, and held the other with one hand and dashed the hatchet through her brain. One squaw with her two children, were on their knees begging for their lives of a dozen soldiers, within ten feet of them all, firing . . . I saw two Indians hold one of another's hands, chased until they were exhausted, when they kneeled down, and clasped each other around the neck and were both shot together. They were all scalped, and as high as half a dozen taken from one head. They were all horribly mutilated. One woman was cut open and a child taken out of her, and scalped. White Antelope, War Bonnet and a number of others had Ears and Privates cut off. Squaw's snatches were cut out for trophies. You would think it impossible for white men to butcher and mutilate human beings as they did there, but every word I have told you is the truth, which they do not deny.

Chivington's men killed some 160 people, most of them women, children, and the infirm. Black Kettle survived (Custer's cavalry would kill him a few years later, at the Washita River), but three other Cheyenne leaders who had been with him at the White House did not. A fifth, Lean Bear, had already been killed earlier that year, also by Chivington's troops, while carrying his peace medal and a note declaring him a friend to whites — signed, *A. Lincoln.*

Soule's report triggered a congressional investigation that forced the colonel to retire and dashed his political aspirations. A few months later, Soule was shot and killed on the streets of Denver, reputedly, though it was never proved, in retaliation for his honesty and courage.

The Cheyenne massacre was an abominable betrayal and a dark stain upon the country. Yet there was no US commemoration of the attack at the site until 2007, when the park service opened the Sand Creek National Historic Site, over the objections of those who viewed it as an insult to the military. Only six thousand people visit the remote location each year, one of the lowest numbers for any National Park Service site. Those who come through Julesburg are more likely to visit the Pony Express Monument than they are to encounter the story of why the town was set ablaze. Coming to terms with stories like Sand Creek, and fully integrating them into the American story, is a frontier we are still just beginning to forge.

— 27 —

Dueling Realities

Although Philip K. Dick never lived in Fort Morgan, Colorado, he's buried here in the family plot. In books like *The Man in the High Castle*, Dick explored the nature of reality and illusion, hallucination and psychosis, and the role of the mind — and the external forces that work upon it — in the formation of identity and the construction of reality. "The two basic topics which fascinate me," he wrote in a 1978 essay, "are 'What is reality?' and 'What constitutes the authentic human being?'" In the essay, he explained the difficulties inherent in these questions that are easy to overlook.

> Maybe each human being lives in a unique world, a private world, a world different from those inhabited and experienced by all other humans. And that led me to wonder, If reality differs from person to person, can we speak of reality singular, or shouldn't we really be talking about plural realities? And if there are plural realities, are some more true (more real) than others? What about the world of a schizophrenic? Maybe, it's as real as our world. Maybe we cannot say that we are in touch with reality and he is not, but should instead say, His reality is so different from ours that he can't explain his to us, and we can't explain ours to him. The problem, then, is that if

> subjective worlds are experienced too differently, there occurs a breakdown of communication . . . and there is the real illness.

Illness isn't just a breakdown of the body or mind. It's the breakdown of dialogue and understanding. And it has spread, like a contagion, all over the land. Earlier this week, to slow the spread of one virus driving the illness, Facebook announced that it would remove all QAnon content from its pages, a week after the House of Representatives passed a resolution condemning the group. Seventeen Republicans and one Republican-turned-independent voted against the resolution, and the Republican congressional candidates who have spoken of it approvingly include Colorado's Lauren Boebert, who told an audience: "Everything that I've heard of Q, I hope that this is real."

Plural realities are not a new challenge to our democracy, but the dangers they heighten — of violence and vigilantism — have brought down many others.

We are heading for Denver today, by way of the Kiowa Creek Sporting Club. Guns have been a frequent backdrop to our journey, from the rifles used at Gettysburg and Homestead and all across the frontier, to the pistols used by anarchists, outlaws, white supremacists, and vigilantes of every kind, to the blanks fired by *Wild West* entertainers, to the semi-automatic handguns used by police officers and criminals, to the AR-15 fired by the shooter at the Tree of Life Synagogue. America's relationship with guns is deeply rooted in our history. In western Pennsylvania, we passed through a town where settlers attacked British forces who had seized their guns — the first colonial attack on the British in America, a decade before the celebrated Battles of Lexington and Concord, motivated by a defense of a liberty we're still fighting over today: the right to bear arms.

Here at the sporting club, a sign covers the window beside the front door. "Attention Customers," it reads, notifying us that because of federal law and the Fourth Amendment, "we cannot legally ask you about your medical condition. Therefore, if we see you without a mask, we will assume you have a medical condition and we will welcome you inside to support our business." The sign is a wink. But we enter with our masks on. When preparing to shoot a gun, it's best to follow all precautions, even those that come from the government. Or so it seems to us.

Inside, we meet Daniel and Katie Moore, in their late twenties and five years married. Katie's family started the shooting club in the 1990s, around the time her father got out of the navy and couldn't put his geology degree to work. She and Daniel now run it, and we sit down on a patio overlooking their rolling hills.

"There were some neighbors around here convinced we were going to shoot the school bus," Katie says of the club's first days. "My mom and dad said, 'Well, our kids will be on it, so we probably won't be doing that.' But we bought enough land — two hundred acres — to avoid having issues with neighbors. We now have 750 in total. You're not in a fenced-in area, so it makes it very natural, without having to drive more than about forty-five minutes from Denver. You have a good amount of land to go out and have the most authentic planted bird hunt you can find."

Authentic planted bird hunt. What a beguiling phrase. What does it mean?

"The birds are raised in Kansas but they are native to the area," says Daniel, who notes that they have very little human contact. "The division of wildlife loves us, because the ones that get away, once they leave our property, they are wild birds, so you need to have a license to hunt them. People say, 'Oh, you raise birds and you shoot them.' But the wild birds that are out there, a lot of them are raised birds." Since the days of Buffalo Bill, it has been difficult to separate the wildness of the west from the westernization of the wild.

People choose the number of birds they want released — pheasant, quail, and chukar — and set out with a guide and dog. "You have to have a guide to hunt," Daniel says. "Some places you don't require it, but here we make you do it, which is a good thing, but some of our customers don't like it."

"There's some people that just want to go out by themselves, and you can understand that," Katie explains. "The biggest reason that the guides are out there is to make sure that everyone's watching what they're doing. And the guides will even say to someone, if they're just continuously unsafe, 'No, you don't get to hunt anymore. Just sit out.'"

"We're pretty strict on safety," Daniel says. They require customers to have taken a hunter's education course. "Since we're private property, we don't have to require it, but we put that in place for ourselves."

"For liability," Katie explains, "and you don't want someone going out there that's never hunted before and has no idea what they're doing."

"Well, it's fine if you've never done it," Daniel clarifies, "but we just want you to take that step."

"Right," says Katie. "We don't require a hunter safety for the sporting clay course, because you're in shooting cages, and we have guys that are down there monitoring you. It's a much more controlled environment."

"We'll watch you, and if you break a rule," Daniel adds, "we're going to say something about it. Not only us, but our customers will do the same. It's a community thing, because we don't want an accident happening." Nothing can ruin a hunt like a bit of irresponsibility. "It's all about having fun," he says. "Politically, the gun talk is mostly negative, but you come out here and realize, 'Oh, there's positives.' I've never had a new shooter come out here and not have fun. And I love it when that happens, because it kind of educates people. This shotgun shooting, it's all for fun."

"The extremists are the squeaky wheels, and then there's the rest of us that are kind of in the middle," Katie says. "There is a lot more common ground than we hear about. I don't really watch the news very much because there's so much Chicken-Little-ing everywhere. Whichever side you're on, it's all Chicken Little."

"What do you think of the idea of safety requirements for gun ownership?" I ask.

"I don't think it's a bad idea to have, say, a course," says Daniel.

"Like a hunter's ed course," Katie adds.

"But," Daniel says, beginning to pull back, "it's a slippery slope." Katie agrees: "Yeah, it's a tricky question. I understand that some people, especially in sad situations, they say, 'We've got to have more legal blocks.' But it's the people that aren't law abiding that work their way around that, and then they make it hard on the people that do go through the proper channels. Felons that have guns in inner cities get them off the black market and the serial number's sawed off. Those are truly the people that frustrate us because they are ruining it for those of us that are doing everything by the book."

"And the common criminal doesn't want you to have a handgun," Daniel says. "So if you implemented a safety course, would that have stopped most of the violence that happened? I doubt it, because most of the time, they have that gun illegally. And would they go through those channels? Probably not. And so do you just make it harder for law-abiding people? How much is that going to help? And does it stop there? Or does it keep going when something else happens? And then all of a sudden, you blink and the Second Amendment is gone. We need to enforce laws we have right on the books right now. And half the problem is that's not happening."

"What about," I ask, "the responsibilities that come with the right to own a gun — not only knowing how to use it but also putting it into safe storage when you're not?"

"I think there could be sensible laws," Daniel replies, "but I think it should be local. It shouldn't be a federal blanket, because what we do out here is totally different from what they do in Denver."

"That's the most frustrating part, the blanket laws that are supposed to apply to everyone, no matter what lifestyle you live," says Katie. "There's farmers that carry a rifle in the back of their truck because you might have a cow that you've come across that broke their leg and you've got to put them down. Should they have to have a trigger lock on it 100 percent of the time? It's locked up in the gun rack in the back of their truck. It's plenty safe. They don't have kids in the truck because it's a farm truck."

"You have to have ammo over here and your firearm over there" — Daniel's gesturing to opposite sides of his body, referring to laws that require them to be stored separately. Katie picks up his point: "People that don't know what they're talking about are making blanket laws that are supposed to protect everybody. But they don't actually apply in a commonsense way to everybody. In the last couple of years, there was a state senator that authored the bill that got the magazine requirement down to ten versus thirty for AR-15s and those kind of rifles. And the thing that makes us conservatives and gun enthusiasts laugh is that that lady in particular, she clearly had no knowledge, because she was convinced that when you use a magazine from a gun, you simply throw it away. That's not the case. It just shows how uneducated they are on the topic, but they're making those kinds of laws."

"But when people can get off so many rounds in a theater," I say, "or another public place without stopping —"

"I understand that point of view," Daniel counters, "but also, I could reload a ten-round clip just as fast as I could shoot. If you have any little bit of training, it takes two seconds. Literally, it's drop a mag; grab a mag off of you; put it in; and you're going. And so if it's ten or thirty, I don't know if that is going to make a difference. I don't think that's going to fix the situation. The AR-15 looks scary and that's what the whole thing is about. But really, if you broke it down and looked at it, it would look like just like any other rifle that you would hunt with."

"So that's the frustration for us here in Colorado," says Katie, "and it does seem like it's a very slippery slope. You have these people at the top that are making those decisions and have no knowledge of it whatsoever. People need to educate themselves before they write laws. A lot of people who are pro-gun-control haven't fired a gun before."

I'm one of them, but not Laurel. She's even fired a gun in Manhattan. Not long after we started dating, she attended an office holiday party at an old Italian social club in Greenwich Village with a shooting range in the basement. While being supervised by a retired police officer, she lifted a rifle to her shoulder and squeezed off six rounds at a paper cutout of a man aiming a pistol at her. She brought the cutout home and proudly showed me the evidence: two bullets square between his eyes, one direct on his nose, one to his throat, one to his chest, and one for good measure to the, as the Italians might say, *coglioni*. She was a regular Annie Oakley. And with a wink, she let me know there was more where that came from if I didn't watch out.

We pick up shotguns in the clubhouse and Katie and Daniel show us how to carry them, muzzles always pointed at the ground. At the clay stations, they give us a lesson on loading a shell, handling the gun safely, and aiming.

"We throw about 2.8 million clays a year," Daniel says, "which is the most in the state of Colorado."

My first shot is high. Then behind. The clay moves fast. I miss all six shots. Laurel takes a turn and finds it harder than shooting a stationary target. Each of us goes another round, missing all our shots. Daniel tells me to keep my eye on the tip of the barrel, not the clay, and move the barrel with the clay. On my next shot — pop! A hit! Everyone cheers. Daniel gives Laurel the same advice, and on her first shot — pop! Another hit! Bigger cheers.

We thank them for their hospitality — we've enjoyed talking with them and listening to them. I've heard a lot of their arguments before — about how carrying guns makes people safer in stores and public places, the danger of slippery slopes, the national security benefits of a well-armed populace, and the fact that criminals will always find a way around laws. But they've also made points we haven't thought much about, including the reluctance of residents in remote areas to rely on law enforcement. "If you have someone breaking into your house and it's ten minutes until police come, what are you going to do?" asks Katie. She posed the question to us, but Daniel answers it: "I'm not going to have someone coming to my house and hurt my children or my wife."

Gun ownership is personal for them. I'm not going to sway them by pointing out that studies show homes with guns are more likely to suffer homicide, suicide, and serious injury from guns than homes without them, including accidental shootings, and that home shootings are far more likely to injure or kill a domestic partner than an intruder. Unlike Daniel and Katie, many people, especially those prone to violence, tend not to be interested in safety protocols and lawful behavior. It makes perfect sense to me that laws should try to account for that aspect of human nature by adopting the same kinds of safeguards that are required here at the club, where hunters must take a safety course, where they must carry their guns responsibly, and where they can lose the right to their gun if they endanger someone's life. And while for Daniel and Katie that aspect of human nature will always find its way around laws, making them wary of government restrictions, I also heard in their words and tone at least some measure of openness to considering ideas they are skeptical of, if more legislators spent more time learning about guns and what matters to gun owners.

As we drive off, my mind returns to something Daniel said: "There should be understanding that we all want well for each other." *We all want well for each other.* That's not something we hear much in politics. Much of political discourse is about how the other side is trying to destroy both you and your way of life and the country — the Chicken-Little-ing that Katie talked about. Politics as apocalypse.

"I just wish people could talk more and not get so offended," Daniel said. "That's why I just can't stand politics, because I don't think we're that far apart. I mean, if we just sit down and talk and understand their point of view, and then you could respectfully disagree." And maybe even inch toward respectful agreement, too.

Twenty miles and a world away from the vast open fields surrounding the shooting club is the Denver suburb of Centennial, which stands between the sites of two mass shootings that made national headlines: Columbine High School in 1999 and an Aurora movie theater in 2012. We park in front of the home of Tom Sullivan, whose son, Alex, was at the Aurora theater for a midnight showing of a new Batman movie. It was his twenty-seventh birthday. He was shot and killed, two days shy of his first wedding anniversary, along with eleven others. Dozens more were wounded.

I used to work with one of the survivors from that night, Stephen Barton, who was shot in the head, neck, chest, and arms with more than twenty rounds. He was on a cross-country bicycle trip after graduating college. During his recovery, he went to work for the organization that became Everytown for Gun Safety, founded by Michael Bloomberg. I told him I'd be coming through Denver, and he put me in touch with Tom, who also turned grief into political action.

"I tried reaching out to my electeds who are in this district, tried to get meetings with them," Tom says, about the aftermath of the shooting, as we sit in his backyard. "They would not meet with me. They wouldn't have time for me. So okay, enough is enough. I ran against them. All of a sudden, now they want to have coffee."

He lost the race but won his second, for state assembly. "The first bill that we ran was an extreme risk protection order. And now, because Democrats have got the Senate, the House, and the governor, we were able to pass that law. But we did it without any Republicans. Not a single one would vote for that."

"What are your conversations with Republicans like?"

"They don't talk to me. This whole persona of a parent of a murdered child who's facing them every single day is a conversation they're incapable of having. They don't have that within them to even attempt it. So they stay away from me. If they would actually listen to my story, it could be their stories. It's only through the grace of God that their kid wasn't sitting in that movie theater the night that Alex was, because gun violence doesn't care about your sex, your gender, your political affiliation. It doesn't care. If they really give themselves an opportunity to think of it in that way, that's what scares them. So they try to avoid it." And when they can't avoid it, they dismiss him.

"Republicans will say to me, 'Oh, I can't imagine what that is like.' Then the very next thing they say is, 'Oh, but because of that, I understand that you probably want to repeal the Second Amendment. You wouldn't want any guns to ever be sold again. And you're probably figuring out where my guns are and how to get them.' I mean, they jump right from that to that. When we're talking to people, I hear: 'Oh, yeah. You're anti-gun. I understand what happened in your life, but you're anti-gun.' No, I'm not. You can have all you want. What I'm asking you to do is be responsible with it. I get women who will see me and just start to cry. They understand who I am and why I'm doing what I'm doing. And from people who don't know me, I will get: 'Oh, well, yeah. Oh, sorry about that.' No. That was my son. There's no, 'Sorry about that.' Guy walked into the movie theater with three pieces of equipment and over three hundred rounds of ammunition and opened fire on people. There's no sorry about that. There's something we can do about that. The guy walked in with a hundred-round drum. You can't tell me that if he had to change out that magazine seven, eight times, because there was a limit of fifteen, that he would have still been able to do what he did, that Alex wouldn't have had an opportunity — each one of those times when he was switching out, Alex would have had an opportunity to get below something and save himself. You can't tell me that, because he opened fire with that hundred-round drum, and it didn't stop until it jammed up after he had fired sixty-three bullets."

It's almost like he's responding to Daniel and Katie — that the magazine limit doesn't stop someone bent on a mass shooting — because he's heard it so many times. But he doesn't believe it and never will. He may well be right. And even if he's wrong, what's indisputable is this: A magazine limit *might* have given Alex and others a fighting chance. "My story," he says, "is to tell people: 'It could be you. And we can figure out a way on this.'"

Tom ticks through some bills he's pushing. "We had one on lost and stolen firearms. All it does is make sure that you have to report if your firearm was lost or stolen. Law enforcement should know. They've done surveys: 95 percent of Democrats and 87 percent of Republicans across the country support it. It's in the high 80s between rural and urban. And what we were going to do is fine you $25 if you didn't report it, hoping that that would make people lock their cars before they left, not leave the firearm on the front seat of the car when they went inside. Because that's what was happening. The kids, they were just opening the car doors and getting them. Here in Denver this year, we've had seven hundred firearms that have been stolen out of cars. We're not taking anything away from anybody. All we're asking you to do is to report that. And they still want to say, 'Oh, that's the beginning of the end.' That's always one of the places that they go, the whole 'Oh, everything's a slippery slope.' Well, no. It's not a slippery slope. Same thing with safe storage. All we're asking you to do is get yourself a safe, get yourself a gun lock. Do something like that, because we're having these kids — we had a seven-year-old, it was an accident, but he murdered his three-year-old sister, because Mom left a shotgun sitting on the kitchen table. Kid picked it up and shot it and killed his sister."

Tom, Daniel, and Katie all want gun owners to be responsible. Tom believes laws will increase responsibility. Daniel and Katie generally don't. Seeing it from the other side may not change minds, but it can increase understanding and empathy — that, in itself, can save lives. Maybe even the life of a man who was just killed in Denver.

In between our shooting clays and arriving at the Sullivan house, an altercation occurred in downtown Denver near the statehouse on the Lincoln Highway. A Patriot Muster rally organized by a conservative group and its militia auxiliary prompted a counter-demonstration by local communist, socialist, and other activist groups. The two competing demonstrations occurred in the shadow of a statue of Kit Carson that had stood until June, when the city removed it following George Floyd protests that toppled two others, a decision that did not sit well with the Patriot Muster crowd.

Carson has long been a celebrated western figure and the embodiment of manifest destiny for guiding John Fremont to the Oregon territory (Buffalo Bill named his youngest son Kit Carson Cody). But his battles with Native Americans and the scorched-earth campaign he waged against the Navajo — forcing them onto a three-hundred-mile Long Walk that left some two hundred dead in 1864 — have led some to call for his honors to be rescinded. Which side has the stronger claim?

Let's ask the two questions we posed about Woodrow Wilson: Why was the monument erected? To celebrate his exploration of the west, his defenders say, not the killing of Native Americans, but it can be hard to separate the two. And did he, on the whole, help advance the nation toward a more perfect union and its promise of equality — or fight those leading the way? It's a question on which, even after a thorough examination of his complicated history, reasonable people of good faith can disagree. The important thing is to keep talking, peaceably.

When the protest and counter-protest ended, a young black man and a middle-aged white man, Lee Keltner, got into an argument. As the black man got animated and loud, Keltner, a Navy veteran wearing a T-shirt that read, "BLM: You're fucking right bikers lives matter," pulled out a can of bear spray and held it by his side, remaining calm — until he saw someone filming the confrontation. "Get the cameras out of here," he shouted as he walked toward him, "or I'm gonna fuck you up!" A security guard stepped between Keltner and the local television producer filming the scene, putting his hand on Keltner's chest to keep him away. "Don't fuckin' touch me," said Keltner, hitting him in the head.

What happened next may never be clear. Keltner's supporters say he backed away. The security guard said he saw Keltner reach for something. A photo captures the two of them about six feet apart, Kelter shooting orange bear spray, the security guard pointing a gun at him — a split second before he fired, killing Keltner.

Keltner owned and ran Crossfire Hats, custom-making each one. His slogan: "Keeping the west alive, one hat at a time." A colleague in the ranch-wear business, Steve Weil, told the *Denver Post*: "He was your quintessential western kind of guy. You know, he lived the western lifestyle. He was the real deal." In the shadow of Kit Carson's dethroned monument, myth and reality collided, leaving a bloody mess. "What has happened to our society that politics has become deadly?" asked Weil. "And how do we come back from that?"

Tom Sullivan has answers to those questions. And however unpopular they are with the Patriot Muster crowd, and whether any law could have saved Lee Keltner, there can be no question that Tom is at least attempting to grapple with an undeniable reality: a dead body. When a college student asked Philip K. Dick to define *reality* in one sentence, he wrote: "I thought about it and finally said, 'Reality is that which, when you stop believing in it, doesn't go away.' That's all I could come up with."

Whatever their beliefs about guns and the western lifestyle, the Keltner family's reality isn't going away. Neither is Tom Sullivan's. And neither is ours. "I mean, it could be you," Tom said.

— 28 —

Beer Break

Our first baseball game of the pandemic comes with a surprise. Our friends Ryan and Tennaly have generously invited us into their Denver home for a break from the road, and as we watch their son Kenan's Little League game, people begin whispering and nodding in the direction of right field, where a tall figure throws batting practice: Peyton Manning. In Denver, seeing the quarterback who brought the city its third Super Bowl championship toss a ball, any ball, is like being in Vatican City and happening upon the pope sprinkling holy water. Laurel notices him before I do — she knows her Manning brothers, and thankfully it isn't Eli, or I might have lost her.

In the final inning, Kenan steps to the plate with runners on, his team trailing. He takes a good swing, and another, but there will be no joy in Mudville. After the game, all the kids on both teams line up and, in lieu of handshakes, hold their hats high and wave them at each other. When Kenan comes over to us, he's terribly disappointed but keeping his chin up. Accepting defeat graciously is one of the hardest and most important lessons youth sports can teach about life, and citizenship. Kenan's handling it like a champ.

Our plan to go for a hike gets scotched — it's snowing in the mountains — so we head downtown and bounce around the same neighborhood where Sal Paradise spent a week "listening to jazz, drinking booze in Negro saloons, and gabbing till five o'clock in the morn" in Jack Kerouac's

On the Road. Our final stop is a brewery in Lincoln Park overlooking the South Platte River: Raices. The name is Spanish for "roots," and it was named the best new brewery of the year by a local magazine, no small feat in a city that's a craft beer mecca. When our family took a cross-country trip in 1983, there were forty-nine breweries in the United States. Today there are about a hundred in Denver alone. I remember being in Colorado during that family trip and watching my father try a local beer he'd never had before: Coors. Usually his favorite beer was whatever was cheapest, although when my mother brought home a six-pack of cans labeled, simply, "BEER," he began requesting the second-cheapest option.

Behind the bar at Raices is José Beteta, forty-one, who arrived in America at age thirteen from Costa Rica with his parents, crossing into the country illegally. As we sample flights of beer, he tells us his story.

"About four and a half years ago, I had the idea of opening a Latino brewery," he says. "I hadn't seen one. And the idea just kind of came to me." Only a tiny fraction of US breweries are Latin-owned, despite the fact that Latino consumers account for almost 20 percent of the beer market. José was not new to entrepreneurship. In Boulder, he ran the county's Latino Chamber of Commerce, growing it from 10 members to more than 150 and starting an outreach program to teach entrepreneurship to students who — because of their gender, ethnicity, race, income, or sexual orientation — rarely saw reflections of themselves among business owners. Young Rebels, he called it — and he's one himself. He got the opportunity to run the chamber only because, after seeing a play featuring unauthorized immigrants telling their stories, he decided to stop hiding. And when the Boulder city council passed a law allowing anyone to serve on boards and commissions, he applied to one and was appointed — maybe the first unauthorized immigrant to serve in a public office in the modern era.

To open the brewery, he saved for years and took out a small-business loan, but he still needed more financing, which he saw as a chance to begin community outreach. "We put out there a $400,000 investor opportunity, but we didn't want to just bring in any investor. We wanted to bring in new investors — people of color, women. And so most of the investments are between $5,000 and $10,000. We have about forty people who are investors here who have never invested in their life, most of them."

He wasn't just opening a business. He was running a master class in community-based capitalism. "That was the other part of the education of the Latino community," he says. "It's not only about becoming an entrepreneur, but it's also learning about ways to make money other than active income. We wanted to teach them about passive income and all these other investment tools." But this wasn't an academic exercise or a philanthropic endeavor. It was his career. In such a competitive market, he knew he needed a strong business plan.

"I brought in my wife, and I brought in Martin, our brewer, and we polished this idea of, 'What does it mean to be a Latino brewery?' And we worked on it, and worked on it, and worked on it, until we came to the realization that we have to be about three important pillars: community, culture, and beer. And all of them are going to come together to celebrate Hispanic and Latino culture — something that's been used against us to make us feel lesser, to make us feel ashamed of ourselves."

Paintings by local artists line the walls. On the patio, a brightly colored mural features figures wearing traditional Latin and Caribbean masks, their bodies growing from tree trunks and roots — *raices*. José points out the symbols: shamans (health and healing), a jaguar (strength and resilience), a maraca (music and dance), and a hummingbird. "In some of the Latin American countries," he explains, "the hummingbird is thought to travel back and forth in time. So it's a connection between the past, present, and future."

The taproom has a stage for events — music and dancing, open mic and karaoke, panels and discussions. "We had a five-part series called Racism Zero. And every week we talked about racial issues because that is something that is taboo in our culture. So we talked about racial issues here in the US, and we talked about racism in Latin American countries, which exists very much, too. And the next series is going to focus on the next step: How do we fix this?"

A lager in our beer sampler is called Vota! "That is a unique collaboration that we're going with the Denver Common Clerk's Office to encourage people to vote," José says. "This Thursday, for example, we have a ballot and beer event in which the clerk's office is going to come, and we're going to talk about each item on the ballot, so they can explain them in case people have questions. People can fill out their ballots, and then they can go and drop them off at the ballot boxes." José will be voting in his first presidential election. He recently became a citizen, after twenty-six years without legal documents. We raise our glasses to that.

In the progressive era, reformers saw bars as a pox on democracy. José is using his brewery and bar to show how capitalism can strengthen democracy.

"What a person who's not Latino gets out of this place aside from great products," he says, "is to experience and immerse yourself in this atmosphere, as if you were traveling to another country. And you feel included, and you feel and taste it, and hear and see everything that is our culture. Instead of you being a spectator, you are taking part in this whole thing."

We walk into their fifteen-barrel brewhouse and meet the head brewer, Martin, from Puerto Rico, who is self-taught. He was working at a local brewery when José found him. "I told him I didn't want an employee," says José. "I wanted a partner. Martin was like, 'Dude, I don't have any money.'"

"I can't contribute for shit," Martin says, recalling the conversation. "I have a truck, and I don't have shit."

"I was like, 'That's fine,'" says José. "'But you're going to put in sweat equity, and don't worry about leaving your job right now, because it's going to take about four years to open it.'"

"That's when I told myself," says Martin, "how in the hell am I going to say no to this?" He gives us a sample of a beer he's working on that features roasted poblano peppers from a local community garden. "Some of the proceeds will go back to the garden," says José, "even though they're not expecting it. We're going to surprise them."

On our way to Fort Collins, we pass a man in Loveland wearing a "Make America Great Again" hat and holding a sign reading, "Defeat Democrats. Save the USA. No on 113." Laurel looks up Proposition 113, and we learn that it asks voters whether they should approve or overturn a law passed by the state legislature that commits Colorado's presidential electors to voting for the winner of the national popular vote. The law will only go into effect once the number of states making the same commitment reaches 270 electoral votes, and the idea is to do an end run around the Constitution's Electoral College to ensure that the popular vote winner is also the electoral college winner — no matter what a state's voters may say. Only states with Democratic majorities have approved it, for the obvious reason: The past two Republican presidents have been elected while losing the popular vote. Elected officials in Democratic states have concluded that while it is politically impossible to amend the Constitution to abolish the Electoral College, since doing so requires ratification by two-thirds of states, it is possible to skirt the Constitution with support from less than half the states.

There is a lot of sense to scrapping the Electoral College. It turns losers into victors. It narrows down general election campaigning to about half a dozen states, making voters in all the other states irrelevant. It is antidemocratic, giving a select group the power to pick a president regardless of how the people vote. And it is — and must be, if the republic is to survive — entirely pro forma. No state's electors have ever, as a group, gone against the wishes of their citizens to elect a different candidate. To do so would be to court insurrection. Yet that is precisely what Proposition 113 proponents are unwittingly doing.

If electors can override voters to support the popular vote, why can't they override voters to elect whoever they please? There are news reports that some Republican state legislatures are considering directing their state's electors to do exactly that. And there is precedent for state legislatures choosing electors without regard for the people.

In August 1876, Colorado was admitted to the union by a Republican Congress. That November, rather than hold a presidential election, the Republican state legislature chose three electors who supported the Republican nominee, Rutherford B. Hayes. In several southern states, each party claimed victory, with each accusing the other of fraud. A congressional commission was created to adjudicate the parties' competing vote totals and slates of electors, handing Hayes the victory — by a single electoral vote.

The outcome, which marked the end of Reconstruction, has been the subject of countless studies, books, and debates. But often forgotten has been the Colorado state legislature's role in deciding the outcome without even asking the people what they thought. That the country survived it is not an argument for repeating it.

The guy in the red MAGA hat holding the sign has a point. Democrats pushing an Electoral College end run ought to be careful what they wish for. For all the rightful concern on the left about respecting and upholding the Constitution, this, too, is an effort to usurp it, one that will only make it easier for Republicans to undertake and justify their own attempts to do so.

— 29 —

Earth, Wind & Fire

We step onto Main Street, USA, or at least the inspiration for Walt Disney's version of it. When Disney wanted to re-create the feel of a 1910 downtown for the opening of his fantasyland in 1955, he hired a movie set designer, Harper Goff, to create it. Goff grew up here in Fort Collins, Colorado, which was founded as a military fort during the Civil War. "For those of us who remember the carefree time it re-creates," Disney said, "Main Street will bring back happy memories." Like his predecessor in mass entertainment, Buffalo Bill, Disney knew that nostalgia, especially for a place that people have idealized but never experienced, sells.

Although we see no historic theater here, Disney placed one on Main Street, USA, with a marquee announcing its feature: *Great Moments with Mr. Lincoln*. As a boy, Walt idolized Abe, and the gauzy film about his life and the Civil War still plays at Disneyland, and still makes no mention of what the war was fought over, allowing audiences to supply their own answers. As battle scenes unfold, a ballad written in 1951 is sung about two brothers who enlist on opposite and seemingly equal sides.

> *One was gentle, one was kind*
> *One came home, one stayed behind*
> *A cannonball don't pay no mind . . .*
> *All on a beautiful morning*

A Veterans of Foreign Wars post stands on the Lincoln Highway in Fort Collins, and inside, at the end of a long wooden bar, an older man sits with a newspaper and a middle-aged woman with a bottle of beer. The stools and tables are otherwise empty, except for a young volunteer, John Carpenter, wearing a baseball cap and face mask. I ask how he got involved in the VFW.

"I was in infantry, took a tour in Iraq, lost seven of our guys," he says matter of factly. He doesn't say anything about the seven men he lost, and I don't interrupt him. "A Vietnam friend of mine — he helped me out when I came back. I was struggling quite a bit. Really angry. Didn't know where to go, couldn't find a job. So he helped me navigate the VA system, get enrolled in community college, trying to better my life."

He says he felt isolated upon his return from service, and when faced with social or professional situations, he would shut down and walk away. "Working here has helped bring me out of my shell a little more. Despite the struggles, and I still have struggles, this organization helps me with my issues — by helping other people."

He works in construction now — odd jobs, word of mouth — and spends a lot of time here managing activities. We are standing near a sign that announces this Friday's dinner: "Kevin, Diana, and Alicia are cooking up something good!"

Covid has kept some members away, especially older ones. John is trying to recruit the younger generation. "They appreciate what we're trying to do, to transition to more wellness. We offer massage therapy on Mondays. We do yoga on Thursdays. Just things that help people relax. When you come through the doors, we treat you like family, and we want you to be acknowledged the minute you walk in and know that we care about you and want to do whatever we can to help you."

A lot of members need help, one way or another. "Maybe they're homeless, they need food, they need gas, books. So our auxiliary does a food pantry and hygiene items." Sometimes, he says, they just need someone to listen to them. I ask if people talk politics here.

"There's a wide variety of different political views, so we try not to keep the national news on. I try to keep it local — to what's pertinent to where we live, because those national debates can get heated. You can't debate someone because they get so hot over an issue. It's like, 'Wait a minute: I thought we were just discussing something here.' You can't really get a full perspective about something unless you can debate actively and listen.

The hard part of that is the listening. There's more waiting to respond than actual listening. I've encountered that a lot in the civilian world. You automatically hate this person — just because they have different views than you? What are you doing to try and understand where that view is coming from? It may be a generational thing. There may be some factual evidence behind why they think the way they think."

"It's a good sign they all keep coming back," I say.

"Yeah. We're all adults here, and we've all been in some horrible situations, so if we can't get over something as trivial as a differing perspective on how things operate — I don't know. Politics are really not my thing."

Listening with an open mind. Being slower to judge. Being more accepting of differences. Through his leadership of this post, he's fighting the war at home, too.

When I ask John what binds the country together, he says, "Our love of freedom, our ability to come and go as we please — except this year." He laughs through his mask. "There's a lot of really wonderful people in the world that just need to get out a little more and become a part of the community, give a hand to help somebody up. We find meaning through each other, helping each other, and being kind to each other. And I think that's one thing Americans do really well, when they do it. And when they don't" — he laughs again — "they do very well at that, too."

Before leaving, I bring the conversation back to Iraq, and I ask him where he served.

"I was —" he pauses "— in Sadr City my first tour. My first year went pretty well. We didn't have much happen. Second tour was kind of a nightmare."

"Second tour was when you lost seven members?"

"Yeah. We had twenty-one guys injured badly enough they had to be sent home. We would get shot at about every other day — about every day for a while. Definitely eye opening. Just the way that I saw some of the women and children — the way they were treated. They were blown up. It's heartbreaking." He tells the story of a kid who picked up an Iraqi improvised explosive device (IED) by the side of the road — Iraqis had concealed it in one of the food bags soldiers handed out. The bomb killed two kids and dismembered their mother, who was still alive when John's vehicle rushed her to get medical attention. "I appreciate going to war just for the understanding of how evil people can be to each other. It just reinforces, like, man — we just really need to be kind to each other, 'cause like, why shoot? If I kill this person, I create generations of people that hate

America and want to kill us. And if I show love and compassion, I may have saved generations. Just based on one decision."

There is no VFW Hall at Disney's Main Street, USA. It wouldn't fit "The Happiest Place on Earth." But we might be a happier country, or at least a more empathetic one, if we left stories of war to veterans like John Carpenter.

Waking up at a KOA in Fort Collins, I step outside Charley and am startled by the strong smell of smoke, which hits me before I see a dark-gray and burnt-orange cloud blocking out the sun. I quickly retreat inside, unsettled by the fiery sky that carries the whiff of apocalypse. I wake up Laurel, and we stare out the windows, never having seen anything like it. We had heard a wildfire was northwest of us but had not been tracking it. It was nearer than we realized, only about thirteen miles, and the wind has carried its smoke to our doorstep. We are a long way from the October days celebrated by the Colorado poet, novelist, and Native American rights activist Helen Hunt Jackson.

O suns and skies and clouds of June,
And flowers of June together,
Ye cannot rival for one hour
October's bright blue weather

As it happens, I have a 9:00 A.M. meeting with the director of the Colorado State University Energy Institute, Bryan Willson — our friend Ryan in Denver had put me in touch with him. When I arrive and say hello, he skips the pleasantries and offers a grim greeting. "You are breathing the worst air quality in the US — it's actually worse than Delhi." He calls the wildfires in the region "a sudden manifestation of a long-term issue" — climate change. "As we've gotten warmer winters," he says, "the pine bark beetles have come in and we've lost tens of millions of acres of forest that are standing" — a mass of kindling wood that has been waiting to go up. The fire started two months ago and is now the largest in state history. The previous record was just set in August. All of the ten largest fires in Colorado history have occurred since 2002. "Our forests are burning and we're seeing displacement related to our warming climate" — people being pushed off the land —"but, I'm a technology optimist."

The center Bryan runs is dedicated to clean energy development, and it's housed in a coal plant that closed in the 1970s. "Our motto is, science to solutions to scale," he says. "What we've tried to do is work to turn that science into real products and then work with companies to get them into production." It's part laboratory and part office space, a modern Bell Labs that connects businesses, faculty, and researchers. "We tend to think of Edison as the innovator," he says. "But the innovation is really the network — the group you bring together to get important stuff done. That's what I like to think we have here — an innovation network."

As we walk around the old coal plant, he shows off an engine to reduce emissions while compressing natural gas, a hydrogen-powered car students have built, a solar-powered microgrid to bring electricity to the billions without it, a machine to allow utilities to deploy wind energy more efficiently and reliably, and a project they're working on with the Gates Foundation: a clean-burning fecal sludge incinerator for the developing world — "the re-inventing the toilet challenge," he calls it. I had no idea this journey would be so full of toilet challenges.

He mentions that CSU is a land grant university that grew out of the Morrill Act, which Lincoln signed in 1862, three years after Darwin's *On the Origin of Species* was published. Science was moving quickly, and the land grant act was the federal government's first major effort to support science-related education, focusing on agriculture and industry. "The land grants were established to solve problems of the common people," Bryan says, and he sees his work as continuing that tradition. And just as his work faces political headwinds, so, too, did the land grants — opponents considered them elitist. As Minnesota senator Henry Rice put it: "We want no fancy farmers; we want no fancy mechanics."

Heading north, we return to October's bright-blue weather only to run into a more immediate danger: high winds. With both hands gripped tight on the wheel, I'm fighting gusts that are jerking and shaking Charley, rattling everything, including our nerves. I slow down to a crawl, but the jerking continues. Stressed and concentrating, I think back to what a neighbor in North Platte had told us about driving in wind: get sway bars. Too late for that. And soon, a thumping starts on the roof. Did something come loose? Finally, just over the Wyoming border, we see our stop for the night: the Terry Bison Ranch Resort, a campground, saloon, steakhouse, and animal zoo with ostriches, alpacas, and camels.

After turning off the engine and breathing a deep sigh of relief, I open the driver's-side door and — whoosh! The wind jolts it forward, testing the strength of the hinge. I force it shut and turn around to see that the wind has ripped the canopy off the roller tube that hangs over the slide-out, and it's been flapping against the roof. Laurel and I move a picnic table beside Charley, climb atop it, and roll the canopy back into place. It holds, but only for a few seconds before the winds pulls it off again. We roll it again, with the same result. I study the roller tube. There's a screw missing! But Laurel notices that it's not just screws — the stopper on the end appears to be broken. The best solution we can come up with is duct tape, which I apply liberally, to no avail. The wind is too strong. Even keeping my balance on the table is difficult. And then it dawns on me: Maybe standing beside an eleven thousand pound vehicle as the wind smashes into it isn't a great idea.

At the check-in desk, the ranch hand is unfazed by the wind — "That's Wyoming," she says — but a woman who just arrived via the interstate delivers some startling news. "We saw two semis blown over," she says. The obvious is now dawning on me. We should not have been on the road. I check the weather report and finally see the bulletin: "High Wind Warning . . . Winds 40 to 50 mph with gusts up to 75 mph . . . a high risk for vehicle blow overs." We dodged disaster, though not entirely unscathed. I have no idea how to fix the canopy, but it's late in the day and I'm drained. Is the saloon open?

It is, the ranch hand tells us, but she has another recommendation: The last train tour of the day is leaving in a few minutes, a one-hour ride through the ranch's bison pasture. For $15, we are welcomed aboard by a cowpoke comedian conductor, Jonathan, whose youthful blond hair spills out of his cowboy hat as he makes wide-eyed crazy claims using an exaggerated stage voice, ostensibly to entertain the two children on the train, but he knows it's a show for those who will fill the tip jar, too — and his auctioneer impression alone is worth the price of admission. He's not wearing a mask and announces that he will not let us open the windows because of his allergies to alfalfa. He assures us that any sneezing he does — and the sneezes come quickly — is not because of Covid, which he's already had. Twice. It's the alfalfa dust blowing in the wind.

As the train creeps down the tracks, Jonathan, who says he has a master's degree in computer science, gives us a bit of history on the ranch, which was bought in 1885 by Francis Warren, the richest man in the state, mayor of Cheyenne, governor, and US senator. One of the ranch's visitors, Theodore

Roosevelt, served as the honorary president of the American Bison Association, which formed in 1905 at the Bronx Zoo and helped save the bison from the extinction. On an 1889 hunt, Roosevelt wrote in his diary, "Few indeed are the men who now have or evermore shall have, the chance of seeing the mightiest of American beasts, in all his wild vigor, surrounded by the tremendous desolation of his far-off mountain home."

We stop at a herd that's waiting for the train, knowing what's coming: alfalfa pellets. Between sneezes, Jonathan instructs us on how to feed them: hold the pellet in the air, wait for a bison to stick out its tongue, and place it on the tongue. "You'll regret it if you don't do it — it's an experience!" He says one of their bison was in the movie *Dances with Wolves* and was so accustomed to being fed that, to get him to run, they had to throw Oreos out of a moving vehicle. Not exactly the wild vigor Roosevelt wrote of, but all the more American.

The train loops briefly into Colorado. In the nineteenth century through the 1950s, telling people that this rickety mini choo-choo would be the only privately operated interstate train in America would have prompted uproarious laughter. It would have been as absurd to them as the idea would have been to Native Americans in the first half of the nineteenth century that the bison, which had numbered somewhere between thirty and seventy-five million, would approach extinction.

Afterward, we head into the Senator's Steakhouse and Saloon and admire its gabled wooden ceiling and the wagon wheel chandeliers that hang above worn wooden floorboards. It's a cavernous barn, mostly empty, except for two small dinner parties and a trio of guitarists on stage. It feels safe to eat inside — our first indoor restaurant meal since the start of the pandemic — and we could not possibly leave the warm glow of the room and soft twang of the band.

I order the bison bacon cheeseburger, Laurel the bison meat loaf. Hers arrives smothered in gravy, mine in barbecue sauce, both with heaping piles of buttery mashed potatoes and vegetables. Compared with beef, bison has lower cholesterol, fewer calories, and less saturated fat, but I don't think this meal is extending our lives — and that's okay. Between the wildfire and wind, we feel we've already cheated death twice today.

"We don't call it winter here — we call it 'winder,'" says Steve Hrkach, a wind energy instructor at Laramie County Community College in Cheyenne, just up the road from the Terry Bison Ranch. Before getting caught in the windstorm, I had asked him if I could sit in on one of his classes. "I was twenty-five years in the air force," he says. "I worked on the Minuteman 2 and Minuteman 3 Peacekeeper weapons systems, so we climbed into a hole. When I retired in 2012, I thought: I'll do something different: I'll climb a tower. Same type of job — electric mechanical work — so it was an easy transition, but I was in my forties so it was a little more difficult physically. This is kind of a younger person's job."

Becoming a wind technician takes two years of hands-on skill development mixed with science, engineering, and critical thinking — brains and brawn, Steve says. "There's a lot of people that go to work in wind that have no experience and so the washout rate is high. They realize, 'Hey, this is a lot tougher than I thought.' And the learning curve is steep. So the companies expect an entry-level technician to have a set of skills, and that's what we're giving them here."

This morning, three students are practicing emergency rescues. "One thing about rescues," Steve says, "there's no two that are the same." Up on the ladder, secure in a harness, weighed down by tools, and handling pulleys and clamps, is Rusty. At thirty-five, he's the oldest in the class. He worked as a heavy-equipment operator for a company that staged concerts and festivals until the live entertainment industry collapsed with the pandemic.

"I really wanted to keep in an industry that was going to allow me to travel, and something that I could take internationally if I wanted to," he says, after successfully completing the rescue. "And coming from a company that has a real focus on environmentalism and conservation" — the events company worked to minimize waste — "I really didn't want to jump into a field that was the antithesis of that — oil or gas or any nonrenewable resources. I've always been mechanically inclined. I've always liked taking things apart and putting them back together. And I think this is going to be a fun thing to go and troubleshoot and have a different problem every day, in a different place every day."

The chance for upward mobility within the profession also appealed to him. "One of my goals for doing this is to be a crew lead so that I can assemble a crew of people that I trust and people that work well together to go and do the best job that we can." And good jobs are not hard to come by.

"One of the things we stress in this program is," Steve says, "I guarantee you're going to get a job. There's tons of jobs. I have companies, recruiters calling me all the time. As a matter of fact, I got an email yesterday asking for names." Steve says the region has some of the best winds in the country — we've learned that the hard way — but controversy around wind farms abounds.

"Some of my family does work in oil," Rusty says. "So there's been some pushback there. There's been some passive-aggressive Facebook posts saying how oil is so much better than wind. But for the most part, a lot of my friends and family have seen this as sort of a natural progression and are very supportive." In Fort Collins, Bryan Willson had said, "Climate is a solvable problem, but it's one that we have to come together in order to solve. And I believe that the next generation can catalyze around that." People like Rusty.

"I know people that work in Pennsylvania coal country — that's where I'm from," Steve says. "There's no way they would ever let anybody know they were wind techs." *We want no fancy mechanics.* "But they're just trying to make a living like everybody else. And here's an opportunity for our young people to stay in Wyoming. We're great at exporting resources. We have wheat, cattle, coal, natural gas. Unfortunately, we're also exporting our people to get jobs at other places. Okay, maybe you're against green energy and wind. I get that. But fifty years ago, if I told you I was going to sell wind to California, you'd think I was a snake oil salesman."

The four states that are currently producing the most wind energy — Texas, Iowa, Oklahoma, and Kansas — all vote Republican. Only California tops Texas in solar energy, and the next two solar states — Florida and North Carolina — also lean Republican. Renewable energy has been great for red state economies, and while some Republican politicians are pushing back against the spread of wind and solar in their states, their voters like the lower energy bills and jobs they bring. As more extreme weather continues to inflict damage on communities, it may be that more Republicans see political value in boasting that red states are doing more to fight climate change than their blue neighbors. Here's hoping that day comes soon.

While wind techs are in high demand around here, RV repair seems like a pretty good career opportunity, too. The main RV dealer in Cheyenne won't take us — too busy — but a mobile repairman agrees to meet us at his shop, and once he gets a look at Charley, the news isn't good. "We can take the canopy off so it won't be a problem," he says, "but we don't have that part and there's not a shop in town that will." My heart sinks. We'll have to fit a five-foot-long canopy roll inside Charley and step around it until we can get it reattached. "Wait a minute," he says. "I think we have that slide canopy. Just took one off someone's RV last week. Might be the same part. Let me check."

I try to suppress my hopes but can't. Laurel is entirely unfazed, the picture of equanimity. As we wait, I notice that we are parked beside Messenger's Old West Museum, which has a collection of wagons and stagecoaches. Breakdowns on the Oregon Trail happened routinely, which is one reason why families rarely ventured west alone, instead traveling in wagon trains with carpenters and blacksmiths who carried tools for fashioning fixes. We no longer travel cross-country in caravans, but we still need others' help along the way. I think of what Bryan Willson had said when I asked him what binds the country together. He leaned back, took a deep breath, and looked up at the ceiling. After fifteen seconds, he said, "America's always been a frontier land. It's always been a land people came to because of possibilities. In a frontier mentality — whether it was coming to the US or wagon trains — people had to work together to survive. And I think that's the moment that we're in."

The repairman returns from the shop with a part. I watch anxiously as he climbs a ladder up to our canopy and . . . it's a match! What luck. We drive off with the wind at our back.

— 30 —

Laramie Legends

"BUFORD, Pop 1." The sign is out of date — the town lost its lone resident a few years ago. We are parked at the gas station and trading post he owned and ran until he put it up for auction on eBay — *Buy a gas station, get a town!* — drawing bids from around the world and fetching $900,000 from a Vietnamese businessman who thought it the perfect place to introduce his coffee business to Americans. "It's an American Dream!" he wrote after winning the auction. He had never visited Buford.

Although Buford is less a ghost town than a shuttered gas station, it does have two ghosts, the brothers Oliver and Oakes Ames. A stone pyramid honoring them stands sixty feet tall and sixty feet wide, built by the Union Pacific following the Crédit Mobilier corruption scandal that had disgraced them and the railroad. The monument is one of the earliest examples of corporate public relations and one of the most successful — tourists still come to see it and read signs mythologizing the brothers. The company understood that history etched in stone is difficult to erase.

We've already seen enough of the Ameses on this trip — having passed through Ames, Iowa, and Ames, Nebraska — so we head for a Lincoln monument instead, a few miles west. It's a thirty-foot-tall granite pedestal topped with a bust, sculpted by local artist Robert Russin. Lincoln's face is gaunt and his cheeks almost skeletal, but his eyes bulge and his hair, beard, and eyebrows are bushy, like an exhausted Zeus. Affixed to it is a quote from Lincoln's 1862 message to Congress, in which he defended his Emancipation Proclamation, which was about to go into effect. "We must think anew and act anew," he urged Americans. The monument originally stood at the highest point on the Lincoln Highway, but when the interstate displaced the old highway, the state moved the monument to a new place of honor — the Sherman Summit Rest Area, making it the most American of tributes. *Let us think anew and act anew, while we stop to use the bathroom.*

Arriving in Laramie, the Lincoln Highway takes us past the University of Wyoming, where a bench on a quad is dedicated to the memory of Matthew Shepard, whose vicious 1998 murder — he was beaten bloody, pistol-whipped, and left tied to a fence in freezing temperatures — made international headlines, not only because of the extreme brutality of the crime but also because of the reason: homophobia. Shepard's murder galvanized and mainstreamed the movement for gay rights, raised awareness of violence against gays and lesbians, and led to one of the most frequently performed plays in America, *The Laramie Project*. But the story was always more complicated than the headlines let on.

Fifteen years after the murder, Stephen Jimenez's *The Book of Matt* revealed that friends and associates of Shepard and his murderer said the killing wasn't a case of gay bashing but rather an issue the prosecution had carefully avoided, drugs. According to them, Shepard used and dealt methamphetamine, the murderer was bisexual, and the two had been intimate partners — not total strangers, as had been claimed by both the prosecution and the defense. In this telling, the murderer had hit Shepard in a rage fueled by his meth addiction and had used homophobia as an excuse — he told police that Shepard had come on to him, setting off his fury — in hopes of winning sympathy from the jury. The book was broadly condemned on the left, and Jimenez was roundly smeared as a right-wing tool and even a self-hating gay, attacked for daring to look more closely at a story that had become an article of faith and inspired so much good. In a preface to Jimenez's book, Andrew Sullivan wrote:

> Shepard was a victim twice over: of meth and of a fellow meth user, driven to a form of madness that sustained meth use invariably produces. Gay men did not want this to be known — because it muddied the narrative of sainthood for Matthew and aired some dirty laundry many in the community wanted

> kept out of sight. Straight people who wanted to display how concerned they were had a unique chance to weigh in with genuine sadness, shock, and pity and were not inclined to ask questions. And then there was the huge pressure not to query a murder that seemed to have no purpose if it didn't advance gay equality. So now we have the body of Matthew Shepard interred, like a martyr to homophobia, at the National Cathedral in Washington, DC. And you begin to understand how saints are indeed made: by legend and by orthodoxy.

Legend and orthodoxy are powerful forces that feed on each other, sometimes for good causes, like gay rights, sometimes for bad ones, like racism, and sometimes for more complicated ones, like westward expansion. If we Democrats can recognize our own resistance to revisiting the Shepard legend, perhaps we can also begin to understand how others have resisted attempts to eradicate the legends that inspired them, whether Kit Cody and manifest destiny or Robert Lee and the Lost Cause. We are no more immune to legends than previous generations. Every age creates its own, so hardwired are we to seek and believe in them. Not all are equal in value and worth, of course — far from it. But all elevate what is held dear out of the reach of inconvenient truth and into the realm of incontrovertible fable.

In a 1962 speech, President Kennedy said, "For the great enemy of truth is very often not the lie — deliberate, contrived and dishonest — but the myth: persistent, persuasive, and unrealistic. Too often we hold fast to the cliches of our forebears. We subject all facts to a prefabricated set of interpretations. We enjoy the comfort of opinion without the discomfort of thought." And it is often that very discomfort that gives rise to myths in the first place.

Shortly after President Kennedy was assassinated, his widow, Jacqueline, asked the author William Manchester, who had written approvingly (critics said adoringly) of her husband, to write the definitive account of the assassination. But when the book was ready for publication, she sued to stop it, upset by some of its revelations, including her disappointment upon hearing that Lee Harvey Oswald was not a right-wing racist but a communist: "He didn't even have the satisfaction of being killed for civil rights. It had to be some silly little communist," she lamented. "It robs his death of any meaning."

It is understandable why she wished that he had been killed for civil rights, just as it is understandable why Matthew was turned into a martyr for gay rights. We want good to come out of tragedy — light and hope and inspiration. But what if, asked Andrew Sullivan in his foreword, the lesson that had come out of Matthew's murder had been about the rising cost of a meth epidemic in gay communities, including the violence and psychosis it can spark — and the need to stop it? Could some lives have been saved? Perhaps not. Perhaps people were not ready for that conversation. But what about now? As the meth epidemic in gay communities rages on, could positioning Matthew's story within it — not so much demythologizing it as remythologizing it — help save lives?

"It seems to me," wrote Sullivan, "that we can honor the memory of Matthew Shepard by refusing to lie about him anymore."

We park downtown, near the bar where Shepard spent his final peaceful hours, which is on a street named for another martyred American: Custer. We pass it by and head for another: the Buckhorn Bar & Parlor, established in 1900 and "the oldest standing bar" in Wyoming. As a few patrons play pool, we take in the taxidermy. The bartender correctly pegs us for out-of-towners and points out the bullet hole in the mirror behind her, telling us the Buckhorn's most famous legend. A man shot into the bar from across the street, she says — a jealous husband. Or maybe it was a boyfriend. Other tellings have the shooter smitten with a bartender who denied his advances. No one seems to know for sure, and it doesn't much matter, since no one died. But the bullet hole isn't a cautionary tale about guns. It's a celebration of their role in the wild west in a town full of stories about outlaws.

Calamity Jane and Frank McCall, who killed Wild Bill Hickock, both spent a night in the town's jail, and murdering thieves once took over control of the city until a group of citizens formed a vigilance committee, confronted four of them, lynched them, and left them hanging for hours as a warning. These stories bring tourists seeking glimpses of the same lawless culture that Buffalo Bill sold so profitably, turning Thomas Hobbes's view on the state of nature — where every person lives for himself in unlimited freedom, producing chaos, war, and misery — into an American utopia. Every western town, it seems, has its own version of this dystopia-as-utopia tale, because it still sells. And I'm not casting judgment. We didn't stumble into the Buckhorn by accident.

Despite the tourism trade in bullets, Laramie's greatest contribution to history lies in ballots. The first woman to cast a legal vote in a US election was a Laramie resident, Louisa Swain, in 1870, after the Wyoming territory became the first government in the Western world to legalize women's suffrage. Democrats pushed it through the legislature at least partly to embarrass the Republican governor. They expected him to veto it, which would allow them to claim he supported elevating blacks over women. Instead he signed the bill — and when Democrats repealed the law two years later after realizing that Wyoming women favored their Republican opponents, he vetoed it. Democrats came within one vote of overriding it.

Voting laws have always been tied up in partisan politics. Each party accuses the other of doing what it does itself: using them to gain advantage. So it has always been, and this year, the pandemic has supercharged a debate over a voting reform that grew out of the partisan angling around Lincoln's reelection campaign: mail-in voting.

In 1864, Republicans feared they could lose the election without soldiers being able to return home to vote, so they pushed state legislatures to enact laws allowing soldiers to cast ballots while in the field. Inevitably, frauds occurred among both parties, and when a scheme by Democratic officials in Baltimore to change the ballots of soldiers was exposed by a Republican operative, a national scandal ensued, and Republicans worried they might be cheated out of the White House and Congress. On the eve of the election, William Seward decried "frauds more fraudulent in conception, more wicked in design, than we have ever encountered." Yet there is no record of Lincoln ever publicly bemoaning fraud or suggesting that it might be to blame were he to lose. To have done so would not only have been beneath his dignity, but it would also have sown doubt where he wished to instill faith.

In the twentieth century, the right to cast a ballot in absentia was extended beyond soldiers to those traveling for business or family reasons, which led some states to go further: allowing anyone to vote by mail for any reason. In 2000, Oregon became the first state to conduct elections entirely by mail. Others have followed, and the pandemic has accelerated the trend. This year, half of all voters will cast their ballots absentee, Laurel and me included.

Wyoming is one of about three dozen states that allow voting by mail without requiring an excused absence, and because of Covid, the Republican secretary of state sent out absentee voter applications to every registered voter in the state. "It's wonderful," says Susan Simpson, president of the Wyoming League of Women Voters, as I sit in her backyard in Laramie a block off the Lincoln Highway. The league's treasurer, Katie Morgan, who lives a short walk away, is here, too. "We are so physically distanced," Katie says of her sparsely populated state, "sometimes it's hard for people to get in to vote. And in November, we can have horrible weather that makes it difficult for older people, or even younger people." Might mail-in voting become permanent? "I'm not optimistic that will happen in the short term," Katie says, "given our current state government. The push-back against some of the voting reforms arise more out of input from the national policy of the Republican Party. That's who's in charge in Wyoming and has been for a while." Nationally, Republicans have increasingly been equating mail-in voting with election fraud, even though instances of it are rare, because they fear it advantages Democratic voters, even though studies suggest otherwise. Older voters who might not make it to the polls tilt Republican.

Throughout this year's campaign, Trump has made repeated attacks on mail-in ballots, telling Fox News's Chris Wallace that "mail-in voting is going to rig the election." It was a baseless prediction, but not a purposeless one. "Are you suggesting," Wallace asked him, "that you might not accept the results of the election?"

"I have to see," Trump replied.

"Can you give a direct answer: Will you accept the election?"

"I'm not going to just say yes. I'm not going to say no."

The league labors to stay above the partisan fray, and while it advocates for legislative reforms, it focuses largely on voter education and hosting candidate debates — "we prefer to call them forums," Susan says. Civility and nonpartisanship have traditionally been points of pride for the league, but in recent years, the increasing intensity of politics has led the league to forfeit some of both. In 2018, the league's national president was arrested for disrupting Brett Kavanaugh's Senate confirmation hearing. The next year, after its Nevada chapter pushed a nonpartisan redistricting reform referendum that Democrats and liberal activists opposed, the national league dissolved it.

Today we can see partisanship nearly everywhere we look, and often when we don't, it just means we aren't looking hard enough. That's true even of historical commemorations. In front of the state capitol in Cheyenne is a statue of Esther Morris, the first woman to serve as a judge in the United States, after the suffrage law made it possible. But that's not why she was honored with a statue.

During the national debate over a constitutional amendment guaranteeing women the right to vote, Wyoming Democrats sought to score political points by taking credit for the state's suffrage law, despite having tried to repeal it. Republicans could counter by pointing to Abe himself, citing a letter he wrote in 1836 when he was a candidate for the Illinois General Assembly. "I go for all sharing the privileges of the government, who assist in bearing its burdens. Consequently I go for admitting all whites to the right of suffrage, who pay taxes or bear arms (by no means excluding females)." Historians tend to believe Lincoln wrote the parenthetical with tongue in cheek, and given his sense of humor and lack of support for women's suffrage throughout the rest of his career, it probably was. No matter. Suffragists knew the power of Lincoln and touted his endorsement on signs reading, "Lincoln said women should vote."

Still, Wyoming Republicans couldn't let Democrats get away with claiming credit for passing the state's landmark suffrage law, so they decided they ought to have a woman hero — a *Republican* woman hero. And who better than Judge Morris? They spread a made-up story about how Morris had co-authored the bill and convinced the legislature to pass it during a tea party she held, making her "the Mother of Women's Suffrage." Mythology was on the move. There was soon a rock cairn marking the spot where her house had stood, and the state later sent a statue of Morris to Congress, even before erecting one in Cheyenne.

In 2018, the *New York Times* ran a much-belated obituary of Morris as part of its series called "Overlooked." It mentioned that "some historians" say her role in passing the suffrage bill is overstated — quite the understatement — but it made no mention of the partisan gamesmanship surrounding her lionization. In celebrating her appointment to the bench, the story also neglected to mention that her judicial philosophy — "justice first, then after that the law" — was the same one adopted by wild west vigilantes and that shortly after her brief stint on the bench (neither party would nominate her for a full term) the legislature rescinded the right of women to serve on juries. Why muddy a heroic narrative?

"After the initial one in 1870, we didn't have another female juror until 1949," says Katie, a trailblazer herself, having been in the first ROTC class at the University of Wyoming to admit women. "So it's an example of how popular history is not always an accurate representation of what happened." That's true even when popular history is rewritten 148 years later to correct for past oversights. One of the *Times*'s omissions is particularly emblematic of our political challenges.

When Morris left the bench, replaced by the same man whose seat she filled when he resigned in protest of the suffrage law, she acknowledged that her tenure had been "a test of women's ability to hold public office," declaring that she had passed. "I feel my work has been satisfactory." The *Times* article quoted those lines but left out the ones that followed, when she spoke with Lincoln's humility about her lack of education — "I have often regretted I was not better qualified to fill the position" — and then with his eloquence: "Like all pioneers, I have labored in faith and hope." Few phrases — *I have labored in faith and hope* — have better captured the essence of American citizenship, then and now. Maybe the *Times* writer didn't see it that way or space didn't allow for it. Whatever the case, the article gave us Morris's pride but not her humility, reflecting more of ourselves than her.

Morris wasn't the Mother of Suffrage in Wyoming, but her legend helped advance it nationally. This is the centennial of the ratification of the Nineteenth Amendment, which barely squeaked through. Alabama, Delaware, Georgia, Louisiana, Maryland, Mississippi, South Carolina, North Carolina, and Virginia — all slaveholding states at the time of the Civil War — voted it down. Had the Civil War not led to the partition of Virginia, and had Lincoln not accepted the tortured legal basis for admitting it to the union, women's suffrage might have been delayed by years. Much of the old Confederacy didn't get around to ratifying it for another half century or longer, during which time both black women and men were routinely denied the right to vote. And of course, suffrage didn't bring equality for women, in law or in culture. That fight would long continue — and still continues, each generation of women building on the progress made by their pioneering mothers, as Queen Latifah and Monie Love sang.

> *We are the ones that give birth*
> *To the new generation of prophets because it's Ladies First*

Before I depart, Katie shares a few memories from growing up on the Lincoln Highway in the little town of Wheatland, Iowa, like the time her mother left her purse on a gas station counter with every cent the family had, infuriating her father, until they returned several hours later and found it still there, untouched. In high school, she says, "The big entertainment was to drive up and down Main Street and honk at people we knew."

I love that the Lincoln Highway still holds a special place in her heart, and the passion she and Susan have for democracy warms mine. Spreading that passion has never been easy, but at least in my lifetime, it's never been harder. Tonight at a rally in Georgia, Trump tells the crowd, "Lock up the Bidens, lock up Hillary," as the crowd chants, "Lock him up!" *Justice first, then after that the law.*

We stay in Laramie an extra day, though not by choice: high winds have trapped us. We leave the next morning at dawn — we have until about 11:00 a.m. before the winds force us off the road — and on our way out of town, we stop at the post office to drop off our ballots. Even though there isn't a single competitive race on our ballot, there was no way we were missing this election. Voting is more an act of faith and hope than one of reason or logic, and it is when the equality of citizenship finds its most perfect expression. John Greenleaf Whittier, an elector for Lincoln in 1860 and 1864, captured its essence in "The Poor Voter."

The proudest now is but my peer,
The highest not more high;
To-day, of all the weary year,
A king of men am I.
To-day, alike are great and small,
The nameless and the known;
My palace is the people's hall,
The ballot-box my throne!

— 31 —

Outliving Fact

Leaving Laramie we enter a barren and brown plain, seeing a herd of antelope but no houses or cars and little else until we reach Rock River, forty miles north. Thinking we might find breakfast at Hostler's General Store, we park beside their 1940s era gas pump, which has a red and green Lincoln Highway inset above the price display. A sign on the door reads, "Closed Went to Church Be Back at 2." Across the street is the Longhorn Lodge, a motor court with a half dozen detached cottages, but its coffee shop is closed.

North of Rock River, past the site where Butch Cassidy's Wild Bunch robbed a Union Pacific train in 1899 and made off with about $50,000, a billboard appears for the Virginian Hotel in Medicine Bow. "Let's stop!" Laurel says with home-state pride, before deadpanning: "But they probably don't allow any damn Yankees."

We pull over at the hotel, named for a 1902 novel set in Medicine Bow, *The Virginian*, which sold a million and a half copies and turned its author, Owen Wister, into a household name. Across the street is a pyramid, about eight feet high, with a plaque that mangles a line from the novel: "When you say that, smile." It's the reply the Virginian gives to a gambler he has never met, Trampas, as they sit at a poker table, after Trampas says to him, "Your bet, you son-of-a—." A friend of the Virginian's had called him that same term only moments earlier, while slapping him on the back, which resulted in the Virginian buying a round of drinks. At the poker table, the Virginian heard it differently, and he offered some advice intended to spare the man's life: "When you call me that, smile." Variations on the line would reappear in western movies, and the Virginian's character became the archetypical hero of Hollywood westerns.

"Lounging there at ease against the wall was a slim young giant, more beautiful than pictures," Wister wrote of the Virginian. "His broad, soft hat was pushed back; a loose-knotted, dull-scarlet handkerchief sagged from his throat; and one casual thumb was hooked in the cartridge-belt that slanted across his hips." In those two sentences, Wister brought to life a cowboy image that Hollywood would replicate time and again. Over the course of the novel, Wister defined the cowboy's character, code, and cultural identity, including his heritage, creating an idealized American: not just white, but Anglo-Saxon and imbued with southern chivalry and aristocratic heritage. Although many cowboys were black, Mexican, and Native American, they were mostly absent from Wister's story, and when Native Americans did appear, they did so as savages, not cowboys. Wister would later attack the "Ellice Island mongrel mobs" who were "invading our shores." *Invading.*

Wister believed, like Buffalo Bill, that he was capturing the essence of the wild west and memorializing it as it died out. He lamented that no novelist had yet done it, writing, "Roosevelt had seen the sage brush true, had felt its poetry; and also Remington, who illustrated his articles so well. But what was fiction doing, fiction, the only thing that has outlived fact?"

The plot of Wister's novel centers on the search for and execution of cattle thieves, a mirror of 1892's Johnson County War, due north of Medicine Bow. It began when wealthy ranch owners hired cowboys to hunt down and kill cattle thieves, paying them per murder. But many of the supposed thieves were homesteaders who clashed with the large ranches over grazing rights and calf ownership. After the hired-gun vigilantes killed two men, the homesteaders organized their own force, cornering the vigilantes and killing their horses to prevent them from escaping. The ranchers appealed to the White House for army assistance, and Republican president Harrison obliged. It just so happened that most of the homesteaders were Democrats and most of the wealthy ranchers were Republicans. The army broke up the standoff and detained the vigilantes, but none were tried. Afterward, Wister wrote in his diary: "The extermination of thieves was most wholesome." Two of his Harvard classmates were among the wealthy ranchers who organized the lynching.

In the novel, the Virginian works for a wealthy ranch owner and local judge and leads the posse that hangs two cattle rustlers. When his love interest from New England, Molly, expresses her concerns about the breakdown of law and order, the judge explains that because juries won't convict the suspects, men have every right to enforce the law themselves. Since the law's authority originates in citizens, "when they lynch," the judge says, "they only take back what they once gave." The judge and Virginian, heroes of the story, embodied the dark side of Esther Morris's homespun judicial philosophy: *Justice first, then after that the law.*

Wister's patrician view of democracy — he believed it should produce an aristocratic ruling class rather than social and political equality, which he disdained as "a great big bluff" — meant that he got the story backward. Had he been a hero worthy of democratic admiration, the Virginian would have been among the homesteaders fighting back against the lynching rather than the posse carrying it out. But generations read and loved his story, and Hollywood did, too, turning it into movies and a television series. In the very last line of the novel, as the Virginian's son rides a horse, the narrator confides to the reader, "Strictly between ourselves, I think his father is going to live a long while." And so he has, but not without rivals.

Other writers have offered competing visions of the west, perhaps none more powerfully than Willa Cather through her strong, gender-role-defying heroines. As *The New Yorker*'s cultural critic Alex Ross wrote: "Wister was a tourist; Cather was the real Virginian. In her rendering of the Great Plains and the West, women achieve independence from restrictive roles; people of many countries coexist; and violence is futile, with guns most often fired in suicidal despair." But women didn't run Hollywood, and, when Cather was writing her masterpieces in the 1910s, in much of the country they couldn't even vote. Although her heroines helped change that, Wister's cowboy myth has lived on, despite efforts by Larry McMurtry and others to recast it.

We enter the Virginian Hotel through the café. Its counter and tables are empty, but its walls are full of old photographs and artifacts hanging beneath a pressed-tin ceiling painted gold. A mural with characters from *The Virginian* is painted above wooden booths, and it contains the famous directive — "When you call me that, smile" — which can be found in the saloon adjoining the cafe, too. We had not planned on sitting down to a meal, just to peek inside, but the cook comes out of the kitchen and tells us to take any table. Leaving would be against the code of the Virginian I'm with. I know better than to fight her. Plus, I would love some pancakes.

We take a table just outside the Owen Wister Dining Room and have the place to ourselves for our first indoor dining breakfast experience of the trip, which couldn't be any more enjoyable. On our way out, a group of men in hunting gear walks in.

"That your RV?"

"Yup, that's us."

"You're a long way from home." They had seen our license plates.

"Yeah, that's for sure."

"How do you like these big open spaces?" I can hear the attack on New York City in his voice, but I can also see — as can the Virginian beside me — that as he says it, he's smiling. And we are, too.

"We love 'em."

As we ride off, we turn on the Outlaw Country radio channel and hear Willie Nelson singing "The Red Headed Stranger," a song about a cowboy who, like the Virginian, lives by the code of the old west, where justice comes before the law, sometimes even for judges.

> *The yellow haired lady was buried at sunset*
> *The stranger went free, of course*
> *For you can't hang a man for killin' a woman*
> *Who's tryin' to steal your horse*

We're heading to Rawlins, Wyoming, and we've been curling northwest with the old Union Pacific line, which followed the Overland Trail to the west coast. A 1913 Lincoln Highway guide listed eighteen gates that motorists had to open and close between Laramie and Rawlins, and a traveler would later write that the route across Wyoming "was defined by the towns it passed more than by the road itself. How a traveler got from town to town, and by which route, was pretty much left up to the imagination." In that sense, the early Lincoln was more like the old Overland Trail than a new highway.

We pass what is left of Hanna, population 783. The Union Pacific once owned it all — the town, the houses, the rail track, and its raison d'être: coal mines. That the town is named for the man who would become one of the nation's leading promoters of corporate power, Marcus Alonzo Hanna, is not an accident.

We met Hanna briefly back in his hometown of Lisbon, Ohio — the Republican kingmaker who helped put William McKinley in the White House. His support for Lincoln in 1864 nearly cost him a bride, owing to her Democratic father, a successful coal and iron merchant who did not want his daughter marrying "a damned screecher for freedom." Hanna entered the family business and politics, too, parlaying his political connections into a seat on the Union Pacific board, a position that dovetailed with his financial interests in the coal industry and his own efforts to exert control over the supply chain in Ohio. Democrats who opposed the appointment called him "a monopolist of labor-crushing propensities." Republicans saw it differently, and still do. In his admiring biography of Hanna, Karl Rove credited him with transforming his father-in-law's company into a "vertically integrated business that owned mines, furnaces, smelters, steamships, and warehouses." More than McKinley's presidency, Hanna's political legacy rests in the rise of corporate consolidation and corporate political influence.

The last shipment of coal rolled out of Hanna, Wyoming, in 2012, and the population is less than half what it once was. The town's annual King Coal Days festival — a parade, mud drags, pie eating, bake-off, and games galore — was canceled this summer. The official reason was the pandemic, but the dethroning happened years ago. US coal production will hit a fifty-year low this year, and 151 mines will idle or close. But the town's old owner, the Union Pacific, is rolling strong, generating billions in annual profits. The company was never interested in the community, of course, only the profits it could wring from it. And so the town it started and named for one of its monopoly-friendly directors has been left to suffer the fate of all monopolies, once technological innovation passes them by.

Approaching Hanna, we passed dozens of wind turbines. Some nine hundred more are coming to the area, the largest onshore wind farm in the United States, which could power nearly one million homes. Transmission lines will carry the power as far as Southern California, just as the trains here had once carried coal. The turbines and transmission lines will create jobs — not as many as the mines once offered, but maybe enough to help keep Hanna alive. Wind now accounts for 10 percent of the state's energy mix, and that number will continue to grow. This is still Carbon County, but soon, perhaps, in name only.

Hanna's nearest neighbor, thirty-five miles west, is Sinclair: another company town built on fossil fuels. The welcome sign is a sprawling refinery complex of warehouses, smokestacks, holding tanks, and silver pipes running every which way, processing eighty-five thousand barrels of crude oil a day, which supply fourteen hundred Sinclair gas stations.

Where the refinery ends, the town square begins. We stop in the center, at a fountain plaza facing a block-long, three-story, sixty-room Spanish Colonial hotel that once welcomed Amelia Earhart and Clark Gable: the Parco Inn, with stucco walls, arched bell towers, and a terra-cotta roof. Other

Spanish Colonial–style buildings bookend the block. Grit and grandeur, cheek-to-jowl, thanks to a Denver oil baron who was one of the nation's wealthiest entrepreneurs, Frank Kistler. In the 1920s, he picked this spot to build a refinery because of its proximity to oil fields and direct access to both the Lincoln Highway and Union Pacific. Rather than let his workers and their families live in shacks, he hired Denver architects to design a town, siting houses west of the refinery to avoid its fumes, running electrical wiring underground, and placing a large park in the center of town, facing the hotel. The town was "truly an oasis in an otherwise drab desert territory," announced the *Rocky Mountain News* when it opened in 1925.

When the Great Depression hit, Kistler couldn't hold on, and Parco entered federal receivership. Snapping up the whole town was Harry Sinclair's Consolidated Oil empire, only five years after he'd served six months in jail for his role in the century's biggest corruption scandal until Watergate. He was accused of bribing a cabinet official to win a secret sweetheart deal to drill for oil in a land reserve in northern Wyoming called Teapot Dome, which the federal government had set aside for use in case of war — the nation's first emergency petroleum reserve.

In 2018, the refinery here began processing renewable diesel, made from vegetable oils and other feedstock, which emits less pollutants and CO_2. A company whose logo is a green dinosaur — from the days when oil was thought to come from dinosaur bones, abundant in this area — Sinclair is proving it can adapt. But survival of the fittest can be cruel to small towns.

The Parco Inn, long closed, has been saved by a Baptist church group, but Sinclair will soon be bought for $1.8 billion by the Dallas-based HollyFrontier. A year after closing the deal, the company will announce layoffs of nearly one hundred people here. For a town of four hundred, it's "devastating," said the state's lone member of Congress, Liz Cheney. The reasoning is always the same: operational efficiency. "As a result of the recent acquisition," a HollyFrontier spokesperson explained, "we are aligning our facilities to reflect best practices for operational excellence." Mark Hanna couldn't have said it any better.

Maybe Sinclair had to sell. Maybe it couldn't have survived otherwise. But maybe it just needed an owner who felt a stronger sense of civic duty to the town that had sustained it for a century. We have yet to see a town that has benefited from an out-of-state entity acquiring its largest employer.

Places like Sinclair and Hanna are the subject of a steady stream of news articles about discontented people who are often left with a feeling that the country as they knew it — or at least as they thought they understood it, or wanted it to be — is being lost, sacrificed to impersonal corporate forces and un-American foreigners. That feeling, however, is hardly new.

"There's nothing united about these States any more than Standard Oil and discontent," wrote Owen Wister in his 1906 novel, *Lady Baltimore.* "We're no longer a small people living and dying for a great idea; we're a big people living and dying for money." The novel was a love letter to antebellum America and the supremacy of Anglo ancestry, before the wretched refuse washed up on our shores and the enslaved cast off their chains. But Wister got it wrong: Money has always been at the heart of the American idea, since the Boston Tea Party and George Washington's land claims, and it has always been both a powerful force for national unity among a polyglot of ethnicities and religions and a challenge to it.

Wister's lament — that the rise of cultural diversity and corporate power led to a tragic national decline that betrayed our founding identity and ideals — is bunk. But it is enduring in part because we are always mistaking it as a new phenomenon. The problems of capitalism faced by places like Sinclair and Hanna are often tragic, but recognizing that they are not new, and that the most common political response to them — lashing out at immigrants and faceless enemies, whether corporations or countries — is not effective, can help us see that other approaches are required, whether renewable energy, place-based economics, or even a more politically fraught idea: helping people move.

Geographic mobility is at its lowest level since records began being kept in 1947. The varied causes of the slowdown, including rising housing costs, are not easy to change, but little effort is being made in part because politicians generally don't like to tell voters that it may be in their best interest to move. Lincoln, whose family moved from Kentucky to Indiana to Illinois in pursuit of economic opportunity, had no such qualms. Addressing striking shoe workers in New Haven, Connecticut, he said, "If you find it hard to better your condition on this soil, you may have a chance to strike and go somewhere else, where you may not be degraded . . . Then you can better your condition, and so it may go on and on in one ceaseless round."

Lincoln knew that economic mobility can require geographic mobility and that America's great promise — democracy, freedom, and equal opportunity for all, including immigrants — is built on faith in the future, not longing for the past. But Wister was right: fiction outlives fact.

— 32 —

Across the Great Divide

The wind shaking and rattling Charley's metal creates a noisy clatter that wakes me up and leaves me wondering if we might tip over. I do what I did much of last evening: check the forecast, hoping for a change. No luck. Even before dawn, winds are twenty-three miles per hour and rising. The only way we'll make it out of Wyoming alive, it seems, is to drive at daybreak and go as far as the winds will allow.

At the crest of a long hill, a road sign announces "Continental Divide, Elevation 7000." There are no dramatic views of the mountains — we're in them, on a massive plateau — and as we slope down the other side of the hill we see little besides sagebrush and prairie grass. After about an hour, a long upward incline brings us to another sign that baffles us: "Continental Divide Elevation 6930." How can there be two Continental Divides an hour apart on the same line of latitude? I later learn we had just driven through the Great Divide Basin, a giant bowl that once was a tropical lake with crocodiles. As Winifred Dixon wrote in his 1921 book, *Westward Hoboes*: "There are about as many Continental Divides in the West as beds in which Washington slept in the East."

As a freight train keeps pace with us, we wind our way along gray sandstone buttes to the town of Rock Springs, where the Lincoln brings us past the butcher shop where, so the story goes, Robert LeRoy Parker got the nickname "Butch." He chose "Cassidy" in honor of his mentor in cattle rustling and horse thieving, Mike Cassidy. Butch Cassidy's outlaw story has long been celebrated here, but as I walk along the rail tracks on Main Street, I'm surprised to see that, amid the monuments dedicated to coal miners and people killed in a bus crash, there is nothing commemorating the town's most notorious crime.

In 1885, anger boiled over among European immigrant miners at Chinese miners who refused to strike and were willing to work for lower wages in dangerous conditions. A fight led to a donnybrook, which led to a march on the Chinese section of town, which led to murder, theft, looting, and an inferno that burned nearly every Chinese house, leaving more than two dozen people dead, their bodies left for hogs and dogs to eat, one of the most horrific ethnic attacks in American history. In his book *Violent Land*, David T. Courtwright wrote, "Chinese men were scalped, mutilated, burned, branded, decapitated, dismembered, and hanged from gutter spouts. One Chinese miner's penis and testicles were cut off and then toasted in a nearby saloon as a 'trophy of the hunt.' This was plainly racial terrorism, and it had its intended effect." The Chinese fled the town.

No one was ever prosecuted, despite widespread awareness of the attackers' identities. What jury would convict them? The newspapers reported the "unanimous opinion of the people" was behind them. *First justice, then the law.* The territorial governor appealed to President Grover Cleveland to send troops, and he did — but as much to protect lives as to ensure that the Chinese could go back to work. Even though some had no desire to do so, and some may have been tricked into returning, they had no choice. But they did make one change. They began to own guns.

It wasn't until 2016 that a small stone memorial appeared in Rock Springs, where Chinatown once stood. It displays the Chinese character for peace and the names of twenty-eight people who were killed. But the town is no longer trying to bury its history. Soon it will choose a local artist, David Alan Clark, to sculpt an eight-foot-tall memorial portraying a Chinese miner holding a dragon banner, standing atop the rubble of the fire. Growing up here, Clark never learned of the massacre in school, but what lay buried for generations is now being unearthed by a city that sees the divide its denial perpetuated — between ignorance and knowledge, bigotry and tolerance, exclusion and equality — and is crossing it.

We soon see why David Alan Clark won the commission. In the center of the next town, Green River, where the high desert plateau begins to give way to mesas and the wonders of the western geology, stands a fine sculpture by Clark of the man who first put the most spectacular western wonder — the Grand Canyon — on the map: John Wesley Powell. We encountered him at the 100th Meridian in Nebraska, as a climate Cassandra. But there is more to his story that matters to ours.

Clark depicted Powell with his right arm missing, having been blown off in the Battle of Shiloh. He had eagerly joined the US Army out of his conviction that preserving the country was a sacred mission. A friend and fellow veteran said of him: "He was not an admirer of Napoleon, or Caesar, or any of the great slaughterers; but oh how illuminated and beautiful became that rugged, bearded face when he talked of Abraham Lincoln."

Powell's other arm holds a paddle, as his foot rests on a rock. It was here in 1869 that he and a crew of nine men with no experience running whitewater rapids set out in four boats in an audacious attempt to see lands known only to natives. A nation that had fixated on connecting its coasts still did not know much of its own interior, but the building of the transcontinental railroad made it possible for Powell to have boats professionally made in Chicago and sent west. Fourteen days after Americans celebrated the Golden Spike that completed the railroad, Powell and his men began voyaging down the Green River for the Colorado River, which — if they could survive its rumored waterfalls — would lead them through the Grand Canyon, covering a thousand miles of territory that remained unmapped and unexplored by the nation that had claimed it for two decades, such was the extreme danger it presented. Kit Carson had passed on such an expedition, as had John Fremont, who wrote from the banks of the Green River in 1843: "No trappers have been found bold enough to undertake a voyage which has so certain a prospect of a fatal termination." The first US citizen to record visiting the bottom of the Grand Canyon, army lieutenant Joseph Christmas Ives, called it "valueless" and "profitless," predicting that no white people would ever again visit and that it "shall be forever unvisited and undisturbed."

Powell, however, was a geology teacher who saw the void in the map as a void in the nation's understanding of itself. His aim, he wrote upon embarking, was "to make collections in geology, natural history, antiquities and ethnology," with the goal of "adding a mite to the great sum of human knowledge." In doing so, he also hoped to advance the nation's interests and what he saw as its missionary calling: to civilize Native Americans.

In his report on the journey, Powell wrote of his interactions with Indians: "I tell them that all the great and good white men are anxious to know very many things, that they spend much time in learning, and that the greatest man is he who knows the most; that the white men want to know all about the mountains and the valleys, the rivers and the canyons, the beasts and birds and snakes." But Powell wasn't much interested in learning from the people who knew those natural wonders best. He wanted to teach them, which required, he believed, removing them from their ancient lands.

In 1888, Powell wrote a letter to Colorado senator Henry Teller, a strident critic of the Dawes Act that had passed the prior year. The act authorized the federal government to break up Indian reservations by transferring land from common tribal ownership into private parcels of 160 acres per family, and 80 acres per individual, with the remaining lands opened to public sale. Senator Teller understood what the act would mean for Indians, saying:

> If I stand alone in the Senate, I want to put upon the record my prophecy in this matter, that when 30 or 40 years shall have passed and these Indians shall have parted with their title, they will curse the hand that was raised professedly in their defense to secure this kind of legislation, and if the people who were clamoring for it understood Indian character, and Indian laws, and Indian morals, and Indian religion, they would not be here clamoring for this at all.

Powell believed he understood all of that, having devoted himself to Indian ethnography. In his letter to Teller, he explained that "Indian religion is localized" in creeks and rivers, valleys and mountains, and thus removing the Indian from the land was to liberate him from savagery: "When an Indian clan or tribe gives up its land it not only surrenders its home as understood by civilized people but its gods are abandoned and all its religion . . . Such a removal of the Indians is the first step to be taken in their civilization." And, he might have added, citizenship. Under the act, any Indian who renounced tribal relations would be granted citizenship. For Congress, that was the heart of the trade: *Give up your land and your ways, and citizenship is yours.*

A House minority report on an early version of the bill scorched the deception behind the trade: "The real aim of this bill is to get at the Indian lands and open them up to settlement. The provisions for the apparent benefit of the Indian are but the pretext to get at his lands and occupy them. With that accomplished, we have securely paved the way for the extermination of the Indian races upon this part of the continent. If this were done in the name of Greed, it would be bad enough; but to do it in the name of humanity, and under the cloak of an ardent desire to promote the Indian's welfare by making him like ourselves, whether he will or not, is infinitely worse . . . We want their lands and we are bound to have them."

And have them we did. In 1887, Native Americans controlled 138 million acres. Within a few years, sales of "surplus" lands to settlers reduced their holdings to eighty-four million acres, and it shrank much further in the decades following it as poverty and government dependence rose.

In asking our two questions about Powell's statue — Why was it erected, and did he, on balance, advance or retard the nation's march toward freedom, democracy, and equality? — the first answer is easy: Its purpose was not to perpetuate and glorify what Powell got so wrong but instead to honor him for risking his life in pursuit of a noble goal — knowledge — in the service of a nation that was still discovering itself, following a brutal war over its identity to which Powell, an abolitionist, had given his right arm.

The second answer is more complicated. Wherever one comes out on it — and I believe there is much to honor in Powell's brave voyages and later efforts to protect the environment — his memory should not be reduced to a daring explorer. It should live through the fullness of what Powell most treasured: expanding knowledge of the nation and filling voids in the public's understanding of it, to help chart a new, more unified, and more prosperous course forward. Today, those voids include Native American culture and history, the persecution of immigrant groups, the lies of the Lost Cause, the terrorism and coups of Jim Crow, and other territory long left abandoned as profitless and valueless.

— 33 —

Mormon Trail

Along the banks of the Green River, the Lincoln bends beneath a high wall of buttes and mesas etched with the carvings of the currents, when the river once ran deep and mighty. This is Toll Gate Rock, named for the toll that Mormons supposedly charged to pass it.

"Can you get some shots of this?" I ask Laurel, who is trying to concentrate on a spreadsheet.

"Okay, Ansel Adams."

The natural beauty gives way to a series of billboards advertising Little America, about the only signs of human life for miles around, precisely what led Stephen Mack Covey to open it in 1934, as a gas station, hotel, cabin court, and café, creating a monopoly on everything travelers needed. He named it after Little America, Antarctica, the polar base camp established that same year by Richard Byrd, the most famous American explorer of his era — the John Wesley Powell of flight, the first person credited with flying over the North and South Poles.

Covey claimed he decided to open Little America after seeing a photo of Byrd's camp, and he had a story to go with it, which he printed on every place mat in his café, about building it in the exact spot where he had gotten caught in a blizzard while herding sheep, forcing him to sleep outside. "Oh how I longed for a warm fireside," he recalled, "something to eat, and wool blankets" — precisely what Little America offered! An entrancing story and, in true western fashion, highly dramatized. Covey understood what sells. His grandson Stephen would, too.

In 1989, Stephen Covey packaged a variety of garden-variety bromides (*Be Proactive! Put first things first! Think win-win!*) into a self-help book with a catchy title, *The 7 Habits of Highly Effective People*, that would sell twenty million copies, turn him into a wealthy leadership guru, and spawn an advice industry — books, lectures, trainings, coaching — that is now approaching half a trillion dollars. The language of corporate and personal coaches is a secular echo of traveling preachers, selling salvation in the form of prosperity. And the more they promise wealth through leisure — *The 4-Hour Work Week!* — the better they seem to do.

We stop at Little America, figuring we'll use the spotless restrooms and have a look around, but there's not much to see. The original version burned down — and with it, apparently, went the offbeat and oddball spirit of the best roadside novelties. This version feels corporate, and it is. After Little America struggled in its early days, the elder Covey sold it to his manager, Robert Earl Holding, who turned it into a chain, which led Holding to buy a refinery to supply his gasoline — vertical integration! — which led to a business empire that included luxury hotels, ski resorts, and the Sinclair oil company. Little America became the foundation of their American Dream, a rags-to-riches story built on the same great American tradition that the Lincoln Highway is part of: marketing gimmicks.

Holding, like the Coveys, was a member of the Church of Jesus Christ of Latter-Day Saints. As we follow the Lincoln along the final leg of the Mormon Trail, we'll see just how far the Mormons would travel in American culture, from hated outcasts who sought salvation outside the United States, to model citizens who, in becoming champions of capitalism, have found great prosperity within it.

We stop for the night about thirty-five miles before the Utah state line at Fort Bridger, Wyoming, which is made up of a motel, bar, general store, and RV park, all on a dirt road. The RV park abuts Fort Bridger State Park, named for Jim Bridger, "America's greatest frontiersman and the West's most gifted scout," a sign here informs us, whose "unerring judgment regarding problems" encountered by travelers "bordered on the miraculous." Not all travelers would have agreed.

The Donner party arrived at Fort Bridger in late July 1846, having left

Springfield, Illinois, with several dozen people, among them the family of James Reed, an Irish immigrant who had served in the Black Hawk War with Lincoln and employed Lincoln for legal services, including the bankruptcy that sent Reed westward. Based on a 1919 interview with Reed's daughter, Patty, who was eight years old at the time of the journey, a reporter wrote, "Abraham Lincoln had half a notion to come to California with the Donner Party." Abe was "very interested" in joining his old friend on the journey, historian Mark Wallis contends, perhaps overstating it, but a pregnant wife and his political hopes — he would win election to Congress that year — kept them in Springfield. "They were in good spirits and trust they will safely reach their anticipated homes," the *Sangamo Journal* reported after the group's April 14 departure, as it drove into the annals of disaster and desperation in made-to-order wagons, including a luxurious two-story "Pioneer palace." Another Reed daughter, Virginia, would later write, "I can say without fear of contradiction that nothing like our family wagon ever started across the plains." It can be fairly said that the American love of traveling cross-country in oversized vehicles traces back to the Donner party. At least it sets a low bar for success.

The Donner-Reed party met up with a larger train of wagons as they moved west on the California Trail, but split off from it in central Wyoming after learning of a shortcut that brought them here, to Fort Bridger. The shortcut was being promoted by Lansford Hastings, who sought to entice more emigrants to choose California over Oregon. He aimed to attract enough settlers to do what Texas had done: break away from Mexico and form an independent republic, catapulting him to power, he hoped, in the process. To lure crowds, he published a travel guide that denigrated Oregon and celebrated California.

Once here, the Donner-Reed party asked Jim Bridger for his opinion of the shortcut. "Mr. Bridger informs me that the route we design to take," wrote James Reed, "is a fine level road, with plenty of water and grass, with the exception before stated" — about forty miles without water. Reed didn't know, however, that friends of his had left letters at the trading post warning him not to take the shortcut, because the terrain was too treacherous for their wagons. Bridger or his partner may have kept the letters from him, in the hope that the route would prove successful, thus bringing their trading post a bonanza of business.

The story of the Donner party is best remembered for its ending: cannibalism, high in the Sierras, while trapped in a blizzard. But it is first and foremost a story about the dangers of politically driven misinformation and those who exploit it for political and financial gain — and the desperate extremes to which its victims can succumb.

Bridger's original trading post is long gone, but there are still remnants of the stone wall Mormons built here, after chasing him out in 1853. Bridger had guided Mormon emigrants westward, but he and others clashed with Utah authorities over their trading rights. When Mormon traders accused Bridger of selling guns and ammunition to Native Americans, Brigham Young, governor of the Utah territory, which then encompassed this part of Wyoming, sent 150 men to arrest him for treason.

Bridger knew he had no judicial recourse. Most of the federal judges appointed to the territory had left, feeling usurped by Young, who admitted to running a dictatorship. "I do dictate and I never expect to see the day while I am Governor amongst this people that I don't do it," he declared. "I am, and will be, governor, and no power can hinder it, until the Lord Almighty says, 'Brigham, you need not be governor any longer.'"

Young was only following in the tradition of his predecessor, Joseph Smith, who created a mini theocratic state in Nauvoo, Illinois, anointing himself "Prophet, Priest, & King," while also holding the titles of mayor, chief justice, and general of the militia. In 1844, when Smith ran for president to secure the rights of religious minorities and "put down mobocracy," it quickly became clear he did not mean all religious minorities: He attempted to suppress a newspaper published by a rival church leader who exposed his support for plural marriage. Smith ordered the city marshal to destroy the printing press, which led the county to bring charges against him, which prompted Smith to declare martial law and order the Nauvoo militia to seal the city from outsiders, fueling allegations of treason and fear of civil war. When Smith surrendered, a mob of two hundred broke into the jail and killed him, the first presidential candidate to be assassinated. No one was ever convicted of the murder.

Mormons came to Mexico in the hope of starting over, re-creating Smith's theocracy far away from the clutches of civil authorities. But their hopes of governing themselves without interference ended with the US acquisition of much of Mexico — and by their embrace of polygamy. Young and church leaders publicly endorsed it as a tenet of their faith in the early 1850s, rooting it in the Old Testament and castigating Americans and Europeans for abandoning it. The Republican Party declared in its 1856 platform that it was "both the right and the imperative duty of Congress to prohibit in the Territories those twin relics of barbarism — Polygamy, and Slavery." But it was not only polygamy that Americans found troubling.

The Mormon Reformation of 1856–1857 included sermons by Young on "blood atonement," the idea that some sins are so grave that God will not forgive them without the person's blood being shed. Thus, to love your neighbors — if they are irredeemable sinners — is to kill them, to save them. Murder could be a religious duty.

Such fanatical rhetoric was disturbing in itself, but the Mormon faithful also believed that the coming destruction of the world would restore their power and dominion over the United States and the Constitution, saving God's favored nation from the infidels running it and establishing Christ's millennial kingdom upon his return to earth. This was a competing vision of manifest destiny, and the two were on a collision course.

Amid rumors that church leaders were enlisting Native Americans to aid them in the event of war with the United States, newly inaugurated James Buchanan dispatched twenty-five hundred soldiers to accompany his gubernatorial appointee, Alfred Cumming, to Utah. "This is the first rebellion which has existed in our Territories," Buchanan would write later that year in his first message to Congress, "and humanity itself requires that we should put it down in such a manner that it shall be the last."

Lincoln wasn't much concerned about polygamy. Instead, he used Stephen Douglas's opposition to Utah statehood because of polygamy as "additional proof" that popular sovereignty "was a mere deceitful pretense for the benefit of slavery." If voters should be able to choose slavery, he argued in laying bare Democrats' hypocrisy, why not polygamy? There was no federal law against polygamy, but most Americans viewed the issue much as Esther Morris viewed cases in her courtroom: first justice, then the law.

As the US Army set out for Utah in 1857 to ensure Cumming's installation as governor, Young and church leaders prepared not merely for battle, but for Armageddon. Young ordered missionaries and settlers from western colonies to return, collected arms and ammunition, and — much like Joseph Smith when faced with arrest in Nauvoo — mobilized the church's militia and attempted to close the Utah territory, banning emigrants from passing through without a permit. At that time, Utah stretched from California to western Colorado and north into present-day Idaho and Wyoming, which meant that Young was threatening much of western emigration and, with it, America's manifest destiny.

The restriction on emigrants came via an August 5 declaration of martial law that began: "We are invaded by a hostile force, who are evidently assailing us to accomplish our overthrow and destruction." It highlighted old grievances ("our houses have been plundered and burned") and touched raw emotions, saying that Mormons have been "scorned, held in derision, insulted and betrayed." As Young stirred fear and anger and prepared residents to burn their homes and march south, a group of Mormons attacked an emigrant wagon train three hundred miles south of Salt Lake, along with Paiute Indians they had enlisted. False rumors had swirled that the emigrants included a man who'd killed a Mormon church leader after his wife left him to join a plural marriage, feeding the hysteria. After a five-day standoff, Mormons raised a white flag and promised travelers safe passage in exchange for turning over their arms. Once done, they slaughtered 120 "gentiles," as they called non-Mormons, sparing only the youngest children. It was September 11, 1857.

Young ordered no investigation for nine months, finally appointing a man to lead it who had also whipped up anti-American fervor. The investigation blamed the emigrants and Paiute. Eventually, two decades later, a single man was convicted and executed. The church continued to blame the Paiute for the massacre until 2007, when Elder Henry Eyring issued a statement expressing "profound regret" to both the descendants of those killed and the Paiute, whose reputation was smeared. Some historians noted that Eyring's statement did not include any notion of seeking forgivingness or even the word *apologize* or *sorry*. Descendants noticed, too. One told the *Salt Lake Tribune*: "Simply saying 'I'm sorry' would go a long way." The absence of those words was not an accident: Eyring was careful not to implicate Young or any other prominent church leaders in the massacre. And how he did it matters.

His statement began by citing the recently published book that forced the church's hand, *Massacre at Mountain Meadows*. It was written by church employees, two of them BYU professors, who were given full access to church archives and retained full editorial control. Eyring, seeming to ground his regret in scholarship, noted "two of the significant conclusions they have reached." First, that Brigham Young's message not to interfere with the wagon train arrived after the massacre had already been carried out; and second, "that the responsibility for the massacre lies with local leaders of The Church of Jesus Christ of Latter-day Saints in the regions near Mountain Meadows." In other words: It wasn't

Young's fault. The crazy locals did it. Except that's not what the authors concluded.

There is a passage in *Massacre at Mountain Meadows* that Eyring didn't mention, summarizing the responsibility Young and other church leaders bear. I include it here because we have heard the echo of its subject — blinding fanaticism — all along our journey, from the World Trade Center to the jailhouse that held the Conestoga Indians, to the Tree of Life synagogue, to Henry Frick's office and William McKinley's receiving line, to the KKK and Sundown Towns, to mob lynchings and threats against Muslims, to massacres of Native Americans and the Chinese.

"Episodes of violence often begin when one people classify another as 'the other,'" the *Massacre at Mountain Meadows* authors wrote, "stripping them of any humanity and mentally transforming them into enemies. Once this process of devaluing and demonizing occurs, stereotypes take over, rumors circulate, and pressure builds to conform to group action to the perceived threat. Those classified as the enemy are often seen as the transgressors, even as steps are being taken against them. When these tinderbox conditions exist, a single incident, small or ordinary in usual circumstances, may spark great violence ending in atrocity."

What can spark them? The authors continued: "The literature suggests other elements are also present when 'good people' do terrible things. Usually there is an atmosphere of authority and obedience, which allows errant leaders to trump the moral instincts of their followers. Atrocities also occur when followers do not have clear messages about what is expected of them — when their culture or messages from headquarters leave local leaders wondering what they should do. Poverty increases the likelihood of problems by raising concerns about survival. The conditions for mass-killing — demonizing, authority, obedience, peer pressure, ambiguity, fear, and deprivation — were all present in southern Utah in 1857."

As these tinderbox conditions and their sparks appear increasingly present today, it's useful to remember not only the Mountain Meadows Massacre but also what followed it.

As the US Army approached this area in 1857, guided by Jim Bridger, the Nauvoo Legion burned seventy-six supply wagons, destroying much of the food, tents, and other supplies, while also stealing cattle and horses and lighting grasslands on fire to deprive the rest of food. To skirt a direct confrontation, Bridger directed the army on a circuitous northern route, which proved both disastrous and fortuitous. Snow made passage impossible, forcing a retreat to Fort Bridger to ride out a brutal winter, short on supplies — and buying time for a mediator, a non-Mormon Philadelphian, Thomas Kane, who had befriended church leaders, to undertake the long journey to Salt Lake.

In Salt Lake City, Kane convinced Young to step aside for incoming governor Cumming, but Young still wasn't ready to call off the militia. Kane then trekked to Fort Bridger, where he convinced Cumming to go with him to Salt Lake without the army or even a military escort. Over the army's objections, Cumming reluctantly agreed. But Young, fearing Kane's mission would fail, set in motion an evacuation of Salt Lake City and its surrounding area, moving about thirty thousand people south. When Kane and Cumming arrived, Cumming assumed office without incident, and he and Young established a working relationship. After the promise of a full pardon for all those who had been involved in what President Buchanan termed "seditions and treasons," Young allowed federal troops to march west unmolested. When the army arrived and appeared to present no threat, the faithful returned to their homes.

The so-called Utah War was resolved without fighting, thanks in large part to Kane's determined diplomacy and a blizzard. Snow had doomed the Donners, but it helped prevent what could have been a calamitous confrontation that might have destroyed Salt Lake City — Young was prepared to burn it — and sent Mormons into exile, again. Young, in agreeing to give up power peacefully rather than fight, saved many lives — and accepted the cornerstone of American democracy: rule by the people.

I stroll around the grounds of Fort Bridger and the buildings that have been preserved and reconstructed from its days as a US army post, and while there is a statue of Bridger (another David Alan Cark work) commemorating his role in exploring the west, I see not even a brief word for Kane, an abolitionist who would go on to fight in the Civil War. Mormons have honored Kane in a variety of ways, but his peacemaking efforts benefited all Americans, which deserves remembrance here and elsewhere. Although I know of no songs written about him, there's one about the triumph of pluralism and national unity that was written by a different Kane, Big Daddy, that is filled with his spirit: "Word to the Mother (Land)."

However, to sever, we could never
So hold up the peace sign and stand together

I've been checking the weather so frequently that it's becoming a nervous tic. Yesterday I noticed that the Lincoln Highway between Laramie and Hanna was closed to RVs and trucks due to high winds and "Extreme Blow Over Risk." The daily stress of driving in potentially dangerous conditions is wearing thin, but we are almost in the clear.

Approaching the Utah border, the Lincoln brings us along what's left of Evanston's historic blocks, past the spot where a dry-goods store once operated under the management of James Cash Penney. His success impressed the store's two owners, who sent him to open a new store and gave him a one-third stake in it. He soon bought them out and turned the franchise, called Golden Rule, into J. C. Penney, but the old name remained at the center of his business philosophy, doing for others what others had done for him, by allowing managers to take a one-third stake in new stores they opened. Other profit sharing and stock incentives followed, and he attributed the company's success — it became one of the nation's largest retailers — to the business model. He wrote several books on ethical living and leadership, prefiguring the genre that launched Stephen Covey to wealth, but with Christian principles at the center of them. "Is not service part and parcel of business?" he wrote in his memoir. "It seems to me so; business is therefore as much religious as it is secular."

Earlier in 2020, JCPenney entered bankruptcy and was bought by Brookfield Asset Management, which owns about 170 malls. Online shopping has been unkind to both malls and the large department stores that anchored them, but Brookfield hopes that owning both will prove profitable. It has also bought Forever 21 and Aeropostale out of bankruptcy, becoming both landlord and tenant. For chain stores, vertical integration can offer a lifeline. I doubt, however, that Brookfield has any interest in reviving what made JCPenney different and important. Sharing profits with workers and incentivizing ownership stakes are not among the Seven Habits of Highly Effective People.

Past the Utah state line, the Lincoln Highway follows the transcontinental tracks through mountain passes that begin to protect us from the wind. As we descend into Echo Canyon at the base of red sandstone cliffs, it's easy to imagine wagon train travelers being mesmerized, as we are, by majestic sights not found in the east. We pull over to take them in at the mouth of the canyon, near where the Donner-Reed party camped in 1846; where the first Mormon emigrants, including Brigham Young, camped the following year; and where Mormon militiamen dug trenches and fortified the cliffs in preparation for making a stand against the US Army, establishing the military advantage that led Jim Bridger to guide the army around the canyon rather than through it, averting what would have been America's first civil war — other than the centuries-long civil war with Native Americans.

We wend our way through the canyon following the Weber River, which opens up to spectacular views of the Rocky Mountains' Wasatch Range and spits us out by an air force base south of Ogden. The base was built after a war that began with a gun designed by an Ogden man, John Moses Browning. It was his 1910 model that a Serbian student used to kill Archduke Franz Ferdinand, setting off World War I. Browning was born here in 1855 to a gun-making father, Jonathan, who knew Lincoln and hosted him at his home in Illinois, so the family story goes. After visiting Nauvoo and converting to the Mormon faith, Jonathan outfitted his co-religionists with guns for the journey west. Upon arriving in Ogden and setting up shop, he supplied guns to the Mormon militia that prepared to battle the US Army at Echo Canyon — the same army his son would supply with guns in the Spanish-American War and First World War.

In the span of one generation, the Brownings personified the shift in the Mormons' relationship with the United States, from preparing to battle it to winning its wars. Whereas Brigham Young had refused to support the US Army during the Civil War, more than twenty thousand church members served in World War I, including six children of church president Joseph F. Smith — and Browning's guns would help them win it. In World War II, nearly all of the two and a half million machine guns used by US soldiers were designed by Browning. Tomorrow we will see how this transformation occurred and what it tells us about ourselves.

— 34 —

Becoming America

Reaching Antelope Island State Park by car requires driving a seven-mile causeway across the Great Salt Lake, but the water level is so low that we see only the sandy lake bed for much of the way. The causeway was built in 1993, back when Antelope Island was still an island. Now it's a peninsula, the lake having shrunk by about two-thirds. Whether it will survive another century has become an open question, thanks to warmer temperatures that produce less snow in the mountains, and more of the snow that does fall evaporates instead of melting into the rivers that feed the lake. Economic growth is also diverting more water from the rivers that feed the lake. At the state park, the marina is dry.

The lower the lake level falls, the more inhospitable to life it becomes, as evaporation leaves behind salt and pollutants that threaten the lake's brine shrimp industry. Winds could eventually blow the crust off the dry lake bed, kicking up the metals and toxins lodged underneath, including high concentrations of arsenic, and depositing them into the lungs of residents — poison dust. A rancher on the north side of the lake who's also a Republican state lawmaker, Joel Ferry, told the *New York Times*: "We have this potential environmental nuclear bomb that's going to go off if we don't take some pretty dramatic action."

When the lake finally appears, hemmed in by mountains under blue skies, the view is majestic, and when we pass two bison grazing, among the seven hundred that roam freely on the island, the image is complete. But its beauty and serenity masks an unfolding environmental catastrophe.

We leave Antelope Island at sunrise — a bison by the side of the road pays us no mind — and head toward Salt Lake City, traveling through what Mormons who first arrived here called the State of Deseret, a word from the Book of Mormon meaning "honeybee," a symbol of the industriousness they prized. In their early days, Mormons petitioned Congress to be admitted as a new state of Deseret, but the idea of naming a state after a word in the Book of Mormon was almost as preposterous as statehood itself, given public suspicion of the emigrants. Nevertheless, the bees got busy building the hive, and as industrial sprawl gives way to the skyline, the scale of the achievement comes into view.

Downtown, the Lincoln runs along Temple Square, the city's geographic, religious, historic, and cultural center, but we see more cranes and construction workers than pedestrians. The pandemic has emptied out the heart of the city, just as it's done in New York. I never thought Times Square and Temple Square would have the same vibe.

We park on an empty street just past the Beehive House, where Brigham Young lived, now a museum. It doesn't look big enough to fit his fifty-six children and the sixteen wives who bore them, no less the other thirty-nine women he married, though he didn't live or even have sexual relations with all them. Fronting it is an archway commemorating Young's control over a creek that flows into the city. The threat of lacking access to fresh water has loomed over the city from its earliest days.

We walk into a corner of the square that's not fenced off for construction, and two young women ask if we are Latter-Day Saints. When we say we are not, they ask our religious affiliation. They are exceedingly friendly and gracious, but I can tell from Laurel's eyes that the possibility of being proselytized has her a bit on guard.

At this point, I will confess to you what I did not say to the young women, since it may not have been taken in the spirit that I trust you, having traveled with us this far, will take it: As a lifelong resident of New York, the possibility that God would reveal the secrets of eternity in our great state is entirely within the realm of believability. But the idea that the Almighty would choose to do so in the Rochester area — instead of, say, Niagara Falls or the Adirondack Mountains or the Saratoga racetrack — makes faith in an All-Knowing Being rather difficult to swallow. The only thing that would make me more skeptical of Joseph Smith is if he had been from Staten Island.

To be clear: I am kidding. Rochester is a lovely place! (Staten Island, too!) And any city that could invent both Genesee Cream Ale and the garbage plate, a local delicacy, has a stronghold on divine inspiration. But I don't say any of this to the two church guides, as I imagine they already put up with a lot of silliness from people who have seen *The Book of Mormon* but not read it.

The Church of Latter-Day Saints and its members deserve great credit for reacting with such good humor to the Broadway show. If a popular musical had satirized the Catholic Church in the same way, the usual scolds would have been up on their high horses demanding a boycott. To laugh along at good-natured parody — or at least to allow others to do it without taking offense — is part of the art of good citizenship. Every group should get its own Broadway parody and respond with the same grace and class as Mormons have.

In that spirit, I would like to beg forgiveness of the members of the Church of Latter-Day Saints for using the word *Mormons*. In 2018, the church began a push away from the term, requesting that its members be called Latter-Day Saints. I have no objections to people calling themselves saints, but asking others to do so doesn't quite seem saintly to me. If not saints, the church has asked people to refer to its faithful as "members of the Church of Jesus Christ of Latter-Day Saints." That's fine on first mention, but writing it repeatedly would test a reader's patience. The church doesn't like *LDS*, and I don't much, either — language is already inundated with too many initials, imho. Since church members have long used *Mormon*, and the church still endorses the name Mormon Trail, I've adopted it, too — not out of disregard for church wishes but only to simplify terminology.

The two young women who approached us to talk are church guides, and they give us a stationary tour of this corner of Temple Square, pointing out two monuments we are standing between. On our one side is the *Handcart Pioneers*, depicting a man pulling a cart with his wife beside him and child in tow. On our other side is the Seagull Monument, a tall column topped by a seagull that represents the "miracle of the gulls," a story about flocks of seagulls swooping in to devour swarms of crickets and grasshoppers that were destroying the crops planted by emigrants during their first season here, a sign of a divine blessing for their new colony.

The episodes that inspired both monuments are like fishing stories.

Over time, exaggeration and dramatization set in. And as with most myths, commemorating their noble truths erases memory of their painful tragedies.

Only about 4 percent of Mormons traveled west via handcarts, which became a central symbol of the hardiness and heroism of the emigrants, whose fortitude and faith has been passed down through the generations. And while a sign notes that 250 handcart emigrants died, left unmentioned is that 250 deaths came in a single calamity, in 1856, after church leaders urged groups onward in August, assuring them that the journey from Iowa would take only seventy days — and Jesus's return would not wait. The emigrants, mostly English and Scandinavian converts, put their trust in the church, whose elders convinced some to sell their wagons to fund handcarts for others, but the journey took much longer than promised. Food vanished, snow appeared, and the suffering was unimaginable. Death came from starvation and hypothermia, but millenarianism had rushed them on the way. That God didn't rescue the emigrants from handcart hell was not taken as a sign of divine opposition. Blessings come from God, curses from the devil — but that's presuming we can tell the two apart. In the case of the seagulls, the emigrants could not.

A 1987 article written by retired University of Utah history professor Brigham Madsen and his son David, "One Man's Meat Is Another Man's Poison" examined the high nutritional value of the crickets and grasshoppers and concluded that the Mormon emigrants should have been eating them — as the Utes, Paiutes, and Shoshones had long done — instead of praying for divine intervention. In other words: What they took for a plague was really a godsend. The Madsens tried placing the article in the *Utah Historical Quarterly* but were rebuffed because it was deemed to be, Professor Madsen wrote in his memoir, "inappropriate for Mormon readers."

When the Seagull Monument was unveiled in 1913, in the same month the Lincoln Highway was dedicated, one of the speakers told a story of how Mormons had banned the killing of seagulls and arrested an Indian for the crime. As art historian Nathan Rees writes, "From the seagull monument's logic, the Mormons taught Indians the proper relationship between humans and the land, not the other way around." Shortly after its unveiling, a church elder, Brigham H. Roberts, took note of the Indian depicted on its base, below the level of a child: "An Indian sits in idle but graceful pose," he said, "looking upon this strange activity that is to redeem his land from savagery and give it back to civilization."

Yet what is most interesting about the Seagull Monument isn't the story it depicts, which even church historians acknowledge is highly exaggerated — there's no contemporaneous mention of the gulls in the diaries of those present in 1847 — or its typically condescending view of Native Americans, but rather the story that gave rise to it. The church commissioned it in the wake of a US Senate investigation into whether Utah senator Reed Smoot could honor his constitutional oath, given his leadership role in the church as one of the Quorum of Twelve, or whether he should be expelled from the Senate. The Smoot hearings inevitably focused on whether the church was still secretly sanctioning plural marriages, as well as its political and commercial activities and emphasis on revelation, all of which cast it in a negative light.

The Seagull Monument was in part an exercise in mass marketing. By promoting a story that carried a universal Christian moral — God answers prayers and survival is a blessing — while rooting it in the landscape that all farmers struggled to tame, and focusing not on revelation but providence, the church was showing unity with Protestant America. In choosing the artist, the church hired a Mormon by birth but not by practice: a grandson of Brigham Young, Mahonri Young. Having studied art in Paris and New York (he would become associated with Robert Henri's Ashcan School of art), and holding strong views against polygamy (he was raised by monogamous parents), he was the perfect messenger for a church trying to win acceptance from eastern elites.

Against this backdrop, the sacred bird atop the pedestal is as much as a dove as a gull, a symbol of peace offered by the church to a nation still warring against it. By elevating the myth of the gull, in both physical and spiritual form, Mormons were seeking to stay true to their roots while also proudly displaying their American identity, which included joining in America's oldest tradition: infantilizing and marginalizing Native Americans. At the unveiling ceremony, three large American flags covered the monument as a band played "The Star Spangled Banner." What is history, the old question goes, but a fable agreed upon?

Our two guides ask us what brought us to Salt Lake and whether — when we tell them we're married — we have any children. We demur — we're still kinda newlyweds, we say — and they talk about how important marriage and family are to their faith.

Marriage has never been far from conversations about Mormons, and polygamy remains a source of public fascination. Laurel is a fan of the shows *Big Love* and *Sister Wives*. When I see her watching them, I'll say, "How interesting!" And she'll invariably laugh and say, "Good luck! You can't even handle one wife." She has a point.

Lincoln laughed about polygamy, too. When one of Brigham Young's sons came to visit him in the White House in 1862, it was reported that Lincoln told him: "It was absurd to talk about polygamy, as 'he never yet heard of a man having a wife who wanted two.'" Polygamy was a plague upon many women, but as we saw in the lead-up to the Utah War, Lincoln didn't see it as a threat to the nation.

One of the reasons for Lincoln's sympathetic view of Mormons was undoubtedly familiarity. When he was in the Illinois state legislature, Mormons came to Illinois after being forced out of Ohio and then Missouri, where a proclamation by the governor declared, "The Mormons must be treated as enemies, and must be exterminated or driven from the state if necessary for the public peace." Three days later, soldiers in the state militia opened fire on a Mormon community, killing seventeen.

Illinois welcomed them, since both Whigs and Democrats felt sympathy for their persecution. Mormons credited Lincoln, a member of the state legislature at that time, with helping to secure passage of a charter drawn up by church leaders for their settlement along the Mississippi River, Nauvoo. Lincoln's law office would also represent Mormons both as defendants and plaintiffs. Nevertheless, many Mormons saw Lincoln's election as president in much the same way enslavers in the south did: an existential threat.

Brigham Young reported that many Mormons were "very much chopfallen at Lincoln's election," believing he would be "hostile to this people," likely because of Lincoln's party affiliation rather than anything he had ever said. Young's private letters from this period included a steady stream of invective against Lincoln, but there is no record of Lincoln denigrating either Young or Mormons, and undoubtedly he was heartened by the message Young sent to the president of the Pacific Telegraph Company in 1861 — the first telegram to travel along the transcontinental line between Utah and Ohio, six days before the line connected Utah and California. It read, "Utah has not seceded, but is firm for the Constitution and laws of our once happy country."

A month after Young sent his telegram, Lincoln requested three books on Mormons from the Library of Congress, as well as the Book of Mormon, to better understand them. When Congress passed the 1862 Morrill Act for the Suppression of Polygamy, Lincoln signed it into law, at about the same time he returned the books, but he had no intention of enforcing it. When a church delegate paid him a visit to inquire about his intentions, he reported that Lincoln told him a homespun parable: "When I was a boy on the farm in Illinois there was a great deal of timber on the farm which we had to clear away. Occasionally we would come to a log which had fallen down. It was too hard to split, too wet to burn, and too heavy to move, so we plowed around it. You go back and tell Brigham Young that if he will let me alone I will let him alone."

To put the matter in modern parlance: Lincoln wasn't a culture warrior. He didn't seek to inflame passions, whether it was slavery or polygamy, but to soothe them. He didn't whip people into a frenzy over differences concerning culture and identity. And he didn't denigrate minority religions as un-American. He knew what mobs were capable of — he remembered the Illinois mobs that murdered Joseph Smith and Elijah Lovejoy, an abolitionist printer — and he understood the power not only of language and tone but also of small gestures of goodwill.

When Mormons sought federal support for fending off Native Americans, Lincoln authorized Young to "raise, arm, and equip" a cavalry company, even though they refused to enlist with the US Army. When Mormons protested a governor they disliked, Lincoln replaced him with someone more accommodating, winning him praise and earning sympathy for the Union cause. By 1864, Lincoln had made converts of many Mormons. When he was reelected, they celebrated with a parade that stretched for a mile and patriotic speeches that toasted his health. When he was assassinated, three thousand came to the tabernacle to mourn, and all businesses closed.

Respect, compromise, understanding, dialogue, humor. Lincoln deployed them all in managing a group that initially held him in contempt. And while it's now easy to recognize the wisdom of this strategy, it isn't hard to imagine another president attempting either to crack down on polygamy or force Mormons into the Civil War, either one of which may have pushed them further away from the Union and resulted in many unnecessary deaths. Instead, by the time Lincoln was assassinated, the people here were more determined than ever to see their petition for statehood succeed, though it would founder for decades on its commitment to polygamy.

The church's decision to give up on that commitment came only after the Supreme Court upheld a federal law revoking its legal incorporation, authorizing the government to confiscate its property, disenfranchising women, and requiring all Utah voters to swear an oath that they would follow an 1882 federal law banning polygamy. The court's 7–2 decision followed unanimous rulings, in 1879 and 1890, finding that polygamy bans did not violate the First Amendment's right to free exercise of religion. Faced with the prospect of losing all its property and assets, and having its members stripped of their democratic rights, the church abandoned polygamy in the United States while quietly suggesting it could be practiced in Mexico and elsewhere.

Never had the federal government made suffrage rights for a minority group dependent upon formal and public renunciation of a specific religious teaching. Coercing a church to change its theology to survive in American society — by revoking its property and its members' political rights — was an unprecedented infringement upon religious freedom. It is easy to imagine Brigham Young, had he still been alive, daring government officials to seize church temples, provoking a standoff. Or leading the faithful to Mexico, where many thousands had already gone to practice polygamy more freely. Or even burning Salt Lake City, as he had been prepared to do in 1857. But after half a century of resistance and persecution, church leaders relented, sacrificing a theological tenet about the afterlife to sustain itself on earth. And once done, they looked for ways to demonstrate that Mormons were good and faithful Americans — including by participating in the 1893 World's Fair, where their agriculture and mineral exhibits won medals, their women won praise for the civic leadership, and their choir — oh, their choir!

The World's Fair was the choir's first out-of-state trip, and it stopped to perform at communities along the route, making positive impressions that built goodwill, just as Notre Dame would do with its football team en route to the 1924 Rose Bowl. Both promoted shared American culture (song and sport) to conquer stereotypes — and both trips were made possible by that great force for broadening horizons, the railroad.

The story of the Mormon Church is one of the nation's great lessons in compromise and conciliation — a case study in overcoming religious intolerance through cultural accommodation and assimilation. The church moved from seeking separation to seeking acceptance. From proclaiming exceptionalism to proclaiming Americanness. From organizing its own political party to joining the two mainstream parties. From preaching millennial fanaticism to practicing market capitalism. And from excluding black people from full church membership to coming to terms, albeit much too slowly, with its history of racism.

On the base of a Brigham Young statue here in Temple Square are the names of the 148 people who first arrived at Salt Lake in July 1847. The last three names on the list are separated from the rest by a solid line, beside the designation "Colored Servants." Green Flake. Hark Lay. Oscar Crosby. They were not servants. They were enslaved.

In an address on legislation authorizing slavery, Brigham Young condemned whippings and beatings but left no doubt where he stood. Said the prophet: "I am a firm believer in slavery." He called it "a divine institution," believing that dark skin was a curse from God. Still, he wasn't entirely happy with the legislation, and he requested that the title be changed from "African Slavery" to "Manual Service," spinning slavery into service to justify it, just as Christians would do across the south — and here, slaves included Native Americans that Mormons took in as "indentures."

Congress banned slavery in the territories in 1862, but to the Mormon Church, blacks remained cursed and excluded from the priesthood until 1978. There was never an apology — just a statement that a new divine revelation had occurred, as the song "I Believe" in *Book of Mormon* satirizes.

I believe that in 1978 God
changed his mind about black people

In 2018, on the fortieth anniversary of the reversal, a black church member told the Associated Press: "A lot of members are waiting for the church just to say, 'We were wrong.'" A Mormon studies professor at the University of Utah, W. Paul Reeve, speculated on the reason the church hasn't yet said those words: "What else are they wrong about? Are they wrong about gay marriage? Are they wrong about female ordination? If they got race and the priesthood wrong, what else could they be wrong about? I think that's part of the fear."

It's hard for people to admit they're wrong. For religious organizations, especially those with leaders who claim the mantle of prophet, it's especially vexing. Nevertheless, in keeping with its long tradition of compromise and conciliation within American culture, the Mormon Church is finding ways to make amends. Its members are erecting a monument to the first enslaved pioneers, Flake, Lay, and Crosby — all Mormon converts who were barred from the highest reaches of heaven because of their skin color.

Oh Lord I want to be in that number
When the saints go marching in

We stop into an auto-shop-turned-roadhouse-bar on the Lincoln Highway, called the Garage, an oasis beside a sprawling oil refinery in an industrial area. We are meeting Laurel's friend Josh and his husband, Thomas, who are sitting on the back patio near a firepit and stage. Laurel and Josh once worked together, before Josh and Thomas moved back home to Salt Lake City. They ask us about New York, as parents might ask about a child. It was hard for them to watch the news when the city shut down and the death toll spiraled up. They've been glad to be in Salt Lake, but they miss New York. Come back, we say. They might.

It's not always easy living as a gay couple in Utah, given Mormon opposition to same-sex relations. The state flag features a beehive, a reflection of how the line separating church and state, brighter than it used to be, can still be fuzzy. Nevertheless, the Mormon Church is trying, in keeping with tradition, to inch toward cultural accommodation. It recently revoked a policy it adopted months after the Supreme Court found that same-sex couples have a constitutional right to marry. The policy had declared same-sex relations an apostasy subject to excommunication and banned children of same-sex couples from being baptized before they turned eighteen, unless they moved out of their homes and renounced same-sex relations. Many church members disapproved of it, showing that even institutions that are guided by divine revelation can recognize that God speaks through protesters, too. The church will later come out in support of a congressional bill revoking the 1996 Defense of Marriage Act and guaranteeing that marriage licenses granted in one state would be valid in others, should the Supreme Court reverse its decision. That the church still strongly opposes same-sex marriage made its support for the bill, which became law, all the more honorable — a recognition of the tolerance that democratic pluralism requires.

Society-wide support for monogamous marriage was long the biggest obstacle to accepting Mormons as Americans. Now, the roles have been reversed: No other religion has had more success promoting marriage than Mormons, who look upon society's softening support for two-parent families as a serious cultural failure that exacerbates social problems. The link between marriage and poverty is one that liberals are often reluctant to acknowledge, but it is not a coincidence that Utah, with the highest marriage rate in the country, also has one of the lowest poverty rates.

Josh and Thomas ask us if we've ever had funeral potatoes. We've never heard of them. It's a Mormon thing, they say. No one knows where they came from. It might have begun as an easy-to-cook comfort food casserole neighbors would bring to grieving families. Recipes vary, but they generally include cheese, sour cream, and cream soup, plus breadcrumbs, crushed crackers, or cornflakes. They're really good here, Josh and Thomas say.

Today, Utah registers a record number of Covid cases, and Governor Gary Herbert warns residents that hospitals are "starting to fill up." He urges everyone to "do your part" by taking basic precautions. Outside and distanced, we take our masks off to eat funeral potatoes, and they're as good as promised.

We have mostly avoided museums thus far, but the title of an exhibit at Brigham Young University's Museum of Art, *Becoming America*, seems to hang over so much of our journey that I decided to contact the curator, Dr. Kenneth Hartvigsen, who kindly agreed to give me a tour. When I arrive, we sit down to talk — he's wearing stylish yellow glasses that match his yellow-and-blue-striped tie — and he begins by explaining how the exhibit came together. "The pieces I was finding," he says of his dive into the museum's collection, "were underscoring the idea that America is always in the process of becoming something new — so that every day, every generation, America is becoming itself."

Becoming itself! What a wonderful phrase. We are a nation in permanent adolescence, which is often painfully obvious, especially when watching reality shows, TikTok, or cable news. And we are a people that, no matter our past failings, believe in our future and commit to creating it. Langston Hughes captured it in a poem that expresses so much of the national experience: "Let America Be America Again."

> *O, yes,*
> *I say it plain,*

America never was America to me,
And yet I swear this oath —
America will be!

At the entrance to the exhibit is the first work, *Immigrants to New York City*, by Minerva Teichert, a Mormon artist whose son was a missionary in Germany in the 1930s and witnessed the rise of Nazism. The letters he wrote home inspired this painting, from 1938, showing a man and woman standing on a ship deck with two girls as they encounter the Statue of Liberty and the Manhattan skyline. Mother, looking down, worried, holding her daughters. Father — or stranger — gazing up, mesmerized, holding a guitar. Germany's wretched refuse. "Here we are on the deck with them," Kenneth says. "And in this moment, these people are not America. When they step off the boat, they are. From the second they step off the boat, they are America."

Inside the exhibit room, the first wall holds paintings of western landscapes: mesas, purple mountains, desert clouds, grain fields, a ghost town, and two landmarks we had passed in Echo — Castle Rock and Witches Rock. Mixed in are scenes from New York — the Hudson River, the subway, and city streets — and photographs of roadside landscapes in between: gas stations, fast-food joints, parking lots, traffic intersections. It's almost as if the artists have been in the back of Charley for our journey.

"We placed works of art in conversation with each other," Kenneth says, "and as a visitor, you get to sort of listen in on the conversation. My hope was that the conversation would always be changing, that people would find connections and associations that I didn't anticipate." I love this way of thinking about the exhibit. Let's listen in.

Here are portraits of upper-class ladies (by Gilbert Stuart and John Singer Sargent) and portraits of down-and-out men (by Claude Buck and Maynard Dixon), talking to each other about economic inequality — its causes, harms, and solutions.

Navajo men on horseback (Carl Oscar Borg) and a Navajo woman with a herd of goats (Mahonri Young) talk about land rights — what they lost, and what they hope to recover — with pioneers in a covered wagon (Minerva Teichert) and loggers clearing a forest (Harvey Dunn).

Native Americans who are raiding pioneers (Teichert) offer a sympathetic word to striking workers who are beating up a policeman (Maynard Dixon), encouraging them to stand up to power.

Annie Oakley (Andy Warhol) and Baby Ruth (John Steuart Curry), a fat lady in Ringling Brothers and Barnum and Bailey Circus, are sharing stories about the power of pop culture with the actress Fay Painter (Robert Henri).

The men and women at Plymouth Rock in *The Landing of the Pilgrims* (anonymous) talk about manifest destiny with an astronaut planting the American flag on the moon (Robert McCall).

A *Mountain Man* (Frederic Remington) talks about the public's love of mythic heroes with *Superman* (Curt Swan and Jack Abel), who wishes people would remember that he is a refugee, giving back to the country that gave him a chance.

Robert Lee, Jefferson Davis, Stonewall Jackson, and Ulysses Grant — all carved in wood (Harry G. Taylor) — are talking to each other about what to do with Confederate monuments, and they are joined by *Yankee Doodle* (Norman Rockwell) and *Uncle Sam* (Mahonri Young).

People fleeing the destruction and burning of their cabins, in *Saints Driven from Jackson County, Missouri* (C. C. A. Christensen), speak about the dangers of mob rule with a man who stands behind a concentration camp's barbed wire, titled *If I Forget Thee, O Jerusalem* (Thomas Hart Benton).

Today marks the anniversary of the publication of another work of art inspired by Nazi Germany, Sinclair Lewis's *It Can't Happen Here*, the story of a lying snake-oil-salesman-turned-politician, Buzz Windrip, who fuels grievance, religious bigotry, and racism to launch himself into power, with support from the clergy, while promising to "make America a proud, rich land again." Before long, the Windrip regime is repressing minorities and creating a brutal dictatorship. The novel endures because its message — scoffing at humanity's susceptibility to demagogues is a constant threat to democracy — endures. The journalist Dorothy Thompson, who lived through the 1920s heyday of the KKK and covered Nazi Germany, noted, "No people ever recognize their dictator in advance. He never stands for re-election on the platform of dictatorship. He always represents himself as the instrument of Incorporated National Will . . . When our dictator turns up, you can depend on it that he will be one of the boys and he will stand for everything traditionally American."

I leave the museum thinking about the man standing on a platform addressing a crowd in a Maynard Dixon painting titled *Free Speech*. I can hear the man saying to every artwork in the room, and all the visitors who come to see them: *Keep talking.*

— 35 —

Somewhere, Nevada

"Do you have a white pie?" I ask the guy behind the counter at a pizza joint by our KOA in Salt Lake City.

"A white?"

"Yeah, a white pizza."

"What's that?"

"Never mind. I'll have a large pepperoni. And do you have any garlic knots?"

"Garlic nuts?"

"Never mind, all set."

I wait outside. Temperatures have dropped into the low forties, and overnight they'll hit the freezing point. I still haven't figured out how to protect Charley's pipes, and while I think we should be fine tonight, there's snow expected in three days, the first of the season, and Nevada will have its first freeze then, too. We had planned to spend another day in Salt Lake and take our time crossing Nevada, but now we'll have to leave in the morning and get over the Sierras to California within three days. Late-October snow doomed the Donner party. Maybe I should have ordered a second pie, or inquired about funeral potatoes.

Tomorrow will be our longest drive of the trip by far: five hundred miles from Salt Lake City to Fallon, Nevada. I had hoped to travel the original Lincoln Highway route to see what remains of Iosepa, founded in 1889 by

Mormon converts from the Hawaiian Islands, before the church encouraged their return to Hawaii in 1915. Every Memorial Day weekend, hundreds of the roughly forty thousand Polynesians living in Utah, most of them Mormon, come to Iosepa to remember those who lived here — and to speak of their own families' experiences in *Becoming America*, including enduring discrimination from Mormons, gentiles, and the US government, which denied them voting rights. I wanted to visit, too, but the original Lincoln Highway route through Iosepa leads through central Utah, and I couldn't find much information about road conditions along the way. While we were in Wyoming, I emailed the leader of the Lincoln Highway Association's New York chapter to ask if he was familiar with the route. He replied:

> Hi Frank. The entire 1913 Lincoln Highway desert route is a very rough gravel road for almost 200 miles. Some portions have steep grades, with blind curves and no guard rails, particularly over Dugway Pass and Shellbourne Pass. (Think of Lucy and Desi in "The Long Long Trailer.") The section from the Dugway entrance to Fish Springs is VERY accordioned and can really tear your vehicle apart. The last time we came across was last year during the 2019 Lincoln Highway Tour that commemorated the centennial of the army convoy tour of 1919. All of us remarked that we would probably never drive that road again. It is very desolate out there, with no traffic and no cell phone reception. If you break down it could be a day or so before somebody comes along. The AAA and tow truck companies do not go out there. Also there are no gas stations or any other kind of services for about 280 miles. Definitely follow the 1928 Lincoln Highway on Interstate 80 to Wendover. (If you REALLY want to take the desert, it's best to have a second vehicle accompany you, in case you need a ride to get help.) Regards, Paul.

Even having browsed the web and looked at Google Maps, I didn't know any of what Paul revealed. He probably saved us from calamity. He certainly spared us a lot of stress. No wonder guides in the old west were so valuable to emigrants.

The original Lincoln Highway route traveled south to Iosepa, because to go west, as the Donners and Reeds did, and as we are now doing, meant crossing the Great Salt Desert at its widest point and through its most treacherous terrain. The desert was once the bottom of Lake Bonneville, the mammoth body of water that filled the Great Basin fifteen thousand years ago. When the water evaporated, it left behind a bed of salt crust covering mud, a quagmire for wagons and early auto travelers, as well as the army's 1919 convoy. The Donner-Reed party lost days pushing through it, lost oxen and cattle to dehydration, and lost supplies to the wagons they had to abandon. When the state and federal government finally built a road straight across it in 1925 — earlier attempts had failed to conquer the terrain — the Lincoln Highway Association reluctantly abandoned its southern route and adopted it.

As we cross the desert, vegetation ends and a mirage appears: snow. The landscape has turned white, like a winter wonderland. Given the overnight freeze, snow seems plausible, but it's salt, as far as the eye can see.

Just over the Nevada state line in Wendover, we fill up the tank — the next gas station is 117 miles south in Ely — and turn south on the Great Basin Highway across a flat desert landscape with sage replacing salt. Cloud wisps stripe the blue sky. The mountains bare cragged lines. There is no wind. There are no cars. A band of wild horses appears. This is driving.

We had planned to spend the night in Ely, before the forecast forced us to push on, so we only stop to see the storefront casinos that line the main drag amid cheap motels and midcentury modern signs. The RV park is on the edge of town, a block from the Stardust Ranch, a brothel. Nevada is the only state that offers legal prostitution, provided it takes place in a brothel licensed by the local government. (The law excludes Clark County, home to Las Vegas.) There has always been demand for the world's oldest profession, including by our noble traveling companion, Honest Abe, or so said his law partner, William Herndon, who believed that Abe frequented prostitutes while traveling the circuit courts before he married. Herndon related a story told by Lincoln's friend Joshua Speed about Lincoln getting into bed with a lady but, before going further, asking her price: $5, she said. When he replied that he only had $3, she offered to accept the rest on credit. Lincoln refused, saying, "I'm poor and don't know where my next dollar will come from and I can't afford to Cheat you." When he offered the girl the $3 anyway, she replied, "Mr. Lincoln, you are the most Conscientious man I ever saw."

It sounds apocryphal, even ridiculous. But Herndon had no reason to doubt Speed and neither had reason to smear Lincoln. Douglas Wilson, whose biography of Lincoln's early years won acclaim, accepts it as credible. And for good reason: It fits with the sympathy Lincoln expressed for such women, including in a poem he wrote in the 1830s, a time when sexually active women could be ostracized from society and left with few options but prostitution, while the men carried no such black mark, offending Lincoln's sense of justice.

Whatever Spiteful fools may Say —
Each jealous, ranting yelper —
No woman ever played the whore
Without a man to help her.

The word *prostitute* is now often replaced with *sex worker*, yet many in the sex trade suffer from conditions that are even more isolating and suffocating than social stigma, by being trapped in the grip of traffickers or drugs, or both. Last year, the Stardust Ranch closed after the overdose death of a thirty-two-year-old woman. But brothels remain open here for one reason: They attract visitors who spend money in the casinos and motels. Whatever spiteful fools may say, the brothel owner is no more a pimp than the mayor and city council.

Beyond the brothel and RV park, the road begins to rise through a canyon parallel to railroad tracks. We are following the old Pony Express trail on Route 50 — "The Loneliest Road in America," a sign announces, a title that sprang from a 1986 *Life* magazine story and became a tourism campaign. In the silence of a vast desert expanse surrounded by distant mountains is a large rust-colored tank, about ten feet tall, with a pipe that leads to a mud-caked pool — a water source for cattle, I presume. On the tank are hand-painted white letters reading, "Nowhere, Nevada." The next town, Eureka, is sixty-five miles west. The middle of Nowhere is a big place.

The ride to Eureka is a succession of stunning climbs and descents through winding mountain passes above seven thousand feet, each one followed by long stretches of desert plains that point us straight to the next set of distant mountains and the ridges that will nestle us in and carry us through. Sagebrush is our constant companion. The occasional car passes. We see a few cattle and, though we can hardly believe it, a man on horseback in a cowboy hat and swinging a lasso.

Past Eureka, the topographic pattern repeats itself: long stretches of desert plains hemmed in by distant mountains that we eventually ascend and descend. At the bottom of the windiest, steepest, and most scenic of the passes is Austin, one of Nevada's "living ghost towns," with a population of less than two hundred. Approaching it, we hit a traffic jam. Road construction. We are stopped near a small stone building the size of a garage. A sign above the front entrance reads, "Gridley Store." This is the Gridley whom Mark Twain wrote about in *Roughing It*, telling a story that was already famous. Today it's mostly forgotten, but it's more relevant than ever.

In short: Democrat Reuel Gridley and a Republican friend placed a wager on the outcome of Austin's April 1864 mayoral election. The loser would have to march through town carrying a fifty-pound sack of flour. Gridley lost, and his Republican friend turned out the town to witness the humiliating procession starting at Gridley's store.

In Twain's telling, upon completing the task Gridley declared he did not need the sack and asked for suggestions of what to do with it, which led someone to suggest auctioning it and donating the funds to the newly formed US Sanitary Commission, to aid wounded Union army soldiers. The winning bidder paid $250 and then offered a suggestion even better than the first: *Sell it again*. And so it was sold again, and again, and again, raising $8,000. When word reached another mining town, Virginia City, the citizens there demanded another auction. Twain, working as a reporter there, helped gin up the hoopla. Gridley had the most valuable sack of flour in the world, and he took it on tour, carrying it to both coasts and raising some $275,000.

What Twain left out of the story, however, is that Gridley was a Copperhead, a southern sympathizer who favored peace with the Confederacy. Part of the bet, at least in other retellings, was that the losing man carrying the flour would be serenaded by the victor's song of choice. If Gridley had won, the band would have played "Dixie." Instead, it played "John Brown's Body." Gridley wasn't the only Copperhead in Nevada, but the territory was solidly for the Union, and Congress was pushing to make it a state.

A month before the mayoral election, Lincoln had signed legislation enabling Nevada to become a state after the adoption of a constitution. Nevada had only about thirty thousand to forty thousand residents at the time, well below the usual threshold to be considered for statehood, and the larger territories of Nebraska and Colorado had yet to be admitted as states. But what mattered was bolstering Lincoln's reelection chances in the event of a tight race, while also providing votes for the Thirteenth Amendment, which Congress was struggling to pass.

Nevadans adopted a constitution, and Lincoln proclaimed Nevada a state only eight days before the 1864 election, enough time for its residents to vote — helping to give Lincoln a second term and sending to Congress

Henry Gaither Worthington, who would cast one of the decisive votes for the Thirteenth Amendment (and serve as one of Lincoln's pallbearers eleven weeks later). Nevada was "battle born," they say here of its Civil War origins, but it was conceived by scheming politicians, Lincoln among them.

Imagine the howls of protest and worse that would now erupt if one party attempted such an effort to "rig" the vote in the immediate run-up to an election. People would wail that the end of the country was at hand. But just as politics ain't beanbag, as Finley Peter Dunne wrote, elections aren't pattycake. They've always been a fight. The important thing is to shake hands when they're over.

In his 1904 book on the history of Nevada, Thomas Wren wrote of the effect Gridley had on the town: "The sack of flour had brought about a change of feeling in Nevada. Men realized they could feel differently about the war and still be friends." Even if this moral is greatly exaggerated, so much of the story's details have been embellished, why not the moral, which could serve such a useful purpose? It is a myth worth recapturing. Although the annual Gridley Days Festival hadn't been held in years, due to popular demand it returned in 2022 — a hopeful sign if ever there was one.

Gridley deserves to be remembered as much for his extraordinary flour fundraising as for his simple acts of citizenship, playing two roles that are crucial to sustaining democracy: the gracious loser and the aisle crosser, supporting an effort to aid a cause that he did not, at least not wholeheartedly, support. He personified what would become the Nevada state motto, in 1866: "All for our country." And in the telling of his story — call it flour power — we can hear the fifth voice and see the central truth about elections: How people respond to the results matters as much as, and often more than, the results themselves.

When traffic begins moving, we roll slowly up to a roadside table with signs reading, "Recall Sisolak," the Democratic governor. A few of the town's two hundred residents are gathering petition signatures and seeking to oust him for a variety of reasons, including his pandemic restrictions and closures of schools and churches. The effort will fail, but the anger will not subside and he will lose 2022 reelection by a narrow margin. In his concession statement, he says, "I believe in our election system, in democracy and honoring the will of Nevada voters. Whether you voted for me or Sheriff Lombardo, it is important that we now come together to continue moving the state forward. That is why I reached out to the sheriff to wish him success." Strike up the band and give that man a sack of flour.

The 110-mile drive from Austin to Fallon continues the pattern we've been seeing since leaving Ely — a long stretch of desert valley leads up and over distant mountains and down to another long valley — yet there is no sense of monotony, only awe.

On the backside of a mountain outcropping, at least a mile off the road, is a mammoth white sand dune, two miles long and six hundred feet high. It's unlike anything we've seen thus far, but it's less surprising than what's at its base: a sea of RVs. What's the occasion? We drive in for a closer look and see what appears to be a huge tailgate party. To our astonishment, dune buggies, dirt bikes, and ATVs ride up and down the side of the dune, Sand Mountain. It finally dawns on us: This is not a special event. It's just Friday at 5:00 P.M. The loneliest road has come to its end.

Sand Mountain is a remnant of Lake Lahontan, which was larger than Lake Ontario. When the lake dried up about ten thousand years ago, the winds blew its sands miles across the lake bed, until the mountains here slowed the winds. The sands that fell formed their own mountain, with a spine that curves back and forth. When the sand shifts, it makes noise — a vibrating hum that can murmur, drone, whistle, and roar. A singing sand dune, it's called, one of only a few dozen in the world.

There is another origin story told about the mountain, by the Paiute and Shoshone. A long serpent buried itself in the sand, hence its sinuous shape, and the noises come from its hisses and movements. For them, it's a spiritual, sacred place. To ATV riders, it's a slice of adrenaline heaven. Tensions between the two groups have simmered for decades, with environmentalists joining the tribes to push for greater protection from motorized vehicles that, they argue, jeopardize plant life, a species of blue butterfly, and the sounds of the singing sands. Between the two groups stands the federal Bureau of Land Management, which is tasked with keeping ATVs off protected parts of the dune. Rangers here do their job with too much or too little vigilance, depending on which side you're asking.

More than 80 percent of Nevada's land is owned by the federal government, most of it controlled by BLM. Friction with residents is inevitable, especially for ranchers who must abide by BLM rules and pay a grazing fee for each head of cattle they own. When Cliven Bundy and his sons staged a standoff against BLM and local police — they refused to pay grazing fees for more than twenty years — they became folk heroes for some on the far right. The Bundys claimed states' rights, arguing that the Constitution does not allow for federal ownership of the land. Turning federal lands over to states is a position many western Republicans have held since the 1970s, but never had an armed rebellion occurred. Members of right-wing militia groups like the Oath Keepers joined Bundy's standoff, and conservative media personalities — particularly Alex Jones and Sean Hannity — fanned the flames. BLM backed down, and two months later, a married couple who had been among the armed militia killed two police officers and a civilian in Las Vegas.

The Bundys are members of the Mormon Church, and Cliven claimed to be receiving messages from God. This wasn't 1857 all over again, but the thread connecting the two situations — the rejection of federal authority, the organizing of a private militia, the claim of divine revelation, the conspiracy-driven paranoia, the mistaking the rule of law for tyranny — is clear enough. The error many of us made wasn't to see Bundy as a kookie old codger with racist ideas, a claptrap legal theory, and wingnut supporters. It was saying to ourselves: *There's only two hundred of them*. More than a decade later, Bundy still isn't paying grazing fees, and the BLM, cowed by the incident, still isn't enforcing the law.

Back the Blue, people say. But BLM rangers are law enforcement officers, too.

Beside the Sand Mountain ranger booth is an ATV with a pole flying the Confederate flag. Maybe it's a middle finger to the rangers, but whatever the case, I wish Nevada hadn't removed the unifying motto from its state flag — "All for Our Country" — and replaced it with a slogan that is easily co-opted by those who would put it to opposite ends: "Battle Born."

Before we left New York, we became members of Harvest Hosts, a collection of family farms, breweries, vineyards, museums, and other places that offer free overnight stays to RVers for a $65 annual fee. We are excited to be pulling into our first host, Lattin Farms, in Fallon, Nevada. The dirt parking lot is nearly full — it's a fall festival weekend — but we see other RVs in a field past the pick-your-own-pumpkin patch, by the corn maze.

"A corn maze! I've never done one," I say to Laurel, who reacts incredulously. It's nearing sundown, so we plan to eat quickly and then do the maze, but by the time we get to the entrance, it's nearly dark. By a tower of jack-o'-lanterns, we are given a map and carefully examine it. I take the lead, and we soon find ourselves back where we began. "Okay, Magellan, let me see the map," Laurel says. She takes the lead and moves us deeper into the maze, but eventually we end up back in the same spot. We abandon the map and follow our sense of direction, but as we lose the last bit of light and the temperature drops, the thought of getting trapped inside no longer seems quite as funny. What happened next would become a matter of dispute. I assert that, as full darkness descended, I somehow sensed the portal of escape, an inspired and heroic discovery. Laurel tells a more dubious story, about us overhearing teenagers speak of knowing the way out and following behind them.

In the morning, as Laurel visits the chickens and goats, I meet up with Rick Lattin, seventy-six, outside the produce stand. "My cousin lives across the street," he says, orienting me. "Her daughter has a house right down here, and my daughter built toward the other end, and my son built over here. We've got our own little family farm here. It's kind of neat." And they're not all that unusual, he says. "We don't have very many farms around here that are more than a couple of hundred acres," he says. "It's all broken up, because people came in and they took 40 acres, 80 acres, 120 acres. You can go sixty miles to Yerington and they have a lot of fifteen-hundred- and two-thousand-acre farms, because they weren't homesteaded. They came in and over time they got bigger, bigger. Ours are small farms."

Rick's grandfather arrived here in 1909 as a homesteader, four years after the completion of a canal that diverted water from the Truckee River to irrigate the region. Homesteaders helped pay for it — their land fees went into a fund for dams and irrigation projects under the 1902 Reclamation Act, named for the idea that desert lands needed to be reclaimed from nature for farmers. No longer able to push the frontier westward, the federal government pushed it inward. Thirty years before the Roosevelt name became synonymous with public works, Teddy's Reclamation Act gave rise to the most ambitious public works agenda ever undertaken, and one of the first projects was the Truckee Canal.

"Right where we're standing here, there used to be a south fork of the Carson River," Rick says. "During the early 1900s, they were building the dam, and building the canal, so they said, 'Okay, we don't need that river. We have a canal running through that area.' So the Carson River south fork doesn't exist anymore. This area was in the riverbeds, so it's very good soil."

His farm's top cash crop has long been one that loves the loamy and sandy soil the river left behind: Hearts of Gold cantaloupe, which has won awards and appeared in *Every Day with Rachael Ray*. Local dairy farmers buy Rick's alfalfa and corn silage. And with visitors buying pumpkins, vegetables, baked goods, and tickets to the maze, business has been good, but he's worried. "We will have another drought next year if it doesn't change," he says of the weather. "We've had no precipitation."

"Aren't you in a drought now?"

"No, because we've got the reservoir. As of today — I check it every day — there's fifty thousand acre-feet. It holds about three hundred thousand, and we need over four hundred thousand to finish a year. If we don't start getting some water, we're going to be in deep trouble. We have to watch for the Sierra runoff and the Sierra has nothing now. So we're already prepping for drought. We put in the drip irrigation, use the water a little bit differently. We'll pull some of the alfalfa out of production and things like that. We're hoping we don't have to do that. It looks like there's a pretty good chance, but you just don't know. And you look around and some places are getting hit with so much rain they don't know what to do with it. And then here we don't have any water at all."

"What's your view on whether climate change factors into it?"

"My view on climate change — and you get in trouble with your views on it — is that any person with an IQ over five knows there's climate change. But when it became a political thing, it makes it very, very difficult. I was sitting with some Sierra Club people at an Indian reservation, and they said: How's this climate change affecting you? And I said, well, for the most part, it's been very good for us because we're a high desert pool place and it's extended our crop seasons. It's allowed us to grow things that we couldn't grow. This year we picked melons until day before yesterday. As a kid — that's 1960, 1955 — we never picked melons past Labor Day."

I can hardly believe it's been a seven-week change in harvest time in the span of one lifetime, but Rick sees the other side of climate change, too. "In another way, it's been brutal," he continues. "Last year or two years ago, I can't remember, we went up to 108 degrees, 107, 105. And it was that way all summer. It's really, really tough. It's not just the water, it's the plants. I have a little raspberry patch, and when that climate change sun hits those raspberries, it's done. I mean, you just can't grow them here."

The raspberries may be the first to go, but they won't be the last. Whether even the melons can survive several more generations is an open question that will depend, in large part, on whether we can find our way through the maze of climate change before darkness sets in.

— 36 —

Reconcilable Differences

I was wrong about the Lincoln Highway not running through any Indian reservations. North of Fallon, it crosses the southern tip of the Paiute Reservation, where the Truckee River bends north to Pyramid Lake, the center of reservation life. We won't be able to see the lake that was once called "the most beautiful desert lake in the United States" by the National Park Service — the road to it remains closed to the public due to Covid — but it's struggling to survive. A dam and diversions to irrigation canals built under the 1902 Reclamation Act have destroyed the wetlands around it, decimated a primary Paiute food source — the Lahontan cutthroat trout — and given rise to toxic algal blooms that are fed by fertilizer and other runoff from irrigated farms. The blooms, which irritate intestines and lungs, recently closed the lake to swimming. No one asked the Paiute what they thought of the dam and irrigation canals. The water was simply taken — or more accurately, given the reservation's legal protections, stolen.

The Reclamation Act was the nightmare inversion of the paradise a Paiute named Wovoka envisioned in 1889, where Native Americans would be reunited with their ancestors and regain dominion over the earth, while whites disappeared and buffalo returned. Fulfilling the vision required native people to live moral and industrious lives in harmony with whites and to perform what came to be called the ghost dance. As word of Wovoka's prophecy spread among native nations, Lakota leaders came to western Nevada to hear it firsthand. Convinced of its authenticity, they brought it home. The more people danced, the sooner the vision would come to fruition.

Wovoka's vision was much like Mormon and other Christian millennialism — the righteous would soon be rewarded and the evil damned — but Americans viewed it as a threat to the nation's peace and security, especially when reports circulated of "wild and crazy" Lakota falling under trances while dancing. The federal government had already banned some traditional religious dances and ceremonies that it believed fed agitation for war, adopting an Indian Offenses criminal code in 1883. As the ghost dance continued — "the messiah craze," news reports called it — the Harrison administration did what the Buchanan administration had done with the Mormons: It called in the army.

"I should let the dance continue," a former Indian agent, doctor, and friend to the Lakota, Valentine McGillycuddy, warned Washington, perhaps influenced by his Catholic mother's tales of religious repression in her native Ireland. "If the Seventh-Day Adventists prepare their ascension robes for the second coming of the Savior, the United States Army is not put in motion to prevent them. Why should not the Indians have the same privilege? If the troops remain, trouble is sure to come."

General Nelson Miles tried to avert trouble by enlisting someone to play the role Thomas Kane had in the Utah War, someone known for treating the Lakota in his employ with decency and respect, including allowing for free religious expression: Buffalo Bill Cody. As the Lakota danced, General Miles hoped Cody could secure the peaceable surrender of his old friend and employee Sitting Bull, the Lakota holy man and one of the leaders of the ghost dance movement. Once again for Cody, life was a stage. But as he traveled west to undertake the act, the army stopped him and instead sent Native American police officers to arrest Sitting Bull. Amid resistance, an officer shot and killed him.

In the aftermath, the Seventh Cavalry rounded up the Lakota and disarmed them. When one man refused to hand over his rifle without being paid for it, a struggle ensued, the gun went off, and the army began indiscriminately firing into camps of families, killing three hundred people. What began as a spiritual and peaceful prophecy here in Nevada ended as one of the worst massacres in American history, the bloodiest episode ever to stain the First Amendment's free exercise of religion, and the final nail in the coffin of Native America's resistance to the armed takeover of its lands.

Until 1970, with the publication of Dee Brown's *Bury My Heart at Wounded Knee*, the episode remained mostly forgotten, and many believed that was how it should stay. Three years later, when a Native American rock band, Redbone, wrote a song with a funk beat about the massacre, CBS Records refused to record it. After the band paid to record it themselves and promoted it to radio stations in Europe, where it was a hit, CBS still refused to release it in the United States, a refusal that — in its fear of history and what it requires of the present — revealed the truth in the song's refrain.

> *We were all wounded at Wounded Knee*
> *You and me / In the name of manifest destiny*

And not just at Wounded Knee, of course. Healing those wounds is a challenge not only for Native America — the Paiute are still in court fighting to secure their Pyramid Lake water rights — but for us all, as citizens and voters.

Casale's Halfway Club is a Lincoln Highway restaurant named for its distance between Reno and Sparks. Inez Casale Stempeck — Mama Inez, born to Italian immigrants — was the owner-operator until three and a half weeks ago, when she died of natural causes at age ninety-three, after having worked there since her parents opened it in 1940. One of her children, Tony, spent decades at the restaurant preparing to succeed her, learning the secrets of her raviolis and sauce, the recipes she never wrote down. Five days ago, and only three and a half weeks after taking over for his mother, Tony died from Covid.

Covid hospitalization rates are up 40 percent from last month. In Nevada, cases are approaching their July peak. Some public health experts are calling for a nationwide mask mandate, using terms like *chaos* and *wildfire* to describe the latest surge. When we pass by, Casale's Halfway Club is closed.

On the Lincoln Highway between Reno and Sparks, buses run with Abe's face emblazoned across them, and each bus stop offers a trip back in time through old photos and historical displays that tell of the lumber mills, breweries, and bottling works that once lined the street and of motels that sprang up with the Lincoln Highway and died with the interstate. The last stop before downtown Reno displays photos from "the Fight of the

Century," Jack Johnson versus Jim Jeffries on Independence Day 1910, a match to determine the champion of the world and something far more important: the validity of white supremacy.

In a hastily constructed arena on what would become the Lincoln Highway, eighteen thousand people — twice the city's population — came to watch Jack, the reigning champ and son of emancipated slaves, take on Jim, who had been retired for six years. Jim had refused to fight Jack or any other black fighter during his day, but when Jack won the belt, Jack London and other journalists pressured Jim to return. "I feel obligated to the sporting public at least to make an effort to reclaim the heavyweight championship for the white race," Jim said. "I should step into the ring again and demonstrate that a white man is king of them all."

The Great White Hope, they called Jim, and bettors overwhelmingly favored him, but Jack beat him from the get-go and knocked him out in the fifteenth round. As the news spread across the country — thirty thousand people waited in Times Square for the telegraph to arrive, and President Roosevelt repeatedly called the telegraph office in the hope of hearing of a Jeffries victory — whites began to attack blacks. The myth of white supremacy lay beaten on the mat — "I couldn't have beaten Johnson on my best day," Jim would later say — but not the attachment to it.

At least ten people were killed in riots around the country, adding to the dozens of black people who would be lynched that year. When film footage of Jack's victory appeared in theaters, more rioting occurred. Cities and states banned the film and Congress banned the interstate transportation of boxing films, but they could not erase the memory of the feeling the triumph brought, as Harlem Renaissance poet William Waring Cuney, a classmate of Langston Hughes at Lincoln University, wrote.

Oh, my lord / What a feeling,
When Jack Johnson / Turned Jim Jeffries'
Snow-white face / Up to the ceiling.

Unable to beat Jack in the ring, whites beat him in the courts, arresting him for violating a law against transporting prostitutes across state lines. An all-white jury convicted him. His real crime? Cavorting with and marrying white women. The year the Lincoln Highway was dedicated, he fled the country and lived in exile for seven years, before returning to serve his year-and-a-day sentence in 1920.

In 2009, Congress passed a resolution calling on President Obama to issue a posthumous pardon to Jack Johnson. He declined. President Trump, whose career included promoting prizefights at his casinos, signed the pardon and chastised Obama for failing to do so, without mentioning one reason why he didn't: Johnson had a history of beating women. That he was railroaded by a racist judicial system was plain. But countless others were racially railroaded without having engaged in violent crimes and spent far more time in prison, and worse. Should the famous be privileged with posthumous pardons denied others? Or is it too cheap and easy a societal penance? And would all the other victims then be more easily forgotten? Reconciliation requires recognizing the reasonable arguments that exist on both sides of these questions.

"You have the audacity to ask that with the pandemic and the Black Lives Matter? Oh my goodness."

I'm in the lobby of the Antique Angel Wedding Chapel, which sits on the Lincoln Highway, just past the arch proclaiming Reno "The Biggest Little City in the World." I had asked the older woman behind the counter how business has been this year. Perhaps I should have put the question more delicately, but I doubt niceties would have dampened her outrage. Having gotten it off her chest, she continues: "We were totally closed for over three months. We were told that we get to open on May the twenty-ninth. May the twenty-ninth, they had Black Lives Matter over in the park. And that night we had eleven windows broken out and two shot out. The only thing that saved our gift shop is that there were four off-duty sheriffs in the crowd, and they stood in front of our windows and wouldn't let them in, or we would have been totally devastated." Across the street, protestors vandalized and set fire to city hall.

Over the summer, some Reno residents organized a more productive protest with a more concrete objective, gathering signatures to remove the name of Francis Newlands from a park that surrounds a house he once owned, along the Truckee River. Newlands, a Nevada senator born in antebellum Mississippi, proposed what he called a "white plank" to the 1912 Democratic Party platform, restricting both suffrage and immigration to whites. "I believe this should be a white man's country," he said, calling blacks "a race of children." Removing his name from the park would be erasing history, his supporters say, yet his house would still stand as a place to explore his historical legacy, good and bad, including the segregation that persisted here through the 1950s not only in the housing he developed but in Reno's restaurants, hotels, and clubs, too. Let the public park carry a name that welcomes all, and let the 1902 Reclamation Act that bears Newlands's name be his public legacy, for better and worse.

Only 3 percent of Reno's population is black. That makes it too easy for politicians to ignore matters of racial justice, which raises the risk of rocks coming through windows. But the woman at the chapel is not just angry at the vandals. "We lost a lot of weddings because people couldn't travel, lockdowns in some cities," she says. Lockdowns have been deeply unpopular in many areas not only because of the hardships they impose but also because of the culture they cut against in a country that worships at the altar of commerce and the human nature they try to suppress. The woman here is not wearing a mask, and I suspect she would have signed the petition we came across in Austin to recall Governor Sisolak. Still, that both left and right take to petition gathering to demand justice is a sign of faith in democracy — and a determination to work through our differences and stick with one another in good times and bad, sickness and health.

Although Covid has canceled many weddings, Nevada still leads the nation in marriages, thanks mostly to Las Vegas but also to Reno. The wedding industry sprang up here in the early twentieth century when Reno began offering easy divorces to anyone with only six months of residence. Facing competition from other states, Nevada reduced the residency requirement to six weeks in 1931, when it legalized gambling. Among the brothels that opened to serve the new arrivals was the Lincoln Bar, which surely would have made Abe smile, and not just for the ladies: He and his partners handled more than 130 divorce cases, representing both women and men and winning more than they lost.

The notion that government might not permit the dissolution of a marriage now seems foreign. As a teenager, I memorized Billy Joel's "Stop in Nevada," about a woman escaping a man, without ever understanding that it was about a woman escaping a government that made it exceedingly difficult to escape a man. But so it was in much of the country until 1969, when California governor Ronald Reagan signed the nation's first no-fault divorce law, perhaps informed by the unpleasant experience of having his first wife claim one of the only acceptable grounds for divorce, "extreme mental cruelty." Under the new law, "irreconcilable differences" was sufficient. Most other states soon followed, a triumph for freedom, especially for women, though it has not been without costs for children of divorced parents, who have been more prone than children in two-parent families to suffer economically, educationally, emotionally, and psychologically, including being at higher risk of depression and suicide. That doesn't make no-fault divorce laws wrong. The old system was oppressive. Many kids come through divorce just fine. But children who struggle often need more help and support from communities than they get.

Preventing those harms led to one of the most interesting proposals of the 2020 presidential campaign, by Andrew Yang, who suggested public subsidies for marriage counseling, a pro-marriage idea both parties ought to be able to get behind. And since constructive communication is no less essential for communities and countries as it is for couples, why not counseling for citizens? Throughout our journey, people have mentioned their fear of the country dividing into partisan camps that don't communicate civilly, that consume news separately, and that think of the other side hostilely. They frequently blamed social media for tearing apart families, friendships, and the country itself. It may be that the breakdown of the nuclear family has extended to the American family for a similar reason: If we don't need to be tied to people we can't get along with, why stay? It's easier to walk away. We can see this retreat in communities' increasingly homogenous political cultures. Self-sorting has come to feel normal and, worse, righteous.

As we retreat from one another, we lose trust. And that extends to our trust in the will of the majority and in the democratic institutions — the justice system, the education system, the media — that both underpin and check it. As trust erodes, so does faith in a shared national culture. Rebuilding trust, like repairing a marriage, isn't easy and doesn't always work. But it can.

In today's *New York Times*, a story looks back on an assembly held a year ago in Dallas, called America in One Room, which brought together 526 Americans from across the political spectrum to discuss common challenges. Stanford University researchers convened it under the theory that, since extremism feeds on feelings of exclusion and disaffection, bringing people into dialogue on common challenges could help reduce tensions, build trust, and reveal common interests. A year later, as the *Times* reports, the experience has left attendees more politically attentive, more open to different news sources, more moderate in their views, and, perhaps most important, more inclined to have positive feelings about members of the other party.

Assemblies of this sort are no panacea, of course, but even small steps forward are worth taking, lest feelings of irreconcilable differences lead one party to take matters into its own hands.

Leaving Reno, we have a choice to make, the same one faced by the earliest Lincoln Highway travelers: head west over the Sierras via Donner Pass, now mostly on I-80, or south to Carson City and then over the Sierras on Route 50. I've heard that both are steep and treacherous in bad weather, and while the forecast is holding up for the moment, I texted a friend, Morrie, who grew up in the Bay Area, to ask which he'd recommend. "I hit some ice and rolled a car onto its roof on Route 50 — not a great place to do that," he replied. "Accordingly, I'd think 80. But maybe I just had rotten luck with 50. Or perhaps I'm thinking about it backward. Neither Colin nor I died" — he was traveling with our friend Colin — "so maybe we had good luck." It was not quite the definitive recommendation I was hoping for.

Since the western route is the interstate, we head south along the Sierras to (Kit) Carson City. The Lincoln takes us past the state capitol, where a portrait of Lincoln has hung above the Assembly Speaker's chair for a century, and to an intersection with a metal sculpture of a bald eagle that has been named *Freedom* by residents. It sits near an old Indian boarding school for the Washoe, Shoshone, and Paiute children, some of whom were removed from their families, a kind of legalized abduction that happened at hundreds of other Indian boarding schools, which were established to "kill the Indian and save the man," in the words of Richard Henry Pratt, one of the earliest school founders. For Indians, American freedom meant conformity, and conformity meant the loss of their lands, their language, and, for many children, their parents and families.

In the county abutting the school, a 1917 law forbade any native people or other non-whites from being on the street after 6:30 P.M., sometimes accompanied by a fire siren half an hour earlier to ensure that no one lost track of time. We have driven through Sundown Towns, but to my knowledge this is our first Sundown County.

The law was repealed in 1974, but a town just south of here, Minden, has continued to blast its 6:00 P.M. siren, despite protests from Native Americans. The siren honors first responders and carries nostalgia, the town board says, but one person's nostalgia is another's nightmare. A year after we pass through, Governor Sisolak will come to the old Stewart school, now a museum, to sign a bill banning sirens and alarms that were timed to racial curfews. Minden's town leaders, however, will resist the law — it's easier to name a bald eagle Freedom than to engage in reconciliation with those who have been deprived of it. In response, the Washoe will show extraordinary graciousness in accepting a compromise: The siren will continue to sound, but an hour earlier.

Up and over the first range of the Sierras, the desert gives way to evergreen forests and the full splendor of Lake Tahoe appears. After an intersection with two casino hotels, the architecture immediately changes from high-rise to low-slung, from bright lights to dark wood, and from glitzy glam to rustic chic. We don't see a "Welcome to California" sign, but the aesthetic — and the price of gas — confirms we've arrived.

Pine trees lead us to the small community of Meyers, and Laurel remembers that Meyers is where eleven-year-old Jaycee Lee Dugard was abducted on her way to the bus stop in 1991, beginning eighteen years of captivity, rape, and trauma in the backyard of a man who had already been convicted of abduction and rape. Although very few children are abducted by strangers each year, it is every parent's worst nightmare — and in recent years, the fear and disgust that accompany it have been unleashed on our politics.

One of the most telling signs about the depth of distrust now permeating and polluting American politics is the consistent polling showing about half of Republican voters believe Democratic leaders are involved in a pedophilia ring. The anonymous partisans who originally spread the loathsome conspiracy online did not pick that crime at random, but rather because it signifies an irredeemable level of both moral bankruptcy and wicked deception — the essence of evil, masked. A documentary about America's most heinous serial pedophile murderer, John Wayne Gacy, is titled *Devil in Disguise*. Labeling Democrats secret pedophiles is an effort not only to destroy their moral standing — that could be done by calling them murderers — but also to remove the possibility that anything they say could be truthful. It's an ugly update of an old story, the one found in the New Testament's Second Corinthians: Satan masquerading as an angel.

It took off in 2016 with "Pizzagate," the vile idea that Hillary Clinton and other Democrats were sexually abusing abducted children in the basement of a Washington, DC, pizzeria. It seemed like a passing lunacy, but as it merged with QAnon, the general pedophile conspiracy moved from 4chan to TikTok, and the madness moved into the mainstream of the Republican

Party. Too many Republican leaders have lacked the courage to forcefully denounce the loathsome conspiracy for what it is: an attack upon democracy. Instead, some have fine-tuned the idea, turning debates over when and how to teach sexuality in schools into accusations that Democrats are homosexual "groomers," pedophiles who manipulate children to sexually abuse them. The accusation is its own manipulation, of course, inflaming the same emotions that can spiral into violence and government repression: disgust, dread, dehumanization, and demonization.

"We are not enemies, but friends," Lincoln said as the nation hurtled toward Civil War. "We must not be enemies." But people don't want to be friends with a pedophile, and that is precisely the point of the conspiracy theory.

While it is easy for Democrats to denounce the vile pedophilia slander, it is harder to apply the same standard to our own thinking about the moral standing of Republicans. The worst part about Hillary Clinton's "basket of deplorables" speech was that after ticking through the problems with "half" of Trump's supporters — calling them "racist, sexist, homophobic, xenophobic, Islamophobic" — she added, "Now some of those folks, they are irredeemable." *Irredeemable.* What a damning accusation, far more so than *deplorable* — so uncharitable in its judgment. Although she apologized for using the word *half*, she stood by the rest of the statement. And while her denigration of some voters as "deplorables" will long be remembered, her most scornful and pietistic indictment — "irredeemable" — was quickly forgotten, even as the belief became more widely shared among Democrats.

Democrats may cry false equivalence at this comparison, but to do so is to misunderstand the principle at stake and its gravity. To see our fellow citizens as so depraved as to be irredeemable, whether as secret pedophiles or paleolithic bigots, is to court danger and disunion and make reconciliation more difficult. Lincoln, who publicly withheld contempt for enslavers who had dragged the country into a war that killed about 750,000 Americans — "with malice toward none, with charity for all" — showed that moral leadership can be most powerful when it is least judgmental.

Charley handles the twisting ascent to Echo Summit (elev. 7,300) with ease, and though I tense up when bending along a cliff, we've beaten the snow here. Driving down the Sierras through Eldorado National Forest continues the feeling we've had since leaving the desert and spotting Lake Tahoe — that we've crossed into a different country. And for twenty-five days in 1846, it claimed to be.

The small group of Californians who rebelled against Mexico were stirred up by the same two explorers we keep encountering, John Fremont and Kit Carson. They adopted a flag with a bear and a star, inspired by the Republic of Texas, that was designed in part by a recent emigrant from Illinois, Mary Lincoln's cousin, William Todd. The navy soon arrived and claimed the territory for the United States, just as the rebels had hoped. But California is so big that talk of it seceding, or splitting into multiple states, has never ended.

Along the old Pony Express route, a house flies a green flag with a gold circular seal announcing the State of Jefferson, made up of northern California and southern Oregon. The seal contains double X's, signifying a belief among its mostly rural supporters that they've been double-crossed by their state governments. It dates back to 1941, when a group of armed men set up a blockade and declared the region "in patriotic rebellion" over the poor state of their roads. "Our roads are not passable, hardly jackassable" they declared. Their Proclamation of Independence read, "Until California and Oregon build a road into the copper country, Jefferson, as a defense-minded State, will be forced to rebel each Thursday and act as a separate State." It was the first rebellion in the history of the world to take six days off each week, which perhaps explains its staying power. What began as a demand for a more active government, however, has turned into a revolt against it, though the source of the frustration remains the same: urban political power.

Over the years, there has been a steady stream of efforts to cleave off rural areas into separate states to increase their political power, usually spearheaded by conservatives. They are unlikely to go anywhere, since the Constitution requires state consent to partition. And while debating the issue is fair play, the mission of the left-wing California National Party is more troubling: secession and independence. It's a tiny fringe party, yet the Trump years have increased chatter about secession on the left. A book published a month before we left, *Break It Up*, chides liberals for "too hastily" dismissing the idea because of its association with slavery. Republicans have also been flirting with talk of secession, and an idea that once seemed to be buried with the bones of 750,000 soldiers has crept back into the public discourse.

Descending through Eldorado National Forest, we are on the El Dorado Freeway in El Dorado County, all named for the mythical city of gold that brought prospectors here during the California gold rush on their way to the Mother Lode — the name given to the vein of rock more than a hundred miles long that held the promise of paradise. Down in the valley, we arrive at another Harvest Host, a winery with a tasting room in a barn where the grapes are pressed, fermented, and aged. The owner pours us each a flight, and I ask how business has been during the pandemic. "The good news is," he says, "people haven't stopped drinking."

Next door to the winery is a brewpub. As we eat dinner on a patio listening to a singer and guitarist play hits from the American songbook, I text our friend Morrie to let him know we've arrived in his home state safely and to an abundance of riches: spectacular views, local wine, craft beer, live music, and friendly hosts. "The mother lode of CA," he replies, "welcomes you with open arms."

— 37 —

Crime & Punishment

"Welcome to Placerville 'Old Hangtown.'"

The sign is part of a debate that has engulfed Placerville since the George Floyd protests, a western echo of the south's reckoning with Confederate monuments and symbols. On one side of the debate is the familiar refrain: Don't erase history. On the other the familiar rejoinder: It's offensive and should be removed.

Placerville sits along the American River just south of where a man found gold while building a sawmill for a Swiss immigrant named Johann Suter. In the first year of the California gold rush, 1849, three men were hanged here for robbery, in what was then called Old Dry Diggins or Ravine City. Stories differ over the hanged men's nationalities — white, Mexican, Chilean, French, Spanish — but not the tree they hung from, the same tree where vigilantes hanged Richard "Irish Dick" Crone the next year for stabbing a man to death in a saloon. Other hangings may have also occurred at the tree, leading people to start calling the place Hangtown. The Methodist Church didn't approve and neither did many residents, who cut the tree down in 1853 and adopted a new name to improve the town's image, a celebration of the placer (surface) gold that prospectors sought. The makeover worked: The state soon named it the county seat. But as time passed, the town began promoting its hangtown history to attract travelers in search of wild west legends.

In the summer of 2020, the city council held a public hearing on whether to change Placerville's logo, which features a man panning for gold in front of a tree with a noose hanging from it. A majority spoke in favor of keeping the noose, fearful of what would come next: the removal of George the Dummy, a mannequin who hangs in a noose from the second floor of the Hanging Tree, a historic saloon-turned-ice-cream-parlor where the stump of the old lynching tree can still be found in the cellar. "First it's the logo, letterhead, and street signs and then," said the first man to speak at the hearing, "it will be George. After George, or maybe before George, it's going to be the sign Old Hangtown . . . I assure you these people do not stop because in their world, outrage has become nothing more than a recreational pastime. If you don't agree with them, then they throw the race card."

Council members stressed they were only considering removing the noose from the logo, not abandoning the Old Hangtown nickname or George the Dummy, but it didn't matter. To opponents, changing the logo would be an irreparable breach in the dam.

"I am a sixty-year resident of this county," began one woman, "and I have never been offended or embarrassed by the name Old Hangtown or the use of a rope. It is a part of our rich history of this area, whether those that are relatively new to our county understand this or not. When we remove everything of history we are starting to repeat it in the future. You know what offends me is when people move into an area and then demand changes." No doubt the Washoe, Maidu, Nisenan, and Miwok who lived here before the gold rush agree with her.

Conflicts between longtime residents and newcomers over differing visions of the future have long been a staple of politics, but more and more, we are seeing those conflicts extend to differing views of history. In both cases, the questions that lower tensions and promote compromise are the same. Are we making a genuine effort to see it from the other side? And in doing so, can we show the compassion and empathy that are hallmarks of good citizenship?

More than 350 people were lynched in California, most of them Latino, Asian, or Native American, yet the mythology that has been built up around wild west outlaws and the men who exact justice often centers on white victims and white perpetrators. In our public discourse, can we acknowledge and discuss both strands of history — the racism and romanticism — without pretending differences don't exist? At the same time, can we see that the discussion is about more than history? Because it's not just tourists who are attracted to stories of vigilante violence.

Before the year is out, a group of Proud Boys will gather on the Lincoln Highway in Placerville, wearing hooded sweatshirts reading, "Hangtown Proud Boy." The group describes itself as a "pro-Western fraternal organization for men who refuse to apologize for creating the modern world, aka Western Chauvinists." *Chauvinism* is a synonym for "superiority," and its members make that clear here in Placerville by flashing the hand gesture for white power.

In 1959, a different fraternal organization placed a plaque near the burial site of the three hanged men, noting the history and making a plea on behalf of the vigilantes who acted in the absence of police and judges: "Let us not judge them too harshly for those were the rough days of the great gold rush." Viewing history with mercy is admirable, but another appeal is necessary: Let us not romanticize, sentimentalize, and commercialize mob violence, for doing so begets it.

In 1838, a twenty-eight-year-old Lincoln gave a speech in Springfield before the Young Men's Lyceum in which he denounced "savage mobs" that "substitute the wild and furious passions, in lieu of the sober judgment of Courts." He decried the hangings they carried out of blacks, whites, and others, whether they were innocent or guilty. When an accused person is not protected by law, Lincoln argued, no one is safe. "Let reverence for the laws," he said, "become the political religion of the nation."

We are parked in front of the Hangtown Cantina, a few parking spaces away from a stone that holds a small plaque honoring John Studebaker: "Pioneer — Blacksmith — Soldier — Inventor — Builder." He arrived here in 1853 after a months-long journey from South Bend, Indiana, carrying visions of gold in his head. Seeing the area overrun with prospectors, he began making wheelbarrows instead, earning him the nickname "Wheelbarrow Johnny" and enough money to return home and buy back into the family wagon business, which would supply the US Army during the Civil War and become a pioneer in the auto industry. While stories of thrift, good sense, service to national unity, and innovative engineering may not attract tourists like a hanging, they carry far more valuable civic benefits.

The foothills of the Sierras lead us to Folsom, home to one of the most famous prisons in the world, thanks to Johnny Cash's song about it and the concert he played in its cafeteria in 1968. At that time, most inmates were white. Today more than 40 percent of inmates are Latino. *Damned immigrants*, some might say, except that only about one in six inmates are immigrants, about half their share of the state's overall population (35 percent). And what's true in California is true in other states, too. Immigrants are less likely to commit crimes than native-born Americans, and that's especially the case for unauthorized immigrants. A study of Texans found that unauthorized immigrants have crime rates that are about half the rates of native-born Americans. If those of us born here had crime rates equal to those who arrive or stay without authorization, the country would be a whole lot safer.

Folsom Prison didn't host another concert for inmates until 2018, when Los Tigres del Norte played the prison in front of the Greystone Chapel. It was the fiftieth anniversary of Cash's show and of the band's arrival in America, on their way to becoming the world's most popular norteño band, playing border ballads called *corridos* that tell stories of laborers living in northern Mexico, with all the usual themes of folk songs. A subgenre of the corrido is the *narcocorrido*, telling stories of the drug trade. Many Mexican radio stations have banned them, and it is illegal in Mexico to play them to live audiences. They were barred from playing any at Folsom, too.

Like some hip-hop songs, narcocorridos are often criticized for glorifying violent criminals, but they are not so different from the genre of outlaw country that Johnny Cash helped popularize. People don't kill simply because they hear a song about it, just as people don't kill just because they visit a place that romanticizes wild west violence. That is not to diminish the cultural influence of music or myth, only to put them in perspective. Attacks on "Old Hangtown" are a liberal echo of conservatives who demonize narcocorridos and hip-hop. Can each side see a bit of itself in the other?

"We have always felt a deep bond with Johnny Cash and his music," said one of the Los Tigres brothers, Hernán Hernández, in a film of their performance. "Johnny Cash's music, like ours, is about those who struggle, the marginalized, and the voiceless," Hernández continued. "No matter their crimes, there is always the chance for hope and redemption for all of God's beings." Los Tigres closed their show at Folsom Prison with "America," their song about the right of all people in North and South America to call themselves Americans.

We follow the Lincoln into Sacramento to the home of Rob Gold, who welcomes me wearing a gray long-sleeved shirt that holds the logo of his alma mater, Lincoln Law School, where he's been teaching after retiring from a thirty-three-year career in the Sacramento district attorney's office prosecuting murder and rape. A neighbor of his and a friend of mine, Nancy, introduced us. We sit on his covered back patio, and though he's soft-spoken, he wants to speak about hard things.

"The quality of life in Sacramento has really suffered. Homelessness, drug use, crime that people don't want to talk about. There's open theft in stores now. People are just going in and stealing things. They know guards aren't going to lay hands on them. Walmart and other stores in certain neighborhoods, they're leaving. Crime has gone up, drug use is out of control. We were at a taco stand the other day — they're shooting up across the street! Homelessness is everywhere. A lot of those individuals used to be in either the criminal justice system or court-ordered drug programs. Now, because drugs are such a petty thing, they don't want to go to a drug program because it's tough. They say, 'I'd rather do my twenty days of a work project,' which they don't do. I'm just talking here."

But it's not just talk, of course. It's frustration and exasperation with a breakdown in the social order, expressed by the kind of voter — moderate, middle-class, white, suburban — that both parties covet.

"You would not want to go and walk around the city at night," he continues. "Our daughter got married at the cathedral right in the heart of Sacramento. The reception was at the Library Galleria right across from Cesar Chavez Park. It was all homeless and thugs. I've never seen Sacramento like this. It's like in *It's a Wonderful Life* — the difference between Bedford Falls and Pottersville. San Francisco has been that way, Seattle, Portland. Possession of drugs — what used to be felonies are all misdemeanors now. Nobody does anything about it, because you're probably not even going to jail." Voters approved a referendum in 2014 making most drug possession cases misdemeanors.

"I certainly embrace the phrase *Black Lives Matter*," he says. "But the organization, at least the Sacramento chapter, they're anti-cop. People say it's just nonviolent protest — some of it is and some of it's not. There's been destruction of property. Our office was vandalized, and somebody threw a Molotov cocktail. We found our window shattered. There's a lot of hate."

Rob isn't much worried about the defund the police movement. He knows most people, especially in low-income neighborhoods, want more officers on the beat, not fewer. But he worries about the spirit that animates it and its effect upon the country. "What I see in the movement is they want to attack things. They want to tear statues down. They want to discredit people. They want to shame people. They want to out people. They want people losing their jobs." Grant Napear, the longtime radio announcer for the Sacramento Kings, was fired after tweeting, "All lives matter . . . Every single one!!"

The righteous intolerance that Rob sees gnaws at him, and so does its source. "Unfortunately," he says, "it's primarily coming from the party that I'm a part of." He's a Democrat, and he feels let down — and worse, disrespected and scapegoated. His thirty-three years of service to crime victims and their communities now place him as an obstacle to progress. His heritage — his grandparents were Jewish émigrés from Hungary and Russia who arrived with nothing — is now dismissed as white privilege. His view of crime — "it starts with the family, which has broken down" — is derided as backward. And his diverging views now put him at risk of being called a racist by his fellow party members.

"I've always liked President Obama," he says. "I voted for him both times. I don't agree on many of the things that he did, but I always felt that he wanted to bring people together and he loved the country, and he would try to be a healer. I can't stand Trump because he's the opposite. Even if I agree with a position or two, he is bad for the country."

He doesn't put much stock in either party. "The older I get, the more I feel that what's really going to make our lives better is someone like Nancy. We have different views, but I love her to bits. She'll have a gathering in her home, and she does these no mic night talent shows, where she invites neighbors to read a poem, do a song. Let's get together, let's talk. All different types of people."

Nancy has just popped by to say hello. "I would just say, Frank, this guy is a relationship builder," Nancy says. "I've been to graduation parties here and birthday parties, and victims' families are at these parties because of the relationships that Rob has with them. I think that says a lot about his character."

Before I leave, Rob pulls two stones out of his pocket. "That's for you," he says, pushing one toward me, "and this one's for your wife." Each has Abe's face painted on it. "This is my retirement hobby. And look at this" — he takes out a wood carving that he's done of Lincoln's bust. I ask him what he admires about Lincoln.

He pauses. "Humility." He pauses again. "Love." Another pause. "And that he saved the union."

"I'll take you by our Johnny Cash mural," Nancy says. "It's by the same artist who did the Obama 'Hope' poster, and it's about raising awareness of criminal justice reform — it faces toward Folsom Prison. I forget exactly where it is but we'll find it." She is giving me a tour of Sacramento, driving us around the elegantly designed homes and old oaks of the Fabulous 40 in East Sacramento, where her mother grew up and where Ronald Reagan lived during his time as governor, though many of the old houses have been knocked down and replaced with larger ones. Public debates over which history to preserve, and whether to tear down and start anew, lie at the center of so much that divides America.

Nancy takes me to see Sutter's Fort State Park, where replica walls surround a replica pioneer community. There is only one original building from John Sutter's time. The rest of it was built in the 1890s to honor him and what he represented: settlement of the west. But long left out of the history was who constructed the original fort — Native Americans whom Sutter enslaved — and his treatment of them, which even at the time was recognized as abominable, based on an account by a mountain man who recorded the conditions, including feeding them from troughs.

Lincoln tried to stamp out native slavery here by appointing an abolitionist as superintendent of Indian affairs for the region, but the practice was centuries old in the west, and it was carried out not only by Europeans, Mexicans, and US citizens but also by the group that, as Andrés Reséndez wrote in *The Other Slavery*, "came to control an ever larger share of the traffic in slaves" — Native Americans. Apaches, Comanches, Kiowas, Navajos, Utes, and others were both victims and practitioners of slavery. They routinely took captive Mexicans and Native Americans, and some whites, too — usually selling them for weapons and horses, but also enslaving them for their own purposes. The California parks department is undertaking a statewide "Reexamining Our Past" initiative that will revise the history told at the fort. It will rightly cover the enslavement of Native Americans, but will it also cover enslavement by them? Historic preservation, if done right, is messy work.

"We're close — I think it may be on the next block over," Nancy says of the Cash mural. When we don't see it, we park and set out on foot, stopping into the Catholic cathedral before walking to a nearby park that honors a Catholic icon many believe to be a saint: Cesar Chavez. The park is a homeless refuge, just as Rob Gold had said. The city would like to move the campers out, but its hands are tied. A federal court decision restricts nine western states from preventing people from sleeping in public places without offering them shelter. There are about four thousand more homeless people in Sacramento than shelter beds, but many would rather live in a tent than in a shelter. In the absence of a solution, the city is installing a public bathroom, as much to aid the homeless as to reduce the unpleasant sights and smells that keep visitors away.

There is a statue here of Chavez that commemorates the 280-mile march of striking farmworkers he led in 1966 from the Central Valley to Sacramento, raising awareness of their demands for union recognition, higher wages, and better working conditions — a Coxey's Army for agricultural workers and immigrants, mostly Filipino and Mexican. Chavez, who kept a bust of Lincoln in his office, became an icon to the labor movement and liberals in the same pantheon as Martin Luther King, but there are some aspects of his legacy that they would rather not discuss: his cozying up to a brutally repressive dictator, Ferdinand Marcos; his autocratic rule of the union, which included purging those suspected of disloyalty and communism, even fanning an anti-Semitic conspiracy about a Jewish takeover of the union; his embrace of cultish practices; and, especially, his crusade against illegal immigration. In addition to demanding tighter border security and supporting deportations, he backed efforts to form a vigilante border force to stop the people he called "wetbacks" and "illegals" from entering the country. It was called a "wet line," and it sometimes employed violence.

Should Chavez's statue come down and his name be removed from the plaza? Should the annual state holiday honoring him be revoked? Let us ask our two questions: Why was he memorialized? For his lifetime of work on behalf of civil rights and economic justice. And did he, on balance, nudge the nation forward in its long march toward its highest ideals? Without a doubt, and all the more so since his views and rhetoric on the border evolved away from vigilantism and denigration. Nevertheless, through him we can see that supporting a border wall and deportations is not inherently racist, in and of itself. It can be something much more mundane: a desire to protect wages and jobs, a reflection of the labor movement's long history of supporting immigration restrictions. About one in three US Latinos support a border wall, a reality often ignored by liberals.

Chavez's statue is a reminder of the importance of forgiveness and the foolishness of holding historical figures to saintly standards. It is also a call for understanding. Can we look upon historical figures — and even more important, our present opponents — with greater humility and sympathy? The answer is etched here in stone below Chavez's feet, in the phrase often attributed to him even though it was coined by his partner in founding the union and organizing the march to Sacramento, Dolores Huerta: *¡Si Se Puede!* The strongest case against the statue of Chavez is this: It should have honored Huerta, too. It's not too late to add another statue — or better, to add her name to the park. Preserving history often starts with filling in its gaps.

Nancy brings me to the oldest part of Sacramento, the neighborhood between the grand state capitol and the docks of the Sacramento River. It had been called the West End until the city demolished much of it in the 1950s in the name of urban renewal, envisioning a broad new boulevard leading to the state capitol surrounded by office buildings and parking garages. Building it required knocking down blocks of storefronts, apartments, and Victorian homes.

We are standing at the entrance to the neighborhood that first met the wrecking ball: Japantown, whose residents were Japanese, Chinese, Mexican, black, and white and whose children attended an integrated elementary school: the Lincoln School. Established in the early 1890s, it was a model working-class community, but not to city officials. The head of the redevelopment agency called it "a full-blown, three-dimensional, horrible, filthy slum." The city's first licensed black lawyer and an NAACP leader, Nathaniel Colley, called the city's claims "the blight of bigotry."

At a public hearing, the first to speak in opposition to the wrecking ball was Henry Taketa, a lawyer and the unofficial mayor of Japantown, who grew up in the neighborhood and attended the Lincoln School. He noted that the planned demolition was especially painful because so many of its residents had been forcibly removed from the neighborhood and sent to internment camps for the duration of World War II. When they returned, they worked to rebuild their lives, businesses, and community organizations — but they could not stop the urban renewal plan that destroyed their community a second time. The census tract that included most of Japantown had 4,467 residents in 1950. By 1970, the number was only 370.

After being kicked out of the West End, non-white residents had limited housing options. The NAACP's Nathaniel Colley found a burning cross on his lawn when he bought into a white neighborhood. When the California legislature passed a law outlawing housing discrimination in 1963, voters overturned it in a referendum by a two-to-one margin. Colley challenged it and won in state Supreme Court, and the US Supreme Court upheld the decision in 1967.

The city won a national prize for its redevelopment plan, and some large corporations moved in, as did government agencies, but the vibrancy of the area is long gone. The old Lincoln Theater is now a parking lot. The Lincoln School is the headquarters of the state's pension fund. The entire block where Henry Taketa's law office stood has long been vacant. "I thought they were gonna make the town look beautiful," April Adachi remarked in a documentary about her old neighborhood. "What happened?"

In 1988, Congress passed a law granting $20,000 to survivors of internment camps, an effort spearheaded by Representative Robert Matsui, who was a toddler when his family returned to Japantown after being sent to a camp, having lost their produce business and almost everything else. The descendants of internees received no money, only an apology, which is more than the victims of urban renewal have received. But tonight, as it happens, the city council will vote to designate as a historic landmark the old law office of Nathaniel Colley, the city's first black lawyer, who hired the city's first black architect to design the modest structure — preserving a small piece of history that helps tell a much larger story about the struggle for equality and the ways governments, often in the name of progress, have been guilty of some of the worst civic crimes: abetting modern segregation and poverty.

"There he is!" Nancy points up to the Man in Black, who is standing outside Folsom Prison, painted in red, orange, and yellow, fifteen stories tall, as if rising from a ring of fire. It's a stencil-and-spray-paint work by Shepard Fairey, based on a photograph by Jim Marshall, completed on the fiftieth anniversary of Cash's concert at Folsom Prison. Above him is the phrase, "United Prisoners Union Bill of Rights." The union formed in 1970 after inmates at Folsom Prison staged a nineteen-day strike, issuing demands for better conditions, more rights, and asylum in foreign countries. But the movement splintered and was doomed by radicals who spoke less about improving conditions than abolishing prison and bringing about a new world order, revolutionary and Marxist.

In the prisoners' failure, it's possible to see Cesar Chavez's efforts to purge his union of communists as something more than merely egomaniacal power-hungry paranoia. He understood the union could succeed only by working within the system, not trying to overthrow it — and that radical or revolutionary rhetoric would destroy it. Concrete objectives framed in rhetoric consistent with American values and history — the same approach taken by Reverend King and other civil rights leaders — were the keys to progress. Today some activists see defunding the police as a first step toward the same goal sought by the Folsom's radical faction: abolishing prison. It's hard to see how they won't meet the same fate.

Nancy and her husband, Tom, kindly invite Laurel and me over for a big dinner that we eat on their patio, which feels like an extension of their indoor living space, the kind of architectural blend that's natural to warm climates and a novelty to New Yorkers. Conversation flows easily: family and friends, politics, the pandemic — Tom is a pediatrician, one of the many unsung heroes of the year — and, of course, the George Floyd protests.

Earlier in the year, Nancy and Tom sat down with their three kids to discuss whether to put up a "Black Lives Matter" lawn sign, treating the controversy as a teachable moment, including about the importance of group deliberations and the value of each person's opinion. The verdict was unanimous, and after putting up the sign, Nancy took the exercise in civic dialogue further, sending an email to neighbors inviting them over to share their own views. People came, pro and con, including her neighbor Rob. She hopes more people will talk face-to-face.

Nancy takes out an anonymous letter she received in the mail a few days ago and gives it to me to read. It's a brief but vicious personal attack that tries to shame and humiliate her for sharing a few news articles about politics on Facebook. In an act of courage and strength, she decided to post the letter, since remaining silent would only empower the persecutor, along with a message. "As we head into the last week of election season," she wrote, "I invite you to remember the feeling of having read that message and do everything in your power not to inflict that feeling on someone else. The way we speak out and disagree can be constructive or destructive."

At the end of the night, they send us off with a generous haul: groceries, local beer, and a throw pillow — Nancy had noticed Laurel's collection in a photo — embroidered with an outline of California and the word "Vote" emblazoned across it. The election is only a few days away.

— 38 —

Ghosts & Ghouls

It's Halloween in Stockton, and we are camped beside an inlet of the San Joaquin River, part of a sprawling delta that feeds the Central Valley's astounding array of table-ready crops — fruits, vegetables, nuts — although the city's annual food celebration, the Asparagus Festival, seems designed to scare off children and many of the rest of us, too.

I spent the day exploring Stockton by foot, and while I saw no children in costumes, the city's downtown blocks had a ghost town feel to them, still suffering from the urban renewal programs that destroyed its thriving immigrant neighborhoods. The few people I encountered were in a zombie-like state outside a homeless shelter under an overpass. At a bus stop beside a vacant dirt lot dotted with tents and a few old motorhomes, someone slept on a bench. When I finally saw two pedestrians, a young black couple pushing two strollers, I felt a sense of relief at the normalcy of sharing a street with a family, but my heart sank when they stopped at a dumpster to dig through it.

In "The Ghost of Tom Joad," Bruce Springsteen sings:

Waiting for when the last shall be first
and the first shall be last
In a cardboard box 'neath the underpass

The case of Tom Joad seems sunny in comparison with the homeless situation here and elsewhere. Joad, John Steinbeck's dust bowl everyman who travels to California in *The Grapes of Wrath*, was out of work in an oversaturated labor market with no safety net and no way to provide for his family — problems government could and did address, to no small extent, through New Deal programs. But it's one thing to hand someone a shovel and a check. It's another to treat the addiction and mental illness that pervade today's street homeless population.

At the bus stop where someone slept, I saw a bumper sticker with a quote attributed to Lincoln: "Corporations have been enthroned . . . and the money power of the country will endeavor to prolong its reign . . . until all wealth is aggregated in a few hands and the Republic is destroyed." Lincoln never said anything like it, but it endures because people on the left want to believe he did — one of the socialists imprisoned in Canton, Ohio, quoted it at his trial — and because, looking at scenes like the one here, corporations and billionaires make easy scapegoats for social problems that the governments are trying and failing to solve.

In the city center, an old brick apartment building beside an empty lot holds a mural by a local artist, Kia Duras. It shows hands holding the trunk of a tree growing atop a city and wrapped in a message, "Plant the S.E.E.D. UBI." It's a reference to the universal basic income program being run by the Stockton Economic Empowerment Demonstration, a pilot project started by Mayor Michael Tubbs that's giving 130 residents $500 a month, no strings attached. Tubbs, one of the city's youngest and most dynamic big-city mayors, has become an evangelist for UBI, and the idea has gained some national popularity thanks to Andrew Yang's 2020 presidential campaign. Although Yang lost, a mini version of UBI began playing out when Congress authorized $1,200 pandemic payments to most Americans, plus $500 per child. Both parties and President Trump support a second round of payments, which soon passes.

Though it has gone little noticed, Democrats and Republicans have come to share a core economic conviction: In a crisis, government's role in addressing unemployment is to offer relief, not work. And yet during the Democratic Party's finest hour in domestic leadership, its leaders and voters believed the opposite.

"Our greatest primary task," Franklin Roosevelt said in his 1933 inaugural address, "is to put people to work." Just four weeks later, Congress adopted his plan for employing unmarried men aged eighteen to twenty-five to live in camps while working to plant trees, build reservoirs, strengthen flood-control systems, stop soil erosion, and improve campgrounds, as part of the newly formed Civilian Conservation Corps. They were paid $30 a month but received only $5; the rest was sent home to their families. When three thousand veterans of World War I showed up at the White House demanding early payment of a bonus due to them in 1945, Roosevelt turned them down but offered them jobs in the CCC. Nearly 90 percent accepted.

Within months, more than four million young men and veterans were repairing streets, building dams, and constructing public works of every kind: schools, playgrounds, pools, post offices, and other facilities. New Deal programs would also employ teachers to conduct literacy and vocational classes for the unemployed, artists to paint murals, actors to stage plays, writers to document the nation's culture and folklore, and musicians to write songs. Woody Guthrie wrote "Grand Coulee Dam" while on the federal payroll to promote it.

Uncle Sam took up the challenge in the year of Thirty three
For the farmer and the factory and all of you and me

In his speeches, Roosevelt made plain his and the public's preference for work over relief: "Continued dependence upon relief induces a spiritual and moral disintegration fundamentally destructive to the national fiber. To dole out relief in this way is to administer a narcotic, a subtle destroyer of the human spirit. It is inimical to the dictates of sound policy. It is in violation of the traditions of America. Work must be found for able-bodied but destitute workers. The Federal Government must and shall quit this business of relief."

Today we do not hear Democratic Party leaders speaking of idleness posing a threat to society, and I suspect FDR would be surprised to learn that we have forgotten something he viewed as fundamental to the New Deal: an understanding that each side had obligations to uphold. Government had an obligation to provide relief, and able-bodied citizens had an obligation to labor for their checks. During the pandemic, the compact between citizen and government has been mostly one-sided: Government provides.

The title of the bill Democrats will pass in 2021 — "American Rescue Plan" — reflects the party's heroic mind-set: Save the helpless. But the voters Democrats are trying to pry from the Republican Party don't want Washington to ride to their rescue. They want to be able to save themselves and their families through their own work, just as those who took New Deal jobs did. Democratic leaders and activists are continually frustrated that so many working people vote Republican, and they usually lay the blame on cultural flashpoints, from abortion to immigration. Those certainly play a large role, but many people are concerned about what they perceive as the country's declining work ethic, and they often lay the blame for that on a Democratic Party that they view as more concerned with providing benefits than promoting work.

This is not a new problem for the party. FDR battled Republicans who attacked the New Deal as nothing but "shovel-leaning" jobs that fostered dependence on government. But FDR countered their attack with results: The American people could see the fruits of the New Deal labor in their own communities, and workers took pride in knowing they had earned their paychecks. Both of those outcomes helped Democrats keep the White House for thirty-five years, interrupted only by the centrist war hero Democrats had hoped would run under their own banner, Dwight Eisenhower.

Today Democrats employ neither FDR's rhetoric on work nor his interventionist strategies to create temporary jobs that could benefit the nation in a wide variety of ways: fighting wildfires; running summer school sessions for the millions of students most harmed by remote classes; creating art that enriches communities; and tackling the $12 billion backlog of deferred maintenance projects in our national parks. Spending the money on jobs rather than relief also would have helped private employers hire for positions they have struggled to fill. But Democrats haven't proposed anything of the sort. The central idea of the New Deal — public work for a public wage — is but a ghost.

In its place, a prevailing consensus reigns among both parties that maximizing the speed of economic recovery calls for cash payments and tax cuts. Had that adherence to macroeconomic efficiency carried the day in the 1930s, FDR might have scrapped public employment in favor of broader and more generous direct relief — and the country would be poorer for it.

Along the San Joaquin River, we have opened Charley's canopy, unfurled our outdoor rug, unfolded our outdoor table, and put out our camping chairs, the better to watch scullers passing by. It's the first time we've had time to fully set up our outdoor living area since Jersey City, and inside,

Laurel strings pumpkin lights and makes a candy bowl, placing our skeleton atop it and surrounding it with small pumpkins and an electric jack-o'-lantern she recently picked up. Covid cannot rob her of the spooky season's joyful climax.

There's a full moon out, and I suppose we should stream *Abraham Lincoln: Vampire Hunter*, or *Abraham Lincoln vs. Zombies*, but behind closed doors, an actual horror movie is playing out: Steve Bannon tells a group of fellow travelers that election night will bring a trick — and, for them, a treat. "What Trump's gonna do is just declare victory," he says, "but that doesn't mean he's the winner. He's just gonna say" — he chuckles ghoulishly — "he's the winner." He explains how more Democrats than Republicans vote by mail, so the election night returns will favor Trump, before the mail ballots are counted. "Trump's gonna take advantage of it — that's our strategy. Trump's going to declare himself the winner." The plan is simple: "At 10 or 11 o'clock, Trump's gonna walk in the Oval, tweet out, 'I'm the winner. Game over. Suck on that.'" Come Monday morning, Bannon says, "Trump's goin' be sittin' there mocking, tweeting shit out, 'You lose, I'm the winner. I'm the king.'"

South of Stockton in the town of Tracy, we pass the high school where the parade began in *The Candidate*, the 1972 film that satirized how politics corrupts idealists, written by a speechwriter for Eugene McCarthy's 1968 presidential campaign, Jeremy Larner. In it, Robert Redford's character, Bill McKay, wins the election because he moderates his positions and rhetoric — a plot that reflected a cultural plot change. Liberalism's great adversary was no longer fascist strongmen, like Buzz Windrip in *It Can't Happen Here*. It was poll-tested centrists who stood for nothing beyond getting elected. In the movie's closing line, McKay asks, "What do we do now?"

During the 1988 presidential campaign, when it became known that the Republican vice presidential nominee, Senator Dan Quayle, found inspiration in *The Candidate* as a young man, Larner wrote a *New York Times* op-ed scolding him: "Sorry, Senator Quayle, you thought we were telling you 'how-to,' when we were trying to say: watch out. You missed the irony. Unless, in a way I never could have foreseen, you are the irony." But maybe Quayle was something else: a person who took from the movie that success in politics required appealing to the center, using rhetoric that, even if prosaic and vacuous at times, was generally unifying. As vice president, he promoted the idea that the party should be a "big tent" that welcomes people of differing ideological positions, including on abortion. And even when he targeted Hollywood during a speech in San Francisco — criticizing the TV character Murphy Brown for "mocking the importance of fathers" by choosing to have a baby on her own — he did not set out to provoke a culture war, and the White House did all it could to tamp down the furor over it. For the next season's premiere, Quayle sent a handwritten card and baby gift (a stuffed elephant) to Brown, and he sat down with a group of single mothers to watch it. He was a good sport.

In reading Quayle's Murphy Brown speech today, what's most noticeable is that, while he offered a familiar lament about the breakdown of traditional values beginning in the 1960s and tied it to poverty and government dependence, he did not demonize or otherize. He applauded diversity and immigration as national strengths. He said it would be "overly simplistic" to blame everything on Great Society programs. And he generally used hopeful and inclusive language in the spirit of Bush's "thousand points of light."

Quayle wasn't *The Candidate*'s irony. Its irony, as we can now see, is that its message —moderation that appeals to a broad base and big tent is empty and useless — has been embraced by extremists. In place of McKay's platitudes, candidates have increasingly adopted bombastic and divisive rhetoric, often focused on the culture war that Pat Buchanan helped ignite in 1992. And so instead of the ghost of Bill McKay hovering over our politics, as he did in 1988, the ghost Buzz Windrip is back.

In 1988, most Democrats agreed with Larner, seeing Quayle as the embodiment of politics at its worst. We were wrong. We didn't know how good we had it.

We are approaching a site that still loomed large over Quayle's San Francisco audience as we begin winding our way through the golden hills of Altamont Pass. Some three hundred thousand young people overran these hills in December 1969, turning the Lincoln Highway and other local roads into parking lots that extended ten miles from the Altamont Speedway and the music festival conceived as a Woodstock West, an opportunity for California's biggest bands to show they could create their own youth utopia of peace, as Joni Mitchell was already singing about it in her song "Woodstock."

I dreamed I saw the bombers / Riding shotgun in the sky
And they were turning into butterflies / Above our nation

At Altamont, an unruly crowd clashed with the Hells Angels who were managing security. As the Rolling Stones played "Under My Thumb," Meredith Hunter — eighteen, black, high on meth, and carrying a gun for protection — climbed atop a speaker box next to the stage. A Hell's Angel tried to drive him off, Hunter tried to shake him, the Angel punched him, and as more Angels converged on him, Hunter tried to escape, pulling out his gun. Did he fire it? A Hell's Angel moved in with a knife, fatally stabbing him in the back. The Angels took his gun, stomping and beating him. The band played on, unaware that a man was being killed.

Altamont is still mentioned next to phrases like "the end of the Age of Aquarius" and "the day the '60s died," but the decade had been full of violence: murder and assassinations, riots and war. Altamont was a more accurate mirror of the decade's zeitgeist than the momentary mirage of Woodstock. What was shattered in these hills was the illusion of a society without violence. Mick Jagger sang of it in "Gimme Shelter," as Meredith Hunter lay dead.

War, children / It's just a shot away

Altamont was a reality check, but it was not a death knell for the spirit of the '60s, which long outlived it. In recent years, however, one of the era's signature achievements has been facing an adversary far more formidable than the Hell's Angels.

Just beyond the Altamont Pass, in a park adjacent to a 1915 auto garage — few early travelers survived the pass without needing to stop for repairs to tires, radiators, transmission, or brakes — I meet Jonathan Min, a sophomore at UC-Berkeley. Born in Seoul, he moved to California with his family when he was six. He arrived on campus in the aftermath of protests that shut down lectures by several right-wing commentators, including Ann Coulter and Ben Shapiro.

When Coulter returned to campus in 2019 in a second attempt to speak, Jonathan was a freshman. He walked by the event and saw hundreds of students blocking the gates so others couldn't get in, chanting, "Nazis go home!" and "Don't let them in!" Jonathan describes the scene as "pretty interesting," which I take as a laid-back California euphemism for "totally insane."

UC-Berkeley gave birth to the Free Speech Movement in 1964, when administrators tried to block students from political leafleting and organizing. The students won, but it would be years before the principle they were fighting for — that the First Amendment protects free speech and expression no matter the political content of the message — would be recognized by the Supreme Court. Eventually, freedom of speech for all — even communists and Klansmen — became not just the law of the land but a proud triumph for liberal culture, part and parcel of the civil rights and antiwar movements. But memories are short.

"The people I've been surrounded with are more progressive than I am," Jonathan says. "I'm more moderate." He and other moderates on campus feel "a bit of 'hold back,' and 'think before you speak,' because we don't want to accidentally set off anything."

"So there's a sense of walking on eggshells?"

"Yeah, at least for me — a bit of self-censorship." In a 1776 rebuttal to an opponent of American independence, Thomas Paine wrote, "He who dares not offend cannot be honest."

"The self-censorship," Jonathan says of his moderate and conservative friends, "can make them feel uncomfortable in some classes," which he calls "quite detrimental," leading people to cluster around those with the same beliefs, reinforcing divisions. And not just at Berkeley.

Colleges have become hotbeds of implicit censorship, but the old roles have been reversed. Where students once protested formal restrictions on speech by administrators, administrators now bow to informal restrictions on speech by students, who have turned against a foundation of the 1960s counterculture revolution: free expression. "It's never easy to foster dialogue about race, class, gender and culture," Erika Christakises wrote, after students sought to have her fired from her post at Yale (she resigned) for daring to suggest that administrators should not try to censor Halloween costumes, "but it will only become more difficult for faculty in disciplines concerned with the human condition if universities won't declare that ideas and feelings aren't interchangeable."

Ideas and feelings aren't interchangeable. That sentence gets to the crux of the matter. If ideas can be limited to protect feelings, who sets the limits? And if language can be equated with violence that necessitates safe spaces, what spaces should be left unsafe? Not the *New York Times*, as James Bennet learned earlier in 2020 when he was forced out of his job as editorial page editor over an op-ed by Senator Tom Cotton calling for the national guard to be deployed in cities facing looting, violence, and other lawlessness. I strongly disagreed with the op-ed's message, but the editor of a page that is ostensibly devoted to viewpoint diversity getting pushed out because a piece made some staffers feel "unsafe" was a triumph of feelings over ideas. The *Times* tried to portray it as a breakdown in editorial standards rather than what it was: a capitulation to ideological censors and a fear of being on the wrong side of those who claim the mantle of racial justice.

The *Times* is hardly the only example of this kind of capitulation. As the George Floyd protests erupted, a leading Democratic data analyst, David Shor, tweeted out research showing that violent protests reduced Democratic turnout while nonviolent protests increased it. Liberal activists attacked Shor as racist and accused him of bullying. His employer, Civis Analytics, faced the same dilemma the *Times* did — staffers at Civis's clients complained of feeling unsafe — and it reacted in much the same way. Shor lost his job. He quickly found a new one, though he didn't reveal the company's name publicly, lest another backlash erupt. Around the same time, the San Francisco Museum of Modern Art fired its longtime curator after he remarked that he wanted to exhibit works from a wider range of people even as they continued to show works by white artists, since to do otherwise would be "reverse discrimination" — a phrase that set off a wave of calls for him to be forced out. He was.

It's not just the coasts where this is happening. Daniel Elder, a Nashville music composer dismayed by mob violence in the wake of George Floyd's murder — people smashed the windows of a courthouse and set it aflame — posted a farewell message on social media: "Enjoy burning it all down, you well-intentioned, blind people. I'm done." After he was attacked as a racist and hate-filled white supremacist — he considered himself a center-left supporter of social justice — his music publisher demanded he sign an apology it wrote for him. When he refused, the company dropped him. In addition to losing his livelihood, he has lost fans and friends, too.

During Senator Joseph McCarthy's blacklisting Red Scare, the smearing of reputations and deprivation of livelihoods came mostly from intolerance on the right. Today they more often come from intolerance on the left. Jonathan is trying to do his part to fight it — he's part of a campus group that organizes debates to encourage open dialogue, and he's interned for the Foundation for Individual Rights and Expression — but many others, both on and off campus, find it easier to keep quiet.

I think back on the Notre Dame students who attacked the Ku Kluxers in South Bend to prevent them from holding a parade and rally, but who — after engaging in a face-to-face mediation — allowed the Klan to proceed so long as they left their guns (and robes) behind. The safest spaces are those where combatants agree that words are the only acceptable weapons. Democracy can withstand a few potatoes being thrown at windows, and even rocks, but without leaders who stand up to mobs and appeal to their better angels, as Father Walsh did with the Notre Dame students, gross injustices can occur — and, as Lincoln knew, people can lose more than their jobs.

When a mob in southern Illinois attacked an abolitionist newspaper editor, Elijah Lovejoy, destroying his printing press, throwing it into the river, and killing him, it stirred Lincoln and helped spark his first major speech outside the state legislature. "Whenever the vicious portion of population," he said, "shall be permitted to gather in bands of hundreds and thousands, and burn churches, ravage and rob provision-stores, throw printing presses into rivers, shoot editors, and hang and burn obnoxious persons at pleasure, and with impunity; depend on it, this Government cannot last."

— 39 —

To Build a Fire

The final stretch of the Lincoln Highway! After passing through Oakland's leafy commuter communities and ragged outskirts, we stop for a picnic lunch downtown at Lake Merritt. Barring catastrophe, we'll reach the Presidio in San Francisco before dusk.

Before lunch, we walk partly around the lake that made national news in 2018, when a white woman called 911 to report two black men barbecuing on a charcoal fire in an area designated for non-charcoal grills. The woman denied being racially motivated. The men believed she was. Lighting a few coals ignited a firestorm about racism and over-policing, though it should've been a story about something else, too: over-regulation. Nevertheless, the response by residents was pitch-perfect: They began holding "BBQing While Black" parties in defiance of the unnecessary regulations. City officials supported the parties but have left the regulations in place, and with them the potential for more arguments and more calls to the police that could leave citizens echoing Brownie McGhee, the great bluesman who made Oakland his home, in his song "Barbeque Any Old Time."

Well, please don't mistreat me, please don't do me wrong

After eating lunch near tennis courts that have been overtaken by tents and rummaged furniture, the Lincoln Highway leads us to more of each

— and more fire. Under a highway overpass, motorhomes line the south side of the street and tents line the median, along with debris and garbage, before they give way to makeshift shanties made of plywood and pallets, with tarps for roofs and walls. The shanties end in blackened wood and ash. It's the starkest and most abject poverty we've seen on the Lincoln Highway.

The Lincoln leads to Jack London Square on the Oakland Inner Harbor, where a ferry took travelers to San Francisco before the Bay Bridge opened in 1936. The old working waterfront is now a dining and shopping district that Covid has mostly emptied out, and the one place we'd want to go is closed: Heinold's First and Last Chance Saloon, a seafarer's watering hole opened in 1883, built from the boards of an old steamer and frequented by Jack London, who grew up poor around these docks.

London referenced Heinold's in his autobiographical novel, *John Barleycorn: An Alcoholic Memoir*, published the year of the Lincoln Highway's dedication, but it was his focus on the primitive nature of humanity in *The Call of the Wild*, *To Build A Fire*, and other works that attracted generations of readers and influenced Hemingway, Steinbeck, Kerouac, and many others. Lately there's been a push to remove his name from the square and replace it with that of Barbara Lee, Oakland's long-serving member of Congress. The reason, of course, is London's racism, which we glimpsed in Reno through his promotion of the Fight of the Century.

London subscribed to eugenics and believed the superiority of the white race could and should lead to the extermination of the others — natural selection at work. But London is not honored here for his racism any more than he is for his politics. He was a fervent socialist who signed his letters, "Yours for the Revolution." During his second run for mayor of Oakland on the Socialist ticket, the *San Francisco Newsletter* wrote of him: "He is a firebrand and red-flag anarchist . . . and he should be arrested and prosecuted for Treason." In neither run did he register much support.

A few years after his second campaign, London wrote *The Iron Heel*, a dystopian novel that foresaw socialists winning elections in the United States and provoking a violent backlash by an oligarchy that would not relinquish power. To place his hero's cause squarely within the American tradition, London included the fake Lincoln quote that we saw on the bumper sticker in Stockton, the same one the socialist jailed in Canton had used, about the republic being destroyed by the concentration of wealth. For London, since socialists would always be cheated at the polls, the only way forward was violent revolution: "It's no use," his hero says. "We are beaten. The Iron Heel is here. I had hoped for a peaceable victory at the ballot-box. I was wrong . . . We shall be robbed of our few remaining liberties; the Iron Heel will walk upon our faces; nothing remains but a bloody revolution of the working class. Of course we will win, but I shudder to think of it."

If Jack London falls to Barbara Lee, Democrats can say that the city has opted to honor a more conservative figure. But Lee, like London, hasn't always kept faith with democracy. After the 2000, 2004, and 2016 elections, she voted to challenge the votes of the Electoral College.

Crossing the Bay Bridge, Laurel and I look at each other in disbelief. After fifty-three days and four thousand miles — through a pandemic, windstorms, freezing temperatures, dirt roads, a run-in with a fire hydrant, and no shortage of small mechanical issues that left us perplexed, but also the owners of a new toilet — we have nearly made it. The elephant we came to see awaits.

We turn onto California Street and have an unobstructed view up Nob Hill, three-quarters of a mile long. There are only two other vehicles on the road, one moving in each direction, a perfect postcard but for the absence of streetcars, which haven't run since the start of the pandemic. The streets here have Manhattan's empty eeriness, but with more foreboding. We see fewer pedestrians than workmen wearing yellow vests and carrying plywood. On each block, storefronts are being boarded up. A saw buzzes through two-by-fours atop a makeshift workbench. Lumber lines the sidewalk and frames out glass windows. It's Election Day eve, and the city is preparing for a firestorm.

Prior to this, San Francisco had been slowly reopening from the pandemic, and its local public health leaders have been hailing their sustained shutdowns for slowing the virus's spread. A comment by a doctor at a university here in a recent news story struck me. "When things are going a little sour," he said, "his job" — referring to San Francisco's public health director — "is to scare the shit out of people." Even if he believed that to be true, I might have thought he'd have kept it to himself, rather than reveal that he so distrusts the public that he favors scaring them into submission.

The Lincoln brings us through Cow Hollow and into the Presidio, the military-base-turned-national-park. On Lincoln Boulevard, we pass Building 35, where Lieutenant General John L. DeWitt signed an order, authorized by President Franklin Roosevelt, to round up residents of the west coast with Japanese heritage, including citizens, for removal to inland locations, out of fear that spies and saboteurs lurked among them. In defending the policy, DeWitt adopted the same tactic the university professor applauded: scaring the shit out of people.

There is a world of difference, of course, between scaring people into accepting government restrictions on individual and economic liberty during a pandemic and scaring them into accepting the rounding up and removal of their neighbors during a war. But government use of fear, especially during emergencies, is a dangerous threat to democratic values and constitutional rights that should not be shrugged off.

As the light holds a late-afternoon glow, the last two miles of local streets bring us to Lincoln Park, which abuts the Golden Gate National Recreation Area. We wind our way up the hill and reach the end of the Lincoln Highway — a museum parking lot! And not even a museum of American art! There is no view of the ocean, just empty parking spaces and an overgrown shrub, which blocks a view of the second hole of the Lincoln Golf Course.

It would be hard to imagine a more anticlimactic ending, except we know that no Lincoln Highway traveler ever ended the journey here. The Pacific is just down the hill, and we are heading there to meet friends, Justin and Tharu, who had suggested an activity they've been wanting to do since moving here a few years ago: building a fire on the beach. At the start of the trip, I had imagined leisurely nights sitting beside campfires, but nights devoted to reading, writing, and planning slipped past, and I didn't build a single one.

We arrive as the sun sets over the Pacific, leaving a red sky that suggests good weather tomorrow, if nothing else. Justin and Tharu have brought supplies: firewood, sandwiches, snacks, drinks. We add a few beers to their cooler, including a Vota! that I've been saving from Raices Brewery in Denver. On a nearly empty beach, Justin crumples newspaper, layers kindling, and strikes a match: a fire beneath a fiery sky.

"I have long desired to see California," Lincoln said twenty days before his death, according to a Californian, "and nothing would give me more pleasure than a visit to the Pacific shore, and to say in person to your citizens, 'God bless you for your devotion to the Union,' but the unknown is before us." And so it is before us now. We watch the horizon fade to black. As the temperature drops and a chill sets in, we draw closer to the fire. It was worth the wait.

— 40 —

Election Day

Our RV "resort" in Pacifica is a tightly packed parking lot, but a well-placed one: We are on the edge of a cliff overlooking the ocean. The views are spectacular, but I'm paranoid that our parking brake will give out and we'll roll off the cliff, about the same feeling the election is giving me.

After watching the morning fog roll out, we hail a ride downtown to face the day. Plywood is still going up to protect windows. A sign on a chained wooden door reads, "Unauthorized Entry Will Be Met with Armed Response." Few people are on the street. One of them is Steven Aragon, a man with gray hair and an orange T-shirt and whose crew is boarding up a shop. "I grew up here and I've never seen anything like this," he says. The last time the city was this quiet and this on edge might have been the 1934 general strike, when some 125,000 workers stayed home after police killed two striking longshoremen. Newspapers called the general strike "civil war" and a "communist insurrection" — a reminder that alarmist and apocalyptic cries have been almost as common in politics as they have been in religion.

I ask Steven what these boards say about us. "People are ignorant," he answers. "You support the president you elect. Disagree, yeah. But you have to support democracy. Violence is not the answer."

"What do you think the night will bring?"

"I really just hope that everyone comes together and supports whatever presidency we get, and let's keep democracy" — he pumps a fist — "number one." God bless Steven Aragon.

The challenges to democracy we've seen on this journey began on Wall Street, where enslaved people revolted, anarchists bombed the JPMorgan building, and young people were beaten up for protesting the Vietnam War. Here in San Francisco, the home stretch of the Lincoln Highway witnessed the worst domestic attack in the city's history. In 1916, a bomb exploded during a Preparedness Day parade organized by the city's business interests to build support for America's entry into World War I. Many workers and labor leaders believed the organizers had ulterior motives — lucrative military contracts — and opposed the parade and its goal: sending them off to war. As crowds watched fifty thousand marchers and dozens of bands, a suitcase loaded with dynamite exploded, killing ten and injuring forty.

The city's district attorney was in the pocket of business leaders and proceeded to investigate with all the diligence of a lynch mob, pinning the crime on their chief antagonist, a labor organizer and socialist, Tom Mooney. A jury sentenced Mooney and an associate, Warren Billings, to death. The obvious miscarriage of justice — witnesses were conjured and coached to perjure themselves, it later came out — led to national protests and an intervention by President Woodrow Wilson that resulted in a commutation of their sentences to life in prison, where they became a cause célèbre for a generation of laborers and leftists, but the two served more than twenty-two years before finally being released in 1939.

All along the Lincoln Highway we have seen injustices, from the colonial period to the present day, often perpetrated by the government. We have hardly scratched the surface, of course, and most injustices never make headlines. In 2013, San Francisco–based musician Thao Nguyen released a song called "We the Common (For Valerie Bolden)," dedicating it to a woman she met while volunteering with the California Coalition for Women Prisoners. Bolden was sentenced to fifty-six years to life for killing her husband in 1996, even though it was in self-defense.

All they wanted was a villain, a villain
And all they had was me

There will be many more injustices in the years ahead, terrible and tragic ones. Injustice is inherent to courtrooms, legislative chambers, and executive offices. The challenge of democracy is keeping faith in debate and peaceful protest even during the most egregious injustices, rather than turning to violence and vigilantism — and keeping faith in the idea that, in the end, "right makes might." Two months before we arrived here, Valerie Bolden was released from prison.

The Lincoln Highway runs uphill on Market Street to the city's Civic Center, which rose from the rubble of the 1906 earthquake that laid waste to 80 percent of the city. It's a collection of government and cultural buildings surrounding open plazas — the very kind envisioned by the architects and designers of Chicago's White City and the City Beautiful movement, though they did not envision what we see here: a man sitting on the sidewalk sticking a needle in his arm outside a plaza fenced off to the public to safeguard a tent encampment.

The fence blocks us from seeing the plaza's centerpiece, the Pioneer Monument, which is surrounded by three statues symbolizing ambition, enterprise, and the desire for health and prosperity. In 2018, the city removed a fourth statue for its depiction of a priest and settler standing over a fallen Native American. Other figures honored by the monument, including Sutter, Fremont, and Father Junipero Serra, continue to stir debate. Many would like to see the monument removed, but the desperation, destitution, and disease of the camping colony around it are a tragic reminder that the noblest values of the pioneer spirit — enterprise, ambition, and the desire for health and prosperity — remain worthy of public acclaim, without being dismissed merely as incidental to the oppressions of colonization. When I take a photo of the monument over the fence, a man screams obscenities at me.

Even in America's most liberal big city, tolerance for street living is stretching thin. Homelessness here has long been a problem, but it has risen in recent years and changed, too, as drug addiction has worsened. Understandably, residents don't want their neighborhood sidewalks to be places of disturbing volatility and hostility, delirium and indecency — screaming obscenities is the least of it — especially when rates of burglary, theft, and robbery are well above those in other large cities. But the mayor is hampered by a federal court decision that restricts the ability of western cities to clear tents from public places without offering alternative shelter. And like Sacramento, San Francisco doesn't have enough shelter beds for all the people sleeping on the street, and many prefer the street anyway.

Republicans have turned San Francisco into a poster child for the dysfunctions of liberalism, a place where tents have overrun sidewalks, open drug use leads to antisocial behaviors — complaints about human feces are not uncommon — and shoplifting goes unprosecuted. The local district attorney, Chesa Boudin, has largely stopped prosecuting petty theft, with conviction rates falling below 10 percent from 50 percent just a few years earlier. (Voters will recall him in 2022.)

The heart of Republicans' critique of San Francisco is a charge leveled decades ago by a Democrat, one of the only Democrats my parents could agree on — the one who pulled pints at his mother's bar on the Lincoln Highway in Manhattan, Senator Daniel Patrick Moynihan. His famous 1992 essay, titled "Defining Deviancy Down," came to be mostly associated with crime, but it also took aim at homelessness. Moynihan argued that both problems, along with other social disorders that had exploded since the 1960s, resulted from society's willingness to tolerate and excuse behavior that for centuries had been stigmatized as unacceptable and restrained through force of law or social mores. His argument helped push Democrats toward the center on crime and street disorder, but the mind-set of treating all antisocial behavior as a result of failed public policies, and denigrating those who disagree as misanthropes and worse, has returned among many Democratic activists.

"These god-damn elitist liberals almost succeeded in running the working man out of the Democratic Party," Moynihan said to a reporter while sitting in the booth of a tavern in 1976, over cheeseburgers and beer. Watching a bus pass, he continued, "They made that bus driver out there feel illiberal. They turned him into a caricature." It's still happening, and it's still costing Democrats votes, as people made to feel *deplorable* and *irredeemable* for being cross-wise with progressive orthodoxy, and who may fear speaking out against it, look for other options.

"The central conservative truth," Moynihan said, "is that it is culture, not politics, that determines the success of a society. The central liberal truth is that politics can change a culture and save it from itself," as it did with abolition, women's rights, labor rights, civil rights, and much more. The essential thing to remember is that a virtuous culture — and the politics that can change and save a depraved culture — has never been the province of one party.

The homeless encampment keeps us from the Pioneer Monument but not what it faces: the steps of city hall and the Lincoln Highway's final statue of Abe. One hand grips a lapel, the other rests on a thigh, as he leans forward and looks down, somber, yet ready to rise. Next month, the city's school board will consider removing his and forty-four other names from schools, and someone will smear his face with red paint, on the anniversary of the day the military executed 38 Sioux fighters, but not the 265 whose sentences Lincoln commuted at considerable political risk. If we cannot honor historical figures who seek to navigate the lesser of two evils with compassion and caution, there is little hope of electing those who would follow in their footsteps.

The defacing of Lincoln here followed the toppling and vandalizing of statues in Golden Gate Park during the George Floyd protests, including of Father Serra ("Stolen Land," "Olone Land," "Decolonize") and Francis Scott Key ("Slave Owner"). I'm sympathetic to the argument for replacing Father Serra. Let one of the city's many Catholic parishes take him and stand him in a churchyard, and let all individual faiths celebrate their evangelizers and saints without imposing them on the public. And there are better ways to honor Key, too.

Key's statue was erected not for the reasons protestors toppled him — he kept slaves, opposed abolition, and prosecuted a doctor for possessing abolitionist literature — but only for the verses he wrote that captured the nation's idealistic self-image: "the land of the free and home of the brave." His greatest monument will always lie in song, not stone — and in the freedom Americans have to express themselves, including the right to silently protest the singing of Key's verses at sporting events.

When two San Francisco 49ers, Colin Kaepernick and Eric Reid, knelt during the singing of "The Star-Spangled Banner" in 2015, they set off the most contentious sports debate in decades, though it had nothing to do with sports. The tradition of singing the national anthem at ballgames was popularized by the Chicago Cubs in a 1918 World Series game against the Boston Red Sox. With America having joined the war in Europe and with a Red Scare under way at home — a bomb had exploded at a federal post office in Chicago the day before, killing four people — the Navy Band at the game played the song during the seventh inning, prompting the crowd to sing along, ending with thunderous applause and cheering. The Red Sox, who won the game behind a Babe Ruth nine-inning shutout, repeated the exercise when the series returned to Boston. In the seasons that followed, teams across the country played the song for special occasions, and during World War II, they began to play it before every game — and have never stopped.

Few now remember that the idea for Kaepernick to kneel during the anthem was suggested by former NFL player and Green Beret Nate Boyer, who had served in Iraq and Afghanistan. Seeing Kaepernick sit on the bench during the anthem upset Boyer, a diehard 49er fan raised in San Francisco. He wrote an open fan letter to Kaepernick that was a model of respectful and thoughtful discourse. He explained why he enlisted in the army, citing the motto of the special forces, *De Oppresso Liber* — To Free the Oppressed. He supported Kaepernick's right to protest. He acknowledged racism exists. He even cited his own objections to the song — its third verse, no longer sung, is most likely an attack on slaves who sought refuge in British promises of freedom.

> *No refuge could save the hireling and slave*
> *From the terror of flight or the gloom of the grave*

What bothered Boyer most, he wrote, was that Kaepernick wasn't with his teammates during the song — he was sitting on the bench, separate and apart. Boyer said he'd keep listening with an open mind and looked forward to the day when Kaepernick would be inspired to stand — and he would be right there with him.

Kaepernick, rather than ignoring the letter, contacted Boyer. They sat down together. Each expressed their feelings. Neither could change the other's mind, and so Boyer came up with a possible compromise. As he later told it, kneeling has never been "seen as a disrespectful act. I mean, people kneel when they get knighted. You kneel to propose to your wife, and you take a knee to pray. And soldiers often take a knee in front of a fallen brother's grave to pay respects. So I thought, if anything, besides standing, that was the most respectful. But, of course, that's just my opinion." When Kaepernick knelt during the anthem, Boyer stood next to him.

Later in the game, when a veteran sang "God Bless America," Kaepernick stood and applauded. "I'm not anti-America," he said after the game. "I love America. I love people. That's why I'm doing this. I want to help make America better. I think having these conversations helps everybody have a better understanding of where everybody is coming from."

Kaepernick remains a lightning rod, but his critics might consider this: He stood and applauded a song that Woody Guthrie turned his back on, a song Guthrie disliked so much that he wrote a protest song in response, penning it on a New York island at the start of the Lincoln Highway. Patriotism is bigger than any one song.

And all around me a voice was sounding
This land was made for you and me

Laurel and I arrive at a beer garden, Zeitgeist, to watch the returns. It calls itself a punk rock bar, but it's positively civilized. On a patio, picnic tables are separated by Plexiglas taped with signs reading, "Do not write on, sticker, or tag glass. Violators will be removed immediately." The punks must be policed. Maybe we'll hear the Dead Kennedys over the stereo, San Francisco's most famous punk band, but I hope the evening's soundtrack isn't their album *Bedtime for Democracy*. I'd much prefer their mocking homage to RVers, "Winnebago Warrior."

We watch the returns trickle in with Justin and Tharu, but last call arrives before the election is called: 8:45 P.M. Punk has never felt so prim. With the outcome still up in the air, we walk to a block party hosted by drag queen Afrika America, who is belting out Whitney Houston and Tina Turner to a mostly deflated crowd watching CNN on a Jumbotron. At 10:00 P.M., with no winner called, the party ends with "Celebration," by Kool and the Gang, but the mood is tense. Soon Trump tweets, "We are up BIG, but they are trying to STEAL the Election. We will never let them do it." Moments later, he tweets again: "I will be making a statement tonight. A big WIN!" It's just as Steve Bannon had predicted.

One of the poets Lincoln admired, and who was one of his electors in both campaigns, John Greenleaf Whittier, wrote of the anxiety of election night 1868, awaiting word on whether Ulysses Grant would triumph over New York governor Horatio Seymour, whom supporters called "the White Man's Candidate." Whittier titled his poem "After Election."

As on the thronged, unrestful town
The patience of the moon looks down,
I wait to hear, beside the wire,
The voices of its tongues of fire.

Tongues have been on fire this year like never in my lifetime, but the fire has consumed us more than it has lit the way. During the George Floyd protests, a statue of Whittier, a devoted abolitionist, was vandalized in the Southern California town that bears his name, the red paint reading "BLM" and "Fuck Slave Owners," the same ignorance, anger, and righteousness that foments extremism and begets violence.

All along the Lincoln Highway, I've asked people the same two questions: What is your biggest fear or concern about the future of the country? And what binds us together as Americans? To the first question, not a solitary soul said China. Or Russia. Or Iran. Or any other country. Not one person mentioned a terrorist group — not a word about another 9/11-style attack, or a dirty bomb, or even a nuclear weapon. A few mentioned climate change. One person cited cyberwarfare. But even those issues were framed as internal challenges — a national complacency that must be overcome.

Every person saw our biggest threat to be lying within us. The most common answer was the divided state of the country — politically especially, but also economically and socially. In those answers I heard the speech Abraham Lincoln gave in 1838, long before civil war lay on the horizon, in which he inveighed against mob violence, including lynching and looting: "If destruction be our lot, we must ourselves be its author and finisher. As a nation of freemen, we must live through all time, or die by suicide."

In that speech, Lincoln had an answer to my second question. The way to hold the country together, he said, and to prevent it being torn apart by inflamed passions, was "reason, cold, calculating, unimpassioned reason." Yet not one person we've met seemed to place their faith in reason, or at least none said so explicitly. Even as many lamented our inability to communicate with one another, they seemed at a loss as to how to overcome it, blaming social and partisan media for fomenting tribalist passions and swamping civil dialogue. More reasoned dialogue would surely benefit us, but there is no basis for believing that unreasonable people will cease to be. So if not reason, what will hold us together?

People we met along the way cited the Constitution and the Creator, our common aspirations, values, and humanity, and our shared faith in the American trinity: freedom, democracy, and equality. All of them are powerfully unifying forces, and underlying all of them is another one — tolerance for diversity — that four people mentioned, all of them religious leaders: a minister, two priests, and an imam. It's tolerance, including tolerance for losing elections and carrying the sack of flour, that lies at the center of the faith that Steven Aragon expressed in democracy as he boarded up glass windows.

The trip across the Lincoln Highway is over, but the election's thin margin means it is ending as it began: with an overriding sense of uncertainty about the future that is leaving the nation on a cliff's edge. Laurel and I could make it back to New York in a week via the interstate, but for what? To be trapped in a one-bedroom apartment in a city still mostly locked down? Besides, we're finally getting the hang of RVing — and the elephant we came to see wasn't Election Day but rather what it leads to, including our most sacred public tradition: the peaceful transfer of power. We have miles still to go, and there is no escaping the two places that loom so large over our national divisions: the Mexican border and the old Confederacy.

— 41 —

National Sins

We're still in San Francisco when the news breaks four days after the election: Biden wins. The fourteen states we passed through on the Lincoln Highway split 7-7. The results are all but official — each state's count still needs to be certified — but it's not over. "I WON THIS ELECTION, BY A LOT!" Trump tweets. Privately he tells aides, "I'm just not going to leave."

Today, too, Stewart Rhodes, the leader of the right-wing militia group Oath Keepers, sends a text message to an associate: "We now must do what the people of Serbia did when Milosevic stole their election. Refuse to accept it and march en masse on the nation's capital." Rhodes had already told the group: "We aren't getting through this without civil war. Too late for that. Prepare your mind, body, spirit."

Others are suggesting a different type of insurrection. The day after the election, former Texas governor Rick Perry texted White House chief of staff Mark Meadows: "HERE's AGGRESSIVE STRATEGY: Why can t the states of GA NC PENN and other R controlled state houses declare this is BS (where conflicts and election not called that night) and just send their own electors to vote and have it go to SCOTUS."

When Stephen Douglas lost the 1860 election, he told Lincoln: "Partisan feeling must yield to patriotism." Every other losing presidential candidate down through history said some version of the same, including Hillary

Clinton in 2016, who told her supporters: "We must accept this result and then look to the future. Donald Trump is going to be our president. We owe him an open mind and the chance to lead. Our constitutional democracy enshrines the peaceful transfer of power and we don't just respect that, we cherish it."

A history teacher I had in high school, Mr. Bley, told our class that Richard Nixon's decision not to contest the 1960 presidential vote, despite the possibility that fraud tipped Illinois to Kennedy and cost Nixon the presidency, was a great act of patriotism, because it ensured the peaceful transfer of power without putting the country through a potential constitutional crisis. Mr. Bley was a bleeding-heart liberal, but he said Nixon was an American hero for that act. It stuck with me — liberals never said nice things about Nixon — but it never occurred to me that it might be an essential lesson rather than a historical footnote.

At no point on the trip did Laurel and I ever talk about where we'd go after San Francisco. There were too many unknowns. Would we tire of RV life? Would the virus still be raging? Would we need to go back to our offices? After the election, we talked of going to Yosemite — Abe signed the bill that led to its creation — but snow is in the forecast, so we do the next best thing: drive Highway 1 south, stopping to gaze at the grandeur of its coastal cliffs, to visit John Steinbeck's cottage in Monterey, to sleep under the redwoods beside the Big Sur River, to detour into Paso Robles wine country, and to eat oysters on the docks of Morro Bay. With no deadline or destination, we are now moving at a leisurely pace, slowing down enough to begin making better use of our outdoor furniture. In San Luis Obispo, we stop for sandwiches at the Lincoln Market and Deli and see the most California of tributes to Lincoln: a mural of him with the line he uttered in *Bill and Ted's Excellent Adventure*: "Be excellent to each other." For a national credo, we could do worse.

As we approach Santa Barbara on the anniversary of Lincoln's Gettysburg Address, former New York mayor Rudy Giuliani and two other Trump lawyers, Jenna Ellis and Sidney Powell, hold a press conference at the national headquarters of the party Lincoln helped found. They claim to have proof of massive and widespread voter fraud orchestrated by a vast "national conspiracy" from "a centralized place" that occurred in cities run by Democrats with support from "globalist dictators, corporations," along with George Soros ("the biggest donor to antifa") and voting machine companies in cahoots with cronies of deceased Venezuelan dictator Hugo

Chavez. "My goodness," Giuliani says to reporters, "what do we have to do to get you to give our people the truth?"

Today, too, Trump summons Michigan's state legislative leaders to the White House for a meeting, brazenly putting his strategy on public display, after he privately pressured two Michigan election officials not to sign the certification of the results. "We've got to fight for our country," he told them in a phone call. "We can't let these people take our country away from us." As Michigan's leaders head to the White House, Utah Senator Mike Lee texts Trump's chief of staff, Mark Meadows: "Please give me something to work with. I just need to know what I should be saying." Trump provides an answer via tweet: "Hopefully the courts and/or Legislatures will have the COURAGE to do what has to be done to maintain the integrity of our elections, and the United States of America itself." It's an explicit endorsement of — and plea for — legislatures to create alternate slates of electors, just as Rick Perry had suggested.

After hiking the hills of Malibu and camping oceanside at Huntington Beach, we reach the end of Highway 1 and keep going. At San Diego's Waterfront Park, I meet Frank Xu, a software engineer who landed here from China with a work visa on Christmas Eve 2005, early in his career. This year, he helped lead the campaign to maintain the state's ban on racial, gender, ethnic, and religious preferences in public contracting, hiring, and school admissions — what supporters call affirmative action and what opponents call discrimination. The state's entire Democratic leadership supported a ballot proposition (Prop 16) to overturn the ban on preferences, yet in one of the country's most liberal states, and in a year that saw massive protests against racial injustice and high voter turnout, the result was not particularly close: 57 percent of voters supported keeping the ban in place.

"You cannot imagine, when the campaign started, how many people reached out to us," Frank says. "They say that they're not to talk. Because whenever they speak up, they will be labeled as white supremacists. And they identify themselves as liberals, Democrats." He found the self-censorship alarming. "The people reach out to me saying, 'I dare not to speak up' — that's a problem. I experienced it in China, and I don't want it to happen here in the United States. It'd make my American dream fade a lot — make my moving here have no sense. I could make much more money in China."

During the campaign, he was disappointed by what he perceived as biased media coverage. "It looks like propaganda media in China," he says. "They just label us, at least label me, as a selfish parent who only cares about his kids getting into college. It's not about my kids' education. It's about our future. Why did we move here? The reason I came into the United States is because I believe this is a land of equal opportunity."

He brings up Thomas Jefferson High School in San Francisco. "Last week they voted to abandon their merit-based entrance program," he says. "That high school is the number one high school in the entire nation because they have a pure merit entrance and very focused on academics. But since more than 60 percent of students are of Asian descent, they said, 'It's not fair.' I don't see any unfairness as long as the entrance program is the same standard for everyone. But they voted to abandon the system. And they even call the opposing Asian parents an Asian supremacy, and they said they make the culture in the school toxic. Well, this now is very important to me. Because if we, as an entire society, abandoned the idea that you should get your job or get your college because you did great, that will be a disaster to the entire nation."

The debate over affirmative action usually centers on equality and justice and what each requires, but there is another aspect to the debate that underlies both: identity. A few days earlier I had spoken with Ward Connerly, a former member of the California Board of Regents and a longtime proponent of race-neutral policies, who was also active in defeating Prop 16. He takes umbrage at preferences as a matter of principle — equality is "the essence of what this country was founded upon," he told me — and at racial categorization as a matter of practice. Such segmentation, he said, "has deepened the belief that there is something inherently within us that represents who we are. Being, quote, black, is in my view, not a real identity. There is no black community. There is no Latino community. And there certainly is no white community. We are thrown into that briar patch by our society and asked to embrace that identity. My own ancestry is imbued by Irish, Creole, and Choctaw on my mother's side, and my father's side, almost the same, except you add in a flavor of an African slave. That's a very complex background, but all of it is America. You can't put me neatly into one of those silly little boxes. And when I rebel against that, I'm told I'm not being authentically black. But that's what it means to be American: to be honest about yourself, to have no fear about your views, to go into the arena and debate issues without regard to those structures of race.

Asking people to pledge their allegiance to their group is a recipe for disaster."

I had heard something similar from a college student, Kevin, when I visited an early polling station at Lincoln High School in Sacramento. "When I was a residential adviser at UC-Davis," he told me, "they divided all the future RAs into caucus groups based on their racial identity, which I thought was really bizarre because isn't the whole idea that in America, we're so many different people, and everyone comes from a different background?" His mother is Mexican; his father is half German and half Filipino. "I'm very mixed and I find it very hard to be able to distinguish — 'Oh, this is an entirely Asian issue or this is an entirely white issue.' That doesn't make any sense to me, and I feel really left out, because I can't align with a single group. And that's something that really concerns me." He felt strongly that such sorting was exacerbating racial tensions and bias, while also fearing — as Frank Xu heard from so many people — what would happen if he spoke out.

There are many stories like Kevin's: discomfort with schools and companies separating people into identity groups in the name of diversity, equity, and inclusion. Many colleges now offer dormitories for "affinity groups" that promote the kind of racial sorting that mirrors and models one of the country's most intractable problems: residential segregation. Bias, inequity, and exclusion are serious and long-standing problems, and overcoming them requires the ability to see them. But we must also be able to see what we share as Americans. For every human resource initiative that focuses on individual differences, the country could use two focused on group commonalities, especially the idea behind our national motto — *E Pluribus Unum*, "out of many, one" — and what it requires of us.

In my conversation with Ward Connerly, he brought up Black Lives Matter. "Yeah, black lives matter," he said, "but blackness does not. And that's the thing we have to get right." Blackness has always mattered, of course — and to him, the challenge is to overcome the social construct of race by diminishing it, rather than perpetuating it by heightening it. For that reason he opposes capitalizing the *b* in *black*, because it "would sort of set us apart from the rest of society" — fortifying the very barriers we are trying to break down, barriers that have done so much harm over the ages, barriers that white supremacists, in capitalizing *white*, seek to uphold.

Much of the media and many corporations jumped on capitalization during the George Floyd protests, some deciding to capitalize *black* but not *white*. It was easier for organizations to adopt it than to argue, and it was done in the spirit of goodwill and empowerment. I've read lots of viewpoints on the question and find the case for capitalization reasonable and well meaning, but not entirely convincing. I have no objection to others doing it, but in wrestling with the question for this book, I found myself persuaded by an interview of the linguist and *New York Times* columnist John McWhorter, who said the issue is a "distraction" that produces anger without leading to progress. "There is activism, there is concern with society, and then there are these issues of gesture and symbol. And once again, if black is going to be capitalized, there you go with one more reason to be offended when someone doesn't do it . . . And I just don't get the appeal of seeking ways to be offended." His words remind me of what the Princeton students had talked about on the first day of the trip: the oppressive emptiness of virtue signaling.

McWhorter also pointed to how racial identity and experience are evolving with bi- and multiracial kids, how a capital letter seems to demand or imply conformity of thought and experience, and how a capital letter is a poor substitute for what black communities need, an echo of why President Obama didn't pardon Jack Johnson: The penance was too cheap.

In deciding not to capitalize *black* in these pages, I also decided not to capitalize *north* and *south* when referring to the two sides of the Civil War. In addition to ignoring contested border states and erasing the millions of people in the south, black and white, who remained loyal to (and in many cases aided and fought for) the United States, capitalization helps perpetuate a political construct that, more than 150 years later, still fosters division. Let north and south reject North and South.

McWhorter summed up capitalization as a political challenge, saying that "our conversation needs to evolve. But it would require openly admitting that racism now is not what it was thirty years ago. Many people just can't do it." But many, including many liberals, are doing it in the privacy of the poll booth. The opponents of Prop 16 were outspent by more than $20 million, which made the victory even more satisfying for them.

"To me," says Frank Xu, "it's reaffirmation of the democratic process and makes me feel so comfortable that the election cannot be bought. The people's voice can still be heard. It's different than in China. I cannot expect that to happen in China when all the officials, all the media advocating for one thing, and people vote other way. So it built my confidence in the system." Frank just became a citizen, and he registered to vote as a Republican because of this issue.

The conventional wisdom on the left, and among some on the right, is that the 2020 election should force Republican party leaders to engage in some soul-searching. But the California experience suggests that Democratic leaders have some thinking to do, too — not only about affirmative action but also about the fear and intimidation that Frank spoke of and the dangers it poses, both to the party and the country.

When the Supreme Court later struck down the use of race as a factor in school admissions as a violation of the Fourteenth Amendment's equal protection clause, Democratic leaders expressed outrage, but the decision reflected the view of the nation's most liberal state. To conservatives, the decision was a victory for racial equality. In his majority opinion, Chief Justice John Roberts cited statistics showing that a black student in the fourth-lowest decile had a better chance of being admitted to Harvard than an Asian student in the top decile. To liberals, it was a loss for racial equality. In dissent, Justice Ketanji Brown Jackson wrote, "Given the lengthy history of state-sponsored race-based preferences in America, to say that anyone is now victimized if a college considers whether that legacy of discrimination has unequally advantaged its applicants fails to acknowledge the well-documented 'intergenerational transmission of inequality' that still plagues our citizenry."

Both views are valid. The issue is a perfect example of Lincoln's dictum that almost all government policy is a mixture of good and evil that requires judgment to determine which holds the preponderance. We can disagree on that judgment and still embrace what Justice Sonia Sotomayor wrote in her dissent: "The pursuit of racial diversity will go on." As it does, it may be that other policies — such as giving a larger boost for economic hardship, requiring public universities to accept top students from every high school, and most of all improving in school systems that have been failing for decades — can achieve similar or better results.

It's strange not to be seeing family on Thanksgiving and even stranger to be in Palm Springs in an RV. Things get stranger still when I chat with Gertie, the woman handling check-in at the RV park. She has short white hair and is wearing hoop earrings and a stylish black T-shirt with a deep V-neck and shoulders cut out.

"I was brought up in Germany," she says with a strong German accent. "I came to the United States in 1953, seventeenth of July. My dad got killed in

Stalingrad, so it was my mom and my three sisters and I, and my brother. We lived in Heidelberg, Hillesheim. One day, I met Hitler."

What?

"One day the teacher said we were having a special guest, and in a half an hour or so, Hitler and three of his men showed up. I had long red hair, and German people hated red hair. I was like an outcast. But he came around my desk and took a curl from my hair and told me I had beautiful red hair. He took the one curl on my right-hand side. All I can remember about him is a big smile on his face looking at me, and it was nice to hear somebody say I had — instead of like everybody else treated me. Even my mom treated me like that. She hated my hair. But I got over that when I came to the United States. It was like a new world."

"What year did he come to your school?"

"1943, '44."

"And you don't remember anything else he said to the class?"

"He didn't say that much. We just had to sing and say, 'Heil Hitler,' put our arm up and stuff. He really didn't talk to us. He talked to the teacher. I can still see his smile on his face."

My head is spinning.

"Do you remember the war?"

"I have good memories of the wartime, but I do have one memory. We were all in a cellar sleeping. Everybody had a cellar. There was eight apartments, and one night the door opened up. We were right where the stairway was, and here comes three or four gestapos down the stairway knocking on somebody's cellar door, wanted to find out where Mr. and Mrs. Hermans were, and nobody wanted to tell them. They were Jewish. Finally, they found out. They were in the last cellar back from us. Luckily, their son stayed overnight with a friend in a different cellar, and that night they took the parents away and never come back. But the son, the people raised him as their own son. Nobody ever told. Nobody ever said anything. His name was Georgie."

"Was he your age?"

"I think he was maybe a year younger than me. I saw the same thing happen next to my grandma's house. They took a whole family away, grandparents. They lived upstairs in a three-story place, and they took them all away. All that came back was two of the younger kids. The rest of them, all got — yeah." She pauses. "I can remember that like yesterday." Another pause. "We were kids. We didn't quite know what it meant. Now I know what it means, what they did. I did go with my aunt and uncle to where the concentration camp is. I couldn't believe it when we got there. It was so hard to see those buildings. I would never want to go back there again."

Though it is little taught in American schools, Hitler's ideas on Aryan supremacy were inspired in part by the US eugenics movement and its twin, immigration restrictions, including Jews. In his book *Hitler's American Model*, Yale professor James Q. Whitman writes that Nazi lawyers "regarded America, not without reason, as the innovative world leader in the creation of racist law." Facing up to that history does not diminish by one iota the US's heroic role in perhaps the greatest military victory ever recorded, but it does help underscore the monstrous injustices that can result, especially in the hands of a demagogue, from using racial identities as a basis for organizing society and defining a nation.

To be clear: This is not to suggest that identity politics leads to genocide, of course. In a diverse and pluralistic society, a certain amount of identity politics is inevitable and often healthy. But too much of it can lead to exclusion and injustice both from the right and, in Frank Xu's and Kevin's experiences, the left. In debates over where to draw the line, the important thing is to keep the Declaration's promise of equality — the nation's "electric cord," as Lincoln called it — front and center, and to recognize, as Lincoln did, that we might be wrong.

My chat with Gertie turns to the pandemic. "I made it to eighty-five years old," she says. "I'm still working. I'm going to work till I'm 115. I'm going to make it, too. I'm stubborn enough."

"I don't doubt it for a second."

"You know what? I don't live like most Americans do. I live day by day. I'm happy today, I'm eating, I have a home. Why worry about what's going to happen tomorrow? If I don't wake up tomorrow, I'll never know."

"Today's Thanksgiving, are you —"

"I'm working. I've got nine people coming, so I'm working."

Gertie's gratitude for her health and life, her perseverance through hardship and deprivation — she spoke about eating one meal a day as a child — and her appreciation for America puts the present crisis in a broader perspective, which is very much in the spirit of what Lincoln hoped to achieve when he established a National Day of Thanksgiving and Praise in 1863, as a way of strengthening national unity. He set the last Thursday of November as the day to thank God "with one heart and one voice by the whole American People." In doing so, he created a holiday that was both religious and patriotic, and he asked that citizens mark it "with humble penitence for our national perverseness and disobedience." It is hard to imagine a president saying anything like that today, but Lincoln understood that acknowledging our "national sins" — a phrase he had used the prior year in issuing a proclamation for a day of national prayer and humiliation — is not to "hate America," as some would now say, but to love it so much as to seek moral self-improvements that will strengthen it.

Many Americans, however, refused to recognize Lincoln's holiday. "After the war," writes historian Judge Glock, "white Southerners remained suspicious of the 'Yankee abolitionist holiday.' When early Reconstruction-era governors proclaimed Thanksgiving Days in the south, white people ignored them, even while black people and Republicans feasted. It took decades before Thanksgiving became a truly national holiday. It also took decades before most of the country layered on a Pilgrims and Indians story as part of that holiday." The Pilgrims and Indians myth, and all the violence it whitewashed, overtook Lincoln's plea for "humble penitence."

Last night, on Thanksgiving eve, Trump pardoned retired general Michael Flynn, one of the most vocal proponents of the conspiracy that the 2020 election was stolen and who also videotaped himself taking a QAnon oath. Flynn had pleaded guilty to lying to the FBI about his contacts with Russian officials after the 2016 election, when Russia was facing sanctions for interfering with it. He expressed his thanks for the pardon by tweeting "Jeremiah 1:19," a Bible verse that promises divine deliverance for those who fight for God. It would be hard to get much further from Lincoln's humble penitence.

For turkey and stuffing and pie, Laurel and I head to Melvyn's at the Ingleside Inn, where waiters still remember when the regulars included the Rat Pack and Hollywood royalty. (The meal is delicious, though the mashed potatoes don't compare to my cousin Mike's.) While we are there, Trump holds a press conference and declares Georgia's Republican secretary of state, Brad Raffensperger, "an enemy of the people" — the same term he has applied to reporters dozens of times, and for the same crime Raffensperger is now committing: refusing to go along with his fabrications — in this case, that Georgia's election was rife with Democratic fraud.

In a 2018 speech, Arizona Republican Jeff Flake decried Trump's use of "enemy of the people," saying, "It is a testament to the condition of our democracy that our own president uses words infamously spoken by Josef Stalin to describe his enemies. It bears noting that so fraught with malice was the phrase 'enemy of the people,' that even Nikita Khrushchev forbade its use, telling the Soviet Communist Party that the phrase had been introduced by Stalin for the purpose of 'annihilating such individuals' who disagreed with the supreme leader."

The right attacked Flake for comparing Trump to a tyrant who killed millions, but that wasn't his point, which was to say that Trump's assault on truth and fact is incompatible with democracy and liberty. And though he didn't mention it, the fact remains: Hitler and the Nazis deployed the phrase, too. "Each Jew is a sworn enemy of the German people," wrote propaganda minister Joseph Goebbels.

Having come one degree of separation from Hitler, on Thanksgiving no less, I'm especially grateful for those who, in standing up for democracy, have been labeled enemies of the people. I just wish there were more of them among elected Republicans and that the ones who do speak out didn't do so only after deciding, like Flake, not to run for reelection.

On Black Friday, a federal judge in Pennsylvania appointed to the bench by President Trump dismisses a lawsuit by the Trump campaign attempting to toss out a million and a half absentee ballots: "Calling an election unfair does not make it so," the judge writes. Over the weekend, one of Trump's lawyers, John Eastman, sends a memo to the White House titled "The Constitutional Authority of State Legislatures to Choose Electors." The plan that Rick Perry suggested the day after the election is well under way.

— 42 —

Where the Hell Is God?

We finally make it to a national park, Joshua Tree, a desert moonscape of monumental rock formations and small cactus-like trees that Mormon emigrants may have named after the man who helped Moses lead the Israelites out of Egypt. Many visitors are less familiar with the Book of Joshua than they are with U2's *The Joshua Tree*, an album full of Old Testament imagery, appearances by Cain and Jacob, and faith in the Kingdom Come. But music lies at the center of the story of Joshua, who followed God's command to attack the city of Jericho and bring its walls tumbling down with the sound of trumpets, allowing the Israelites to slaughter its inhabitants.

In Stephen Vincent Benét's epic 1928 poem, *John Brown's Body*, Brown imagines himself as Joshua, praying to God before launching his attack on the federal arsenal at Harpers Ferry, which he believes will earn him a place in heaven beside Joshua. Today, others are again imagining themselves as Joshua. While we are here in Joshua Tree, a group of Pentecostal ministers, some claiming prophetic powers, are drawing inspiration from Joshua to organize "Jericho March," a national rally in Washington in support of Trump's claim that the election was stolen. The trumpets are set to blow on December 12.

Lincoln drew inspiration from Joshua, too, but in a very different way. In February 1861, shortly before he left Springfield for Washington, he received a gift from a Jewish immigrant in Chicago, Abraham Kohn, who saw Lincoln as a Moses figure who would lead the country out of slavery. He sent the president-elect a painting of an American flag, with lines from the Book of Joshua on the white stripes, not about blowing trumpets but about God's omnipresence: "Be strong and of good courage; be not affrighted, neither be thou dismayed; for the Lord thy God is with thee whithersoever thou goest." When Lincoln departed Springfield, he gave a brief speech to local well-wishers. "Without the assistance of the Divine Being who ever attended him," Lincoln said, "I cannot succeed. With that assistance, I cannot fail." According to Lincoln biographer Harold Holzer, those words were "clearly inspired by Kohn's present." Lincoln was expressing uncertainty about God's view of his endeavors, even as his faith in the nation and its sacred principles didn't waver. Once in Washington, he hung the painting in the White House.

From our campsite, we watch a nearly full moon rise over the mountains and illuminate the desert floor. It's bright enough to read by, though the dropping temperatures necessitate gloves and a hat. We haven't needed to turn on the furnace, because Charley's walls do a good job of trapping the sun's warmth. As long as the sun streams in during the day, Charley is comfortable until bedtime. Given my near-freezing experience in Boone, Iowa, I have become rather militant about keeping the doors and windows closed as evening approaches. This sometimes requires clandestine actions so as not to alert Laurel, who enjoys a late-afternoon breeze and has taken to telling me I should seek therapy for PTSD. I assure her that all is fine as I put on my military-grade thermal undershirt.

Over several days, we take hikes that bring astonishing views across the desert, its barren desolation carrying a sense of eternity. It's not hard to see why Gram Parsons, maker of what he called "cosmic American music," wanted his body burned here. On our last day, some seemingly important news arrives: Attorney General Bill Barr announces that there is no evidence of widespread voter fraud. At the same time, however, a group that includes Michael Flynn calls on Trump "to immediately declare a limited form of Martial Law, and temporarily suspend the Constitution and civilian control of these federal elections, for the sole purpose of having the military oversee a national re-vote." Flynn's group also demands that Trump shut down the media: "You must also act, like Lincoln did, to silence the destructive media's one-sided propaganda designed and proven to influence the election outcome, and end the unlawful censorship of Big Tech, to restore the confidence of the American People in our electoral process or we cannot continue as a nation." *Or we cannot continue as a nation.* "Failure to do so," the statement continues, "could result in massive violence and destruction on a level not seen since the Civil War. Limited Martial Law is clearly a better option than Civil War!"

Flynn's call for a shutdown of the media is especially notable given the credence conservative media has been giving to claims of fraud. "It's remarkable how weak ratings make good journalists do bad things," Fox News executive director Bill Sammon texts the network's political director, Chris Stirewalt, the next day, our last at Joshua Tree. "It's a real mess," Stirewalt replies. "What I see us doing is losing the silent majority of viewers as we chase the nuts off a cliff." On the same day, December 2, Fox CEO Suzanne Scott writes to an executive after an on-air fact-check of baseless voter fraud claims. "This has to stop now," she demands. "The audience is furious." And the fury is growing.

December 2 is the anniversary of the Senate's condemnation of Republican Joseph McCarthy, by a vote of 67–22, not for his Red Scare tactics that destroyed so many lives and inflamed so much hatred — there weren't enough votes for that — but for failing to cooperate with the Senate's investigation of his conduct, which he called a "lynch party." It was a half measure — not even an official censure — that came four years after the only woman in the Senate, Maine's Margaret Chase Smith, delivered a speech condemning the anti-democratic nature of his anti-communism campaign. "I don't want to see the Republican Party ride to political victory on the Four Horsemen of Calumny: Fear, Ignorance, Bigotry and Smear," she said. "I doubt if the Republican Party could, simply because I don't believe the American people will uphold any political party that puts political exploitation above national interest. Surely we Republicans are not that desperate for victory."

From Joshua Tree, we're heading to another national park: the Grand Canyon. For much of the way we'll be on Route 66, whose fame has long eclipsed the Lincoln Highway's, thanks partly to *Easy Rider* and *The Blues Brothers*. The Lincoln Highway never got the full Hollywood treatment — just a couple of silent films, a radio show, and a line in the Woody Guthrie song "Hard Travelin'" — and even then, Route 66 overtook it.

I've been walking that Lincoln Highway, I thought you knowed
I've been hittin' that 66, way down the road

The drive is a jaw-dropping, eye-popping, head-shaking, desert-mountain experience. Across the Colorado River in Arizona, we stop in Oatman, a collection of souvenir shops masquerading as an old west town. Burros wander the street hoping for food handouts as tourists browse for trinkets at shops like Classy Ass Gifts. We catch the tail end of a high-noon shootout, but the highlight of our visit is watching a burro snatch a bag out of a woman's hand immediately after she stepped out of a fudge shop. The modern version of *Wild West* is as ridiculous as it is hard to pass by, but myths that celebrate lawless violence can seem to validate it, too, as with the Proud Boys gathering in Old Hangtown. Here, a Confederate flag is emblazoned with a machine gun and the slogan "Come and Take It."

Halfway to the Grand Canyon, we stop in Kingman at a Route 66 saloon with RV hookups. As we settle in for the night, an election worker in Georgia, Ruby Freeman, calls 911, telling the dispatcher that she had received a torrent of "threats and phone calls and racial slurs." The Trump campaign had showed a heavily edited video purporting to reveal Freeman and her daughter, Wandrea "Shaye" Moss, with suitcases full of illegal votes. Sean Hannity called it a "bombshell," *The Gateway Pundit* smeared the women as crooks, and Rudy Giuliani declared that the video proved "beyond doubt" that Democrats stole the election. An investigation would show the charges to be baseless, but the mob wasn't waiting for facts. "It's scary," Freeman says to the 911 operator, "because they're saying stuff like, 'We're coming to get you. We are coming to get you.'"

The next morning we meet Emmett and Lori Sturgill at their ranch north of Kingman, a vast desert floor hemmed in by mountains and the western rim of the Grand Canyon. A dirt road leads to their house, between a cattle pen and horse corral. "Welcome!" Lori says, walking out to greet us. "And you don't have to wear those things — we're not big into that Covid thing." They have a lot of company. At a Kingman motorcycle shop flying the Confederate flag, a sign advertised "Kung Flu Commie Scamdemic Masks."

Lori invites us into the house. Feeling ungracious, I ask if we can talk on their porch, and they readily agree. Having kindly met us halfway, we take off our masks and settle in to hear their story.

"When I was growing up," Emmett says, "the people that owned ranches had a TV. I told my dad when I was fifteen years old" — his dad was a cowboy — "I want to own a ranch. I don't want to work on the ranch because I want to have a TV." He learned the trade from his father, but it took thirty years working in law enforcement for him to save enough to begin buying land. After days spent on drug trafficking cases, ranch work began, but he isn't complaining. "The good Lord has just been really good to me. So many people don't get to realize their childhood dreams. I've been very lucky, and I've worked really hard to make that happen."

Their ranch, which runs to the base of the Grand Canyon, is 180,000 acres — twelve times the size of Manhattan. It's hard for Laurel and me to fathom how a single piece of property could be that big, but it's not even the biggest ranch in the county. "Just to check our waters" — making sure the water feeders for the cattle are full — "is about a hundred miles," Lori says. Much of their ranch is federal land overseen by the Bureau of Land Management, which limits the size of their herd. They have a permit for five hundred mother cows, but because of the drought and their desire to prevent overgrazing, they've kept the number below four hundred. They have virtually no fences — all open range. "We put reflective ear tags in our cattle, and we still lose about eight or ten a year," Emmett says. The neighboring ranch, which has more exposure to the road and does not use reflectors, loses thirty.

The road that runs through their ranch leads to the Grand Canyon Skywalk, a $30 million horseshoe-shaped glass walkway cantilevered seventy feet over the canyon's rim, opened in 2007 by the Hualapai. Some tribal members opposed it, seeing it as a desecration of a sacred place. If they controlled the canyon their ancestors long roamed, along with other tribes, they would not have needed to build it: They could have just charged admission, as the federal government does. Instead, they are creating their own tourist attraction, complete with hotels and helicopter rides over the canyon.

"We used to have a dirt road," Emmett says. "No problem. Now they paved the road. They built the skywalk. They bring a million people here a year and they run over our cattle — and they want me to fence the road. Arizona is an open-range state. I was here before they were, but that doesn't seem to matter." Of course, the Hualapai were here thousands of years before him, but his real beef isn't with them. It's with state legislators from Phoenix and Tucson who are "trying to do away with the open-range laws here, which will put all the ranchers out of business. I don't have a million and a half dollars to fence the road."

"A million and a half?" I ask, dumbfounded.

"I could actually finish it for $70,000," he says. "The $1.6 million that I'm talking about is to comply with the regulations. Because if I do that, everywhere there's a turnout I have to put in a $70,000 cattle guard. They won't let me put in a gate, and it has to be county-approved, state-approved — this, that, and the other thing." His problem is less with the fence than with the government that's fencing him, giving a new twist to the old Cole Porter–Robert Fletcher song, "Don't Fence Me In."

It's not just the fence. Lori wanted to put up shades on their water feeders. "That way," she says, "the water's cool, and that helps prevent moss and algae from growing on it, and cattle can drink it better. They don't want to sit and drink water that's 130 degrees. When they don't have proper water in their system, they're not digesting correctly." The water feeders sit on BLM land, and the BLM won't let her do it, or plant trees that would provide shade, without going through a National Environmental Policy Act (NEPA) process, which can take years and cost a lot of money. "So I went and bought forty acres right next to that, so that I could put up my own shade on my own property."

It's not just the shade. Lori put up a note on Facebook offering an opportunity to a local butcher to start her or his own business. She'd build a butcher shop and buy all the equipment, and the butcher could use it free of charge, in exchange for butchering some of their cows. Emmett explained what happened next: "It wasn't twelve hours before the Department of Agriculture started inundating us with, 'You can't do that. And this is the regulation.' Sent us five books full of regulations, hundreds of pages."

Lori could not believe it. "I even have a relationship with the Department of Ag, but right away, that's their first response. As opposed to: 'Here's what you can do,' it's all about what you can't do. And I think: Why have we gotten to that point in our life?"

Time and again they return to examples of government bureaucracies being devoid of flexibility and common sense, yet still always thinking they know best. "I don't have a college education, she doesn't have a college education," Emmett says. "So we must be idiots because they went to college and they know better. They haven't been out here on the land."

The Endangered Species Act is another headache. In 1987, the federal government added the Mexican vole, a rodent, to the endangered species list. The decision, says Emmett, was based on a single study that lacked a proper taxonomy. Subsequent studies cast doubt on whether it was in fact a distinct subspecies or merely a common vole. He says someone lost a ranch when the vole was found to be present on it — the government took it away — and it cost taxpayers millions of dollars in added expenses to design roads and other infrastructure to protect the vole. "I'm all about protecting the panda bear and whatever else. But for God's sakes, let's be reasonable. And number one is: Let's make sure that it is endangered." The US Fish and Wildlife Service considered removing it from the list during the Obama administration, as the state of Arizona had petitioned, but never acted. The Trump administration did.

"There's a wash right here" — Emmett points behind the house to a creek bed that carries runoff during a monsoon. Most of the year it's bone-dry. "Under Obama, that was a navigable waterway, and all of the regulations concerning navigable waterways applied to that — and on our private property. Now think about this for a minute. When Congress passed the navigable waterway act, navigable waterways meant a barge would move commerce. But for a rancher, if I wanted to put a road there, I'd have to go through the Army Corps of Engineers and get permits. And they would have to do NEPA studies, which take an average of four years."

The Sturgills say they are not anti-government. "I think there's a place for them," Emmett says. "I don't think that we should eliminate them. I'm going to make a living off of public land — I've got a million dollars invested here, and they have a role to play. If there are guys who don't manage the land — there are very, very few, but there are some — there should be someone to come in and stop them."

It's easy to understand their frustrations with government. Up-close-and-personal experiences with bureaucracies tend to leave people feeling the same way. When a friend from New York built a deck in his backyard, the city's Department of Buildings ordered him to remove it because it wasn't code-compliant. He had spent a paycheck building it, and a lot of time, too. His politics are liberal, but months of tangling with the agency to resolve the issue left him deeply frustrated. "I can see why people become Republicans," he said, only half joking.

At various points in the conversation, Emmett refers to his faith in God. "I don't know a farmer and I don't know a rancher that isn't a Christian," he says. "Why do you suppose that is? I know lots of college-educated people that are atheists. I don't know any people that work the land — there's got to be some, there's exceptions to every rule, but if you live like I live, almost every day we see new babies being born. We see deer, we see elk, we see anything you can imagine here. Baby calves. Every year, we're privileged to watch a lot of babies being born. I mean the miracle of life and all of that."

They see God all around them, both in the animals they sell for slaughter and those that are extended members of their family. As we've been sitting with them, horses wander a corral, pigs roam the yard, a pheasant sits atop a trailer, and half a dozen cattle dogs have come on and off the porch, as does Heiney, a seven-week-old burro they rescued. Laurel is smitten with Heiney and wishes we could bring her with us.

Eventually, of course, talk turns to the election. Lori is hopeful the outcome will be reversed, while Emmett says it's a done deal, much to his regret. Five days earlier, Arizona officials certified Biden's victory, by about ten thousand votes, backed by the state's Republican governor, Doug Ducey. But as we say good-bye to the Sturgills, President Trump is in the midst of a hundred-minute speech in Georgia, claiming victory: "They cheated and they rigged our presidential election, but we will still win it," he says. The crowd chants, "Stop the steal!" The president is ignoring the plea made days earlier by a Republican election official in Georgia, Gabriel Sterling, who urged him to stop making baseless claims of voter fraud and to condemn the death threats, harassment, and intimidation being directed at state employees, their families, and others. Sterling was especially disturbed by a noose left outside the home of someone who works for the voting machine company Dominion.

"Mr. President, you have not condemned these actions or this language," Sterling said angrily. "Stop inspiring people to commit potential acts of violence. Someone's gonna get hurt, someone's gonna get shot, someone's gonna get killed. And it's not right . . . Tell your supporters: Don't be violent. Don't intimidate. All that's wrong. It's un-American."

The next night, as we camp on the south rim of the Grand Canyon, the election worker Ruby Freeman hears banging on her door, fears for her life, and calls 911 again. She's received more than four hundred emails and text messages, most of them threats. "Lord Jesus, where's the police?" she asks the 911 operator. "I don't know who keeps coming to my door."

Reservations for mule rides to Phantom Ranch at the bottom of the Grand Canyon are usually sold out at least a year in advance, but thanks to Covid, we were able to book a night's stay just a few weeks ago. When we meet our guides, the assistant livery manager with a bushy goatee, Don, assures us the mules are extremely sure-footed and not to be alarmed when they follow the trail's outer edge along cliffs. "That's their happy place," he says. I hadn't known about this curious instinct, and maybe I would have been more comfortable with it had I not been given a mule named Fooler, which does not inspire a great deal of confidence in his maturity and judgment.

Early on, we stop to see the image of a face in the rock at the rim: the Keeper of the Canyon, says our lead guide, Simmon, who grew up on the Navajo reservation east of here and tells us the story of the grandfather sending his granddaughter into the canyon for water. She never returned, and he has kept watch ever since. Simmon says a prayer in his native Navajo language, which he translates for us: "The Keeper of the Canyon is going to keep us safe with an eye on us on our way down to Phantom Ranch, all the way back out tomorrow, and on your journey home. God bless all of us."

Descending to the bottom of the Grand Canyon on a mule is six hours of awe and exhilaration, but also, at least for anyone with a fear of heights, mild terror. The trail is a cliff's edge for much of the way, including up and around "Oh Jesus Corner," so named because of the religion people find when rounding it and staring into the abyss, which brings me face-to-face with the reality that I've entrusted my life to a half ass named Fooler. But my faith in him was repaid. Even after hours spent gazing in wonder at the canyon's vast beauty, the sight of the Colorado River flowing green as an emerald, cutting through the canyon's sedimentary rocks for millions of years, astonishes us.

After dinner at Phantom Ranch, I read a short book that I had stashed under Charley's dinette bench seat before leaving on the trip — *Where the Hell Is God?* — a gift from a close family friend, Sister Mary, whom my mother met in her early days in the convent. It's by a Jesuit priest whose answer to the title question is much like the line from the book of Joshua that Abraham Kohn inscribed on the flag for Lincoln: that God is always by our side, though not to protect us as an all-powerful being, a Keeper of the Canyon, but to support us as a friend. Whatever one's conception of the divine, being surrounded by natural beauty can make it easier to see it, an idea Bob Dylan wrote about in "Last Thoughts on Woody Guthrie," which unfolds as a search for hope that ends with finding God in houses of worship and Woody Guthrie in Brooklyn State hospital, before it concludes with Lincolnian humility.

And though it's only my opinion
I may be right or wrong
You'll find them both
In the Grand Canyon at sundown

As best I can tell, he was right.

As we ascend the canyon's walls the next morning, Utah senator Mike Lee texts White House chief of staff Mark Meadows: "If a very small handful of states were to have their legislatures appoint alternative slates of delegates, there could be a path." Meadows responds, "I am working on that." Our mules are not the only ones walking the outer edge of a path along a cliff.

— 43 —

Borderlands I

As we passed through Phoenix yesterday, a federal judge there dismissed a lawsuit by the Trump campaign, writing, "Allegations that find favor in the public sphere of gossip and innuendo cannot be a substitute for earnest pleadings and procedure in federal court. They most certainly cannot be the basis for upending Arizona's 2020 General Election."

Today a group of leaders representing an assortment of conservative activists, evangelical leaders, and former Republican members of Congress release an open letter: "There is no doubt President Donald J. Trump is the lawful winner of the presidential election. Joe Biden is not president-elect." They urge Arizona and other states where the vote was close to "exercise their plenary power under the Constitution and appoint a clean slate of electors to the Electoral College to support President Trump. Similarly, both the House and the Senate should accept only these clean Electoral College slates and object to and reject any competing slates in favor of Vice-President Biden from these states." The idea proposed by Rick Perry the day after the election is gaining public traction — and tomorrow, the Trump campaign will acknowledge in a court filing that the effort to create independent slates of electors in various states is being orchestrated by the campaign itself, with Rudy Giuliani, the former New York mayor who tried to extend his own expiring term after the attacks of 9/11, at the center of the push.

Just before sundown we arrive in Tombstone, where the main drag is a dirt road, the better to convey an old-timey feel. Covered wooden sidewalks run along western-style buildings, some that are historic and some made to look like it — saloons, souvenir shops, and stages for shows. We park Charley at a municipal RV lot behind the Gunfighters Hall of Fame in the Old Tombstone Western Theme Park, where a sign advertises "Shoot-Outs Daily / Shooting Gallery / Pan For Gold / Mini-Golf Course." We have entered the heart of the mythic wild west, a place where six men hung here for murder in 1884 — one of them lynched by the townsfolk after a judge sentenced him to life in prison rather than death — don't even rank among the town's most celebrated outlaws.

At the Four Deuces Saloon, a large back patio decked with garlands and holidays lights appears warm and welcoming. As we approach, a woman smoking a cigarette outside the front door greets us. "Those things are finally good for something," she says. "They keep your face warm." We laugh through our masks and comment on the cold weather — temperatures have dropped into the forties — but she doesn't seem amused. The patio is empty, so we head inside to order. The young woman bartending greets us with the same message, but in friendlier terms: "Oh, you don't have to wear those in here," she says, which is clear from a glance at the patrons, who are giving us the stink eye, "but whatever you're comfortable with."

We take our drinks to the patio, where Alabama's "Christmas in Dixie" is playing over the outdoor speakers. We are technically in Dixie now, since leaders in the region voted to secede, and the territory was formally admitted to the Confederacy and given a non-voting delegate. We drink quickly — it's too cold not to be moving — and after returning our glasses to the bar, we walk back out the front door. The same woman is still outside smoking, now with a friend. "Have a merry Christmas," she says, but her words have an edge to them, almost a snarl. It sounds like she's testing the masked outsiders — laying a trap to see if we'll say "Happy Holidays" in return. So I offer a joyful reply that conceals a joust: "And Merry Christmas to you!" Sure enough, as we walk away, we hear her complain that the phrase is being taken away by political correctness. It would be hard to say which is less in the Christmas spirit: her attempt to bait us or the small pleasure I take in disappointing her. "Merry Christmas from Dixie," the Alabama song goes, "to everyone tonight."

On the next block, we walk past the town's main attraction: the O.K. Corral, a re-creation of the place where the world's most famous gunfight occurred. Assistant US Marshal Virgil Earp and the small posse he deputized — his brothers Wyatt and Morgan and their dentist-turned-gambling-and-gunslinging friend, John "Doc" Holliday — squared off with cattle rustlers and horse thieves who were part of the Cochise County Cowboys. In the shootout, three cowboys were killed: Billy Clanton and Frank and Tom McLaury. The drama is now restaged three times daily.

Tombstone's celebration of guns has been going on since Ned Buntline and other dime novelists began dramatizing the incident shortly after it occurred, but it is an artifice for tourists concealing two issues that remain at the center of national political debates.

The first concerns the US-Mexico border. Cowboys like the Clantons and McLaurys routinely crossed into Mexico to steal livestock. "The inhabitants of Northern Sonora and Chihuahua have suffered," wrote the US attorney for Arizona three months before the O.K. Corral shootout, "and are daily suffering outrages and indignities at the hands of these outlaws." Mexican officials were furious. They deployed three hundred soldiers to the border and urged the US government to send troops, too. Cattle rustlers like the Clantons and McLaurys weren't just a local menace. They were undermining Mexican national security and US-Mexico relations.

When the United States finally began to patrol the Mexican border with civilian agents, it was not to keep out Mexicans. It was to stop Chinese immigrants from evading the 1882 Exclusion Act by arriving in Mexico and traveling north. In the 1880s, there were two efforts to drive the Chinese out of Tombstone, both fueled by electoral politics: one by an Anti-Chinese Political Party, and one by the successful mayoral campaign of John Clum, editor of the *Tombstone Epitaph*, which is still publishing. The anti-Chinese tales are not much told to tourists here, but leaving them out of the experience makes it harder to recognize parallels in modern politics.

In 2002, another local newspaper publisher — a kindergarten-teacher-turned-gunfight-reenactor who purchased the *Tombstone Tumbleweed*, Chris Simcox — ran a front-page headline: "ENOUGH IS ENOUGH! A PUBLIC CALL TO ARMS! CITIZENS BORDER PATROL MILITIA NOW FORMING." The volunteers adopted the name the Minutemen, likening themselves to Revolutionary War heroes, and chapters formed across the southwest. Simcox became a national figure, raised funds for a border fence that never much materialized (prompting lawsuits), and, like the publisher of the *Tombstone Epitaph*, tried to parlay fear and bigotry into political office. Eventually, the law caught up with him, though not for vigilantism or fraud: He is currently serving a nineteen-and-a-half-year sentence for molesting a five-year-old girl. But to see his call for vigilante militias to patrol the border only as an echo of wild west gunslinging is to miss the xenophobia that has always run through it, and to see the O.K. Corral shootout as only a conflict between outlaws and lawmen is to miss that Americans were regularly crossing the border to commit crimes in Mexico.

The second issue the O.K. Corral myth conceals is that gun laws were often much stricter in the old west than the new west. The 1881 shootout began, at least ostensibly, because the cowboys refused to obey the town's prohibition on carrying guns. Now guns can be carried in the street, openly or concealed, thanks to a state law that blocks localities from adopting local gun measures. And while signs are posted at various businesses, including saloons, notifying customers that guns are not permitted on their premises, it can be hard to separate romance from reality. Not long ago, an O.K. Corral reenactor was shot in Doc Holliday's Saloon by a friend who had drunk ten beers and didn't remember loading the gun. "I didn't even know I was hit till the karaoke guy came out and said I was spurting blood," he told a local reporter.

Overnight at the municipal RV lot, Laurel is woken by howling coyotes that give her a fright. But it's other coyotes that many in the region fear, and we're heading to meet people who track them.

Thirty miles south in Bisbee, an old mining town high in the Mule Mountains, Sergeant Tim Williams leads me to a conference room to meet Cochise County sheriff Mark Dannels, an army veteran with thirty-seven years of law enforcement experience and a master's degree in criminal justice. When he began in the sheriff's office in the 1980s, the county was acquiring the nickname "Cocaine Alley" for all the drugs coming over its eighty-three-mile border with Mexico, mostly ranchland. The county, like the Cochise Cowboys, is named for the Chiricahua Apache leader famed for his daring in crossing the border, raiding Mexican communities, and returning home with horses, cattle, and captives. Mexican troops could not follow the Apache back into the United States, just as they could not follow raiding cowboys, adding to Mexico's frustrations with Washington. Border challenges are not new here.

"Cochise County has always been on the front line of smuggling," the sheriff says. "The Sinaloa cartel is south of us. It's a profit-greed game for them. Anything they can smuggle in the United States, they will do for a dollar bill." He says people are paying about $6,000 for three attempts to cross, along with head-to-toe camouflage for the journey. "These people don't have $6,000, so they're servants to the cartels, whether it's sex, gang labor, drug labor, whatever it may be," he says, likening it to modern-day slavery. "The torture these people go through is just incredible, and that's where the humanitarian side comes from." He sees that side — protecting the human rights of those being smuggled and exploited — as a core part of his mission, in addition to protecting public safety for local residents and protecting national security for all Americans.

"We watch them every day," he says of the drug traffickers picked up by the camera system his office has developed and deployed. "They go around Cochise County every day to New Mexico and the counties adjacent to us." One reason why is Dannels's crackdown on a favorite cartel tactic: enlisting teens as smugglers. About five years ago, youth smuggling was chronic. "We had twenty-two juveniles in forty-five days that were bringing drugs into this county," he says — a majority of them Mexican, but some American kids, too. "Not one prosecution. The US attorney's office would not prosecute them. They released them, no consequence" — exactly why the cartel kept recruiting them.

"They would go right back" to Mexico, says Sergeant Williams. "If they lost their drugs, they would get a severe beating and then be sent right back to the border. We would catch them the next day, if not sooner. We have numerous pictures of kids that are beat with two-by-fours on their backside. They're completely black and blue, or even possibly tortured."

Sheriff Dannels developed a local program to prosecute juveniles. "We went from one or two in our facility right next door here" — the county jail — "to thirty-six a day. One hundred percent of those kids went to prison for 1.5 years." Today they are down to one juvenile a year. "When you run a 100 percent conviction rate, you see the reduction in drugs."

Dannels has a message for those who extol sanctuary cities. "When local leaders and state leaders say, 'Come see us, get through that border, break the law, and we'll take care of you,' that's offensive to what we've done here," because it puts his officers at greater risk. But he recognizes that law enforcement is only one piece of the puzzle. "Immigration reform is so needed. It truly is. What is the process to get in this country? It takes years. Come on — can we look at that? But people are so afraid of their parties. I blame Congress hard on this, all sides. I mean, Republicans will blame Democrats,

Democrats will blame Republicans, but remember: Republicans had the House, Senate, and the presidency and didn't fix a damn thing."

His nonpartisanship is refreshing — patriotic pragmatism on an issue sorely lacking it. "We have to have a balanced progressive plan," he says. "We also need a balanced plan of border security, which is a balance of technology, staffing, physical — all that needs to come into play. One doesn't fix it all. We all know that's common sense, but can you get them to agree on any of that? Of course not. You've got from open borders to close it all. Folks, the answer's in the middle. We all know that. Politics, emotions, sensation have no business in policing. It truly doesn't."

Sergeant Williams — Tim, he says — takes me for a drive in his truck to have a look at the border, ten miles south. On the way, we pass the Warren Ballpark, one of the oldest baseball stadiums in America, built by one of the nation's largest copper concerns for its employees. It opened in 1909, a year after Jack Norworth was inspired to write "Take Me Out to the Ballgame" while riding the New York City subway and spotting a sign for the Polo Grounds. The ballpark's most notable history is also tied to a train ride — and to the deportation of immigrants.

In 1917, Bisbee miners struck for better conditions and wages, including an end to a tiered wage system that discriminated against immigrants. The United States had just entered World War I, and disruptions to industrial production were attacked as treasonous, especially when the disruptors were immigrants led by a socialistic union, the International Workers of the World, a group Theodore Roosevelt had called "undesirable citizens," which led IWW members to wear buttons reading, "I am an undesirable citizen." The first proud Deplorables.

The mining companies demanded that the Cochise County sheriff round up strikers and their sympathizers, and after news broke of the Zimmermann Telegram — Germany's offer to support Mexico if it invaded the United States to reclaim its lost territory — the sheriff acceded. He organized a posse of "deputies" who were deemed "loyal Americans," and they marched two thousand people at gunpoint to the Warren Ballpark, where they demanded the "undesirables" renounce the strike and pledge allegiance to the company. About eight hundred did so. The others — about 90 percent of whom were immigrants, about half Mexican and Slavic — were placed in boxcars in sweltering heat with little or no water, sent 180 miles east into New Mexico, and left to fend for themselves in the desert. They were rescued by the army, but few ever came back.

Buy me some peanuts and Cracker Jack
I don't care if I never get back

One of the mine executives had served as a Rough Rider with Theodore Roosevelt in Cuba, and the former president gave his full support to the sheriff and mine owners. "No human being in his senses," Roosevelt declared, "doubts that the men deported from Bisbee were bent on destruction and murder." No one involved in the deportation was ever convicted of a crime, but in one way, the deportees were lucky: They were not among the twenty-three hundred people, most of them German immigrants or of German heritage, sent to internment camps for the duration of the war, on the flimsiest of pretexts. When a nation is in a wartime mentality and the word *invasion* is on people's lips, loyal immigrants can be turned into treasonous enemies and calls for deportation and imprisonment can find broad support.

We arrive at the border town of Naco and see construction crews installing a thirty-foot steel-beamed fence directly behind a twenty-foot steel-beamed fence.

"That's the Obama-era fence," Tim says, pointing to the smaller one. The two fences back-to-back are a jarring sight that call to mind King Canute and the futility of trying to stop the tide from coming in.

"Has anyone tried to scale the new one yet?" I ask.

"Absolutely. We catch them all the time."

"Ropes?"

"No, you literally grab it like this" — he extends his arms in a circle — "and they just shimmy right up. I think border patrol's already had quite a few fall off it. They got seriously injured. The top of the fence is supposed to be sharp enough to where you can't grab it, but they just throw a blanket over it." Often, however, they don't need to climb it at all. I'm astonished to learn the fence includes storm gates that are open half the year.

"During monsoon season, all these gates will be wide open and they'll leave them open," Tim says, "and there's thousands of these gates across the border. You can see where they lift up. They'll walk right through that. For months at a time, those will just be open, because if they aren't, the water will rip the whole fence apart — take it right off."

When they're open, I ask, doesn't that make the rest of the fence moot?

"Yeah. And that's where our camera system comes into play, because we can see them coming across and go after them." Tim built the camera network the sheriff proudly touted, which uses AI to filter out non-human images and provide real-time data to the team. On the ride to the border, he told me: "Every time you hear that phone go ding" — he pointed to his cell phone — "that's another group of illegal aliens or drug smugglers coming across." He had no experience building a camera and communications network, so he taught himself how to bounce signal with radio waves. "One of the border patrol supervisors said that my unit and our camera system does 80 percent of their work," he says, meaning that the cameras were identifying 80 percent of the people they are going after.

He shows me a house where they found a tunnel and several thousand pounds of marijuana. "It was a very well-built tunnel. I'm just under six foot five and I couldn't stand up in it, but I could move pretty easily." Even with occasional tunnels and open gates, the fence has made an enormous difference, he says. "Several years ago, you would be standing right here and a group of thirty would run right into the community. So the residents here, they really wanted to secure the town and push them out to where the rural population was. But then you also have US citizens that live out in the rural part. They're just as important as anybody that lives inside the city."

Leaving town, we turn west toward the Huachuca Mountains. "This is a corridor that they'll get on and then they're gone — to New Mexico or Tucson or wherever. This is a main highway, Highway 92. It's only three miles from the border to here. They get their products" to a waiting car, "and then go back."

"So without that fence, it's extremely easy to get on the highway?" I ask.

"With the fence, more difficult. And that's why we're so adamant that you got to have something because it gives us a fighting chance to try to get them. Even if they're going back, they'd still have to climb that, versus what you're about to see when we cross the pass over here, there's nothing."

For most of American history, there was nothing, just an open border. The first significant fence to go up didn't come until 1948, in California. It was chain-linked, under a mile long, and built with posts and wire recycled from their original use: securing Japanese internment camps. "You don't build a nine-foot fence along the border between two friendly nations," former California governor Ronald Reagan said while campaigning for the presidency in 1980. "You document the undocumented workers and let them come in here with a visa." Reagan's view of immigration led to a 1986 law that provided a pathway to legal status for three million people, most of them from Mexico, and sought to discourage future unauthorized crossings by imposing fines on employers who hired people without legal status. In the Senate, majorities in both parties supported it. It was the last comprehensive immigration bill Congress has adopted.

We pass a ranch that belongs to John Ladd, whose family has owned the land for more than a hundred years. "He has over $50 million worth of border infrastructure on his ranch," Tim says, mostly fencing built during the Obama administration. It did little to deter migrant and smuggler traffic, until Tim installed the camera system. "He has not had drug smuggling on his property in close to three years. We put so many drug smugglers in prison off of his property that they won't run drugs on it anymore, but he still has a lot of the human immigration going on" — and that creates problems, too. "Every day his cattle troughs are getting broken, his fence is getting cut. Every day he deals with that." Ladd wants more agents patrolling the border. "If they build a wall and do what they did to us," Ladd said of the federal government, "it isn't going to work."

We are entering Coronado National Memorial, a wilderness area in the Huachuca Mountains overseen by the National Park Service and named for Francisco Vásquez de Coronado, the Spanish explorer whose expedition came through here in 1540. We stop at the Montezuma Pass Overlook. "The Arizona Trail starts right here," Tim says. "It goes from Mexico all the way to Utah. But the trail is heavily used by smuggling. They'll come up over the peaks and then come down, or they'll follow the peaks and keep going up north."

"I see why people would want to hike up here — it's beautiful," I say as we look many miles across a Mexican valley. "Is it safe to camp?"

"That was one of the things that I wanted to make sure could happen again. Everybody should be able to enjoy the beautiful scenery we have here. You shouldn't go up in the mountains, try to camp, and be overrun by illegal aliens or drug smugglers, to the point you don't even feel it's safe. So this is one of the areas that we have really hit hard, where we have said, 'The general public shouldn't have to walk up there and run into forty illegal aliens tramping down the trail.'"

"Do hikers ever report seeing them?"

"Absolutely, yes. A lot. They get scared. Several of them have been assaulted." He mentions a worker at the Chiricahua National Monument — northeast of Naco — who was badly beaten by a drug smuggler who had returned after being deported, and who stole her vehicle.

From where we are standing, the view of Mexico is essentially the same one Coronado had when passing through, but it's changing. Tim drives me down the other side of the mountain, back to the border.

"See that gray up there?" he asks. "They're blowing road to get the fence up the mountain" — using dynamite to blast a gash through the national monument's pristine wilderness, flattening cliffs and widening passes to allow construction vehicles to drive through areas that have been accessible only by foot or hoof for millennia. Construction companies call the blasting "pioneering." The new frontier is walling it off. To do it, the Department of Homeland Security has waived a slew of environmental protections, including the Endangered Species Act. Environmentalists are irate about the damage, fear its effects on wildlife, and argue it will cause floodwaters to back up, even with the floodgates. Not all neighboring ranch owners are happy, either. But contractors are racing against the clock and adding overnight shifts to finish as much of the wall as possible before January 20.

The road brings us along the border to a wooden slat fence a few feet off the ground.

"They call this Normandy fencing. It's supposed to be a vehicle barrier but smugglers just cut it, move it, and drive through it. That's the only thing stopping you from crossing into Mexico. This goes almost all the way to Nogales, about forty-five miles west. They're over this in seconds."

"How many crossings are you guys trying to chase down?"

"Right now, we're averaging right around twenty-seven hundred a month."

"How many do you think are getting through?"

"We're at a 39 percent apprehension rate. Every time we put new cameras out, we've seen more and more. It's like, 'Oh, crap. We didn't even know there were people running in this area.'"

When we cross back into cell service, Tim's phone lights up in a stream of dings. "You hear all that?" he asks. "That's how many groups have crossed since we've been over there. How many was that, thirty dings?"

It's easy to seize on the gaps in the border wall to treat it as an object of ridicule: *People can walk around it! Or under it! Or even right through it!* Officers here see it as something else: an essential tool that makes it harder to cross into population centers and buys law enforcement time to respond. Even if it doesn't solve the nation's problems, it helps address the local communities'.

That night, Laurel and I walk into Bisbee from our RV park overlooking an old copper mine. After I try to convey what I saw and heard, she draws a connection to the prior night in Tombstone. "It's just like the mask issue," she says, "but reversed." She's right. Border walls are to Democrats what masks have been to Republicans: objects of dismissal and derision because neither is capable of solving the entire problem, yet neither side wants to admit that each could play a constructive role — however flawed and limited — in tackling a complex and difficult problem. Instead, each side views the other's position as an offensive infringement on our national character because it strikes at the heart of values we cherish: societal openness by liberals, individual freedom by conservatives.

Of course, assessing the wisdom of each requires weighing costs and benefits, but the scale is usually tipped by partisan loyalties. For liberals, acknowledging that border walls have some public safety benefits would risk appearing to be sympathetic to Trump's attacks on foreigners. For conservatives, acknowledging masks can have some health and safety benefits would risk appearing sympathetic to Democratic attacks on Republicans. Can we see some of ourselves in the other side? And if we can't, that, too, means we share more in common with the other party than we would like to admit. We don't need to take off our blinders — it's awfully tough to do — to at least recognize their existence.

Over our few days in Bisbee, Laurel and I fall for its narrow, hilly streets and the artsy vibe that took root after the mines closed in 1975. We take a jeep tour and learn a good deal of its history — its saloons and brothels, art and architecture, mansions and celebrities, cultural traditions and landscape oddities — but our guide says nothing of the Bisbee Deportation or its time as a Sundown Town for the Chinese. Many who grew up here never learned of them, either. Our guide does mention the Warren Ballpark, but only to note that Babe Ruth played there. There is no proof he did, but it's more fun to imagine the Bambino trotting the bases than boxcars loaded with immigrants.

As our tour wraps up, thousands are gathering in DC for various Trump rallies, including the evangelical-led Jericho March, whose speakers show the crossover between militant Christianity and militant nationalism. In addition to Michael Flynn, there's Alex Jones, who propagated the conspiracy theory that 9/11 was an inside job and who tells the crowd that "the state has no jurisdiction over any of us; our relationship with God is sacred and eternal." Mike Lindell, the pillow salesman, says we're living in "end times." Roger Stone, the dirty tricks political consultant, says that Jesus gave Trump the courage and compassion to pardon him. And Stewart Rhodes, the Oath Keepers founder, again urges Trump to invoke the Insurrection Act and speaks of a coming "bloody war." They've all been egged on by Trump, who tweeted this morning, after approving of the "thousands" of people arriving for the rallies: "WE HAVE JUST BEGUN TO FIGHT!!!" By the end of the night, more than thirty people will be arrested, including six for assaulting police officers. Four people are stabbed. Proud Boys maraud through the streets, attacking people and tearing down "Black Lives Matter" banners, setting one aflame. The Electoral College will meet in two days.

— 44 —

Borderlands II

Crossing New Mexico, about the only vehicles we see are US Border Patrol, and even in the largest town — Columbus, population eleven hundred — we see no people, just some of the same buildings the Bisbee deportees saw when they ended up here after being rescued by the army. At that time, the army had a large presence in Columbus because a Mexican revolutionary, Pancho Villa, had recently attacked the town, stealing guns and horses. The raid — the first foreign attack on US soil since the War of 1812 — left nearly twenty Americans dead, while Villa lost about eighty men. In response, and without consulting the Mexican government, President Wilson sent General John Pershing and ten thousand troops into Mexico to disband Villa's army and capture him. After a year of marching through Mexico, they mostly succeeded in the former but failed in the latter, elevating Villa to folk-hero status in Mexico.

Today, as Republicans talk of again sending the army across the border over Mexico's objections to kill and capture enemies, this time drug traders, the failed attempt to capture Pancho Villa has faded from public memory, but not here. One Columbus resident whose great-grandfather was killed in Villa's raid has been waging a lonely decades-long effort to change the name of Pancho Villa State Park, viewing it as an insult. His brother has taken a different tack: turning the town's annual commemoration ceremony into an exercise in cross-border healing, by inviting Villa's descendants to attend.

The population of Columbus is about 85 percent bilingual, and there is regular traffic across the border from Puerto Palomas, including by schoolchildren who are American citizens. Often one or both of their parents has been deported. Columbus has allowed them to attend school for free since the 1950s, mostly out of self-interest. "They are going to more than likely live in the United States," explained the principal of the elementary school, Armando Chavez. "We want to get them to the highest level of education possible, so they can be successful, and so they can become productive members and contribute back." In recent years, however, American kids crossing from Mexico have faced increasing antagonism from classmates who don't think they belong on this side of the border. "It seems like it's more acceptable to be able to say things that you couldn't say a couple years ago," the superintendent, Arsenio Romero, said.

We had hoped to camp in Pancho Villa State Park, but since New Mexico is requiring all travelers except those from Hawaii to quarantine for fourteen days upon arrival, we press on to the next option, also the site of a deadly raid, this one "a response to the Hispanic invasion of Texas," wrote the killer. *Invasion.*

We park in the back of the lot at the El Paso Walmart, near a memorial to the twenty-three people murdered at the store in 2019 by a man bent on killing as many Mexican immigrants as he could. The memorial is called Grande Candela. It consists of twenty-three aluminum vertical pipes in a circle. At night, it glows like a candle, giving off a light that "transcends borders and connects our hearts as one community," the plaque says. The pipes stand thirty feet tall, the same as the new border fence. I wish they were a foot taller.

The next morning, I walk over the Rio Grande to Juárez, Mexico, on a bridge flanked by a wall and barbed wire. There is no identification check to leave the country, only a 50-cent toll, but the massive effort to prevent illegal entry makes it easy to forget that many of the early American settlers in Texas arrived here illegally, claimed land, built homes, and became a public nuisance. "A great number of the foreigners who have entered the frontier are vicious and wild men, with evil ways," wrote a Mexican army general. "Some of them are fugitive criminals from the neighboring republic; within our borders they create disturbances and even criminal acts."

The city is named for President Benito Juárez, who is sometimes called the Lincoln of Mexico for his success in liberating the country from French rule, an effort that Lincoln aided through moral and diplomatic support.

There is a statue of Lincoln here, one of at least four in Mexico — four more than exist in Texas, from what I've been able to gather. In fact, there are more Lincoln statues in Mexico than there are in all the Confederate states combined.

When the United States wished to offer a gift to Mexico to celebrate the 150th anniversary of its independence, US senators proposed a statue of Miguel Hidalgo, who had inspired the independence movement. Mexican officials offered a different suggestion: Lincoln. It was Abe, after all, who had opposed the Mexican-American War and rejected a Confederate proposal for the north and south to join forces in invading Mexico. At the statue's dedication in Mexico City, on the 101st anniversary of Lincoln's death, President Lyndon Johnson said, "What Abraham Lincoln stood for is what binds our two nations — and indeed, this entire hemisphere — together." Johnson declared those binds to be "common values and shared beliefs." Freedom. Equality. Democracy.

Returning to the border, a US agent with a Mexican surname and accent asks me: How long were you there? Are you carrying any drugs or weapons? How much money do you have with you? About $100, I tell him. "Don't worry, we're not going to take it — this isn't Mexico." We both laugh, but he isn't kidding and tells a story about corrupt federales extorting Americans. Law enforcement in the wild west — *first justice, then the law* — is romanticized only at a safe distance.

We were not prepared for the vast emptiness of west Texas, and we're taken in by it. We stop for a night in Marfa, an old railroad and army town that has become a magnet for artists and tourists. When it became a Covid hot spot, two local artists decided to send a message to us out-of-towners, placing a neon sign in a window, declaring, "Everyone Here Hates You." While the artists blame visitors for the spread, contact tracing suggests a different story, with local interactions — in homes, bars, and workplaces — the more common culprit. Tourists are easy villains, as outsiders always are. The artists' view of visitors is not so different from the way many Americans view those who cross the border illegally: If only we could keep them out, everything would be better.

As we're eating dinner, the Electoral College wraps up its voting. There are no faithless electors: Biden 306, Trump 232. Nevertheless, Trump-organized electors also met today in five states: Arizona, Georgia, Michigan, Nevada, and Wisconsin. They declared themselves the "duly elected and qualified electors." In two other states, New Mexico and Pennsylvania, alternate slates made the same declaration with a caveat that they might *later be found* to be qualified electors. Tomorrow, Senate majority leader Mitch McConnell will finally congratulate Biden, recognize him as president-elect, and urge Republicans not to object to the election results when the House certifies them on January 6. House Republican leader Kevin McCarthy, like many other Republican members of Congress, will not take any of those steps.

After one night in Marfa, we drive south to the border, passing desert ranches and little else. About the only face we see is Abe's. "Profile Of Lincoln," a road sign reads, and sure enough, off in the distance, the Cuesta del Burro mountaintop bears a passing resemblance to him. Just because Texans have never built a monument to Abe doesn't mean they don't claim the biggest one in the world.

On the border, we follow the meandering Rio Grande, so slender one could almost jump across it with a running start. There is no wall or fence, just a gorge the river has cut through over millennia. We stop for a few nights in Terlingua, an abandoned mining town that was reincarnated as a refuge for offbeat bohemians, inspiring the title of Jerry Jeff Walker and the Lost Gonzo Band's cosmic country album, *¡Viva Terlingua!* The town's full-time population is less than one hundred, and its economy relies on visitors, just like Marfa's, but its vibe is more welcoming. At the village entrance, a handmade sign reads, "Everyone Here Loves You."

We are the only ones at the Lost Gringo RV Park, a small dirt parking lot tucked into the hills near the town's old mines. While sitting in Charley, I catch a momentary glimpse of the back half of a running animal that is too big to be a dog. *I think I saw a mountain lion*, I tell Laurel. She dismisses it as an aberration until, a little later, she sees it, too — just the back half. It slightly unnerves us, since we both spotted it near the road into town, but we're willing to risk walking the road to have dinner outside at the Starlight Theatre, so-named because a storm once blew off its roof. Besides, there are more dangerous threats afoot than mountain lions.

Today the militant right-wing group Three Percenters issues a statement: "We stand ready and are standing by to answer the call from our President should the need arise that We The People are needed to take back our country from the pure evil that is conspiring to steal our country away from the American people. We are ready to enter into battle with General Flynn leading the charge. We will not act unless we are told to."

Terlingua is a jumping-off point for Big Bend National Park, which runs along the Rio Grande for 118 miles. We were lucky to land a last-minute campsite for two nights, long enough to explore a few corners of the park, hike several canyons, and stare at the darkest night sky in the continental US. As we watch the sunset over the Rio Grande and the Mexican village of Boquillas del Carmen, two young men cross in a canoe to retrieve cash that hikers leave beside handmade goods Mexicans have placed in the park: walking sticks, crafts, and beer koozies. They'll take the money home, replace their stock of goods, and return tomorrow to do it again.

The river is low, easy to cross. The Trump administration plans to build a wall through the park, though it's hard to believe Texas Republicans would allow this unspoiled landscape to be so desecrated, especially given the park's economic impact on the region. A wall would also block wildlife — bobcats and mountain lions, black bears and mule deer, big-horned sheep and white-nosed coatis — from the river, their primary water source.

I take a walk into Boquillas Canyon and see Americans swimming in the Rio Grande. On the other side, a Mexican man beside a horse yells out to me: "Tamales!" I'm standing near a group of hikers eating them, who tell me they're six for ten bucks — and delicious. I dig into my pockets and realize I'm short. I yell back to the man in the other country: "I've only got $4. Can I buy two?" He mounts his horse, fords the river, comes to America to make the delivery, and returns to his native land. I don't imagine Democrats are his only customers, especially after tasting the tamales.

Around the same time, Army Secretary Ryan McCarthy and Chief of Staff James McConville issue a statement in response to calls by Michael Flynn and others for the president to institute marshal law, seize ballots, and rerun the election. "There is no role for the US military," they write, "in determining the outcome of an American election." The statement infuriates Trump, who dispatches an aide, Johnny McEntee, to relay a message to the acting Secretary of Defense, Chris Miller. (Trump fired Secretary Mark Esper days after the election in retaliation for Esper's opposition to sending the army into cities in the aftermath of George Floyd's murder.) After delivering the message, McEntee reported back in a note on White House stationery: "Chris Miller spoke to both of them and anticipates no more statements. (If another happens, he will fire them.)"

That night, as I cook hot dogs on the campsite's grill and we wait for the stars to emerge, a wild scene happens in the White House, what would come to be called "the craziest meeting of the Trump presidency." The group includes Flynn, Giuliani, Overstock CEO Patrick Byrne (who flew a group of Proud Boys on a private jet to Washington so they could attend a post-election rally that turned violent), and the lawyer Sidney Powell, who is pushing the conspiracy theory that voting machines were rigged by Venezuela. The group urges Trump to confiscate voting machines, and Trump considers appointing Powell as a special counsel to investigate voter fraud. White House counsel Pat Cipollone wages a valiant effort to debunk the group's unsubstantiated and unconstitutional claims. Amid shouting and insults, the meeting stretches on for hours, with no resolution. Shortly before 2:00 A.M., Trump tweets, "Big protest in DC on January 6. Be there, will be wild!"

North of Big Bend, in the little desert town of Marathon, Texas, a street sign warns people to beware of UFOs. Two out of three Americans believe in aliens, according to polls. An even higher percentage of Trump voters believe the 2020 election was stolen from him.

Heading east on Route 90 brings us through Langtry, where Judge Roy Bean held court in his saloon beginning in 1882, the year the Southern Pacific Railroad came through and turned the area into a den of debauchery. The state needed a lawman, and Bean got the job, despite a past shrouded in mystery and rumors of murder. The bandanna he wore around his neck concealed the rope marks from the time he escaped a hanging, goes one story.

We step inside the weathered-wooden walls of his saloon-courthouse and see the pistol he used as a gavel, sometimes interrupting proceedings to allow people to refill their drinks, and sometimes sentencing the guilty to buy a round for the judge and jury. Bean called himself "the law west of the Pecos" River, and a sign says he was known for "dispensing hard liquor and harsh justice." There is no record of the judge ever executing anyone, and since there was no jail in town, every offense was met with the same type of sentence: confiscated property and fines, which often ended up in Bean's pocket. In one case, he imposed a fine on a dead man for carrying a concealed weapon: $40, the same amount the man had in his pocket. Bean took his pistol, too.

Bean rarely consulted his 1879 statute book, and when updated law books arrived, he used them as kindling. *First justice, then the law.* When his Irish patrons demanded the exoneration of an Irishman accused of killing a Chinese railroad worker, the judge obliged, saying that he consulted his law book and found laws against killing a person, but none against killing the Chinese, whose humanity he and many others denied.

Bean was credited with taming the town, and by embellishing his life story, he joined the pantheon of mythic western figures he carved into his walking stick, including Buffalo Bill Cody, Wild Bill Hickock, Texas Jack Omohundro, and D. L. Payne, a leader of the Oklahoma "boomers" who sought to illegally open Indian lands, leading to arrests and trials. But part of the Roy Bean legend often forgotten ought to be recovered: He was a bad loser. He lost his 1885 reelection bid but harassed the winner into resigning. A decade later, he lost again — a rival saloon owner was declared the winner after Bean received more votes than there were qualified voters — but Bean refused to concede. In the next election, Bean chased voters from the polls at gunpoint until the sheriff arrived. He lost the election, but he refused to give up his seat on the bench.

Romanticizing rogues is an American tradition, as we have seen across our journey. But when romance overtakes reality and myth blinds us to truth, we can wake to find justice discarded and democracy denied. When it occurs in a small town, the harm is regrettable but endurable. When it spreads across the nation, catastrophe looms.

Earlier today, Michael Flynn retweeted a plea by the chair of the Arizona Republican Party, Kelli Ward: "Mr. President," she wrote, "We are working every avenue to stop this coup & to stop our Republic from crumbling. Patriots are united." She ended it with "#CrossTheRubicon," a reference to Julius Caesar's decision to cross the river separating Gaul from Rome in defiance of the law, a treasonous insurrection that began a civil war and led to Caesar naming himself dictator for life of the Roman Empire. The phrase *cross the Rubicon* is now making the rounds on the right, since the phrase attributed to Brutus, *Sic Semper Tyrannis*, is only useful when an opponent is in power. Today Trump tweets, "GREATEST ELECTION FRAUD IN THE HISTORY OF OUR COUNTRY!!!"

East of Langtry is Del Rio, across the Rio Grande from its much larger sister, Ciudad Acuña. A mile from the border, we stop at an assistance center being run out of a shuttered school by the Val Verde Humanitarian Border Coalition. A volunteer who helped set it up, Tiffany Burrow, shows me around, pointing out where they keep donated clothes and coats. "An amazing lady," she says, "held a clothing drive for winter clothing: scarves, gloves, hats, and coats. But they go so fast. We're always in need of coats. Men's coats, but also coats that fit a nine-month belly for pregnant women. And over there" — she points to a shelf — "are the shoes."

"People arrive without shoes?"

"Yeah. This week we had somebody in socks. Fuzzy socks."

"And what are people typically coming with?"

"The Bible. Or another set of clothes. Jewelry. Could be something sentimental. Never enough to fill a suitcase."

The number of individuals apprehended at the border here has soared because of asylum seekers. Border patrol repatriates many of them, but some are released into the United States pending a hearing, after being processed through a short-term holding facility. "That can mean a couple of days. It can mean ten days. The longest I've ever heard in our area has been twenty-three." She has visited the facility. "It's very, very cold. And it's like a cell. There's nothing in there. Nothing."

Border patrol was dropping them at the Del Rio bus station by the hundreds, but many lacked the money or language skills needed to arrange their travel. "Border patrol reached out to all of the pastors within our city," Tiffany says. "Only one responded and said, 'I think we can do something.'" The pastor enlisted other churches to join him, and border patrol has been dropping families here, where they can use the phone, buy bus tickets, and get some food and clothing.

"There's a lot more folks that come through than what we're seeing," Tiffany says, "and they're also filtering out the human traffickers, the drug smugglers. Most of the folks that we see will cross over the Rio and then give themselves up to border patrol before they ever reach the fence." She points to flags lining the walls. "Those are where the families have come from. I think we have twenty-two countries, although one flag is not up yet."

"I'm surprised to see all the African nations."

"It's a huge, huge portion. They come over to Brazil, they travel through the jungle" — a dangerous, harrowing journey. "And we're also getting a ton of people from Haiti. And then sprinkle in some Central American countries — Honduras, Panama, El Salvador."

"Are Mexicans less likely to be released on this side than others?"

"I don't see any Mexicans."

"And do you hear from them about ending up in trafficking situations?"

"A little. You can tell when there's been some trauma. We don't get all the stories, but oh my goodness — some of them, yes, it's crazy. Some of them have traveled with people who have died along the way. I've been in the hospital with a pregnant mother, and the father passed on the journey."

Pregnancy is a common trait. "We see a lot of women in their third trimester. They're either having babies here at our hospital or they're having babies right after. That's what drives them to cross" — citizenship for the child. One day last week, they saw four adults: "Two couples and they were both due. One was thirty-nine weeks and the other was thirty-eight weeks."

Conservatives have lambasted this phenomenon, calling the new Americans "anchor babies" and their mothers "baby tourists." Democrats generally try to avoid the subject, and while the terms are crass and compassionless, the activity itself is real. "We're the only country in the world where a person comes in and has a baby, and the baby is essentially a citizen," Trump said in 2018, as he declared that he would issue an executive order banning birthright citizenship. He was wrong — similar laws are on the books in nearly every country in the Western Hemisphere and some in Europe — and lawyers talked him out of issuing the order, since there is a long-held legal consensus that such a change requires a constitutional amendment. It might also require putting an asterisk on the plaque at the base of the Statue of Liberty: "Give me your tired, your poor, your huddled masses* yearning to breathe free."

Tiffany began volunteering here when her church became involved. "We take the politics out of it," she says. "There's no left or right, because it's all faith-based — you're showing God's love to everyone. I'm a mom and wife and I wanted my kids to be a part of volunteering and to see what was happening in their community."

She wants to show me the border wall, so we get in her car and drive the mile south. "We have a really strong partnership with border patrol," she says, "and it's unusual because you'd think we'd be on opposite sides. It's not the case at all. I just have tremendous respect for them. They put their heart into their job, and it is dangerous. They're so essential to keeping out the bad stuff, and then on top of that, they're trying to deal with this migration issue. It's pretty crazy."

Before we get to the wall, I ask if there is talk of a larger fence going up behind the existing one, like I saw in Arizona. "No," she says. "There's so many spots in our Texas border without a fence that you can't put it

* Just don't send any pregnant women.

here. At least, I wouldn't want my money to go into it." When we reach the border and see a construction site, she's not sure what it's for.

"It looks like they might be building the second fence," I say.

"This is insane," she says. "What is the point? All you do is walk around it. This is brand new."

"It's the exact same fence I saw in Arizona."

"Really? I cannot believe I'm seeing this."

After Tiffany drops me back at Charley, I want to show Laurel the new fence, since she had missed it in Arizona. We drive there and quickly get stopped by border patrol.

"Are you lost?" the officer asks, smiling. He knows why we're here. "That's the new wall. Not much to see."

"How far does it go?" I ask.

"Only as far as the other wall," which ends not far from where we are. "And it might not even go that far, depending on what happens." I think he's referring to what happens after President-elect Biden takes office — but it occurs to me he might be referring to *whether* Biden takes office.

We drive to an RV park a mile from the border, but I make a wrong turn and we end up at a spot where a smaller border fence ends. I stop and walk up to it, to take a closer look. I could easily step around it — and would have, if only someone were selling tamales on the other side.

— 45 —

Holiday Road

Good friends in Austin, John and Jennifer, have kindly offered to take us in for Christmas, and as we've driven across Texas, we've been listening to John's welcome gift: a playlist of native artists, from old blues (Lightnin' Hopkins), classic country (George Strait), and Texas swing (Bob Wills), to genre-benders of every kind, many needing only a first name (Willie, Janis, Townes, Guy, Blaze, Lyle), some needing a middle name (Stevie Ray, Jerry Jeff, Billy Joe, Ray Wylie, Robert Earl), and only a few needing a last name, including one (Steve Earle) I've seen more times than I can count. It's a great mix, but he's left off a Texan who's often overlooked, even though he's a national treasure, the artist-writer-musician Terry Allen. His latest album, released just before the pandemic, includes a song, "Sailin' on Through," that I have played repeatedly because of the tumoil it envisions and the perseverance it inspires.

There's storms in the gulf, fires on the plains
Half the world is screwed, the other half's insane

Today a lawyer connected to Michael Flynn named Ivan Raiklin shared on Twitter a two-page memo explaining "Operation Pence Card," intended to create the appearance of a legal basis for Pence to reject electors from states where Trump alleges fraud took place. Trump retweets it.

After getting rapid Covid tests at a clinic — we're negative and relieved — we visit a liquor store to buy bottles of the good stuff for our hosts, as Terry Allen had suggested.

So better break out the bottle, bring on the glass
Fill it up with the good stuff, 'cause everything must pass

John takes us downtown in his Tesla. After nine thousand miles in Charley, it feels more like a SpaceX rocket than a car. As we drive past tent encampments along the highway, he tells us about Mobile Loaves and Fishes, a homeless organization that he, Jennifer, and their two boys have volunteered with. Its founder, retired real estate entrepreneur Alan Graham, has kindly agreed to meet us at his latest housing development, which began in 2004 with a single RV for one homeless person. It has since burgeoned into Community First! Village, a fifty-one-acre neighborhood with two hundred residents living in a mix of trailers and tiny houses.

When we arrive, Alan brings us inside one of the recently completed small homes, beautifully decorated and furnished, like something from an Instagram account. But he cautions us. "Don't walk away with the cute tiny house idea in your brain," he says. "It has nothing to do with that. It has everything to do with community." The reason people end up without homes, he says, is "a profound, catastrophic loss of family." He mentions other obstacles they may face: "physical health issues, addiction issues, affordable housing, trauma, adverse childhood experiences, the criminal justice system, the foster care system — I could go on and on." But most people who face these difficulties don't end up homeless. He cites his mother, who was mentally ill and institutionalized much of her life. "Never in a billion years was she homeless," he says, because of the love and assistance she received from her extended family.

That extended family is what Community First! Village works to re-create. "The system is depending on housing to solve homelessness," Alan says. "But there's a complete misunderstanding as to what home means. If my house were to burn down, I would try to save my family — my wife first, and then the dogs — before I ever tried to save the house. We believe that housing is necessary, don't get me wrong, but it's insufficient."

He feels much the same way about government, seeing it as a critical partner, but a junior one. "We believe the government is very valuable and important, but we can't go and take all the human shit of the world" — he's talking about problems, not people — "and then shovel it over to city hall and demand that they fix it, which is what we do right now. We're pointing our finger at the mayor and the council or the governor or the president of the United States. Well, stop. We the people are responsible for this deal. So Community First is actually a philosophical invitation to the entire community" — all of Austin, and beyond — "to come join with us."

Most residents here had been homeless for at least a year, but the village is open to all. "About fifty of the people on-site have never been homeless before in their life, including titans of industry, physicians, nurses, and schoolteachers," Alan says. They come to live out their faith at a place whose mission is rooted in the gospel, but Alan doesn't talk like a preacher and instead peppers his sentences with cuss words. "We make no bones about the fact that we are fueled by our faith, but we're not proselytizers here," he says. "We welcome everybody of every walk of life. I believe I live in the most diverse neighborhood anywhere. Everything that you could imagine that God created lives here: gender ID, color, religious preferences. We all live here in predominant harmony with a side salad of tension."

There is tension in all communities, and Alan welcomes it. "There's no backyards — everybody's got a front porch pushed right up to the roadways so that people are interacting with each other, and into relationship with each other. That includes the conflicts. The only conflict we have now is just yelling 'F you!' on Facebook to each other. It's nonsense, man, because we wouldn't do that if we were face-to-face."

His original vision for the village was inspired by his own experience as a kid at KOAs. "There was this inherent sense of community inside of the deals" — *deal* is a favorite word of his, along with *bro*, his term of endearment: *I love you, bro. What's goin' on, bro?* At the KOAs, he says, "I've seen a $12,000 Jayco fifth wheel next to a million-dollar Prevost, and these families come out and they're cooking burgers together. One's a millionaire. The other's trying to make $179.95 a month payments on the fifth wheel. The kids, they're all integrating — so that's where the philosophy came from." Laurel and I have seen this ourselves. There is no social hierarchy at campgrounds.

Many residents also interact through their work for the village, often in business ventures the village supports. "I'm an entrepreneur," Alan says. "I have zero fear of failure. Most of everything that you're going to see — like an outdoor movie theater, a bed-and-breakfast, a blacksmith shop — no human on the planet would put that on a business plan in a neighborhood that lifts the chronically homeless crackheads, glue sniffers, and prostitutes up off the streets. But unless we look at it as a community effort, where we're willing to take that risk, we're never going to move the needle in this country."

We hop into Alan's golf cart, and he takes us to an entrepreneur hub where residents make art and crafts to sell — jewelry, pottery, leather, dog chains — earning them an income of about $1 million in 2020. Alan explains the idea behind the investment in the arts workshop. "We have to meet people where they are. So that the guy that came off the streets who's a glassblower — why should we make him work at McDonald's? Blow glass and sell." He mentions an artist we meet: "Don't try to fix and repair him. Go get him on the art deal. And if you want to ride around on your wheelchair cleaning things up" — we had met a gentleman doing that, who told us Alan saved his life — "do it."

The entrepreneur hub is run by Carlos Guerra, who left a corporate career to pursue this calling. Whatever people want to make, his response is: "Great. Let's do it. Let's find what your skill set is and give you the opportunity to earn some income" — not for the money alone, but for what the work provides: dignity, confidence, self-worth, hope.

Getting people to the hub can be difficult, Carlos tells us, because new residents often withdraw into the security of their new houses. Tim Shea, who lives in a beautifully furnished 3-D printed house, one of the first Americans to do so, talks about holing up. "I always isolated — windows shut, curtains down," he says. "That's what drug addicts do." He's overcome a lifetime of heroin addiction, in and out of rehab. Now? "I got flies in my house because I can't keep my door shut. Got to keep it open — that's a mentality change that comes from feeling safe. Not to mention, I actually feel rich. I'm proud of what I have here."

Not every resident is sober. We ride past a small group drinking beer and smoking marijuana on a porch. Alan's voice goes into high drama, as though he's shocked. "Oh God! Oh no! Michael, what are you smokin' over there?" They erupt in faux protest, as though they're worried about having been caught. Alan continues, "I smell it! You can't fool me!"

There's a lot of carrying on, and the residents promise to clean up the beer cans in the yard. As we drive away, Alan explains, "They're my neighbors. They're not threatened by me and I trust them and they can smoke dope right in front of me, I don't give a shit. We have no problem with the potheads here. Only the other stuff" — hard drugs — "and the alcohol."

There are no rules prohibiting drug use. He tells addicts: "If you want out of this deal, let me know and we'll figure that deal out together. They all want out — every addict I've ever met, and I've been around a billion. They hate it, but they're medicating themselves against pain that you and I can't even begin to understand. So it's loving on people, man, that's what it is. Letting them know we care for them."

I ask about drug-counseling programs. "We find all of that a failure. What I believe actually works is being in a community and what we call harm reduction. We've done five studies and we believe there's about an 80 percent drop in drug use from the streets to here and a 60 percent drop in alcohol use. It's working all day and going home and being tired."

Occasionally, drugs will lead to crime here, as they do everywhere, but the village has no paid security officers. "We tell people we have 250 full-time security officers" — the residents and staff. "You want a nice neighborhood, you make it a nice neighborhood." There are responsibilities that come with being a member of the community, including paying rent, which most residents do through their Supplemental Security Income (SSI). Occasionally, people need to be evicted if they repeatedly become a problem. "Be who you are," Alan says. "Just don't be a dick. It's not complicated."

Community First! Village is a direct challenge to all the conventional approaches to dealing with homelessness: temporary shelter, transitional housing, drug counseling, mental health services, and employment referrals. Alan's answer is simpler and utterly more difficult: "Love your neighbor."

He's purchased another 125 acres and has plans to expand the village to about two thousand residents, larger than many small towns. Sitting on the porch of his trailer — he sold his big house a few years ago and lives here with his wife — I ask him what the public response should be to all the people living in tents across America. He pulls out a pen and paper.

"Let's say there are a hundred thousand. And there's 330 million Americans that live in the United States." He writes 330,000,000 above 100,000. "You take away the zeros — remember fifth-grade math? And you have thirty-three hundred people to one person." He's made his point: Imagine if even a small percentage of those thirty-three hundred people got together to bring the one person into community with them. "It actually turns out to be not that big of a deal, when you really do the math."

The simplicity of the theology behind Community First! Village reflects the radicalness of Christianity at its most elemental. But the courage it takes to practice it as fully as Alan and others here do reflects the rarity with which we see it. Alan, maybe more than anyone else in the city, is being faithful to its unofficial motto: Keep Austin Weird.

Toward the end of our golf cart tour, we return past the group that had been smoking and drinking. One of the guys flags us down to tell Alan that he's picked up the beer cans, but also to air a grievance.

"I do have a complaint about the dude from Assisi," he says. "Someone stole him."

"No, a cat knocked it out," Alan says, of the missing statue of St. Francis, who renounced his family's wealth to live among the poor. "We have it on video."

"Oh yeah?"

"Yeah. We've got another one being made right now."

At the entrepreneur center, we saw a woman molding a new St. Francis statue out of clay.

"Okay," the man says, relieved. "I'm going to screw that one in."

"That's a good idea. Hey, thanks for picking up, bro. Love you, man."

"Love you, too."

We drive off. Alan smiles and shakes his head. "The dude from Assisi."

It would be hard to imagine a better Christmas gift than visiting Community First!, but the generous hospitality that Jen, John, and their extended family show to Laurel and me is greater still. Our cup runneth over, including at their Christmas Eve brisket feast. The next morning arrives exactly as Laurel and I imagined it would in Texas, based on our understanding of it from the singer-songwriter Robert Earl Keen.

> *Someone put the coffee on and find the Tylenol*
> *Merry Christmas everyone, Happy Holidays y'all*

The news on Christmas morning, however, is grim. Someone has detonated an RV in downtown Nashville next to an AT&T building, injuring people and badly damaging businesses and homes. A conspiracy theory has already begun spreading that the attack was intended to destroy fraudulent ballots held in the building. It later emerges that the perpetrator was deeply distrustful of government and captive to a broad range of conspiracy theories himself, including one that holds that the world is run by alien lizards who take human form, which is rooted in anti-Semitism and gaining adherents among QAnon believers.

We head out from Austin two days after Christmas, skirting Dallas and the site of the most dissected conspiracy theory of all, the assassination of John F. Kennedy as he rode in a Lincoln Continental. JFK was set to deliver a speech that afternoon that now sounds fresh and urgent: "There will always be dissident voices heard in the land, expressing opposition without alternatives, finding fault but never favor, perceiving gloom on every side and seeking influence without responsibility. Those voices are inevitable. But today other voices are heard in the land — voices preaching doctrines wholly unrelated to reality . . . We cannot expect that everyone, to use the phrase of a decade ago, will 'talk sense to the American people.' But we can hope that fewer people will listen to nonsense." But hope has never been enough.

While we are at a Harvest Host alpaca farm outside Dallas — Laurel falls hard for the furry creatures and is inspired by the owner's story of quitting a high-powered corporate job to start the farm — Trump pressures acting attorney general Jeffrey Rosen to take action on voter fraud. "You guys may not be following the internet the way I do," he tells Rosen over the phone. Rosen assures him he will look into his complaints. "But understand," Rosen says, "that the DOJ can't and won't snap its fingers to change the election — doesn't work that way." Trump replies, "Don't expect you to do that. Just say that the election was corrupt and leave the rest to me and the Republican congressmen." As we turn in for the night, Trump tweets, "See you in Washington, DC, on January 6th. Don't miss it. Information to follow!"

In his undelivered speech in Dallas, Kennedy was set to say, "We in this country, in this generation, are — by destiny rather than choice — the watchmen on the walls of world freedom." And the watchmen now include watchwomen. Vice President Mike Pence's former homeland security and counterterrorism adviser, Olivia Troye, a Texas native and lifelong Republican who has worked at the Pentagon and in Iraq, is standing on the wall and ringing an alarm. "I'm actually very concerned that there will be violence on January 6th," she says, "because the president himself is encouraging it. This is what he does. He tweets, he incites it, he gets his followers and supporters to behave in this manner, and these people think that they're being patriotic because they are supporting Donald Trump."

When Rudy Giuliani appears before the Georgia legislature, he compares a video of election workers doing their job to the Zapruder film of JFK's assassination. "If you can watch that and not realize that this was a major situation of voter fraud," he says, "then you're a fool or a liar." Meanwhile, another lawyer working for Trump complained to a colleague: "When our research and campaign legal team can't back up any of the claims made by our Elite Strike Force Team" — Giuliani, Sidney Powell, Jenna Ellis, and others — "you can see why we're 0–32 in cases. I'll obviously hustle to help on all fronts, but it's tough to own any of this when it's all just conspiracy shit beamed down from the mother ship." And conspiracies, once born, are hard to kill.

Just before our campground in Hawkins, a sign proclaims the town "The Pancake Capital of Texas." We're surprised to see no restaurant in town save a Sonic and come to learn the title doesn't derive from a local diner. Hawkins was the hometown of Lillian Richard, one of the women long featured on Aunt Jemima–branded products, before PepsiCo decided earlier in 2020 to end the brand, citing racial stereotypes. In news stories about the cancellation, her great-niece Vera Harris was pitted against Black Lives Matter activists. In fact, Vera tells me when I reach her by phone the next day that she supported the company's decision, up to a point.

"I don't want anybody that's a person of color to be looked at in a negative light, because I know where we have been and there was nothing we could do fifty, sixty, seventy years ago," Vera says. "We just don't want PepsiCo, we don't want Quaker Oats, to forget the legacy of those women that made them what they are today, made them their beans. We know that the women were cheated out of the money. I know how they did black people back then."

Lillian Roberts was working as a domestic in Dallas when Quaker Oats discovered her. "She was a young twenty-one-year-old woman that wanted to make a living for herself," Vera says. "She was not ashamed that she did domestic work. She wasn't ashamed that she cooked. She wasn't ashamed of the job opportunities that were available for her back then." Vera, a thirty-year army veteran and children's book author, knows how few and far between those opportunities were for black women. Working for Quaker Oats, Lillian toured the state and beyond, giving product demonstrations until she got sick, at which point the company dropped her back home in Hawkins, where she died. She was long buried in an unmarked grave, which led Vera's family to ask Quaker Oats and Pepsi for help in providing a marker with her name on it. "After all she did for them," Vera says, "they denied our request."

Instead of ending the brand, Vera hoped the company would put the names of the women who served as Aunt Jemima models somewhere on the packaging. "Just don't erase those people from history. Those were real live people — so their names, their faces should still be there. Even if it's a hashtag, remember these names. For them not to do anything is saying that those women didn't matter."

Across America, we've seen graffiti art with the message "Say their names." That is what I hear in Vera's words, too — a plea for simple recognition, so victims of injustice are not forgotten, so that their stories are told. It's the same plea that leads people to gather every September 11 in Lower Manhattan to listen to the reading of nearly three thousand names. But saying names is rarely only about memorializing individuals. It's about honoring something larger — a cause, a purpose, an idea.

Approaching the Louisiana state line, we park at the old county courthouse in Marshall's town square, where there are three names inscribed on stone monuments along with their biographies. All are Confederate leaders, including Edward Clark, "Texas' First Confederate Governor," who attempted to prevent "the invasion of Texas." There is no mention of his fleeing to Mexico at the end of the war and returning only after he was secure in the knowledge that he would not be executed or even prosecuted, owing to the victors' desire for reconciliation. The individual monuments surround a much larger Confederate monument erected by the United Daughters of the Confederacy, dedicated on Robert Lee's birthday in 1906. This year, black residents organized a drive to remove the monument, but county commissioners opted to keep it.

Marshall was the slave capital of Texas — this was cotton country — but during Reconstruction, blacks held power. In 1878, the first of the state's White Citizens Parties formed. Through fraud and intimidation, party members stole the election, took power, and — through more fraud, intimidation, and force of law — held it for nearly a century. In Marshall, as in many other places, Jim Crow wasn't just segregation. It was a coup d'état. The two plaques that give a brief historical review of Marshall and Harrison County make no mention of this, nor of the lynchings that occurred, nor of the Klan march around this square that drew thousands of white people. Instead, we learn of "a strong heritage of slavery" and, as an aside, that "an influx of many slaves after the war resulted in a large black population, as well."

Culture is shaped as much by history unwritten as written, and civil wars do not always play out on battlefields. For a hundred years, whites in the south waged a de facto civil war by stealing elections, through the disenfranchisement of voters and by enforcing the results through legislative action combined with vigilante fear, intimidation, and violence.

Marshall is represented in Congress by Representative Louie Gohmert, the first Republican it has elected since Reconstruction. Since November, his Twitter feed has been almost entirely about "rampant fraud" and "stop the steal." Two days after we pass through his district, he tweets, "The country is at stake. Once an election is established by fraud, there's no coming back." He should try telling that to his black constituents, whose ancestors fought and clawed their way back over generations — and who are still fighting. In 2018, the Supreme Court approved, in a 5–4 vote, congressional and state legislative district maps that a panel of three federal judges had found, in a unanimous ruling, racially discriminatory.

Today the leader of the Proud Boys announces, "The Proud Boys will turn out in record numbers on Jan 6th." President Trump does not ask them to "stand back," or even to refrain from violence. They are no longer standing by. They are mobilizing for a fight.

In the deserted village of Gibsland, Louisiana, we pull over at the Bonnie and Clyde Ambush Museum. It was near here where police staked out the road to catch the bandits Bonnie and Clyde, who were suspected of murdering thirteen people, nine of them police officers. As their car approached, police decided to take no chances. Arrest them and put them on trial? *Justice first, then the law.* They emptied their guns, firing about 130 rounds, killing them.

The museum displays a replica of their bullet-riddled 1934 Ford, and since it's said that their ghosts still haunt the area, the museum recently hosted a paranormal investigation led by — there's no making this up — Stormy Daniels, America's most famous porn star. Her attempt to sell her story of having had sex with a married Donald Trump led to a ham-handed cover-up that helped send Trump lawyer Michael Cohen to prison and will later lead to criminal charges against Trump. If she encountered the ghosts of Bonnie and Clyde here, it would not have been her first run-in with outlaws.

Almost half of Americans believe in ghosts, surveys show, which helps explain how both conspiracy theories and religions take hold — we often put more trust in intuition and faith than evidence and reason. The local congressman here, Mike Johnson, has lately been seeing a ghost of his own: Hugo Chavez, the dictator who died in 2013. "When you have a software system that is used across the country that is suspect because it came from Hugo Chavez's Venezuela," he said recently, "it begs to be litigated and investigated." No software used in the election came from Venezuela; nor did a British-based software company founded by Venezuelans, Smartmatic, have any ties to the corrupt regime (its owners spoke out against Venezuelan fraud in 2017); nor was their software used in the 2020 election outside of Los Angeles County. No matter — people looking for ghosts tend to find indications of their existence. Today Trump tweets, "JANUARY SIXTH, SEE YOU IN DC!"

Today, too, Missouri senator Josh Hawley announces he will join a group of House members in challenging the certification of presidential electors on January 6. In response, one of his Republican colleagues, Nebraska senator Ben Sasse, posts a message on Facebook explaining why he will not join Hawley. "Let's be clear what is happening here: We have a bunch of ambitious politicians who think there's a quick way to tap into the president's populist base without doing any real, long-term damage. But they're wrong — and this issue is bigger than anyone's personal ambitions. Adults don't point a loaded gun at the heart of legitimate self-government . . . When we talk in private, I haven't heard a single congressional Republican allege that the election results were fraudulent — not one. Instead, I hear them talk about their worries about how they will 'look' to President Trump's most ardent supporters . . . All the clever arguments and rhetorical gymnastics in the world won't change the fact that this January 6th effort is designed to disenfranchise millions of Americans simply because they voted for someone in a different party. We ought to be better than that. If we normalize this, we're going to turn American politics into a Hatfields and McCoys endless blood feud — a house hopelessly divided."

When the year began, we had not expected to wake up on New Year's Eve morning in a Walmart parking lot in Lincoln Parish, Louisiana, but there has been little precedent for much of the year. Campaign signs here promote Luke Letlow, a Republican who was elected to Congress last month and who died three weeks ago, of Covid. He was forty-one years old, with a wife and two young children.

We cross the Mississippi River at Vicksburg and take a driving tour of the battlefield where US Army forces under General Grant lay siege to Confederates in what Lincoln called "the key" to eventual victory and what Sherman called the war's "most decisive event." At the Kentucky monument honoring its soldiers who fought for the United States and Confederacy, there are statues of Lincoln and Jefferson Davis — both Kentucky-born, only eight months apart. Yet in standing side by side, they appear as equals, as though martyr and traitor deserve the same honor. It was here in Vicksburg that Davis, who enslaved more than a hundred people, told a crowd that if an abolition president were elected in 1860, he "would rather appeal to the God of battles at once than to attempt to live longer in such a Union." During the war, the contrast between Lincoln's and Davis's rhetoric could not have been sharper. Where Lincoln conciliated, Davis demonized — referring to the north as "dirty Yankee invaders" and "savages" who were "the offscourings of the earth" and who compared unfavorably with hyenas.

A little farther on we stop at the Illinois Memorial, a domed and columned Greek temple that quotes Lincoln's first inaugural address ("The mystic chords of memory . . ."). We walk into it, and our guide tells us to find the name Albert Cashier. "He was only five feet and weighed a hundred pounds. But they wrote in their diaries about him, 'Albert is the strongest little guy you'll ever meet, and if you give him a hard job to do he'll never complain and he'll get it done.' Well, about forty years after the war, Albert was living in Chicago and got run over by a neighbor, broke his leg. Doctor looked and said, 'Oh my gosh, Albert — you're a woman!' Albert said, 'Yes I am. My name is Jennie Hodges but please don't tell anybody because the government might try to take my $15 a month pension away from me.' Well, the government tried to take it away but they couldn't because she had served and served honorably."

Our guide has the story mostly right. Albert Cashier, an immigrant from Ireland, was born a girl and began wearing boys clothes as a child. Almost no one knew Albert's secret, not even the soldiers who served in these trenches with him. When Albert was captured by Confederates here, he broke free by attacking a guard, wrestling away his gun, and beating his pursuers in a footrace. He identified as a man throughout his life, a war hero forced to keep his cross-dressing a secret by a society that would not tolerate it for another century, until rock 'n' roll and its gender-bending king, Little Richard, helped launch the liberation. Richard's song "Long

Tall Sally," one of rock's biggest hits, hinted at the hiding that he — in bright boas and blouses and heavy makeup — would not do.

Well, I saw Uncle John with bald-head Sally
He saw Aunt Mary comin'
And he ducked back in the alley, oh baby

When Albert's secret was discovered in the hospital, doctors and nurses forced him to wear skirts. Unaccustomed to walking in them, a trip and fall broke his hip, killing him. *Albert Cashier — say his name.*

In 2017, President Trump announced a ban on transgender people enlisting in the armed forces, over the opposition of military leaders. The battle over trans rights has only intensified since then, as some Republicans have sought to turn elections into referenda on trans bans for bathrooms, youth sports, and medical treatment. While the issues can be thorny, the debate over them should begin with a recognition of people like Albert Cashier, who fought honorably and deserved better from the nation he helped save — and Albert was far from the only transgender American to serve in the Civil War and other wars. The promise of America for which they fought — that all people are created equal — is our responsibility to carry forward. Progress can be slow, but change can come fast. Last month, after months of protests over the murder of George Floyd, the voters of Mississippi voted to remove the Confederate flag from their state flag.

We spend New Year's Eve in a casino parking lot in Vicksburg. We have no noisemakers, streamers, or silly hats, but we stay up to watch the ball in Times Square drop and sing along to Robert Burns, the "Ploughman Poet," whose verses Lincoln memorized and often recited. A member of New York City's Public Design Commission recently suggested removing a statue of Burns that has long stood in Central Park to make way for statues honoring women. "I don't think that there are many people who will miss the Burns statue," the commissioner said, perhaps correctly, despite the countless people who sing his song each new year. Burns might well understand: Old acquaintances are indeed forgot. His is worth remembering.

We'll take a cup o' kindness yet,
For auld lang syne

— 46 —

Highway 61 Revisited

New Year's Day. We leave Vicksburg on Highway 61, the cradle of the blues that tracks the Mississippi River from Minnesota to New Orleans, the same road we crossed in Iowa in late September. We have plans to meet friends in the French Quarter for dinner on January 5, which leaves time for visiting a few musical ghosts along the 250-mile drive there.

First stop: Port Gibson, where Grant's army defeated Confederates on its way to laying siege to Vicksburg. A century later, another siege occurred: a black-led boycott of white businesses that refused to integrate. It went on for years, and when whites eventually lost, many left. Today, the town is 85 percent black. On Market Street, shops are boarded up and the movie theater is in ruins.

Across from the old theater in a vacant lot, a Blues Trail sign notes that Port Gibson was home to the Rabbit Foot Minstrels, a traveling troupe that mixed music, comedy, dancing, and carnival acts — the Greatest Colored Show on Earth, it was billed by its owner, F. S. Wolcott, who also owned a plantation here. Levon Helm remembered the Foots playing "the dark outskirts" of his Arkansas hometown up the Mississippi River when he was a boy, which gave rise to the song "W. S. Walcott Medicine Show." The Foots gave Ma Rainey her big break and over the years featured Big Joe Williams, Brownie McGhee, Arnold "Gatemouth" Moore, and Louis Jordan, who became a national star in the 1930s and 1940s by reveling in minstrel tropes and antics for white and black audiences alike — not as the usual slow-moving lazy country bumpkin but as the wild, uninhibited, and manic city slicker, a transition that, Yuval Taylor and Jake Austen argue in their history of the minstrel tradition, *Darkest America*, "led directly to the birth of rock-n-roll."

To see more of its birth, we cross the Mississippi River at Natchez to visit Ferriday, Louisiana, where one of the Rabbit Foots, Leon "Peewee" Whittaker, often played Haney's Big House, a club that attracted stars traveling the chitlin circuit: Ray Charles, Fats Domino, B. B. King, Bobby Bland, and countless other greats. It was a black-only club — admitting whites could lead to trouble — but a couple of white kids from the neighborhood couldn't stay away.

"My friend Jimmy Swaggart and I would listen from out on the sidewalk to the singers and the juke box," Jerry Lee Lewis said in 1958. "Then we'd run right home and try to play the same kind of great blues music." Eventually, Jerry Lee began sneaking in to hear the music, and then asking to sit in with Peewee Whittaker and the band. "I sure heard a lot of good piano playin' down there," Lewis said.

Jerry Lee Lewis and Jimmy Lee Swaggart were not just friends who learned how to play piano together. They were cousins, and their lives ran on parallel tracks. Jerry Lee got expelled from college for giving a church hymn a boogie-woogie beat, after having earned the nickname "the Killer" for trying to choke a man with his necktie in Ferriday. Jimmy Lee turned down a recording deal with Sun Records in order to preach, but he'd sell seventeen million records as part of a lucrative business empire saving souls. *Newsweek* dubbed him the King of Honky Tonk Heaven in 1982.

Jerry Lee played with the reckless abandon and uninhibited wild energy he saw at Haney's Big House, which turned him into the face of rock 'n' roll, while Jimmy Lee's theatrical showmanship, emotional histrionics, fire-and-brimstone theology, and use of gospel music made him an heir to Billy Sunday and the world's most popular televangelist. While Jerry Lee raised hell, Jimmy Lee crusaded against it, blaming moral decay on his cousin's calling. "Rock-n-roll is one of the most destructive forces in the country and world today," Jimmy Lee said. "Drug addiction, venereal disease, homosexuality, you name it. I think it denigrates every value. And rock stars are heroes to kids." That was a year before Jimmy Lee began getting caught with prostitutes by a rival pastor out for revenge, after Jimmy Lee had publicly exposed and shamed him for adultery. "We all got our urges," said Jerry Lee, expressing more grace and understanding than his cousin ever had.

Before his fall, Swaggart's televangelism empire boasted of fifty million viewers globally and annual revenue above $100 million. "You've got to keep people's attention," he told a reporter, repeating it a second time for emphasis, an echo of what Phil Donahue said ("No one wants to be a dead hero") in defending the tawdry spectacles he staged. Swaggart kept people's attention by preaching about the coming Rapture, when God will lift up believers and spare them from seven years of hell on earth — the reign of the antichrist, the horrors of Armageddon, and the Great Tribulation — before Jesus returns with the believers to establish a new Millennium reign of paradise.

End-of-world theology has always presented a challenge to democracy. If you believe in the imminence of the Rapture or the Second Coming, there is less reason to keep faith in the American trinity. The country has long survived messianism, but never before has it mixed quite so thoroughly with extreme partisan polarization and the political demagoguery of a charismatic leader.

During the 2016 campaign, when a leading Southern Baptist theologian, Russell Moore, remarked that "Trump is leading the 'Jimmy Swaggart wing'" of the evangelical movement, he was castigated by many evangelicals as an elitist. When Trump won, Swaggart said it was "of the Lord," while Moore saw it differently. "The religious right," he observed, "turned out to be the people the religious right warned about." Perhaps he should have seen it coming, as did another evangelical leader, James Dobson. "What has alarmed me, throughout this episode," Dobson said, "has been the willingness of my fellow citizens to rationalize the president's behavior, even as they suspected, and later knew, that he was lying. I am left to conclude that our greatest problem is not in the Oval Office. It's with the people of this land." He said that in 1998, about President Clinton. In 2016, he endorsed Trump and has supported him since. Partisanship is powerful as hell.

In 2016, Democrats did not believe evangelicals could possibly support Trump, a twice-divorced cad who has had multiple affairs, engaged in sexual harassment and worse, seemed to have little grasp of the Bible, and routinely got caught in lies. Yet none of that was new for evangelicals. Jim Bakker, who survived a sex scandal, admitted he had never read all the way through the Bible before going to prison for stealing millions from his followers. Jerry Falwell often exaggerated the size of his audiences and made up stories that he passed off as true, calling them allegories, a religious precursor to "alternative facts." Falwell and other leading evangelical preachers also opposed the civil rights movement and veered into anti-Muslim bigotry and fear-mongering. Trump, in his mastery of media, manipulation of emotions, obsession with celebrity, penchant for stoking religious and racial resentment, and declarations about End Times for America — he's prone to saying, "We won't have a country" if voters elect Democrats — is far and away the most televangelist-like president we have ever had.

The merger between evangelical Christianity and Republican Party politics, begun in the 1970s, has reached its apogee under Trump, who personifies what historian Richard Hofstadter in 1963 called "the paranoid style in American politics," capturing the national predilection for thinking — in "overheated, oversuspicious, overaggressive" terms — that the last days are near. "The paranoid spokesman sees the fate of conspiracy in apocalyptic terms — he traffics in the birth and death of whole worlds, whole political orders, whole systems of human values," Hofstadter wrote. "He is always manning the barricades of civilization. He constantly lives at a turning point: it is now or never in organizing resistance to conspiracy. Time is forever running short." And this week, time is running especially short.

Today White House chief of staff Mark Meadows sends a memo to Vice President Pence outlining a plan for Pence, on January 6, to announce that six states have disputed electoral votes and to ask each state's legislature to rule on which is valid. The memo was written by Trump campaign lawyer Jenna Ellis, who is affiliated with two Christian organizations, Liberty University and the Thomas More Society. That a religious organization attempting to overturn the election is named for Thomas More, who was executed for his refusal to accept a merger of church and state under Henry VIII, only further highlights how morally bankrupt the effort is.

Here in Ferriday, we see historical markers for both Jimmy Lee and Jerry Lee. The one for Jerry notes what he told an old college classmate when they saw each other many years later: "You know it's strange, the same music they kicked me out of school for is the same kind of music they play in their churches today. The difference is, I know I am playing for the devil and they don't." There has always been lots of overlap between juke joints and revival tents — the search for salvation happens in each — and now the line between entertaining and evangelizing, always thin, has been erased by electioneering and worse: refusal to accept the results. "The BIG Protest Rally in Washington, DC, will take place at 11.00 A.M. on January 6th," Trump tweets today. "Locational details to follow. StopTheSteal!"

We return to Natchez to explore its quiet streets and see its stately and well-preserved antebellum homes, though few traces remain of the industry that financed them: the country's second largest slave market, which helped turn it into one of America's wealthiest cities. We stop for dinner at the Natchez Brewing Company, where we sit outside as fireworks explode over the Mississippi River, and online, too. "January 6th. See you in DC," Trump tweets. It's almost as if Jerry Lee Lewis is here singing to us:

Goodness gracious, great balls of fire

January 2. Walking around the Woodville town square, we see a sign noting that it's the birthplace of Jefferson Davis. His family plantation, now a museum, is closed for repairs. It will reopen, but much of Main Street is permanently shuttered. The only open shop we see is a small burger-and-fry stand, across the street from a school district office. Schools are a main reason for the town's eerie quiet.

When federal courts forced Mississippi's districts to integrate in 1970 — sixteen years after *Brown v. Board of Education* — white families opened a private Christian academy. "If Chief Justice Warren and his associates had known God's word and had desired to do the Lord's will, I am quite confident that the 1954 decision would never have been made," the Reverend Jerry Falwell said. "The facilities should be separate. When God has drawn a line of distinction, we should not attempt to cross that line." On the first day of classes after integration at the Woodville public elementary school, only two white children, a brother and sister, appeared among the 1,389 black children. "We just couldn't afford a private school," their mother said.

Today the public schools remain 99 percent black. Other communities across the south have experienced similar abandonment, often led by Christian churches, the beginning of the rise of the religious right in politics. "What galvanized the Christian community," recounted Paul Weyrich, a co-founder of the Heritage Foundation and coiner of the term *moral majority*, "was not abortion, school prayer, or the ERA. I am living witness to that because I was trying to get people interested in those issues and I utterly failed. What changed their mind was Jimmy Carter's intervention against the Christian schools, trying to deny them tax-exempt status on the basis of so-called de facto segregation." Woodville's native son had seen it all coming: "The principle for which we contended is bound to reassert itself," Jefferson Davis said after the Civil War, "though it may be at another time and in another form." The form took many shapes, including one just a little farther down Highway 61: the Louisiana State Penitentiary.

In the aftermath of the Civil War, as Confederate states passed black codes that became pretext for arresting out-of-work former slaves and forcing them into labor, a former Confederate officer who had a prison contract with the state bought a former slave plantation named Angola, a tribute to a slave-trading African nation or the traders who plied it, and moved prisoners there to work it, housing them in slave shacks and leasing out others as laborers to build railroads and levees and work the fields, pocketing the lucrative profits and not caring how many men died. Unlike enslaved blacks, imprisoned blacks could be had for free. "One dies, get another," as a businessman put it. It was another form of slavery, in some ways worse, masked as penitence. The prison developed a reputation for ruthless brutality — floggings and whippings were common, work conditions often deadly — that lasted for nearly a century.

When John Lomax and his son Alan visited the prison to record and preserve songs for the Library of Congress in 1933, they encountered Lead Belly, who was serving time for attempted murder, after being kicked by a white man and slashing him with a knife, one story goes. He had already sung himself out of prison in Texas, and here he was released early for good behavior after four years. Back then, the warden had a policy: Even those serving life sentences could be released in ten years and six months if they worked hard and stayed out of trouble. The policy remained in place until the 1970s, when the state began mandating twenty-year minimums for life sentences before becoming eligible for parole, which quickly became forty-year minimums, which became life without parole in 1979.

Today the prison, still called Angola, is the nation's largest maximum-security prison, and of its more than five thousand prisoners, some four thousand are serving life sentences, three-quarters of them black. In recent years, support has been bubbling up for "geriatric parole," the practice of allowing older prisoners to become eligible for release, since recidivism rates decline as years advance. The warden here supports it, but district attorneys do not, and the legislature hasn't taken it up. It's one thing to tell the story of Jesus pardoning a criminal on the cross, as Jimmy Swaggart will do at Jerry Lee Lewis's funeral in 2022. It's another to do it ourselves.

Lead Belly became one of the most influential bluesmen of his era, King of the 12 String Guitar, his songs widely covered, many of them of unknown origin, passed down and changed over time, like "Goodnight, Irene." Others were social commentary, like "Scottsboro Boys," about the eight black teenagers sentenced to death in Alabama in 1931 for allegedly raping two white women, despite the absence of medical evidence and the recantation of the allegation by one of the women. After a national uproar, legal support from the Communist Party, and a Supreme Court ruling that excluding black citizens from jury pools was a violation of the Fourteenth Amendment, the accused eventually went free, though not before many years in prison. "I advise everybody be a little careful when they go along through there," Lead Belly said of Scottsboro in a recording of the song. "Best stay woke, keep their eyes open."

Stay woke. Lead Belly's is one of the earliest documented uses of a phrase that has become a political lightning rod. For many Republicans, it is a catchall for everything that is wrong with liberalism, especially the sense that racial, gender, and sexual orientation identities can be used as proxies for putting people into categories of oppressor and oppressed, with the former deserving flagellation and the latter favoritism. The excesses of what has been termed woke-ism can be disturbing to Democrats, too, who often fear speaking out publicly, lest they be cast as racist Neanderthals — a serious political problem the party has yet to reckon with.

Without rehashing the drama surrounding the term *woke*, it's worth remembering that the concept is rooted in religious teaching, which is likely how Lead Belly came to use it. In the Garden of Gethsemane, Jesus instructs his disciples to "stay awake," and much of Christianity is a warning to stay awake for the Second Coming, hence the "Great Awakenings" that periodically swept across the United States, their tent revivals becoming a regular feature of the landscape. The notion of being awake is also found in the Hebrew Bible, and the name Buddha means "the one who waked up." In a sense, awakening is what this whole journey has been about — to more of our history and culture, more of ourselves and our fellow citizens, and more of what faith in the American trinity requires of us.

While *woke* has become a bugaboo for the right, its nearest synonym is *vigilant*, a Spanish word meaning "watchful, wide awake." The young people who marched for Lincoln in the 1860s called themselves the Wide-

Awakes because of their determination to awaken their generation to the need for national unity and social change, including — for some of them — abolitionism. The name may have even come from Lincoln himself. According to one account, after a speech in Hartford, Connecticut, in 1860, young men lined up in military order to escort him to his hotel, prompting Lincoln to remark to the mayor: "The boys are wide awake. Suppose we call them the Wide-Awakes."

Being vigilant — watchful, wide awake, woke — is a mark of good citizenship, so long as it's restrained. But when it is overtaken by unbridled passion and righteousness that disregards the facts and the rule of law, whether on the left or the right, it becomes democracy's most dangerous enemy.

Today President Trump calls Georgia secretary of state Brad Raffensperger. In an hour-long conversation, joined by White House chief of staff Mark Meadows, conservative activist Cleta Mitchell, and several lawyers, he repeatedly pressures Raffensperger to "find" him votes, arguing that votes had been stolen from him in every imaginable way. "Mr. President," Raffensperger replied, "the challenge that you have is the data you have is wrong."

Toward the end of the call, Trump summed up his request: "So look. All I want to do is this: I just want to find 11,780 votes, which is one more than we have because we won the state . . . So what are we going to do here, folks? I only need 11,000 votes. Fellas, I need 11,000 votes. Give me a break . . . All we have to do, Cleta, is find 11,000-plus votes."

Before hanging up, Trump accused the Georgia officials of a crime — covering up the real vote count — and suggested they might face prosecution, saying, "You know what they did and you're not reporting it. That's a criminal offense. And you can't let that happen. That's a big risk to you." Afterward, Trump, Rudy Giuliani, and the lawyer John Eastman — a professor at the conservative Claremont Institute, founded by devotees of Lincoln scholar Harry Jaffa — convened a call with three hundred state legislators from states where phony electors had declared themselves the real electors. "You are the real power," Trump told them. "You're more important than the courts . . . and you're the ones that are going to make the decision."

As that was going on, Ted Cruz and ten other senators released a statement calling on Congress to appoint an electoral commission to conduct a ten-day audit of the election returns in the states Trump was disputing — setting the stage for Congress to "certify a change in their vote, if needed," they wrote. Mitt Romney called it an "egregious ploy" and "nonsense" that "dangerously threatens our democratic Republic." He talked about his own experience nobly carrying the sack of flour. "Look, I lost in 2012. I know what it's like to lose. I have people today who say, 'Hey, you know what, you really won,' but I didn't, I lost fair and square. Of course there were irregularities — there always are — but spreading this kind of rumor about our election system not working is dangerous for democracy here and abroad."

As January 6 approaches, best stay woke.

January 3. We stop in Baton Rouge to see the monument of Huey Long that faces the nation's tallest state capitol, 450 feet high, which he built as a monument to his own reign. He is buried here under a tall marble tombstone topped by a bronze statue of him. Critics called him a communist for pushing a redistribution plan that would guarantee everyone a basic income, an idea that is popular again on the left, but his promise to make "every man a king" came with an unspoken caveat: The people would need to accept him as *the* king. In the song "Kingfish," Randy Newman captured Long's campaign pitch in a single verse, with the first two lines reminding voters of the good he's done for them.

Who built the highway to Baton Rouge?
Who put up the hospital and built your schools?

The third reminds them that he protects the common people from the rich and powerful.

Who looks after shit-kickers like you?

And the fourth answers all their questions.

The Kingfish do

Long inflamed crowds; called opponents "thieves, bugs, and lice"; and used his political machine to register phantom voters and rig returns. In 1935, as he prepared to run for president as a US senator, he was in the state capitol to orchestrate passage of a bill to gerrymander a judge out of office. The judge's son-in-law, a doctor, confronted him and shot him, the first sitting senator to be assassinated. He died a victim to what he had trafficked in throughout his career: vigilantism.

Long's life and death inspired the 1946 novel *All the King's Men* by Robert Penn Warren, the story of a humble, teetotaling country lawyer, Willie Stark, whose run for governor generates little support until he tastes the power to move a crowd, which transforms him into a modern Machiavelli, cutting dirty deals to win the race and descending into corruption and decadence. In the end, as he faces impeachment from a legislature that has had enough, his loyal supporters stand outside the state capitol, waiting to storm it should the trial go the wrong way, threatening the kind of violence that leaves Stark assassinated.

The *New York Times* hailed a film version of the novel for portraying "the potential of demagoguery in this land" to incite "howling political mobs," highlighting "the dim but dreadful aspect of ignorance and greed when played upon by theatrics, eloquence and bluff." Its director, Robert Rossen, had offered the lead role to John Wayne, but Wayne was disgusted by the script, seeing it as an un-American smear against government. He told his agent to "shove it up Robert Rossen's derriere." The film won three Academy Awards, including Best Picture and Best Actor.

Wayne's denunciation of the script was an early shot in the battle conservatives would wage against Hollywood, always over the same dominant themes: morality and patriotism. The difference between *All the King's Men* and the movie Wayne chose to make instead, *Sands of Iwo Jima*, captures the tension in American culture over the meaning of patriotism and its obligations. Wayne wanted to glorify soldiers even though (and perhaps partly because) he had sat out World War II, unlike other stars of the era. When Wayne visited troops during the war, they booed him.

Wayne would become one of the most ardent hawks of the Cold War and a staunch supporter of the Vietnam War, including through his 1968 film *The Green Berets*. As the Watergate scandal began to surround President Nixon, and as Bob Woodward and Carl Bernstein undertook the reporting that would lead to *All the President's Men* — the title a play on Warren's novel — Wayne sent Nixon a telegram that could have been written by the supporters of Willie Stark: "Dear sir, nobody has lost faith." As investigators closed in on the White House, he sent Nixon a second telegram: "don't give up the ship."

Having angrily rejected the role of Willie Stark, Wayne could not recognize himself among Stark's supporters. But neither would he join the most rabid of them.

Wayne campaigned for Gerald Ford in 1976, but when Ford lost to Jimmy Carter, Wayne sent a congratulatory note, as he had to other Democratic presidents. And when Carter invited him to the inauguration, he accepted. At a pre-inaugural ball, Wayne gave a speech that, whatever one may think of his movies and politics, is worth remembering and honoring: "I'm pleased to be present and accounted for in this capital of freedom to witness history as it happens — to watch a common man accept the uncommon responsibility he won fair and square by stating his case to the American people — not by bloodshed, beheadings, and riots at the palace gates. I know I'm considered a member of the loyal opposition — accent on the loyal. I'd have it no other way." Neither would we, Duke.

Tonight Trump retweets a post by a conspiracy theorist suggesting that the inauguration could be postponed, and one promoting the January 6 protests, while adding his own message: "I will be there. Historic day!"

January 4. We spent last night at a Harvest Host plantation on the Mississippi River, where a woman in antebellum dress led a house tour, telling us in detail about the white family who owned it but almost nothing of the enslaved who worked it. Today we are visiting two more plantations. At Oak Alley Plantation, we start to get closer to the slave experience: Replica slave cabins hold exhibits about life for their inhabitants, their names written on the wall: Adam. Adeline. Adonis. Albert. Alexandre. Alexis. Alfred. Alfred. Andre. Anne. Antoinette. Angela. Anthony. Antoine. Argus. Armantine. Augustine. Augustine. Avril. Azaire. Those are the A's. *Say their names.* The guide who brings us through the house mentions a few details about how the enslaved were treated, and I ask him if that information had always been part of the tour. "No," he says. "A few years ago we stopped wearing period dress and got rid of the *Gone with the Wind* stuff."

Just down the road, we visit the Whitney Plantation, the first to tell the story of plantation life from the perspective of those enslaved. It is an entirely different experience. The savage brutality of the institution — and the monstrous physical violence, often sexual, that underpinned it — finally begins to come into view.

"The point of a plantation is to enslave people for their labor," Ashley Rogers, the executive director, tells me, "but we have this narrative that this"

— she points to the big house — "is the plantation. So sometimes people come here and they go, 'Where's the plantation?' And I'm like, 'You're on it.'"

She isn't interested in being a house museum and is doing something other plantations wouldn't dream of: liquidating the house's antiques. "The more that we have that stuff," she says, "the more it distracts people." She wants to convert the house into program space "so people can sit down and talk and have conversations. I want them to be able to reflect and think about" what they have seen and felt and learned, with facilitators helping to draw people into discussion. "I think that this year shows us that it's necessary," she says.

I ask Ashley what kind of reactions people have to the experience. "A friend of mine came here and he brought his mom, very sweet old southern lady, very conservative," she says. "She did the whole tour and came up to me afterward, and she was in tears. She said, 'I just never knew this.'" A man in a MAGA hat had a similar reaction. "He came up afterward and said, 'I grew up without a lot of money, and I just didn't know that this happened.' This really changed his perspective." He was *awakened*. Less than half of their visitors are white, and only now it dawns on me: We didn't see a single black person on the other plantation tours.

The Whitney's story doesn't end with the Civil War. It operated until 1975, and like other plantations, it attempted to approximate the slavery system as closely as possible. After the collapse of Reconstruction, plantation owners formed the Louisiana Sugar Planters' Association to fix wages, which ended competition for labor and the little bargaining power the newly freed people had acquired. "That ensures nobody's going to run away from the plantation," Ashley says. Chattel slavery gave way to systematic exploitation, another affirmation of Jefferson Davis's prediction that the principle for which Confederates had contended would reassert itself in other forms.

There are several memorials on-site. One includes the names of the 107,000 people recorded as slaves in Louisiana — a small fraction of the total. Another honors the 1811 slave revolt, the largest in US history, which started just across the river and was put down by a local militia backed by federal troops. Dozens of rebels were executed, some without trials, their heads placed on pikes stretching for many miles along the river, a warning to others.

Around the time we are at the Whitney Plantation, Henry "Enrique" Tarrio, the leader of the Proud Boys, is arrested in Washington, DC, on a misdemeanor charge of destruction of property, for burning a church's

"Black Lives Matter" flag in December. His arrest was preceded by a warning the FBI delivered to the city's police: The Proud Boys are planning to come to DC to protest the certification of the election on January 6 and could use violence to do so. When the officers arrest Tarrio, he is charged with additional crimes: unlawful possession of two high-capacity firearm magazines, emblazoned with Proud Boys insignia. As a condition of his release, he is ordered to stay out of Washington, DC.

Our third and final plantation of the day doubles as an RV park. We're too late for a house tour, but we've seen enough of white antebellum life anyway. As we settle in for the night, Trump is holding a rally in Georgia, ostensibly to stump for the two Republican Senate candidates ahead of tomorrow's runoff election, but he spends much of his hour-plus speech rehashing false claims of voter fraud, falsely asserting he won the election, and urging resistance: "The Democrats are trying to steal the White House. You can not let them . . . When you win in a landslide and they steal it and it's rigged, it's not acceptable. Not acceptable." He preaches that the country is nearing end times and the election of two Democrats would seal our fate: "America as you know it will be over. And it will never, I believe, be able to come back again. It will be too far gone. Your vote tomorrow . . . could be your last chance to save the America that we love." The Supreme Court, which has refused to indulge his baseless claims of fraud, is "bent on destroying our Constitution and overthrowing America's founding."

"In just about every case of democratic breakdown we have studied," write Steven Levitsky and Daniel Ziblatt in their book, *How Democracies Die*, "would-be authoritarians — from Franco, Hitler, and Mussolini in interwar Europe to Marcos, Castro, and Pinochet during the Cold War to Putin, Chávez, and Erdoğan most recently — have justified their consolidation of power by labeling their opponents as an existential threat."

Trump pins his hopes on Vice President Mike Pence, whose ceremonial role as president of the Senate is to count the electoral votes: "I hope Mike Pence comes through for us, I have to tell you. I hope that our great vice president comes through for us." He doesn't mention it, but earlier in the day at the White House, John Eastman presented a legal memo outlining the steps Pence could take to deny the electors from seven states and to count the phony electors instead. Once done, Eastman writes, "Pence then gavels Trump as re-elected."

Not all Republicans are on board with this plan, even if they don't say it publicly. Today Tucker Carlson sends a text message full of excited anticipation: "We are very, very close to being able to ignore Trump most nights. I truly can't wait. I hate him passionately." It's among the private communications Carlson has had with colleagues disparaging Trump and lamenting his effort to overturn the election, even as Carlson has fanned the flames of the conspiracies on his show. "I've got four more years here," he wrote in a text message, referring to his contractual obligations. "I'm stuck with Fox. Got to do whatever I can to keep our numbers up and our viewers happy." Nobody wants to be a dead hero.

January 5. Highway 61 carries us into New Orleans, past the cheap motels where Jimmy Swaggart met prostitutes. It ends at the Orleans Parish Criminal District Court, its stone facade reading, "This Is a Government of Law Not of Men."

Today Ohio congressman Jim Jordan, who so angered the farmer we met in September, Chris Gibbs, that Gibbs left the Republican Party to run against him as an independent, forwards a text message to White House chief of staff Mark Meadows: "On January 6, 2021, Vice President Mike Pence, as President of the Senate, should call out all electoral votes that he believes are unconstitutional as no electoral votes at all." Jordan is only saying privately what Trump is saying publicly, including in a tweet today: "The Vice President has the power to reject fraudulently chosen electors."

We follow the Mississippi River south, through the 9th Ward to the St. Bernard State Park campground. As we arrive, Trump tweets, "Washington is being inundated with people who don't want to see an election victory stolen by emboldened Radical Left Democrats. Our Country has had enough, they won't take it anymore! We hear you (and love you) from the Oval Office. MAKE AMERICA GREAT AGAIN!"

The people Trump is referring to are participating in rallies that, like the Jericho March, mix militant Christianity with militant nationalism — bound, as usual, by fear. "They want your Bible, they want your babies, and they want your bullets," says one speaker. "We serve a mighty, powerful God," says another. "He wants everybody to know it's by His might, by His hand, that Donald J. Trump will serve four more years." The conspiracy-obsessed pillow producer Mike Lindell says much the same: "Donald Trump was picked for eight years by God, not four."

"I will be speaking at the SAVE AMERICA RALLY tomorrow on the

Ellipse at 11AM Eastern," Trump tweets during the rally. "Arrive early — doors open at 7AM Eastern. BIG CROWDS!"

One of those who answers Trump's call will be Ashli Babbitt, a thirty-nine-year-old air force veteran from San Diego. Today she tweets, "Nothing will stop us. They can try and try and try but the storm is here and it is descending upon DC in less than 24 hours . . . dark to light!" Her reference to the "the storm" is QAnon terminology for the day when Trump would unmask the imagined cabal of pedophiles — Democrats, bureaucrats, tycoons, Jews, Hollywood stars, medical experts — who are secretly pulling the nation's strings, Oz-like, and execute them. In QAnon theology, the storm will follow "the Great Awakening," the process of the nation awakening — getting *woke* — to The Truth of QAnon. This connects QAnon to America's long tradition of "Great Awakenings" that date to the 1730s, making the movement "not so much aberration," writes Jeff Sharlet in *The Undertow*, "as the continuity of feverish dreams twisting through the American mind since the beginning" — the kind of feverish dreams that Jimmy Swaggart and many other End Times preachers have tapped into so effectively, and profitably.

On the Facebook page Red State Secession, a person posts that people should be "prepared to use force to defend civilization." The page states, "Trump has sent at least four tweets asking his followers to be in DC on [January] 6. His Twitter account uploaded a militant video that seems like agitprop. What are the addresses of the residences of our political enemies in DC? . . . We predict that the vote will be against us and the crowd will be looking for enemies."

Tonight someone posts a photo of a cache of weapons "blocks away from the Capitol," under the tagline "2021is1776." Trump's former campaign manager and White House adviser Steve Bannon says on his podcast, with the certainty and hope of a zealous believer, "All hell is going to break loose tomorrow. Just understand this. All hell is going to break loose tomorrow."

Trump's most faithful followers are ready to rock 'n' roll. But unlike the hell-raising Jerry Lee Lewis, who recognized the demons within him, they believe they are carrying out God's will. Turn up the Killer and hold on tight.

You shake my nerves and you rattle my brain

— 47 —

January 6

A text arrives from our friend Barry Lemoine, who lives in St. Bernard Parish near our campground in the wetlands: "Good morning. Hope the alligators and mosquitoes didn't get you." We saw him and his wife, Katherine, last night at the French Quarter apartment of mutual friends. Over shrimp and oyster po'boys, he kindly offered to take today off to bring me on a driving tour of the Mississippi River Delta. It would be hard to imagine a better guide. He's a teacher, playwright, screenwriter, actor, and impresario — the Bard of St. Bernard, they call him — who has a gift for making strangers smile and laugh, to say nothing of friends. Among the plays he has directed and acted in is a parody called *The Complete Works of William Shakespeare (Abridged)*, which features farcical snippets of thirty-seven plays, including Lincoln's favorite, *Macbeth*.

Why did Lincoln so enjoy and admire *Macbeth*? Surely its political plot attracted him — a nation descending into civil war — but Shakespeare's genius lay in language, which was of such importance to Lincoln, and psychology, which lay at the center of his career, politics. And like Macbeth, Lincoln was a man of great ambition, whose dreams were haunted by death and who bore great mental pressure uneasily. Surely he saw some of himself in Macbeth — and, by extension, those who had launched the bloody Civil War. When he read aloud long passages of the play while on a ship leaving Richmond for Washington in the war's final days, those with him noted that he dwelled particularly on Macbeth's lines about the murdered Duncan.

Treason has done his worst

Before the Bard of St. Bernard arrives at our campground, I spend some of the morning looking at news and commentary. "Today is 1776," Colorado congresswoman Lauren Boebert tweets. Trump's messages have taken a sharper turn. Overnight and this morning, he tweeted, "If Vice President @Mike_Pence comes through for us, we will win the Presidency. Many States want to decertify the mistake they made in certifying incorrect & even fraudulent numbers in a process NOT approved by their State Legislatures (which it must be). Mike can send it back!" In another tweet, he wrote, "States want to correct their votes, which they now know were based on irregularities and fraud, plus corrupt process never received legislative approval. All Mike Pence has to do is send them back to the States, AND WE WIN. Do it Mike, this is a time for extreme courage!"

Double, double toil and trouble

When Trump reaches Pence on the phone, the call gets heated. And when Pence rejects Trump's pleas and reiterates that he doesn't have the constitutional authority to reject the electoral votes, Trump tells Pence that he can either be "a patriot or a pussy," according to aides.

Fire burn, and cauldron bubble

Around the same time the Bard of St. Bernard arrives at our campsite bearing coffee for Laurel, Trump tells staff to remove the magnetometers from the rally he's about to speak at, despite the fact that some people are carrying weapons. "I don't care that they have weapons," he says, according to White House aide Cassidy Hutchinson. "They're not here to hurt me. Take the fucking mags away. Let my people in. They can march to the Capitol from here."

By the pricking of my thumbs
Something wicked this way comes

Under a blue sky, with temperatures approaching sixty degrees, the Bard and I lower the windows and head south on Judge Perez Drive, which honors a local judge, Melvyn Perez, at least officially. The Bard tells me that until the 1990s, it honored a different Judge Perez, Leander Perez, a powerful local political boss who ruled the parish for nearly half a century beginning in 1919, enriching himself with graft, adding fictitious names to the ballot rolls, blocking blacks from registering to vote, and rabidly opposing school desegregation. In *Travels with Charley*, John Steinbeck was left "sick with weary nausea" when he witnessed the fury of white parents in New Orleans screaming "bestial and filthy and degenerate" words at four black six-year-old girls who entered public schools in 1960 under the protection of US marshals. More than anyone else, it was Leander Perez who incited the ugliness.

As white parents began a school boycott, Perez spoke at a rally of five thousand people, whipping up the crowd into a frenzy of fear and bigotry: "Don't wait for your daughter to be raped by these Congolese. Don't let these burr-heads into your school!" Perez urged the crowd to "take matters into your own hands" and march on the school board and city hall the next day. Many did, and when they couldn't break into the mayor's office — the mayor was locked inside — they rioted, attacking and beating black residents, stabbing at least one. Perez died in 1969, but his ghost still floats above us, like the vision that appears before Macbeth as he begins to execute a bloody coup.

Is this a dagger which I see before me,
The handle toward my hand? Come, let me clutch thee

The Bard drives us through open gates in a concrete wall designed to hold in water twenty-eight to thirty-two feet above sea level. "We call that the Great Wall of Chalmette," he says. It was built after Hurricane Katrina, part of a sprawling network of floodwalls, levees, and gates that now surrounds New Orleans, trying to do what King Canute could not, nor the walls we saw along the Mexican border: stop the tide from coming in.

The Bard has lived his whole life in New Orleans, except for when Katrina forced him to move to Alabama for four months. His home was underwater, as was virtually every other home in St. Bernard Parish, and it wasn't just water: An oil tank burst at a local refinery, spilling millions of gallons of crude that coursed through streets and houses, the nation's largest residential oil spill. Nearly all the parish's sixty-eight thousand residents were left homeless. About half moved away. The Bard returned when his school eventually resumed classes in trailers.

On the other side of the Great Wall of Chalmette, we head south to a fishing village, Delacroix, the one Bob Dylan sang about in "Tangled Up in Blue," a song about a breakup and the long road to reunification. "A friend of mine said the song had new meaning after Katrina," the Bard says, "because the blue tarps on the roofs ended up tangled in the dead trees."

We park where the road dead-ends into the Gulf. "They call this 'the End of the World,'" the Bard says. A house on fifteen-foot stilts looks abandoned. Half its siding is gone, revealing plywood. Detritus litters the lot, including a boat filled with junk, in front of a trailer that's tipped over and half crushed. The only sign of life is a black cat walking toward us. The witching hour has arrived.

> *Thrice the brinded cat hath mewed.*
> *Thrice, and once the hedge-pig whined.*
> *Harpier cries "'Tis time, 'tis time!"*

I have mostly stayed off my phone since leaving the campground, but when I take it out here in Delacroix, I see a news alert on my home screen: "All US Capitol Buildings Go Into Lockdown Due To Protests." Text messages from friends have piled up: *This could get ugly. Fucking nuts. I believe they evacuated the chamber and the vote is now on hold. Where do we live? They're in.*

Said Banquo, after seeing the witches' apparitions that set in motion Macbeth's murderous path to power:

> *Have we eaten on the insane root*
> *that takes the reason prisoner?*

Many protestors storming the Capitol are coming from a "Save America" rally, where an assortment of Trump loyalists riled up the crowd. Alabama congressman Mo Brooks, wearing a camouflage hat, criticized Republicans for lacking the courage to fight and die for the country. "The fight begins today!" he exhorted the crowd. "Today is the day American patriots start taking down names and kicking ass!"

Campaign lawyer John Eastman shouted, "We no longer live in a self-governing republic if we can't get the answer to this question!" — the question being how the machines were rigged and election stolen from Trump.

Rudy Giuliani told the crowd that it's "perfectly legal" for Vice President Pence to take the electoral count and "cast it aside," saying there was "conclusive evidence" of massive fraud, calling it "a matter of scientific proof." After alleging that Democrats were criminals for stealing the election, he thundered, "So!" — banging his hand on the lectern — "let's have trial by combat!" He urged people to "fight to the very end."

Texas attorney general Ken Paxton, whose lawsuit over illegal voting in other states had been endorsed by a majority of Republican congressmen before being unanimously dismissed by the Supreme Court, attacked Republicans in Georgia: "They capitulated, they consented. We kept fighting in Texas."

The prosperity-preaching televangelist Paula White, who gave the invocation at Trump's inauguration, and who spoke in tongues following the election while claiming that "demonic conspiracies" were attempting to steal it from Trump, offered the prayer: "May your people rise up and stand strong," she said, asking God to "give us a holy boldness in this hour."

Those and others were the warm-up for Trump, who covered the same ground he has been harping on for months: a rigged election stolen by Democrats who hate freedom and America. But to an audience that included Proud Boys and other members of militant groups, he went further.

"We will never give up, we will never concede," he said. "Our country has had enough. We will not take it anymore and that's what this is all about." Having failed to convince state legislatures to submit phony electors, having failed to persuade a single member of the Supreme Court of his claims, having failed to persuade his own appointees to the Justice Department to call the election into doubt, he turns to his *last best hope*: "I hope Mike is going to do the right thing. I hope so. I hope so . . . Because if Mike Pence does the right thing, we win the election. He has the absolute right to do it." Said Macbeth:

> *False face must hide what the false heart doth know*

"All Vice President Pence has to do is send it back to the states to recertify and we become president and you are the happiest people. And I actually,

I just spoke to Mike. I said: 'Mike, that doesn't take courage. What takes courage is to do nothing. That takes courage.'"

Trump is correct, in one way: Standing up to him will indeed take courage, or at least more courage than other Republicans are showing. Congress is in the process of certifying the electoral votes over the formal objection of more than 130 Republican House members, an effort spearheaded by Louisiana congressman (and future House Speaker) Mike Johnson, after his legal effort to overturn the election failed. "This is a very weighty decision," he had told his colleagues. "All of us have prayed for God's discernment," as if upholding democracy requires discernment. In the Senate, eight Republicans joined them, including Louisiana's John Kennedy and the ringleaders, Ted Cruz and Josh Hawley.

"And Mike Pence is going to have to come through for us," Trump continued, "and if he doesn't, that will be a sad day for our country because you're sworn to uphold our Constitution . . . So I hope Mike has the courage to do what he has to do. And I hope he doesn't listen to the RINOs and the stupid people that he's listening to."

After Trump's public plea to Pence, he urged the crowd to take the gloves off: "Republicans are constantly fighting like a boxer with his hands tied behind his back. It's like a boxer." The past two months have been a depressing affirmation of Paul Simon's "The Boxer."

All lies and jest
Still a man hears what he wants to hear
And disregards the rest

"And we want to be so nice. We want to be so respectful of everybody, including bad people. And we're going to have to fight much harder." *Fight much harder.* "And after this, we're going to walk down, and I'll be there with you . . . And we're going to walk down to the Capitol, and we're going to cheer on our brave senators and congressmen and women . . . Because you'll never take back our country with weakness. You have to show strength and you have to be strong."

Over the past few days, aides pleaded with Trump to urge his followers to be peaceful at the rally. He refused. Today he used the word *fight* twenty times. He describes the state of the country in militant terms, as "under siege," calling the members of Congress who support him "warriors" and speaking in bombastic tones. Over the course of seventy-five minutes, he brings himself to utter the word *peace* once: "I know that everyone here will soon be marching over to the Capitol building to peacefully and patriotically make your voices heard." It was a passing sentiment, a checking of the box.

"Today we see a very important event," Trump says. "And I'm going to be watching. Because history is going to be made. We're going to see whether or not we have great and courageous leaders, or whether or not we have leaders that should be ashamed of themselves throughout history, throughout eternity they'll be ashamed. And you know what? If they do the wrong thing, we should never, ever forget that they did. Never forget. We should never ever forget."

Never forget. We left Lower Manhattan on 9/11 to the sound of those words, and now they have returned in a nightmare echo. "And we fight," Trump continues. "We fight like hell. And if you don't fight like hell, you're not going to have a country anymore . . . So let's walk down Pennsylvania Avenue."

Said Macbeth, after sending men off to murder Banquo and Fleance, which he believes necessary to uphold his treachery and remain in power:

Things bad begun make strong themselves by ill

Minutes after he finished speaking, Trump is informed that the Capitol is under attack. Various staff, family, and allies urge him to condemn the attack and call on protestors to leave, but he refuses. As the mob descended on the Capitol, Mitch McConnell spoke on the Senate floor. "We're debating a step that has never been taken in American history," he said. "Whether Congress should overrule the voters and overturn a presidential election. I've served 36 years in the Senate. This'll be the most important vote I've ever cast . . . The Constitution gives us here in Congress a limited role. We cannot simply declare ourselves a National Board of Elections on steroids. The voters, the courts, and the stage have all spoken. They've all spoken. If we overrule them, it would damage our Republic forever. This election, actually, was not unusually close. Just in recent history, 1976, 2000 and 2004 were all closer. The Electoral College margin is almost identical to what it was in 2016. If this election were overturned by mere allegations from the losing side, our democracy would enter a death spiral. We'd never see the whole nation accept an election again. Every four years would be a scramble for power at any cost."

As the Bard and I are in Delacroix standing at the End of the World, Trump tweets, "Mike Pence didn't have the courage to do what should have been done to protect our Country and our Constitution, giving States a chance to certify a corrected set of facts, not the fraudulent or inaccurate ones which they were asked to previously certify. USA demands the truth!" Five minutes later, a Proud Boy leader sends a group text message: "Civil War started."

On the first day of this journey, we passed Cooper Union, where Lincoln presciently warned that some were threatening to "rule or ruin in all events" — that is, to get their way or "destroy the government." It has come to pass, again. Rioters smash windows, break down doors, storm lines of police, attack officers with chemical sprays, wreak havoc, shout threats, and hold aloft Confederate flags. A gallows is set up outside, with a noose. The "QAnon Shaman" — Jacob Chansley, a man wearing a horned hat, body and face paint, and no shirt — enters the Senate chamber and sits in the same chair that Pence occupied just minutes earlier as he tried to carry out his duty of announcing the electoral results. From Pence's chair, Chansley leads a group in prayer: "Thank you heavenly Father," he begins. His ridiculous getup and association with QAnon make it easy to dismiss him as a kook, but he is a Christian who believes he is doing God's will, and he has plenty of company. Some in the mob hold flags carrying Christian symbols and messages, and someone carries a wooden cross. A yellow banner on the Capitol steps reads, "Jesus Saves."

The closing lines of Dylan's "Tangled Up in Blue" seem to hold what's missing among the rioters: the humility to recognize that people can share something precious — Dylan sings of personal love, but it could be love of nation — while having conflicting perspectives. The danger lies in realizing it too late.

We always did feel the same
We just saw it from a different point of view
Tangled up in blue

As we leave Delacroix, Trump reluctantly agrees to send a tweet in support of law enforcement, but he doesn't condemn the riot or tell anyone to leave the Capitol. At the same time, Ashli Babbitt is leading a mob trying to force its way onto the House floor. Mike Pence has just been evacuated from the Capitol, but about a hundred lawmakers are still in the chamber.

Several officers barricade the doors to the House floor. The mob circles the chamber, looking for another entrance, and they find the same hallway where some lawmakers are being evacuated, while others are trapped in the balcony overlooking the House chamber, ducking under their seats, wearing gas masks — tear gas has been set off in the Rotunda — and murmuring prayers. The mob breaks through the glass in the doors. An officer yells to stand back. Ashli Babbitt tries to climb through. The officer fires, killing her.

Said Macduff, in patriotic despair, fearing what Macbeth's bloody coup will mean for his fellow citizens:

> *Bleed, bleed, poor country*

Trump's son Don Jr. fires off a text to White House chief of staff Mark Meadows, with understandable misspellings: "He's got to condem this shit. Asap. The captiol police tweet is not enough." But Trump doesn't. Nor does he direct the secretary of defense to call in the army or National Guard to retake control of the Capitol. Pence did that, in consultation with the Joint Chiefs of Staff, after being steps away from being attacked by a mob that included people chanting, "Hang Mike Pence!" When Trump is told of the chant, according to aides, he suggests Pence deserves it.

"They are in possession of the very Capitol, rioting and reveling in the sacred halls of American legislation, without fear or without danger," a news account reads. It was published in 1814, the last time the Capitol was violently overrun, when the British burned it during the War of 1812.

Late in the afternoon, after visiting a friend of the Bard's, he takes me to the Chalmette Battlefield, the site of the last great battle of the War of 1812. Beside it is a national cemetery created during the Civil War, where some twelve thousand US Army soldiers are buried, more than half of them unidentified. As we pass it, President-elect Biden speaks to the nation, decrying the assault on democracy and the rule of law: "I call on President Trump to go on national television now, to fulfill his oath and defend the Constitution and demand an end to this siege."

Inevitably, Biden also turns to Lincoln, quoting from his 1862 message to Congress: "Here's what Lincoln said. He said: 'We shall nobly save or meanly lose the last best hope on earth.' He went on to say: 'The way is plain, peaceful, generous, just — a way, which if followed, the world will forever applaud and God must forever bless.' The way is plain here, too.

That's who we are. It's the way of democracy, of respect, of decency, of honor and commitment as patriots to this nation."

The quote fits the moment, but there is a better one to explain it. In 1863, Lincoln wrote a letter to a faction of Missouri abolitionists at loggerheads with other groups. He noted that the difference of opinion "may be sincerely entertained by honest and truthful men," but in a time of war, "blood grows hot, and blood is spilled. Thought is forced from old channels into confusion. Deception breeds and thrives. Confidence dies, and universal suspicion reigns. Each man feels an impulse to kill his neighbor, lest he be first killed by him. Revenge and retaliation follow. And all this, as before said, may be among honest men only. But this is not all. Every foul bird comes abroad, and every dirty reptile rises up. These add crime to confusion." And so it has come to pass.

In his first inaugural address, Lincoln said that when democratic elections and the rule of the majority is rejected, "anarchy or despotism is all that is left." He was speaking of secessionists but also of mobs. In the weeks preceding his inauguration, a plot to delay, disrupt, or deny the Electoral College vote prompted General Winfield Scott — a native Virginian — to send troops to the capital to preserve order. "*Unquestionably* it was at one time the purpose of the seceders to have prevented the counting of the votes for president," one observer noted, "but finding that they would be ignominiously whipped if they attempted to execute their treason, they wisely concluded that it were better not to [try]." The outgoing vice president charged with certifying the election, John Breckenridge, had finished third in the race for president, but he performed his duty "with Roman fidelity," Massachusetts congressman Henry Dawes reported, "and the nation was saved." Today Mike Pence is playing the role of Breckenridge.

The Bard and I gaze upon the open expanse of the Chalmette Battlefield, an empty field that conceals what was once a thriving black community, Fazendeville, until the National Park Service cleared it out in 1966, a final act of violence performed here in the name of historic preservation. There is still some blue in the sky, but we are now mostly under a cover of clouds, taking in the battlefield's peaceful stillness.

So foul and fair a day I have not seen

While we're here, Trump asks people, finally, to go home. In a video, he begins with an expression of solidarity and empathy: "I know your pain.

I know your hurt." He moves to repetition of his grievances: "We had an election that was stolen from us. It was a landslide election, and everyone knows it, especially the other side." He shifts briefly to the ostensible purpose of the video — "But you have to go home now. We have to have peace. We have to have law and order. We have to respect our great people in law and order. We don't want anybody hurt" — before returning to solidarity, empathy, and grievance: "It's a very tough period of time. There's never been a time like this where such a thing happened, where they could take it away from all of us, from me, from you, from our country. This was a fraudulent election."

He briefly returns to his request: "But we can't play into the hands of these people. We have to have peace. So go home." Then the coup de grâce: "We love you. You're very special." He closes with more solidarity, empathy, and grievance. "You've seen what happens. You see the way others are treated that are so bad and so evil. I know how you feel. But go home and go home at peace."

He delivered no condemnation nor even criticism of violence, lawbreaking, and the attempt to hijack democracy, nor did he say anything to those who had gathered in state capitals around the country. In Georgia, Republican secretary of state Brad Raffensperger was evacuated earlier in the afternoon. In Ohio, Proud Boys started fights outside the statehouse. In Washington State, protestors crashed through the gates of the governor's mansion. In Arizona, they cracked a window in the capitol and demanded the governor come outside.

"I see that some, at least, of you are of those who believe that an election being decided against them is no reason why they should sink the ship," Lincoln said to Democrats in New York on his way to his inauguration. "I believe with you, I believe in sticking to it, and carrying it through. And, if defeated at one election, I believe in taking the chances next time."

The Bard drops me back at Charley, and I thank him for guiding me through a tragedy that I'm only just beginning to absorb. Shortly after the Bard departs, Trump tweets his final message of the day: "These are the things and events that happen when a sacred landslide election victory is so unceremoniously & viciously stripped away from great patriots who have been badly & unfairly treated for so long. Go home with love & in peace. Remember this day forever!"

Never forget.

January 6 will long haunt us, and while what's done is done, an overarching question looms: Will the coup's failure spell the end for its architects? When Lady Macbeth fears their coup has failed, she realizes it would be their ruin, as the king would surely have their heads. "The attempt and not the deed confound us," she says. For Americans, the question will be answered by the people — the same people celebrated by Carl Sandburg, a man born on January 6 in a three-room home in Galesburg, Illinois, a voice of America who never lost faith in its citizens and the promise of the American trinity.

The people will live on.
The learning and blundering people will live on.
They will be tricked and sold and again sold
And go back to the nourishing earth for rootholds,
The people so peculiar in renewal and comeback,
You can't laugh off their capacity to take it.

— 48 —

Aftermath

January 7. "I was wrong, I am deeply sorry, and I ask for your forgiveness," writes Jeremiah Johnson on Facebook, one of at least forty Christian leaders who had prophesied, based on claims of direct communications from God, that Trump would be reelected. For his humble penitence, he "received multiple death threats and thousands upon thousands of emails from Christians saying the nastiest and most vulgar things I have ever heard toward my family and ministry. I have been labeled a coward, sell-out, a traitor to the Holy Spirit, and cussed out at least 500 times. We have lost ministry partners every hour and counting . . . I have been flabbergasted at the barrage of continued conspiracy theories being sent every minute our way and the pure hatred being unleashed."

As the Civil War entered its final month, Lincoln understood that accepting defeat would be difficult for the Confederates. "Men are not flattered by being shown that there has been a difference of purpose," he wrote, "between the Almighty and them."

The more that trust declines in traditional institutions — including governments, news organizations, and churches — the more those claiming prophetic powers can step into the breach, and they have. Prophetic Pentecostalism has become one of the fastest-growing Christian sects, and despite its lousy track record this year — in addition to getting the election wrong, no leading prophets saw Covid coming, and many prophesied its quick demise — its popularity shows no sign of abating. One evangelical leader who believes in prophecy, the activist and author Michael Brown, calls the rise in those claiming prophetic powers "an embarrassment to the movement" and the prophecies about Trump's victory "the largest-scale deception I've seen in 49 years of following Jesus."

Congregations and Christian media have become hotbeds of political conspiracy theories and misinformation, often pushed by pastors who dress up grift as grace. Today the doomsday televangelist and prophet-profiteer Jim Bakker, who hawked Covid cures for $125 as soon as the pandemic started, denounces those seeking Trump's impeachment as "the demons of hell." He called Trump's 2016 election "the greatest miracle I have ever seen."

It's become increasingly difficult to distinguish prophets from partisans, and few of either are backing down from claims that Trump was defrauded. "What happened at the Capitol yesterday was incredibly restrained from my perspective," John Guandolo says on a Christian television network called the Dove. "I was there, I watched it, I was in and amongst it." Guandolo is a former marine and FBI agent and one of the nation's most virulent Muslim fearmongers and conspiracy theorists, seeing a Muslim takeover of the country being orchestrated from hostile forces foreign and domestic. "It's amazing to me that patriots haven't strung up these traitors," Guandolo continues, the traitors being Republican politicians and others who held the country together yesterday. "This is the 2021 Boston Massacre," he adds, equating Ashli Babbitt to the early revolutionaries who were gunned down by the king's soldiers.

"I trust in God and I know that I didn't do anything wrong," says Jacob Chansley, the QAnon Shaman. Peter Montgomery, a journalist who has long covered the Religious Right, explained how there could be so many like him: "The relentlessness of apocalyptic spiritual-warfare rhetoric and pro-Trump propagandizing by right-wing Christian leaders and media outlets helped create what religion scholar Peter Manseau has called a 'permission structure' for the violent insurrectionists to believe they were acting righteously."

The next day the Bard's wife, Katherine, brings me to an anniversary commemoration of the Battle of New Orleans, held on the street median that holds the only structural remnant remaining from the battle. As about two dozen of us shiver in the cold, a marine band and reenactors in uniform provide some pomp, various dignitaries give ceremonious remarks, and then William Hyland steps to the microphone and says something important. The Bard had introduced me to him on January 6, when we stopped by Los Islenos Museum, which Hyland runs and which celebrates the heritage of the Canary Islanders who settled this area.

"The victory helped to redefine the identity of an American citizen," Hyland says of the Battle of New Orleans. "Can you imagine, for the very first time, you had people speaking French, Spanish, Native American dialects, Tagalog — because there were Filipinos — all of these people fighting as American citizens, or fighting *for* the American cause, even if they were not American citizens." The national motto Congress adopted in 1782, *E Pluribus Unum* — out of many, one — now stretched beyond the peoples of Northern Europe. It would go on stretching ever wider, slowly and never without a struggle, with victors long denied and victims long forgotten.

After the ceremony finishes, Katherine and I meet the Bard and Laurel at Rocky and Carlo's, a local institution famed for its mountainous heaping of baked macaroni and cheese with brown and red gravy. Some reenactors beat us there, and as we all feast, Biden is asked at a press conference about elected officials who fed the "stop the steal" fury that led to the insurrection, particularly its most prominent ringleaders, two Harvard Law grads, Senators Ted Cruz and Josh Hawley, the latter having raised a fist in solidarity with the protesters as he entered the Capitol on January 6 — riling them up, a police officer on the scene said.

"They're part of the big lie, the big lie," Biden says of Hawley, Cruz, and others who joined them in fanning Trump's flames. "Goebbels and the great lie — you keep repeating the lie, repeating the lie . . . There are decent people out there who actually believe these lies, because they've heard it again and again . . . This is the human condition."

It was Hitler in *Mein Kampf*, not Goebbels, who described "the big lie." People, he wrote, "more readily fall victims to the big lie than the small lie, since they themselves often tell small lies in little matters but would be ashamed to resort to large-scale falsehoods. It would never come into their heads to fabricate colossal untruths, and they would not believe that others could have the impudence to distort the truth so infamously. Even though the facts which prove this to be so may be brought clearly to their minds, they will still doubt and waver and will continue to think that there may be some other explanation."

Hawley and some other Republicans attacked Biden for connecting their conspiracy-mongering to Nazi propaganda, but Biden is hardly alone in drawing the connection. On January 10, California's former Republican governor Arnold Schwarzenegger delivers one of the most powerful speeches of the era, one I never expected to hear in my lifetime.

> I grew up in Austria. I am very aware of Kristallnacht, or the Night of Broken Glass. It was a night of rampage against the Jews carried out in 1938 by the Nazi equivalent of the Proud Boys. Wednesday was the Day of Broken Glass right here in the United States. The broken glass was in the windows of the United States Capitol. But the mob did not just shatter the windows of the Capitol. They shattered the ideas we took for granted. They did not just break down the doors of the building that housed American democracy. They trampled the very principles on which our country was founded. Now, I grew up in the ruins of a country that suffered the loss of its democracy. I was born in 1947, two years after the Second World War. Growing up, I was surrounded by broken men drinking away their guilt over their participation in the most evil regime in history. Not all of them were rabid anti-Semites or Nazis. Many just went along, step-by-step, down the road. They were the people next door.
>
> Now, I've never shared this so publicly because it is a painful memory. But my father would come home drunk once or twice a week and he would scream and hit us and scare my mother. I did not hold him totally responsible because our neighbor was doing the same thing to his family, and so was the next neighbor over. I heard it with my own ears and saw it with my own eyes. They were in physical pain from the shrapnel in their bodies, and in emotional pain from what they saw — or did. It all started with lies, and lies and lies, and intolerance. So being from Europe, I've seen firsthand how things can spin out of control. I know there is a fear in this country and all over the world that something like this could happen right here. Now, I do not believe it is — but, I do believe that we must be aware of the dire consequences of selfishness and cynicism. President Trump sought to overturn the results of an election — and of a fair election. He sought a coup by misleading people with lies. My father and our neighbors were misled also with lies, and I know where such lies lead.

This week, George Orwell's *1984* tops the bestseller list. "In the end the Party would announce that two and two made five," Orwell wrote, "and you would have to believe it."

A week after the assault on the Capitol, the House impeaches Trump a second time, the first president ever twice impeached. Only ten Republicans voted to impeach. More would have joined them, but as some told colleagues privately, they feared not only for their careers but also for their family's safety. And no wonder: Franklin Graham, Billy's son, compared the ten Republicans to Judas: "It makes you wonder," he wrote, "what the thirty pieces of silver were that Speaker Pelosi promised for this betrayal." Jesus cured the blind, but never the partisan.

Some Republicans are blaming the whole episode on antifa, claiming that all the insurrectionists were socialists masquerading as Trumpers. It would be hard to invent a more perfect example of Richard Hofstadter's description of the "paranoid mind" that has long stalked American politics. Inspiring the paranoia, Hofstadter wrote, is an "appeal to a lost America," which he explained in terms that broadly apply to the insurrectionists and their leaders. "America has been largely taken away from them and their kind, though they are determined to try to repossess it and to prevent the final destructive act of subversion," he wrote. "The old American virtues have already been eaten away by cosmopolitans and intellectuals; the old competitive capitalism has been gradually undermined by socialistic and communistic schemers; the old national security and independence have been destroyed by treason plots," orchestrated by "major statesmen who are at the very center of American power."

Hofstadter was more prophet than today's Pentecostal preachers, and his vision came not from claiming a direct line to God but simply by studying American history, including Alexander Hamilton's *Federalist Papers*, in which Hamilton warned against ambitious panderers who sow distrust for political gain, "commencing demagogues, and ending tyrants." Lincoln, too, had warned against the "mobocratic spirit" that led to vigilantism and threatened the nation. He knew as well that democracies are inherently susceptible to such spirits. "It is to deny what the history of the world tells us is true, to suppose that men of ambition and talents will not continue to spring up amongst us," he said in his 1838 Lyceum speech. "And when they do, they will as naturally seek the gratification of their ruling passion, as others have so done before them," he continued, citing Caesar, Alexander, and Napoleon as examples. When such a person arises, "it will require the people to be united with each other, attached to the government and laws, and generally intelligent, to successfully frustrate his designs."

A few days before Biden's inauguration, I meet Justin Nystrom, a Loyola University history professor who wrote a book on Reconstruction in Louisiana. We sit down at a café in the Roosevelt Hotel in New Orleans, where Huey Long once sipped gin fizzes. Justin picked the spot because it's the site where, five months after Lincoln endorsed at least limited black suffrage in his final speech, hopes for a peaceful national reconciliation died, along with more than thirty black men who were massacred while attempting to attend a state constitutional convention convened by Republicans to extend suffrage to blacks. Democrats, many of them Confederate veterans, opened fire and brutally attacked black marchers. In the bloody aftermath, many arrests were made — of *black* citizens, by police officers who had carried out the attack. There is no monument here to those killed.

There was more violence in the years that followed, as Democrats sought to wrest power from Republicans during Reconstruction. "They had this contested election in 1872 with a Democratic fusionist ticket," Justin says. "The fusionists lost, but they actually had an argument that perhaps the election was stolen from them. They set up a shadow government. You could imagine them chanting, 'Stop the steal.' They made all kinds of legal challenges, lots of racialized language. It doesn't work. It's not enough." And so they attempted to overthrow the Republican government. They failed, but no one was punished, which emboldened them. Months later, when Republicans attempted to seat a local judge, whites attacked the courthouse and massacred more than a hundred black men. The Supreme Court later ruled that the federal government could not prosecute the killers. The mob then organized itself into a White League militia and tried again to overthrow the government, launching a frontal assault on the city's police force, which was commanded by Confederate-general-turned-Republican James Longstreet. The Battle of Liberty Place, as Democrats called it, ended with more than thirty dead — and this time, the coup was successful. Once again, no arrests were made.

"If you don't arrest people who do this," Justin says of those who would overturn elections, "they'll be back, because they always come back." And their violence grows.

The conversation turns to the George Floyd protests, and he laments that the primary slogan for racial justice has ended up being divisive. "I always contend that BLM should have requisitioned 'law and order'" as a rallying cry, he says. "Because ultimately it's about the Fourteenth Amendment, and their theme should have been, 'We want law and order,' because that's only fair — equal protection under the law is what they seek. And I thought stealing that, appropriating that from the right, would have been a twist, but nobody asked me." Swords into plowshares, dog whistles into peace pipes.

Instead, we have tribalistic flags, Black Lives Matter versus Blue Lives Matter, that have ended up pushing people into making a false choice: Stand with black Americans or stand with police officers — one or the other, as though we can't do both. All across the country, I saw countless BLM signs and countless thin blue line American flags. I never saw one house, one business, or one RV displaying both. Most Americans do stand with both groups. But in front yards and storefronts, we see only division, centered on that hardest and hottest of topics, race.

To some extent, the division is an inevitable part of the national reckoning over race that has only just begun. Justin mentions that his profession, long dominated by whites who have downplayed racial injustice, has been part of the problem. "I think there's a lot of questioning about the American mission," he says, "and I think this reckoning that we're doing with our history — whether it's the monuments, whether it's finally coming to grips with *Birth of a Nation* — there's a lot of the country that's just not ready for that. Every country believes its own myths. That's what kind of holds it together, right?"

Without me asking it, he's answered the question I've put to every person I've met along my journey — What holds America together? — and he's gotten right to the heart of it. "I don't mean to be cynical," he says, "but when you quit believing, when a country no longer agrees on the story," the bonds of union begin to slip. "And we're a long way from agreement on the story of what the country means."

There has always been loud and heated disagreement on the story, of course, and tolerance for disagreement is, in so many ways, the story itself. But can we see that? Can we help others see it? "I can't think of a lower point of what *E Pluribus Unum* might mean to Americans," says Justin. It may be the bleakest statement I've heard the entire trip. "I'm hoping that in this hour where we seem so divided, that we can look at that old Latin saying and say, 'Yes, that is who we are. And that is who we need to be.'"

I ask him what he fears most about the future of the country ten years from now. "As the father of two sons, I most fear that they will have to fight for their country against their own countrymen. I think that's a fear shared by many. Our children shouldn't be fighting each other in the streets of this country to preserve it."

Laurel and I eat our way across the city — jambalaya, gumbo, char-grilled oysters, po'boys, rice and beans, étouffée, king cake — and stop by Galatoire's, the Bourbon Street institution where I asked her to marry me. Lincoln referred to his marrying as a "matter of profound wonder," and I feel much the same, especially after the past four months in Charley, which have been the best four months of our years together.

Galatoire's is closed, Bourbon Street is eerily quiet, and the music clubs on Frenchmen Street are shuttered, though one runs an outside bar with jazz on weekend afternoons, which helps lift the funeral pall hanging over the city, but only slightly. As we watch the Treme Brass Band, my mother calls to tell me that her cousin John — the brother she never had, beloved by my sister and me as a fun-loving uncle — has suddenly entered hospice. He recently contracted Covid, possibly at a restaurant. The coronavirus is spiking, just as the vaccine is starting to become available. January will be the deadliest month of the pandemic, claiming an average of thirty-three hundred lives a day, including, to our great shock and sorrow, our cousin John.

Late afternoon on January 19, we visit a spot the Bard recommended: Dixie Brewery. On the first day of this journey, we had passed near the site in Manhattan where blackface minstrels first performed "I Wish I Was in Dixie's Land," later shortened to Dixie. Its lyrics are usually credited to Dan Emmett of Ohio, the son of an abolitionist and a Union supporter who knew William Sherman as a boy. "If I had known to what use they were going to put my song," Emmett reputedly said of Confederates, "I will be damned if I'd have written it." But others also claimed authorship, including the Snowden Family Band, a group of siblings whose parents had been enslaved and who taught it to their fellow townsman Emmett — or so it is written on their gravestone. In the hands of minstrels, it romanticized a freed person's view of slavery, but it may have been born of a more subversive sentiment.

In Dixie's land, I'll take my stand to live and die in Dixie

Lincoln loved the song — "one of the best tunes I have ever heard," he told a crowd the day after Lee's surrender at Appomattox. He asked a band to play it, saying that "our adversaries over the way attempted to appropriate it." He wanted it back, declaring it "fairly captured." But it never fully returned.

The brewery is now rebranding itself, dropping Dixie for Faubourg, the name of one of New Orleans's earliest neighborhoods. Months earlier, the Dixie Chicks had dropped Dixie, too, inspired by the George Floyd protests and NASCAR's decision to ban the Confederate flag at its races. The impulse behind the name changes is honorable. I just hope a song that children of enslaved people claimed to have authored, and that Lincoln loved, can someday be reclaimed for the cause for which they stood. That day, if it ever comes, will be determined by black Americans. Until then, I'm fine drinking a Faubourg and listening to the Chicks.

The sun sets on the Dixie Brewery. Tomorrow it will rise on a new era. Trump will not be in attendance at Biden's swearing-in, the first sitting president to skip an inauguration in protest. "So destructive," Tucker Carlson says of it, privately. "It's disgusting. I'm trying to look away." He's not alone. Tomorrow Rupert Murdoch will write in a private message: "Trump insisting on the election being stolen and convincing 25 percent of Americans was a huge disservice to the country. Pretty much a crime. Inevitable it blew up Jan. 6th. Best we don't mention his name unless essential and certainly don't support him."

Of course, Trump isn't going away, nor is the threat of future political violence and insurrection. But this election and its aftermath has underscored what Ronald Reagan said in his 1981 inaugural address, when he spoke a profound truth that seemed so banal that most major newspapers didn't bother to mention it in their coverage. "The orderly transfer of authority as called for in the Constitution routinely takes place, as it has for almost two centuries," Reagan said, "and few of us stop to think how unique we really are. In the eyes of many in the world, this every four-year ceremony we accept as normal is nothing less than a miracle."

Over the course of our journey, we have seen a wide array of what Americans have perceived to be dire threats to the nation, and we have survived them all, a testament to the strength and resilience of our democracy.

We've survived attacks by enemies foreign and domestic
Left-wing bombings and right-wing bombings
Murders by police and of police
Mass shootings and gun control.

We've survived enslavers and nullifiers
John Brown and Jim Crow
Black Codes and white leagues
Lynch mobs and race riots.

We've survived imperialist adventures and isolationist retreats
World wars and proxy wars
Cold Wars and culture wars
Draft resisters and flag burners.

We've survived Chinese Exclusion and Japanese Internment
Open borders and border walls
Sundown Towns and Supreme Court injustices
The KKK and IWW.

We've survived massacres by Indians and massacres of Indians
Indian removal and slum clearance
Western outlaws and southern carpetbaggers
Redlining and white flight.

We've survived communists and socialists
Anarchists and populists
Red Scares and Black Lists
Red Summers and Black Lives Matter.

We've survived corruption by the poor and by the rich
Looting and wage theft
Labor strikes and boycotts
Trade wars and free trade.

We've survived illegal abortion and legal abortion
Women's suffrage and women's lib
Interracial marriage and gay marriage
Plural marriage and single motherhood.

We've survived welfare queens and robber barons
Tent encampments and tent revivals
Messianism and atheism
Eugenicists and jingoists.

We've survived rock 'n' roll and gangsta rap
Censorship and smut
Prohibition and the War on Drugs
Holy rollers and sin cities.

We've survived yellow journalism and trash TV
The Great Depression and the Great Society
The New Deal and the Old Boys Club
Watergate and Russiagate.

We've survived vertical integration and disruptive innovation
Monopolists and trust-busters
Factory closures and farm foreclosures
Off-shoring and out-sourcing.

We've survived the Lost Cause and White Man's Burden
Conspiracy theories and alternative facts
Mass hysteria and mass incarceration
Internment and reparations.

We've survived assassinations of presidents and prophets
Poll taxes and stolen elections
Even secession and Civil War
But never this:

A commander in chief refusing to concede defeat
Dismissing voters and the College of Electors
Inciting militias and demonizing the law-abiding
Fomenting insurrection by legislators and citizens.

We have now survived that, too — a coup from the top down, unprecedented and previously unthinkable — and are stronger for it. But the virus that gave rise to it and that has spread across the land — a contagion that weakens our collective bonds through resentment, animosity, and end-times talk — still lives. And the challenge that Lincoln wrote of in his message to Congress on July 4, 1861, still remains.

Maintaining the nation "against a formidable attempt to overthrow it," he wrote, required demonstrating "to the world that those who can fairly carry an election can also suppress a rebellion; that ballots are the rightful and peaceful successors of bullets, and that when ballots have fairly and constitutionally decided there can be no successful appeal back to bullets . . . Such will be a great lesson of peace, teaching men that what they can not take by an election neither can they take it by a war; teaching all the folly of being the beginners of a war."

In Charley, we watch the inauguration on Fox News, the only channel that comes in. In his speech, Biden strikes a conciliatory tone: referencing Lincoln, mentioning the word *unity* or *unite* more than ten times, and calling for "tolerance and humility" and an end to "this uncivil war." It's a fine speech, but the best lines of the day belong to a twenty-two-year-old poet, Amanda Gorman, who makes the same scriptural reference George Washington did in writing to the Jews of Newport, about sitting under our own fig and vine trees, unafraid, before she speaks to the challenge that has run through our whole journey: understanding the nature and obligations of American identity. Though she performs her poem solo, it rings with the sound of the fifth voice.

> *It's because being American is more than a pride we inherit.*
> *It's the past we step into*
> *and how we repair it.*

The ceremony ends. A new presidency begins. Sound the bells and swell the chorus: We've seen the elephant — and it's nothing less than, as Reagan said, a miracle.

CODA

— 49 —

Remember the *Clotilda*

Laurel and I had planned to split the driving when we left New York, but she ended up having second thoughts and I grew comfortable behind the wheel. After nearly ten thousand miles, however, she found inspiration in the seaside town of Port Aransas, Texas. Golf carts are street legal there, so we rented one — and Laurel jumped into the driver's seat, cruising us around the town and the beach. I'm not sure which of us enjoyed it more.

We spent the month of February in Port Aransas to regroup and wait out the winter. On March 1, we got our first dose of the vaccine, which was available to us only because not enough local residents wanted it, a harbinger of things to come. We celebrated by picking up Whataburger Honey Butter Chicken Biscuits, but a realization was sinking in: Our employers would be wanting us back in the office soon. We began sketching out a route back to New York based on the proverb James Joyce cited in *Ulysses*, his odyssey through Dublin that challenged a nation's view of itself: "Longest way round is the shortest way home." And as it happens, our departure coincides with the anniversary commemoration of the Battle of the Alamo.

Neither Laurel nor I have been to San Antonio, so we head there on a tourism route called the Texas Independence Trail, which leads us to Goliad and the Spanish colonial fort where the first Texas Declaration of Independence was signed in 1835, and where, the following year, Mexican forces imprisoned hundreds of soldiers under the command of James Fannin, who had surrendered. Under the take-no-prisoners wartime policy of Mexico's president Santa Anna, they were executed and their bodies burned and left for vultures. The Goliad Massacre is commemorated each year and its victims lionized as martyrs to the Texas revolution. Less well remembered: Fannin committed a series of strategic blunders, including a failure to follow an order to retreat until it was too late, dooming his men.

Before leaving Goliad, we walk around the town square surrounding the county courthouse and see its "Hanging Oak," whose limbs were used for executions, including lynchings of Mexicans. Goliad was the center of vigilante activity during the so-called Cart War of 1857, when Anglo-Texans in the carting industry attacked and killed dozens of Tejanos and Mexicans who were outworking them and undercutting their prices. The Cart War was less a war than a lynch mob, but calling it a war lessens the perpetrators' culpability. Victors write history not only to consecrate their cause and erase their errors but also to cover up their crimes.

We visit a succession of Spanish missions on our way to San Antonio, where the Alamo takes me by surprise: I had not realized that what remains of it is little more than a small stone church, or that it stands smack in the middle of downtown. It's San Antonio's Times Square, and in many ways it's an extension of the tourist attraction it faces: a Ripley's Believe It or Not! museum.

At a predawn commemoration, about five hundred people watch reenactors fire rifles, a band plays "The Battle Hymn of the Republic," and dignitaries give speeches glorifying the two hundred men who "paid the ultimate price" in defending the fort from the Mexican army in 1836. The ceremony carries the same type of solemnity found at the World Trade Center Memorial each September 11, and the same phrase heard there is spoken here, too: "Never forget." But when we remember the Alamo, what are we remembering?

From the day it fell, the Alamo has been celebrated as a glorious defeat in much the same way the Battle of Little Bighorn was: an atrocity committed by an aggressor that required avenging. And like Little Bighorn, it got the Hollywood treatment, with John Wayne playing Davy Crockett in a script that wiped away historical inconveniences. Generations of Americans, especially Texans, have grown up learning an Alamo fable that echoes the tale of both the early colonists and later the Confederates. In short: After a despotic tyrant mobilized the military against a liberty-loving people, a group of courageous men fighting for independence took a stand against a larger and more powerful army and heroically fought for the principles they believed in. And here, their sacrificial defeat helped secure victory by slowing the tyrant's army, making them martyrs to the cause of independence and liberty. Believe it or not?

The mythic version of the Alamo contains falsehoods, of course, not only that Mexico was the aggressor but also the idea that the defeat helped secure ultimate victory. As University of Texas historian H. W. Brands put it: "Regardless of what the defenders contributed to the mythology of Texas, their contribution to the strategy of the Texas revolution was nil or negative." But the myth is built less on falsehoods than half-truths that reflect intentional omission and obfuscation.

For instance: The men certainly were courageous in fighting to the death, but they were also reckless in their passions, more Ned Buntline than General Washington, whose retreats during the Revolutionary War were essential to success. Sam Houston had wanted to "blow up the Alamo and abandon the place," he wrote, since it was of little value to the war effort. While his directive to retreat went unheeded, he refused to send reinforcements to avoid getting drawn into what he saw as a pointless battle. "The battle should never have been fought," wrote Brands. And while it's true that the men here fought for liberty, some — including William Travis, Davy Crockett, and James Bowie — owned and traded slaves, and the fear that Mexico would outlaw slavery was "part of the reason" for the war, wrote Brands. Even if only a small part — and the debate over that is fierce — slavery has been entirely written out of the history here.

At this morning's ceremony, there is no mention of slavery, and there are many who want to keep it that way. Efforts to carve the names of the enslaved people who were present for the battle into the monument outside the Alamo have been rejected. The president of This Is Texas Freedom Force, labeled an extremist militia group by the FBI, tells the *Washington Post*: "If they want to bring up that it was about slavery, or say that the Alamo defenders were racist, or anything like that, they need to take their rear ends over the state border and get the hell out of Texas."

Secession from Mexico is not the only war where the role of slavery has long been denied. Only in the past few years have education standards in Texas required students to be taught that slavery was the primary cause of the Civil War. Previously, standards listed the main issues as states' rights and sectionalism. Slavery was a "side issue," explained a member of the board of education in 2015.

A $500 million renovation of the Alamo and plaza surrounding it has long been stalled over which version of history should be told here: only the mythical tale of the battle itself, or also the more complex story of the revolution, as well as the role of indigenous people who lived here. A similar debate has been playing out at the state's board of education, which has rejected a push to remove the word *heroic* from its mandate that students be taught about the Alamo's "heroic defenders." While the word *heroic* may reflect good intentions — instilling in children an appreciation for the courage and sacrifice that liberty requires — the effect can be blinding. After all: Was a refusal to obey a directive to retreat, in a battle that cost the Texas army dearly, in a war fought partly to sustain slavery, heroic? Students should discuss and debate the question rather than have the answer dictated to them by government. In its endless complications, it's a powerful opportunity to engage young minds in critical thinking, reasoning, and argument.

A few weeks after our visit here, Texas adopts a law banning schools from teaching any history that suggests "an individual should feel discomfort, guilt, anguish, or any other form of psychological distress on account of the individual 's race or sex." But history without discomfort is not history at all, just a security blanket — or as Peter Carmichael put it to me at the Gettysburg Battlefield, a bedtime story. Other Republican-controlled states have passed similar "discomfort laws," and their defenders say they seek to prevent indoctrination. But the laws can lead teachers and schools to avoid material that might prompt complaints and expose them to legal or professional risk. After Oklahoma passed a discomfort law, some teachers have shied away from covering the systematic murder of Osage Indians by whites seeking their oil revenue during the 1920s, and invitations to Osage speakers have been rescinded. In other southern states that have adopted discomfort laws, many worry that schools will shy away from the long shadow of Jim Crow.

Discomfort laws seem to be less about avoiding indoctrination than avoiding truths and the responsibility we have for coming to terms with them. In this way, they mirror the driving force behind many Confederate monuments. When New Orleans erected a statue of Robert Lee in 1884, the *Daily Picayune* explained its purpose: "We must show to all coming ages that with us, at least, there dwells no sense of guilt."

Excising guilt from public memory is why a variety of foreign governments have enacted "memory laws" that sanitize the past, and why Vladimir

Putin has moved to erase the history of Soviet genocide and Nazi cooperation. In doing this, governments are playing to the natural human tendency to distort memory in self-serving ways. "That which we remember is, more often than not, that which we would like to have been; or that which we hope to be," wrote Ralph Ellison. In his magisterial book on American myth, *Mystic Chords of Memory*, Michael Kammen called this the "heritage syndrome," which he defined as "an impulse to remember what is attractive or flattering and to ignore all the rest."

Ignoring all the rest — the mistakes that cause regret and shame and call for amends and reconciliation — can be done in public, but it is much harder to do in the privacy of our consciences. In *The Road*, Cormac McCarthy's novel about a post-apocalyptic America, when all that's left is the remnants of family and memory, the father says to the son: "You forget what you want to remember and you remember what you want to forget."

So yes: *Remember the Alamo*. But not just the courageous men killed here.

Remember the reasons some of the men here and elsewhere fought: not just independence and liberty, but also land and slavery.

Remember that Mexicans were fighting to preserve and protect their country.

Remember that the Coahuiltecans, who built the Alamo mission, have long been seeking recognition for the sacred burial grounds that remain unmarked here.

Remember the hatred of Mexicans and Tejanos that the celebration of the Alamo helped perpetuate, and the lynchings and repression they experienced in the years after the war, with thousands of Mexicans and Mexican Americans lynched by vigilante groups.

Remember that viewing the Alamo as a good-and-bad morality play — and elevating it to the realm of a secular passion play — runs counter to mercy and forgiveness and engenders ill will among both white and Mexican Americans.

And remember the value in teaching students that, as Shakespeare wrote in *Henry IV*, "The better part of valour is discretion" — a lesson that could have saved many lives here *and* strengthened Texas's fight for independence, had it been heeded.

The letter that William Travis wrote while here has long been required teaching in Texas schools, with its vow to "never surrender or retreat" and its celebrated cry of "Victory or death." Ted Cruz's frequent citing of that cry led Ted Olsen, who served as solicitor general during George W. Bush's first term in the White House, and whose wife died on the hijacked plane that flew into the Pentagon on 9/11, to rebuke him. "Conservatives who love liberty more than political death ought to forget the Alamo," Olsen wrote. "Far better to follow the words and deeds of prudent men of principle like Reagan and Houston, who knew what it took to win." At a DC rally on January 5, Ali Alexander, who is from Fort Worth and founder of a Stop the Steal organization, led a crowd in a chant of "Victory or death!"

Education, Lincoln said in his first campaign speech as a twenty-three-year-old candidate for state legislature, is "the most important subject which we as a people can be engaged in." Not just for its own sake, but so that every person could "read the histories of his own and other countries, by which he may duly appreciate the value of our free institutions." It's a sentiment on which both liberals and conservatives agree, and though neither trusts the other to write those histories, democracy is strengthened when we remember what we want to forget.

We have one more stop to make on the Texas Independence Trail, and we leave San Antonio on Route 90, one of the nation's oldest transcontinental roads. After pulling over in Seguin to admire the world's largest pecan — even the nuts are bigger in Texas — we drive through Houston to the San Jacinto Battlefield. It was here that Texan forces attacked Santa Anna's troops — and kept attacking after they surrendered, in retribution. An obelisk honoring the victory mimics the Washington Monument, except that it's taller, since this is Texas. "With the battle cry 'Remember The Alamo! Remember Goliad!' the Texans charged," reads the inscription. "The slaughter was appalling, the victory complete, and Texas free!" We had seen similar language on signage at the Alamo: "With the capture of Santa Anna, the Independence of Texas was won. The Republic of Texas was born." The battle here, however, did not end the war or set Texas free, as H. W. Brands points out: "Mexico continued to claim Texas for another decade and in 1842 succeeded twice in reoccupying San Antonio. What finally settled the Texas question was the intervention of the United States, which annexed Texas in 1845 and defeated Mexico in the war of 1846–1848."

As we drive away, I start to feel little jabs on my ankles. I flick at my feet, figuring it's a mosquito, but when the jabs get worse I pull over and see the problem: I've been attacked by fire ants. Laurel immediately takes command of the situation and orders me out of Charley — she's familiar with these little devils and aims to take no prisoners. She throws the floor mats out my door, and as I wage a defensive war, she issues another order: "Take off your clothes!"

I do as I'm told and find myself standing in the road wearing nothing but boxer shorts. People in passing cars stare, but the tactical maneuver works. After making a careful inspection of Charley, Laurel comes out to inspect me. Finding no ants, she brings me fresh clothes, seals my discarded clothes in a bag, and allows me to reenter Charley. The victory is complete, and we are free.

Route 90 leads us back through New Orleans and along the Gulf to Biloxi, where we pass Beauvoir, Jefferson Davis's final home. In the 1990s, the Mississippi Sons of Confederate Veterans added a library with Davis's books and papers, making it a "presidential library." It continues to promote Lost Cause mythology and the image of the happy slave, with help from state funds. We skip it and head to a small community on the outskirts of Mobile, Alabama: Africatown.

At Union Baptist Church we meet Darron Patterson, who grew up down the street. A career in journalism brought him to Detroit — "I was the first African American in the country to cover NASCAR and IndyCar for a major metropolitan daily," he says — before he found his way back to Mobile. "Growing up, I didn't know anything about any of this African stuff," he says. "My family never told me anything."

"Was the name Africatown even here?"

"No, it was Plateau. And Henry Williams was an old man who tried to tell all the young people who we were, and people said, 'Don't listen to Henry Williams. He's crazy.'" Williams was old enough to remember the people who had been brought here on the last slave ship to leave Africa for the US, in 1860, fifty-two years after federal law prohibited the importation of slaves. As Darron began uncovering his past, he learned that his great-great-grandfather, Pollee Allen, was aboard the *Clotilda.*

"Remember, when the *Clotilda* happened, the penalty for importing enslaved people was death. Now, Frank, when I think about it, maybe the reason my folks didn't say a lot about my ancestry was so I wouldn't get out here and run my mouth to a lot of people who might not have wanted to hear that, because the penalty was death and there still could have been some repercussions against the Meaher family."

Timothy Meaher, a cotton plantation owner, made a bet with a New Yorker over drinks on Meaher's steamboat, which he named the *Roger B. Taney* in honor of the chief justice who had written the *Dred Scott* decision. Meaher wagered his northern visitor $1,000 that he could get a load of Africans to America without getting caught, no less hanged. It must have seemed like a safe bet: No one had ever been hanged for the crime, convictions were exceptionally rare, sentences were light, and presidential pardons were common. Given the high cost of purchasing an enslaved person, there was a growing movement in the south to reopen the African market, where a person could be bought for a small fraction of the price fetched here. A boat had just returned to Georgia with 471 Africans, and the man who orchestrated it went unpunished. Meaher wanted in on the action.

"Timothy Meaher's family still owns that land" — Darron points in one direction — "and that land," pointing in another direction. "We can't get the Meaher family to talk to us. They're still here. They're very wealthy. We just want to talk. I don't have anything against them. I just want to talk to them, because they're part of this story. Maybe they're worried about some reparations against the estate, I don't know." The wealth that enslaved people created for the Meahers not only continues to enrich them but also incentivizes them not to talk. "I understand now that there's a younger generation of the family coming to the forefront, and I've heard they have a different view of this thing, and we may end up having some dialogue."

Darron started the Clotilda Descendants Association two years ago to tell the story of what happened here, before it faded from memory. "It's a very well-documented story," he says. "The Dahomey king, Glele, decided to get rid of his rivals and to make money, he just enslaved some of his own African people." The kings of Dahomey, now the West African nation of Benin, captured and sold millions of people into bondage, killing those deemed too old or too young to sell. "My folks were a part of a rival tribe. Glele started just enslaving them and selling them to white slavers from America. Got rich."

The vast majority of Africans sold into bondage went to South America and the Caribbean. Only about 5 percent came to the United States. The shame of the African slave trade is hardly borne by America alone.

"The *Clotilda* was a merchant cargo schooner that had been built for speed," Darron says, "and they put 110 Africans they bought from Glele into a cargo hold a little bit bigger than this RV you got. They were butt naked. And for two months on the Atlantic Ocean, they were stuffed into this cargo hold. Only let out to walk around on deck a few at a time, once a week, so their muscles wouldn't atrophy. They had to eat where they shit, they had to sleep where they shit, women with cycles, young girls — the squalor, for two months." When two people died, their bodies were dumped overboard, and when the captain feared detection by the British, who patrolled the coast to stop the slave trade, he made plans to dump everyone else, too. He would not have been the first to do so.

"We don't ever want people to forget about the inhumanity of this story. Never. We don't ever want you to forget that. That's part of America's history." *Never forget.* "No matter how much some people would like to sanitize America's history and not understand that it was Africans that built the Capitol, Africans that built the White House, Africans that built America." As state legislators in Alabama consider passing an education "discomfort" law, the importance of Darron's work grows.

"There's a philosophy called Sankofa in the African culture," he says, "and the symbol is a bird with a ball in its mouth representing the future. But the bird's looking back over his shoulder as to not forget where he came from. And that's the theory of Sankofa. You have to go forward, but don't forget where you came from."

The remains of the *Clotilda* were discovered in 2019, thanks in large part to the determined efforts of a local journalist, Ben Raines. "Of the twenty thousand ships used in the global slave trade," he wrote in his terrific book, *The Last Slave Ship*, "just thirteen have been found, and the *Clotilda* is the only ship ever found that brought enslaved people to America." Meaher was caught but never punished. He and his brothers took charge of about sixty of the captives, while the ship's captain took sixteen and the rest were sold at a Montgomery slave market.

When the Civil War ended, some of the newly freed people wanted to return to Africa. The issue of whether black Americans should return to Africa had long divided both black and white anti-slavery leaders. Lincoln supported colonization but preferred blacks be sent to Central America and the Caribbean, because transportation would be less costly and they would make better trading partners. Lincoln and other anti-slavery whites saw support for colonization as complementary to emancipation — a way, as historian Benjamin Quarles wrote, to "accomplish a dual purpose: rid the south of human bondage and rid the country of the colored man." And yet, as Quarles noted, "the man most responsible for the failure of negro emigration was Lincoln himself," because emancipation meant black interest in it mostly evaporated. But not for the newest arrivals. Darron explains, "They said, 'We're done now, can we have a boat to go home? You're not going to give us a boat? Well, give us some land so we can build a house since we got to stay here.'" As Raines notes in *The Last Slave Ship*, "this moment was likely the first instance of freed slaves anywhere in the nation demanding reparations from their former masters." But the answer here would be the same everywhere: *No.*

Meaher and his descendants became slum lords, renting substandard housing to their former cargo and employing them in their fields. During Reconstruction, he tried to block them from voting, a problem solved by the 1901 Alabama Constitution, which cut the number of registered black voters from 181,000 to 5,000. But they persisted, eventually attracting the attention of Booker T. Washington and Zora Neale Hurston, who wrote a biography of one of the last survivors, Cudjo Lewis, *Barracoon*, which went unpublished until 2018. "All these words from the seller," she wrote. "Not one word from the sold."

Word is finally getting out. In 2020, Shemekia Copeland released a song about the *Clotilda* that mentions Africatown.

> *Clotilda's on fire / Off the Alabama coast*
> *Clotilda's on fire / We're still livin' with her ghost*

"We just broke ground on a temporary museum," Darron says, "near Mobile County Training School." Schools for blacks were often called training schools to reinforce class divisions, and this one was built on the very same property where Cudjo Lewis asked Timothy Meaher for land. Although the land was never granted, the school was built thanks to Booker T. Washington and Julius Rosenwald, the president and co-owner of Sears Roebuck, who helped black communities construct and staff five thousand schools across the south between 1917 and 1932, a time when schools for black children, where they existed at all, were starved of resources. Rosenwald was born a block from Lincoln's home in Springfield in 1862, and it may be fairly said that, after emancipation and Reconstruction, nothing did more to advance the cause of black equality than the Rosenwald schools. But the bar was low.

Darron believes that Africatown can be an international tourism destination and finds inspiration in another new memorial nearby. "I've been to Montgomery many times, and now you step off the curb wrong and you might get hit by a tour bus. I was sitting in a restaurant up there and a guy said, 'We're from San Diego. We came for the Lynching Memorial.'

Another guy was from Los Angeles, came for the Lynching Memorial. Unreal. Have you seen it?"

"No, but we hope to."

"You gotta go."

We follow Darron's car around Africatown's small homes, passing a church food pantry line and empty lots. In the late 1960s, to reduce their property taxes, the Meahers knocked down hundreds of houses they had built, part of a downward spiral many other communities experienced: Factories closed, small businesses shuttered, people moved away, drugs moved in, and a highway cut through the neighborhood. Darron points out the modest home of Cleon Jones, who caught the final out of the 1969 World Series for the Miracle Mets, when the Mets had an all-Mobile outfield: Jones, Tommie Agee, and Amos Otis. Jones and Agee played together in high school. (Hank Aaron was from Mobile, too.)

As we pass Jones's yard, he's outside cutting grass. We stop and get out. Darron shouts, "Cleon, we got some New Yorkers here!"

"You're from New York?" Cleon asks, over the engine noise.

'Yeah, the city," I say.

"Then we can be friends."

He has a large Africatown sign on his porch, and he's been active in the movement to keep its history alive. He knows from experience that miracles can happen, but saving the *Clotilda* and the story of Africatown doesn't require a miracle — just greater public resolve to lift it out of the mud in which it's long been buried.

After detouring into the Florida panhandle to avoid the path of a tornado, and barely, we pilgrimage to Hank Williams's childhood home in Georgiana, Alabama, where he learned to play guitar from a black street musician, listened to recordings of black blues singers, and learned the gospel music he sang at his family's church. We follow his family's trail north to Montgomery, walking past the auditorium that hosted his funeral at age twenty-nine, in 1953. It was a segregated affair that relegated blacks to the balcony, as twenty-five hundred white people below sang, with no sense of irony, Hank's song of revelation and redemption.

Now I have traded the wrong for the right
Praise the Lord, I saw the light

Montgomery is teeming with civil rights history, but only recently has it become part of the landscape. A statue of Rosa Parks arrived in 2019, but the Lost Cause still hovers over the city, especially at the state capitol, which sits perched on a hill. Inside, the Senate chamber has been restored to its appearance in 1861, when southern delegates met here to organize the Confederate States of America. It's now a tourist attraction, which strikes me as unfortunate. Better for it to be a living monument to democracy than a deadened shrine to the Confederacy.

Outside, at the top of the capitol steps, is a statue of Jefferson Davis, still looking down on Reverend King's Dexter Avenue Church, near another Confederate monument inscribed with paeans.

The Knightliest of the knightly race
Who since its days of old
Have kept the lamp of chivalry
Alight in hearts of cold

In 1963, George Wallace stood by Davis's statue and invoked the Confederacy, declaring to wild applause from a white-only audience: "Segregation now! Segregation tomorrow! And segregation forever!" Cross burnings and racial attacks increased after Wallace's speech, including murders and bombings. "The governor said things and did things," said Reverend King, "which caused these people to feel that they were aided and abetted by the highest officer in the state." When Attorney General Robert Kennedy visited the statehouse to meet with Wallace on voting rights, Wallace removed the American flag from atop the capitol dome and replaced it with a Confederate flag, which flew until the 1990s, when black legislators brought suit and a court ordered it removed.

Wallace had begun his career as a liberal on race, and in his first campaign for governor, he ran with the support of the NAACP. After he lost the Democratic primary to a candidate backed by the KKK, he learned his lesson: "I'm never gonna be out-nigguhed again," he said. Four years later, he ran again and won in a landslide. Party primaries have long incentivized and rewarded extremism in candidates, and Wallace became the nation's leading trafficker in racial grievance and resentment, painting protestors as anarchists and denouncing liberals as godless socialists. In his 1968 presidential campaign, he won five Confederate states and was competitive across the south, winning nearly enough electoral votes to send the election to Congress, where he could have played kingmaker. When he ran in the 1972 Democratic primary, his strength in the north — he won Maryland and Michigan — might have propelled him to the nomination had a fame-seeking white man not shot and paralyzed him, ending his campaign.

Earlier in 2020, Peggy Wallace told the *New York Times*: "In the presidential campaign of 1968, my father, Governor George Wallace, understood the potential political power of downtrodden and disillusioned working-class white voters who felt alienated from government. And Donald Trump is mining the same mother lode." It's the lode Pat Buchanan mined, too. "I don't think the governor owes anyone an apology," Buchanan said in a 2000 documentary about Wallace. "Maybe you can say the cause was wrong" — *maybe?* — "but I think the man in many ways was right." Wallace disagreed. Unlike many of his followers, he ended up repudiating his racism and bigotry and seeking forgiveness from black Americans. When he ran for governor in 1982, he won a significant share of the black vote in the Democratic primary and 90 percent of it in the general election.

As we drive away from the capitol, "The Night They Drove Old Dixie Down" comes on the radio, with Levon Helm singing about the last days of the Civil War — but only, as Jeff Davis gazes down on us, for the army.

A mile and a half and a world away stands the National Memorial for Peace and Justice, also known as the Lynching Memorial, which opened in 2018. Though Darron told us of its power, Laurel and I are overwhelmed by it. Eight hundred weathered-steel blocks — many of them hanging from steel poles that drop like ropes — hold the names of the nearly forty-four hundred black Americans lynched between 1877 and 1950. And how many lynchings are unaccounted for? In his 1838 Lyceum speech denouncing mobs, Lincoln remarked that lynchings had become so common that "dead men were seen literally dangling from the boughs of trees upon every road side; and in numbers almost sufficient, to rival the native Spanish moss of the country, as a drapery of the forest." A century before Billie Holiday sang "Strange Fruit," Lincoln had painted a similarly ghastly image.

As we move through the gallows, Laurel is shocked to see the town where she went to high school, Warrenton, Virginia, written on one of the memorials. Arthur Jordan was lynched there in 1880, for eloping with a white woman. In New York, a lynching happened in 1892 in the county neighboring the one I grew up in: Robert Lewis was brutally beaten and killed by a mob, even though the woman he supposedly assaulted stated that they had the wrong man. "I am not the man!" Lewis kept repeating. More than half of the victims memorialized here were accused of sexual assault or murder, but often the reason was more mundane: leaving work without permission, drinking from a white man's well, addressing a white man without using "mister," marrying a white woman, reprimanding white children for throwing stones, rejecting a white merchant's bid for cottonseed, organizing a union, striking, voting, and more.

The memorial was built by the Equal Justice Initiative, an organization founded by civil rights attorney Bryan Stevenson, and its purpose is not merely to increase awareness of what happened. It is to open hearts in ways that make possible political and social change that heals and repairs the damage done not only by mobs but also by the politicians who incited them — and still incite them.

Two months before our arrival here, the University of Alabama, where George Wallace stood in the schoolhouse door to stop integration, removed his name from a campus building in Birmingham. Wallace's daughter Peggy supported the decision, but others raised an alternative idea: adding beside Wallace the name of a native Alabaman who devoted his life to civil rights, Congressman John Lewis, and rededicating the building in honor of the reconciliation Wallace had sought and the forgiveness Lewis had shown. "With all his failings, Mr. Wallace deserves recognition for seeking redemption for his mistakes, for his willingness to change and to set things right with those he harmed and with his God," Lewis wrote when Wallace died in 1998. "George Wallace should be remembered for his capacity to change . . . for his effort to redeem his soul and in so doing to mend the fabric of American society."

Maybe leaving Wallace's name on a building is a bridge too far even if paired with Lewis's. But such stories of repentance and forgiveness need to be told — and honored — if we hope to prevent political leaders from believing that Wallace had nothing to apologize for, from asserting, whether directly or through dog whistles, that *maybe* his cause was wrong, and from succeeding by playing to people's fears and biases, rather than embracing our common struggles. Those who say it can't be done haven't listened to enough John Lewis speeches or Hank Williams songs.

Then like the blind man that God gave back his sight
Praise the Lord, I saw the light

— 50 —

Marching Through Georgia

Kaaryn Walker was a Democrat for much of her life, having been a child of the civil rights generation. Her father was shot by law enforcement during a protest against a segregated bowling alley in Orangeburg, South Carolina, in 1968, while he was a college student. The governor had called in the National Guard, tensions escalated, and police fired into the crowd, wounding more than twenty and killing three, including her father's roommate. Two years later, the National Guard's killing of four white students at Kent State sparked national protests and became lodged in our collective memory. Through media, song, and textbooks, generations have grown up knowing about the shooting at Kent State — "Four dead in Oh-high-Oh," Neil Young sang — but until meeting Kaaryn, I'd never heard of the shooting in Orangeburg, which led to no charges for the officers involved but a seven-month stint in prison for one of the student activists, Cleveland Sellers.

Kaaryn is still a strong believer in civil rights, but she is no longer a Democrat. "There are far more black conservatives than people know or understand — they just don't want to talk about it," she says, as we sit on the Abernathy Greenway north of Atlanta. She founded a Facebook group called Black Conservatives for Truth, and the response has been affirming. "I have people reach out to me all the time and say, 'I'm conservative, I did not know there were so many other black conservatives in Atlanta. I thought I was the only one.' And some of the people say, 'Well, we are not willing to talk about it the way you are, so just keep us posted.'" Frank Xu had said much the same in California, except of liberals.

Why are people not willing to talk? I ask her.

"They have all said the same thing — that they are not allowed to have their thoughts around liberal family members. I don't know one conservative person, whether you're black or white, that this does not happen to. Liberals go on and on about how terrible Republicans are, and then you say something about the Democrats and they just get so offended and they don't want to talk anymore. That's not equitable, but it happens over and over again. I have lost some friends, but here is what I have noticed: I did not leave them. They left me. I have never unfriended anyone for being liberal but I get so many people who unfriend me for being conservative. Liberals fight about voter suppression, but they suppress speech, and I don't think they realize it. I don't think they see that, by ridiculing people for what they believe, they're really trying to suppress their speech. Democrats really are what they accuse Republicans of being. They're just intolerant. They are suppressive."

I'm glad she brought up voter suppression. As we speak, the Georgia state legislature is considering a bill that Democrats around the country have blasted as an attempt to block black voters from the polls and deny them their right to vote, calling it Jim Crow 2.0. Kaaryn doesn't see it that way.

"There is a difference between being suppressed and being inconvenienced," she says. "People are too lazy, and then want everything to be very convenient. The same inconvenience one person has, the other person has, too, regardless of their party or their race. Some of the reasons they have for calling it voter suppression are really insulting to me as a black person. Even if we pass everything, it's still more liberal than New York's voting laws."

Don't I know it. New Yorkers can only dream of the bill being debated in Georgia, which soon becomes law. For example: New York has no early voting at all, while Georgia's new law requires at least seventeen days of it, including weekends. New York does not permit any drop-boxes for ballots, while Georgia's new law requires at least one in every county. New York prohibits voters from receiving absentee mail-in ballots unless they will be out-of-state or have another good excuse, while Georgia allows all voters to receive them. New York State's board of elections rejected 3.6 percent of all absentee ballots, while most states, including Georgia, rejected less than 1 percent. New York does not allow its three million independents (who outnumber Republicans) to participate in primary elections — voter suppression begins with eligibility — while Georgia does. But Georgia is Jim Crow and New York is not?

New York's laws are designed to achieve the same purpose as Georgia's: to protect incumbents from voters who might unseat them. Democrats in New York have been at least as willing as Republicans in Georgia, if not more so, to use election laws to help them hold on to power.

To be clear, many Republican-controlled states have spent years trying to make it harder to vote while claiming they are only attempting to protect election integrity, including by passing laws requiring voters to show a driver's license or other proof of identity at the polls. They have adopted such laws for partisan purposes, but there are racial implications to them, since the vast majority of black voters vote Democratic. This has led some Democrats to villainize Republicans as racists for doing what Democrats often do: writing election laws that protect and advance their power.

The biggest problem with pretending that voter suppression is only a red state racial problem isn't only that it lets blue states off the hook for worse activity, or that it inflames racial tension. It's that, in close elections, it can lead Democrats to view losses as thefts.

When Stacey Abrams lost the 2018 gubernatorial race by fifty-five thousand votes, Democrats charged that it was stolen through racially driven voter suppression, despite record-high turnout (far higher than New York's gubernatorial race that year). Abrams refused to concede and sued, alleging illegal and suppressive acts. A black federal judge appointed by President Obama eventually ruled against her. And while Stacey Abrams is not Donald Trump, of course, and the situations are not equivalent, her case illustrates how a political party can come to wrongly believe that the other party has stolen an election even when the evidence doesn't support it — and how its rhetoric can deepen partisan resentment. There is a long and shameful history of suppression against black voters, but Democrats who exploit those memories risk engaging in their own version of what Republicans have been doing: fearmongering about rigged elections.

As long as we're touching on racially sensitive issues, I ask Kaaryn about reparations.

"No, no, no," she says, shaking her head. "It's not going to work. And the problem I have with reparations is that it's seen as a settlement. But whenever you have a settlement, it's designed to make you whole. Does anyone think having what some see as an oppressive government, an oppressive race, give reparations is going to be enough to stop the complaining? No, because when you have reparations and you accept it, no one wants to hear about your injustice, or slavery, or Jim Crow. Because you have settled. I've never understood: 'Well, white people have to do this, and they have to give us that.' I don't understand how you look to your 'oppressor' as the problem *and* solution. And maybe it works. I've not found that to happen."

Over the course of our conversation, Kaaryn sounds like a fairly traditional Republican, socially and fiscally conservative and a believer in self-reliance. It's important for Democrats to hear people like her, to avoid casually equating Republicans with racism. And it's important for Republicans to hear people like her, to avoid thinking they have no racial problem. "We do have racial issues within the Republican Party," she says, "and I think for people to say there's no racism is disingenuous." Wouldn't the Republican party be better able to attract black voters, I ask her, if it stopped defending Confederate monuments?

"When I see a statue, I don't pay any attention to it. I grew up on *Dukes of Hazzard*. I had a General Lee with a Confederate flag on the roof. Didn't affect me." I can see Republicans nodding along. "But I know that in the south, the Confederate flag was put up as a thumbing to the civil rights movement. So you do have segments of people who use it for racism. You also have some people who say that it's heritage. I do believe it's both. But I also believe that the heritage, the purpose of that civil war, was to keep slavery — and your heritage is going to be there without that statue. If having that statue is important to your heritage, then erect a statue on your property. I know they say that it's just history, and I think the history belongs in the museum. In Germany, you cannot have Nazi statues. So I see it both ways, but I think it would go a long way to take them down. Get rid of them."

Looking at each side's argument and making a reasoned judgment without fear of differing with and challenging allies. Both parties could learn from Kaaryn Walker.

Following Robert E. Lee Boulevard to Jefferson Davis Drive to Stonewall Jackson Drive, we arrive at our campsite looking out on the backside of Stone Mountain. It was atop the mountain in 1915 on Thanksgiving Day, the holiday Lincoln created as a day of atonement and national unity, that a handful of men revived the KKK. They burned a cross so the whole region could see it, announcing their intention not to seek forgiveness but to spread terror among blacks, Jews, Catholics, and others. Several months earlier, an anti-Semitic lynch mob had stormed a nearby state prison and hung Leo Frank for a murder he likely did not commit.

A Klan member who owned the mountain gave permission to the United Daughters of the Confederacy to carve into it a monument to both the Klan and the Confederacy. The former group was dropped, but not the reason why it was first included: to honor white supremacy. And so the UDC set out to carve three icons of the Confederacy — Robert Lee, Jefferson Davis, and Thomas Jackson — on horseback, across three acres, the largest bas-relief sculpture in the world. The carving stalled for logistical and financial reasons until 1954, after *Brown v. Board of Education*, when Georgia gubernatorial candidate Marvin Griffin vowed that, if elected, he would have the state buy the mountain and complete the monument — and he did, after changing the Georgia state flag to incorporate the Confederate battle flag. When Griffin returned to Stone Mountain in 1962 to again campaign for governor, he boasted of keeping his promise in a speech largely devoted to denouncing Reverend King for being "dedicated to violence and lawbreaking" and threatening to jail him.

Three years later, as Georgia's senators opposed the voting rights bill being advanced through Congress, Stone Mountain State Park was dedicated on April 14, 1965 — the hundredth anniversary of Lincoln's assassination, a not-so-subtle dance on his grave, a way of showing that the Confederacy's commitment to racial oppression had long outlived him. Sheffield Hale, CEO of the Atlanta History Center, put the matter plainly: "This mountain is about massive resistance to desegregation. It's not about the Civil War."

From the park's education center, Confederate Hall, Laurel and I walk toward the sculpture down a long sloping lawn, along a path that leads past tributes to each state in the Confederacy. I was prepared for the sculpture, but not for the signage. Reading it leaves us gobsmacked.

"North Carolinians loved the old Union and were reluctant to leave . . . As Lincoln prepared to invade the Confederacy, a state convention voted . . ." Virginia's sign carries a similar message: its people were "reluctant to secede . . . After Lincoln called for troops to invade the Confederate states, Virginia's convention voted . . ." I'm stunned that the word *invade* is still here. "Arkansas was not anxious to secede. However, when Lincoln called for volunteers to overturn the new Confederate government . . ." Each sign paints the state as a victim, drawn into a battle it had no choice but to fight — just as white Americans had long done with Native Americans.

Mississippi's sign tells us that residents viewed the 1860 election "as a threat to their rights and property" — *property* being a euphemism for enslaved people — even though a majority of residents were enslaved. Florida's sign calls Lincoln's election "a direct threat to their interests." The people of Tennessee "hoped for a conciliatory policy toward the seceding states. But like the others, they would not stand for coercion" — as if slavery was not the most abominable form of coercion.

We see only one mention of slavery in any of the signs: "Missouri was one of the northernmost of the slaveholding states," with a "substantial population from the north and abroad." Slavery is mentioned here to implicate the north and the entire world in the practice — and so it was. But Missouri's population had a lower percentage of slaves (10 percent) than any state in the Confederacy. Like Mississippi, a majority of residents in South Carolina were enslaved, and the enslaved made up more than 40 percent of the population in Alabama, Florida, Georgia, and Louisiana. In North Carolina, Texas, and Virginia, the figure was at least 30 percent. There is no mention on Missouri's sign of Senator Thomas Hart Benton, Missouri's enslaving senator who, in supporting manifest destiny, fiercely opposed the spread of slavery westward — and secession, too.

At the base of the sloping lawn are stones engraved with quotations by Jackson and Lee set beside quotations from George Washington, Thomas Jefferson, George Mason, and other southern heroes from the founding era, pairing them to claim that Confederates kept faith with the founders. The sight of Patrick Henry's immortal lines — "give me liberty or give me death" — bowls me over. It's as if enslaved people didn't exist.

We see only one quotation from a black person, not an artist or activist — not Harriet Tubman or Ida B. Wells, not Frederick Douglass or Reverend King, not Ralph Abernathy or Medgar Evers, all born south of the Mason-Dixon Line — but a man who was criticized for being too much of an accommodationist to racism, Booker T. Washington: "No race can prosper until it learns that there is as much dignity in tilling a field as in writing a poem." Its placement here sends an unmistakable message to black visitors: *Know your place.*

Beside the lawn is a shopping plaza in the form of an old-timey town with faux facades, which fits: The whole experience here is an exercise in make-believe. The commercial signs at least advertise truthfully — ice cream, funnel cakes, miniature golf, laser tag, scenic railroad, a 4-D theater — but all are closed for the pandemic. Running a for-profit theme park for children to help bring people to a whitewashed shrine to the Confederacy that grossly distorts history and erases enslaved people and their contribution to victory is the polar opposite of what Confederate sympathizers claim these memorials are about: upholding honor.

A tram runs over the lawn to the peak of the mountain, affording close-up views of the Confederates on horseback. I've seen enough of the sculpture, but I'd like a view from the top. Laurel has work to do, so I hike up the mountain alone, soon seeing an array of four Confederate flags flying. As I stand there in amazement, a black man walks by me wearing a US Navy hat. I pardon the imposition and ask if he's a veteran. He is. I thank him for his service and ask what he thinks of the display here. "The flags should come out," he says. "They should put them in a museum where people who wanna go see it can see it. As a taxpayer, this mountain should be a place for all people. You shouldn't have to see that rebel flag, knowing what it stood for. No."

At the summit, I can see the Atlanta skyline in the distance and hear the words Reverend King spoke from the Lincoln Memorial in 1963: "Let freedom ring from Stone Mountain of Georgia!" A month after our visit, the state will remove the Confederate flags here. Perhaps the signs will be next — and maybe even the carving. Sandblasting the carving would not destroy the mountain, and an even simpler interim step is possible: Stop cleaning it, which costs money, and allow moss, lichen, and other plants to grow out of its cracks and begin covering it.

Opposition to the monument isn't new. When it was being planned and debated, the Daughters of the Union Veterans of the Civil War wrote that it "deserves an unmistakable and unqualified rebuke by the loyal people of the American republic, and by them stand forever disapproved." That verdict still stands.

General William Sherman had gazed upon Stone Mountain after capturing and leveling Atlanta in 1864, never imagining it would hold such a colossal monument to the men who had betrayed their oaths to the Constitution and initiated a war that killed so many. His daring March to the Sea began here, and we follow it south, tracking the railroad his men ripped up to destroy the Confederate supply lines. "This movement is not purely military or strategic," Sherman wrote before setting off, "but it illustrates the vulnerability of the South. They don't know what war means." By "they" he didn't mean the poor. In directing his men to freely appropriate livestock and other necessities on the march south, he ordered them to "discriminate, however, between the rich, who are usually hostile, and the poor and industrious, who are usually neutral or friendly."

Sherman recognized a reality that, generations later, the UDC would work hard to erase: In a rich man's war for slavery, many poor whites never supported it — and still more were tired of it and resented the planters who continued to grow cotton to maximize their profit despite food shortages. So it had been in other states. The lack of support for the Confederacy among poor whites, and the social divisions it sowed, weakened the war effort, yet that story proved no match for the pride of heritage that took root among succeeding generations. Through statues and ceremonies, movies and music, novels and textbooks, southern elites achieved the kind of unity among whites in the twentieth century that had eluded their forebearers during the Confederacy.

Sherman split his troops into two columns. We follow the left (northern/eastern) column, stopping in each town along the way. At no point do we see any monuments celebrating the liberation of enslaved people, who joined the march "frantic with joy," Sherman observed, or honoring their liberators — only monuments dedicated to Confederates. Too often, the debate over them takes place without considering the words inscribed on them. Let's take a look.

In Madison, where Sherman's troops destroyed slave pens and killed a hound famed for tracking the enslaved, a monument references the "Unconstitutional Invasion" and the war "to perpetuate forever the sovereignty of the states." It further reads, "No nation rose so white and fair, none fell so pure of crime . . . Their unchallenged devotion and matchless valor shall continue to be the wonder and the inspiration of the ages." So the monument aimed to make it.

In Eatonton, a monument contains a tribute to Confederate women "whose patriotism will teach their children to emulate the deeds of their Confederate sires." *Patriotism.*

In Milledgeville, home of the state capitol at the time of the Civil War, representatives passed a law requiring all able-bodied men to take up arms against Sherman's army, but they made an exception: themselves. They fled on a train. We see no state historical sign marking that flight, but one sign does note the arrival of a "carpetbag" government after the war. A Confederate monument pays tribute to the soldiers "whose fame is as imperishable as the everlasting hills; whose courage is unrivalled since the dawn of civilization; whose name shines in undying glory on the pages of history."

In Warthen, a small monument notes the spot where Aaron Burr was incarcerated "en route to trial for treason," but the state historical sign noting where Jefferson Davis camped while running from Union forces makes no mention of the treason for which he was sought.

Just before arriving at our campground in Warthen, we hear Shemekia Copeland's "Uncivil War" on satellite radio. It's the first time I've heard it, and it's one of the many times that the DJs on SiriusXM seem to be riding along with us.

> *How long must we fight this uncivil war*
> *The same old wounds we opened before*
> *Nobody wins an uncivil war*

The Warthen RV park is one of the only black-owned RV parks in the country. We've seen hardly any black, Latino, or Asian campers across our whole journey. I can't say whether we met any Jews, but a man in Pittsburgh told me his last name, Markowitz, was Yiddish for "no camping." The lack of diversity at RV parks is unfortunate, because life happens outdoors, people tend to be chatty, and as Alan Graham had said in Austin, there's no social hierarchy. "Doesn't matter whether you're a millionaire or poor," a neighbor had told me in Florida, after inviting me over to sample some of his moonshine and before the tornado bore down on us. "Everyone's on the same level here. That's what I love most about it." We've loved it, too. But the RV community would benefit from more diversity — and as people find themselves parked next to neighbors from different backgrounds, so would the whole country.

The next morning in Louisville, a majority-black town of twenty-five hundred, we stop at an old slave market with original timbers that still stands in the center of town. In the wake of the George Floyd protests, the city council approved a citizens' petition to relocate it, but state legislators have objected. For now, it still stands here, against the will of the people.

In Millen, where Confederates held more than 10,000 prisoners and left behind a burial pit with 650 bodies, a monument stands "In honor of our Confederate soldiers, whom power could not corrupt, whom death could not terrify, whom defeat could not dishonor." It pays tribute to "their adherence to the strict principle of right." We don't see any monument to the Union soldiers who died here while living in conditions "barely fit for swine," a Union army chaplain wrote.

In Sylvania, a Confederate flag flies beside a monument: "They fought bravely for local self government and the rights of the states" in "The war between the states." At least the monument is in a cemetery, not in front of a courthouse or in a public park. As some towns considered moving their monuments to cemeteries, Georgia governor Brian Kemp signed a law in 2019 blocking them. He did so on April 26, Confederate Memorial Day — still a state holiday in Alabama and Mississippi, as are the birthdays of Jefferson Davis and Robert Lee.

In Statesboro, a Confederate monument at the county courthouse reads, "How many a glorious name for us, how many a story of fame for us." It was dedicated on April 26, 1909.

We reach Savannah and walk its streets, admiring its stately homes and public squares, one of the earliest examples of urban planning in America, and still one of the best. At Madison Square, we stop at a historical sign that reads, "Green-Meldrim House — Sherman's Headquarters." The sign provides details on the length of Sherman's stay in the house (forty days), its owner (Charles Green, a British immigrant), its architecture (Gothic Revival), its interior ("sumptuous"), its cost in the 1850s ($93,000), and its subsequent owners. Yet it leaves off the most important fact, the same fact long left out of most school textbooks: It was here that Sherman met with a group of twenty black leaders, all of them ministers, and asked them what they wanted for their communities. Land, they said: forty acres per household, "to turn it and till it by our own labor" and gain economic independence, one minister explained. Sherman granted the request through Special Field Order No. 15, designating much of the coast from Charleston south, four hundred thousand acres. He also offered the assistance of army mules — hence forty acres and a mule, the seminal promise of reparations. Lincoln's administration approved of the order, and forty thousand free black people flocked to the land. But shortly after Lincoln's assassination, President Johnson overturned it; black families lost their land, and America lost its best hope of building a just postwar society.

Savannah's Confederate monument stands in a popular square, and while there is no statue of Sherman in the city, there should be, given the liberation he led on the way here. There would be no need to come up with an inscription, since Herman Melville has already done it, in his poem "March to the Sea."

Was it Treason's retribution —
Necessity the plea?
They will long remember Sherman
And his streaming columns free —
They will long remember Sherman
Marching to the Sea

— 51 —

Amazing Grace

It would have been a preposterous April Fools' joke only thirteen months ago, had someone told us we would need to make an appointment at a supermarket in a small town in Georgia to get a potentially lifesaving shot. But here we are on April 1, rolling up our sleeves at a Kroger in Rincon, twenty miles outside of Savannah. Vaccine appointments have been hard to come by, though maybe less so here. A sign at another supermarket read, "Covid shots Half-priced ham." The shots brings a sense that the pandemic cloud is finally lifting, and as we head north for the last leg of the journey, we begin to sense for the first time that we are not far from completing the circle.

Approaching Charleston, we cross the Stono River, where the largest slave revolt in colonial America occurred in 1739, leaving some sixty people dead, most of them trying to break the chains of slavery. Afterward, a law prohibited the enslaved from assembling in groups, earning money, and learning to write, and it remained on the books long after America won independence from England. More than 250 slave revolts occurred in America, but there is no national park or battlefield to draw people to that history, and it has long gone hardly mentioned in public schools.

The *New York Times*'s 1619 Project aimed to draw attention to historical gaps like Stono, a noble undertaking undermined by its over-reaching contention that "one of the primary reasons the colonists decided to declare their independence from Britain was because they wanted to protect the institution of slavery." In an *Atlantic* article correcting that error and other distortions, including a portrayal of Lincoln that seems designed to cast him in the most unflattering light possible, Princeton historian Sean Wilentz explained his motivation for writing, "No effort to educate the public in order to advance social justice can afford to dispense with a respect for basic facts. In the long and continuing battle against oppression of every kind, an insistence on plain and accurate facts has been a powerful tool against propaganda that is widely accepted as truth." Democrats who rightly criticize "alternative facts" must be willing to call them out when they appear within their own party, or be rightly accused of hypocrisy.

The controversy surrounding the 1619 Project overshadowed a simpler point that should have had unifying effects: The fight for freedom on American soil began with black people. Every child learns the colonists' cry: *No taxation without representation!* Let them also learn the cries that went up long before that, from Stono and elsewhere, announcing: *No labor without liberty!*

In Charleston, the visitor center garage offers a luxury: spaces for RVs, allowing us to park in the city center, explore its streets, and walk home after dinner. The next morning, however, Laurel wakes with a 101-degree fever and no energy to get out of bed, done in by the vaccine. She kindly tells me to go out and enjoy the day without her. I feel terrible leaving her behind in a dark garage, but as she sleeps, I slip out to take a nearby walking tour of African American history. In exploring the city on our own yesterday, we had encountered lots of white supremacist history but almost no black history.

We saw, for example, a monument celebrating Lucius Mendel Rivers, a "Statesman and Patriot" who voted Dixiecrat in 1948, signed the Southern Manifesto, and was close to George Wallace. "He spoke for his neighbors," it says. We saw a stone inscribed with a prayer by an Episcopal bishop thanking God for bringing "a patriotic and courageous people" through the Civil War with "nothing to regret in our defense of the rights and honor of our Southland." And we saw an obelisk dedicated to Confederates who fell in "the war between the states" inscribed with the phrase *fortuna non mutat genus* — fortune does not change our nature. But we saw, too, the spot where a statue of John C. Calhoun, the slavery champion and father of secession, had stood. A month after George Floyd's murder, the city removed it. Time, at long last, is beginning to change what fortune did not.

The walking-tour guide, Franklin, begins with a question: "You wanna know the impact African Americans had on this city?" He spreads his arms wide. "All of it." Although there is virtually no monumentation noting it, Charleston was built by and is imbued with black labor and culture. Franklin says books teach us about plantation slaves, but not city slaves — often skilled artisans (carpenters, blacksmiths, masons) who hired themselves out to make money, acquire property (in someone else's name), buy their freedom, and even buy slaves. He's touching on something we have seen all across our trip. The closer one looks at history, the murkier the story gets, with contradictions and complications that defy neat categorizations of right and wrong, guilt and innocence.

Franklin tells us the story of Denmark Vesey, who purchased his freedom out of bondage and planned a slave revolt that aimed to seize the city's arsenals, kill whites, and sail to freedom in Haiti. But an enslaved man leaked the plot — his Christian faith led him to abhor killing — and the authorities rounded up the suspects, executed thirty-five of them, including Vesey, and burned the church. When Frederick Douglass rallied free blacks to join the army during the Civil War, he invoked Vesey's name: "Remember Denmark Vesey of Charleston!" And when black troops were among the first to enter Charleston after its surrender in 1865, they were singing "John Brown's Body" and carrying Denmark Vesey's spirit.

In the 1970s, Franklin says, when blacks wanted to honor Vesey with a statue, the powers that be refused, calling him a murderer, even though Vesey had been the one murdered. A Vesey statue finally went up in 2014, not downtown, where workers, residents, and tourists would see it, and where black leaders wanted it, but far off the beaten path, in a park that holds a mass burial site for some 250 Union soldiers that, in the twentieth century, was named in honor of one their opponents, Confederate general Wade Hampton, a plantation owner who held three thousand people enslaved and who rode to election victories in the post-reconstruction era on the back of white vigilantes, the Red Shirts.

At a 150th anniversary commemoration of the Civil War in Hampton Park, the pastor of Vesey's church, Mother Emanuel AME, spoke. "It was in 1822 that Mother Emanuel was standing strong," Reverend Clementa Pinckney said, "and one of its members and ministers, Denmark Vesey, had this wonderful, crazy idea that the Constitution actually was correct that freedom was for all people." Three weeks later, a twenty-one-year-old enthralled with white supremacy and the Confederate battle flag sat down in a pew during a Bible study meeting, before pulling out a gun. "I have to do it," he told the group. "Y'all are raping our white women and taking over the nation." He killed nine people, including Reverend Pinckney.

President Obama delivered Reverend Pinckney's eulogy, the most beautiful and moving address of his tenure, a meditation on God's grace and how we can express it to our fellow citizens. "Reverend Pinckney once said," Obama recalled, "'Across the south, we have a deep appreciation of history — we haven't always had a deep appreciation of each other's history.' What is true in the south is true for America. Clem understood that justice grows out of recognition of ourselves in each other . . . He knew that the path of grace involves an open mind — but, more importantly, an open heart." Obama ended the eulogy by quietly and slowly breaking into song. "A-maaaay," he started in, "-zing grace." People jumped to their feet.

How sweet the sound
That sav'd a wretch like me

Hearts opened after the massacre, and the Confederate flag came down from the statehouse — a momentous change, but an isolated one. A month after we leave Charleston, Vesey's statue will be vandalized over Memorial Day weekend, a holiday begun to honor US soldiers who died in the Civil War. *Remember Denmark Vesey? Appreciate each other's history?* Without leaders who speak of the power that lies in expressing grace, more will look for power in expressing or indulging hatred.

After checking on Laurel — she's still running a fever and still telling me to enjoy the day — I walk to Gadsden's Wharf, where about 40 percent of the people who arrived from Africa to be sold into slavery disembarked. A new International African-American Museum is opening here, a project championed by the city's longtime mayor, Joe Riley, after reading a book about the city's deep connection to the African slave trade, a connection that had long been buried under the weight of figures like Calhoun and Rivers. And it wasn't just Africans. Between 1670 and 1720, there were more enslaved Native Americans sent out of Charleston, mostly to the Caribbean, than there were Africans imported into it.

Charleston's history is finally coming to the surface, the romance of its cobblestone streets no longer able to cover it up. And one of the city's most important long-buried stories is what occurred here a year before Confederates attacked Fort Sumter.

In 1860, northern Democrats chose Charleston for the party's national convention in the hope of promoting party unity, and they proposed a platform meant to appease southerners by making several major concessions on slavery, but it wasn't enough. Southerners drafted their own platform and refused to budge. Much of the convention consisted of speeches by northern delegates imploring southerners to compromise. Northerners even offered a platform that merely reaffirmed the one from four years prior. No deal. Southerners also rejected the majority's preferred presidential candidate, Senator Stephen Douglas, because he was not sufficiently supportive of slavery's expansion, and they walked out.

Slavery did not lead to war, in and of itself. War came after a series of political overreaches by southern political leaders. First, by insisting on the unfettered spread of slavery in the west, then by walking out of the 1860 party convention, then by rejecting a constitutional amendment backed by Republicans prohibiting federal interference with slavery, then by attempting to create their own country, and then by attacking Fort Sumter. Each was a strategic blunder born of extreme intransigence. The nation was better for the war, ultimately, but Americans north and south paid a cataclysmic price. And no state bore more responsibility for it than South Carolina, the first to secede and the first to attack the US Army, despite the words in its state seal meant to signify the unity of the states: *Quis separabit* — Who shall separate?

In 2017, historians took White House chief of staff John Kelly to task for saying that "the lack of an ability to compromise led to the Civil War," because he seemed to blame the north and south equally for failing to compromise. In fairness, however, he was correct, just not in the way he meant it. It was the unwillingness by southern whites to compromise that led to war. The lack of understanding of that fact — even by a retired four-star general like Kelly — helps perpetuate the Lost Cause and the monuments that celebrate it.

From Gadsden's Wharf, I ride a ferry to Fort Sumter, where I'm amazed to see bricks that still show evidence of the Union shelling of the fort when Confederates controlled it. Even more amazing is a stone tablet placed into the bricks by the United Daughters of the Confederacy in

1919, paying tribute to the Confederates who faced "continuous siege and constant assaults" and who "defended this harbor without knowing defeat or sustaining surrender." While Confederates didn't "surrender" at the fort, they fled it in the face of Sherman's advancing army. And the word *defended* turns history upside down: They attacked their own nation's army. Even here, where Confederate cannonballs began the Civil War, a white southern attempt to sanctify its cause remains. If there is a plaque noting that Denmark Vesey's son was among those here on April 14, 1865, to re-raise the Stars and Stripes, ending a war his father's memory helped win, I don't see it.

Laurel's fever breaks in the morning, and as she begins to recover her spirit, I show her photos of my ferry ride across the harbor under sunny skies, which was perhaps a mistake. "Oh, how nice for you!" she says.

We are heading west across the state to see friends in Anderson. Along the way in Orangeburg, we stop at the segregated bowling alley that led to protests that brought out the National Guard and ended with three black students killed by state troopers, and others, including Kaaryn Walker's father, shot. It appears to be long closed — the roof is caving in — and we don't see any marker of its history, though in the center of town an 1893 Confederate monument stands as "A grateful tribute to the brave defenders of Our Rights, Our Honor, and Our Homes." Defending the bowling alley would come later.

At the state capitol in Columbia, the Confederate flag is gone, but there is still a towering Confederate monument that honors those "who have glorified a fallen cause." There are still statues of Wade Hampton and Pitchfork Ben Tillman, "the friend and leader of the common people," a plaque reads, though there is no mention of the lynching of common black people he fomented. And lo and behold, there's a statue of Strom Thurmond, the Dixiecrats' 1948 presidential nominee, who never apologized or sought forgiveness for his racial bigotry — but here he stands, facing a Confederate woman turned into an angel and striding toward her.

In recent years there has been an effort to pass a bill to erect a statue of Robert Smalls — an illiterate enslaved man who commandeered a Confederate steamship, sailed it out of Charleston Harbor past Fort Sumter's unsuspecting guards, handed it over to the Union navy, helped convince Lincoln to allow blacks to enlist as soldiers and sailors, joined the navy, returned to Fort Sumter to re-raise the Stars and Stripes, won election to the state legislature, helped establish universal education, and served in Congress before losing in white-controlled elections to Hampton and Tillman. The bill has failed.

In Anderson, we see a Confederate monument bearing an inscription that, even after weeks of reading these romantic paeans, astonishes me — and we soon see it again in Greenville.

The world shall yet decide
In truth's clear, far-off light
That the soldiers who wore the gray, and died with Lee,
Were in the right

I'm saddened to learn that the verse was written by a Catholic priest, Abram Joseph Ryan, who makes an appearance in Margaret Mitchell's *Gone with the Wind* as "the poet priest of the Confederacy" for his glorifying odes. Between the two monuments in Anderson and Greenville we had passed a modern echo of Father Ryan: Bob Jones University, an evangelical school founded with financial support from the Ku Klux Klan. It was still fighting desegregation into the mid-1970s and still banned interracial dating in 2000. Father Ryan would likely have cheered for the university, until he learned it was also anti-Catholic. Throughout history, no rule has seen more exceptions carved out of it than the Golden Rule.

We pick up the Blue Ridge Parkway in Asheville and ride atop mountain waves to Boones Mill, Virginia, where we spend the night across the road from an old brick church that has been converted into a Trump store. The pews and religious icons have been replaced with Trump-branded merchandise: hats, clothing, signs, flags, bumper stickers, magnets, knives, and other collectibles, including a flashlight that doubles as a Taser, which a customer eagerly demonstrates, after warning me to step back. One yard sign for sale carries a message we have seen many times on this trip: "Jesus is my savior. Trump is my president." Here in this old church, like so many others across the country, it can be hard to tell the difference, as faith in Jesus merges with belief in Trump and talk of his Second Coming.

I once was lost, but now am found
was blind but now I see

Just south of Boones Mill in Rocky Mount, Bridgette Craighead is styling hair in her beauty salon. A young mother, she had never been involved in politics before George Floyd's murder, but after it, she became a leader in the push to relocate the Confederate monument in front of the Franklin County courthouse, a few blocks from her shop. Local officials decided to put it to a countywide vote. Only 8 percent of the county is black. "They made the decision to put it out there," she says as she works with hair extensions. "They need to make the decision to take it out — and put it in a place where they can admire it on their own and not in front of the place of justice. That was a coward move for them to put it to a referendum, knowing that we were outnumbered."

Southern states put secession to a vote in the run-up to the Civil War, and Jim Crow state constitutions, too. Now it is happening with monuments to those eras — a modern echo of Stephen Douglas's popular sovereignty. In the November 2020 election, the referendum here lost 2–1. It was one of six countywide votes in Virginia on removing Confederate monuments. All lost.

Bridgette was born and raised here in Rocky Mount, and I ask her if she experienced racism growing up. "Oh my goodness," she says, sounding almost overwhelmed. "In school it was ridiculous. I got called the N-word all the time. I think my first fight was outside a football game. Somebody called me the N-word. I stayed fighting."

That wasn't your only fight?

"There was one guy I would never forget. I was going to class, leaving lunchroom, and I guess I was in his way and didn't move fast enough. He called me the B-word and then he was like, 'You stupid nigger.' And when I say I beat him, I did. I had him in a headlock so close they could not get me off him." Usually, her fights resulted in ten-day suspensions. That time, because her aunt got the NAACP involved, she only got three days.

"My first encounter with a racist person — I think I was maybe seven. We had these next-door neighbors. My sister is about your complexion. She's really light-skinned, pretty hair. I'm dark-skinned, nappy hair, as they would call it. And she could always go to our friend's house, Caitlin's, and play, but I could never. They were like, 'No, Bridgette, you can't go.' And they never told me why. So one day, I got curious. I'm like, 'You know what? I'm going to go over there anyway because I want play, too.' And as soon as I crossed their yard, I got probably halfway over, Caitlin ran to me and was like, 'Bridgette, you need to turn around right now.' And I was like, 'Why can't I come over?' And she said, 'Well, my papa said no niggers allowed. And he got a shotgun.' I didn't even know what that meant. So I told my family and they were like, 'Well.' And that was it. Nobody went over there and said anything. And I remember crying because I was like, 'I'm a nigger.' I didn't know what that was. But like I said, my sister, she could always go over there. And I feel like sometimes my family played us against each other because she was so light-skinned and I was so dark. And it was like, 'Well, Whitney got this pretty hair. I don't know what to do with Bridgette's hair.'"

"Maybe that inspired this salon."

"Yes. I honestly felt like I was the wrong color. I mean, think about as a kid: Santa Claus, white. Jesus, white. I was like, 'Oh my God, I'm going to hell already.' Seriously, I thought that."

Thro' many dangers, toils, and snares,
I have already come

She's running for state representative now, focusing on education, transportation, and jobs. It's a long-shot campaign in a solidly Republican district, but she decided to run after two Rocky Mount police officers were arrested at the Capitol on January 6, as they joined the mob. Rather than enforce the law while in uniform, they tried to overturn it wearing gas masks and brandishing a stick. When Bridgette demanded that the town take action, elected officials demurred, but after the men were arrested on federal charges, they were fired. A month before Laurel and I arrived here, one of the two, Jacob Fracker, pleaded guilty to conspiring to obstruct the election and agreed to cooperate with the probe of his partner, Thomas Robertson, who will eventually be found guilty and given more than seven years in prison. At his sentencing, he will express no contrition.

I ask Bridgette what binds the country together.

"Oh my goodness," she says, again sounding almost overwhelmed. "That we're here stuck with each other."

She won't win her campaign for office, but that's no reason to give up hope.

'Tis grace hath brought me safe thus far
And grace will lead me home

We are heading to Laurel's sister's home in Richmond, but first, there's a place I've been wanting to go: the Floyd Country Store, which opened in 1910. In the 1980s, the owners belonged to a bluegrass band and held practice sessions in the store on Friday nights. People walking by would ask to be let in, and soon the band opened the doors to everyone, giving birth to a tradition. When the store closed in the 1990s, as big boxes took business away from Mom and Pop, the owners kept running the Friday-night music sessions. The music saved the store — and in many ways the town. Visitors who come from far and wide to hear the music also patronize local restaurants, shops, and inns.

On a Friday afternoon, Laurel and I meet Dylan Locke inside the store, which he bought with his wife in 2014. "We own the store, but we don't really own it," he says. "We just assumed stewardship of this incredible community gathering place." He had worked at a local performing arts center but grew disillusioned with the expensive seats and big artist fees, which priced out many people and turned music into a transaction. There is no admission fee here, only a suggested donation. Before the pandemic, Friday nights would draw a crowd of about six hundred, about half inside the store and half outside. "The street would be full of people playing music," he says. "I'd give a hat away to the person who comes from the farthest away. It's hardly ever the US."

We head upstairs, where the great banjoist and singer Charlie Poole used to sleep and where a string band is practicing. He nods to the woman playing stand-up base. "Rhoda Kemp, the queen of old-time music, she's from Roanoke," he tells me. She's ninety-years-old and playing with three young kids. "It's about generation sharing," he says. "It's raw and simple and sincere. We just open the doors and let it happen."

As a young girl sings a Carter Family song, Dylan offers a little history. "A. P. Carter was one of the biggest early song catchers — got songs from people and learned how to copyright them and call them his own," he says. "He took credit for music that wasn't his. He had a guy, Leslie Riddle, by his side, who was African American, who helped him collect the songs. There's just a lot of African Americans behind the scenes who never got credit." He talks about the banjo having African roots and how artists like Rhiannon Giddens and the Carolina Chocolate Drops are helping to reclaim that history. Country music is as black as it is white, but the music industry long refused to accept black musicians and audiences as equals. That's changing, slowly.

Before arriving, Laurel and I saw a Confederate monument in front of the courthouse, and I ask Dylan if the debate over it filtered into the store. "There's this unwritten rule of checking politics at the door," he says. "People don't get into heated debates. Now, is that good? Maybe not. It'd probably be healthy for us to break some of that open and talk about it and have hard conversations, but quite honestly, I don't know how to get to that place where it's a healthy dialogue. There might be someone who might have an opposite political point of view from me who I know would do anything for me and my family, and I would do anything for them. It's about 90, 95 percent of our values are pretty aligned. I think if we were able to really talk about the differences, I think we'd probably agree on a lot of points. It's just unfortunate that we can't have those conversations and figure out how close we are, because it really feels like red-blue, black-white — you are either this or that. We had a guy on a horse with a Confederate flag on a Friday night when people were trying to play music — I was like, 'No.' I have friends who go to Richmond and protest, and it's just not my style. I'm not going to be good going into the streets. My version of fighting is to do what we do here."

"Bringing people together?"

"Yeah. You're going to feel something a little bit different here, and you're going to get touched by it and hopefully take it out there" — back into the world, back home.

Laurel and I sit on the lawn with about two dozen other people and watch a string band quartet play from a back porch. An old man shuffles his feet in time. A couple dances. Children romp. The music is scheduled to end at eight o'clock, but the band plays until nearly nine, and everyone sticks around, pulled in by the sound of the fifth voice that graces us all.

— 52 —

Both Sides Now

In the replica village in the replica house where Lee surrendered to Grant, a national park ranger explains how Confederate forces were surrounded and trapped by a Union army that included black infantry units with formerly enslaved soldiers. We are here on April 10, the day after the anniversary of the surrender, when Lee expected to be taken prisoner. He was not. Grant extended amnesty to soldiers for their treason and permission to return home with their pistols and horses. "Were such terms ever before given," one US Army officer later commented, "by a conqueror to a defeated foe?" Lee later acknowledged as much, saying that the terms were "without a parallel in the history of the civilized world."

The surrender sheet was prepared by Grant's aide Ely Parker, the army's highest-ranking Native American. Lee mistook him for being part black, and when told otherwise, he said with relief: "I'm glad to see one real American here." Parker replied, "We are all Americans." There is no record of Lee's response, but it was made clear the next day, when Grant and Lee met again and Grant implored him to persuade the remainder of the Confederate army to surrender. Lee refused. It was the first sign of southern resistance to accepting defeat. At a centennial ceremony in 1965, there was no mention of Confederate surrender, only of a "re-united nation."

In the town of Appomattox, there is no monument to Union soldiers or what was won here — the preservation of the nation and the freedom of the enslaved — just a towering statue honoring Confederate soldiers and a stone monument listing Confederate units, giving the lie to the idea of an unconditional surrender. In the parking lot behind the courthouse, an old wooden sign is propped up against the building's back wall, where few people see it. Maybe that's for the best, since its message is a myth that has long hindered true reconciliation: "Appomattox: Where Our Nation Reunited."

A real reunion is the purpose of our next stop: Richmond, to see Laurel's family. At her sister's house, we sit outside with their parents and share stories of a strange year. We are socially distanced, but at least without masks hiding smiles. In our final few days before returning home, life is starting to feel almost semi-normal.

Laurel has toured me through Richmond before, but neither of us is prepared for the sights we encounter walking down Monument Avenue. The large pedestals that long held imposing statues of Stonewall Jackson, J. E. B. Stuart, Jefferson Davis, and Matthew Maury (a US Navy commander who resigned his position to join the Confederacy) are empty. All came down in the weeks following George Floyd's murder. Stuart and Jackson were removed by the city, Davis by people who pulled him down with a rope. Those who believe these statues honor southern heritage have no good answer for why a statue was never erected to General James Longstreet — not here or across the south, until one went up in 2001 in Gainesville, Georgia, at his birthplace. The answer, of course, is that he became a Republican and supported Reconstruction and black voting rights. Not all southern heritage was celebrated.

Still standing here on Monument Avenue is a statue of Robert Lee on horseback, in a traffic circle that has been fenced and barricaded, though that hasn't stopped people from covering it with colorful graffiti. A BLM group is setting up two tents in the avenue's median across from it, and there are about ten Black Panthers in black uniforms on the sidewalk. One of them is holding an assault rifle strapped across his chest, despite a sign declaring that carrying guns is illegal during protests and public events, and despite the presence of three police officers steps away. As at Appomattox, Lee is penned in and there will be no escape: Democratic governor Ralph Northam has ordered the statues' removal.

Lee's defenders cite his allegiance to his home state as evidence of his honor, but many other southerners remained loyal to the United States, including Lee's cousin, Samuel Phillips Lee, a naval officer who declared, "When I find the word Virginia in my commission, I will join the Confederacy." More than one-third of Virginia's military officers stuck with the United States, including General Philip St. George Cooke, who remarked, "I owe Virginia little; my country much." That both Cooke's son and son-in-law, J. E. B. Stuart, chose the Confederacy did not sway him.

Of the six Virginia colonels in the US Army in 1861, only Lee resigned his commission. One of those who kept his oath was Lee's close friend George Henry Thomas, a cavalry instructor at West Point while Lee was superintendent. Thomas came from a slaveholding family, but the two men viewed the institution — and their obligations — differently. Lee was regarded by some of those he enslaved as cruel — "the worst man I ever see," said one of his enslaved men, perhaps for the whippings Lee reportedly ordered, or his attempts to override his father-in-law's will that the family's enslaved be freed within five years, or his decision to split up families in selling them off. Or perhaps all three. Lee's apologists often point to a letter he wrote referring to slavery as a "moral and political evil," but he considered it a necessary evil beneficial to an inferior race, and in 1860 he advocated for its expansion. Even after the war, he signed a manifesto denying that southerners had ever oppressed blacks and calling for a restoration of the "'kindness and humanity' of their former social system."

As a boy, Thomas broke Virginia law by teaching his family's enslaved people how to read. When he declined a Confederate army position and kept his oath to the United States, he said of Lee and secessionists: "There was no excuse whatever in a United States officer claiming the right of secession." Thomas became one of the most important figures of the Civil War. Under his command, outnumbered blue coats secured the first major Union victory in January 1862, which kept Kentucky mostly in US control, a paramount objective of Lincoln's. His later successes in Tennessee played a central role in bringing the war to a close.

After the war, Thomas remained in the army and became one of the first to sound the alarm about a new secret society of marauders, the Ku Klux Klan. In November 1868, he wrote a report to his superiors that forewarned so much of what was to come, referring to the "lawless and diabolical nature" of the Klan's acts, having learned of the "oppression and outrages committed by these midnight prowlers," whose attacks targeted "especially that class of colored people who, by their energy, industry, and good conduct are most prominent."

The *New York Times* printed his report in full, and reading it today provides a glimpse of the century that would follow — and a window into terrible epiphanies that must have visited US Army veterans like Thomas as they began to realize that the war they had sacrificed so much to win was only just beginning. The spirit that inspired the rebellion, "far from having died out," Thomas wrote, remained "a latent fire, ready to burst forth with violence upon the least occasion," with southern whites "establishing a grand political society" by force of law. He foresaw Jim Crow and urged his superiors to take the threat seriously.

In the same report, Thomas wrote presciently of the southern effort to rewrite history by promoting "the idea that the cause of liberty, justice, humanity, equality, and all the calendar of the virtues of freedom, suffered violence and wrong when the effort for southern independence failed." He was describing what came to be called the Lost Cause, "whereby the crime of treason might be covered with a counterfeit varnish of patriotism, so that the precipitators of the rebellion might go down in history hand in hand with the defenders of the government." He called it "a species of self-forgiveness amazing in its effrontery, when it is considered that life and property — justly forfeited by the laws of the country, of war, and of nations, through the magnanimity of the government and people, was not exacted from them."

One year earlier, Thomas's forces had arrested men in Rome, Georgia, who displayed Confederate flags. When their supporters wrote in protest that they meant no disrespect, Thomas directed a letter to be published that read, "Everywhere in the States lately in rebellion treason is respectable and loyalty odious. This the people of the United States, who ended the rebellion and saved the country, will not permit." He led the charge against the flag until his dying day, in 1870, without ever receiving his due. Even his family, who had disowned him for not joining the Confederates, refused to acknowledge him in death. Yet he expressed no bitterness about the way he had been overlooked in the public eye, only optimism about the future, writing, "Time and history will do me justice." They have not, at least not yet.

There is no statue of Thomas in his native Virginia, and his name is mostly forgotten to Americans. When Lee is gone, why not replace him with a statue of Thomas? And replace Jefferson Davis with Lincoln. And J. E. B. Stuart, Stonewall Jackson, and Matthew Maury with Virginians who sided with the Union, like Philip St. George Cooke, William Rufus Terrill, and David Farragut, whose cry in the last days of the war — "Damn the torpedoes! Full speed ahead!" — came during the battle for Mobile in August 1864. It was Farragut's victory there, combined with Sherman's capturing of Atlanta days later, that helped save Lincoln from electoral defeat and the nation from a ruinous capitulation.

Those men are hardly the only good candidates for the newly empty pedestals. To better reflect the nature of the battle for freedom and equality, which extended far beyond four years, consider any number of other southerners who played instrumental roles in fulfilling the promise in the 1776 Declaration penned by a Virginian, such as Nat Turner, who led a slave revolt; Elizabeth Van Lew, a Richmond abolitionist who was an invaluable spy for the US Army; Mary Richards Bowser, who worked for Jefferson Davis and leaked plans to the north; and Mildred and Richard Loving, whose love led the Supreme Court to strike down the state's law against interracial marriage more than a century after Lincoln had spoken in support of it. "If a white man wants to marry a negro woman," he said in 1858, "let them do it — if the negro woman can stand it."

We have parked Charley at the American Civil War Museum along the James River. Tucked behind it is the first statue of Lincoln we have seen in the south, save the one at Vicksburg where he stands beside Jefferson Davis. Here he is sitting on a bench with his arm around the shoulder of his son Tad commemorating their visit to Richmond on April 4, 1865, two days after the Confederate capital fell. At its dedication in 2003, protestors in the front row stood and turned their backs, wearing shirts that read, "Booth was right." Someone held a sign reading, "Jefferson Davis Was Our President." The Sons of Confederate Veterans sang "Dixie." Above, an airplane flew a banner: "*Sic Semper Tyrannis.*" Etched in stone behind father and son are the words that Lincoln had spoken one month before arriving here, a challenge to all Americans that still echoes today: "To bind up the nation's wounds."

We leave Richmond for a city still nursing an open wound, Charlottesville. At dawn, I walk through a deserted pedestrian mall to Lee Park, where a black man sleeps on the street in the shadow of Robert Lee on horseback, a bronze sculpture dedicated in 1924. It was the city council's decision to remove the Lee statue that prompted protests by a variety of white supremacist groups and culminated in the 2017 "Unite the Right" rally, when neo-Nazis, neo-Confederates, neo-fascists, Klu Kluxers, and other bigoted groups marched by torchlight, chanted racist and anti-Semitic slogans, instigated attacks on peaceful counter-protestors, and inspired a man who admired Hitler to drive his car into a crowd, injuring dozens and killing thirty-two-year-old Heather Heyer.

When President Trump referred to the "very fine people on both sides," the most charitable interpretation was that he was referring to, as he later said, the "many people in that group other than neo-Nazis and white nationalists." But the fact was: There weren't many, if any. It was a white supremacist rally through and through. And while many of Trump's supporters waved off his comments, the bigots understood it as endorsement and were emboldened by the moral equivalence it conferred upon them — a nightmare inversion of Joni Mitchell's song of humble self-awareness, "Both Sides Now."

A few blocks from Lee Park, down Heather Heyer Way, is a makeshift memorial with messages written in chalk on the side of a building. "Gone but not forgotten." "Not In Vain." "Love + Action = Change." As in Richmond, the Lee monument will be removed before the end of the year, but this one will be melted down by a local group, called Swords Into Plowshares, and transformed into a new piece of public art. Maybe the new art will also help melt down the pedestal on which the monument stood, the Lost Cause, reflecting the truth spoken by W. E. B. Du Bois: "All art is propaganda and ever must be."

In the foothills of the Virginia's Blue Ridge Mountains, the Silverback Distillery in Afton is run by the only mother–daughter master distillers in the country, Christine and Lauren Riggleman — Hooch Mama and Baby Hooch — who have won some of the industry's most prestigious awards. As I peer into a vat of bourbon mash from atop a ladder, Christine explains how a distilling tower works, including how it produces a head, a heart, and a tail, and how most distillers will use a little of the head and tail to increase their volume, but the heart is the purest part, and they use that exclusively. The head contains methanol, and too much of it can lead to blindness.

The name of the distillery, Silverback, is the teasing nickname Lauren and her two sisters gave to their father, Denver, likening him to a gorilla. But that's not Denver's only connection to a hairy and human-like creature, which is one of the reasons why I came to see him.

As a child, Denver's grandfather told him he'd seen Bigfoot, which began his lifelong fascination with why people — with no credible evidence whatsoever of its existence — believe in it. Some even believe that Bigfoot is a supernatural force — an "energy-being" — that can bring enlightenment. After going on a couple of Bigfoot hunting expeditions to learn more about the Bigfoot underworld, Denver wrote a book about the subject, and the topic became a running joke with his old army buddies. But when he ran for Congress in 2018, recruited by local Republican leaders who liked his background as an air force intelligence officer, it became something else entirely.

"I was sitting in my distillery when our former congressman resigned because of alcoholism. So it's a little ironic that I got a call to run," he says with a smile. In the general election, he faced the television journalist Leslie Cockburn, whose campaign did its research and found a tweet Denver had sent of a Bigfoot-like animal with a black bar running from its crotch to its knees with the word *censored* over it, suggesting a prodigious appendage. Cockburn sent a tweet saying that Denver had been "exposed as a devotee of Bigfoot erotica."

"I was viral by the next morning and talking to the *New York Times* about how I wasn't involved in Bigfoot pornography. What the . . ." His voice trails off. "She called me a Bigfoot Eroticist Nazi. I fought ethnic cleansing in Kosovo! So un-fucking-believable." The late-night comedians mocked him. *Saturday Night Live*, too. Democratic activists ran with it. "They put me on Bigfoot porn pictures and taped them up all over Charlottesville. On the one hand, it was awful, but it was also sort of funny. I would lose sleep while I was laughing. It was a bizarre thing. I mean, who would even believe it? But people did."

He won the election, but once in office he quickly lost the support of the local Republican Party, though not over Bigfoot. "First I voted to open the government, which was anathema to the far-right conservative base here," he says. "And then when I voted against a lawsuit to get rid of Obamacare's protections for preexisting conditions — I was only one of eight Republicans to do that. Forget about it, man. And then the gay marriage." Two of his campaign volunteers asked him to serve as the officiant of their wedding, and he gladly agreed. "I got my face ripped off. People who knew I was right, that I considered friends, absolutely ran away from me after the gay wedding."

From his days in the military and bouncing at his father's bar, he's not afraid of a fight, but he wasn't prepared for this kind of fight. "I was called fag lover. This is when I started knowing about QAnon. And I started warning the Republican Party, because QAnon said I was funded by George Soros to change the sexual orientation of children. They said I take it in the ass by Jewish people. It was awful. I was called a pedophile. Death threats. They were going to send a group of BLM people to rape my family."

"Was this being said on Twitter?

"This was official mail to my congressional office. And the phone calls were worse."

A few Republicans stood by him, but not many.

"They ran away from me on the QAnon stuff. I still talk to them. I'd still help them out. But I will tell you this: I'm not making a long-distance trip if they're on fire. And what I found was that people who behind closed doors said, 'Denver, you're one of the bravest dudes,' in public would say, 'Denver's an idiot,' more or less. Pretty hurtful."

Denver's congressional district was first represented by James Madison, who played a leading role in drafting the Constitution just months after Shays' Rebellion, when a group of about fifteen hundred armed Massachusetts residents — angry about taxes and property seizures resulting from debts — attempted to take over a state armory and overthrow the state government. Shays' "Rebellion" was actually an insurrection, and several thousand participants confessed to treason, surrendered their arms, and swore an oath of allegiance — the terms for receiving amnesty for their crime. Two men were hanged.

The adoption of the Constitution did not end insurrections. A variety of other efforts tried and failed to use force to overturn governments, in Pennsylvania, New York, and Rhode Island, and of course at Harpers Ferry, Virginia. Madison understood that in democratic societies, human nature can be constrained through the rule of law, but the public's natural susceptibility to a demagogue will always persist. In urging passage of the Constitution in Federalist 55, Madison warned of the tendency of mass democracy to degenerate into violence, writing, "Passion never fails to wrest the sceptre from reason." He was likely thinking of the Greek ruler Cleon, the original demagogue, who gave bombastic speeches, smeared opponents in coarse language, advocated brutality against enemies, and won the loyal following of the people. "Had every Athenian citizen been a Socrates," Madison wrote, "every Athenian assembly would still have been a mob." Populist mobs are inherent to democracy. They cannot be eradicated, only constrained.

Denver's apostasy cost him his seat in 2020. Virginia's parties nominate their candidates by convention, not primary, and Republicans chose someone more popular with the party's right-wing base, Bob Good, but Denver didn't go quietly. After the November election, he blasted the Stop the Steal movement, saying there was "more proof of alien abductions." He knew it wasn't just QAnon who believed in it, though. "If you sat down with close friends of mine that are professionals, they still believe the election was stolen. And the only way I can talk them out of it — not all the facts and the data — the only argument that's worked is, 'Then why did the Republicans pick up seats in the House on the same ballot?' That argument actually stops people in their tracks. And then they get very angry. 'You're a piece of shit,' they say."

"And given your background as an intelligence officer," I ask him, "did this look familiar to you?"

"Well, the language is the same. It's messianic. Good against evil. They're taking away our way of life. Facts are malleable. You have sort of carte blanche to utilize any tool at your disposal — whether it's hate, misdirection, political tools, disinformation, conspiracy theories, propaganda — in order to further an agenda where God told you: 'This is where you need to go.' There's certainly a racist underpinning to some of this. I think a lot of it is based on racism and fear and xenophobia and things like that. And how do I know that? Because it's been said to my face." He recounts an incident from a firehouse where someone suggested that a second day should be added to the Martin Luther King holiday, "for the guy who shot him."

He brings it back to Bigfoot. "When I went on that first Bigfoot expedition, the leader had forty people there that all paid $2,000 apiece to go look for a mythological creature. And you have the different Bigfoot belief systems, one of which is that Bigfoot is a Harmonic Universe Being that can see into the future and is an energy-being: an interdimensional long jumper that can give you prophecy. That is a huge belief system in the Bigfoot world. And that is the same shit as QAnon. It's the same apocalyptic, messianic crap. QAnon is a mythological creature. This is no different from people paying for a Bigfoot expedition. It's a grift. It is not real. It's bullshit. And it's always about this good-against-evil, unprovable, unverifiable theory that there's beings that we can't understand that are manipulating our existence. God dang, that was pretty good."

I must admit: He's definitely the most eloquent Bigfoot expert I've ever met.

He makes a point of saying that these theories don't become mass political movements without the participation of what he calls "little Stalins" — the hacks and hangers-on who elevate the conspiracies around a charismatic leader, often profiting from them. "There's a lot of money to be made in crazy and ignorance, man." And he's not letting the left off the hook, either. "I think the crazy on the left goes to this abiding belief that somehow fallible people in government have the answer for you. And I keep telling people: 'If you've done your studies and been around the world, if you look at fascism and Marxism, they sort of meet at the same place.' I got a lot of anger in my heart toward the far left, because they're as inconsiderate and as fanatical as the far right when it comes to winning. And truth and facts don't matter. It's the political message — trying to paint somebody as evil as possible."

In two months, Denver's successor in Congress, Bob Good, will be among twenty-one Republicans — along with Trump loyalists like Lauren Boebert, Matt Gaetz, Louie Gohmert, Paul Gosar, Marjorie Taylor Greene, and Chip Roy — to vote against awarding medals to police officers who defended the Capitol on January 6. *Back the blue*, just not when they are defending democracy.

Before I leave, Denver suggests trying some whiskey. I'd love to, I tell him, but since I'm driving, I'll buy a bottle instead. Also, it's still morning and I missed breakfast. As he rings me up in the taproom, he insists on a tiny taste, pouring a drop of straight bourbon whiskey, which is smooth but also as advertised: "chest-thumping." For good measure, he also pours a drop of honey rye, which is sweet without being too sweet. In gratitude for the time Denver has given me, and not wanting to offend Hooch Mama and Baby Hooch, I buy a bottle of that, too.

Back at Charley, after telling Laurel about the great discussion we had, I confess that I also had the tiniest of tastes.

"We haven't had breakfast!" she says, fairly.

"It would've been rude to decline!"

"You call that working? Some job you got."

I have no defense but no regrets, either, as the old bluegrass song goes:

Lord protect us, saints preserve us
We've been drinking whiskey 'fore breakfast

Near the distillery, we return to the Blue Ridge Parkway at the spot where it becomes Skyline Drive, and we spend a night in Shenandoah National Park. Laurel has fond childhood memories of Shenandoah but hasn't been back since high school. I've never been, but after taking a mini hike to a lookout along the Appalachian Trail, I'm already thinking about a return. When Franklin Roosevelt came in 1936 to dedicate the park, he spoke of the need to "give to men and women of moderate means the opportunity, the invigoration, and the luxury of touring and camping amid scenes of great natural beauty like this." And not merely for recreation's sake. "There is merit for all of us in the ancient tale of the giant Antaeus, who, every time he touched his Mother Earth, arose with strength renewed a hundredfold."

So it has been for us. We have touched more of the earth over the past seven months than we had in our combined lifetimes, and it has renewed our strength and our faith in the nation's, too, thanks partly to the simple act of seeing more of the land and its history — all the violence and divisions that generations have endured — but especially to the conversations we've enjoyed and the kindness we've been shown. We've met an awful lot of good people and been shown great hospitality by strangers, to say nothing of friends. As we begin the homestretch, I'm hoping to see two more old friends, both from summers working in the Adirondacks, and both with stories that are important to ours.

The first, Joey, lives in Alexandria. We haven't been in touch in years, and I hadn't told her we'd be coming through, but when we arrive there in the late afternoon, I text her to ask, after apologizing for the extremely short notice, if she might be free for dinner. She quickly responds with a yes and asks if she can bring her son, Mac. Even better.

Joey works as a counselor at a boarding school here, and she takes us for a drive through the campus, as well as the historic Episcopal seminary adjoining it. The seminary has recently begun a first-of-its-kind project: paying reparations to the descendants of enslaved people who built the campus and those who suffered discrimination and exploitation in the generations that followed. The seminary has begun sending about fifteen people annual payments of about $2,000, from a $1.7 million fund it set aside, and dozens of others may become eligible. In 2022, Evanston, Illinois, will become the first city in the nation to begin making reparation payments to black residents: $25,000 for housing costs. Wherever one falls on the debate over dollars, and I share the concerns that Kaaryn Walker expressed in Georgia, the recognition of past wrongs and the desire to right them is noble — and it can take many forms. Earlier this year, the Confederate monument here in Alexandria — the city that was a major slave trading center and knit the noose for John Brown — came down.

Over wood-fired pizza in a heated dining tent, Mac tells us about making the high school baseball team. Joey talks about the strength of her school community and her oldest daughter, Abby, who's in medical school. Laurel and I share some of the details of RV life (minus the toilet troubles), and eventually the conversation turns to Joey's daughter Ellie.

When Laurel and I were in Sacramento, we learned from Nancy, who is close to Joey, that Ellie had developed a severe breathing problem and tests revealed heart failure. Only twenty-two, Ellie had been active all her life, a runner and musician like her father, who was one of my favorite camp counselors as a kid, beloved by all. Joey had lost him six years ago to a heart attack, when he was only fifty-one. The doctors believed Ellie's condition was treatable, but a few weeks after we left Sacramento, news came that Ellie had passed away. I was in shock. Nancy was deep in grief. And Joey — I couldn't even imagine. I was devastated for her. Here at dinner, she is a tower of strength, but I know she has suffered more than we can fathom.

A journey that has followed the spirit of Abraham Lincoln could not end without recognizing and honoring the resilience of parents who have lost children. The Lincolns lost two of their four boys in childhood: Eddy, aged four, and Willie, aged eleven. In the weeks that followed Willie's death, Abe would shut himself in a room in the White House so that he could weep alone. "Did you ever dream of some lost friend," Abe asked a friend, "and feel that you were having a sweet communion with him, and yet have a consciousness that it was not a reality? That is the way I dream of my lost boy Willie." After Mary lost Abe, she lost another son, Tad, aged eighteen.

Ellie was only twenty-two years old when she died, the same age I was when I began a year of living with an order of Catholic brothers while teaching at a high school. At the start of the year, one of the brothers told our volunteer group that when we grew frustrated, exasperated, and stressed out by the students — and we would — we should remember this: *Each day is a gift.* To a cynic, it's a trite message, but here with Joey and Mac, during a still-unfolding pandemic, it's a powerful truth.

This is the first time Laurel has met Joey, and back in Charley, she raves about her kindness and graciousness, her down-to-earth warmth, and her incredibly resilient spirit — all of which we can see in Mac, too. It's one of the best meals we've had in a long while, and it didn't hurt that it included the best pizza we've had since leaving New York. We're ready for more of it. But we still have another friend to see.

— 53 —

Ruination Day

The cherry trees are in full bloom at Arlington National Cemetery, as we walk uphill past memorials to John and Robert Kennedy to the plantation house where Robert Lee once lived and where he made the decision to decline Lincoln's offer to lead the army and instead join the insurrection. In 1864, the US Army decided to bury its dead around the house so that, should the Lee family members ever return, they would be surrounded by reminders of his choice. "We must never forget," Frederick Douglass said at a Memorial Day event here in 1871, "that the loyal soldiers who rest beneath this sod flung themselves between the nation and the nation's destroyers." *Never forget.* He was speaking to — and denouncing — the rising notion that, in the name of patriotism, Americans should "forget the merits" of the war and offer those on both sides — *both sides* — "equal admiration." For many, so it came to be.

In 1906, the United Daughters of the Confederacy were permitted to erect a monument to the Confederate dead here, and as usual, they sought less to memorialize the fallen than to glorify why they fought. The base, which includes depictions of enslaved people loyal to their enslavers, is adorned with a line from a play about Julius Caesar written fifteen hundred years before Shakespeare.

We encountered Julius Caesar on the first day of this journey in Manhattan, at the spot where John Wilkes Booth and his two brothers staged

Shakespeare's Roman tragedy to raise money for a statue of the Bard in Central Park, only to be interrupted by Confederates trying to burn the city. We have carried the play's central themes around the country: the nature of power and the struggle for it, the violence that can arise from internal strife, the competing notions of tyranny that can fuel it, and the fragility of even the strongest republics. We have seen those themes course through the conflicts that lay along our route, and here on April 15th, the anniversary of Lincoln's death at the hands of a man inspired by an ancient cry — *Sic Semper Tyrannis!* — we encounter them again, this time in the words of Roman poet Lucan: "*Victrix causa diis placuit sed victa Caton.*" It means "The victorious cause was pleasing to the gods, but the lost cause to Cato."

The Lost Cause, written in stone, here in a national cemetery. In 1862, Friedrich Engels had seen it coming, writing in a letter to Karl Marx that southerners "abide by the outcome of the big battles and console themselves with *victrix causa diis*, etc."

The Daughters of the Confederacy adopted Cato as a patron saint because he took a hard line against Caesar's tyranny, just as they believed Confederates had done with Lincoln. Cato sought conciliation after Caesar invaded, just as they believed Confederates had done with the invading Lincoln. And Cato's forces were defeated after fighting a noble war for liberty, just as they believed Confederates had done.

Cato's Lost Cause was the Confederate's, or so the Daughters told the world — not only in monuments but also in classrooms and living rooms. They hoped that linking Confederates to Cato would allow them to live together in glory for another two thousand years and longer. Yet myths survive through the ages only through evolution. When the world overtakes them, they must adapt or fade away — or get hauled away. In 2023, the Department of Defense will order the monument removed, as the family of the sculptor's descendants had called for in the wake of the killing of Heather Heyer at Charlottesville. But as one lost cause begins to be dismantled, another — that the 2020 election was stolen — has been taking root.

"Let's go see Old Abe," Langston Hughes wrote in his poem "Lincoln Monument: Washington." It's time.

From Lee's mansion we walk down the hill to the Potomac River and cross the Arlington Memorial Bridge, where there are monuments to

Sacrifice and Valor — virtues frequently celebrated in public statuary, along with liberty. Long may they stand, but missing from our town squares are symbols of a virtue essential to holding the country together: tolerance for pluralism, including the pain of suffering defeats at the ballot box. Although ancient Greece and Rome did not give us a mythological figure to represent that virtue, that should not stop us from creating our own. Failure to do so is to court the fate of those republics.

Just beyond the bridge is the Lincoln Memorial, which might have been built in the cemetery surrounding Lee's mansion had House Speaker Joe Cannon gotten his way, but when Democrats won control of the House in 1910, the new House Speaker, Champ Clark of Missouri, dismissed the idea. "I, for one," Clark said, "will never consent to the erection of the Lincoln Memorial in any part of the South." The Great Emancipator would have to stay on the north side of the river, and not just physically.

The Lincoln Memorial's 1922 dedication was a segregated affair, with black attendees seated in the rear, some leaving in protest. Former president William Taft, head of the memorial commission, urged the lone black speaker, Robert Moton, president of the Tuskegee Institute, to cut the part of his speech that called for civil rights, which Taft deemed "propaganda." Moton reluctantly obliged, and attendees were denied the chance to hear what would have been the most Lincolnian expression of the day.

> So long as any group is denied the fullest privilege of a citizen to share both the making and the execution of the law which shapes its destiny — so long as any group does not enjoy every right and every privilege that belongs to every American citizen without regard to race, creed or color, the task for which the immortal Lincoln gave the last full measure of devotion — that task is still unfinished.

Unfinished. The word is inscribed in stone on the memorial wall, part of the Gettysburg Address, and part of what makes Lincoln, in Langston's Hughes's phrase, "a voice forever."

In that brief address, Lincoln twice urged Americans to be "dedicated" to "the unfinished work" and "the great task remaining before us." That work, and that task, was winning the war. In his second inaugural, which is also etched onto the walls here, he swapped out war for peace and reconciliation, but he remained focused on the work: "Let us strive on to finish the work we are in to bind up the nation's wounds." The work of securing liberty and justice for all, of protecting the unity of the nation, and of healing deep and painful wounds, isn't over. It never will be. It is the burden and blessing of American citizenship.

At the bottom of the steps to the Greek temple, we look upon Lincoln sitting God-like, his alert eyes gazing down on us, his right fingers grasping the chair's arm and his right leg stretched forward, as if he's ready to rise in defense of the nation's sacred principles and beckoning us to join him. We would not be the first.

Under Lincoln's eye in 1939, on the anniversary of Lee's surrender, Marian Anderson performed for a crowd of seventy-five thousand people, about half black and half white, after being denied use of Constitution Hall by the Daughters of the American Revolution. She opened with "My Country 'Tis of Thee," and fourteen years later, standing in nearly the same spot in front of a crowd more than twice as large, Reverend King recited the first verse as he spoke at the March on Washington for Jobs and Freedom.

While King's speech is best remembered for its soaring poetry, his diplomacy deserves remembering, too. He embraced the spirit of the civil rights movement's "new militancy" while also renouncing what some of its leaders were calling for: a rejection of nonviolence. "We must forever conduct our struggle on the high plane of dignity and discipline," King said that August day, in words that echoed Lincoln's abhorrence of violent mobs. "We must not allow our creative protest to degenerate into physical violence. Again and again, we must rise to the majestic heights of meeting physical force with soul force."

My friend Mike Riccardi meets us here, a son of Atlanta like Dr. King and a sergeant with the Capitol Police. It's been more than a decade since I've seen him, and despite the gray flecks in his beard, he still has his boyish face, and the old nickname he earned for his stocky build still fits: Tank. He's in uniform and on duty, just as he was on January 6. I asked him if he would be willing to share his story from that day, and he kindly agreed.

"The morning was quiet, but a little after noon, we got a call that a pipe bomb had been found outside the Republican National Committee," he says. "So we began closing streets, evacuating townhomes, restaurants, offices, and creating a perimeter. We're holding the perimeter for about twenty minutes when a call came in — an identical-looking pipe bomb at the Democratic National Committee, a few blocks away. So we decided to expand the perimeter to encompass both buildings. And as we were getting set up for the DNC, they also found an unoccupied vehicle with multiple pipe bombs on the floor. So this has definitely jumped up a notch. And as we're setting this big perimeter, the chatter on the radio at the Capitol is they are now becoming overrun. People are coming up over the fences, they're not obeying any of the officers' directions, they're getting physical, and all hell is breaking loose. But we can't just rush over there because you have what appear to be live bombs, and we found out the next day they were in fact live bombs." Among those raising hell were evangelicals who had participated in December's Jericho March, inspired by the biblical destruction of Jericho.

"All I'm hearing now on the radio is 10-33 codes, which is 'Officer down.' Any other day, you're going to have fifty cops show up. But today, you can't really send anybody — whoever's there has to handle it. Everybody is stretched thin. We get the whole perimeter set up, and my lieutenant and I were in a closed street, and we literally almost got run over by the vice president's motorcade, because they are coming out full force, guys out the window with assault weapons. And meanwhile, they're driving through our bomb perimeter.

"Eventually MPD [Metropolitan Police Department] and some other agencies come. I find an MPD guy, and I was like, 'Listen, you got to hold down this perimeter,' because I'm thinking, 'There's no way I can live with myself if I'm just standing out here in a perimeter when all these guys are getting their asses kicked in the Capitol.' So I respond into the House office building, the Longworth Building. On my way there, I hear on the radio, 'Shots fired on the House floor.' And then someone else came back and said, 'Shots fired in the Speaker's Lobby,' which is essentially the House floor. And that's when that one woman got shot and killed coming through the Speaker's Lobby." Ashli Babbitt. "A college friend's wife texted me as I was getting over to the Capitol. I replied, 'Melissa, there's a good chance I'm going to die today.' And I think of my entire twenty-four-and-a-half years on the force, that was the only day I thought I was going to die.

"When I get to the Capitol, I see my captain and he said, 'Are you ready to go in?' I was like, 'I'm ready to go in.' And I took seven guys with me, through the tunnels, and our goal was to make it up to the House floor, find any other members of Congress, and bring them back through the tunnel and pass them off to another group, who would bring them to shelter in place in one of the committee rooms. We were basically an extraction team. The Capitol can be very confusing — the basements are like catacombs, you could get lost, but I knew my way. So we get to the Speaker's Lobby off the House floor. We grab one member, one of the last ones there, bring him back through the tunnel, hand him off. We go back in again. There are officers everywhere, all through the halls, on different stairwells. All their guns are drawn, and they are just kind of holding down the area. So as I'm coming upstairs and rounding the corners, I got to be yelling, 'Blue! Blue! Blue!' so we don't get shot.

"No other members were there, so I took my team into the Rotunda, which is the dome. I would say there were maybe five hundred people inside the Rotunda, about half protesters and half police. Capitol Police, MPD, US Park Police. Some state troopers. And there was this haze over the entire area because you were overwhelmed with fire extinguishers going off, because the protesters were spraying fire extinguishers, and then the sting instantly hits you of Mace and pepper spray and other types of chemical spray. So we're coughing and everybody's eyes are tearing up, and it was like a mosh pit, shoulder-to-shoulder — shoving, pushing, shouting, trying to get these people out of the set of double doors that faces east, which would be toward the Supreme Court. Our goal is to push all these people out, but you can't just push two hundred people out of two double doors. It's a bottleneck. And outside on the steps, you had another thousand people who were trying to come in. I remember seeing some fully loaded magazines on the floor. Some were clear, some were green. And we knew that Capitol Police only carries black. And a lot of these guys that you're pushing and shoving, sometimes you take a break because you're both exhausted, and I had guys tell me, 'Hey, I'm law enforcement too.' Or, 'I'm military.' One guy's like, 'I served four tours in the Marine Corps, Afghanistan, Iraq.' And he specifically told me, 'You know what? I fought for this House. I didn't fight for these 535 motherfuckers that are in this House.' And I was like, 'I get it. I do, but you got to go.' And other guys are like, 'You know we're armed, right?' And I was like, 'Yeah, I can figure you're armed, absolutely.' And you hear later on the next day or the day after like, 'Why didn't you just start shooting all these people?' And the thing is, my instructors on Capitol Police, most of them are prior military. And that training is, if you see someone with a gun and you have to use deadly force, we are trained to shoot twice to the chest and reassess. And if I drew my gun and shot twice, well, I might have another easily twenty, thirty officers on either side of me seeing what I'm going to do, and those thirty are now going to draw their guns and shoot twice — and now you have sixty rounds in a round room made out of granite and marble. They're all going to ricochet. There was going to be a tremendous amount of bloodshed. And all the protesters, a lot of them were military and law enforcement, they're going to do the same thing. So people had asked me, 'Were you ordered not to shoot?' No. It was just an unspoken rule. Like, we're all going to die if somebody starts shooting. So you have to take your punch and your sprays and everything else, you just got to suck it up.

"We worked probably an hour to clear the Rotunda. And there was a lot of tension. I did have a conversation with a guy in the Rotunda when the pushing and shoving stopped, and he's part of a militia down in Arkansas. He's like, 'Yeah, most of us are here. I have my whole group.' I'm like, 'Oh, okay. Sweet.'"

In the rotunda is a life-sized painting of George Washington as he resigns his commission as head of the army. The artist, John Trumbull, selected that scene because of the meaning it held for future generations. "I have thought that one of the highest moral lessons ever given to the world," he told James Madison, "was that presented by the conduct of the commander-in-chief, in resigning his power and commission as he did, when the army, perhaps, would have been unanimously with him, and few of the people disposed to resist his retaining the power which he had used with such happy success, and such irreproachable moderation." Madison replied, "I believe you are right; it was a glorious action." How many in the rotunda on January 6th had ever heard that story?

"It was like a bad movie," Mike continues. "People still coming through windows, and I'm on the second floor. And I remember thinking to myself: 'This is like *The Walking Dead*, where they're coming in from every open area — doors, windows, scaling the walls. It doesn't stop. And I even remember this woman, a white female, she was probably late forties. She asked me to help her get down from the window as she's climbing in, essentially breaking and entering through a broken window. And I'm like, This is nuts. I could shoot you, really, but my brain is like, 'Help her down.' And that's what you do. I helped her down and said, 'Ma'am, you can't be in here.' It was so weird that it wasn't a reality.

"I went to what is called the set of north doors. It's the north door of the Capitol. There's two sets of double doors, and they're trying to break down the first set. We have officers in this little vestibule area between them. So I try to get into that fight, and I'm in there for like thirty seconds, and I got sprayed in the face, and I couldn't even open up my eyes. I couldn't breathe. I kind of blacked out. I went onto one of the little hallways, and I'm just throwing up and trying to blow my nose, and somebody's pouring water on my face. And I remember thinking, 'I am blowing snot all over these beautiful Minton tile floors where I used to be posted and worked' — it was just surreal.

"There was this haze in the air that you've never seen before, because when you work there, nothing really changes. Anything that changes in the building has to be an act of Congress. I remember walking through the building when I was posted there and thinking, 'Oh my gosh, that's a new light switch. They updated the light switches!' It was a shocking moment. So to go in there and see broken glass on the floor, the haze in the air, debris all over the floor, and I'm spitting up on the floor — it was surreal.

"From there we went over to the Crypt, which is the center of the building on the first floor, and they were calling for help at the Lower West Terrace door. And if you've ever seen those videos of where that MPD guy was getting crushed and sprayed, that's where he was, Lower West Terrace door. There's a big staircase outside it — the staircase that the president walks down when he's going to get inaugurated every four years. He comes out the Lower West Terrace door onto the platform. We get about ten feet from the door, and you are just stopped by this chemical wall. And then officers are kind of retreating back up the steps, and they're saying, 'Gas masks only.' And some of us are like, 'No, no, I can handle it.' No. You get hit with this chemical wall, and it was so thick and strong, if you didn't have a gas mask, you couldn't even make it to the door. So we went back up to the Crypt and posted up between the Crypt and the north door, because there's a long hallway with windows that people were still trying to come through.

"We just held down the inside because a lot of state troopers had shown up on the grounds outside in their riot gear, and they just cleared people out. Probably around 6:00 P.M., I get back to my House detail office, and we're all just kind of sitting around thinking, 'What the hell just happened?' I did some reports on some found property and one was this can wrapped in black electrical tape that was used to spray us. It was brake cleaner. We learned the next day that brake cleaner is the poor man's pepper spray and Mace. So if you get sprayed with that, it could blind you, but it also opens up your pores, so when you do get hit with pepper spray or Mace, it burns even more. It's something that's taught in these militias.

"I worked all these other protests over that last year or so, the antifas and the Black Lives Matter, and they would come and they would spray paint, and they'd show up with chains and hooks wanting to pull down statues, throwing bricks and rocks, and really just complete assholes to the point where they would just want to swear just to swear. You're on a police line, and they would be like, 'You fucking cock-sucking cowardly pussies,' and just berating you nonstop because maybe the cell phones are rolling, and they're able to just swear at cops all day long. They were coming in to just destroy things. I viewed them, the very left, as unruly children that had no direction or purpose but to break stuff and create anarchy. And I guess I'm saying that because, with this protest, they knew what they wanted. They did not destroy the building. All the priceless paintings hanging in the Rotunda, untouched. The snack room, untouched. All the busts and statues, untouched. The grandfather clocks, untouched. They knew what they wanted. They wanted those members of Congress. They wanted Pelosi and Schumer and Pence, and if they got them, yeah, I think they would've beat the shit out of them. I really do." Some protestors were caught on tape saying, "Where's Nancy?" — just as the man who later broke into her San Francisco home asked, before viciously beating her husband.

"I'm a conservative Republican, but I remember when I first started, I worked on the Senate floor for a while, and the first time I was listening to Dianne Feinstein, around 2000, I'm thinking, 'God, her viewpoint on everything is terrible.' But I totally respected the way she said it. She loves this country and she wants to do the best for this country. It's just that she wants to get from A to B, and she wants to take this path, and while somebody else wants to go from A to B, the exact same endpoint, but wants to take another path, and you could see that. I totally disagree with your opinion, but the way you formulated it was amazing. And I kind of miss that type of politician."

I ask him if he's seen the vibe at the Capitol change over the course of his career.

"It absolutely changed as soon as Trump won. Because they're like, 'Oh my God, he did all this, and now he's president of the United States.' Do you remember Howard Dean? I thought he was an intelligent, motivated, great guy, and he got railroaded for saying, 'Yeah!' Horrible. But everybody had to watch what they said. And then Trump's just basically like, 'Hey, you're a fucking idiot.' They're like, 'Oh my God, he just said that.' And his poll numbers would go up, and then once he won, yeah, you saw it left and right on these politicians saying crap and just being as abrasive and obnoxious as possible. Because like, oh, that could work. So yeah, the whole Hill changed when Trump won."

Did that filter into the police department?

"For all these years with Capitol Police, a lot of times you're coming in the day after an election, and no one says a word. Even Bush–Gore. No one mentions the election or politics unless you specifically know that person, and you're going to say it to them one-on-one, but you're not coming in to a roll call with eighty people and be like, 'Woo-hoo — Gore won, Bush won.' You just don't do it, because when that president's motorcade comes up the Hill, it doesn't matter who's in there. Republican, Democrat, white, black, male, female, it doesn't matter. Your security procedure is the exact same. So I give a lot of guys credit that we did not talk about politics, unless you were friends with that other person and you're alone. But there is not a single officer in my department, including the most conservative Republican ones like myself, that were happy about what happened on January 6. Many of them that have twenty-plus years on were saying things like, 'I never thought I'd see a day worse than September 11 in my lifetime.' I felt the same way."

We began this journey in Lower Manhattan on 9/11, and now we are ending it in Washington, DC, remembering an insurrection that carries echoes of 9/11. Both were attacks on democracy, but only one was planned and perpetrated by Americans, and it might well have been far more deadly — and far more damaging to the life of the nation — but for the restraint that Sergeant Riccardi and his fellow officers showed. Even so, in the days after the trauma of the attack, two Metropolitan Police officers killed themselves. Another died of a stroke hours after being assaulted at the Capitol. More than 150 officers were injured.

QAnon believers and Trump loyalists would canonize Ashli Babbitt as a martyr, sanctifying their cause. An Oath Keeper called her "the first Patriot Martyr of the Second American Revolution," a sentiment that abolitionists had once applied to John Brown — and therein lies the trouble with glorifying those who use vigilante violence. For every cause that is right and just, there is another — and more — that is wrong and evil. We saw it all across the country, in the acts of anarchists, nativists, cowboys, religious fanatics, and even urban reformers, so intertwined with heroical righteousness is the American sense of self, no matter how often we mistake Lincolns for Caesars. In Shakespeare's play, shortly after Brutus kills Caesar, Cassius asks:

How many ages hence
Shall this our lofty scene be acted over
In states unborn and accents yet unknown?

Tomorrow, Jon Ryan Schaffer — a heavy-metal musician and founding lifetime member of the Oath Keepers who grew up in Fort Wayne — will plead guilty to a variety of federal crimes arising from his actions on January 6. In 2009, his band, Sons of Liberty, released an album full of conspiratorial lyrics ("Hail Caesar!") about the United States falling victim to a tyrannical global dictatorship and the need for people to fight to save their freedom. He was one of the first insurrectionists to force his way into the Capitol, where he used bear spray against Capitol Police officers, according to the Justice Department. More than a thousand people will be arrested for crimes committed on January 6. More than half will plead guilty. Dozens more will be convicted at trial, some receiving substantial prison sentences. Proud Boys and Oath Keepers, including their founders, Enrique Tarrio and Stewart Rhodes, will be convicted of seditious conspiracy, with Rhodes getting an eighteen-year sentence. Trump has said that, if reelected, he will pardon "a large portion" of them, and apologize to them.

Passing through the Vietnam Veterans Memorial — *Say their names*, it implores visitors — Laurel and I make our way to Ford's Theatre, where a National Park Service guide is telling a family about Lincoln's assassination and death, providing many details but not a central part of the story. Lincoln's last speech, two days after Robert Lee's surrender, concerned the burning question on everyone's mind: how to bring the country back together. In it, for the first time, he publicly expressed his support for conferring voting rights on at least some black men — "the very intelligent, and on those who serve our cause as soldiers." John Wilkes Booth, after listening in the audience, declared, "That is the last speech he will ever make." He was murdered, at least in part, because of his support for voting rights and black political power — the same reason that, for a century to come, many black Americans would be murdered and terrorized.

Lincoln had seen Booth perform onstage several times and admired him so much that he invited him to the White House, but Booth declined. He shot Lincoln on April 14, the same day the Donner party set out from Illinois in 1846, the same day the *Titanic* struck an iceberg in 1912, and the same day that dust covered the country on Black Sunday 1935 — events that inspired a song by Gillian Welch, "Ruination Day."

And the iceberg broke and the Okies fled
And the Great Emancipator took a bullet
in the back of the head

April 14 is also the date I asked Laurel to marry me. My father believed in doing big things on big days — he asked my mother to marry him on Shakespeare's birth and death day — and April 14 is not lacking for them. It's the day the first abolitionist society in America was founded in Philadelphia, that the first Pony Express rider arrived in San Francisco in 1860, that the Union army under General Robert Anderson raised the American flag back over Fort Sumter, that James Cash Penney opened his first store in 1902, that the Lincoln Highway Association incorporated in 1914, that John Steinbeck published *The Grapes of Wrath* in 1939, that parents of Mexican American children won a federal lawsuit challenging school segregation in 1947, that the Yankees finally broke the color line with Elston Howard in 1955, that Berry Gordy incorporated Motown Records in Detroit in 1960, and that Lincoln, on the last day of his life, wrote in a letter how he sought to create "a Union of hearts and hands as well as of states." No day, not even Ruination Day, is irredeemable.

A block from Ford's Theatre is the site of the old Columbia Theatre, long gone, where *The Melting Pot* was first staged in 1908. Its hero is a Jewish émigré from Russia whose parents were killed in a 1903 anti-Semitic mob attack on Easter Sunday that left forty-nine Jews dead and many Jewish women raped. The melting pot became a metaphor for American assimilation, and while its critics correctly note that immigrants' ethnic traditions do not quickly melt away, the play is not really about a melting pot but rather an orchestral symphony — one the protagonist dreams of performing on the Fourth of July. With its polyglot sounds — brass, string, percussion, and woodwind — performing a symphony that creates harmony out of diversity remains our shared national calling, and as with all the finest orchestras, it requires a commitment to continual practice.

From Ford's Theatre, we walk past the Willard Hotel, where Lincoln stayed under guard in the days leading up to his inauguration, where Julia

Ward Howe wrote "The Battle Hymn of the Republic," where the Reverend Martin Luther King crafted his "I Have a Dream" speech, and where insurrection plotters took rooms and set up a "war room" in the days leading up to January 6, 2021, a group that included Steve Bannon, John Eastman, Rudy Giuliani, and Roger Stone — some of whom were in direct communication with the president. Just across the street, between the White House and the Ellipse, where the January 6 rally was staged, are statues of Alexander Hamilton and William Sherman. Hamilton had seen it all coming back in 1792. In a letter to George Washington, he wrote:

> When a man unprincipled in private life desperate in his fortune, bold in his temper, possessed of considerable talents, having the advantage of military habits — despotic in his ordinary demeanour — known to have scoffed in private at the principles of liberty — when such a man is seen to mount the hobby horse of popularity — to join in the cry of danger to liberty — to take every opportunity of embarrassing the General Government & bringing it under suspicion — to flatter and fall in with all the nonsense of the zealots of the day — It may justly be suspected that his object is to throw things into confusion that he may "ride the storm and direct the whirlwind."

Sherman's words, inscribed on the base of his statue, are no less vital. He wrote them in 1861, while serving as superintendent of the military academy that would become Louisiana State University, to inform the Louisiana governor that he would resign his position immediately should the state secede: "On no earthly account will I do any act or think any thought hostile to or in defiance of the old government of the United States." In the same letter, Sherman wrote, "I prefer to maintain my allegiance to the Constitution as long as a fragment of it survives."

That a plot to subvert the Constitution and overthrow the government was planned so near to statues of Hamilton and Sherman — and amid the ghosts of Lincoln, Howe, and King — shows both the limits of monuments and the importance of continuing to honor those who, flaws and all, devoted their lives to bringing forth the nation, defending its unity, and keeping faith with its trinity: freedom, democracy, equality.

The question facing us today is: Can we inspire a revival of that faith? The concept of a faith revival is deeply rooted in the American experience

— periods of awakening that open eyes and hearts. A new spirit of revival is needed — not Christian but civic, not exclusionary but pluralistic, not centered on celebrity showmanship but ordinary citizenship, not preaching righteousness but humility, not seeking miracle cures but everyday healing, and not speaking in tongues but debating in civil terms, all the while propagating faith in the American trinity.

There are many civic groups nobly toiling in this vineyard. They deserve greater support and participation, and to succeed, they need greater leadership from the institutions most responsible for the formation of our shared faith: public schools. Students across the country once read and studied Washington's prophetic farewell address. Why not start there? And add in Trumbull's painting, and Hamilton's letter to Washington, and the warnings he issued against demagogues in the Federalist Papers, and make the study of civic faith more integrated into school and college curricula. And what if local civic organizations sought new opportunities to emphasize our shared faith? And if elected leaders spurred more dialogue about it, as Mayor Sadaf Jaffer of Montgomery Township has done with Montgomery Mosaic?

These and other efforts could help form a firewall against those who fan the flames of insurrection and vigilantism, bigotry and fear. They can help move us toward a common basis for examining our past, including monuments and the myths on which they are often built. And they can help us see where there is need for new monuments and myths that honor the trinity and bring us into closer communion with it.

A revival of civic faith can occur in schools and colleges, in homes and houses of worship, in community organizations and town halls, and even in media, but only if citizens in each area step forward to lead and participate. Such a revival would be patriotic but not jingoistic, awakening us to the responsibilities of our sacred calling and inviting us to be, in the phrase's most universal sense, *born again* — to find new life in the promise of our trinity. It was that faith in new life that led Lincoln to speak of "a new birth of freedom" at Gettysburg, so that "government of the people, by the people, for the people, shall not perish from the earth." The unfinished work, as ever, awaits.

— 54 —

Home

Representative Lynne Cheney tweets photos this morning with a caption: "Sunrise today at the Lincoln Memorial, marking 100 days since the attack on the U.S. Capitol." She was among the few Republicans who voted to impeach Trump for inciting the January 6 mob and will serve on a congressional committee that pulls the curtain back on the insurrection and its planners. "We must never forget the duty we all have, above partisanship," she writes today, "to defend the Constitution and the freedoms so many have fought and died to secure." *Never forget.* For her role in that defense, she will lose to a Republican challenger in the 2022 elections. "Nobody wants to be a dead hero," Phil Donahue had said. But the country has survived and advanced because some are willing to be.

After spending the night with friends outside DC — we slept in their driveway, which we now think of as normal — we stop in Baltimore to see my cousin Rip, whose father died of Covid while we were in New Orleans. Like millions of Americans, Rip has mourned without being able to gather with loved ones to embrace and remember, to laugh and cry, in rituals and ceremonies that help hold us together as families and communities. He says they hope to hold a funeral later in the spring. We'll be there, but we are grateful to have the chance to see him today.

Our last night on the road is at a Harvest Host brewery on the Lincoln Highway in Malvern, Pennsylvania. After a beer, we begin to pack up our stuff while the turmoil of the past year continues: Protesters in Oregon smash the windows of the Portland Historical Society and spray-paint a message on the building: "No More History" — as if history could be destroyed, or even ignored. "Fellow citizens, we cannot escape history," Lincoln wrote in closing his 1862 message to Congress, after defending the Emancipation Proclamation he was about to issue. His message culminated in a rejection of "the dogmas of the quiet past" but not its central values, and not its heroes, either.

"The duty of keeping in memory the great deeds of the past and of transmitting the same from generation to generation," Frederick Douglass wrote, "is implied in the mental and moral constitution of man." Not only can we not escape history; we need it. We don't need to see it the same way, and we don't need to share all the same heroes. But we need to be able to see that the common bond we share — the one that extends from the Declaration of Independence, the one that calls us to keep faith in the American trinity, the one that has been preserved through the sacrifice of generations, the one that represents the last best hope of earth — is not unbreakable.

The next morning, we clean out Charley, emptying all the bins of food and donating it to a community cupboard. Laurel had been right about the bins. They kept stuff from sliding around and kept me from making too much of a mess, which also kept our marriage intact. She was right about the solar shower, too: We never used it. But summer is coming and we already have plans to take Charley to Maine. The country is still calling.

Our final stop is a retirement home for nuns north of Philadelphia. In an outdoor gazebo, we sit with our dear family friend Sister Mary, ninety years young — the nun who gave me the book I read at the bottom of the Grand Canyon, *Where the Hell Is God?* A number of her friends here have died from Covid, and she has been in lockdown for much of the past year, confined to a small room with a single bed, hardly big enough to fit a chair. And yet she is in her usual good spirits with nary a complaint, asking about our well-being, telling us she kept us in her prayers, expressing hope that she'll be able to come to the Adirondacks for her annual stay with my mother, giving us a snack bag she's packed us for the ride back to New York, and thanking us for the bottle of Irish cream whiskey we sent her for her ninetieth birthday last month, which she shared with other sisters — and which didn't last long, she says. Selfless, gracious, humble, giving, loving, joyful. Where the hell is God? The answer is right in front of us more often than we realize.

After more than seven months on the road, we wish we could do seven more. For now, though, we leave Charley at a nearby RV service center — we've ordered a new back bumper — and take a rental car back to Manhattan. Laurel drives the homestretch, and as we approach New Jersey, a bald eagle swoops down in front of our windshield so close we almost hit it. Thankfully, Laurel pumps the brakes and it flies ahead of us down the road, as if leading the way home. Her first hour of driving has saved the whole trip, sparing us from having to tell people that although we didn't make it to Yellowstone, we did kill a bald eagle near the Jersey border.

When the Manhattan skyline appears, some of the sadness of leaving Charley fades. Approaching the Lincoln Tunnel, our final passage, we cannot see Emma Lazarus's New Colossus, but we know she is out there in the harbor welcoming us home, the Mother of Exiles lifting her lamp to a couple of tempest-tost travelers.

We arrive home on Saturday evening and spend Sunday unpacking, cleaning, and running errands, including my first trip to a barber in fourteen months, to deal with the mop that runs past my shoulders.

"What do you want me to do with this?" the barber asks.

"I don't know," I shrug, "but leave at least a little."

On Monday morning, I head to Bloomberg headquarters. Thirteen months after the start of the pandemic, Times Square and Midtown Manhattan are still much as we left them, ghost towns, and the silence of an empty office building that usually holds thousands of employees is surreal. Almost no one else is here today except, of course, Mike Bloomberg, who comes in at 7:00 am every morning and is greatly relieved when he sees me, though not because I'm back. "Frank," he says, "you finally got a haircut!"

The Bloomberg office is just a few blocks from Trump Tower. The only time I've set foot inside it was on June 16, 2015. It was my birthday, and on a lark, I decided to go watch Trump's announcement about whether he would run for president. I hadn't pre-registered as a member of the press, but his campaign staff gave me a media pass anyway. About 150 people were gathered in a small room, many of them reporters and camera crews. I was late, so rather than stand in the back, I went behind the escalator, where there was plenty of space, not realizing I was walking into the VIP section. No one stopped or questioned me. Just before Trump descended the escalator, security came by and shooed away anyone who wasn't family, friends, or campaign staff. I was wearing my media badge around my neck, but "Media" was printed only on one side. The other side was blank and facing out, though

I didn't realize it. Security let me be but escorted out the gentleman to my right. As that happened, the guy to my left elbowed me. "I was wondering who that was!" he said. I responded the most honest way I could: "Me, too."

Trump walked past us to take the stage, and his speech began as a vintage Trump promotion: "Wow! Whoa! That is some group of people — thousands!" At other announcement speeches, he said, candidates had failed to ensure the air-conditioning worked — "They sweated like dogs" — and had ordered rooms too big for their small crowds. "How are they," he asked, "gonna beat ISIS?" It all seemed like fun and games until he started talking about Mexican rapists. The era that began that day is not over — far from it.

At the end of today's workday, as a jury begins deliberating whether to convict Derek Chauvin of murdering George Floyd, I bike home through Central Park. Pedaling past a grandiose gold statue of William Sherman and past the statue of Shakespeare the Booth brothers raised money for during their one-night performance of *Julius Caesar* in 1864, I stop at a statue of Daniel Webster. On the pedestal is an inscription I had never noticed, from a speech Webster gave in 1830 during a Senate debate on slavery and the right of states to nullify federal laws, a speech Lincoln requested when crafting his first inaugural address. Webster was rebutting a colleague from South Carolina who argued for "liberty first, and Union afterward." Webster closed with words that are inscribed here, words that inspired Lincoln and have echoed through the ages, yet remain contested: "Liberty and Union, now and forever, one and inseparable."

Before we part, I'd like to extend my heartfelt gratitude to you for coming along and sticking with us. "One's destination is never a place," wrote Henry Miller, "but rather a new way of looking at things." And as Steinbeck wrote in *Travels with Charley*, "many a trip continues long after movement in time and space have ceased." Having come this far, I hope you'll keep going, further exploring what we've encountered and what we haven't, drawing up your own routes and sharing your own stories of a nation whose identity defies all captors and eludes all hunters, as Stephen Vincent Benét wrote in *John Brown's Body*.

Never the running stag, the gull at wing
The pure elixir, the American thing

The Lincoln Highway is only one of countless roads into the American thing, and what the army concluded about it after its 1919 cross-country convoy remains true today and always will: It exists "largely in the imagination." If we can keep imagining new ways to connect the country, and keep believing in the importance of that mission, and keep encouraging others not to lose faith in it, we'll be able to keep going, no matter how difficult the terrain, to see the elephant — and to keep listening, no matter how hopeless it seems, for the sound of the fifth voice that leads us there. That sound can often be awfully hard to discern at times, but on occasion it comes bursting through the heavens, as Laurel and I experienced the year after our return, when we made our annual pilgrimage to the Newport Folk Festival.

The festival takes place at a massive granite and shale fort that, for a few months during the Civil War, was commanded by General Robert Anderson, who had commanded Fort Sumter when it was attacked by Confederates and who returned to raise the flag over it at the end of the war. As the sun began to set on the stage in front of the fort, Paul Simon made a surprise appearance. During his set, he invited out Rhiannon Giddens, the folk singer, banjoist, and musicologist Dylan Locke mentioned at the Floyd Country Store. She has made a career out of digging through the roots of American music and revealing how the sounds of West Africa merged with Celtic and other traditions. With Simon playing guitar, Giddens sang "American Tune," which Simon wrote in the aftermath of Watergate — the scandal of a power-drunk president abusing his office in an attempt to subvert democracy and stay in power.

Many's the time I've been mistaken
And many times confused
Yes, and I've often felt forsaken
And certainly misused

The melody of the song comes from a German hymn composed in the 1600s to accompany a Latin poem from the Middle Ages about Christ on the cross. In translating the poem into German, words were changed, altering the meaning — and so it would be again and again, as different German and English translations appeared over the next three centuries. Simon, working in the same tradition — revisiting our understanding of the past to imbue it with new meaning, new relevance, and new power —

changed the first two lines of his climactic verse for Giddens, the daughter of a white father and black mother. In the original, he sang of the mythic American experience, as he understood it.

We come on the ship they call The Mayflower
We come on the ship that sailed the moon

Simon changed only a few words in that couplet, but in doing so he transformed the song, while still leaving the couplet after it untouched. As Giddens sang the verse, new lines and old, with the defiance of someone staking a rightful claim to her own country, a claim that belongs to all of us, an electric sensation ran through me — and based on the crowd's reaction, I was hardly alone.

We didn't come here on the Mayflower
We came in a ship in a blood red moon
We come in the age's most uncertain hours
And sing an American tune

There it was, in one verse, the whole of our journey: The mystic chords of memory, touched by our better angels, swelling the chorus of the union and sustaining our bonds of affection, ever-strained by passion, through our most uncertain hours, so that the soul of the nation, given life by a trinity both sacred and secular, will go marching on.

Acknowledgments

"Ain't it hell the way a book walks up to you and makes you write it," Carl Sandburg wrote of his biography of Lincoln. Some books won't take no for an answer. This was one of them, but it happened only because so many good people said yes.

When I first mentioned the idea of driving the Lincoln Highway to colleagues at Bloomberg, all embraced it, especially Kevin Sheekey, Patti Harris, David Shipley, Katherine Oliver, Lyndsay Firestone, Kim Molstre, and Allison Jaffin. Without their enthusiasm and assistance, and especially the blessing and backing of Michael Bloomberg — whom I have had the great good fortune of learning from for more than twenty years, and whose spirit of nonpartisan bridge-building and patriotic pragmatism lies at the heart of this book — the journey would not have been possible. I also owe a special thanks to Howard Wolfson, who emailed words of encouragement in July 2020, when I had all but given up the idea because of the pandemic. I began looking at the RV market that night. Others at Bloomberg also helped make the trip a success, especially Greg Fullam, Suzanne Foote, Alex Gittleson, and Madison Mills. In writing columns for Bloomberg from the road, I was fortunate to have exceptional editors in Mary Duenwald, Tracy Walsh, Brooke Sample, and Jessica Karl.

I relied on a great many distinguished Lincoln biographers and scholars whose works were indispensable to placing Abe and his spirit along the Lincoln Highway and beyond. In guiding me across the landscape and some of its myths, histories of Native America by Pekka Hämäläinen and David Treuer; of the west by Katherine Benton-Cohen, H. W. Brands, Greg Gandin, Louis S. Warren, and Richard White; of the Lincoln Highway by Brian Butko, Drake Hokanson, and the Lincoln Highway Association; and of American memory by Caroline E. Janney and Michael Kammen were especially vital. I'm no less indebted to the many songwriters and poets I've quoted, whose works are inseparable from our national story.

Many individuals at a wide variety of organizations assisted with research, including at the National Park Service, Buffalo Bill Center of the West, Texas State Historical Association, Nevada Historical Society, Milwaukee Public Library, Fulton County Historical Society (PA), Burke County Historical

Society (GA), Austin Chamber of Commerce (NV), Stories in Place (NV), and University of Georgia professor of religion J. Derrick Lemons. And my New York Public Library card never lacked for use.

Throughout our travels, many people were incredibly generous with their time, including those whose stories, to my regret, I was not able to include. All informed the perspective that shaped this book, and all have my gratitude. (Some names were changed to protect anonymity, and some conversations were lightly edited for brevity and clarity.) A special thanks to Doug Morrison for showing me his lab at Notre Dame's incubator, as well as to San Diego mayor Kevin Faulconer, Fort Collins mayor Wade Troxell, Sophia Aguilar, Jay Bianchi, Michael Capaldi, Maggie Feinstein, Zeke Flores, Josiah Gilliam, Aaron Lehman, Brian Pepin, Esther Terry, Friends of Germantown, and others whose pardon I beg for leaving off this list.

Friends who generously put Laurel and me up in their homes, driveways, streets, and parking lots — Terry Barthel, Matt and Joelle Kellam, Ryan Smith and Tennaly Fortier, Zack Dalton, Colin Devenish, Nancy and Tom Fitzpatrick, John and Jennifer McEwan, Paul and Jiyeon Paparella, Marshall and Anne Enos — touched us with their hospitality and made the trip all the more fun, as did seeing family along the route: Aunt Susan and Michael and Jenny Barry in Austin, the Cahills in the Bay Area — Jeanmarie, Des, Dylan, and Emma (we missed Sinéad) — and Rip Jeppi in Baltimore. And I'm grateful to many friends, colleagues, and strangers — including Stephen Barton, Paul Browne, Emily Clark, Saul Markowitz, Jeremy Robbins, Mo Kantner, Dan Wallace, Chelsie Kramer, Leani García Torres, Tim Wolff, and Chase Zreet — for introducing us to people along our route, and to Morgan Pehme, for his early support.

My good friend and agent Giles Anderson was tireless in helping me find the right home for this project. Chip Fleischer at Steerforth Press believed in it from the beginning and offered instrumental guidance and edits, while also showing great patience. I'm grateful to him and the extended Steerforth team for all their good work, including David Goldberg, Laura Jorstad, Anthony LaSasso, Helga Schmidt, Devin Wilkie, and Victor Mingovits, who designed the bold cover, and to Maddy Grubbs, for creating the beautiful map that begins the book, and for making the collaboration on it such a pleasure.

I was fortunate to have readers who provided essential feedback, including Rosie Barry, Matt Barthel, Mike Blood, Mary Duenwald, Nancy Fitzpatrick, John Feinblatt, Suzanne Foote, Greg Fullam, Sam Koppelman,

Jennifer McEwan, Mitchell Moss, Michael Newman, Michael Peppard, Eleanor Randolph, Ted Widmer, and Sean Welsh, whose commitment to writing and rewriting, and our conversations and commiserations about it, helped me keep pen to paper. Sean Nolan was invaluable in challenging me to sharpen the book's core ideas and tighten their connective tissue, as was William Freeman, a talented musician, singer, and lyricist for the band Heckuva who dug deep into the story and provided a wealth of incisive comments and criticisms that strengthened and elevated it. David Shipley's clear-eyed guidance on how to approach cuts made a world of difference.

I owe a particularly large debt to my sister, Julie, a superb writer and editor, who was my most frequent reader and sounding board, giving generously of her time to offer unfailingly wise and thoughtful comments, critiques, and edits. Especially in the final stages, her willingness to reread chapters and to respond sagely to the endless stream of questions I put to her was an incredible gift and a saving grace. And my mother, Kate Barry, offered constant encouragement, while also giving me the chance to revisit memories of my father, whose love of language and literature he shared with generations of students, especially Julie and me.

My greatest debt is to Laurel, for embracing the adventure with such gusto. Fearless, flexible, and forgiving, she was easy-going through the hardest traveling, endlessly patient through trying times, and always a voice of reason. Throughout the writing, we enjoyed reliving memories of the people and places we encountered. It will come as no surprise that, in reading the manuscript and providing perceptive comments, her recollection of events sometimes differed from mine, such is the nature of memory. Her reactions affirmed, in real time and in personal terms, one of the book's main ideas: how much personal perspective shapes collective history.

Notwithstanding this outpouring of support and assistance, I have made errors, of that I am sure — of both omission and commission. There is no history without them. What Lin-Manuel Miranda said in response to attacks on his musical *Hamilton,* which I quoted as we set out on the Lincoln Highway, goes for me, too. "Did my best," he remarked. "It's all fair game." It was a Lincolnian expression of humility. If this book helps foster more of them in the service of national unity, or even just one, I will judge it a success.

Selected Bibliography

(Additional sources can be found at fsbarry.com.)

Armitage, David. *Civil Wars: A History in Ideas*. New York: Alfred A. Knopf, 2017.

Avlon, John. *Lincoln and the Fight for Peace*. New York: Simon & Schuster, 2022.

Beeman, Richard, ed. *Lincoln Speeches*. New York: Penguin Books, 2012.

Benet, Stephen Vince. *John Brown's Body*. Chicago: Ivan R. Dee, 1927.

Benton-Cohen, Katherine. *Borderline Americans: Racial Division and Labor War in the Arizona Borderlands*. Cambridge, MA: Harvard University Press, 2009.

Beschloss, Michael. *Presidential Courage: Brave Leaders and How They Changed America, 1789–1989*. New York: Simon & Schuster, 2007.

Bourne, Jenny. *In Essentials, Unity: An Economic History of the Grange Movement*. Athens: Ohio University Press, 2017.

Boritt, Gabor S. *The Gettysburg Gospel: The Lincoln Speech That Nobody Knows*. New York: Simon & Schuster, 2006.

———. *Lincoln and the Economics of the American Dream*. Urbana: University of Illinois Press, 1978.

Brands, H.W. *Dreams of El Dorado: A History of the American West*. New York: Basic Books, 2019.

———. *The Zealot and the Emancipator: John Brown, Abraham Lincoln, and the Struggle for American Freedom*. New York: Doubleday, 2020.

Buck, Rinker. *The Oregon Trail: A New American Journey*. New York: Simon & Schuster, 2015.

Burns, Robert E. *Being Catholic, Being American: The Notre Dame Story, 1842–1934*. Notre Dame, IN: University of Notre Dame Press, 1999.

Butko, Brian. *Greetings from the Lincoln Highway: A Road Trip Celebration of America's First Coast-to-Coast Highway*. Mechanicsburg, PA: Stackpole Books, 2013.

Campbell, Joseph, with Bill Moyers. *The Power of Myth*. New York: Anchor Books, 1991.

Carwardine, Richard. *Lincoln's Sense of Humor*. Carbondale: Southern Illinois University Press, 2019.

Chernow, Ron. *Grant*. New York: Penguin Press, 2017.

Churchwell, Sarah. *Behold, America: The Entangled History of "America First" and "The American Dream."* New York: Basic Books, 2018.

Comm, Joseph A. *Rock Springs Park*. Charleston, SC: Arcadia Publishing, 2010.

Cone, James H. *The Cross and the Lynching Tree*. Maryknoll, NY: Orbis Books, 2020.

Cotter, Tom. *Ford Model T Coast to Coast: A Slow Drive Across a Fast Country*. Minneapolis: Quarto Publishing Group, 2018.

Cox, Karen L. *Dixie's Daughters: The United Daughters of the Confederacy and the Preservation of Confederate Culture*. Gainesville: University of Florida Press, 2003.

Crawford, Jack. *The Poet Scout: A Book of Song and Story*. New York: Funk and Wagnalls, 1886.

Cuomo, Mario M. *Why Lincoln Matters: Today More Than Ever*. Orlando: Harcourt, Inc., 2004.

Cuomo, Mario M., and Harold Holzer. *Lincoln on Democracy: His Own Words, with Essays By America's Foremost Historians*. New York: A Cornelia & Michael Bessie Book, 1990.

Davis, William C. *The Cause Lost: Myths and Realities of the Confederacy*. Lawrence: University of Kansas Press, 1996.

de Tocqueville, Alexis. *Democracy in America*. Chicago: University of Chicago Press, 2000.

Dew, Charles B. *Apostles of Disunion: Southern Secession Commissioners and the Causes of the Civil War*. Charlottesville: University of Virginia Press, 2001.

Donald, David Herbert. *Lincoln*. New York: Touchstone, 1995.

Dray, Philip. *There Is Power in a Union: The Epic Story of Labor in America*. New York: Anchor Books, 2010.

Emerson, Ken. *Doo-Dah! Stephen Foster and the Rise of American Popular Culture*. New York: Da Capo Press, 1998.

Fairclough, Adam. *Race and Democracy: The Civil Rights Struggle in Louisiana, 1915–1972*. Athens: University of Georgia Press, 2008.

Fehrenbacher, Don E., ed. *Abraham Lincoln: Speeches and Writings 1832–1858*. New York: Library of America, 1989.

———, ed. *Abraham Lincoln: Speeches and Writings 1859–1865*. New York: Library of America, 1989.

Ferguson, Andrew. *Land of Lincoln: Adventures in Abe's America*. New York: Grove Press, 2004.

Fitzgerald, F. Scott. *The Cruise of the Rolling Junk*. London: Hesperus Press Limited, 1924.

Fitzgerald, Frances. *The Evangelicals: The Struggle to Shape America*. New York: Simon & Schuster, 2017.

Foner, Eric. *A Short History Of Reconstruction: 1863–1877*. New York: Harper Perennial Modern Classics, 1990.

Foner, Eric, ed. *Our Lincoln: New Perspectives on Lincoln and His World*. New York: W. W. Norton & Company, 2008.

Fox, Richard Wightman. *Lincoln's Body: A Cultural History*. New York: W. W. Norton & Company, 2015.

Frank, Thomas. *What's the Matter with Kansas: How Conservatives Won the Heart of America*. New York: Metropolitan Books, 2004.

Freeman, Joanne B. *The Field of Blood: Violence in Congress and the Road to Civil War*. New York: Farrar, Straus, and Giroux, 2018.

French, David. *Divided We Fall: America's Succession Threat and How to Restore Our Nation*. New York: St. Martin's Press, 2020.

Gallagher, Gary W., and Alan T. Nolan, eds. *The Myth of the Lost Cause and Civil War History*. Bloomington: Indiana University Press, 2001.

Ginsberg, Gary. *First Friends: The Powerful, Unsung (And Unelected) People Who Shaped Our Presidents*. New York: Twelve, 2021.

Goldman, Samuel. *After Nationalism: Being American in an Age of Division*. Philadelphia: University of Pennsylvania Press, 2021.

Goodwin, Doris Kearns. *Team of Rivals: The Political Genius of Abraham Lincoln*. New York: Simon & Schuster, 2005.

Gordon, John Steele. *An Empire of Wealth: The Epic History of American Economic Power*. New York: HarperCollins Publisher, 2004.

Gordon, Linda: *The Second Coming of the KKK: The Ku Klux Klan of the 1920s and the American Political Tradition*. New York: Liveright, 2017.

Grandin, Greg. *The End of Myth: From the Frontier to the Border Wall in the Mind of America*. New York: Metropolitan Books, 2019.

Grossman, James R., ed. *The Frontier in American Culture: Essays by Richard White and Patricia Nelson Limerick*. Berkeley: University of California Press, 1994.

Guthrie, Nora, and the Woody Guthrie Archives. *My Name Is New York: Ramblin' Around Woody Guthrie's Town*. Brooklyn: powerHouse Books, 2012.

Finan, Christopher M. *Alfred E. Smith: The Happy Warrior*. New York: Hill and Wang, 2002.

Haidt, Jonathan. *The Righteous Mind: Why Good People Are Divided By Politics and Religion*. New York: Pantheon Books, 2012.

Hämäläinen, Pekka. *Indigenous Continent: The Epic Contest for North America*. New York: Liveright Publishing Corporation, 2022.

———. *Lakota America: A New History of Indigenous Power*. New Haven, CT: Yale University Press, 2019.

Harcourt, Felix. *Ku Klux Kulture: America and the Klan in the 1920s*. Chicago: University of Chicago Press, 2017.

Heat-Moon, William Least. *Blue Highways: A Journey into America*. New York: Back Bay Books, 1982.

Helm, Levon, with Stephen Davis. *This Wheel's on Fire: Levon Helm and the Story of the Band*. Chicago: Chicago Review Press, 1993.

Hendrick, George and Willene, eds. *Carl Sandburg: Selected Poems*. San Diego: Harcourt Brace & Company, 1996.

Hertz, Daniel Kay. *The Battle of Lincoln Park: Urban Renewal and Gentrification in Chicago*. Cleveland: Belt Publishing, 2018.

Hodes, Martha. *Mourning Lincoln*. New Haven, CT: Yale University Press, 2015.

Hogan, Michael. *Abraham Lincoln and Mexico: A History of Courage, Intrigue, and Unlikely Friendships*. Amissville, VA: Henselstone Verlag, 2016.

Hokanson, Drake. *The Lincoln Highway: Main Street across America*. Iowa City: University of Iowa Press, 1988.

Holzer, Harold. *Lincoln and the Power of the Press: The War for Public Opinion*. New York: Simon & Schuster, 2014.

Holzer, Harold, and Norton Garfinkle. *A Just and Generous Nation: Abraham Lincoln and the Fight for American Opportunity*. New York: Basic Books, 2015.

Howe, Ben. *The Immoral Majority: Why Evangelicals Chose Political Power Over Christian Values*. New York: Broadside Books, 2019.

Horwitz, Tony. *Spying on the South: An Odyssey Across the American Divide*. New York: Penguin Press, 2019.

Hubbell, John T., ed. *On Lincoln*. Kent, OH: Kent State University Press, 2014.

Jackson, Joe. *Black Elk: The Life of an American Visionary*. New York: Farrar, Straus, and Girioux, 2016.

Jaffa, Harry V. *Crisis of the House Divided: An Interpretation of the Issues in the Lincoln – Douglass Debates*. Chicago: University of Chicago Press, 2009.

Janney, Caroline E. *Remembering the Civil War: Reunion and the Limits of Reconciliation*. Chapel Hill: The University of North Carolina Press, 2013.

Jennings, Chris. *Paradise Now: The Story of American Utopianism*. New York: Random House, 2017.

Jones, Robert C. *Retracing the Route of Sherman's March to the Sea*. Kennesaw, GA: Robert C. Jones, 2013.

Kammen, Michael. *Mystic Chords of Memory: The Transformation of Tradition in American Culture*. New York: Vintage Books, 1991.

Kennedy, John F. *Profiles in Courage*. New York: Harper Perennial Modern Classics, 2003.

Kerouac, Jack. *On the Road*. New York: Penguin Books, 1959.

Ketcham, Christopher. *This Land: How Cowboys, Capitalism, and Corruption Are Ruining the American West*. New York: Viking, 2019.

Kreitner, Richard. *Break It Up: Secession, Division and the Secret History of America's Imperfect Union*. New York: Little Brown & Company, 2020.

Kunhardt, Philip B. III, Peter W. Kunhardt, and Peter W. Kunhardt Jr. *Looking for Lincoln*. New York: Alfred A. Knopf, 2008.

Kunhardt, Philip B. Jr., Philip B. Kunhardt III, and Peter W. Kunhardt. *Lincoln: An Illustrated Biography*. New York: Alfred A. Knopf, 1992.

Kurtz, William B. *Excommunicated from the Union: How the Civil War Created a Separate Catholic America*. New York: Fordham University Press, 2016.

Jimenez, Stephen. *The Book of Matt*. Lebanon, NH: Truth To Power, 2020.

Journal of the Abraham Lincoln Association. Champaign: University of Illinois Press.

Landrieu, Mitch. *In the Shadow of Statues: A White Southerner Confronts History*. New York: Viking, 2018.

Leerhsen, Charles. *Blood and Smoke: A True Tale of Mystery, Mayhem, and the Birth of the Indy 500*. New York: Simon & Schuster, 2011.

Lepore, Jill. *This America: The Case for the Nation*. New York: Liveright, 2019.

Leonard, Richard S.J. *Where the Hell Is God?* Mahway, NJ: HiddenSpring, 2010.

Levitsky, Steven and Daniel Ziblatt. *How Democracies Die*. New York: Broadway Books, 2018.

Lewis, Sinclair. *It Can't Happen Here*. New York: New American Library, 1935.

Lewis, Tom. *Divided Highways: Building the Interstate Highways, Transforming American Life*. Ithaca, New York: Cornell University Press, 2013.

Lincoln Highway Association. *The Complete Official Road Guide Of The Lincoln Highway*. Detroit: The Lincoln Highway Association, 1916.

———. *The Lincoln Highway Forum*.

———. *The Lincoln Highway: The Story of a Crusade That Made Transportation History*. New York: Dodd, Mead & Company, 1935.

Loewen, James W. *Lies Across America: What Our History Sites Get Wrong*. New York: Touchstone, 2000.

———. *Sundown Towns: A Hidden Dimension of American Racism*. New York: The New Press, 2005.

Loewen, James W., and Edward H. Sebesta. *The Confederate and Neo-Confederate Reader: The "Great Truth" about the "Lost Cause."* Jackson: University Press of Mississippi, 2010.

Lomax, John A., and Alan Lomax, eds. *American Ballads and Folk Songs*. Mineola, NY: Dover Publications Inc., 1994.

———. *Our Singing Country: Folk Songs and Ballads*. Mineola, NY: Dover Publications, 2000.

Madison, James H. *The Ku Klux Klan in the Heartland*. Bloomington: Indiana University Press, 2020.

Mansfield, Stephen. *Lincoln's Battle with God: A President's Struggle with Faith and What It Meant for America*. Nashville, TN: Thomas Nelson, 2012.

McNally, Dennis. *On Highway 61: Music, Race, and the Evolution of Cultural Freedom*. Berkeley: Counterpoint, 2014.

Meacham, Jon. *And There Was Light: Abraham Lincoln and the American Struggle*. New York: Random House, 2022.

———. *The Soul of America: The Battle for Our Better Angels*. New York: Random House, 2018.

Meacham, Jon, and Tim McGraw. *Songs of America: Patriotism, Protest, and the Music That Made a Nation*. New York: Random House, 2019.

McPherson, James M. *Embattled Rebel: Jefferson Davis as Commander in Chief*. New York: Penguin Press, 2014.

Miles, Jim. *To the Sea: A History and Tour Guide of Sherman's March*. Nashville, TN: Rutledge Hill Press, 1989.

Miller, William Lee. *Lincoln's Virtues: An Ethical Biography*. New York: Vintage Books, 2002.

Mitchell, Elizabeth. *Liberty's Torch: The Great Adventure to Build the Statue of Liberty*. New York: Atlantic Monthly Press, 2014.

Mounk, Yascha. *The Great Experiment: Why Diverse Democracies Fall Apart and How They Can Endure*. New York: Penguin Press, 2022.

Nissley, D. Lowell. *The Lincoln Highway: The Road My Father Traveled*. Sarasota, FL: Robert B. Abel, 2010.

Nussbaum, Jeff. *Undelivered: The Never-Heard Speeches that Would Have Rewritten History*. New York: Flatiron Books, 2022.

O'Dowd, Niall. *Lincoln and the Irish: The Untold Story of How the Irish Helped Abraham Lincoln Save the Union*. New York: Skyhorse Publishing, 2018.

Orwell, George. *All Art Is Propaganda: Critical Essays*. Boston: Mariner Books, 2008.

Peraino, Kevin. *Lincoln in the World: The Makings of a Statesman and the Dawn of American Power*. New York: Broadway Books, 2013.

Percoco, James A. *Summers with Lincoln: Look for the Man in the Monuments*. New York: Fordham University Press, 2008.

Peterson, Merrill D. *Lincoln in American Memory*. New York: Oxford University Press, 1994.

Philbrick, Nathaniel. *Travels with George: In Search of Washington and His Legacy*. New York: Viking, 2021.

Putnam, Robert D. *Bowling Alone: The Collapse and Revival of American Community*. New York: Simon & Schuster, 2020.

Raines, Ben. *The Last Slave Ship: The True Story of How* Clotilda *was Found, Her Descendants, and an Extraordinary Reckoning*. New York: Simon & Schuster, 2022.

Reid, Carlton. *Roads Were Not Built for Cars: How Cyclists Were the First to Push for Good Roads & Became the Pioneers of Motoring*. Washington: Island Press, 2015.

Reynolds, David S. *Abe: Abraham Lincoln in His Times*. New York: Penguin Press, 2020.

Richardson, Heather Cox. *To Make Men Free: A History of the Republican Party*. New York: Basic Books, 2017.

Rogers, Fred. *Fred Rogers: The Last Interview and Other Conversations*. Brooklyn: Melville House, 2021.

Rove, Karl. *The Triumph of William McKinley: Why the Election of 1896 Still Matters*. New York: Simon & Schuster, 2015.

Sandburg, Carl. *The American Songbag*. San Diego: Harcourt Brace & Company, 1990.

———. *Chicago Poems*. Digireads.com Publishing, 2019.

———. *The People, Yes*. San Diego: Harcourt Brace & Company, 1990.

Schlesinger, Arthur M., Jr. *The Disuniting of America: Reflections on a Multicultural Society*. New York: W. W. Norton & Company, 1998.

Schmidt, James M. *Notre Dame and the Civil War: Marching Onward to Victory*. Charleston, SC: The History Press, 2010.

Select Committee to Investigate the January 6th Attack on the United States Capitol. *Final Report*. Washington, DC: U.S. Government Printing Office, 2022.

Sharlet, Jeff: *The Undertow: Scenes from a Slow Civil War*. New York: W. W. Norton & Company, 2023.

Smith, Stephen B. *Reclaiming Patriotism in an Age of Extremes*. New Haven, CT: Yale University Press, 2021.

Spann, Edward K. *Gotham at War: New York City: 1860–1865*. Wilmington, Delaware: SR Books, 2002.

Steinbeck, John. *Travels with Charley: In Search of America*. New York: Penguin Books, 1961.

Sykes, Charles J. *How the Right Lost Its Mind*. New York: St. Martin's, 2017.

Taylor, Nick. *American-Made: The Enduring Legacy of the WPA: When FDR Put the Nation to Work*. New York: Bantam Books, 2008.

Taylor, Yuval, and Jake Austen: *Darkest America: Black Minstrelsy from Slavery to Hip-Hop*. New York: W. W. Norton & Company, 2012.

Treuer, David. *The Heartbeat of Wounded Knee: Native America from 1890 to the Present*. New York: Riverhead Books, 2019.

Trudeau, Noah Andre. *Lincoln's Greatest Journey: Sixteen Days that Changed a Presidency, March 24–April 8, 1865*. El Dorado Hills, CA: Savas Beatie, 2016.

Tucker, Todd. *Notre Dame Vs. The Klan: How the Fighting Irish Defied the KKK*. Notre Dame, IN: University of Notre Dame Press, 2018.

Twain, Mark. *Life on the Mississippi*. Victoria, BC: Heritage Illustrated Publishing, 2014.

———. *Roughing It*. New York: Signet Classics, 2008.

Vance, J. D. *Hillbilly Elegy: A Memoir of a Family and Culture in Crisis*. New York: Harper, 2016.

Wallace, Chris. *Character: Profiles in Presidential Courage*. New York: Rugged Land, 2004.

Wallis, Michael. *The Best Land Under Heaven. The Donner Party in the Age of Manifest Destiny*. New York: Liveright, 2017.

Walter, Barbara F. *How Civil Wars Start: And How to Stop Them*. New York: Crown, 2023.